The Principle of Effective Legal Protection in Administrative Law

This collection presents a comparative analysis of the principle of effective legal protection in administrative law in Europe. It examines how European states consider and enforce the related requirements in their domestic administrative law. The book is divided into three parts: the first comprises a theoretical introductory chapter along with perspectives from International and European Law; part two presents 15 individual country reports on the principle of effective legal protection in mostly EU member states. The core function of the reports is to provide an analysis of the domestic instruments and procedures. Adopting a contextual approach, they consider the historical, political and legal circumstances as well as analysing the relevant case law of the domestic courts; the third part provides a comparative analysis of the country reports. The final chapter assesses the influence and relevance of EU law and the ECHR. The book thus identifies the most important trends and makes a valuable contribution to the debate around convergence and divergence in European national administrative systems.

Zoltán Szente is a professor of law and the Head of the Institute for Public Law at the National University of Public Service, and holds a Research Chair at the Institute for Legal Studies of the Hungarian Academy of Sciences, Budapest.

Konrad Lachmayer holds a research chair at the Institute of Legal Studies, Centre for Social Sciences at the Hungarian Academy of Sciences. He is a senior lecturer at the Department of Constitutional and Administrative Law at the University of Vienna–Faculty of Law and is an independent researcher in Vienna.

The Principle of Effective Legal Protection in Administrative Law

A European comparison

Edited by
Zoltán Szente
and
Konrad Lachmayer

Routledge
Taylor & Francis Group
LONDON AND NEW YORK

This edition published 2017
by Informa Law from Routledge
2 Park Square, Milton Park, Abingdon, Oxon OX14 4RN

Simultaneously published in the USA and Canada
by Informa Law from Routledge
711 Third Avenue, New York, NY 10017

Informa Law from Routledge is an imprint of the Taylor & Francis Group, an Informa business

British Library Cataloguing in Publication Data
A catalogue record for this book is available from the British Library

Library of Congress Cataloging-in-Publication Data
A catalog record for this title has been requested

ISBN: 978-1-4724-7565-7 (hbk)
ISBN: 978-1-315-55397-9 (ebk)

Typeset in NewBaskerville
by Apex CoVantage, LLC

Contents

Figures

Tables

Abbreviations

ABRvS	Administrative Law Division of the Council of State (*Afdeling bestuursrechtspraak van de Raad van State*) (The Netherlands)
AC	Aarhus Convention (Convention on Access to Information, Public Participation in Decision-making and Access to Justice in Environmental Matters)
ACA	Federal Administrative Court Act (*Verwaltungsgerichtsgesetz*, VGG) of 2005 (Switzerland)
ACC	Administrative Court Code (*Verwaltungsgerichtsordnung*) (Germany) of 1960
ACPA	Administrative Courts Procedure Act (*Verwaltungsgerichtsverfahrensgesetz*) of 2013 (Austria)
ADA	Administrative Disputes Act (*Zakon o upravnem sporu*) of 2006 (Slovenia)
ADR	alternative dispute resolution
APA	Federal Act on Administrative Procedure (*Verwaltungsverfahrensgesetz*, VwVG) of 1968 (Switzerland); Administrative Procedure Act (*Verwaltungsverfahrensgesetz*) of 1976 (Germany); Administrative Penal Act of 1925 (Austria)
BVerfGE	Federal Constitutional Court (*Bundesverfassungsgericht*) (Germany)
BVerwG	Federal Administrative Court (*Bundesverwaltungssgericht*) (Germany)
CAA	Administrative courts of appeal (*Cours administratives d'appel*) (France)
CAP	Code of Administrative Procedure (*Kodeks Postepowania Administracyjnego*) of 1960 (Poland)
CE	Council of State (*Conseil d'État*) (France)
CEE	Central and Eastern European
CFR	Charter of Fundamental Rights
CJA	Code of Administrative Justice (*Code de justice administrative*) of 2001 (France)
CRvB	Central Appeal Tribunal (*Centrale Raad van Beroep*) (The Netherlands)
DDHC	Declaration of Human and Civil Rights (*Déclaration des Droits de l'Homme et du Citoyen*) of 1789 (France)
DWP	Department for Work and Pensions (United Kingdom)
ECHR	European Convention for the Protection of Human Rights
ECJ	European Court of Justice
EComHR	European Commission of Human Rights
ECtHR	European Court of Human Rights
EU	European Union
FAPA	Federal Administrative Court Procedure Act (*Verwaltungsgerichtshofsgesetz*) (Austria)

GAL	global administrative law
GALA	General Administrative Law Act of 1994 (The Netherlands)
GAPA	General Administrative Procedure Act of 2005 (Macedonia); General Administrative Procedure Act (*Zakon o splošnem upravnem postopku*) of 1956 (Slovenia); General Administrative Procedure Act of 1925 (Austria)
GRASP	General Rules of Administrative Services and Procedures (*törvény a közigazgatási hatósági eljárás és szolgáltatás általános szabályairól*) of 2004 (Hungary)
HR	Supreme Court (*Hoge Raad*) (The Netherlands)
HRA	Human Rights Act of 1998 (United Kingdom)
LAD	Law on Administrative Disputes of 2006 (Macedonia)
LADC	Law on Administrative Dispute Commissions (Lithuania)
LAP	Law on Administrative Procedure (*Administracinių bylų teisenos įstatymas*) (Lithuania)
LJCA	Administrative Courts Act (*Ley de la Jurisdicción contencioso-administrativa*) of 1998 (Spain)
LPA	Law on Public Administration (*Viešojo administravimo įstatymas*) (Lithuania)
NGO	non-governmental organization
PAA	Public Administration Act of 1985 (Denmark)
PASC	House of Commons Public Administration Select Committee (United Kingdom)
PELP	Principle of Effective Legal Protection
PHSO	Parliamentary and Health Service Ombudsman (United Kingdom)
PIA	Public Information Act (Denmark)
REP	Judicial review of administrative acts before an administrative court (*recours pour excès de pouvoir*) (France)
SAC	Supreme Administrative Court (*Naczelny Sąd Administracyjny*) (Poland)
SCA	Federal Supreme Court Act (*Bundesgerichtsgesetz*, BGG) of 2005 (Switzerland)
TEU	Treaty of European Union
TFEU	Treaty on the Functioning of the European Union
TA	Administrative tribunals (*Tribunaux administratifs*) (France)
TAR	Regional Administrative Tribunal (*tribunali amministrativi regionali*) (Italy)
UDHR	Universal Declaration of Human Rights
UK	United Kingdom
UN	United Nations
VfSlg	Official Compilation of Constitutional Court's rulings and decisions (*Sammlung der Erkenntnisse und Beschlüsse des Verfassungsgerichtshofes*) (Austria)

Contributors

Karianne Albers is an Associate Professor of Constitutional and Administrative Law at the Open Universiteit Heerlen (Netherlands). She has published on various general aspects of Dutch administrative (procedural) law, punitive administrative sanction law and state liability.

Marten Breuer is a Professor holding the Chair for Public Law with reference to European Law and Public International Law at the University of Konstanz. He is the author of three reports submitted on behalf of the German Ministry of Justice on the case law of the European Court of Human Rights in non-German cases. In 2014, he attended meetings of the Drafting Group F on the Reform of the Court (GT-GDR-F) as an ad hoc expert. His main fields of research are human rights law (especially the European Convention on Human Rights), the law of international organisations and state liability.

Sylvia Calmes-Brunet is an Associate Professor of Public Law at Rouen University (France), and is a Member of the *Centre Universitaire Rouennais d'Etudes Juridiques CUREJ, EA 4703* (Rouen) and of the *Société de Législation comparée* (Paris). She teaches constitutional and administrative law and has been directing the Master 2 *Services et Politiques publics* since 2007. She has published in French, German and English on French and German constitutional and administrative law, and her main areas of interest are legal certainty, protection of legitimate expectations, local government, regional languages and bioethics.

Fulvio Cortese is a Professor of Administrative Law at the Faculty of Law of the University of Trento, where he teaches Institutions of Public Law and Judicial Review of Administrative Action. He is a member of the European Group of Public Law. The main topics of his research work are the comparative study of liability of public administration and the analysis of methods and tools used by public bodies to coordinate themselves. He has written a series of articles on administrative justice, school law, regional and local law and European administrative law. His fields of interest also include federalism, history of public law and memory and the law.

Fruzsina Gárdos-Orosz is a Research Fellow at the Institute for Legal Studies, Centre for Social Sciences of the Hungarian Academy of Sciences since 2007 and Associate Professor at the National University of Public Service, Faculty of Political Science and Public Administration since 2014. Previously she worked at the Hungarian Constitutional Court as a law clerk in different positions and was a regular visiting lecturer at ELTE Faculty of Law. She published extensively in Hungarian on separation of powers with regard to constitutional review and on the protection of human rights. She published a book, book chapters and several articles mainly in Hungarian and English, but also in Slovakian and Russian. She is an elected member of the Advisory Board of the Hungarian Association of Constitutional Lawyers and of the Organizing Board of the Central and Eastern European Forum of Young Legal, Political and Social Theorists. Since 2015 she has been editor for the peer-reviewed law journal of the Hungarian Academy of Sciences, Acta Juridica Hungarica.

Ulrike Giera is working at the Independent Austrian Energy Agency (E-Control). She wrote her Ph.D. on 'Individual Rights in Environmental Law'.

Christoph Görisch is a Professor of Law at the University of Applied Sciences for Public Administration and Management of North Rhine-Westphalia (FHöV NRW, Hagen), Department of General Public Administration, and a Senior Lecturer (Privatdozent) at the University of Muenster, Faculty of Law. He has published widely on German, European and comparative constitutional and administrative law in German, English, Indonesian and Turkish.

Diana zu Hohenlohe-Oehringen is a Senior Lecturer (Privatdozent) at the University of Frankfurt/Main, Faculty of Law and teaching public, comparative and international law at Jena University. She has published widely on German, European and comparative constitutional and administrative law in German and English.

Erik Kerševan is a Judge of the Supreme Court of Slovenia and a Professor of Law at the Faculty of Law, University of Ljubljana. He has also performed a function of the Secretary General to the Constitutional Court and has been a part of several working groups aimed at modernisation of public administration and administrative law in Slovenia. His main focus of research has been administrative procedural law as well as several aspects of constitutional law.

Lise Kjellevold defended in 2011 at the Radboud Universiteit (Netherlands) her comparative thesis on legal protection against administrative actions in the Netherlands, Norway and Sweden. She has been a lawyer and works currently as a staff lawyer at the Dutch Bar Association.

Konrad Lachmayer is Research Chair at the Hungarian Academy of Sciences, Institute for Legal Studies, Budapest and Research Fellow at the Durham Law School (UK). He is an independent researcher in Vienna. His research and teaching focuses on International Constitutional Law, especially the methodology of constitutional comparison, counter-terrorism activities, especially data protection, and Austrian and European public law, especially democratic legitimation, rule of law and human rights.

Joanna Lemańska is a lecturer at Jagiellonian University in Krakow, Poland, Chair of Administrative Law at the Faculty of Law and Administration. She is also a member of the Regional Bar of Legal Advisors (*Okręgowa Izba Radców Prawnych*), Attorney at Law. He is currently employed in the Polish Ministry of Justice.

Søren Højgaard Møerup is a Professor of Public Law at Aarhus University, Department of Law, and has published mainly on Danish administrative law and law pertaining to property rights. He was a member of the committee set up by the Danish Ministry of Justice in 2014 to examine the rules on whistleblowing and the right to free speech for public employees and is currently serving on another committee examining how to strengthen the effort biker gang club houses/headquarters within the boundaries of human rights.

Angel-Manuel Moreno is a Professor of Administrative Law at Carlos III University of Madrid, Spain. His teaching and research career covers different topics in the domain of public law: administrative law in general, environmental law, EU law and local government law, especially from a comparative perspective. He has published widely on those topics (in the form of books, articles and chapters in collective works) in Spanish, English and French. He is a member of the Group of Independent Experts of the Council of Europe on the European Charter on Local Self-Government and of the 'Avosetta' European network of environmental lawyers.

Jurgita Paužaité-Kulvinskiené is a Professor of Administrative Law and Administrative Procedure Law at Vilnius University, Lithuania. Since 2014, she has been a Director of the Law Institute at the Ministry of Justice of Lithuania. Since 2010 she has been a member of the AEAJ (Association of European Administrative Judges). For several years, she was appointed as a Member of the Ethic Commission for Prosecutors in Lithuania. She has published widely on Lithuanian, Eastern European and comparative public law, especially in constitutional law, administrative and administrative procedure law, judicial review and administrative justice in Lithuania, English, German and Russian.

Raymond Schlössels is a Professor of Constitutional and Administrative Law at the Radboud Universiteit Nijmegen (Netherlands). Before 2002 he was an associate professor at Maastricht University (Netherlands). He has published widely on Dutch administrative (procedural) law and comparative administrative law. He has also published on damage compensation for unlawful administrative acts in French and English.

Gordana Siljanovska-Davkova is a Professor of Constitutional Law and Political System(s) at the University of Ss. Cyril and Methodius, Skopje and Head of the Institute for Juridical and Political Sciences. She is a member and former Vice-President of the Group of Independent Experts for the European Charter for Local Self-Government in the Council of Europe, as well as a former member of the Venice Commission (2008–2016), and former Vice-President of its Sub-Commission for Minorities (2012–2016). Her last (co)author's books are: *Civic and Uncivic Values in Macedonia*, 2013, (eds) S. Ramet, Palgrave Macmillan, and *Key Developments in Constitutionalism and Constitutional Law*, 2014, (eds) L. B. Fleiner, and T. Marinkovic, Eleven Int. Publishing, The Hague.

Zoltán Szente is a Professor of Law at the National University of Public Service, Department for Constitutional Law, and is a Research Chair at the Institute for Legal Studies of the Hungarian Academy of Sciences, Budapest. Since the mid-90s, he has been a member (since 2013 the vice-chairman) of the Group of Independent Experts (for monitoring local and regional democracy), Council of Europe. He has published widely on Hungarian and comparative constitutional law, constitutional theory, parliamentary law, local government and European constitutional history in Hungarian, English, German, Russian and Croatian.

István Temesi is an Associate Professor of Law at the National University of Public Service, Institute of General Administrative Law. He has published on Hungarian and comparative administrative law, local government and administrative sciences in Hungarian, English and French as well as in German and Russian. He is member of the Association EUROPA (*Entretiens Universitaires Réguliers pour l'Administration en Europe*).

Robert Thomas is a Professor of Public Law at the School of Law, University of Manchester. He has published widely on UK constitutional and administrative law, in particular judicial review and administrative justice. His publications include: *Public Law*, which is co-authored with Mark Elliott (Oxford University Press, Oxford 2nd edn, 2014) and *Administrative Justice and Asylum Appeals* (2011).

Renata Treneska-Deskoska is a Professor of Constitutional Law at the Law Faculty 'Iustinianus Primus' at the University 'Ss Cyril and Methodius' in Skopje. She obtained a doctoral degree at the Law faculty Ljubljana in 2002. She worked as a consultant or researcher on several projects funded by UNDP, DIFID, RSS, ABA/CEELI, EAR, LGI, OSCE etc. Since 2012, she has been a member of the Advisory Panel of Experts on Freedom of Religion or Belief of ODIHR, on the proposal of the Venice Commission. She has published widely on Macedonian and comparative constitutional law, parliamentary law and human rights.

Felix Uhlmann has been a Professor of Law at the University of Zurich, Switzerland since 2006. Together with Ulrich Häfelin and Georg Müller he edits a standard treatise on Swiss administrative law, encompassing administrative procedure. He is also an active member of the bar, representing cases before the Swiss Administrative Court and the Swiss Supreme Court.

Stephan Wittich is a Professor of Law teaching international law at the University of Vienna, Faculty of Law in Austria. His research focuses on international courts, international procedural law, immunities, international treaty law and responsibility.

Introduction

After the wave of comparative studies inspired by the Europeanisation of national administrative systems,[1] and by the emergence of 'global' rules and proceedings of administration, comparative administrative law got a new impetus in recent years[2] when the comparison has been focused on particular administrative principles like legitimacy,[3] or protection of legitimate expectations.[4] In this book, we want to continue this work studying the principle of effective legal protection, another fundamental principle of administrative law. Procedural fairness is a substantial requirement of the rule of law principle whenever public power is exercised. According to this principle, the government – and its agencies – are bound by law, and it can prevail only if procedural rules are respected by all public authorities. It has significance not only for the better acceptance of the individual decisions of state institutions, but also for building a democratic consensus and legitimacy in society.

We explore this principle at European and national levels as well, but our main objective in this book is to study the various national understandings and practices of effective legal protection in administrative law. For this purpose, we examine how this principle has been developed and used by the European Court of Justice and the European Court of Human Rights, and what it means in the general international law. Then, the institutions, procedures and rights of effective legal protection are analysed in 14 national jurisdictions. These countries represent all legal cultures, administrative systems and regions of contemporary Europe.

Studying our topic, we use a comparative and legal method. By a general comparison of the national situations we examine if there are general trends in the development and the application of this principle. In order to compare the relevant legislation and practice of the various countries, all authors of these chapters used a common analytical framework. It meant the use of certain standard elements and, as far as it was possible, similar methodology in describing and analysing the national situations. Thus, each country report follows more or less the same structure describing the historical development of this principle, the current constitutional landscape

1 E.g. Karl-Heinz Ladeur (ed.), *The Europeanisation of Administrative Law: Transforming National Decision-Making Procedures* (Ashgate, Aldershot 2002).

2 Susan Rose-Ackerman and Peter L. Lindseth (eds.), *Comparative Administrative Law* (Edward Elgar, Cheltenham, Northampton 2010).

3 Matthias Ruffert (ed.), *Legitimacy in European Administrative Law: Reform and Reconstruction* (Europa Law Publishing, Groningen 2011).

4 Kari Anneken Sperr and Diana zu Hohenlohe-Oehringen (eds.), *The Protection of Legitimate Expectations in Administrative Law: A Comparative Study* (Hart Publishing, Oxford 2016 [forthcoming]).

analysing the most important domestic instruments and procedures, and the relevant effects of European law. Secondly, we apply a legal approach to public administration, rather than a managerial-organisational or political outlook.[5] This follows from the inherently legal nature of the procedural fairness that is the subject of this enterprise.

In the course of our research project, we combined two approaches of the system of effective legal protection of individual rights and legitimate interests. The so-called 'rights-based perspective' has provided a conceptual framework for expounding the available rights of individuals to legal remedy in national jurisdictions. For this objective, we have defined and elaborated those rights which have relevance here. Since there are significant differences between the examined countries in defining these rights, and in their importance, we did not give a closed list of the 'relevant' rights, rather, we used a 'functional' approach to assist the identification of them.

Apparently, the effective legal protection of rights in administrative law presupposes an institutional system guaranteeing or enforcing individual rights. The 'institutional approach' relates to mechanisms of institutional settings existing in the various countries. In this part of the research, the organisation, the scope of responsibility, or the working method of the various courts, tribunals or other institutions were relevant, but only as far as they have importance for the protection of individual rights of the citizens.

This book follows in three major parts the research project as introduced above. Part I begins a conceptualisation of the principle of effective legal protection in administrative law, defining core issues and elaborating the conceptual framework of our research. The other studies of this part analyse this principle on a European level, mainly in the jurisprudence of international/European courts. Part II includes collections of the country studies analysing the present situation of this imperative in the national administrative jurisdictions of the Western and the CEE countries. As a matter of fact, characteristic differences have not been revealed between these groups of countries. In the last section, Part III, we finally provide comparative studies and share some conclusions.

After all, this book does not only present a detailed study of a core principle of the administrative law in Europe, but can also contribute to a general scholarly debate on the minimum requirements of basic rights in those situations, when individuals come into contact with governmental authorities, and when the exercise of public power directly affects their rights and interests.

This book is based on a research project of the Institute for Legal Studies of the Hungarian Academy of Sciences, and was partially financed by the National University of Public Service, Budapest. The first drafts were discussed by the participants of the research project in an international seminar held in Budapest in June 2014.

We would like to thank all contributors to this book and participants of the Budapest conference. Moreover, we thank Alison Kirk for her professional support in publishing this book with Routledge.

Zoltán Szente and Konrad Lachmayer
Budapest/Vienna

5 For these possible approaches of administrative studies see David H. Rosenblom, 'Public Administration Theory and Separation of Powers' in Julia Beckett and Heidi O. Koenig (eds.), *Public Administration and Law* (M. E. Sharpe, Armonk 2005) 7–21.

Part I

Conceptual basis and international background

1 Conceptualising the principle of effective legal protection in administrative law

Zoltán Szente

1 The concept of effective legal protection

The principle of effective legal protection as such is primarily known from, and seems to be the product of, European supranational law. As we will see in the following chapters, this fundamental requirement has been developed by the jurisprudence of the European courts, with some of its elements codified by the primary legislation of the European Union.

However, this book does not focus on the supranational approach of this principle; rather, it explores its meaning and application in the national administrative law systems all over Europe. Despite the great diversity of the national legal systems in this respect, it is generally accepted that this principle is one of the major tenets of the principle of the rule of law as enshrined in many European constitutions.

The elasticity and versatility of this term makes its conceptualisation particularly important. For this purpose, we begin by briefly examining what this concept means within European law, and then investigate its basic characteristics in the national systems of administrative law, attempting to provide a working concept to be used throughout this book.

1.1 The principle of effective legal protection in European supranational law

The concept of effective legal protection is deeply entrenched in the European Union's legislation and in the case law of the European Court of Justice, and is also familiar in the jurisprudence of the European Court of Human Rights. Art. 19(1) of the Treaty on European Union states that the 'Member States shall provide remedies sufficient to ensure effective legal protection in the fields covered by Union law'. The Charter of Fundamental Rights of the European Union, in its Art. 47, again in the fields covered by EU law, provides the right to an effective remedy and to a fair trial for everyone whose rights guaranteed by the law of the Union have been violated.

In the absence of a general code of common European administrative law,[1,2] the most important procedural guarantees have been developed by the European courts.[3] While the founding treaties contain some substantial and procedural principles for EU administrative law, the secondary legislation of EU law relates mostly to sectoral areas. The ECJ, on the basis of the legal traditions of the Member States, has therefore had a prominent role in elaborating the administrative principles which are more general in nature. The Court has created a positive obligation of the member countries to evolve efficient mechanisms and procedural conditions for safeguarding remedies intended to provide legal protection of interested parties who have been adversely affected by the infringement of EU law.[4] Thus, the principle of effective judicial protection is so deeply entrenched in EU law that some think it has a quasi-constitutional status.[5] In spite of the lack of a European code of administrative law or a separate and specialised system of administrative courts in the continent,[6] several attempts have been made so far to summarise the common standards of administrative law and procedures.[7]

1 The term 'European administrative law' can be used in two different ways. First, it indicates the administrative rules of the European Union (including direct administrative implementation of EU law by the EU institutions, and the indirect application of these norms by the national authorities of the Member States); secondly, the concept can express the body of a commonly used European administrative law (*ius commune*). Jürgen Schwarze, *Europaisches Verwaltungsrecht: Entstehung und Entwicklung im Rahmen der Europaischen Gemeinschaft* (2nd edn., Nomos, Baden-Baden 2005) 51.

EU administrative law is discussed in a huge range of literature, see in particular Jürgen Schwarze, *European Administrative Law* (Sweet and Maxwell, London 2006); Paul Craig, *European Union Administrative Law* (Oxford University Press, Oxford 2006); Herwig C. H. Hofmann, Gerard C. Rowe and Alexander H. Türk (eds.), *Administrative Law and Policy of the European Union* (Oxford University Press, Oxford 2011); Jean-Bernard and Jacqueline Dutheil de la Rochère (eds.), *Traité de droit administratif européen* (2nd edn., Bruylant, Bruxelles 2014).

In recent years, the administrative *ius commune* – focusing on the national administrative law systems and their common features – has become a fashionable topic in academic literature. See Armin von Bogdandy, Sabino Cassese and Peter M. Huber (eds.), *Handbuch Ius Publicum Europaeum: Band V Verwaltungsrecht in Europa: Grundzüge des Verwaltungsrechts in Europa* (C. F. Müller, Heidelberg 2014).

2 Schwarze (n. 1) 40.

3 Alexander H. Türk, 'Oversight of Administrative Rulemaking: Judicial Review' (2013) 19 *European Law Journal* 126, 129.

4 Linda Maria Ravo, 'The Role of the Principle of Effective Judicial Protection in the EU and Its Impact on National Jurisdictions' in Edizioni Universitá di Trieste (ed.), *Sources of Law and Legal Protection* (Edizioni Università di Trieste, Trieste 2012) 101, 108.

5 Trakis Tridimas, *The General Principles of EU Law* (Oxford University Press, Oxford 2007) 4. For the history of the principle in EU law, see Brunessen Bertrand and Jean Sirinelli, 'Le principe du droit au juge et à une protection juridictionnelle effective' in Jean-Bernard and Jacqueline Dutheil de la Rochère (eds.), *Traité de droit administratif européen* (2nd edn., Bruylant, Bruxelles 2014) 568–587.

6 Martin Shapiro, 'The Institutionalization of European Administrative Space' in Alec Stone Sweet, Wayne Sandholtz and Neil Fligstein (eds.), *The Institutionalization of Europe* (Oxford University Press, Oxford 2001) 95.

7 *Recommendation Rec(2004)20 of the Committee of Ministers to Member States on judicial review of administrative acts*; *Recommendation CM/Rec(2007)7 of the Committee of Ministers to Member States on good administration*; For the EU law: René Seerden and Frits Stroink (eds.), *Administrative Law of the European Union, Its Member States and the United States: A Comparative Analysis* (Intersentia, Antwerpen-Groningen 2007); Anne Meuwese, Ymre Schuurmans and Wim Voermans, 'Towards a European Administrative Procedure Act' (2009) 2 *Review of European Administrative Law* 3–35. The most important initiative is the Research Network on EU Administrative Law, founded in 2009, which is a research network of over 100 scholars, academics and practitioners in the field of European administrative and regulatory law. For its major

Without denying the autonomous development and innovative role of European law-making and judicial practice, the central argument of this book is that the whole process of the Europeanisation of administrative law is based on values and principles of the national administrative law systems. All the relevant parts of EU law, the ECHR or the jurisprudence of the ECJ as well as the ECtHR originate in the common constitutional traditions of the Member States, as is explicitly recognised both by the founding documents of European integration and in the practice of European courts.

1.2 Effective legal protection in national legal systems

In fact, the principle of effective legal protection in this form does not appear in the constitutions of the European countries. However, as we will see in the chapters about the various national administrative systems, it is regarded in all countries as an abstract constitutional principle in itself, or as a conglomerate of several guarantees and requirements with constitutional status. Indeed, what are mostly judicially inspired guarantees at European level are deeply-rooted and well-established constitutional principles and legal safeguards in the national legal systems.

The concept of legal protection originates from the different manifestations of the idea of rule of law; it is a core idea in the doctrine of the German *Rechtsstaat* and the Anglo-Saxon tradition as well as in their equivalent concepts in some Western European countries (*Stato di diritto, État de droit, Estado de derecho*). Despite the diversity of the path-dependent development of the national administrative laws, it was a common feature that, as the extended powers of the executive branch of government were taken for granted, there was a natural need for establishing guarantees for personal freedoms, rights and legitimate interests *vis-à-vis* state intervention.

To conceptualise this principle, it is advisable to examine all of its definitive elements separately.

1.3 Legal protection

The legal protection of individual rights against illegal state intervention is a key issue in all modern democracies. There is no doubt that it is a very general concept. However, the claim for legal protection may always arise whenever the exercise of public power adversely affects the rights or interests of the citizens. Therefore, it must exist in all branches and areas of law. The general functions of legal protection are: (1) to defend the rights and legitimate interests of citizens (and their groups and organisations) against arbitrary actions of government agencies, and (2) to monitor the objective legal order.

Thus, the first goal of legal protection is always to protect the individuals' rights, freedoms and legitimate interests against overarching and unlawful state intervention, while the second is to ensure the general legality and rule of law by providing external checks of the public authorities. These two sides of legal protection can be

---

contributions see www.reneual.eu. See in particular Herwig C. H. Hofmann, Jens-Peter Schneider and Jacques Ziller (eds.), *ReNEUAL Model Rules on EU Administrative Procedure*, http://www.reneual.eu/images/Home/ReNEUAL-Model_Rules-Compilation_BooksI_VI_2014-09-03.pdf.

conceptualised as a subjective and an objective aspect of the same phenomenon: the protection of individual rights and for guaranteeing the objective legal order.

The various instruments of legal protection may be used to defend the subjective rights and the objective legal order to a different extent; for instance, in some countries, the *ex officio* procedures of public prosecutors are useful mechanisms for promoting public interests, whereas the constitutional right of the citizens to appeal against governmental actions is a valuable instrument for protecting and enforcing the individual rights.

In this context, the protection has a legal character which means that it is realised by institutions and via proceedings laid down by law. Of course, certain individual rights and interests may also be defended by other means, such as through democratic accountability, moral obligation or other informal rules. The classic form of this principle is judicial protection, but the concept has a wider scope than this, since the enforcement of individual rights also has non-judicial tools, such as general principles, substantive and procedural rights during the administrative (or other kinds of) procedure and other institutional guarantees (e.g. ombudsman-type protection).

1.4 'Effective' legal protection

While legal protection has long been a well-established concept in the national systems of administrative law, the requirement of 'effectiveness' had, for a while, distinctive implications in EU law, where in its original form, this principle related to the Community institutions and the Member States' obligation to ensure the effective implementation (*effet utile*) of EU law, rather than the protection of individual rights.[8] Recently, however, there has been a shift of its meaning from the requirements of equivalence and effectiveness[9] towards a human rights-based approach using the principles of necessity and proportionality for balancing the rights of individuals and the justification of the relevant provisions.[10] According to a more permissive approach, there is only a difference in degree of the strictness of the relevant requirements, in that the new concept of effective judicial protection demands more sophisticated procedural guarantees for the rights of individuals conferred on them by EU law than the old standard of effectiveness and equivalence.[11] In any case, the principle of effectiveness in EU law imposes duties on the Member States 'to ensure judicial protection of an individual's rights under Community law',[12] and it means 'that a national procedural rule should not make it in practice impossible or excessively difficult to exercise EU law rights'.[13] Accordingly, legal protection is effective if individuals have effective access to courts enforcing the rights conferred on them by EU law and these

8 Ravo (n. 4) 113.
9 For these concepts see the Görisch report in this volume.
10 Ravo (n. 4) 112.
11 Sacha Prechal, 'Redefining the Relationship Between "Rewe-effectiveness" and Effective Judicial Protection' (2011) 4 *Review of European Administrative Law* 31–50.
12 Case C-286/06 *Impact* [2008] ECR I-2483. para 47–48, and Case C-63/08 *Pontin* [2009] ECR I-10467.
13 Johanna Engström, 'The Principle of Effective Judicial Protection After the Lisbon Treaty' (2011) 4 *Review of European Administrative Law* 62.

courts have at their disposal effective remedies to eliminate the violation of law.[14] It is worth noting that, as the Charter is legally binding for the member countries, they all have to ensure effective judicial protection of the rights recognised by the Charter.

However, the national legal systems know and apply this principle not only because EU law requires it, but primarily as a result of their own organic development. Although it is very difficult to come up with a unified definition of effectiveness from the different conceptions of national administrative laws,[15] it can surely be said that it involves the real availability of legal remedies for the parties of administrative procedures. Thus, the first criterion of effectiveness is that the use of these tools cannot be impossible or excessively difficult for those whose rights are negatively affected by an act of an administrative authority. In other words, legal protection cannot be merely a theoretical possibility for those involved, and they must be able to resort to its institutions and processes.

Furthermore, in its modern approach, legal protection, whatever specific instruments it consists of, must be more than the mere possibility to take action against the activities of state agencies. It must provide, in theory at least, feasible tools for protecting individual rights and legitimate interests. Certainly, the legal protection of rights may not guarantee that private parties will attain their goals in administrative or judicial proceedings, or that any decision making body should decide in their favour. However, the available institutions and processes must be able to give remedy against the illegal actions of governmental agencies when this unlawfulness violates individual rights or legitimate interests.

In summary, the exercise of public power imposing sanctions or duties on people cannot be immune to any legal review, but it must be subject to controlling mechanisms to protect individual rights and the objective legal order.

1.5 Effective legal protection in administrative law

According to a famous and catchy quotation, 'administrative law is a concretised constitutional law'.[16] Nevertheless, if we focus on the principle of effective legal protection in the field of administrative law, first, it must be clear exactly what the object of that protection is, and secondly, it should also be clarified what threatens the protected values. In this book, we use the concept of administrative law in its most common sense, presenting it as a special area or branch of law which is a set of legal principles and rules governing the powers, organisations and procedures of public administration, as well as the remedies against illegal administrative actions to protect individual rights and public interests.[17]

14 For a comparative view, see Rob Widdershoven, 'European Administrative Law' in René Seerden and Frits Stroink (eds.), *Administrative Law of the European Union, Its Member States and the United States: A Comparative Analysis* (Intersentia, Antwerpen-Groningen 2007).

15 Certainly, effectiveness may also be used in different connotations in administrative law. Most frequently, it means a condition of a capable and well-functioning government or, alternatively, an efficacious administrative action that achieves its goals.

16 Fritz Werner, 'Verwaltungsrecht als konkretisiertes Verfassungsrecht' (1959) 74 *Deutsches Verwaltungsblatt* 527–533.

17 John S. Bell, 'Comparative Administrative Law' in Mathias Reimann and Reinhard Zimmermann (eds.), *The Oxford Handbook of Comparative Law* (Oxford University Press, Oxford 2006) 1262.

The substance and forms of effective legal protection are deeply influenced by the major development paths of European administrative law, that is, according to mainstream literature and widely-held opinion, the traditions of French *droit administratif*, English administrative law and German *Verwaltungsrecht*.[18] Although all of them are based on a specific concept of the rule of law, and have special legal institutions and administrative cultures, the essential components of legal protection are similar.

First and foremost, legal protection is mostly suitable for defending constitutional and legal rights. Evidently, those rights that are explicitly or implicitly recognised by law can be legally protected. Presumably, the more specific the legal claim, the more effective the protection, in particular in administrative law, where the exercise of public power is most noticeable in everyday life. Administrative authorities most often decide in individual cases and they impose obligations or take action on rights as concrete legal entitlements (in legal phraseology: to do or not to do something, or to require the same from others). However, this may not always be true. As we will see in the country reports, normative acts may also be reviewed by courts in many countries, while the respect of general principles of law, like proportionality or the equal treatment of citizens, may be controlled as well.

While the protection of fundamental (constitutionally or legally recognised) rights is straightforward, the concept of legitimate interest is not so clear-cut: a legal right is itself a legally protected private interest, but in general, administrative law provides some protection for private interests even if they are not specified as a particular legal entitlement. It is much more a legal standard where the subject of a procedure or an action has a tangible stake for the affected persons. As parties in all legal procedures must be treated as persons of equal dignity, public authorities must always consider all of the relevant circumstances of the case and find a solution which respects the individual rights and personal interests to the greatest extent. A private interest is 'legitimate' if it is worthy of protection, that is as far as it exceeds the public interest or other private interests.

In reality, not only individuals or groups of people but also legal persons can be involved in administrative procedures, as far as they may also have certain rights and legitimate interests recognised by law. Thus, most procedural principles are applied to them as well. Perhaps the provision of legal aid is the only due process instrument from which legal persons may not benefit.

The next basic question concerns what encroachments these rights and legitimate interests should be protected against. Legal remedies may be given mainly against administrative acts. Normally, administrative authorities have to formalise their actions when they affect the rights and obligations of any private person. Otherwise, public authorities could decide at will whether to issue a formal act or not in the case, and, as only the formal administrative acts may be submitted for legal control, the scope of legal protection would depend on decision making of the public authority.

Although there is a great variety of definitions of administrative acts in the various countries, in the most general terms, these are legal acts – including individual and

18 Bernardo Sordi, '*Révolution, Rechtsstaat*, and the Rule of Law: Historical Reflections Ont He Emergence of Administrative Law in Europe' in Susan Rose-Ackerman and Peter L. Lindseth (eds.), *Comparative Administrative Law* (Edward Elgar, Cheltenham, Northampton 2010) 23.

normative ones – of administrative bodies, which are passed in the exercise of public authority and which may affect the rights and legitimate interests of citizens and legal persons. These are legal acts having a public law character (which means that they can be enforced by legitimate force) with the aim of having a legal effect. They must be enacted in the course of a formalised law-making process (regulations, normative acts) or administrative procedure[19] (individual decisions). In this respect, the interested parties are the persons and their groups and organisations whose interests are directly affected by an administrative act. Paradoxically, as far as legal protection is concerned, the absence of a decision – either because of a refusal to act, or an omission to do so – is also to be considered as an act, when an administrative body is obliged by law to make a decision in a case before it. The 'silence' of public administration, after a time specified by law, must be open to judicial review. In this case, the competent agency has to explain the reasons why it has not conducted the appropriate procedure or made a decision. It is also to be noted that certain fields of administrative activity are exempt from the accepted forms of legal protection. The actions of public authorities having a purely civil law character do not fall within the category of appealable decisions. Policy guidelines, concluding public contracts, public service delivery, organisational measures, management decisions and internal processes of governmental authorities are usually also exempt from legal challenges within the scope of administrative law, as these administrative actions do not normally directly affect individual rights or private interests. Yet this does not mean that even these actions are entirely immune from any external control. Civil law claims may be enforced by civil litigation, while internal actions can be subject to administrative supervision. But these actions and processes do not fall within our field of interest here, as they do not belong to the sphere of public power and are beyond the scope of administrative law.

One of the primary elements of the rights of fair process is surely the administrative procedure. This is a legally established mechanism of administrative decision making, adjudication and regulation concerning the rights and duties of private parties (natural persons or corporate organisations). The administrative procedure is understood as the decision making process of administrative bodies as defined by law.

The other domain of procedural rights is the judicial review of administrative acts. In this context, a judicial review involves the checking of the legality of an administrative act by a court with the power to adopt appropriate measures for restoring lawfulness, if necessary. A judicial process is also a legally binding procedure, but it has a lot of features that are distinct from those of the administrative procedure. First of all, the administrative authority and the court exert various kinds of powers and exercise different state functions. The administrative procedures usually have a non-adversarial character, this being the main difference from the judicial process. Sometimes the same sub-principle or right of legal protection is treated or used differently

19 Although the terms 'administrative process/procedure/proceeding' are usually used indiscriminately to refer to the formal and legalised way of decision making of public authorities in individual cases, in this book, we prefer the term 'administrative procedure', distinguishing it from the law-making process and judicial proceeding. It is to be noted that in some languages, the administrative and judicial proceedings are designated by different notions (like *Verwaltungsverfahren* versus *Verwaltungsprozess* in German).

in the administrative procedure and in the judicial process. The hearing, for example, does not form part of a cross-examination in the former, but it can be used instead for consultation or cooperation between the decision making body and the affected private parties. It is another distinctive characteristic of administrative procedures that they have two equally important objectives, as they are designed not only to protect individual rights and legitimate interests, but also to realise public interests. The latter must be achieved not only by defending the objective legal order, irrespective of the benefits of the private parties, but also through the most rational, effective and efficient administrative conduct. Although this dualistic rationale of administrative procedure is also characteristic of the judicial process, its mechanism is usually set in motion at the initiative of the directly interested parties in order to achieve their individual aims. In contrast, the administrative procedure is obligatory under certain circumstances, and can often be launched *ex officio*.

The dual purpose of administrative procedures is reflected in the multifunctional character of some fair process rights. Thus, while the participatory rights of the private parties are an important means for achieving the individual aims and protecting the clients' rights, they also provide tools for the fact-finding process of the administrative authority to ascertain the relevant circumstances of the given case. Furthermore, the indispensable right of the parties to represent their interests might also effectively contribute to the finding of the proper legal arguments necessary for the correct administrative decision.

In this book we explore all tools of effective legal protection in administrative law. While mainstream literature has for a long time concentrated on the judicial protection of rights, we examine the relevant instruments in all areas of administrative law, including the administrative decision making process itself, and other forms of rights-protection (like the ombudsman-type protection). Only the parliamentary accountability of government agencies is not discussed here, although it might have some legally relevant mechanisms, or might be able to promote individual rights. But the political control of administrative policy or decision making do not fall within the scope of administrative law, so it is not part of our focus here.

2 Justifications for the principle of legal protection

2.1 Rule of law justifications

For our purposes, the principle of effective legal protection means procedural fairness requiring the respect of a certain set of procedural rights. This is a requirement and component of the underlying principle of rule of law: the fundamental premise of this tenet is that the exercise of the public power is legitimate only if it is exerted according to and within the limits of the law. Although the classical versions of the rule of law (like the German *Rechtsstaat*, or the English rule of law) have some specialities, all manifestations of the principle have a common basis: public power is bound by law, and the rights of individuals must be protected against the illegal encroachment of the state. The major requirements of the principle of rule of law in administrative law are to keep public authorities within the sphere of their powers and responsibilities, and to ensure that they follow the relevant rules of decision making procedures. They require that a balance has to be struck between the individual rights and legitimate interests of all parties of the administrative procedures and the public interest for the efficient and effective operation of public administration. This balance appears, albeit with different emphases, throughout the whole process of administrative cases both in their administrative and judicial phases.

The principle of rule of law has direct implications for the justification of these rights, since in functional terms the procedural rights seem to have merely an instrumental role for guaranteeing the substantive rights of the private parties. Thus, if the desired outcome has been reached in a proceeding, the possible procedural irregularities do not make sense. Or even when the procedural error has apparently not influenced the final decision (whatever that may be), the faulty act should not be quashed. It might be said that in such cases the private or public interest for whose safeguard these guarantees were required have been ensured in another way. But the fair and due process has an inherent value for the rule of law, especially for legal certainty, as one of its most essential components. If this is so, this value must be irrespective of the particular outcome of a procedure, at least in the case of a serious breach of these principles.

Certainly, the proper application of procedural requirements itself does not make the decision legally valid or correct, as the substantive principles or rules might have been violated. Observing the requirements of fair process is a necessary, though not always satisfactory, condition for the right decisions in administrative law.

Even within their scope of responsibilities, administrative bodies can have a different degree of freedom to act. However, the procedural justice preserves its full importance when discretionary power (*freies Ermessen, pouvoir discrétionnaire*) is exercised. This is the case when no single right answer (or a sole legally binding decision) follows from the situation and, within the legal framework, some degree of choice is allowed to the administrative body. Discretionary powers can be conferred on public authorities for several reasons, for example, when the relevant circumstances cannot be foreseen, or the factual situation is so complex that the right decision can be taken only after the due consideration of all relevant facts of the case. The significance of compliance with fair process is particularly appreciated to avoid the arbitrariness of the administrative decision.

The importance of procedural fairness comes from the intrinsic position of the citizens and other private parties facing the administrative body, which acts in the administrative procedures as a representative of the state exercising public power. In administrative cases, the decision maker and the addressees are in a hierarchical relationship, as the former may make actions of its own imposing duties on the latter in a one-sided manner. This asymmetry needs to be counterbalanced in a fair trial, and the procedural rights of the clients are appropriate tools for this purpose. Nevertheless, there must be a delicate balance between the efficient and effective work of administration and the affected basic rights.

2.2 Human rights-based justifications

The other possible form of justification comes from a rights-based approach,[20] with the administrative procedural rights claiming that human dignity is only respected if

20 See e.g. Eva Storskrubb and Jacques Ziller, 'Access to Justice in European Comparative Law' in Francesco Francioni (ed.), *Access to Justice as a Human Right* (Oxford University Press, Oxford 2007) 178–204.

the individuals are treated fairly by the public authorities of the state. Those persons who cannot present their views in the procedure, or cannot rely on the impartiality of the public authorities in the course of the administrative adjudication in which their rights and interests are affected, are deprived of equal respect of dignity.[21]

The compliance of the administrative decision making with the requirements of both the standards of rule of law and fundamental rights is necessary to accept the adoption of administrative acts as the legitimate exercise of public power.[22] Even though a properly conducted procedure is only a necessary condition of legitimacy, though not sufficient on its own, the term of 'procedural legitimacy' seems to have become a widely-used autonomous concept.[23]

Legal protection has a particular significance in administrative law where the persons who are the addressees of the decisions of public authorities are inherently in a non-equal position with the decision maker. So the core value of this principle is that the affected citizens and corporate entities must be treated fairly in the processes of administrative activities.

3. What rights make up procedural fairness?

Procedural fairness is a set of procedural rights available to citizens for defending their rights against illegal actions of administrative bodies. These rights have different characters and importance even for the same people, depending on their position and the nature of the proceedings in which their cases are being settled.

In this book, we are interested in those 'procedural rights' which are employed to protect private rights and interests *vis-à-vis* the public authority or the adversarial party.

3.1 Substantive versus procedural rights

Effective legal protection as a basic entitlement encompasses a whole series of rights and procedural requirements. These rights can have different relevance, or the same rights can have more or less different functions in the various processes of administrative law. For our purpose, the 'relevant' rights are the so-called procedural rights, rather than substantive ones. Although this sort of differentiation is widely-used in subject literature,[24] these two categories often emerge without distinction, as a conglomerate of fundamental principles having different characteristics.[25] In fact, both

21 Sérvulo Correia, 'Administrative Due or Fair Process: Different Paths in the Evolutionary Formation of a Global Principle and of a Global Right' in Gordon Anthony, Jean-Bernard Auby, John Morison and Tom Zwart (eds.), *Values in Global Administrative Law* (Hart Publishing, Oxford 2011) 321.

22 For a discussion of the legitimating function of decision making procedures in general terms, see Niklas Luhmann, *Legitimation durch Verfahren* (Suhrkamp, Frankfurt am Main 2001).

23 Matthias Ruffert, 'Comparative Perspectives of Administrative Legitimacy' in Matthias Ruffert (ed.), *Legitimacy in European Administrative Law: Reform and Reconstruction* (Europa Law Publishing, Groningen 2011) 353–360.

24 See e.g. Hanns Peter Nehl, 'Administrative Law' in Jan M. Smits (ed.), *Elgar Encyclopedia of Comparative Law* (Edward Elgar, Cheltenham, Northampton 2006) 24–25.

25 See for example: *European Principles for Public Administration.* SIGMA Papers No. 27. OECD Publishing, Paris 1999. 8., which enumerates the most important principles of an imaginary 'European

European and national courts frequently refer to all of them together as the principles of administrative procedures without such a differentiation.

Conceptually, substantive rights are frequently held to exist for their own sake, constituting the 'material' part of administrative law.[26] In other words, they involve core values and interests of the relevant parties, and relate to the substance of the measures, like equality before the law, the right to sound (or good) administration, the principle of accountability, or such requirements as the principles of proportionality or the protection of legitimate expectations and vested rights.

Our work focuses on procedural rights of private parties enabling them to represent their legitimate rights and interests. The basic function of these rights is to enforce the substantive rights, providing formal tools and procedures for those who are affected by administrative decisions. These rights have a procedural character inasmuch as they influence administrative actions regardless of the merit of the particular cases.[27] As a matter of fact, they have an instrumental role as far as they provide tools for achieving and enforcing individual rights or other interests. These rights not only prevent administrative agencies from going beyond the boundaries of their legal mandate (i.e. they cannot do anything *ultra vires*), but also ensure the fair treatment of the parties throughout the whole decision making process.[28]

There is sometimes a differentiation between the thin and thick meaning of rule of law, that is between formal and substantive rule of law. In this project, the thin or formal aspects of rights, that is to say procedural rights, are highlighted. There are other classifications of rights and principles of administrative justice, placing due process rights under the heading of 'sound' or 'good' governance,[29] or differentiating 'material' and 'formal' principles.[30] Others postulate a new or 'fourth' generation of human rights as requirements or principles of 'good administration', on the grounds that the most important rights are entrenched in the European Charter of

---

Administrative Space' as follows: the principle of administration through law; the principles of proportionality, legal certainty, protection of legitimate expectations, non-discrimination, the right to a hearing in administrative decision making procedures, interim relief, fair conditions for access of individuals to administrative courts, non-contractual liability of the public administration. For the commonly shared 'European' principles of administrative law, see: Martin Shapiro, 'The Institutionalisation of European Administrative Space' in Alec Stone Sweet, Wayne Sadholtz and Neil Fligstein (eds.), *The Institutionalisation of Europe* (Oxford University Press, Oxford 2001) 99–110; Peter M. Huber, 'Grundzüge des Verwaltungsrechts in Europa – Problemaufriss und Synthese' in Armin von Bogdandy, Sabino Cassese and Peter M. Huber (eds.), *Handbuch Ius Publicum Europaeum: Band V Verwaltungsrecht in Europa: Grundzüge Grundzüge des Verwaltungsrechts in Europa* (C. F. Müller, Heidelberg 2014) 15–18.

26 However, some scholars claim that the principles of administrative law 'are largely procedural in character'. Carol Harlow, 'Global Administrative Law: The Quest for Principles and Values' (2006) 17 *The European Journal of International Law* 187, 192.

27 Anna Simonati, 'The Principles of Administrative Procedure and the EU Courts: An Evolution in Progress?' (2011) 4 *Review of European Administrative Law* 45, 46.

28 Shapiro (n. 25) 94.

29 See e.g. Mark I. Aronson, Bruce D. Dyer and Matthew Groves, *Judicial Review of Administrative Action* (3rd edn., Law Book Co, Sydney 2004) 1; Carol Harlow, 'Global Administrative Law: The Quest for Principles and Values' 195.

30 Karl-Peter Sommermann, 'Prinzipien des Verwaltungsrechts' in Armin von Bogdandy, Sabino Cassese and Peter M. Huber (eds.), *Handbuch Ius Publicum Europaeum: Band V Verwaltungsrecht in Europa: Grundzüge Grundzüge des Verwaltungsrechts in Europa* (C. F. Müller, Heidelberg 2014) 878–889.

Fundamental Rights.[31] Nevertheless, the classification of individual rights according to their substantive or procedural nature can better serve our undertaking of a wide-ranging comparison of the existing systems of rights-protection in administrative law than any other theoretical framework.

Certainly, it is often difficult to differentiate between 'substantive' and 'procedural' rights, and other conceptualisations may, of course, be plausible. Due or fair administrative process[32] could also be used for a conceptual framework. Whenever these concepts are explored or analysed, very similar components are discussed, like the principles of *audi alteram partem* or *nemo iudex in causa sua*, which are crucial issues in this book as well, since the right of the parties to participate in the proceedings where their rights and obligations are determined, or the impartiality of adjudication plays an important role in the system of procedural rights as they are understood here. However, we abandoned the general use of the term 'due process' as it primarily refers to the American constitutional terminology insofar as the Fifth and Fourteenth Amendments of the US Constitution require 'due process of law' for protecting the 'life, liberty or property' of citizens. It is worth noting that its American concept embodies not only procedural requirements but also substantive rights which fall outside the field of interest of this book.[33]

Another conceptual problem raises the question of how to distinguish the various procedural rights from each other. The particular rights can interrelate with each other, and do so in a complicated way. There is no authentic order of these rights, so the same lists of rights do not appear in national administrative law. The most usual procedural rights are:

- the right to be a party (and right to intervention);
- the right to be heard;
- the right to access to the relevant documents;
- the right to legal counsel;
- the duty to give reasons (for administrative decisions);
- the right to an administrative act within a reasonable time (as a guarantee against the 'silence' of the administrative body);
- the right to access to the court;
- the right to appeal.

A special category of these rights are 'participatory' in their nature, as they provide direct involvement of the parties in the decision making process.[34] Other rights enable the interested parties to seek justice via various institutions, so we refer to this collection of rights as 'access to justice'. In reality, these two groups of rights are closely

31 Klara Kanska, 'Towards Administrative Human Rights in the EU: Impact of the Charter of Fundamental Rights' (2004) 10 *European Law Journal* 296.

32 Correia (n. 21) 313–361.

33 Jerry L. Mashaw, 'Administrative Due Process: The Quest for a Dignitary Theory' (1981) 61 *Boston University Law Review* 885–931, and Jerry L. Mashaw, *Due Process in the Administrative State* (Yale University Press 1985); Peter L. Strauss, *An Introduction to Administrative Justice in the United States* (Carolina Academic Press, Durham 1989) 32–33.

34 Sabino Cassese, 'A Global Due Process of Law?' in Gordon Anthony, Jean-Bernard Auby, John Morison and Tom Zwart (eds.), *Values in Global Administrative Law* (Hart Publishing, Oxford 2011) 20–48.

linked, and indeed are often meaningless without the other. The simple entitlement to get involved in litigation without any more participatory rights, for example, does not provide real protection for the parties.

Sometimes, other procedural rights (or, alternatively, the public authorities' duties) are claimed, like the notice of the bringing of proceedings, the right to present evidence, the right to be notified of the final decision, etc. But the precise and complete list of the relevant rights depends on the criteria applied for identifying them, as they are of different levels of abstraction. The rights listed above are all 'composite' in the sense that they absorb many other accessory rights and instruments. Moreover, not all of these rights are available in each case, even when all of them are recognised by a national legal system. Their application can depend on the nature of the affected interests or can vary in the different phases of the various administrative proceedings. In certain cases, for example, the decision making body, balancing the competing interests, may determine which procedural requirements can be used and to what extent. Sometimes the costs of the administrative procedure, or the benefits to be expected, are more significant than providing a special tool for the private parties to promote their own rights or interests.

A lot of procedural principles and rules are not discussed in this book, even if they can be significant in the relevant proceedings. However, despite the fact that they are 'procedural' in their nature, they fall outside our field of interest since they have no protective function for private rights and interests, promoting instead effectiveness, efficiency or some other property of the administrative machinery. In addition, the majority of procedural rules are technical requirements imposing duties on administrative bodies to conduct affairs in a rational and transparent way, as well as on the private parties in order to ensure their cooperation with the decision making body during the whole process.

As has been mentioned, procedural rights can be divided into two groups. On the one hand, some of them ensure the effective participation of the citizens and other private parties in the administrative procedure. On the other, they open the way for parties to seek administrative justice by enforcing administrative acts in the cases affecting the clients' rights and legitimate interests, and to access to court as external controller of administration.

3.2 Participatory rights

Although the right of standing is especially important for access to legal remedies, and thus to administrative justice, it should not be forgotten that the right to be a party also has great significance for the original decision making process as well. Frequently, people may promote their interests and attain their goals by submitting an application to the competent body, requesting the legal recognition of an existing relationship or legal entitlement for doing (e.g. using or possessing) something. In this way, the administrative procedure itself often has a function of protecting or facilitating individual rights or private interests. In addition, this right also matters in the case of *ex officio* procedures or in any other administrative decision making processes when rights and legitimate interests of parties (be they citizens, groups or corporate organisations) are affected by an administrative act.

As we have seen above, the principle of rule of law requires that public authorities exercise their powers in a transparent way, complying with the related procedural rules and issuing legal acts. This requirement allows citizens to represent their interests by becoming parties in those procedures which directly influence their own lives. To support this kind of rights-protection, the operation of competent administrative authorities must be transparent for the public, and they must be obliged to notify all possible interested parties about the ongoing procedures, as well as clearly designating their administrative procedures or acts as such.

It is another matter how conditions are set by law for standing. Just as in review proceedings, the competent body has to check whether these conditions are met. However, once the right to be a party in the relevant procedure has been refused by a public authority, this must be considered in the same way as if the competent administrative body refused to make a decision in an ongoing case, and as such, it must be open to judicial review.

The law-maker may also provide this right for other people than those directly involved, if an administrative action affects a lot of people or has a great impact on their general interests, even though it only indirectly influences their lives. Thus, the law may allow certain social groups or organisations representing collective interests to take action against administrative acts that affect the protected area of life. Similarly, public authorities (mainly public prosecutors and ombudsmen) might be permitted to intervene in administrative procedures in order to protect public interests.

For the sake of effective legal protection even in this early stage of administrative cases, the right to be a party should be supported by some other sub-principles and rights. Thus, 'equality of arms' and the right to use the mother tongue (or at least the language that the client understands well) are indispensable elements of the principle of fair trial or procedural fairness.[35] While the former means that all parties have equal opportunity for access to the documents of the case or to submit evidence, the latter is a precondition for exercising participatory rights in the procedure. It is worth noting that the principle of equality of arms, on account of the inherent unequal position of the persons involved in the process compared to the decision making body, has a special significance in administrative disputes before the court. Thus, the proceeding is only to be considered fair if equal opportunities have been provided for the affected parties to influence the final administrative decision,[36] which is a prerequisite for fair and equal treatment of persons.

The right to be heard also belongs to the group of participatory rights. This appears to be so self-evident that one may be surprised that its general recognition in the national systems of administrative law only occurred in recent decades in many countries: in Austria in 1925, in Germany in 1978 and in Italy in 1990, while in France and the UK it has not yet been recognised by any statute.[37] Nevertheless, it might apply in administrative law, since the legal maxim of *audi alteram partem* or *audiatur et altera pars* ('listen to/hear the other side as well' or 'no man should be condemned unheard') was known already in ancient collections of legal maxims and law books.[38]

35 See e.g. Bruno Oppetit, *Philosophie du droit* (Dalloz-Sirey, Paris 1999) 117. For the jurisprudence of the ECtHR, see Pieter van Dijk, Godefridus J. H. Hoof, *Theory and Practice of the European Convention on Human Rights* (Martinus Nijhoff Publishers, The Hague, Boston 1998) 430.

36 Correia (n. 21) 327.

37 Cassese (n. 34) 59.

38 See e.g. Herbert Broom, *A Selection of Legal Maxims, Classified and Illustrated* (T. & J. W. Johnson & Co., Philadelphia 1874) 113–116; George Frederick Wharton, *Legal Maxims, with Observations and Cases*

This participatory right involves a guarantee that, if an administrative authority takes a decision, it must hear the view of the interested parties and it has multiple benefits. On the one hand, the parties may present their proposals and legal statements on the merit of the case and they may submit evidence in support of their position. Furthermore, this right enables the parties to check whether the facts in the case have been correctly established or described. Equally, the parties' statements allow the authority to obtain relevant information about the facts of the case and about the interests and legal opinions of the clients. The right must imply the obligation of the administrative authority to give due consideration to these opinions and suggestions – which must be reflected in the statement of reasons for the final decisions of the administrative authority in such a way that the appellant body or the court may check whether due consideration has taken place and the information and arguments of the parties have been correctly taken into account.

The active participation of the private parties is usually not required. However, if the applicant (or in a later phase, the complainant) refuses to take part in the procedure (e.g. refusing to make information available to the competent body), he or she has to bear the consequences of this, including the possible rejection of his/her application or appeal.

The hearing of the parties may be omitted in the case of a favourable decision, except when they possess information relevant to the final decision.

There are some special and additional functions of the right to be heard in the law-making process that are involved in administrative rule making. In such cases, persons or organisations who represent general interests or other values for the sake of many people might also be given this right. In this regard, there are mutual interests of cooperation for the decision making authority and the addressees of the administrative act, since the active participation of the parties gives the chance for the rule maker to estimate the possible impact of the various options and it may enhance the effectiveness of the normative acts by gathering relevant information, policy alternatives and suggestions. The legislator has, notwithstanding this, a wide range of appreciation to determine the entitled groups or corporate bodies.

The right to access to the relevant documents is also an indispensable ingredient of procedural fairness. This right rests on the assumption that a person is only able to protect effectively his or her rights and interests if he/she knows the relevant circumstances and facts of the case. It embraces access to the documents containing information about the matter. Normally, it also extends to the possibility to look into and make a copy of them. As with all other procedural rights, it may also be subject to certain restrictions imposed by law, such as for reasons of national security.

The right to use of the assistance of legal counsel should also be included among the tools available to citizens whose concern is under investigation by public authorities. In most administrative procedures, this is not necessary for the successful participation of the clients, whereas in judicial proceedings it may not be required by the court. At the same time, it cannot be prohibited, and the parties may not be sanctioned because of the use of a legal representative. So it is really a procedural right, rather than an obligation.

(Voorhis and Co. Law Publishers, New York 1878) 74; Seymour S. Peloubet, *A Collection Of Legal Maxims in Law and Equity – With English Translations* (New York 1880) 20.

The right to legal aid is another aspect of this privilege. It can be provided for those who lack sufficient resources to resort to the assistance of a lawyer. In parallel with the jurisprudence of the ECtHR,[39] legal aid can usually be provided both for legal representation or to cover the costs of proceedings. This right, or, conversely, the absence of legal aid is closely related to the principle of effective legal protection, because the poor financial situation of the potential or real parties of administrative procedures or litigation can result in denial of justice for them, preventing rightful claims from being submitted to court.

3.3 Access to administrative justice

3.3.1 Administrative protection

The right to the administrative act within a reasonable time is an essential component of legal protection of individual rights. The decision is the outcome of the whole process, by which the administrative body may resolve the case. No claim by citizens can be satisfied without it, because only a formal act may have a legal (and practical) effect. Thus, the right of individuals in their own case to an administrative decision is a guarantee against the 'silence' of the administrative body.

The silence of the administration means that the competent public authority, for whatever reason, fails to resolve the case, that is it does not make any decision on its merit within a reasonable time. The basis for legal protection in these cases is the legal fiction that the interested party's application has been virtually rejected or refused. One of the major requirements of the rule of law is the transparency of the decision making process of public authorities. It is an indispensable condition of the accountability of state agencies that they have to make their decisions in compliance with the relevant substantive and procedural rules. Otherwise, those who are directly affected by these decisions could remain unprotected.

If there is no administrative act to be challenged, another option for legal remedy is the private law claim referring to state liability. But even if this route is open for citizens who have been adversely affected by the behaviour of an administrative body, it is not an effective form of rights protection for several reasons. First, the civil law claim has its own prerequisites, as the claimant has to prove the damage, the unlawfulness of the behaviour of the administrative body and the causal relationship between the former and the latter. Secondly, civil litigation might be much longer and more costly than an administrative trial when the subject of the proceeding is only to ascertain whether the reviewed administrative act is legal or not. Then, the conduct of public administration can do non-material harm in individual rights or legitimate interests of citizens, so the redress provided by this sort of judicial procedure cannot be satisfactory.

In the absence of the adequate regulation, the court may consider all relevant circumstances to determine what is the reasonable time in a particular case. Several different conditions can be considered, except the lack of capacity (e.g. sufficient personnel) of the administrative body – the rights and legitimate interests of the citizens cannot depend on the equipment of administrative organs. In many countries,

39 Engström (n. 13) 57.

during the judicial process, the courts may issue interim rulings in order to eliminate or resolve procedural barriers, or to seek alternative ways to resolve the case. The purpose of these provisional judicial injunctions is to preserve the legal position of the parties in question without deciding the merit of the case.

The formal act of the administrative body is a necessary condition, though not sufficient in itself, for the correct and lawful closure of a procedure. The decision making authority has a duty to give reasons for its decisions. The objective of this requirement to give reasons is, first, that it makes it less likely that an administrative agency will act arbitrarily and capriciously, knowing that its decision can be reviewed based on these reasons. Secondly, this duty makes the review of the original decision easier for the appellate body and, furthermore, it has an additional function of legitimising the administrative act. Finally, it is an indispensable prerequisite for the effective legal protection of individual rights, because the lack of information about the reasons why the particular act has been adopted may make the right to defence impossible, or at least much more difficult. Thus, it is a precondition for the appellant to try to show that the reasons that have been given are unsatisfactory or mistaken.

The statement of reasons must be expressed in the decision, and it must include the grounds on which the court bases its decision. It would be exaggerated to require the administrative body to report on all relevant circumstances of the case, or the court to react to every piece of evidence or argument raised by the parties during the proceeding. However, the reasoning must be specific enough to enable understanding as to why the decision maker has decided the case in a certain way; the facts that have been determined and taken into account, as well as the legal grounds of the decision, are indispensable elements of the statement of reasons. If only legal issues are examined in the judicial appellate proceedings, the requirement to give reasons may be stricter for courts, specifying not only the established facts and legal acts on which the decision has been based, but also the evaluation of evidence and the reason why the court has not upheld the claims of the complainants. While the failure to give notification of the reasons can usually in itself provide grounds enough for the annulment of the administrative act, it is not necessary when the decision is favourable to the applicant and no adverse party takes part in the procedure.

As has already been mentioned, the adoption of the administrative act, that is to say the settlement of the issue at hand, may by itself be sufficient to satisfy the applicant's claim. When this is not the case, that is the decision is unfavourable to the applicant, the formal act becomes the object of all remedial processes.

In theory, administrative appeal is not necessary for the constitutional right of citizens to appeal against all public acts that adversely affect their rights and interests, provided that they may request a judicial review of those acts. Furthermore, it could be argued that it is not a real appeal, as the recourse to the same body or to a higher-level organ keeps the matter within the administrative hierarchy, where the appellate body is not really an independent forum, so one of the basic requirements of the right to appeal is not met (except when independent administrative tribunals adjudicate the recourses). It is easy to see that the original decision maker is the last one from whom real legal protection can be expected. As far as the superior body is concerned, as the argument may go, it represents and pursues the same interests or policies as the first instance authority, and therefore real remedy cannot be expected of it.

However, administrative remedy itself can be made a constitutional requirement for several reasons. First and foremost, it might be posited as a guarantee for the careful consideration of the applicant's claim. Apparently, the pure possibility of reconsideration of the case can promote the correct and lawful resolving of the matter. So the administrative appeal as an ordinary legal remedy available to all persons affected by a particular administrative decision can hardly be replaced by the judicial route, as administrative bodies use different standards in resolving the day-to-day problems of clients from the courts, which may only check the legality of the decision. This mechanism can then be an effective tool for filtering out those cases which – for whatever reason – should not go to courts, so it serves also to prevent an excessive caseload for the courts. For this purpose, the exhaustion of all available administrative recourse should be a precondition for starting a judicial review process.

It is a sub-principle of legal protection that all those persons who have been parties in an administrative procedure have the right to appeal to another body for review. Moreover, an administrative appeal cannot cause any irrational delay in the whole process, and the applicants must have a reasonable time to lodge a complaint with the court.

3.3.2 Judicial protection

The principle of effective judicial protection requires that natural and legal persons who have been adversely affected by an administrative decision must be able to enforce their rights before a court in a fair trial. Following from the principle of rule of law, all administrative acts should be subject to judicial review, including individual acts and administrative regulations when they might have direct effects on citizens' rights and interests. The scope of judicial review should extend to all questions of legality, so the courts must be able to check any breach of law, including misapplication of law, procedural errors and abuse of power. Judicial review must inspect not only the result of administrative procedures, but also the decision making process itself, as public authorities are bound to both substantive and procedural rules of law. Access to judicial review must be available without unreasonable burdens (e.g. high costs) to all citizens and legal persons whose rights and legitimate interests are directly affected.

Certainly, as with other rights of procedural fairness, access to courts can also be limited, if this is necessary for other legitimate reasons, and when the limitation is imposed in a way proportionate with that objective. Despite the basic principle of the general availability of the judicial route, there may be exceptions, as certain kinds of administrative acts may be excluded from the scope of judicial review. In this regard, the ancient legal maxim of *exceptio est strictissimae interpretationis* should prevail, so exceptions must be narrowly defined and need strong justification. Typically, governmental acts of a political nature (policy guidelines, statements), internal measures (organisational or management instructions) and contractual or other civil law actions and measures count among the non-reviewable administrative acts. This does not necessarily mean that these measures are completely exempt from any external control, but they do not fall within the scope of administrative judicial review.

A separate issue is the judicial review of normative rules (statutory instruments, administrative regulations, ordinances, etc.) of administrative bodies. Where administrative regulations are also subject to judicial control, this task is often (but not always) carried out by different courts and is based on different procedural rules.

According to some scholars, the use of special provisions is justified, as the application of the same procedural rules that were developed for the judicial review of individual acts would be impractical and inappropriate for reviewing normative measures.[40]

As for the procedural limitations, the requirement of the exhaustion of all available remedies is a rational precondition for the judicial route; however, in this regard, only real appeals should be taken into account, when the appealing authority has a power to provide redress. Furthermore, the legislator, for the sake of legal certainty, may determine a time-limit for access to court. In doing so, different deadlines may be set by law for launching an administrative dispute before the court, depending on the subject of the claim. The initiation of the judicial process may be subject to reasonable charge determined by law. Court fees have twofold functions; first, to obtain financial resources for the judicial proceedings; and secondly, to weed out the apparently unestablished requests or petty cases which could overburden the courts. But the payment obligation should not impose an impossible burden on those who seek justice against administrative decisions which have an adverse effect on their rights and interests.

In a judicial appeal, the applicant may ask the court to declare an administrative act illegal and annul it (partially or completely); to forbid the administrative body from carrying out an illegal activity; to recognise or declare a legal relationship, an entitlement or a right of the claimant; or to order the administrative agency to pay compensation for damages caused by an unlawful action. In fact, the courts may have different powers depending on the nature of the matter concerned in the judicial review process. In Anglo-Saxon systems, for example, the judicial review and the 'merit' review are often distinguished from one another.[41] Another distinction is also made in terms of whether the court has full power to change, annul or confirm the examined administrative act, or if it may only annul the illegal decision and send back the case to the administrative body that made the decision at first instance. The return of the case and the repetition of the whole procedure may cause a waste of time. However, the logic of this form of legal protection is that it might be better for both the related private and public interests if the administrative body, which is closest to the parties and has expertise and local knowledge, conducts the decision making process to repair the legal defects of its own first act, too.

4 The institutions of legal protection

4.1 Administrative bodies, ombudsmen and tribunals

Administrative justice needs institutions through which effective legal protection can be realised. As we do not simplify legal protection to the judicial protection, administrative bodies which have the competence to settle the cases of individuals, or to issue administrative regulations, belong to our field of interest. We understand

40 Türk (n. 3) 126.

41 Peter Cane and Leighton Macdonald, *Principles of Administrative Law* (2nd edn., Oxford University Press, Oxford 2012) 209–237; Peter Cane, 'Judicial Review and Merits Review: Comparing Administrative Adjudication by Courts and Tirbunals' in Susan Rose-Ackerman and Peter L. Lindseth (eds.), *Comparative Administrative Law* (Edward Elgar, Cheltenham, Northampton 2013) 426–448.

administrative authorities[42] as entities or persons entitled to issue administrative acts in their own range of responsibility. These bodies are governmental authorities (other than legislative bodies or courts), which affect the rights of private parties through adjudication, rule-making, investigating and other forms of behaviour.[43] Notably, the exercise of public power can be conferred by law to private organisations. Since the power to take legally enforceable decisions or measures is the prerogative of the public authorities (as agencies of the state), such an entitlement must be exceptional and requires serious reasons.

Ombudsmen do not have the power to invalidate administrative acts or to oblige administrative authorities to do or to refrain from doing something. Instead, they use persuasion, publicity and commitment to fair and transparent public administration. They usually hold wide-ranging investigatory powers and the right to initiate different sorts of procedures (supervisory, disciplinary, civil or criminal) and to make recommendations for law-making bodies. However, they may only make non-binding suggestions, as the administrative agencies concerned are not bound to accept their solution proposals in case of maladministration. On account of the relatively weak powers of the ombudsmen, they do not represent the most effective tools for legal protection. Moreover, this institution is more suitable for the redress of infringements of legitimate interests, rather than for the remedy of the violation of rights, as the ombudsmen in most countries deal with maladministration and not (or only indirectly) with the legality of administrative acts.

Legal protection is also provided by independent tribunals and other special commissions, however they are classified; they may be considered as parts of the administration, or as independent (mostly quasi-judicial) bodies. The procedures of administrative tribunals are usually cheaper, quicker and more flexible than those of the courts, and they may be mandated to adjudicate recourses against administrative decisions. Since they specialise in a particular area of administration or public service, they have the necessary expertise for the proper judgment of the facts of the case before them. They can be efficient and effective enough to manage a high volume of similar cases and are thereby able to disencumber the courts.

4.2 Courts

As a matter of fact, judicial review is the primary field of legal protection, and in most countries, the courts are the protagonists of legal protection in administrative law. They can be organised completely independently from the ordinary courts, or they can constitute a separate branch of the general judicial system, or administrative acts may be reviewed by ordinary courts. It does not really matter which model is followed by a country. The point is the admissibility to the judicial route (conditions of standing), as access to courts is a fundamental part of the principle of rule of law. Moreover, the scope of judicial review of administrative acts is much more important than the organisational system in which these disputes may be

42 The terms 'administrative authorities/bodies/agencies/organs' are used interchangeably throughout the book acknowledging that the different names might signify distinct legal or administrative status in the various countries (see e.g. the special legal standing of the regulatory agencies).

43 Kenneth Davis, *Administrative Law and Government* (West, St Paul 1975) 6.

settled. Whatever organisational arrangements exist in a country, the guarantees of the judiciary (like impartiality or the irremovability of judges) and the accessories of judicial processes (like adversarial process, legal expertise) must prevail.

Traditionally, the administrative procedure and judicial review of administrative acts have taken place consecutively, as the subject of the judicial process is the review of the final decisions of administrative bodies, having legal force according to administrative law. It is true that, in frequent cases, when the court annuls the administrative act and instructs the competent public authority to take a new (lawful) decision, the administrative procedure may begin again, but the administrative and the judicial procedures still remain intact and separate from each other. Today, the administrative and judicial phases are often intertwined, as the court may usually issue interim actions or injunctions requiring the administrative bodies to take missing decisions or to correct a procedural irregularity in order to prevent an apparently illegal final decision.

Similarly to that of the administrative procedure, the judicial process also has a double function, once its mechanism has been activated. The mission of the courts in administrative trial cases is to remedy administrative offences against individual rights as well as to remove the unlawful acts. The role of the courts in the protection of the objective legal order can be demonstrated by the mechanism of the annulment of an illegal action, as not only the unlawful violation of individual rights, but also any serious breach of the relevant law can lead to the repeal of the erroneous administrative acts.

Courts may adjudicate on not only the requests of the applicants to review an administrative act, but the extraordinary appeals as well. These recourses may be submitted against enforceable judicial decisions. This is not, however, a normal or usual form of legal protection; on the contrary, it is exceptional, and it serves primarily for the protection of the objective legal order (legality), rather than of individual rights and legitimate interests. Thus, it is a device to ensure the uniform application of law by courts, or to establish precedents for resolving legal problems of major importance. Nevertheless, this route might offer legal protection, even if that is not the main function of this proceeding.

4.2.1 The intensity of judicial control of administrative acts

The courts may be bestowed with reformatory or cassatory powers by law. While the former means full power for the administrative judge, including the ability to change the administrative act, the latter extends only to the annulment of the unlawful decision, when the case typically cannot be settled or closed by the court.

The degree of judicial intervention is a crucial problem of administrative justice. It can be formulated as a normative claim that the greater the power that is bestowed on public authorities, the more strictly the judicial review of administrative acts should be implemented.[44] The question is how far the courts may intervene in the merit of the case. The answer is not as simple as it seems to be at first glance. When only one possible solution follows from the statutes, for example, it can be practical to conclude

44 For a similar claim in European administrative law, see Jürgen Schwarze, 'Judicial Review of European Administrative Procedure' (2004) 68 *Law and Contemporary Problems* 105.

the whole proceeding instead of sending it back to the administrative body (which could lawfully only make the same decision) for reconsideration. However, according to conventional wisdom, the function of the courts is only to guarantee the lawfulness of the administrative acts, not to make decisions instead of public authorities.

One possible extreme option is judicial minimalism[45] using a 'manifest error test', accepted by EU administrative law,[46] annulling an administrative act only in the case of grave and evident factual mistake or error in law. This kind of judicial behaviour can be encouraged by statutes restricting the administrative judge's jurisdiction to the annulment of an illegal decision. This approach is grounded in the principle of separation of powers: the assessment of facts might be a matter of judgment guided by policy considerations, but the courts have no right to substitute their own policy choices for those of the responsible administrative agencies.

In contrast to the deferential approach, the law may entrust the courts to check whether the contested decision of the administrative body is based on reliable and accurate proof, and whether the decision maker has evaluated them in a correct manner. But if the court is able to check even the correctness of the exercise of administrative discretion, in most cases, it can be empowered to settle and close the dispute itself, without taking on the role of administration.

Behind these alternatives are two different philosophies about the true function of the (administrative) court;[47] whether they are expected to find the right solution to the underlying legal question, seeking substantive administrative justice, or whether the function of judicial review is simply to verify the procedural fairness of the administrative decision making process while disregarding the merit of the case.

It is very difficult to determine the limits of legitimate judicial intervention concerning the merits of administrative cases. The separation between administrative and judicial functions is particularly difficult in those cases where the administrative authority has a discretionary power. The wider this power is, the more careful the judicial encroachment is into the sphere of public administration. It is a widespread view that the court may not review the outcome of the discretionary power of the administrative authority. According to this approach, it is the sphere of public administration to balance the public and private interests in individual cases. The administrative bodies, which promote and implement public policy, are equipped with appropriate resources and expertise to consider all relevant circumstances of the particular situations and to make decisions that best serve policy goals and the common good. However, it is also beyond any doubt that administrative discretionary power must be exercised only within the framework of certain substantive principles, like proportionality, equal treatment or legitimate expectations. It is nevertheless strange to say that the courts should not review the administrative balancing of the rival interests of the case, as long as the outcome of such a balance is not contrary, for instance, to the proportionality principle. While checking compliance with the procedural rules seems to be a purely legal question and does not raise any problems of the separation between the administrative activity and judicial authority, a delicate

45 Cass R. Sunstein, *Legal Reasoning and Political Conflict* (Oxford University Press, Oxford 1996).

46 Craig (n. 1) 409.

47 Jean-Marie Whoerling, 'Judicial Control of Administrative Authorities in Europe. Toward a Common Model' (2006) 6 *Hrvatska Javna Uprava* 39.

balance between judicial activism and self-restraint is needed for the judicial examination of the administrative decision regarding whether all relevant facts of the particular situation have been taken into consideration, the choice of the applied sanctions by the administrative body is correct, or the limitation of the legitimate expectations of the appellant is proportionate to the public interest under the given conditions.

Whatever powers are vested in the administrative court, if it finds an administrative act unlawful, it must at least be able to redress the situation by repealing it partly or fully and, if necessary, to refer the case back to the administrative body for reconsideration and for a new decision that complies with the judicial ruling. The court should also have the power to award compensation for damages caused by an illegal act.

It is to be noted that, in general, the breach of a procedural rule itself may not be enough reason to quash an administrative decision; it is also necessary that the irregularity has resulted in a violation of an individual right or legitimate interest whose protection is the objective of the procedural rules. In other words, the general measure of the invalidation of an administrative act is that its content would have been different (supposedly, more favourable for the applicant), if the omitted procedural rule had been followed. At the same time, there are certain procedural guarantees that are considered so substantial that their breach leads in any case to the invalidation of the act. For example, the duty to give reasons for an unfavourable decision is strongly binding in all cases, so the lack of the statement of reasons represents serious illegality and is sanctioned by annulment.

4.2.2 Basic procedural features of administrative litigation

Administrative litigation, like any other sort of judicial proceeding, must take place under strict procedural conditions. It is not a principal issue, however, whether or not these processes have special procedural rules; they may be conducted by applying the general (e.g. civil law) rules. Such disputes may be settled in an inquisitorial or adversarial process, even though these forms cannot be sharply separated from each other. In the first case, the judge oversees the conflict between the parties, seeking arguments and establishing the relevant facts of the case. In the alternative model, he/she is a neutral arbitrator listening to the evidence and arguments submitted by the parties during the process.

Other procedural principles will also be discussed in this book. The *non ultra petita* principle means that the powers of the court are limited to what is conferred upon it by the parties, so the court may not go beyond the framework of the plea submitted by the plaintiff. *Ultra petita* means the opposite; the court is not tied to the claim of the plaintiff. There is a clear link between the use or non-use of the *ultra petita* principle and the basic functions that are attributed to the courts. Where the defence of public interest and objective legal order is just as important as the protection of individual rights, *ultra petita* judgments have a greater chance. But if the judicial review serves primarily as a tool of effective legal control in defence of individual rights, the principle of *non ultra petita* is more plausible, since the only objective of the complaint is to seek justice.

For the aim of effective legal protection, the principle of *reformatio in peius* also has implications for both administrative procedures and judicial processes. By this principle, the second instance administrative body is not bound by the decision of the public authority delivered in first instance, in the sense that it may place the complainant in a worse position than he or she was in beforehand. This power can be given for a more effective provision of public interest, even at the expense of the claimant's private interests. Of course, with regard to the inherent nature of the right to appeal/court, the law-maker may prohibit the appellate administrative organ or the court from making a decision which adversely affects the claimant's position.

All these definitions and requirements may facilitate the wide-ranging comparison that is attempted in the following chapters. However, we must not forget that all concepts, institutions and procedures have to be examined in its own context, and all comparisons have serious inherent limits. But this should not discourage us: the principle of effective legal protection in administrative law is important enough to be studied in a comparative perspective.

2 Effective legal protection in the European legal order

Christoph Görisch

1 Foundation of the principle of effective legal protection in European union law

The principle of effective legal protection is mentioned explicitly in the primary law of the European Union in Art. 19 para 1 subpara 2 TEU (Treaty on European Union): 'Member States shall provide remedies sufficient to ensure effective legal protection in the fields covered by Union law.'[1] But it follows already from the first subparagraph of the same provision, according to which the European Court of Justice has got the general obligation to 'ensure that in the interpretation and application of the Treaties the law is observed', that the principle not only applies to the Member States when they are implementing Union law, but also to the Union itself.[2]

More specifically, Art. 47 CFR (Charter of Fundamental Rights) – in conjunction with Art. 6 para 1 TEU – as 'perhaps the most important provision of the Charter'[3] guarantees the right 'to an effective remedy and to a fair trial' as a basic right within 'the scope of Union law' according to Art. 51 CFR.[4] The explanations to the Charter, which were 'drawn up as a way of providing guidance in [its] interpretation' and

1 Cf also the declaratory emphasis of the requirement of 'necessary provisions on legal safeguards' in the fields of the Common Foreign and Security Policy and the Area of Freedom, Security and Justice according to Arts. 75 para 3 and 215 para 3 TFEU ([Treaty on the Functioning of the European Union] in connection with Declaration [No 25] on Arts. 75 and 215 TFEU, annexed to the Final Act of the Intergovernmental Conference which adopted the Treaty of Lisbon); furthermore – with regard to the particular field of civil matters and therefore largely without relevance in the field of administrative law – Art. 67 para 4 TFEU, according to which the 'Union shall facilitate access to justice, in particular through the principle of mutual recognition of judicial and extrajudicial decisions in civil matters', and Art. 81 para 2 TFEU, according to which the Union 'shall adopt measures [for the purpose of development of judicial cooperation in civil matters] aimed at [. . .] (e) effective access to justice'.

2 Failing to take account of the connection between both subparas, A. Arnull, 'The Principle of Effective Judicial Protection in EU Law: An Unruly Horse?' (2011) 36 *EL Rev* 51, 53 n. 19 comments that the first subpara 'seems out of place in Art. 19' and 'should really have been included at the end of Art. 4 (3) TEU' instead.

3 D. Shelton in S. Peers, T. Hervey, J. Kenner and A. Ward (eds.), *The EU Charter of Fundamental Rights* (Hart, Oxford and Portland 2014) para 47.42 (from a comparative perspective).

4 Cf the explanations of the Charter, OJ 2007 C 303, p. 32 with reference to Case 5/88 – *Wachauf* [1989] ECR 2609; Case C-260/89 – *ERT* [1991] ECR I-2925; Case C-309/96 – *Annibaldi* [1997] ECR I-7493; consenting Shelton (n. 3) para 47.49; disagreeing T. Tridimas, *The General Principles of EU Law* (2nd edn., Oxford University Press, Oxford 2006) 456, assuming a more restrictive interpretation of Art. 51 CFR; as to this discussion more generally, e.g., M. Borowsky in J. Meyer (ed.), *Charta der Grundrechte der Europäischen Union* (4th edn., Nomos, Baden-Baden 2014) Art. 51 paras 24–30b (with numerous references).

'shall be given due regard by the courts' (Art. 52 para 7 CFR),[5] refer to Arts. 6 and 13 ECHR (European Convention for the Protection of Human Rights) and to the ECJ case law as 'sources' of the basic right. It is emphasised that 'in Union law the protection is more extensive' compared to the Convention rights. The Charter guarantees in Art. 47 para 1 the right to an effective remedy not only before any 'authority' (Art. 13 ECHR), but 'before a court'; this corresponds with the inseparable connection between legal and judicial protection according to Art. 19 TEU. Furthermore (unlike Art. 6 para 1 ECHR), the right to a fair hearing according to Art. 47 para 2 CFR 'is not confined to disputes relating to civil law rights and obligations', but is generally applied. 'Nevertheless, in all respects other than their scope, the guarantees afforded by the ECHR apply in a similar way to the Union.'[6]

Even before the Lisbon Treaty with the codification of the principle of effective legal protection in the aforementioned provisions of primary law came into force on 1 December 2009, specific contents of the principle were 'widely acknowledged by secondary law', i.e. in the fields of consumer law or public procurement legislation or the right of free movement within the territory of the Union.[7] As 'a general principle of Union law', the right to an effective judicial remedy was originally 'enshrined' by the case law of the ECJ in 1986.[8] The seminal judgment of the ECJ in the Case *Johnston* also originated in the application of a secondary law provision. The 1976 directive (76/207/EEC) on equal treatment for men and women as regards access to employment provides in Art. 6 that all persons who consider themselves wronged by discrimination must be able to pursue their claims by judicial process. The court pointed out that the 'requirement of judicial control stipulated by that article reflects a general principle of law which underlies the constitutional traditions common to the Member States'.[9] This was a decisive shift of approach from a dogmatic point of view. The court had already referred to the requirement of effective legal protection at an earlier date, but from a different perspective.[10] In its former judgments in the Cases *REWE-Zentralfinanz* and *COMET* in 1976, the Court mentioned a duty of

5 Cf ECJ Case C-129/14 PPU – *Spasic* [2014] ECLI:EU:C:2014:586 paras 54–55; Case C-583/11 P – *Inuit* [2013] ECLI:EU:C:2013:625 para 97 with further references; see also the opinion of Advocate General Kokott in ECJ Case C-17/10 – *Toshiba Corporation and others* ECLI:EU:C:2011:552 points 41, 54; more detailed K. Lenaerts, J. A. Gutiérrez-Fons, *To Say What the Law of the EU Is*. EUI Working Paper AEL 2013/9 (European University Institute, San Domenico di Fiesole 2013) 41–46.

6 OJ 2007 C 303, pp. 29–30; as to the ECHR-guarantees in particular, cf in detail the report of *Marten Breuer* in this volume.

7 L. M. Ravo, 'The Role of the Principle of Effective Judicial Protection in the EU and Its Impact on National Jurisdictions' in Edizioni Universitá di Trieste (ed.), *Sources of Law and Legal Protection* (Edizioni Università di Trieste, Trieste 2012) 101, 106, with reference to Directives 93/13/EEC, 89/665/EEC and 2004/38/EC; more detailed and with further examples A. Arnull, 'The Principle of Effective Judicial Protection in EU Law: An Unruly Horse?' (2011) 36 *EL Rev* 51, 63–68; as to the field of environmental law in particular, see below, around ns. 40–47.

8 See the explanations of the Charter, OJ 2007 C 303, p. 29 with reference to ECJ, Case 222/84 – *Johnston* [1986] ECR 1651 and further references to ECJ Case 222/86 – *Heylens* [1987] ECR 4097; Case C-97/91 – *Borelli* [1992] ECR I-6313. With regard to Art. 19(1) subpara 2 TEU cf also Arnull (n. 7) 51, 53 with reference to ECJ Case C-50/00 *P – Unión de Pequeños Agricultores* [2002] ECR I-6677 para 41.

9 ECJ, Case 222/84 – *Johnston* [1986] ECR 1651 para 18 (with additional reference to Arts. 6, 13 ECHR).

10 For a detailed analysis of the relationship between both approaches see S. Prechal and R. Widdershoven, 'Redefining the Relationship Between "Rewe-effectiveness" and Effective Judicial Protection' (2011) 4–2 *R.E.A.L.* 31–50; Ravo (n. 7) 101, 111–122; cf also, e.g., D. J. Rhee, 'The Principle of Effective

'ensuring the legal protection which citizens derive from [. . .] Community law'. But the court based this duty with regard to the obligations of the Member States on the 'principle of cooperation' [now Art. 5 para 3 TEU] in conjunction with the 'direct effect of the provisions of Community law',[11] not on the principle of effective legal protection as a separate requirement as was later acknowledged in *Johnston* (which also concerned Member States' obligations).[12] In the end, the general principle of effective legal protection 'to which expression is now given by [Art. 47 CFR]'[13] is rooted in the (even more general) rule of law as a framework principle according to Art. 2 TEU.[14]

2 Institutional system of legal protection

The explanations of the Charter emphasise that the 'inclusion of this precedent (*scilicet* the aforementioned case law starting from *Johnston*) in the Charter has not been intended to change the system of judicial review laid down by the Treaties'.[15] This system constitutes the institutional framework within which the principle of effective legal protection is valid. Instead of providing for the creation of 'Union courts' in the single Member States,[16] Art. 19 para 1 TEU is based on the premise that 'the guardians of [the] legal order and the judicial system of the European Union are the Court of Justice and the courts and tribunals of the Member States'. The ECJ assumes that this 'system [. . .] is [. . .] a complete system of legal remedies and procedures designed to ensure review of the legality of acts of the institutions'.[17] At the 'core' of this system, the action for annulment provided in Art. 263 TFEU allows the 'direct review of the legality of binding Union measures before the Union courts', whereas 'the national courts are the bodies to which individuals may turn whenever action or failure to act on the part of national authorities or other individuals infringes rights conferred on them by Union law'.[18] The supremacy of the ECJ over the national courts within the

---

Protection' (2011) 16 *JR* 440, 443–444; A. Ward in S. Peers, T. Hervey, J. Kenner, A. Ward (eds.), (n. 3) paras 47.247–251.

11 ECJ, Case 33/76 – *Rewe-Zentralfinanz* [1976] ECR 1989 para 5; Case 45/76 – *Comet* [1976] ECR 2043 para 13.

12 As to this development cf. e.g. – more or less detailed – K. Lenaerts, I. Marselis and K. Gutman, *EU Procedural Law* (Oxford University Press, Oxford 2014) paras 4.02 (n. 4), 4.05, 4.07; Ravo (n. 7) 101, 103–108.

13 ECJ Case C-69/10 – *Samba Diouf* [2011] ECR I-7151 para 49 with further references.

14 ECJ Case C-354/04 P – *Gestoras Pro Amnistía* [2007] ECR I-1579 para 51; C-355/04 P – *Segi* [2007] ECR I-1657 para 51; cf also, e.g., C. Görisch, *Demokratische Verwaltung durch Unionsagenturen* (Mohr Siebeck, Tübingen 2009) 381–382 with numerous further references to the ECJ case law; furthermore the explanations of the Charter, OJ 2007 C 303, p. 30 with reference to ECJ Case 294/83 – *Les Verts* [1986] ECR 1339; consenting Shelton (n. 3) para 47.49. As to the additional competence of the Union to monitor compliance with the principle on the national level according to Arts. 7, 49 TEU, which will not be examined here, cf more generally European Commission, MEMO/16/2017 (1 June 2016) on the Rule of Law Opinion concerning the situation in Poland.

15 OJ 2007 C 303, p. 29.

16 Cf the reflection on this issue by Lenaerts, Marselis, Gutman (n. 12) para 2.02.

17 ECJ opinion 1/09 [2011] ECR I-1137 para 66, 70.

18 Lenaerts, Marselis, Gutman (n. 12) paras 2.02 (with reference to ECJ Case 26/62 – *Van Gend & Loos* [1963] ECR 1, 12), 7.02. As to the complementary function of Arts. 258, 265 TFEU with respect to Art. 263 TFEU see below, n. 23.

system[19] is guaranteed by the procedure of preliminary ruling according to Art. 267 TFEU. Although this provision contains no explicit obligation to make a reference for such a preliminary ruling for those national courts against whose decisions there is still a judicial remedy under national law, the ECJ held in *Foto Frost* that no national court has 'the power to declare acts of the Community institutions invalid'. The Court argued from the 'purpose' of the preliminary ruling procedure 'to ensure that Community law is applied uniformly by national courts'. Additionally, the ECJ refers to Art. 263 TFEU and assumes that this provision 'gives the Court exclusive jurisdiction to declare void an act of a Community institution'. Consequently, 'the coherence of the system requires that where the validity of a Community act is challenged before a national court the power to declare the act invalid must also be reserved to the Court of Justice'.[20]

3 Substance of the principle

On substance, concentrating on the legal protection in a narrow sense (judicial protection),[21] access to a court has to be regarded as the basic question (concerning the question whether judicial proceedings take place at all),[22] followed by the determination of minimum standards of the court procedure as a 'fair trial' (concerning the question how judicial proceedings take place) and additional procedural aspects (including rights under the administrative procedure).

3.1 Access to a court

In the compound judicial system of the EU constituted by Art. 19 TEU in conjunction with Arts. 263 and 267 TFEU in particular,[23] access to a court means access either to the Union or to the national courts. In addition to the grant of access in substance as described in the following, the 'realisation of access to justice'[24] demands legal aid where necessary according to Art. 47 para 3 CFR; this right, which may also apply to

19 Cf also the formulation in ECJ Case 294/83 – *Les Verts* [1986] ECR 1339 para 23: 'the treaty established a complete system of legal remedies and procedures designed to *permit the court of Justice* to review the legality of measures adopted by the institutions' (emphasis added).

20 ECJ Case 314/85 – *Foto Frost* [1987] ECR 4199 paras 15, 17; cf. also Lenaerts, Marselis, Gutman (n. 12) para 10.01, more detailed paras 3.59–60.

21 As to the particular role of *judicial* protection in the complex system of legal protection see – from a comparative point of view – M. Kayser, 'Rechtsschutz und Kontrolle' in A. V. Bogdandy, S. Cassese and P. M. Huber (eds.), *Handbuch Ius Publicum Europaeum V* (C. F. Müller, Heidelberg 2014) § 91 paras 37–39.

22 Cf the opinion of Advocate General Jääskinen in ECJ Case C-509/11 – *ÖBB-Personenverkehr* ECLI: EU:C:2013:167 point 76: the 'right of access to a Court, [. . .] forms the heart of the principles established by the Court under the rubric of effective judicial protection'; consenting K. Pabel, 'Justizgrundrechte' in C. Grabenwarter (ed.), *Europäischer Grundrechteschutz* (Nomos, Baden-Baden 2014) § 19 para 35.

23 As to the possibility of individual legal protection by an action for failure to fulfil obligations under Art. 258 TFEU and as to the action for failure to act under Art. 265 TFEU as a counterpart to the action for annulment see, e.g., T. v. Danwitz, 'Rechtsschutz in der Europäischen Union' in A. Hatje and P.-C. Müller-Graff (eds.), *Europäisches Organisations- und Verfassungsrecht* (Nomos, Baden-Baden 2014) § 13 paras 8–9,

24 L. Holopainen in S. Peers, T. Hervey, J. Kenner and A. Ward (eds.), (n. 3) para 47.226.

legal persons, 'may cover both assistance by a lawyer and dispensation from payment of the costs of proceedings'.[25]

3.1.1 Union courts

As already mentioned, at the 'core' of the judicial system of the EU the action for annulment allows direct protection even for individuals against Union measures on the Union level according to Art. 263 para 4 TFEU.[26] On several occasions, the more narrowly formulated predecessors of this provision have been interpreted in a broad sense by the ECJ to ensure effective judicial protection. The famous seminal case *Les Verts* dealt with an action for annulment of a political party against a decision of the European Parliament concerning the allocation of appropriations in the General Budget. The ECJ recognised the Parliament as a potential defendant due to the 'complete system' of judicial protection drawn up by the Treaties although the Parliament was not yet explicitly mentioned in the enumeration of potential defendants against an action for annulment at that time.[27] With reference to this landmark decision the General Court (resp. in old terms: the Court of First Instance) accepted an action for annulment against detrimental measures of Union agencies (as institutions which are now mentioned in Art. 263 para 1 clause 2 in conjunction with para 5 TFEU, but have not been mentioned in the Treaties at all before Lisbon).[28] Equally, the ECJ recognised in *Kadi* the admissibility of actions for annulment against restrictive Union measures, like freezing of funds and economic resources, in the area of common foreign and security policy even before Arts. 24 para 1 subpara 2 clause 6 TEU, 275 para 2 TFEU explicitly established the respective jurisdiction of the ECJ under particular circumstances.[29]

Still, despite numerous requests in the judicial literature and beyond[30] for a change of evaluation due to the principle of effective legal protection, the ECJ maintains in the recent *Inuit* judgment its strict interpretation of the rules on the admissibility of individuals' actions for annulment as regards the specific classification of the contested act. A number of *Inuit* seal hunters brought to the European courts an action for annulment against a Parliament and Council regulation containing new rules on seal hunting which the *Inuit* considered incompatible with the fundamental freedoms

25 ECJ Case 279/09 – *DEB* [2010] ECR I-13849 paras 27–62 (quote: 48). See also n. 40.

26 As to the foundations of the concrete Treaty provisions on the judicial system of the Union see also below, around n. 34.

27 ECJ Case 294/83 – *Les Verts* [1986] ECR 1339 para 23; cf also – in turn – the recognition as a privileged applicant in ECJ Case C-70/88 – *Parliament/Council* [1990] ECR I-2041 paras 13–27.

28 CFI Case T-411/06 – *Sogelma* [2008] ECR II-2771 paras 33–57; GC Case T-70/05 – *Evropaïki Dynamiki* [2010] ECR II-313 paras 61–75.

29 ECJ Joined Cases C-402/05 P and C-415/05 P – *Kadi and Al Barakaat* [2008] ECR I-6351 paras 281–327; see however, speaking of more than just marginal irregularities ('*mehr als nur marginale Schönheitsfehler*') in the system of judicial legal protection of the EU with regard to Arts. 275 para 1, 276 TFEU Danwitz (n. 23) Art 13 paras 21–22; cf also – with regard to the jurisdiction of the ECJ to give preliminary rulings in the area of police and judicial cooperation in criminal matters (Art. 35 TEU in the pre-Lisbon version) – ECJ Case C-354/04 P – *Gestoras Pro Amnistía* [2007] ECR I-1579 paras 49–54; Case C-355/04 P – *Segi* [2007] ECR I-1657 paras 49–54.

30 Cf – with regard to the pre-Lisbon version of the Treaties – the opinion of Advocate General Jacobs in ECJ Case C-50/00 P – *Unión de Pequeños Agricultores* ECR [2002] I-6677) point 2 with numerous references; consenting CFI Case T-177/01 – *Jégo-Quéré* [2002] ECR II-2365 paras 22–54.

of the Treaties. The admissibility of this application has to be examined according to Art. 263 para 4 TFEU again. The conventional requirement of an 'act [. . .] of direct and individual concern' to the applicant (if not addressed to him directly) continues to be assessed by the Court on the basis of the *Plaumann*-test which was established already in 1963:[31] 'According to that case law, natural or legal persons satisfy the condition of individual concern only if the contested act affects them by reason of certain attributes which are peculiar to them or by reason of circumstances in which they are differentiated from all other persons, and by virtue of these factors distinguishes them individually just as in the case of the person addressed'. As usual the abstract regulation in *Inuit* did not meet this requirement. But the Lisbon treaty amended this rule on admissibility and now also permits an action for annulment against a 'regulatory act which is of direct concern' to the applicant 'and does not entail implementing measures'. Still, despite an individual concern no longer being required under this variant, the ECJ understands the term 'regulatory act' in a narrow sense as strictly opposed to 'legislative acts', so that Parliament and Council regulations as acts of the Union legislator continue to be excluded from individuals' actions for annulment. This was the case in *Inuit*, and therefore the application was declared inadmissible by the ECJ. A broader interpretation due to the principle of effective legal protection was rejected by the court for 'such an interpretation cannot have the effect of setting aside the conditions expressly laid down' in the Treaties (based on the assumed strict distinction between regulatory and legislative acts).[32]

3.1.2 National courts

As regards the involvement of national courts, the principle of effective legal protection is mixed up partially with the previously established principle of effectiveness derived from the (direct or at least binding) effects of Union law in the Member States. The distinction between both principles remains elusive in the ECJ case law.[33] In theory, this distinction is quite clear: The principle of effectiveness aims at ensuring the full implementation (or *effet utile*) of Union law in the Member States, whereas the principle of effective legal protection aims at the availability of remedies against alleged violations of subjective vested Union rights caused by acts of public authority either of the Union or of the Member States.[34] In the latter case the more general

31 Cf ECJ Case 25/62 – *Plaumann v Commission* [1963] ECR 95, 107.

32 ECJ Case C-583/11 P – *Inuit* [2013] ECLI:EU:C:2013:625 paras 45–62, 68–77, 89–107 with reference to the explanations of the Charter, OJ 2007 C 303, p. 29 which are formulated more or less ambiguously with respect to Art. 47 CFR, stating that the 'inclusion [of the recognised general principle of judicial protection] in the Charter has not been intended to change the system of judicial review laid down by the Treaties, and particularly the rules relating to admissibility for direct actions before the Court of Justice of the European Union. The European Convention has considered the Union's system of judicial review including the rules on admissibility, and confirmed them while amending them as to certain aspects, as reflected [. . .] in particular in the fourth paragraph of Art. 263' TFEU; cf also P. Craig, *European Union Administrative Law* (2nd edn., Oxford University Press, Oxford 2012) 315–318; see furthermore below, around ns. 66–67.

33 As to a detailed analysis cf the references in n. 10.

34 Summarising, e.g., J. Berkemann, 'Der slowakische Braunbär im deutschen Prozessrecht' (2013) 128 *DVBl* 1137, 1146; as to the ancillary nature of the principle of effective legal protection in particular see also H. C. H. Hofmann in S. Peers, T. Hervey, J. Kenner and A. Ward (eds.), (n. 3) paras 47.53,

principle of effectiveness[35] also applies on the basis of the additional 'principle of equivalence' according to which the national procedural rules governing actions for safeguarding an individual's rights under Union law must be no less favourable than those governing similar domestic actions. According to the 'principle of effectiveness' the national procedural rules must not render practically impossible or excessively difficult the exercise of the rights conferred by Union law.[36] The requirements of equivalence and effectiveness contain limitations of the principle of national procedural autonomy. The national courts are obliged to interpret the national procedural law as favourably as possible as regards access to justice in Union law matters. Taking into account the principle of effective judicial protection in particular, this may even result in an obligation to create new remedies in the national courts *praeter legem*,[37] even if not *contra legem*.[38]

This obligation was put in concrete terms, for instance, in *Unibet* concerning a reference for preliminary ruling by a Swedish court. A British internet betting company had brought an action against the Swedish State demanding, firstly, a declaration that the Swedish Law on Lotteries violated its freedom to provide services within the Union (now Art. 56 TFEU), secondly, a compensation for the damage suffered as a result of that alleged violation and, thirdly, interim relief. Under Swedish law, only the claim for damages was fully admissible. The ECJ decided that legal remedies must be available to ensure effective judicial protection of the rights under Community law. It would not be sufficient in this context if the party concerned was forced to be subject to administrative or criminal proceedings and to any penalties that may result as the sole form of legal remedy for disputing the compatibility of the national provision at issue with Community law. But the principle of effective judicial protection does not require the national legal order to provide for a free-standing action for an examination of

47.55, referring to the principle *ubi ius ibi remedium* with the requirement of 'another right arising from EU Law to be protected before it will become operative'; furthermore, e.g., C. Nowak, 'Europäisches Verwaltungsrecht und Grundrechte' in J. P. Terhechte (ed.), *Verwaltungsrecht der Europäischen Union* (Nomos, Baden-Baden 2011) § 14 para 16.

35 Cf the opinion of Advocate General Kokott in ECJ Case C-75/08 – *Mellor* [2009] ECR I-3799 point 28: 'A specific expression of the principle of effectiveness is the principle of effective legal protection'; disagreeing Arnull (n. 7) 51, 55 n. 30.

36 Cf, e.g., ECJ Case C-268/06 – *Impact* [2008] ECR I-2483 para 46 and the case law cited; additionally, also with respect to the tension between both requirements, T. v. Danwitz, *Europäisches Verwaltungsrecht* (Springer, Berlin/Heidelberg 2008) 483–489; Danwitz (n. 23) § 13 paras 49–59, with further references to the ECJ case law.

37 Cf J. Gundel, 'Judicial and Procedural Fundamental Rights' in D. Ehlers (ed.), *European Fundamental Rights and Freedoms* (De Gruyter, Berlin 2007) § 19 paras 48, 50 with reference to the case law of the French Conseil d'Etat; furthermore Hofmann (n. 34) paras 47.56–62; J. Saurer, *Der Einzelne im europäischen Verwaltungsrecht* (Mohr Siebeck, Tübingen 2014) 371–374.

38 D. Krawczyk, 'The Slovak Brown Bear Case' (2012) 14 *Env L Rev* 53, 61 (without a proper distinction between EU law enforcement *praeter* and *contra legem* in relation to the national statutory law; as to this distinction cf also ECJ Case C-268/06 – *Impact* [2008] ECR I-2483 paras 54–55 on the one hand, 100 on the other hand; see furthermore below, around n. 64, and, however, the opinion of Advocate General Jääskinen in ECJ Joined Cases C-401/12 P, C-402/12 P and C-403/12 P – *Council and others/Vereniging Milieudefensie and Stichting Stop Luchtverontreiniging Utrecht* ECLI:EU:C:2014:310 point 137 with reference to ECJ Case C-282/10 – *Dominguez* [2012] ECLI:EU:C:2012:33 para 25); additionally, e.g., M. Eliantonio, Case Note (2012) 49 *CMLR* 767, 783; accordingly the judgment of the German Federal Administrative Court (Bundesverwaltungsgericht), Case 7 C 21/12 (2014) 33 *NVwZ* 64, 67.

whether national provisions are compatible with Union law. Thus, an indirect possibility of challenging the compatibility of national law with Union law by a claim for damages might be sufficient. Nonetheless, the principle of effective legal protection of individuals' rights under Union law requires the national courts to grant the interim relief necessary to ensure that those rights are respected on the national level.[39]

Strict and far-reaching requirements for the interpretation of the national procedural law concerning the access to the national courts have been established by the ECJ in the context of environmental law in particular.[40] In *Lesoochranárske zoskupenie* (the so-called 'Slovak Brown Bear Case') the ECJ had to decide about the general impact of the Convention on Access to Information, Public Participation in Decision-making and Access to Justice in Environmental Matters, known as 'the Aarhus Convention' (AC), which was signed on 25 June 1998 and approved on behalf of the European Community by Council Decision 2005/370/EC, on the Member States' procedural law. According to Art. 9 para 3 AC, 'each Party [of the Convention] shall ensure that, where they meet the criteria, if any, laid down in its national law, members of the public have access to administrative or judicial procedures to challenge acts and omissions by private persons and public authorities which contravene provisions of its national law relating to the environment'. A Slovak association concerned with environmental protection ('WOLF Forest Protection Movement', *Lesoochranárske zoskupenie VLK*) lodged an action against a ministerial decision granting a hunting association's application for permission to derogate from the protective conditions accorded to the brown bear. According to national law, environmental associations were classed as 'interested parties' which could not directly initiate proceedings to review the legality of decisions. On this basis the claim had to be declared inadmissible. The Slovak Supreme Court referred the case for a preliminary ruling to the ECJ to ascertain whether Art. 9 para 3 AC has 'the direct applicability or direct effect of Community law'. The ECJ found that 'the dispute in the main proceedings concerns whether an environmental protection association may be a »party« to administrative proceedings concerning, in particular, the grant of derogations to the system of protection for species such as the brown bear. That species is mentioned in Annex IV(a) to the Habitats Directive [92/43/EEC], so that, under Art, 12 thereof, it is subject to a system of strict protection from which derogations may be granted only under the conditions laid down in Art. 16 of that directive. It follows that the dispute in the main proceedings falls within the scope of EU law.' Although Art. 9 para 3 AC 'does not have direct effect in EU law', the ECJ has ruled with reference to the *Unibet* judgment that 'it is for the referring court to interpret, to the fullest extent possible, the procedural rules relating to the conditions to be met in order to bring administrative or judicial proceedings in accordance with the objectives of [Art. 9

39 ECJ Case C-432/05 – *Unibet* [2007] ECR I-2271 paras 36–77; cf, e.g., the analysis of Arnull (n. 7) 51, 54–56; see also ECJ Case C-268/06 – *Impact* [2008] ECR I-2483 paras 37–55; furthermore however, refusing a general *pari passu* status of the legal protection on the primary and secondary level (with regard to the field of public procurement law in particular) S. Harms, *Unionsrechtliche Vorgaben für den Recht[s]schutz im Vergabeverfahren unterhalb der EU-Schwellenwerte* (Nomos, Baden-Baden 2013) 230–235.

40 As to the transferability to other fields of law see, e.g., S. Schlacke, 'Zur fortschreitenden Europäisierung des (Umwelt-) Rechtsschutzes' (2014) 33 *NVwZ* 11, 17; disagreeing W. Frenz, 'Individuelle Klagebefugnis zwischen Bürgerprotest und Umweltverbandsklagen' (2012) 127 *DVBl* 811, 813. But see also – with regard to Art. 47 para 3 CFR (cf above, around ns. 24-5) – the opinion of Advocate General Kokott in ECJ C-260/11 – *Edwards and Pallikaropoulos* ECLI:EU:C:2012:645 point 39: 'legal protection under the Aarhus Convention goes further than effective legal protection under [Art. 47 CFR]'.

para 3 AC] and the objective of effective judicial protection of the rights conferred by EU law, so as to enable an environmental protection organisation, such as the *zoskupenie*, to challenge before a court a decision taken following administrative proceedings liable to be contrary to EU environmental law'.[41] Based on this preliminary ruling, the Slovak Supreme Court (*Najvyšší súd Slovenskej republiky*) has decided that 'the judicial power needed to grant the individual the right of access to justice' conferred by Art. 9 para 3 AC.[42] Correspondingly, the limitation of the judicial enforceability to subjective public rights, which can 'only be established by those norms which do not merely serve to protect the general public, but at least, in some way, intend to protect the individual as well'[43] in German administrative law according to the so-called *Schutznormtheorie* ('protective provision theory') needed to be modified in the context of environmental law. In accordance with the legal literature[44] the German Federal Administrative Court (*Bundesverwaltungsgericht*) has extended the right of environmental organisations to bring proceedings before the courts with reference to *Lesoochranárske zoskupenie.*[45] Nevertheless, the ECJ demands a further extension of this right, at least in the special context of Art. 9 para 2 AC. The German administrative procedural law has been respectively amended in reaction to the *Trianel* judgment[46] already. However, the amendment has been considered insufficient by the ECJ.[47]

3.2 Basic standards of the court procedure

With regard to the court procedure, basic particular standards can be derived to varying degrees from the principle of effective legal protection.

3.2.1 Binding decision

As regards the binding effects of judgments without which judicial protection would not be effective,[48] the ECJ has the power to annul the contested Union measure as a

41 ECJ Case C-240/09 – *Lesoochranárske zoskupenie* [2011] ECR I-1255 paras 37–38, 51–52.

42 D. Krawczyk, 'The Slovak Brown Bear Case' (2012) 14 *Env L Rev* 53, 60 with reference to the judgment of the Slovak Supreme Court in Case 5Sžp 41/2009 and analogous judgments.

43 Summarizing B. Wegener, 'Subjective Public Rights – Historical Roots Versus European and Democratic Challenges' in H. Pünder and C. Waldhoff (eds.), *Debates in German Public Law* (Hart, Oxford and Portland 2014) 219, 220; cf also, e.g., M. Eliantonio, Case Note (2012) 49 *CMLR* 767, 777; as to a comparative overview of the divergent systems throughout the EU Member States see Kayser (n. 21) Art 91 paras 42–44, 93–100.

44 Cf, e.g., J. Berkemann, 'Der slowakische Braunbär im deutschen Prozessrecht' (2013) 128 *DVBl* 1137, 1141–1148; for further references, also for dissenting voices, see Schlacke (n. 40) 12 n. 27.

45 Case 7 C 21/12, 33 *NVwZ* (2014) 64, 65–68 with additional reference to ECJ Case C-237/07 – *Janecek* [2008] ECR I- 6221 para 3; cf also above, n. 38 already.

46 ECJ Case C-115/09 – *Trianel* [2011] ECR I-3673; for an overview of the other ECJ case law (and the national judges' responses) concerning the special guarantees of legal protection related to the first and second pillars of the Convention according to Art. 9 AC and the implementation provisions in EU law see L. Lavrysen, *Access to Justice in Environmental Matters* (UNEP 2014) (available at http://hdl.handle.net/1854/LU-4426506) 8–13; as to the limited relevance of the general principle in this area with respect to the concrete settlement of the secondary law provisions M. Eliantonio, Case Note (2012) 49 *CMLR* 767, 790: 'probably no need [for the ECJ] to mention this [general] principle'.

47 Cf ECJ Case C-137/14 – *Commission/Germany* [2015] ECLI:EU:C:2015:683.

48 Cf Pabel (n. 22) § 19 para 57 with further reference. As to the obvious reconcilability of the general principle of *res judicata* with the principle of effective legal protection see GC Case T-341/07 – *Sison/Council II*

consequence of a successful action for annulment. In contrast, the court has no power to decide the original case as such in the case of a reference for a preliminary ruling; this final decision continues to be reserved to the referring national court. The difference is reflected, e.g., in the diverging formulation of the legal consequences: An unlawful act is declared void in an action for annulment procedure according to Art. 264 TFEU, and, in contrast, invalid – meaning: inapplicable – according to Arts. 267, 277 TFEU in a preliminary ruling procedure. Nevertheless, in both cases the final judgment of the Union Court with regard to the assessment of Union law has a congruent (factual and legal) binding effect not only *inter partes*, but *erga omnes*.[49]

As regards the question of different levels of jurisdiction, primary law contains binding basic rules for the system of Union courts in Arts. 256–257 TFEU. However, the principle of effective legal protection does not absolutely require such different levels of jurisdiction.[50]

3.2.2 Duration of court procedure

The principle of effective legal protection includes the 'right to fair legal process within a reasonable period'. The ECJ has held, for example, a duration of proceedings of 'about five years and six months' before the General Court as a violation of this principle.[51]

With regard to the extraordinary complexity of the preliminary rulings procedure, certain temporal extensions resulting from this particular mechanism of cooperation are accepted in principle.[52] Furthermore, a general delay caused by the requirement of 'additional steps [of extrajudicial legal protection] before access to a Court can be granted' is regularly accepted by the ECJ.[53] That applies all the more as the possibility of interim measures is an important element in the context of duration of proceedings as already mentioned.[54]

[2011] ECR II-7915 para 23; see furthermore (dealing with the limitations of the first-mentioned principle), however, R. Widdershoven, 'European Administrative Law' in R. J. G. H. Seerden (ed.), *Administrative Law of the European Union, Its Member States and the United States* (3rd edn., Intersentia, Cambridge 2012) 245, 301 with reference to ECJ Case C-2/08 – *Fallimento Olimpiclub* [2009] ECR I-7501 paras 22–31.

49 Cf in detail Lenaerts, Marselis, Gutman (n. 12) paras 6.27–32, 7.219–223, 10.18–21.

50 ECJ Case C-169/14 – *Sánchez Morcillo and Abril García* [2014] ECLI:EU:C:2014:2099 para 36; cf also Pabel (n. 22) § 19 paras 47–48 with further references.

51 ECJ Case C-185/95 P – *Baustahlgewebe/Commission* [1998] ECR I-8417 paras 26–49 (with the final limiting conclusion, that 'in the absence of any indication that the length of the proceedings affected their outcome in any way, that plea cannot result in the contested judgment being set aside in its entirety'); cf also ECJ Case C-270/99 P – *Z/Parliament* [2001] ECR I-9197 para 24; Case C-500/10 – *Belvedere Costruzioni* [2012] ECLI:EU:C:2012:186 paras 23–28.

52 Cf, e.g., Gundel (n. 37) § 19 para 39 with regard to the respective ECtHR case law.

53 Hofmann (n. 34) para 47.85 with reference to ECJ Joined Cases C-317/08 to C-320/08 – *Alassini and others* [2010] ECR I-2213 paras 58–66 (62 in particular); as to the requirement of a preliminary administrative procedure cf with regard to judicial protection against the measures of Union agencies, e.g., C. Görisch, 'Die Agenturen der Europäischen Union' (2012) 34 *Jura* 42, 50–51 (also with regard to the admissibility of an exclusion of direct appeal against factual or preparing acts).

54 See above, around n. 39. As to the important harmonising effect of the respective case law according to which 'the suspension of enforcement of administrative measures based on a Community regulation, whilst it is governed by national procedural law, in particular as regards the making and examination of the application, must in all the Member States be subject, at the very least, to conditions which are

Finally, whereas time-limits have an accelerating effect on the duration of court procedure on the one hand, they must be long enough 'to ensure that interested parties have sufficient time within which to bring an action against published measures and, consequently, to observe the right to effective judicial protection'[55] on the other hand. Although only with regard to abbreviated procedures as rather exceptional cases, the ECJ has decided that even 'a 15-day time limit for bringing an action does not seem, generally, to be insufficient in practical terms to prepare and bring an effective action and appears reasonable and proportionate in relation to the rights and interests involved'.[56]

3.2.3 Liability claims

As regards liability claims, the ECJ has held already in the seminal case *Francovich* that the 'protection of [conferred] rights [. . .] would be weakened' without the possibility of state liability in case of their violation.[57] Correspondingly, the principle of state liability might be called a 'necessary extension of the general principle of effective judicial protection'.[58] Additionally, the principle includes exhaustive Union liability beyond Arts. 340 paras 2, 3 TFEU, 41 para 3 CFR (in connection with Art. 268 TFEU). Therefore, for example, an action for unjust enrichment brought before the ECJ, although not mentioned explicitly in these provisions, has been declared admissible.[59]

4 Additional procedural rights

The basic standards of the court procedure are complemented by additional procedural rights (including rights under the administrative procedure, in particular as guaranteed by the right to good administration according to Art. 41 CFR).[60] According to explicit primary law provisions, these rights comprise, among others,[61] the right to access to documents (Arts. 15 TFEU, 41 para 2 lit b, 42 CFR), the right to refer to the European Ombudsman cases of maladministration in the activities of the (non-judicial) institutions, bodies, offices or agencies of the Union (Arts. 24 para 3, 228

uniform so far as the granting of such relief is concerned and which it [*scilicet* the ECJ] has defined as being the same conditions as those of the application for interim relief brought before the Court' cf Kayser (n. 21) § 91 para 137 with reference to ECJ Joined Cases C-453/03, C-11/04, C-12/04 and C-194/04 – *ABNA* [2005] ECR I-10423 para 104.

55 ECJ Case C-625/11 P – *PPG and SNF/ECHA* [2013] ECLI:EU:C:2013:594 para 35.

56 ECJ Case C-69/10 – *Samba Diouf* [2011] ECR I-7151 para 67. As to the equally affected principle of *res judicata* see already above, n. 48.

57 ECJ Joined Cases C-6/90 and C-9/90 – *Francovich* [1991] ECR I-5357 paras 32–33, 42 (concerning a breach by the Italian Republic of the obligation to implement the directive on the protection of employees in the event of the insolvency of the employer).

58 See the opinion of Advocate General Léger in ECJ Case C-224/01 – *Köbler* [2003] ECR I-10239 point 35; consenting Nowak (n. 34) § 14 para 18.

59 ECJ Case C-47/07 P – *Masdar/Commission* [2008] ECR I-9761 paras 48–50.

60 As to the close link between the 'requirements of good administration and [. . .] the principle of effective legal protection' see Hofmann (n. 34) para 47.67 with reference to ECJ Case C-362/09 P – *Athinaïki Techniki/Commission* [2010] ECR I-13275 para 70.

61 As to more exhaustive enumerations and examinations see, e.g., Nowak (n. 34) § 14 paras 19–28; Pabel (n. 22) § 19 paras 44–75.

TFEU, 43 CFR), the right to petition the European Parliament (Arts. 24 para 2, 227 TFEU, 44 CFR), the right to be heard (Arts. 41 para 2 lit a, 47 para 2 clause 1 CFR) resp. to intervene (Art. 40 Protocol [No. 3] on the Statute of the Court of Justice of the European Union in conjunction with Art. 51 TEU), the right to counsel (Art. 47 para 2 clause 2 CFR) and the duty to give reasons (Arts. 296 TFEU, 41 para 2 lit c CFR) respectively the right to the reasoning of judicial decisions (Art. 36 clause 1 Protocol [No 3] on the Statute of the Court of Justice of the European Union in conjunction with Art. 51 TEU).[62]

5 Conclusions

For some time now, legal protection has been one of the central issues of legal doctrine in European administrative law.[63] Even on the level of European Union law in particular, it raises a number of interesting questions. Regarding the complementary system of legal protection by Union and national courts, perhaps the most interesting one in the present context is whether the ECJ applies higher standards to the national courts' jurisdiction than to that of the Union courts (i.e. its own). The ECJ, as mentioned before, has been heavily criticised for regularly excluding direct access of individuals to an action for annulment against legislative acts on the one hand, but imposing heavy restrictions on the procedural autonomy of the Member States on the other hand. However, a deeper analysis of the case law in *Les Verts* and its successors reveals that the ECJ interprets even Union law *contra legem* if this is necessary to enable access to justice at all.[64] The limitation of direct access to the ECJ for individuals in an action for annulment procedure mainly rests on the procedural primacy of judicial protection in the Member States,[65] corresponding to the principle of subsidiarity (Art. 5 para 3 TEU). Furthermore, it has to be pointed out that even in the highly discussed field of environmental law the ECJ would not promote a 'dual standard' if it declared an action for annulment against legislative EU acts inadmissible due to a restrictive interpretation of Art. 9 para 3 AC[66] as long as it does not require a different interpretation of the Convention from the national courts.[67]

62 Cf also the related explanations to the Charter, OJ 2007 C 303, pp. 28–30.

63 Kayser (n. 21) § 91 para 1.

64 Explicitly M. Breuer, 'Die Klagebefugnis von Umweltverbänden unter Anpassungsdruck des Völker- und Europarechts' (2012) 45 *Verw* 171, 191.

65 Cf Danwitz (n. 23) § 13 paras 15–16.

66 Corresponding to the opinions of Advocate General Jääskinen in ECJ Joined Cases C-404/12 P and C-405/12 P – *Council and Comission/Stichting Natuur en Milieu and Pesticide Action Network Europe* ECLI:EU:C:2014:309 points 18–66 (left open in the judgment [2015] ECLI:EU:C:2015:5 para 54), and Joined Cases C-401/12 P, C-402/12 P and C-403/12 P – *Council and others/Vereniging Milieudefensie and Stichting Stop Luchtverontreiniging Utrecht* ECLI:EU:C:2014:310 points 100–11 (left open in the judgment [2015] ECLI:EU:C:2015:4 para 62), in the latter cases furthermore promoting an extensive interpretation of the term 'administrative act' [points 123–37] and stressing the uniform standard of interpretation and application of the Union Law in the context of Arts. 2 para 1 lit. g) 10 Regulation (EC) No 1367/2006 with reference to Case 104/81 – *Kupferberg* [1982] ECR 3641 para 14 [point 135]; cf also M. Breuer, 'Die Klagebefugnis von Umweltverbänden unter Anpassungsdruck des Völker- und Europarechts' (2012) 45 *Verw* 171, 198–199; J. H. Jans, 'On Inuit and Judicial Protection in a Shared Legal Order' (2012) 21 *EEELRev* 188, 190–191.

67 Apparently disagreeing D. Krawczyk, 'The Slovak Brown Bear Case' (2012) 14 *Env L Rev* 53, 64; similarly (with sweeping criticism of the existing ECJ case law) M. Eliantonio, Case Note (2012) 49 *CMLR* 767,

Additionally, it must be taken into account that an 'extension of the direct legal protection, which at first sight seems to be favourable for the citizens, could also have adversarial consequences. If the concerned party does not use the existing possibility of an action for annulment against a known [Union] legal act, a subsequent indirect review, as for instance in the proceedings of a preliminary ruling, would be denied according the ECJ *Textilwerke Deggendorf* case law' to avoid a circumvention of the time-limit set out in Art. 263 para 6 TFEU.[68] This shows that even a restriction of access to justice sometimes might work for the benefit of effective legal protection – although it has to be admitted that this surprising consequence will occur only in rare and exceptional cases.

Finally, as regards the advancement of the principle of effective legal protection, it is worth noting the observation that '[amongst] the issues which might require further clarification in the future is the question of the intensity of judicial review. So far, the case law interpreting the right to effective judicial review, while acknowledging that that right is linked to the intensity of judicial review, has only rarely addressed this issue. [. . .] To date, the Court of Justice has always held that its own standards of review of legality, especially under the action for annulment (Art. 263 TFEU), satisfy the demands of the principle of effective judicial review, without giving further explanations as to why that might be so'.[69] However, an explanation for the limited intensity of review by the ECJ concerning the strict application of the applicants' burden of proof and the principle of *ne ultra petita* can be found in the Romanist legal traditions,[70] whereas the assumed 'limited judicial review' with regard to discretionary decisions of administrative authorities does not exclude the Union judicature from establishing 'whether the evidence relied on is factually accurate, reliable and consistent' as well as 'whether that evidence contains all the information which must be taken into account in order to assess a complex situation and whether it is capable of substantiating the conclusions drawn from it',[71] i.e. from an intensive review in substance.[72]

786–791; cf also, e.g., J. H. Jans, 'Who Is the Referee?' (2011) 4–1 *R.E.A.L.* 85, 96–97. As to the similar discussion about a 'double standard' of the ECJ in the review of the principle of proportionality, see, e.g., F. G. Jacobs, 'Recent Developments in the Principle of Proportionality in European Community Law' in E. Ellis (ed.), *The Principle of Proportionality in the Laws of Europe* (Hart, Oxford and Portland 1999) 1, 21.

68 J Gundel (n. 37) § 19 para 32 (with reference, among others, to ECJ Case C-188/92 – *TWD* [1994] ECR I-883): 'This preclusion rule [. . .] has so far only been important for individual measures, such as for decisions of the Commission against Member States ordering the reversed transaction of unlawfully granted national state-aids. [. . .] If the [direct] judicial review [of legislative acts before the ECJ] is opened by an extensive interpretation of [Art. 263 para 4 TFEU] the question of whether the corresponding '*Deggendorf*-Rule' should be extended to such cases arises as well.'

69 Hofmann (n. 34) para 47.91, with reference to ECJ C-272/09 P – *KME Germany and others/Commission* [2011] ECR I-12789 paras 91–94; Case C-386/10 P – *Chalkor/Commission* [2011] ECR I-13085 paras 45–57. As to the admissibility of an exclusion of direct appeal against factual or preparing acts cf already above, n. 53.

70 Cf Danwitz (n. 23) § 13 para 42.

71 CFI Case T-187/06 – *Schräder/CPVO* [2008] ECR II-3151 paras 59–61.

72 Cf more detailed C. Görisch, 'Die Agenturen der Europäischen Union' (2012) 34 *Jura* 42, 49–50.

3 Creating a European-wide standard of effective legal protection

The European Convention on Human Rights

Marten Breuer

1 Historical background

The Convention for the Protection of Human Rights and Fundamental Freedoms, commonly referred to as the 'European Convention on Human Rights' (ECHR),[1] has arisen out of the disastrous events of World War II. At a time when the project of European integration under the auspices of the (then) European Communities had not even been launched,[2] the Convention was a first response of European states (mainly of the Western hemisphere) to the atrocities of Nazism and Fascism. This necessitated a fundamental change of thinking in public international law: until the end of World War II, the individual had almost no place in international law whatsoever.[3] The lesson learned from the Nazi era was that it did not suffice to leave protection of fundamental rights to national constitutions. What was needed was a second level of protection, this time being an international one. As a consequence, the individual became a subject (though only a partial one) of international law.[4] The first step in this direction was made, at UN level, by the Universal Declaration of Human Rights (UDHR) of 10 December 1948.[5] Important as it undeniably was, the Universal Declaration lacked a legally binding character and it was no earlier than almost 20 years later, in 1966, when legally binding instruments were set up at the universal level.[6] Against this background, one cannot but praise the Member States of the Council of Europe for having achieved consensus on a strong human rights catalogue as early as 1950 when the Convention was opened for ratification.

1 ETS No 5.

2 The European Coal and Steel Community was founded in 1952, the European Atomic Energy Community and the European Economic Community in 1958 respectively.

3 cf L. Oppenheim, *International Law, Vol. I: Peace* (Longmans, Green, and co., London, New York [etc.] 1905) 346: '[The so-called rights of mankind] do not in fact enjoy any guarantee whatever from the Law of Nations, and they cannot enjoy such a guarantee, since the Law of Nations is a law between States, and since individuals cannot be subjects of this law.'

4 cf generally C. Tomuschat, *Human Rights: Between Idealism and Realism* (3rd edn., 2014).

5 GA Res 217 (III); for further reading, see G. Alfredsson and A. Eide (eds.), *The Universal Declaration of Human Rights: A Common Standard of Achievement* (1999).

6 International Covenant on Civil and Political Rights and International Covenant on Economic, Social and Cultural Rights, both of 19 December 1966.

The Convention entered into force in 1953, and the European Court of Human Rights (ECtHR) was established six years later.[7] However, the human rights protection of the early days significantly differed from the level of protection guaranteed today: First, as for the substance, the Convention contained only the core of (mainly liberal) rights. Other guarantees were added in the course of time by means of additional (and facultative) protocols, such as the right to property (Art. 1 Protocol No 1)[8] or the prohibition of death penalty in times of peace (Protocol No 6)[9] and war (Protocol No 13).[10] Secondly, the enforcement machinery significantly differed from the way it looks like today: the Court's jurisdiction was facultative and subject to a separate declaration of acceptance.[11] In cases where a state had not made such a declaration, it was for the Committee of Ministers – i.e. for a political body within the Council of Europe – to establish whether or not there had been a violation.[12] What is more, even the individual complaint procedure was not compulsory but subject to another (facultative) declaration of acceptance.[13] As a consequence, some Council of Europe Member States hid for years in the shadow since no individual could blame them at the European level for not complying with their Convention obligations.[14] Lastly, even in cases where a state had accepted both the Court's jurisdiction and the individual complaint procedure, the potential victim of a human rights violation had no direct access to the Court. Instead, complaints were lodged with the then European Commission of Human Rights (EComHR) which decided on the admissibility. If the complaint had been found admissible, the case was brought before the Court (mainly) by the Commission which set up a (confidential) report on the merits.[15]

The new era began in November 1998 when Protocol No 11 entered into force.[16] This Protocol brought about a number of innovations which are still central to today's design of the Convention machinery. The right to individual complaint which is nowadays the centrepiece of the Convention[17] became obligatory for all states (Art. 34 of the Convention), as well as the Court's compulsory jurisdiction. Today, it goes without saying that the victim himself or herself has direct access to the Court.[18] The former Commission has been abolished in favour of a Court which is now composed by full-time judges (under the old system, the judges met only irregularly on part-time basis). The role of the Committee of Ministers has been reduced to the surveillance

7 J. A. Frowein, 'Einführung' in J. A. Frowein and W. Peukert (eds.), *Europäische Menschenrechtskonvention: EMRK-Kommentar* (3rd edn., 2009) MN 2, 4.

8 ETS No 9.

9 ETS No 114.

10 ETS No 177.

11 Former Art. 46 of the Convention.

12 Former Art. 32 of the Convention.

13 Former Art. 25 para 1 of the Convention.

14 Turkey e.g., being one of the original Parties to the Convention, made the declaration only in 1987.

15 Former Art. 31 of the Convention.

16 ETS No 155.

17 cf C. Tomuschat, 'Individueller Rechtsschutz: das Herzstück des "*ordre public européen*" nach der Europäischen Menschenrechtskonvention' (2003) 30 *Europäische Grundrechte-Zeitschrift* 95.

18 The direct access to the Court had been introduced by Protocol No 9 (ETS No 140) which was, however, an optional protocol. Hence, it was only by Protocol No 11 that direct access to the Court became obligatory for all Contracting Parties.

of the states honouring their obligations after a finding of a violation (Art. 46 para 2 of the Convention). Protocol No 11 saw the introduction of a new Court formation, the Grand Chamber which decides on serious questions affecting the interpretation or application of the Convention or the protocols thereto, or serious issues of general importance (Art. 43 para 2 of the Convention). Although there have been subsequent procedural innovations (Protocols No 14,[19] which entered into force in June 2010, and Protocols No 15[20] and 16,[21] not yet in force), the fundamental nature of the change brought about by Protocol No 11 cannot be overestimated.

Another factor which had an immense impact on today's functioning of the system was the enlargement of the Council of Europe after the fall of the iron curtain. When the Convention was opened for signature in 1950, the Council of Europe consisted of thirteen Member States, most of them belonging to the Western hemisphere (except for Turkey). Within this part of Europe, there was a large consensus about central human values. After the end of the cold war in 1990, the Council of Europe decided to open its gates and to let in the newly established democracies.[22] This decision, understandable as it might have been, had strong repercussions on the Convention system. Today, the Council of Europe consists of 47 Member States, some of which are facing systemic problems in safeguarding the rule of law. This has led to an immense influx of incoming applications up to the number of 160,000 pending cases, a number which severely endangered the functioning of the system as a whole. Although the Court managed to reduce the number of pending cases to just under the mark of 100,000 by the end of 2013 and even further to 70,000 by the end of 2014, the long-term functioning of the Convention system is still one of the most pressing – and, one might add, still unanswered – questions.[23]

2 Rights-based perspective

It might be rather unusual to cite the European Court of Justice (ECJ) in a contribution dedicated to the European Convention on Human Rights. However, this is exactly what shall be done here. The ECJ has held in a long-standing jurisprudence that the right to effective judicial protection is 'one of the general principles of law stemming from the constitutional traditions common to the Member States', a right that has also been 'enshrined in Arts. 6 and 13 of the European Convention for the Protection of Human Rights and Fundamental Freedoms'.[24] One aspect is striking: The ECJ mentions, in the same breath, both Arts. 6 and 13 of the Convention as if there was no difference between them. Indeed, from a Union law perspective, this is exactly the case since nowadays, both Convention articles have been merged together into what is now Art. 47 of the Charter of Fundamental Rights (CFR). From a genuine

19 CETS No 194.
20 CETS No 213.
21 CETS No 214.
22 cf V. Djerić 'Admission to Membership of the Council of Europe and Legal Significance of Commitments Entered Into by New Member States' (2000) 60 *Zeitschrift für ausländisches öffentliches Recht und Völkerrecht* 605; J. F. Flauss, 'Les conditions d'admission des pays d'Europe centrale et orientale au sein du Conseil de l'Europe' (1994) 5 *European Journal of International Law* 401.
23 Figures according to ECtHR, *Annual Report 2013* (2014) 9; *Annual Report 2014* (2015) 5.
24 Case 50/00 P Unión de Pequeños Agricultores v Council [2002] ECR I-6677, para 39.

Convention perspective, however, things are quite different. Arts. 6 and 13 of the Convention follow different dogmatic concepts. This has strong repercussions on the subject under consideration, namely, the effective legal protection in administrative law matters. Therefore, as a first step, it is necessary to address the respective dogmatic concepts of Art. 6 para 1 and Art. 13 of the Convention.

2.1 Dogmatic concept of Art. 6 para 1 and Art. 13 of the Convention

Art. 6 para 1 of the Convention is at the same time both larger and narrower in scope, compared to Art. 13.[25] It is larger in scope because it does not only apply to alleged breaches of other Convention rights, as Art. 13 does. Instead, it applies to rights protected under national law alone. However, Art. 6 is narrower in scope in that it applies only to disputes concerning 'civil rights and obligations' and 'criminal charges' respectively. This might give rise to the impression that Art. 6 para 1 does not apply to administrative law matters at all. This, however, would be misconceived. The ECtHR has developed an autonomous concept of what is meant by 'civil rights and obligations' and by 'criminal charges'.[26] Large parts of the law which at the national level are regarded as belonging to the administrative branch of law are covered by Art. 6 para 1 as interpreted by the ECtHR.[27] E.g., if a person is denied a building permission by the relevant authority, this would be regarded under many – if not most – national laws as an administrative law matter. In Convention terms, however, Art. 6 para 1 of the Convention applies since the right to property is at the heart of this dispute and the right to property is regarded a 'civil right' by the ECtHR.[28] This is not to say that Art. 6 para 1 of the Convention applies to all administrative law matters. Cases concerning the expulsion of aliens, e.g., are not regarded as being 'civil' in nature.[29] Here, Art. 13 steps in.[30]

There is yet another difference between Art. 6 para 1 and Art. 13 of the Convention. Supposed, Art. 6 para 1 applies, the wording of the provision requires that the dispute be settled by a 'tribunal'. This is different for Art. 13, here, the wording requires only a 'national authority' (in French: '*une instance national*'). The Court has acknowledged that a 'national authority' must not necessarily be a court.[31] In other words, Art. 13 is less strict than Art. 6 para 1 in that it does not require in all cases a judicial remedy. From this, it is generally concluded that Art. 6 para 1 is *lex specialis*

25 cf M. Breuer, 'Art 13' in U. Karpenstein and F. C. Mayer (eds.), *EMRK: Kommentar* (2nd edn., 2015), MN 5. Art. 6 para 1, first sentence of the Convention reads: 'In the determination of his civil rights and obligations or of any criminal charge against him, everyone is entitled to a fair and public hearing within a reasonable time by an independent and impartial tribunal established by law.' Art. 13 of the Convention reads: 'Everyone whose rights and freedoms as set forth in this Convention are violated shall have an effective remedy before a national authority notwithstanding that the violation has been committed by persons acting in an official capacity.'

26 C. Grabenwarter, 'Art 6' in idem, *European Convention on Human Rights: Commentary* (2014), MN 3 et seq.

27 J. Gundel, 'Art 146. Verfahrensrechte' in D. Merten and J. Papier (eds.), *Handbuch der Grundrechte in Deutschland und Europa* (2010) volume VI/1, MN 21 et seq.

28 *Allan Jacobsson v Sweden (No 2)*, Appl no 16970/90 (ECHR, 19 February 1998), paras 38 et seq.

29 *Maaouia v France* [GC], Appl no 39652/98 (ECHR, 5 October 2000), paras 33 et seq.

30 *Infra* at n. 66.

31 *Klass and Others v Germany*, Appl no 5029/71 (ECHR, 6 September 1978), para 67.

with regard to Art. 13 of the Convention.[32] There is only one exception to this, which will be dealt with later, namely the cases of unduly long proceedings.[33] Against this dogmatic background, one might now deal with the different facets of the principle of effective legal protection from a rights-based perspective.

2.2 Right of access to court

The right of access to court is at the very heart of any effective legal protection. From the Convention perspective, an anomaly comes into play. Whereas Art. 13 expressly requires an 'effective remedy before a national authority', Art. 6 para 1, surprisingly, remains silent on the question of access to court. In fact, Art. 6 para 1 enshrines a number of procedural guarantees once a tribunal has been seized, like fair and public hearings, that the tribunal be independent and impartial or that it be established by law. According to the strict wording of the provision, however, it would not be forbidden to deny access to court altogether. Yet, there is a long-standing jurisprudence of the ECtHR going back to the Golder judgment in 1975 where the Court convincingly held that it:

> would be inconceivable . . . that Article 6 para. 1 should describe in detail the procedural guarantees afforded to parties in a pending lawsuit and should not first protect that which alone makes it in fact possible to benefit from such guarantees, that is, access to a court. The fair, public and expeditious characteristics of judicial proceedings are of no value at all if there are no judicial proceedings.[34]

From that, the Court concluded that 'the right of access constitutes an element which is inherent in the right stated by Article 6 para. 1'.[35] This interpretation was heavily criticised, at the time, by judge Sir Gerald Fitzmaurice.[36] Meanwhile, however, it is a well-established and, one might add, a well-accepted jurisprudence.

2.3 Right to appeal

Art. 6 para 1 enshrines a right of access to court but no more than that. In particular, it does not recognise a right to appeal as such. To quote from the Court's jurisprudence:

> The Court reiterates that Article 6 of the Convention does not compel the Contracting States to set up courts of appeal. However, where such courts do exist, the requirements of Article 6 must be complied with, so as for instance to guarantee to litigants an effective right of access to court for the determination of their 'civil rights and obligations'. The 'right to a court', of which the right of access is one aspect, is not absolute; it is subject to limitations permitted by implication, in

32 Grabenwarter (n. 26), Art. 13 MN 8.
33 *Infra* at n. 51.
34 *Golder v United Kingdom*, Appl no 4451/70 (ECHR, 21 February 1975), para 35.
35 Ibid. para 36.
36 Ibid. Separate Opinion of Judge Sir Gerald Fitzmaurice.

> particular where the conditions of admissibility of an appeal are concerned, since by its very nature it calls for regulation by the State, which enjoys a certain margin of appreciation in this regard. However, these limitations must not restrict or reduce a person's access in such a way or to such an extent that the very essence of the right is impaired.[37]

There is, in fact, a right to appeal under Protocol No 7.[38] Art. 2 para 1 of this Protocol gives 'everyone convicted of a criminal offence by a tribunal' the right to have 'his conviction or sentence reviewed by a higher tribunal'. Again, one might conclude at first sight that this provision is automatically inapplicable in administrative law disputes. However, the concept of autonomous interpretation has lead the Court to apply this provision in administrative law cases as well.[39] Administrative sanctions, therefore, might be regarded a conviction of a 'criminal offence' in terms of Protocol No 7. If, in such a case, the decision at first instance has been issued by an administrative authority, it follows from the right of appeal under Art. 2 of Protocol No 7 that there must be two more levels of jurisdiction by an independent tribunal.[40]

2.4 Right to intervention

With respect to stakeholders' right to intervene into proceedings, the application of Art. 6 para 1 to administrative law disputes becomes highly relevant. This is so because Art. 6 para 1 *inter alia* guarantees a 'fair hearing' and the Strasbourg Court has interpreted this as encompassing the principles both of equality of arms and of adversarial proceedings. The principle of equality of arms implies that each party is given 'a reasonable opportunity to present its case under conditions that do not place it at a substantial disadvantage *vis-à-vis* its opponent'.[41] According to the principle of adversarial proceedings, 'the parties must have the opportunity not only to make known any evidence needed for their claims to succeed, but also to have knowledge of, and comment on, all evidence adduced or observations filed, with a view to influencing the court's decision'.[42]

This concept has put considerable pressure on long-established institutions like the '*commissaire du gouvernement*' under French administrative law. The *commissaire du gouvernement*, who is today called '*rapporteur public*', is a member of the *Conseil d'Etat*. His or her task is to present concluding observations (*les conclusions*) at the end of the oral proceedings, very much like the Advocate General does before the ECJ. He does so in full independence. The problem is that the parties to an administrative law dispute have no opportunity to comment on the conclusions. The ECtHR did not see a problem of equality of arms, given that the conclusions were presented orally during the public hearing and neither party had access to them beforehand.[43] Nor did it find a violation of the principle of adversarial proceedings, although this aspect was

37 *Anghel v Italy*, Appl no 5968/09 (ECHR, 26 June 2013), para 50.
38 ETS No 117.
39 *Grecu v Romania*, Appl no 75101/01 (ECHR, 30 November 2011), paras 81 et seq.
40 Grabenwarter (n. 26) P7–2, para 2.
41 *Krčmář and Others v Czech Republic*, Appl no 35376/97 (ECHR, 3 March 2000), para 39.
42 Ibid. para 40.
43 *Kress v France* [GC], Appl no 39594/98 (ECHR, 7 June 2001), para 73.

more delicate. The Court held that the possibility of filing a so-called *note en delibéré* in advance to the oral presentation of the conclusions 'helps to ensure compliance with the adversarial principle'.[44] What the Court did criticise, however, was the fact that the *commissaire du gouvernement* took part in the private deliberation of the judgment, although without a vote.[45] As a consequence, French administrative procedural law was amended to the effect that in cases before the *Conseil d'Etat*, any party, at the beginning of the oral proceedings, might object to the commissaire's taking part in the deliberation of the judgment.[46]

It was already mentioned that the Advocate General at the ECJ was modelled after the French *commissaire du gouvernement*. Hence, it has been questioned whether the Luxembourg proceedings live up to human rights standards. The Luxembourg Court itself has found no breach of the fair trial principle, given the possibility of having the oral proceedings reopened if it considers that it lacks sufficient information, or that the case must be dealt with on the basis of an argument which has not been debated between the parties.[47] In the subsequent Strasbourg proceedings, the applicant company failed for formal reasons.[48]

2.5 Right to an administrative act within reasonable time

With respect to legal protection against inactive administrations, there is a remarkable difference between the Convention and the Charter of Fundamental Rights.[49] The Charter contains, in Art. 41, the right to good administration. This includes that a matter be handled, by the administration, within reasonable time (Art. 41 para 1 CFR). Under the Convention, no such guarantee is expressly acknowledged. This does not mean that there is no legal protection whatsoever against an administration which remains silent. Such protection, however, can be construed only indirectly, by means of an extensive interpretation of Art. 6 para 1 of the Convention.

What Art. 6 para 1 actually does guarantee is a court trial within reasonable time. The question remains, however, what is the temporal scope of this guarantee. Does the 'trial' begin at the time when the claim is lodged with the administrative court? Or does Art. 6 para 1 also encompass proceedings before the administrative bodies preceding the administrative court trial? The Strasbourg Court has decided in the latter sense, thereby extending the temporal scope of Art. 6 para 1 well beyond the sole court trial.[50] As a consequence, the Convention grants an indirect right that an administrative act

44 Ibid. para 76.

45 Ibid. paras 77 et seq.

46 Décret n° 2006–964 du 1er août 2006 modifiant la partie réglementaire du code de justice administrative, JORF n°178 du 3 août 2006 page 11570.

47 Case C-17/98 *Emesa Sugar* [2000] ECR I-665, para 18; see R. Lawson, 'Case C-17/98, Emesa Sugar (Free Zone) NV v Aruba, Order of the Court of Justice of 4 February 2000, nyr. Full Court' (2000) 37 *Common Market Law Review* 983; T. Schilling, 'Das Recht der Parteien, zu den Schlußanträgen der Generalanwälte beim EuGH Stellung zu nehmen' (2000) 60 *Zeitschrift für ausländisches öffentliches Recht und Völkerrecht* 395.

48 *Emesa Sugar NV v the Netherlands*, Appl no 62023/00 (ECHR, 13 January 2003); see M. Breuer, 'Offene Fragen im Verhältnis von EGMR und EuGH' (2005) 32 *Europäische Grundrechte-Zeitschrift* 229.

49 Gundel (n. 27) MN 43.

50 *König v Germany*, Appl no 6232/73 (ECtHR, 28 June 1978), para 98; *Nowicky v Austria*, Appl no 34983/02 (ECtHR, 24 February 2005), para 47.

be issued within reasonable time. This right, it is to be noted, has no standing of its own. The proceedings before the administrative bodies form part of Art. 6 para 1 only insofar as they are a precondition for seizing the administrative courts. If no court proceedings are initiated, Art. 6 para 1 of the Convention is inapplicable.

Art. 6 para 1 enshrines the right to a court trial within reasonable time as such. Another question is whether the Convention also guarantees a national remedy against unduly delayed proceedings. The answer to this question is to be found in Art. 13 of the Convention. In its famous Kudła judgment, the Court has held that there must be a national remedy against unduly long proceedings.[51] This has been expressly acknowledged in cases of unduly long administrative court proceedings as well.[52] Here, Art. 13 applies in addition to Art. 6 para 1 of the Convention. It has been mentioned above that normally, Art. 6 para 1 is deemed to be *lex specialis* with regard to Art. 13.[53] This is not so for length of proceedings cases.[54] The Convention does not only protect the right to proceedings within a reasonable time, it also requires a national remedy against undue delays.

The Court's jurisprudence has led to a number of changes in legislation introducing a national remedy against unduly long court proceedings (be they administrative or otherwise).[55] In some states, the internal law was brought in line with the Convention requirements by way of a change of jurisprudence, a noticeable example being the Magiera judgment of the French *Conseil d'Etat*.[56] The Strasbourg Court has acknowledged the effectiveness of this jurisprudential affiliation.[57] In Germany where the implementation of the Court's jurisprudence took the form of a legislative enactment, the Supreme Administrative Court at least partly seceded from the Strasbourg jurisprudence. The Court found that the administrative proceedings preceding the administrative court trial should not be considered when calculating the length of proceedings.[58] This is not in line with the Strasbourg Court's jurisprudence which held in the opposite direction.[59]

2.6 Locus standi of persons no longer affected

It is in the very nature of police measures that they are typically of only short endurance. The assembly has been dissolved, the house search has been carried out, the surveillance measure has ended well before the person concerned had the chance to go to court. In those situations, the question comes up whether the potential victim still has *locus standi* before the national courts. In the Camenzind case, the Swiss Federal Court

51 *Kudła v Poland* [GC], Appl no 30210/96 (ECtHR, 26 October 2000).

52 *Rumpf v Germany*, Appl no 46344/06 (ECtHR, 2 September 2010); *Vassilios Athanasiou and others v Greece*, Appl no 50973/08 (ECHR, 21 December 2010).

53 *Supra* at n. 33.

54 cf T Vospernik, 'Das Verhältnis zwischen Art 13 und Art 6 EMRK – Absorption oder "Apfel und Birne"?' (2001) 56 *Österreichische Juristenzeitung* 361.

55 cf *Taron v Germany*, Appl no 53126/07 (ECHR, 29 May 2012); *Techniki Olympiaki AE v Greece*, Appl no 40547/10 (ECtHR, 1 October 2013).

56 CE Ass, judgment of 28 June 2002, Recueil Lebon p 247; see Calmes-Brunet in this book.

57 *Broca and Texier-Micault v France*, Appl nos 27928/02, 31694/02 (ECtHR, 21 October 2003), paras 19 et seq.

58 BVerwGE 147, 146 para 24.

59 *Supra* n. 50.

denied *locus standi* on account of the fact that the applicant was no longer affected by the police measure in question. This was arguable from the national point of view because under section 28(1) of the Federal Administrative Criminal Law Act, an investigative measure could be appealed in court by anyone who was affected by it and had an interest worthy of protection in having it quashed or varied. According to settled Swiss jurisprudence, the 'interest' had to be a present one in the sense that persons had only *locus standi* when they were still affected by the impugned measure.[60] This result, however, did not live up to Convention standards. Since neither 'civil rights and obligations' nor 'criminal charges' were directly at stake, the application did not come in the ambit of Art. 6 para 1 of the Convention.[61] Instead, Art. 13, taken in conjunction with Art. 8 of the Convention, was the applicable yardstick. The Court pointed to its longstanding jurisprudence according to which Art. 13 required for an 'effective remedy before a national authority'.[62] Since the applicant was denied, by the interpretation of the national law, any form of judicial remedy, the Court found a violation.

It is interesting to note that the German Constitutional Court changed its case law quite at the same time.[63] Although the Strasbourg Court had not yet given judgment, it is arguable that the ruling of the German Constitutional Court was at least influenced by the Strasbourg proceedings, given the fact that the (then) Commission had already submitted its report and equally found a violation of Art.13.[64]

2.7 Suspensive effect

The effectiveness of legal protection may require that an administrative act not be executed as long as the court trial is pending. However, this requirement contradicts states' interest namely in cases concerning the expulsion of aliens. Typically, national law used to provide that legal remedies against deportation orders are without suspensive effect. What is more, the European asylum system used to exclude, as a rule, suspensive effect in cases where the asylum seeker was to be deported to another Member State where he or she had first entered the European Union.[65] In the widely-noticed MSS judgment, the Strasbourg Court found that this was not in line with the Convention. The Court recalled its established jurisprudence according to which 'in view of the importance [of] Article 3 of the Convention and the irreversible nature of the damage which may result if the risk of torture or ill-treatment materialises, the effectiveness of a remedy within the meaning of Article 13 imperatively requires [. . .] that the person concerned should have access to a remedy with automatic suspensive effect'.[66]

60 BGE 103 IV 115.

61 *BC v Switzerland*, Appl no 21353/93 (EComHR 27 February 1995).

62 *Camenzind v Switzerland*, Appl no 21353/93 (ECtHR, 16 December 1997), para 53.

63 BVerfGE 96, 27.

64 *BC v Switzerland*, Appl no 21353/93 (EComHR 3 September 1996); see Gundel (n. 27) MN 82, n. 717.

65 Art 19 para 2, fourth sentence of the so-called Dublin II Regulation (Council Regulation (EC) No 343/2003 of 18 February 2003 establishing the criteria and mechanisms for determining the Member State responsible for examining an asylum application lodged in one of the Member States by a third-country national, OJ L 50/1).

66 *MSS v Belgium and Greece* [GC], Appl no 30696/09 (ECtHR, 21 January 2011), para 293, citing *Čonka v Belgium*, Appl no 51564/99 (ECtHR, 5 February 2002), paras 81–83 and *Gebremedhin [Gaberamadhien] v France*, Appl no 25389/05 (ECtHR, 26 April 2007), para 66.

This judgment was echoed by the ECJ in the NS case.[67] The ECJ mainly subscribed the findings of the Strasbourg Court in MSS as for the deficiencies of the Greek asylum system but avoided to pronounce itself on the question of suspensive effect.[68] Meanwhile, a new regulation has been set up which provides for a differentiated system of suspensive effect.[69]

2.8 Execution of national judgments

In administrative law, execution of (national) judgments at first sight seems to pose no serious problems: whenever the administrative court decides in favour of the claimant and quashes the impugned administrative act, no question of execution arises. Things are different, however, in cases where e.g. social security benefits are concerned: here, a mere court judgment that the administrative body has to pay a certain amount of money does not suffice to settle the claim since the administrative authority has to become active. In a functioning *Rechtsstaat*, it is not worth mentioning that binding court decisions must be executed. From the Convention perspective, however, non-execution of national court judgments is one of the pressing problems, at least in certain (mostly Eastern European) countries.[70]

In Convention terms, the first question to be assessed is which right is at stake when a binding court judgment is not being executed. Given that most of those cases concern the payment of money, it is arguable to hold that the non-execution of the court judgment infringes the right to property (Art. 1 Protocol No 1). On the other hand, the non-enforcement concerns a procedural aspect. Therefore, the Court in those cases finds a violation not only of Art. 1 Protocol No 1 but also of Art. 6 para 1 of the Convention.[71] This presupposes that Art. 6 para 1 applies even after the national court has given judgment. This is exactly what the Court found in Hornsby:

> However, [the right to a court] would be illusory if a Contracting State's domestic legal system allowed a final, binding judicial decision to remain inoperative to the detriment of one party. It would be inconceivable that Article 6 para. 1 should describe in detail procedural guarantees afforded to litigants – proceedings that are fair, public and expeditious – without protecting the implementation of judicial decisions; to construe Article 6 as being concerned exclusively with access to a court and the conduct of proceedings would be likely to lead to situations incompatible with the principle of the rule of law which the Contracting States undertook to respect when they ratified the Convention (. . .). Execution of a

67 Case C-411/10 *NS and others* [2011] ECR I-13905.

68 cf K. Hailbronner and D. Thym, 'Vertrauen im europäischen Asylsystem' (2012) 31 *Neue Zeitschrift für Verwaltungsrecht* 406, 408 et seq.

69 Art 26 paras 3 and 4 of the Dublin III Regulation (Regulation (EU) No 604/2013 of the European Parliament and of the Council of 26 June 2013 establishing the criteria and mechanisms for determining the Member State responsible for examining an application for international protection lodged in one of the Member States by a third-country national or a stateless person, OJ L 180/31).

70 F. Jacobs, R. White and C. Ovey, *The European Convention on Human Rights* (6th edn., 2014) 262.

71 *Burdov v Russ (No 2)* [GC], Appl no 33509/04 (ECtHR, 15 January 2009), paras 65 et seq.

> judgment given by any court must therefore be regarded as an integral part of the 'trial' for the purposes of Article 6.[72]

It goes without saying that in the administrative law context, Art. 6 para 1 of the Convention applies only where the dispute concerns a 'civil right and obligation' or 'criminal charges' respectively.[73]

2.9 State liability

Many procedures in administrative law aim at eliminating the unlawful decision of the administrative authorities.[74] There are situations, however, where the mere quashing of the impugned decision does not suffice because a non-reparable damage has been caused. In those circumstances, the issue of state liability is at stake. According to the Court's settled case law,

> where an individual has an arguable claim that he has been ill-treated by agents of the State, the notion of an 'effective remedy' entails, *in addition to the payment of compensation where appropriate*, a thorough and effective investigation capable of leading to the identification and punishment of those responsible and including effective access for the complainant to the investigatory procedure.[75]

From that, it might be concluded that Art. 13 of the Convention does not in all circumstances require a compensatory remedy but only 'where appropriate'. On the other hand, the interplay between primary and secondary remedies has become particularly clear in cases of unduly long proceedings. The Court has held that 'where length-of-proceedings violations already exist, a remedy designed to expedite the proceedings – although desirable for the future – may not be adequate to redress a situation in which the proceedings have clearly already been excessively long'.[76] In those cases, Art. 13 of the Convention requires for a compensatory remedy at national level. This has led many states to introduce compensatory mechanisms.[77]

3 Institutional perspective

3.1 The notion of 'tribunal'

It is not necessary for the States Parties to the Convention to set up administrative courts. The ECtHR has accepted that a full examination of administrative acts by civil courts is in compliance with the requirements under Art. 6 para 1 of the Convention.[78] In fact, the Court is cognisant of the reluctance with which states

72 *Hornsby v Greece*, Appl no 18357/91 (ECtHR, 19 March 1997), para 40.

73 *Supra* at n. 25.

74 Cf '*Anfechtungsklage*' in German Law, '*recours pour excès de pouvoir*' in French Law.

75 *El-Masri v the Former Yugoslav Republic of Macedonia* [GC], Appl no 39630/09 (ECtHR, 13 December 2012), para 255 with further references (emphasis added).

76 *Scordino v Italy (No 1)* [GC], Appl no 36813/97 (ECtHR, 29 March 2006), para 185.

77 cf M. Breuer, *Staatshaftung für judikatives Unrecht* (2011) 554 et seq, with further references.

78 *Oerlemans v the Netherlands*, Appl no 12565/86 (ECtHR, 27 November 1991), paras 54 et seq.

have reacted to the demand of their administrative authorities being subjected to any kind of judicial review. To use the words of the Court:

> Admittedly, the very establishment and existence of administrative courts can be hailed as one of the most conspicuous achievements of a State based on the rule of law, in particular because the jurisdiction of those courts to adjudicate on acts of the administrative authorities was not accepted without a struggle. Even today, the way in which administrative judges are recruited, their special status, distinct from that of the ordinary judiciary, and the special features of the way in which the system of administrative justice works [. . .] show how difficult it was for the executive to accept that its acts should be subject to review by the courts.[79]

Irrespective of this general sympathy and understanding, the Court's jurisprudence has brought about some far-reaching changes in the institutional structure of legal protection in administrative law. Again, this is due to the extensive application of Art. 6 para 1 to administrative law cases. This Article requires that each dispute covered by it be settled by a 'tribunal' showing certain characteristics like impartiality, independence and establishment by law. In Austria, traditionally the only court having jurisdiction in administrative law matters used to be the Supreme Administrative Court. The problem, however, was that its jurisdiction was confined to questions of law, as opposed to questions of fact. As a consequence, the Austrian legislator created the so-called 'Independent Administrative Panels' (*Unabhängige Verwaltungssenate*), which are administrative authorities enjoying independence and having full jurisdiction on questions of fact and of law.[80] The Court has accepted those entities as being 'tribunals' for the purposes of Art. 6 para 1.[81] However, the debates about the issue of effective legal protection did not come to an end in Austria. By the year 2014, Austrian administrative law saw the creation of fully-fledged administrative courts of first instance.[82] This is only one example of institutional changes induced by Art. 6 para 1 which could be supplemented by others from the Netherlands, Sweden and Switzerland.[83]

3.2 Judicial review of administrative regulations

According to settled case law, Art. 13 of the Convention does not go so far as to guarantee 'a remedy allowing a Contracting State's laws as such to be challenged before a national authority on the ground of being contrary to the Convention or to

79 *Kress* (n. 43) para 69.

80 Bundes-Verfassungsgesetz-Novelle 1988, Bundesgesetzblatt Nr 685/1988, introducing Art. 129a et seq Bundes-Verfassungsgesetz (Austrian Constitution); see Ulrike Giera & Konrad Lachmayer in this book.

81 *Baischer v Austria*, Appl no 32381/96 (ECtHR, 20 December 2001), para 25.

82 H. P. Lehofer, '"Verwaltungsgerichtsbarkeit neu" – die wichtigsten Änderungen im Überblick' (2013) 68 *Österreichische Juristenzeitung* 757, 759.

83 cf Gundel (n. 27) MN 28; R. Hofmann, 'Erweiterung des verwaltungsgerichtlichen Rechtsschutzes in Schweden' (1990) 17 *Europäische Grundrechte-Zeitschrift* 10; Kley-Struller, *Art 6 EMRK als Rechtsschutzgarantie gegen die öffentliche Gewalt* (1993) 86; A. Knutsson, 'Some Aspects of the Jurisdiction of the European Court of Human Rights and Its Influence on Swedish Law' in P. Mahoney et al. (eds.), *Protecting Human Rights: The European Perspective: Studies in Memory of Rolv Ryssdal* (2000) 715 et seq; see also Karianne Albers, Lise Kjellevold & Raymond Schlossels (concerning the Nethelrands) and Felix Uhlmann (concerning Switzerland) in this book.

equivalent domestic legal norms.'[84] In other cases, the Court formulates that 'Article 13 cannot be interpreted as requiring a remedy against the state of domestic law'.[85] This jurisprudence, however, is concerned with acts of Parliament. It reflects the situation that in many European states, judicial review of acts of Parliament used to be, and partly still is, unknown, due to separation of power arguments. With respect to administrative regulations, this rationale does not hold true. Therefore, it can generally be deduced that under Art. 13, there must be some kind of remedy to a national 'authority' against administrative regulations, capable of challenging their conformity with Convention standards.[86]

4 Conclusion

The Convention sets standards for the effective legal protection in administrative law matters. This is mainly due to the autonomous understanding of Art. 6 para 1, which has lead the Court to apply this guarantee to many administrative law cases in a way definitely not anticipated by the Contracting States in 1950. The overview of the Court's jurisprudence has shown a certain preponderance of Art. 6 para 1, compared to Art. 13 of the Convention, which results from the *lex specialis* character of the former. Still, a full picture of the principle of effective legal protection under the Convention requires that both Articles be taken into account.

From a Convention perspective, strengthening of legal protection at national level is a demand for at least two reasons: First, it is well in line with the principle of subsidiarity, which underlies the whole Convention machinery.[87] According to the principle of subsidiarity, the State concerned should have the opportunity first to wipe out the consequences of a Convention violation. This is so because the national authorities are usually better-equipped to do that, compared to the judges in Strasbourg. Hence, the principle of subsidiarity serves an effective protection of human rights.

Secondly, strengthening national remedies is also in the Court's own interest. National systems where the legal protection is deficient lead to hundreds and thousands of applications being lodged with the Court in Strasbourg. It is common knowledge that the long-term functioning of the Court mainly depends on the improvement of the legal protection at the national level. Hence, the importance of the issue of effective legal protection cannot be overestimated.

84 *James and Others v the United Kingdom*, Appl no 8793/79 (ECtHR, 21 February 1986), para 85.

85 *IG and Others v Slovakia*, Appl no 15966/04 (ECtHR, 13 November 2012), para 156.

86 Breuer (n. 25), Art 13 MN 16.

87 Kudła (n. 51), para 152; see also the Preamble of the Convention, as amended by Protocol No 15 (n. 20).

4 Effective legal protection in international law

Stephan Wittich

Introduction

The idea of effective legal protection in administrative law, while certainly at the heart of any given legal order and as such not alien to public international law as well, is nevertheless very difficult to grasp in the latter field. The conceptual problems one faces in attempting to approach the question are manifold, and it is no exaggeration to say that virtually every single word in the phrase 'effective legal protection in administrative law' raises a host of unresolved problems when applied to international law. For one, assuming for good reason that legal protection in the present context means protection of the rights of individuals, the problem is that individuals only rarely and exceptionally have rights directly under international law. While the time-honoured concept of diplomatic protection admittedly provides for a more or less effective means of protecting the interests of individuals, most notably in the law concerning the treatment of foreigners, the rights at issue do not pertain to the individuals but to their respective home state. The individual merely is the beneficiary of these norms which are owed to the state of nationality. It follows that this 'dependency' of the individual on his/her state of nationality equally applies procedurally on the level of judicial enforcement.[1] Still today, the law of diplomatic protection generally only allows for an invocation by the state of nationality in case of breach of the norms on the treatment of foreigners.[2]

1 This was already made clear by the Permanent Court of International Justice in *The Mavrommatis Palestine Concessions*, Judgment of 30 August 1924 (Objection to the Jurisdiction of the Court), PCIJ Ser A No 2, at 12:

'It is an elementary principle of international law that a State is entitled to protect its subjects, when injured by acts contrary to international law committed by another State, from whom they have been unable to obtain satisfaction through the ordinary channels. By taking up the case of one of its subjects and by resorting to diplomatic protection or international judicial proceedings, a State is in reality asserting its own rights – its right to ensure, in the person of its subjects, respect for the rules of international law. The question, therefore, whether the present dispute originates in an injury to a private interest, which in point of fact is the case in many international disputes, is irrelevant from this standpoint. Once a State has taken up a case on behalf of one of its subjects before an international tribunal, in the eyes of the latter the State is sole claimant.'

2 As the Court stated in *Ahmadou Sadio Diallo (Republic of Guinea v Democratic Republic of the Congo)*, Preliminary Objections, Judgment of 24 May, ICJ Reports 2007, 582, at 615 para 89: 'The Court, having carefully examined State practice and decisions of international courts and tribunals in respect of diplomatic protection of *associés* and shareholders, is of the opinion that these do not reveal – at least at the present time – an exception in customary international law allowing for protection by substitution . . .'. The

To be sure, international law has gone a long way from that situation. Today, there is no doubt that in particular areas, such as human rights, investment law, or the employment law of international organisations, the individual may well enjoy rights directly under international law as will be discussed below. These developments have also mitigated the general problem of effectiveness inherent in international law due to its decentralised structure. While in general international law, legal protection before international courts and tribunals is only possible if and to the extent the parties to the dispute have consented to the jurisdiction of the relevant court or tribunal, in those areas where the individual possesses rights directly under international law, one frequently finds courts or tribunals having quasi-compulsory jurisdiction. Even if one still faces immense difficulties when it comes to enforcing international decisions, these developments have no doubt increased the possibilities of access to legal protection of the individual. Before looking at the various meanings of international administrative law, I will give a few examples on the increased significance of the individual in terms of legal personality. I will not address the most obvious field, namely human rights, as this is covered in detail elsewhere in this book.[3]

1 The legal protection of the rights of individuals

In the discussion of problems concerning the legal protection of individuals in international law the focus usually lies on the relevant substantive rights, and the question of enforcement is generally viewed as being merely ancillary or supplemental to the existence or not of a specific substantive right. However, the situation is much more complex and while it is true that a substantive right exists whether or not it is enforceable, enforcement will always be the ultimate test of effectiveness of the given legal order.

For various reasons, international law very often defers the enforcement of international law by individuals to the domestic level, at least temporarily. The rule on the exhaustion of local remedies which applies in both diplomatic and human rights protection is the classic example of this. In the field of diplomatic protection where, as already noted, the individual does not possess rights on his/her own, the local remedies rule is inextricably linked with the substantive obligation of the host state not to commit a denial of justice.[4] The idea that a person's individual rights (notably under private law) must be enforceable is considered to be a kind of general principle of law,[5] but while under international law this privilege was formerly confined

Court, however, left the question open as to 'whether customary international law contains a more limited rule of protection by substitution, such as that set out by the ILC in its draft Articles on Diplomatic Protection, which would apply only where a company's incorporation in the State having committed the alleged violation of international law "was required by it as a precondition for doing business there" (Art. 11, para. *(b)*)'. Ibid., para 91 and 616 para 93.

3 See the contribution by Breuer in Chapter 3, this volume.

4 J. Paulsson, *Denial of Justice* (Cambridge University Press, Cambridge 2005) 100–130.

5 This was e.g. expressed by the European Court of Human Rights in *Golder v The United Kingdom*, Appl. No. 4451/70, ECtHR, Judgment of 21 February 1975: 'The principle whereby a civil claim must be capable of being submitted to a judge ranks as one of the universally "recognised" fundamental principles of law; the same is true of the principle of international law which forbids the denial of justice. Art. 6 para. 1 (Art. 6–1) must be read in the light of these principles.'

to foreigners, human rights law has in many ways extended the scope of that idea and turned it into a 'real' right of the individual. At least on the European level, the human right of access to justice and due process (especially Art. 6 ECHR) has largely supplanted the 'old' law on the treatment of foreigners.

But the idea that international law may not only create direct rights of individuals but also provide for their enforcement is not as new as one might think. Already in 1928 the Permanent Court of International Justice addressed this idea in its advisory opinion concerning *Jurisdiction of the Courts of Danzig*. The case concerned a dispute between the Free City of Danzig and Poland on the question whether railway employees who had passed from the service of the Free City into the Polish railway administration were entitled to bring actions against the Polish administration in respect of pecuniary claims, even if these claims were based on an international treaty, namely the Danzig-Polish Agreement (the so-called *Beamtenabkommen*). The *Beamtenabkommen* regulated the employment conditions of the Danzig railway employees who were now under Polish administration. Poland disputed such a possibility and argued that the Agreement, as an international treaty, could only create rights and obligations between the parties but not direct rights for the individuals concerned who are to be viewed as mere beneficiaries of these rights, the more so as the Agreement was not incorporated into Polish legislation. The Court however rejected these arguments and held:

> It may be readily admitted that, according to a well established principle of international law, the *Beamtenabkommen*, being an international agreement, cannot, as such, create direct rights and obligations for private individuals. But it cannot be disputed that the very object of an international agreement, according to the intention of the contracting Parties, may be the adoption by the Parties of some definite rules creating individual rights and obligations and enforceable by the national courts. That there is such an intention in the present case can be established by reference to the terms of the *Beamtenabkommen*.[6]

At the time it was expressed that view was quite progressive and the resemblance with the International Court's decision in *LaGrand* more than 70 years later is striking. In *LaGrand* the question arose whether the right of a foreigner to consular assistance by his/her state of nationality was a direct, individual right of the person concerned. The Court closely looked at the wording of the relevant provision of the Vienna Convention on Consular Relations and held:

> 'The Court notes that Article 36, paragraph 1 (b), spells out the obligations the receiving State has towards the detained person and the sending State. It provides that, at the request of the detained person, the receiving State must inform the consular post of the sending State of the individual's detention "without delay". It provides further that any communication by the detained person addressed to the consular post of the sending State must be forwarded to it by authorities of the receiving State "without delay". Significantly, this subparagraph ends with the following language: "The said authorities shall inform the person concerned

6 *Jurisdiction of the Courts of Danzig*, Advisory Opinion of 3 March 1928, PCIJ Ser. B No. 15, at 17–18.

> without delay of his rights under this subparagraph". Moreover, under Article 36, paragraph 1 (c), the sending State's right to provide consular assistance to the detained person may not be exercised "if he expressly opposes such action". The clarity of these provisions, viewed in their context, admits of no doubt. . . . Based on the text of these provisions, the Court concludes that Article 36, paragraph 1, creates individual rights, which, by virtue of Article 1 of the Optional Protocol, may be invoked in this Court by the national State of the detained person.'[7]

Here again, the Court, after carefully analysing the text and the wording used, reached the conclusion that the international treaty included a provision in favour of third parties and thus established direct rights of the individual. There are of course significant differences between the two examples. Thus while the *Jurisdiction of the Courts of Danzig* opinion was concerned with employment law, particularly the possibility to bring legal actions for acts of the administration, the *LaGrand* case involved consular rights towards the host country rather than the state of nationality. Furthermore, in terms of enforcement, the Permanent Court allowed for direct enforcement by the individual in domestic courts whereas the International Court applied a modified concept of diplomatic protection for the violation of consular rights on the interstate level. Genuine and progressive as this *dictum* was, it still upheld the legal fiction according to which the individual depends on the state of nationality for protection.[8]

2 The many meanings of 'international administrative law'

Even more difficult than to ascertain the idea of (effective) legal protection of the rights of individuals in general public international law is the task of identifying or delimiting, let alone defining, what may be understood as international administrative law. Since international law has not (yet) endorsed the idea of a clear separation of powers and given its continuing decentralisation, accompanied by a lack of institutional differentiation and of a clear assignment of roles and functions, the notion of a distinct and uniform branch of international administrative law (as part of public international law and not merely some kind of conflict rules concerning domestic or transnational administrative law)[9] has not yet developed. However, the term has been in use for quite some time, albeit by different people with different meanings at different times in different contexts. But what they all have in common is the idea that administration is concerned with regulatory decision making in the general or public interest. The various understandings, which totally differ from the meaning of administrative law as understood in national jurisdictions, will be briefly set out in the following.

A rather unique meaning of international administrative law implies a territorial or spatial understanding. One may identify two different aspects of this understanding. The first, more general one, refers to the law governing spaces that are not – or not

7 *LaGrand (Germany v United States of America)*, Judgment, ICJ Rep 2001, 466, at 494 para 77.

8 A. Vermeer-Künzli, *The Protection of Individuals by Means of Diplomatic Protection: Diplomatic Protection as a Human Rights Instrument, Dissertation* (University of Leiden 2007); id., 'As If: The Legal Fiction in Diplomatic Protection' (2007) 18 *EJIL* 37.

9 See, eg, Stephan W. Schill, 'Transnational Legal Approaches to Administrative Law: Conceptualizing Public Contracts in Globalization' (2014) 1 *Rivista trimestrale di diritto pubblico*.

exclusively – under the jurisdiction of specific states. Examples of this very loosely circumscribed and heterogeneous, even patchy understanding include large parts of the law of the sea, the norms regulating international or internationalised rivers, canals, the polar regions, or the outer space. A more palpable and much narrower – yet still very broad – understanding of the territorial approach to international administrative law describes the law concerning international territorial administration. Again, this covers a broad variety of understandings ranging from the mandate system under the League of Nations succeeded by the trusteeship system of the United Nations up to distinct administrations established on an *ad hoc* basis, usually in post-conflict situations.[10] Nowadays such administrations are either established and conducted by an international organisation, notably the United Nations;[11] or the international administration is created by individual states. The latter case is generally covered by the international law of belligerent occupation, but the applicable law may well be modified if and to the extent the administration is authorised by the UN Security Council.[12] For present purposes, international territorial administrations raise the question as to the legal accountability of the administration authority towards the rights of the inhabitants of the territory. This concerns e.g. the right to freedom or other fundamental rights of the person. It is usually up to the given authority to establish review mechanisms in order to guarantee some form of protection to persons concerned.[13] The attitude by UN-led administrations has been inconsistent and quite reluctant and the control exercised usually is confined to mere political accountability. Judicial control, e.g. in the form of claims commissions, is the exception. Access to independent institutions such as ombudspersons may provide an alternative forum for review of acts of the international territorial administration.[14]

A third understanding of international administrative law denotes the various aspects of the internal law of international organisations. Unlike the former notions of administrative law, this branch of law is largely unrelated to territory; what it however

10 See generally D. S. Smyrek, *Internationally Administered Territories – International Protectorates? An Analysis of the Internationally Administered Territories with Special Reference to the Legal Status of Post-War Kosovo* (Duncker & Humblot 2006); C. Stahn, *The Law and Practice of International Territorial Administration: Versailles to Iraq and Beyond* (Cambridge University Press, Cambridge 2008); B. Knoll, *The Legal Status of Territories Subject to Administration by International Organisations* (Cambridge University Press, Cambridge 2008); R. Wilde, *International Territorial Administration: How Trusteeship and the Civilizing Mission Never Went Away* (Oxford University Press, Oxford 2008); E. de Brabandere, *Post-Conflict Administrations in International Law: International Territorial Administration, Transitional Authority and Foreign Occupation in Theory and Practice* (Martinus Nijhoff, Leiden 2009); M. Benzing, 'International Administration of Territories' in R. Wolfrum (ed.), *Max Planck Encyclopedia of Public International Law* (Oxford University Press, Oxford 2012) volume V, at 316.

11 Examples include the UN Transitional Administration in East Timor (UNTAET), the UN Administration Mission in East Timor (UNAMET), the UN Interim Administration Mission in Kosovo (UNMIK), the UN Transitional Administration for Eastern Slavonia (UNTAES), or the UN Transitional Authority for Cambodia (UNTAC). See H. F. Kiderlen, *Von Triest nach Osttimor: Der völkerrechtliche Rahmen für die Verwaltung von Krisengebieten durch die Vereinten Nationen* (Springer, Heidelberg 2008).

12 This was for instance the case in Iraq under the administration by the Coalition Provisional Authority after March 2003, which was based on the law of occupation as modified by Security Council Resolution 1483 (2003). See R. Wolfrum, 'Iraq – from Belligerent Occupation to Iraqi Exercise of Sovereignty: Foreign Power Versus International Community Interference' (2005) 9 *MaxPlanckUNYB* 1.

13 See Knoll (n. 10) 339–403.

14 See in detail Stahn (n. 10) 598–644.

has in common with them is the fact that it is intrinsically linked with international organisations as it governs their internal relations and functioning.[15] On the one hand it consists of the rules dealing with the institutional setting, notably the organisational structure, comitology, relations between organs, or law making. On the other hand, it regulates the 'international bureaucracy' by providing rules and regulations on employment of the staff of an organisation. This law of the international civil service has developed over decades and nowadays constitutes a distinct branch of international institutional law usually designated 'international administrative law'.[16] It not only lays down the substantive rules governing the employment relations between the organisation as employer and its staff as employees, but also contains procedural and institutional arrangements, such as tribunals, to ensure legal protection and enforcement of the rights of the organisation's personnel. Given its high significance in practice, this understanding will be dealt with in greater detail below (3.1).

Finally, the most comprehensive and sophisticated understanding of the term international administrative law is that of Global Administrative Law (GAL) as a form of transnational law governing the processes of administration by international actors 'in ways that implicate more than purely intra-State structures of legal and political authority'.[17] The conceptualisation of GAL presumes the existence of global or transnational administration.[18] GAL is an inclusive concept that views all regulatory activity, particularly decision making, from a transnational perspective, without distinction as to the applicable law (international or domestic), the 'type' of actor (private or public, although states and inter-governmental organisations still are the main 'administrative' actors) or the area of concern. In fact, global regulatory regimes cover a vast array of different subject-areas, just as in domestic administrative law (e.g. environmental protection, financial or commercial activity, telecommunication technology, security matters, medical and sanitary standards, or transportation and shipping facilities). Furthermore, the exact character of the norms at issue is often unclear,[19] with a great number of possible 'candidates' for sources (public international law,

15 See e.g. J. Klabbers, *An Introduction to International Organizations Law* (3rd edn., Cambridge University Press, Cambridge 2015) 207–263.

16 For a recent account see O. Elias (ed.), *The Development and Effectiveness of International Administrative Law: On the Occasion of the Thirtieth Anniversary of the World Bank Administrative Tribunal* (Martinus Nijhoff, Leiden 2012). See also C. F. Amerasinghe, *The Law of the International Civil Service (as Applied by International Administrative Tribunals)* (2nd edn., Clarendon Press, Oxford 1994) 2 volumes; *id*, 'The Future of International Administrative Law' (1996) 45 *ICLQ* 773; *id, Principles of the Institutional Law of International Organizations* (2nd edn., Cambridge University Press, Cambridge 2005); C. de Cooker (ed.), *International Administration: Law and Management Practices in International Organisations* (Martinus Nijhoff, Leiden and Boston 2009).

17 B. Kingsbury and M. Donaldson, 'Global Administrative Law' in R. Wolfrum (ed.), *Max Planck Encyclopedia of Public International Law* (Oxford University Press, Oxford 2012) volume IV, at 468–482.

18 See the seminal article by B. Kingsbury, N. Krisch and R. B. Stewart, 'The Emergence of Global Administrative Law' (2005) 68 *Law and Contemporary Problems* 15. The literature on the topic is abounding, hence a few references will suffice: Kingsbury and Donaldson (n. 17) and the literature cited there at 480–482; 'Symposium on Global Governance and Global Administrative Law in the International Legal Order' (2006) 17 *EJIL* 1–278; A. von Bogdandy et al. (eds.), *The Exercise of Public Authority by International Institutions: Advancing International Institutional Law* (Springer, Heidelberg 2010).

19 B. Kingsbury, 'The Concept of "Law" in Global Administrative Law' (2009) 20 *EJIL* 23; B. Kingsbury and L. Casini, 'Global Administrative Law Dimensions of International Organizations Law' (2009) 6 *IOLR* 319.

transnational law, international public law, national administrative or public law, or 'autonomous systems' generating internal norms).[20] However, the relevant point is that these regulatory measures on the transnational level have a direct – in the rare case that the regulatory authority has supranational powers – or, more commonly, an indirect bearing on individuals through national implementation.

It is important to note that the focus of GAL is not the specific content of substantive rules, but the operation of existing or possible principles, procedural rules review and other mechanisms relating to accountability, transparency, participation, and assurance of legality in global governance. The emerging principles of GAL are said to include: procedural participation and transparency, reasoned decisions, the possibility of review, and certain basic substantive standards when individual rights are the main object of administrative action (proportionality, means-ends rationality, avoidance of unnecessarily restrictive means, or legitimate expectations).[21]

The parallel here to domestic administrative law is obvious, even though in most cases the accountability at issue is merely political and the result of the procedure is non-binding and recommendatory only. A good example of the latter is the World Bank Inspection Panel which may, as a result of a complaint procedure initiated by individuals affected, hold the World Bank accountable for failing to adhere to its own policies and procedures in financing projects.

In the following section, I will look at three selected areas in terms of protection of the rights of individuals. These are the system of protection of the rights of employees of international organisations; the protection of the rights of foreign investors; and the protection of the rights of persons subject to sanctions by the UN Security Council. Disparate as these three selected examples may appear as to their substantive content, they nevertheless have commonalities for present purposes in that they involve legal remedies and other forms of protection against regulatory acts and, more generally, may be considered as forming part of GAL.

3 Selected examples of legal protection in international law – where protection works and where it does not

3.1 Legal protection of employees of international organisations

International organisations not only have become key players in international relations but also important employers. The United Nations alone has a workforce of over 40,000 specialised men and women. Each international organisation has its own employment law (staff regulations and rules) which is distinct from municipal law. What is more, given their far-reaching immunities under international law, municipal courts have no jurisdiction over disputes between an international organisation and their staff. To avoid a gap in the legal protection, organisations provide for their own judicial systems, or at least accept the jurisdiction of an existing tribunal, to decide such employment disputes. The jurisdiction, procedure, available remedies and many other features of such dispute settlement vary from tribunal to tribunal, and the law is very heterogeneous in this regard. Apart from these quasi-judicial bodies there are also

20 Kingsbury and Donaldson (n. 17) 468.
21 Kingsbury et al. (n. 18) 37–41.

more informal systems of conflict resolution. The United Nations, for instance, have created a single integrated and decentralised Office of the Ombudsman for the Secretariat as well as a Mediation Division within the Office of the Ombudsman.[22] While the Ombudsmen provide confidential and impartial assistance through good offices, the Mediation Division shall act as facilitator making proposals for negotiated settlements.

Administrative tribunals are competent to hear and decide disputes between a current or former staff member and the organisation. International organisations generally exercise their powers vis-à-vis their staff through administrative decisions. When a staff member disputes an act or omission of the administration, he/she usually questions a decision taken by the administrative authority. These decisions must be taken in the exercise of the powers of the organisation which vary from organisation to organisation. Likewise, the jurisdiction *ratione materiae* of administrative tribunals varies, depending on their statutes. Therefore the picture is very fragmented and resists generalisation. Generally, however, the review by tribunals concerns cases where it appears that the decision was based on a mistake of fact or law (breach of the employment contract or of the staff regulations and rules), on abuse of discretion, on discrimination and inequality of treatment or on procedural irregularity.[23] As to the remedies available, where a tribunal considers a complaint well-founded in fact and law, it may annul the contested decision, remand the case back to the original decision maker, or order the specific performance of the obligation which may also include reinstatement. Furthermore, administrative tribunals have the power to award financial compensation if the injury cannot be made good otherwise.

The two most important administrative tribunals are the International Labour Organization Administrative Tribunal (ILOAT) and United Nations Dispute Tribunal (UNDT).[24] The ILOAT dates back to the Administrative Tribunal of the League of Nations which was transferred to the ILO in 1946.[25] In 1949, the Statute of the ILOAT was amended so as to permit other organisations to recognise the jurisdiction of the ILOAT. The ILOAT may be considered the most important of the existing administrative tribunals, as currently more than 60 international organisations have accepted the jurisdiction of ILOAT for their own staff disputes.[26] The UNDT was established in 2007 and replaced the previous United Nations Administrative Tribunal (UNAT).[27] In contrast to the ILOAT whose judgments are final and without appeal,[28] the UN

22 UNGA Res A/RES/62/228 of 22 December 2007 ('Administration of justice at the United Nations'), paras 25–30.

23 See in detail Amerasinghe (n. 16), volume 1, at 277–401. See also A. Riddel, 'Administrative Boards, Commissions, and Tribunals in International Organizations' in R. Wolfrum (ed.), *Max Planck Encyclopedia of Public International Law* (Oxford University Press, Oxford 2012), volume I, 66, at 69.

24 Mention must also be made of the World Bank Administrative Tribunal, established in 1980.

25 F Gutteridge, 'The ILO Administrative Tribunal' in Cooker (n. 16) 655.

26 For the list of organisations see http://www.ilo.org/tribunal/membership/lang—en/index.htm.

27 GA Res 62/228 (n. 22). See A. Reinisch and C. Knahr, 'From the United Nations Administrative Tribunal to the United Nations Appeals Tribunal- Reform of the Administration of Justice System Within the United Nations' (2008) 12 *Max Planck Yearbook of United Nations Law* 447; M. Struyvenberg, 'The New United Nations System of Administration of Justice' in Elias (n. 16) 243.

28 Art. VI(1) ILOAT Statute. Note, however, that Art. XII ILOAT Statute provides that in any case in which the Governing Body of the ILO or the Administrative Board of the Pensions Fund challenges a decision of ILOAT, the question shall be submitted to the International Court of Justice for an advisory opinion

decided to establish a two-tier formal system of administration of justice. It consists of the first instance, the UNDT, and an appellate instance, the United Nations Appeals Tribunal.[29] Grounds for appeal are that the UNDT has exceeded its jurisdiction or competence, failed to exercise jurisdiction vested in it, erred on a question of law, committed an error in procedure, such as to affect the decision, or erred on a question of fact, resulting in a manifestly unreasonable decision.[30] The Appeals Tribunal may affirm, reverse, modify or remand the judgment of the Dispute Tribunal.[31] Also part of the UN justice system which is of great practical importance is the Office of Staff Legal Assistance whose main task is to provide professional legal assistance for staff in their relations to the UN as employer.[32] With the establishment of the two-tiered system and the numerous other improvements, the United Nations have accommodated most of the criticism voiced against the previous system,[33] and the current internal justice system of the UN can readily be described as an example of effective legal protection of the rights of individuals in a limited, yet important field of international law.

3.2 Investment protection

Apart from human rights protection, international investment protection is the single most important area of international law where individuals not only are beneficiaries of significant substantive rights but also have an array of remedies available to enforce these rights in case of alleged violation.[34] Investment law comprises the legal norms on the treatment of foreign direct investments by the host country. These standards are regularly contained in bilateral investment treaties (BITs) between the state of nationality of the investor and the host country and include protection from unlawful expropriation, fair and equitable treatment, or full protection and security.[35] A distinctive feature of BITs is that in case of breach the investor may bring a claim against the host country before an international arbitral tribunal.[36] The tribunal may be established under various institutions or regimes, such as the International Centre for the Settlement of Investment Disputes (ICSID), the Permanent Court of

which shall be binding. To date only two such advisory opinions were given by the International Court, and the Court appears to be very critical towards such an odd review procedure, see J. A. Frowein and K. Oellers-Frahm, 'Art. 65' in A. Zimmermann et al. (eds.), *The Statute of the International Court of Justice: A Commentary* (2nd edn., Oxford University Press, Oxford 2012) 1623 MN 49.

29 GA Res 62/228 (n. 22) paras 39–45.

30 Art. 2(1) UN Appeals Tribunal Statute.

31 Art. 2(3) UN Appeals Tribunal Statute.

32 GA Res 62/228 (n. 22) paras 12–21.

33 See Report of the Redesign Panel on the United Nations System of Administration of Justice, Doc A/61/205, 28 July 2006.

34 See generally R. Dolzer and C. Schreuer, *Principles of International Investment Law* (2nd edn., Oxford University Press, Oxford 2012).

35 M. Jacob, 'Investments, Bilateral Treaties' in R. Wolfrum (ed.), *Max Planck Encyclopedia of Public International Law* (Oxford University Press, Oxford 2012), volume VI, at 317; A. Reinisch (ed.), *Standards of Investment Protection* (Oxford University Press, Oxford 2008).

36 C. Schreuer, 'Investment Disputes' in R Wolfrum (ed.), *Max Planck Encyclopedia of Public International Law* (Oxford University Press, Oxford 2012) volume VI, at 309.

Arbitration (PCA), the International Chamber of Commerce (ICC), or the United Nations Commission on Trade Law (UNCITRAL).[37]

International investment arbitration has become a very prominent example of effective legal protection of individuals against sovereign regulatory acts in international law. Conceptually, investment law is a hybrid branch of law in various respects.[38] First of all, it consists of several layers of legal norms pertaining to different legal systems. The applicable law in a given investment dispute may include public international law (the BIT, other treaties, customary international law), international contracts between the investor and the host country, and domestic law of the latter. Furthermore, these layers belong to different areas of law. In fact investment law uses concepts from both public and private, notably commercial, law. This is also evident on the enforcement level[39] since investment arbitration shows features that are more akin to commercial arbitration than to arbitration between states or states and international organisations because it governs claims of private individuals. Procedurally it is fashioned along the rules of commercial arbitration, and the enforcement of investment arbitration awards operates in a manner almost identical to that in commercial arbitration. And yet, investment law is part of the broader picture of public international law and, more importantly, investment law and arbitration invariably involve the host country's regulatory powers, such as public services of general interest, infrastructure facilities, energy supply, labour standards, considerations of environmental protection, or medical and sanitary regulations.

All these considerations have prompted a distinct strand in the doctrine arguing that international investment law, particularly investment arbitration, is predominantly public law[40] and as such part of GAL.[41] Although investment law is largely based on bilateral treaties and enforced through arbitration, the effect of its application, interpretation, and operation in practice (notably by strong reliance on *de facto* precedent) has led to a 'multilateralisation' of international investment law.[42] Given that investment protection affects important common or public interests over which

37 Ibid. 315–316 MN 45–50.

38 See generally Z. Douglas, 'The Hybrid Foundations of Investment Treaty Arbitration' (2003) 74 *BYIL* 151.

39 C. Knahr, C. Koller, W. Rechberger and A. Reinisch (eds.), *Investment and Commercial Arbitration – Similarities and Divergences* (Eleven, Utrecht 2010); G. Cordero Moss, 'Commercial Arbitration and Investment Arbitration: Fertile Soil for False Friends?' in C Binder, U. Kriebaum, A. Reinisch and S Wittich (eds.), *International Investment Law for the 21st Century* (Oxford University Press, Oxford 2009) 782. See also the separate opinion of Thomas Wälde in *International Thunderbird Gaming Corporation v The United Mexican States*, 1 December 2005, notably at para 13.

40 G. Van Harten, *Investment Treaty Arbitration and Public Law* (Oxford University Press, Oxford 2007).

41 G. Van Harten and M Loughlin, 'Investment Treaty Arbitration as a Species of Global Administrative Law' (2006) 17 *EJIL* 121.

42 S. Schill, *The Multilateralization of International Investment Law* (Cambridge University Press, Cambridge 2009). This *de facto* application of precedent was nicely described by the tribunal in *Saipem v Bangladesh*, ICSID Case No. ARAB/05/7, Award of 20 June 2009, para 90 as follows (footnotes omitted):

> 'The Tribunal considers that it is not bound by previous decisions. At the same time, it is of the opinion that it must pay due consideration to earlier decisions of international tribunals. It believes that, subject to compelling contrary grounds, it has a duty to adopt solutions established in a series of consistent cases. It also believes that, subject to the specifics of a given treaty and of the circumstances of the actual case, it has a duty to seek to contribute to the harmonious development of investment law and thereby to meet the legitimate expectations of the community of States and investors towards certainty of the rule of law.'

the host state has sovereign powers of regulation, these have to be taken into consideration in adjudicating investment claims.[43]

Therefore, investment arbitration is viewed as an administrative review mechanism against regulatory interference with private rights and as such has 'transplant[ed] the procedural framework and enforcement structure of commercial arbitration into the public realm'.[44] This public law approach towards investment law that is so common nowadays[45] is also recognised in arbitral practice. Thus the tribunal in *Wintershall v Argentina* stated that the Convention on the Settlement of Investment Disputes 'combines a public law system of State liability with private arbitration'.[46]

All these considerations show that investment arbitration is a very effective means of protecting interests against regulatory measures interfering with the rights an investor enjoys towards the host country. The level of protection is further increased by the fact that awards of investment tribunals may in general be challenged or reviewed. While awards are final and not subject to any appeals procedures, it is possible that an award is challenged if it suffers from a serious deficiency. In non-ICSID arbitration review of awards is carried out by national courts pursuant to domestic law. The result of a successful challenge is that the award is set aside and not subject to enforcement. Setting aside may be requested in the country in which, or under the law of which, the award was made. Essentially the same result may be achieved if recognition and enforcement of the award is sought from a competent domestic authority, and the other party requests the refusal of recognition and enforcement. The most important source for such a procedure is laid down in Art. V of the 1958 New York Convention.[47] Awards made under the ICSID Convention are not subject to annulment or any other form of review by domestic courts.[48] The ICSID Convention provides for its own system of annulment which is triggered upon the request of a party to the arbitration. The exhaustive list of grounds for annulment is contained in Art. 52(1):

- the tribunal was not properly constituted;
- the tribunal has manifestly exceeded its powers;
- there was corruption on the part of a member of the tribunal;
- there has been a serious departure from a fundamental rule of procedure; or
- the award has failed to state the reasons on which it is based.

If the *ad hoc* annulment committee finds in favour of the request, the award is set aside. The committee cannot replace the tribunal's award by its own decision on the

43 See T. Treves, F. Seatzu and S. Trevisanut (eds.), *Foreign Investment, International Law and Common Concerns* (Routledge, London and New York 2014).

44 Van Harten and Loughlin (n. 41) 147.

45 See S. W. Schill (ed.), *International Investment Law and Comparative Public Law* (Oxford University Press, Oxford 2010).

46 *Wintershall Aktiengesellschaft v Argentine Republic*, ICSID Case No. ARB/04/14, Award of 8 December 2008, para 160. See also *Glamis Gold Ltd v US*, UNCITRAL/NAFTA, Award of 8 June 2009, para 5, stating that 'Chapter 11 of the [North American Free Trade Association] contains a significant public system of private investment protection.

47 Convention on the Recognition and Enforcement of Foreign Arbitral Awards, New York, 10 June 1958. See also UNCITRAL Model Law of 1985, Arts. 34 and 36.

48 Art. 53(1) ICSID Convention.

merits of the dispute.[49] This makes it clear that there is no room for appeal even if the award is erroneous or incorrect in points of law.

Furthermore, awards may be enforced on the initiative of the investor. How this is to be achieved again depends on the institution under whose rules the arbitral proceedings were conducted. In non-ICSID arbitration, enforcement must be sought in domestic courts. This again is governed by domestic law, and the parties to the New York Convention are under an obligation to grant recognition and enforcement. As mentioned, Art. V of the Convention lists a number of grounds on the basis of which recognition and enforcement of a foreign (including non-national) arbitral award may be refused at the request of a party to the arbitration. In ICSID proceedings, Art. 54 of the ICSID Convention obliges parties to 'recognize an award rendered pursuant to this Convention as binding and enforce the pecuniary obligations imposed by that award within its territories as if it were a final judgment of a court in that State'. This makes it clear that the domestic court where enforcement is sought is not entitled to examine or review the award. It may not even scrutinise whether the award is in conformity with the forum state's *ordre public*.

Finally, unlike in other arbitral proceedings, the ICSID Convention also provides for the possibility of revision that is a regular remedy to standing courts.[50] The party requesting revision of the award must furnish the discovery of some fact of such a nature as decisively to affect the award, provided that when the award was rendered that fact was unknown to the tribunal and to the applicant and that the applicant's ignorance of that fact was not due to negligence (*nova reperta*).

In sum, therefore, international investment law provides for an overall highly effective system of legal protection of the rights of individuals against administrative, that is regulatory, acts by states. Even though the system of investment law is overwhelmingly based on bilateral treaties and contracts, it has assumed a public law-like character through the process of multilateralisation particularly in the framework of investor-state arbitration.

3.3 Legal protection against targeted sanctions

The increasing imposition by the United Nations Security Council (SC) of targeted sanctions against individuals in the fight against transnational terrorism has raised issues of legal protection that were unknown 20 years or so ago.[51] Targeted sanctions are measures taken by the SC under Chapter VII of the UN Charter which are directly aimed at designated individuals. The sanctions employed are mainly freezing of assets and funds as well as travel bans. As is well-known, in particular cases these sanctions are a severe interference with individual rights of the persons or entities concerned leaving them without any remedy to have the particular sanction reviewed.

49 C. Schreuer, L. Malintoppi, A. Sinclair and A. Reinisch, *The ICSID Convention: A Commentary* (2nd edn., Cambridge University Press, Cambridge 2009) 890–1095; R. D. Bishop and S. M. Marchili, *Annulment Under the ICSID Convention* (Oxford University Press, Oxford 2012).

50 Art. 51 ICSID Convention.

51 See generally A. Pellet and A. Miron, 'Sanctions' in R Wolfrum (ed.), *Max Planck Encyclopedia of Public International Law* (Oxford University Press, Oxford 2012) volume IX, at 1.

This disregard of fundamental norms of due process resulted in a complete lack of protection of the individuals concerned.[52]

The administration of these sanctions is regularly conferred to a special 'Sanctions Committee' as a subsidiary organ of the SC, which monitors the observance and implementation of the sanctions regime. It is in charge of registering individuals and entities in an updated list, the so-called 'Consolidated List'.[53] The most prominent of these sanctions committees is the 1267 Sanctions Committee concerning Al-Qaida and associated individuals and entities.[54] Each state is entitled to propose individuals or entities to be included on the Consolidated List, but it is the Committee which decides whether a name is to be put on the list or not. Initially, the 1267 sanctions regime did not offer a delisting procedure; rather, any delisting process had to be started by the person or entity concerned who had to ask the state of residence or citizenship to request a review before the Sanctions Committee. This situation, which left the petitioner completely dependent on its own state and without any remedy to have his situation reviewed, met with strong criticism from various sides. Therefore, the SC established a 'Focal Point' which should provide a clear procedure for delisting. However, the Focal Point only operates as a facilitator; its main task is to receive requests for delisting and to forward the requests to the relevant governments.[55] But neither can it carry out an independent review, nor can it even forward the delisting request to the Sanctions Committee.

It was only after continuing criticism that the SC established formal delisting criteria,[56] and that it subsequently set up an independent and impartial Office of the Ombudsperson to assist the petitioner in the delisting process. The procedure for requests for delisting that are submitted to the Office of the Ombudsperson has been improved and enhanced since the establishment of the Office and consists of three phases.[57] Phase one deals with information gathering and lasts over four months with a possible extension to six months.[58] The Ombudsperson forwards the delisting petition to the Committee, relevant states and UN bodies (including the Monitoring Team),[59] requests information from these entities and gathers any relevant information obtained from these entities and through own research. Furthermore, the Ombudsperson informs the petitioner of the steps involved in the procedure. Phase two is concerned with dialogue lasting for two months with a possible extension to four months. Here the Ombudsperson informs the petitioner of the gathered information and engages in a dialogue with him/her. The petitioner has an opportunity

52 Criticism in the doctrine was accordingly very fierce, and literature on the topic is abundant. For further references see A. J. Kirschner, 'Security Council Resolution 1904 (2009): A Significant Step in the Evolution of the Al-Qaida and Taliban Sanctions Regime?' (2010) 70 *ZaöRV* 585 and the literature cited there at 586 in n. 2.

53 An overview of the existing sanctions committees may be found at http://www.un.org/sc/committees/.

54 See e.g. SC Res 1267 (1999), subsequently extended and modified by numerous SC resolutions.

55 SC Res 1730 (2006), Annex.

56 See e.g. SC Res 1735 (2006) para 14.

57 SC Res 1904 (2009), Annex II, as amended by SC Res 1989 (2011) and most recently by SC Res 2083 (2012). See Kirschner (n. 52) 597–599.

58 SC Res 2083 (2012), Annex II, paras 1–4.

59 The Monitoring Team consists of eight experts appointed by the Secretary General to support the Committee, see SC Res 1526 (2004) para 7.

to be heard, to address the information gathered and to answer relevant questions. At the end of phase two, the Ombudsperson drafts and submits a 'Comprehensive Report' to the Sanctions Committee with a summary of the relevant information gathered and, most importantly, with a recommendation on the delisting request.[60] The third phase includes the discussion in the Committee and its decision.[61] The Committee has thirty days to review the report and the Ombudsperson will then present the report to the Committee in person and answer any questions the Committee might have regarding the request. If the Ombudsperson recommends retaining the listing, the petitioner remains on the list; if however the Ombudsperson recommends delisting, the petitioner is removed from the list unless the Committee decides by consensus to retain the listing, or the matter is referred to the SC for a vote. The decision must be taken 60 days after the Committee completes consideration of the Comprehensive Report. The Committee shall convey the decision to the Ombudsperson, setting out its reasons and including relevant information. If the Committee rejects a delisting request, the Ombudsperson shall inform the petitioner accordingly and provide him/her with all relevant and publicly releasable information.

There is no doubt that the appointment of an Ombudsperson as an independent and impartial authority constituted a great improvement in relation to the situation existing earlier – which was somehow comparable to the procedure under the Spanish Inquisition. However, as can readily be seen from the above presentation, the procedure hardly meets reasonable criteria of effective legal protection. As was stated in its recommendations prior to the establishment of the Ombudsperson, the Watson Report considered such an institution as having only '[l]imited ability to provide [an] effective remedy, since although recommendations [of the Ombudsperson] may be made public, they are non-binding' and that they 'therefore may not fully satisfy court concerns'.[62] Likewise, in 2008 the Parliamentary Assembly of the Council of Europe found that 'the procedural and substantive standards currently applied by the UNSC . . ., despite some recent improvements, in no way fulfil the minimum standards laid down above and violate the fundamental principles of human rights and the rule of law'.[63]

The procedural changes that have been made since the creation of the Ombudsperson have certainly improved the process and supplemented it with aspects of due process required by the rule of law. This concerns for instance aspects of fair hearing of the petitioner or rudiments of an effective remedy by providing a review mechanism with power to grant *de facto* effective relief. And indeed, under the enhanced procedure, the Ombudsperson's recommendations have to date prevailed in every case. No recommendations to delist have been overturned by the Committee nor referred to the SC, although there have been several contentious cases.[64] This is viewed by some, including the Ombudsperson, that the Ombudsperson's current

60 SC Res 2083 (2012), Annex II, paras 5–7.

61 Ibid. paras 8–17.

62 T. J. Bieersteker and S. E. Eckert, 'Addressing Challenges to Targeted Sanctions: An Update of the "Watson Report"', October 2009, at 28 (available at http://www.watsoninstitute.org/pub/2009_10_targeted_sanctions.pdf).

63 Council of Europe, Parliamentary Assembly, Resolution 1597 (2008), United Nations Security Council and European Union blacklists, 23 January 2008, point 6.

64 S. E. Eckert and T. J. Biersteker, 'Due Process and Targeted Sanctions: An Update of the "Watson Report"', December 2012, at 18–19 (available at http://www.watsoninstitute.org/pub/Watson%20Report%20Update%2012_12.pdf).

mandate adequately safeguards the rights of listed persons to a fair, independent, and effective process.[65] To be sure, the Ombudsperson is not a judicial authority and the process is no judicial review of acts of the SC (and its subsidiary organs). It is true that not even European courts have required a fully-fletched judicial review in the formal sense of listing decisions but have demanded that the review process meet standards of effective judicial protection (in the sense of protection equivalent to judicial processes);[66] however, it is difficult to see how the current procedure meet these standards. Thus, in his 2012 report, the UN Special Rapporteur on the promotion and protection of human rights and fundamental freedoms while countering terrorism 'acknowledges and welcomes the significant due process improvements brought about by resolution 1989 (2011), but nevertheless concludes that the Al-Qaida sanctions regime continues to fall short of international minimum standards of due process'.[67] This view was, unsurprisingly, also shared recently by the European Court of Human Rights in *Al-Dulimi v Switzerland*.[68]

It will have to be seen whether the SC is willing in the future to further improve the delisting procedure in favour of strengthening the due process rights of the individuals concerned. As it stands at present, one can certainly not speak of an example of effective legal protection in a context that involves interference with fundamental human rights.

4 By way of conclusion

This brief and rather selective analysis leaves a fragmented picture. There is no overarching legal framework in international law that would provide for and guarantee the effective legal protection of individuals against regulatory acts and decisions, whoever the acting sovereign (states, international organisations or other). Given the generally decentralised structure of international law that is furthermore based on consensualism, the situation in general international law will hardly change in the near future. However, there are branches or areas of international law where the decision makers involved have agreed on some sectorial system of legal protection that may meet minimum standards of due process and thus result in relatively effective legal protection. The internal justice system of international organisations and

65 See the references ibid. 22–23.

66 This is e.g. the constant case law of the European Court of Human Rights, see *Case of Bosphorus Hava Yolları Turizm ve Ticaret Anonim Şirketi v Ireland*, Application no. 45036/98, Judgment of 30 June 2005, paras 108, 155–156; *Behrami and Behrami v France* and *Saramati v France, Germany and Norway*, Applications no. 71412/01 and 78166/01, Grand Chamber, Decision of 2 May 2007, paras 80 and 145. In its notorious decision in the *Kadi* case, the ECJ followed the approach of the ECtHR, see *Yassin Abdullah Kadi and Al Barakaat International Foundation v Council of the European Union and Commission of the European Communities*, Joined Cases C-402/05 P and C-415/05 P, at para 256; *Kadi v Commission*, Case T-85/09, Judgment of the General Court, 30 September 2010, at para 90; *European Commission and others v Kadi*,C-584/10P, Judgment of the Court (Grand Chamber) 18 July 2013, at paras 97–134. The first *Kadi* decision was among the reasons for the SC to establish the Office of the Ombudsperson.

67 Promotion and protection of human rights and fundamental freedoms while countering terrorism, annual report of the UN Special Rapporteur on the promotion and protection of human rights and fundamental freedoms while countering terrorism, 26 September 2012, UN Doc. A/67/396, at para 59.

68 *Al-Dulimi and Montana Management Inc. v Switzerland*, Application no 5809/08, Judgment of 26 November 2013, para 119.

investment protection are such examples of effective legal protection. The situation of individuals affected by targeted sanctions of the UN SC, on the other hand, shows that in areas that are politically highly sensitive, the key players are not willing to concede too much *Rechtsstaatlichkeit*. The invocation of the rule of law then becomes pure lip service and policy needs prevail over legitimate interests of effective legal protection.

Part II

The principle of effective legal protection in national administrative jurisdictions

5 The principle of effective legal protection in Austrian administrative law

Ulrike Giera and Konrad Lachmayer

1 Historical development: from the monarchy towards Europe

1.1 The beginnings in the nineteenth century

The Austrian idea of effective legal protection has its roots in the political liberalism of the nineteenth century. In the time of absolute monarchy, the administration was not bound by law and there was subsequently no legal possibility to appeal before a court in administrative matters. In the second half of the nineteenth century, this situation underwent significant change. The individual was not longer regarded as an object of governmental action, but as a legal subject with (subjective) rights against the state to protect his or her legally protected interests.[1]

This concept was promoted by the Revolution of 1848 that initiated constitutionalism in the Habsburg Empire and finally led to the adoption of a constitution consisting of five State Basic Laws (*Staatsgrundgesetze)* in 1867.[2] Most importantly with regard to our topic, these developments then resulted in the establishment of the (High) Administrative Court in 1876. The new Administrative Court introduced a new system of judicial control of the administration. The Court was competent to declare an administrative ruling void if the decision was unlawful and infringed the rights of the person concerned and thus initiated legal protection against administrative acts.

Due to the fact that the administrative procedure was not codified by the parliament, the progressive case law of the Administrative Court became very important. The Court developed several substantive rule of law principles that an administrative procedure had to be in accordance with and that administrative bodies had to follow if they did not want to risk their decision being declared unlawful by the Administrative Court.[3] Nevertheless, the margin of appreciation for the government and the administration remained very great.

1 R. Thienel and E. Schulev-Steindl, *Verwaltungsverfahrensrecht* (5th edn., Verlag Österreich, Wien 2009) 43.

2 The so-called 'Constitution of December' consisted of five separate acts. The Act on General Rights of the Citizens contained a catalogue of fundamental rights which is still in force today (*StGG über die allgemeinen Rechte der Staatsbürger, RGBl 1867/142*).

3 See R. Walter, D. Kolonovits, G. Muzak and K. Stöger, *Grundriss des österreichischen Verwaltungsverfahrensrechts* (9th edn., Manz 2011) para. 22.

1.2 From the Austrian constitution 1920 to the abolishment of any rule of law

After World War I, the Austrian state was created as a democratic republic (the so-called 1st Republic). The Austrian Constitution, which in its core is still in force, was enacted in the 1920. With regard to administrative procedure, the intentions for a consistent codification were realised as a result of the international pressure regarding the dramatic economic situation in the country, which led to the adoption of several procedural acts in 1925, including the General Administrative Procedure Act (GAPA) and the Administrative Penal Act (APA). These administrative procedural acts are still in force today, although they have been amended several times over the years.

Since the enactment of the Austrian Constitution in 1920, the Austrian system of judicial protection has been based on three supreme courts: the Constitutional Court, the Administrative Court and the Supreme Court. There is no formal hierarchy between these three courts and each of them is competent for a different substantive area of law.

The Austrian rule of law was abolished in 1933 with the introduction of an Austrofascist regime, when the democratic constitution lost its force. This situation finally led to Austria's participation in the NS regime, which perverted any form of rule of law, rights and legal protection. After World War II, the so-called 2nd Republic was proclaimed and re-established the Austrian Constitution from the year 1920 as amended in 1929. The official government position on the NS regime, however, was based on the 'first-victim' thesis (*Opferthese*), ignoring the context of Austria's accession to Nazi Germany.[4] This position goes along with a reluctance on the part of the Austrian government to grant transitional justice to the victims of the NS regime. Effective legal protection was not guaranteed; restitutions were quite limited. It actually took until the late 1990s for certain forms of restitutions to be offered.

1.3 Enfolding the rule of law: From the ECHR to EU law

After World War II, judicial protection in administrative law was still the domain of the Administrative Court and Constitutional Court.[5] An appeal against an administrative body had to be filed before another – in the hierarchy, 'higher' – administrative authority before the Administrative Court decided in the final instance. Austria's accession to the European Convention of Human Rights in 1958 had an important impact on the organisation of legal protection and the conceptualisation of rights. The ECHR made significant changes to the Austrian system of legal protection over the next decades.

The Austrian system of non-independent administrative authorities and of having only a 'reviewing control' of the Administrative Court did not comply with the European Convention on Human Rights (ECHR).[6] The case law of the European Com-

4 In 1945, however, an anti-NS principle was integrated into the Austrian Constitution, and this does not allow any political party or political movement or even an individual to express National Socialist ideas.

5 See K Lachmayer and H Eberhard, 'Rule of Law in Austria' (2011) *Understandings of the Rule of Law in various Legal Orders of the World, Rule of Law Wiki* (available at http://wikis.fu-berlin.de/display/SBprojectrol/Austria) accessed 1 October 2015.

6 Thienel and Schulev-Steindl (n. 1) 54–55.

mission/Court of Human Rights made clear that Art. 6 ECHR requires a decision by an independent and impartial tribunal in matters concerning civil rights and obligations as well as criminal charges. The Austrian system of legal protection adopted the standards of the ECHR step by step. The acknowledgment of the ECHR as Austrian Constitutional Law in 1964 was an important move towards giving authority to the ECHR in the Austrian legal system. The application of Art. 6 ECHR furthermore strengthened the role of the Constitutional Court in deciding on procedural questions in administrative matters.

In 1989, Austria established so-called Independent Administrative Tribunals (*Unabhängige Verwaltungssenate*), which represented a major amendment of the Austrian Constitution. The Independent Administrative Tribunals met the requirements of the ECHR. Although they were classified as administrative bodies, they were independent and could be classified as tribunals with regard to Art. 6 ECHR.[7] The intensity of (quasi-)judicial control was therefore significantly enforced.

With the accession to the European Union in 1995, several other independent tribunals were established in order to comply with the standards and requirements of legal protection of European law.[8] EU law furthermore demanded the creation of legal protection, even in cases in which the legal system of the Member State did not thus far provide any legal protection. The effectiveness of EU law required a certain legal protection. The Constitutional Court, in particular, created new concepts to enable the enforcement of these principles of EU law.[9]

1.4 The fundamental reform of administrative justice in 2014

The Austrian legal system's adoption of European standards finally led to the introduction of administrative courts of first instance in 2014,[10] which is a decisive change to the overall constitutional system of judicial protection in Austria. The concept was obviously inspired by the German model of legal protection in administrative law. This new system changes the understanding of the Administrative Court, in so far as the control of the administration is primarily the duty of the administrative courts of first instance, and no longer that of the Administrative Court. The function of the Administrative Court is now to ensure the objective legality and a uniform case law of the administrative courts of first instance.[11] Although the new system of administrative courts of first instance has brought and will continue to bring an improvement to judicial protection, the Austrian legal system still does not provide fully effective legal protection in administrative law, which will be discussed in this paper.

7 Theo Öhlinger, *Verfassungsrecht* (6th edn., Facultas WUV 2005) para 653.

8 E.g. in the context of telecommunications or energy liberalisation and regulation.

9 See Konrad Lachmayer, 'Country Report: Austria' in Anneli Albi (ed.), *The Role of National Constitutions* (T. M. C. Asser Press, The Hague 2016 [forthcoming]).

10 See the Administrative Justice Amendment 2012 (Verwaltungsgerichtsbarkeits-Novelle 2012); Administrative Justice – Implementation Act 2013.

11 See Rudolf Thienel, 'Die Kontrolle der Verwaltungsgerichte erster Instanz durch den Verwaltungsgerichtshof' in Michael Holoubek and Michael Lang (eds.), *Die Verwaltungsgerichtsbarkeit erster Instanz* (Linde Verlag 2013) 331–379.

2 Constitutional framework

2.1 The constitutional foundation of effective legal protection

The core document of the Austrian Constitution does not explicitly mention the principle of effective judicial protection. This is only contained in Art. 13 ECHR, which is part of Austrian constitutional law. It provides an effective remedy in case of the violation of rights and freedoms of the ECHR. Nevertheless, the Constitution guarantees effective judicial protection through several other legal institutions. Effective legal protection is, for example, constitutionally ensured by the principle of legality, various fundamental rights, the separation of power principle and the system of independent judicial review. Effective judicial protection constitutes an implicit constitutional principle as part of the rule of law principle.[12] In this context the jurisdiction of the Constitutional Court was and is very important. The Court has determined different aspects of the principle of effective legal protection.

2.2 The case law of the constitutional court

First of all, the Constitutional Court developed according to and relies on the rule of law principle. Since the 1980s, the Constitutional Court has increasingly based its constitutional reasoning on the rule of law principle and promoted the principle of effective legal protection.[13] The Court understands the principle of effective legal protection as an essential aspect of the rule of law principle.[14] Based on the rule of law principle, the Court has derived the more specific principle that the legal order must provide sufficient and efficient legal protection.[15]

Based on its landmark case, in which the Constitutional Court qualified the rule of law principle for the first time as a fundamental principle of the Austrian Constitution in the 1950s, the Court developed its settled case law according to which the sense of the rule of law principle is that all governmental acts must be based on law and indirectly on the constitution (principle of legality in Art. 18 Austrian Constitution). The Court claims that a system of institutions for legal protection must be provided. This, however, only means that administrative acts adopted in accordance with laws higher in legal hierarchy (*Stufenbau der Rechtsordnung*) are legally binding.[16]

Nowadays, settled case law dictates that legal protection requires a minimum of 'factual efficiency' for the person concerned. 'Factual efficiency' means not only the enforcement of an administrative decision by legal means, but also the actual implementation of this decision in social reality. The word 'protection' – as part of the term

12 Martin Hiesel, 'Die Rechtsstaatsjudikatur des Verfassungsgerichtshofes' (1999) 53 *Österreichische Juristenzeitung* 522; Martin Hiesel, 'Die Entfaltung der Rechtsstaatsjudikatur des Verfassungsgerichtshofs' (2009) 63 *Österreichische Juristenzeitung* 111.

13 See Konrad Lachmayer, 'Constitutional Reasoning in the Austrian Constitutional Court' in András Jakab, Arthur Dyevre and Giulio Itzcovich (eds.), *Constitutional Reasoning* (Cambridge University Press, Cambridge 2016 [forthcoming]).

14 VfSlg 17.340/2004.

15 VfSlg 14.702/1996.

16 VfSlg 2455/1952; 2929/1955, 8.279/1978; 11.196/1986; 13.003/1992, 13.182/1992, 13.223/1992, 13.305/1992, 14.374/1995, 14.548/1996, 14.671/1996, 14.765/1997, 15.218/1998.

'legal protection' – also refers, in its constitutional sense, to the timely guarantee of a factual position. Therefore, the purpose to actually implement the right is inherent in institutions for legal protection.[17] Furthermore, the Court stated that the purpose of institutions for legal protection is to ensure a (certain) minimum of efficiency for the person seeking legal protection.[18]

According to the principle of effective judicial protection, the Constitutional Court declared several statutes unconstitutional.[19] Some conclusions of the Court can be listed as follows:

- A general elimination of suspensive effect of an appeal is unconstitutional.
- Burdening a person seeking legal protection generally and exclusively with the negative effects of a potentially illegal administrative decision should be avoided until his or her request for legal protection is taken care of.
- Not only the person's positions have to be taken into account, but also the purpose and the content of a regulation, the interests of any third person and the public interest. The legislative authority must find a balance between those circumstances, but the principle of factual efficiency of a legal remedy does take priority and it is only possible to limit that principle if objectively necessary and important grounds exist.[20]
- The general exclusion of a legal remedy is illegal in a court procedure.[21]
- A time limit for a legal remedy must be adequate in relation to the content of a decision and to the procedure and must guarantee an appropriate possibility to appeal against the decision.[22] A time limit of two days to file an appeal is therefore contradictory to the rule of law principle in an asylum proceeding because effective legal protection is not ensured for an asylum seeker, who normally does not speak German.[23]
- The possibility to gain knowledge about judgments of the Supreme Court is a requirement for the efficiency of legal protection.[24]
- An excessive time limit for an administrative ruling can contradict the principle of effective legal protection. In the concrete case, the Constitutional Court declared a time limit that was four times longer than the normal time limit to be unconstitutional.[25]
- If a legal remedy necessitates high fees, it can also contravene the principle of effective legal protection.[26]

In conclusion, the Constitutional Court identifies in a case-to-case strategy several elements of effective legal protection, such as the balance of interests when eliminating

17 VfSlg 11.196/1986.
18 VfSlg 11.196/1986, 15.218/1998, 15.369/1998.
19 See Hiesel (n. 12) (1999) 522; Hiesel (n. 12) (2009) 111
20 VfSlg 11.196/1986.
21 See Hiesel (n. 12) (2009) 113.
22 VfSlg 15.529/1999.
23 VfSlg 17.340/2004, see also VfSlg 15.218/1998; 15.369/1998; 15.529/1999.
24 VfSlg 12.409/1990.
25 VfSlg 16.751/2002; see also Hiesel (n. 12) 114.
26 VfSlg 17.783/2006.

suspensive effect of a legal remedy, the possibility to appeal against a decision, time constraints or appropriate fees. A legal remedy must not only exist in theory, but also has to fulfil effectively its purpose. Based on an overall idea of a rule of law and a certain understanding of access to justice, the Court expands its understanding of effective legal protection step by step.

2.3 Specific constitutional challenges

2.3.1 The constitutional concept of administrative acts

Although the new system of administrative courts of first instance brought and will bring an improvement to judicial protection, the Austrian legal system still does not provide full effective legal protection in administrative law. One of the most obvious deficits is the restriction of legal protection to certain forms of administrative action. The scholarly debate hypothesises that the Constitution is based on an exclusive enumeration of sources of law that existed when the Constitution was adopted in 1920 ('*Relative Geschlossenheit des Rechtsquellenssystems*'). The ordinary legislator must not create new sources of law because effective legal protection is ensured only against legal acts provided by the Constitution.[27] Judicial protection in Austrian administrative law is bound to a certain number of forms of action. Thus, an administrative authority that wants to adopt a legally binding act is limited to the forms of action the Constitution provides. However, in the scholarly debate, it has been demonstrated that the exclusive enumeration of sources of law is merely relative because there are also forms of action, that are implicitly accepted by the Austrian Constitution, although they are not mentioned in the text of the constitution.[28]

Due to the rule of law principle, administrative acts that have an extensive legal effect on an individual person must be legally defendable. Otherwise, the constitutionally guaranteed system of legal protection would be suspended.[29] In the underlying case, a statute, qualified as an administrative act, did not grant financial aid, as a non-binding expertise and not as a binding administrative issue. As already mentioned, in the Austrian constitutional framework, effective judicial protection is only possible against those forms of administrative action which are provided by the Constitution. Ordinary federal and state legislation must not create new sources of law because otherwise effective legal protection would not be ensured. Every administrative act that potentially infringes an individual person's rights must be enacted in a form of action that provides effective legal protection. However, the examination of the Constitutional Court stops at that point. It seems the Constitutional Court implies that every action is in accordance with the constitutional system of forms of action. But what happens if the system of forms of action provided by the Austrian Constitution is too narrow and some acts adopted by an administrative authority do not fit in? In such a case, the Austrian Constitution does not provide legal protection at all.

27 Heinz Schäffer, *Rechtsquellen und Rechtsanwendung* (Manz 1973) p. 34.
28 See Ibid. 34, 42; Harald Eberhard, *Der verwaltungsrechtliche Vertrag* (Springer 2005) 264.
29 VfSlg 13.699/1994.

2.3.2 EU law's challenges and potential for the constitution

Due to the influences of EU law, the link between certain forms of action and judicial protection becomes more and more difficult.[30] Within the scope of Union law, the strong constitutional link between effective legal protection and certain forms of action become problematic, because not all regulations provided by EU law fit into the Austrian system of administrative forms of action. In this case, the Austrian legal order does not provide effective judicial protection.[31]

An example from environmental law regarding air quality plans clearly shows the deficits of this system. Such air quality plans are implemented in the form of ordinances by administrative authorities. According to the case law of the ECJ, a person directly affected by air pollution is entitled to require the competent national authorities to draw up an action plan.[32] In general, a subjective right to an ordinance does not exist in the Austrian legal system. If a person who is concerned by air pollution exceeding permitted values requests the competent administrative authority to release an air quality plan and if the authority does not react to the application, the right to an air quality plan cannot be enforced effectively.[33] The right to an administrative decision within a reasonable timescale is only enforceable concerning administrative issues. The Austrian legal system does not provide legal remedies to challenge inactivity regarding ordinances.

EU law, however, also creates new potential for the effective legal protection in the Austrian constitutional system. The Constitutional Court declared in its leading case on the EU-CFR in 2012[34] that 'it follows from the equivalence principle [as a general principle of the EU][35] that the rights guaranteed by the Charter of Fundamental Rights may also be invoked as constitutionally guaranteed rights'. The Court thus strengthened the possibilities for invoking the rights of the Charter before the Constitutional Court. The Court opened the possibilities for legal protection in other cases too, by arguing with EU law.[36]

2.3.3 The principle of reasonableness

According to the established case law of the Constitutional Court, which is based on a mere interpretation of the wording, the Austrian Constitution does not contain any provision[37] that recognises parties' rights in an administrative procedure at all or to a

30 See Harald Eberhard, 'Altes und Neues zur "Geschlossenheit des Rechtsquellensystems' (2007) 61 *Österreichische Juristenzeitung* 679.

31 See Ulrike Giera, 'Individualrechte aus Unionsrecht' in S. Schmid, V. Tiefenthaler, K. Wallnöfer and A. Wimmer (eds.), *Auf dem Weg zum hypermodernen Rechtsstaat?* (Jan Sramek 2011) 183–213.

32 Case C-237/07 Dieter Janecek v Freistaat Bayern [2008] ECR I-6221.

33 See Giera (n. 31) 183–213.

34 VfSlg 19.632/2012; see also Konrad Lachmayer, 'The Austrian Approach Towards European Human Rights, VfGH 14 March 2012, U 466/11 et al.' (2013) 7 *ICL-Journal* 105–107.

35 See Takis Tridimas, *The General Principles of EU Law* (2nd edn., Oxford University Press, Oxford 2007) 424.

36 Konrad Lachmayer, 'Country Report: Austria' in Anneli Albi (ed.), *The Role of National Constitutions* (T. M. C. Asser Press, The Hague 2016 [forthcoming]).

37 An exception is of course Art. 119a para 9 Austrian Constitution that provides parties' rights to municipalities in a supervisory procedure initiated by the federal or state authority.

certain extent. It lies within the scope of the statute to provide parties' rights. Thereby the legislator is bound by the principle of legality and the principle of equality.[38] The Court explicitly stated that the rule of law principle does not require granting of locus standing.[39] Only in rare cases does the Constitutional Court derive from the rule of law principle the obligation to grant parties' rights to a person concerned.[40] Instead, the Constitutional Court usually relies on the principle of equality (Art. 7 Austrian Constitution), which the Court tends to interpret loosely.[41] Thus, the Court has derived from the principle of equality a general principle of reasonableness.[42] In some cases the Court uses this principle of reasonableness to determine whether a statute grants locus standing or not. The statute from which individual rights are derived is bound to the general principle of objectivity. In general, granting subjective rights requires at the same time granting locus standing. Depending on the purpose of the procedure and on the peculiarity and the importance of the rights concerned, the exclusion of parties' rights can be appropriate, if the procedure will primarily guarantee the interests of another person.[43] The Constitutional Court examines case by case whether a differentiation concerning parties' rights is on the one hand essential in relation to the regulation and on the other hand founded on actual differences regarding the interests considered in the procedure.[44]

The reference to the principle of equality has to be viewed critically.[45] In licensing procedures concerning industrial facilities, for example, neighbours have subjective rights granted by the particular statute (Industrial Act) and are thus parties to the procedure. They can claim that they are adversely affected in their life, health or property by the facility. Due to deregulation a simplified procedure was introduced, in which neighbours – although their substantive rights are the same – are no longer parties to the administrative procedure. The Constitutional Court, however, did not classify this provision as a violation of the principle of equality. The purpose of speeding up procedures is legitimate. In the case of licensing an industrial facility for which granting permission is the rule, neighbours can be excluded from the procedure. The administrative authority is obliged to take care of the public interest – which also lies in the neighbours' interest and therefore the rights protected under the Industrial Law Act are not violated.[46]

In general, the non-reference to the rule of law principle in the context of establishing rights is surprising considering the fact that effective legal protection in administrative law depends on the participation in an administrative procedure which requires locus standing. Individual rights are only effectively protected if the beneficiary participates in the procedure.

38 VfSlg 6664/1972, 10.605/1985, 14.512/1996, 15.545/1999; 17.593/2005.

39 VfSlg 15.123/1998.

40 For example VfSlg 13.646/1993.

41 Lachmayer (n. 13).

42 Manfred Stelzer, *The Constitution of the Republic of Austria* (Hart Publishing 2011) 242–243.

43 VfSlg 11.934/1988; 19.617/2012.

44 VfSlg 15.545/1999, 17.389/2004.

45 See Bernhard Raschauer, 'Anlagenrecht und Nachbarschutz aus verfassungsrechtlicher Sicht' (1999) 13 *Zeitschrift für Verwaltung* 506–520, see also Rudolf Thienel, 'Verfassungsrechtliche Grenzen für das vereinfachte Genehmigungsverfahren nach Art 359b GewO' (2001) 15 *Zeitschrift für Verwaltung* 718.

46 VfSlg 14.512/1996, see also VfSlg 16.103/2001.

3 Rights-based perspective

3.1 Constitutional rights

The Austrian Constitution contains several fundamental procedural rights that are linked to the principle of effective legal protection: the right to a lawful judge (Art. 83 para. 2 Austrian Constitution), the right to a fair trial (Art. 6 ECHR) or the right to an effective remedy (Art. 13 ECHR and Art. 47 CFR).[47,48] The scope of the right to a lawful judge is quite broad. Every governmental authority that makes legally-binding decisions is regarded as a lawful judge. Hence Art. 83 para. 2 Austrian Constitution also comprises administrative bodies. The right to proceed before the lawful judge is infringed if an authority exercises a power it does not have or if it wrongly rejects its competence and thus refuses to decide on the merits,[49] if an improperly constituted tribunal deals with the case[50] or if a court does not request a preliminary ruling of the ECJ although it is obliged to.[51] The right to a fair trial (Art. 6 ECHR) is usually applied in accordance with the ECtHR case law as well as Art. 13 ECHR, which guarantees an effective remedy before a national authority if someone alleges the violation of rights and freedoms of ECHR.

3.2 Individual and procedural rights

3.2.1 Individual rights as structural precondition to effective legal protection

In Austrian administrative law, access to justice and effective legal protection crucially depends on individual rights (*subjektives Recht*). Without an individual or subjective right, a person does not enjoy legal protection. The right to access administrative authorities, the right to appeal to an administrative court or the right to a decision within a reasonable timescale requires a subjective right. The most common and accepted doctrine defines subjective rights as the legal power that an individual person derives from a regulation of public law to claim his/her interests against the state.[52] The difficult and still not fully answered question is when and how a subjective right can be derived from administrative law. There is a scholarly consensus that not every statute provides subjective rights for individuals. On the contrary, administrative statutes regularly contain objective duties for authorities and do not grant rights to an individual. If an interest concerned is recognised as a legally protected interest by law, a subjective right can be derived and subsequently enforced. Economic or environmental interests are usually not regarded as legal interests, but as factual interests that the administrative authorities have to consider *ex officio* without granting legal protection in an administrative procedure. Moreover, legal interests are usually narrowly defined.

47 See, regarding the application of the CFR, Chapter 2.3.2.

48 See, regarding the overall situation of fundamental rights in Austria, Anna Gamper, 'A "Bill of Rights" for Austria: Still Unfinished Business' (2010) III *Percorsi costituzionali. Quadrimestrale di diritti e libertà* 211.

49 VfSlg 12.889/1991.

50 VfSlg 10.022/1984.

51 VfSlg 14.390/1995.

52 VwSlg 14.750 A/1997; see W. Antoniolli and F. Koja, *Allgemeines Verwaltungsrecht* (3rd edn., Manz 1996) 283.

3.2.2 How are individual rights determined?

Some statutes explicitly grant subjective rights to individuals, but other laws have to be interpreted. According to the case law of the Administrative Court and the so-called 'impairment of rights doctrine' (*Schutznormtheorie*) a person has a subjective right if a statute protects not only public interests, but also interests of a specific person. The specific interest of a person must be distinguishable from the interests of the general public.[53] Whether a statute grants a subjective right or not depends on the purpose and objectives of the statute.[54] The interests that are protected under the 'impairment of rights doctrine' are traditionally limited to the subjective interests and concerns of a person, for example life or property.[55] Various cases have dealt with these disputed questions. However, the case law of the courts does not fully resolve the question. The result of the interpretation of the statute also tends to be part of a free decision on the part of the relevant administrative authorities and courts. The distinction between legal and factual interests is very contingent and to a certain extent arbitrary. It is often unclear or disputed, whether a statute grants a subjective right or not. Due to the narrow interpretation of subjective rights, access to justice in administrative law is more limited than open. In the light of effective legal protection, the uncertainty about whether an individual right exists or not is unsatisfactory, and the negative result that no individual right exists is – at least in certain cases – highly problematic.

3.2.3 Locus standing of parties

Granting locus standing to parties makes subjective rights enforceable. According to the General Administrative Procedural Act (GAPA), a person who is involved in an activity of an authority by a legal title or legal interest is party to a procedure. In other words, the party to the administrative procedure is a person whose rights are affected by the procedure. The GAPA does not constitute a subjective right for the parties itself, but refers to the substantive administrative law. Substantive statutes must again be interpreted in order to deduce subjective rights (regarding the theories described above). If a person is granted a subjective right in an administrative statute, he or she normally has locus standing in an administrative procedure to defend his or her rights. Some laws explicitly specify persons whose legal interests are recognised by law and are therefore considered as 'parties' in administrative procedure.

Subjective rights and locus standing in an administrative procedure are closely linked, but the two terms are not equal. On the one hand, some statutes grant locus standing without a corresponding subjective right (several environmental statutes for example grant locus standing to governmental organs or NGOs), on the other hand, as already mentioned, in some cases statutes do not grant locus standing although

53 J. Hengstschläger and D. Leeb, *Kommentar zum Allgemeinen Verwaltungsverfahrensgesetz I* (Manz 2004) Sec. 8 GAPA para 6.

54 C. Grabenwarter and M. Fister, *Verwaltungsverfahrensrecht und Verwaltungsgerichtsbarkeit* (4th edn., Verlag Österreich, Wien 2014) 24.

55 Eva Schulev-Steindl, 'Vom Wesen und Wert der Parteistellung' in C. Jabloner, G. Kucsko-Stadlmayer, G. Muzak, B. Perthold-Stoitzner and K. Stöger (eds.), *Vom praktischen Wert der Methode, FS Mayer* (Manz 2011) 694.

a subjective right is affected (neighbours for example do not have locus standing in procedures regarding certain industrial facilities that have minor effects on the neighbourhood).[56]

3.2.4 Procedural rights

Once someone is recognised as a party in an administrative procedure according to the GAPA, he or she has various rights, such as the right to access the files, the right to be heard, the right to remedies, the right to service of process or the right to an administrative decision within due time. These rights ensure an effective participation in the procedure and enforcement of the subjective rights.

If the administrative procedure ends with a negative administrative ruling, a person who alleges infringement of his or her rights has the right to file an appeal before the competent administrative court.[57] The right to appeal requires the anterior position as party to the administrative procedure. If a party does not have a subjective right, he or she can neither participate in the administrative procedure nor in the procedure before the court. Subsequently, an appeal against a decision of the administrative courts before the Administrative or the Constitutional Court can be filed by the parties to the procedure. Once again, only the parties to a procedure are entitled to file an appeal before the two supreme courts. While before the Administrative Court the allegation of the violation of an individual right granted by an ordinary statute is sufficient, the appeal before the Constitutional Court requires the alleged violation of a constitutionally guaranteed fundamental right.

3.2.5 Individual rights which cannot be enforced in an administrative procedure under the GAPA

As already mentioned, effective judicial protection in Austrian administrative law is focused on subjective rights and the participation in an administrative procedure according to GAPA and the obtaining of an administrative ruling. If a person is party to an administrative procedure and therefore gains an administrative ruling, his or her rights are effectively protected – first, by participating in the procedure, and second, by filing an appeal before the competent administrative court.

The reality is different when it comes to subjective rights which are not the subject of an administrative procedure to which the GAPA applies. In this case, effective judicial protection is not ensured, due to the fact that the right to appeal requires the participation in the preceding administrative procedure. If a person requests the application of an ordinance or a so-called 'factual act' like for example, the submission of information or the conducting of inspections, then neither the GAPA, nor the ACPA nor any other general procedure act is applicable.

56 Bernhard Raschauer, *Allgemeines Verwaltungsrecht* (4th edn., Verlag Österreich, Wien 2013) para 1105–1109.

57 Art. 132 para. 1(1) Austrian Constitution.

- Ordinances

Ordinances are adopted in an internal procedure where the persons concerned or interested do not have locus standing.[58] In order to ensure effective judicial protection it is necessary to obtain an administrative ruling which opens access to justice for the parties of the procedure. If the GAPA cannot be applied because a person files an application for an ordinance or a factual act, effective judicial protection is not guaranteed in Austrian administrative law, which constitutes a breach of Art. 47 CFR.[59]

- Acts of law enforcement

Against acts of law enforcement and police powers – although the administrative authority does not issue an administrative ruling, due to the fact that it does not conduct a formal procedure – effective judicial protection is ensured. A person who claims infringement of his or her rights because of the exercise of law enforcement has the right to appeal before the administrative courts of first instance.[60] The aim of an appeal against the exercise of direct administrative power is to declare the act unlawful and, should it still be taking place, to terminate it. Acts of direct administrative power or compulsion include the arrest of a person, towing away of cars or seizure of goods.

- Further (factual) acts

The administrative courts of first instance can still only review those forms of actions the Constitution provides. However, the limitation to certain legal acts was softened by the constitutional amendment establishing the administrative courts of first instance.[61] The Constitution opens up the possibility of introducing new forms of legal protection regarding other (factual) acts of administrative authorities, including the submission of information or the conducting of inspections. Federal or state laws can provide complaints for illegality of the 'conduct of an administrative authority in executing the law' ('*Verhalten einer Verwaltungsbehörde in Vollziehung der Gesetze*').[62] It remains to be seen whether and how the ordinary federal or state legislator will make use of this option.

3.3 Rights of administrative authorities or groups to intervene

The right to intervention exists in some limited cases. It may be granted to administrative authorities which are then formal parties in an administrative procedure. According to Art.132 para. 1(2) Austrian Constitution, the competent Federal Minister has

58 Raschauer (n. 56) para. 789.

59 See Bernhard Raschauer, 'Realakte, schlicht hoheitliches Handeln und Säumnisschutz' in Michael Holoubek and Michael Lang (eds.), *Rechtsschutz gegen staatliche Untätigkeit* (2011) 265.

60 Art. 130 para. 1(2) Austrian Constitution.

61 See Chapter 4.1.

62 Art. 130 para. 2(1) Austrian Constitution.

the right to appeal before an administrative court of first instance against an administrative ruling in certain matters that are regulated by federal law, but executed by the states, for example matters concerning citizenship or environmental impact assessment. With this right, the federal state supervises the execution and performance of the states.[63] Furthermore, federal and state laws can grant the right to appeal against administrative rulings to certain persons[64] or organs.[65] The Ombudsman for the environment, for example, is entitled to appeal against administrative rulings of certain environmental or nature protection proceedings. Several statutes grant locus standing to environmental organisations. Locus standing is explicitly granted to such organs or groups.

Such 'administrative parties' do not have their own subjective rights that they are defending. They participate in the procedure without being directly and personally affected. Their task is to observe and ensure objective legality in administrative or court procedures. The Ombudsman for the Environment, for example, is entitled to represent the concerns and interests of the environment as a public interest. He can challenge compliance with environmental laws and regulations in an administrative procedure. For the purpose of ensuring objective legality, 'administrative parties' have procedural rights, but no substantive rights. They can only file an appeal in the case of an alleged infringement of procedural rights.

3.4 Right to challenge inactivity as an essential aspect of effective judicial protection

Judicial protection is only efficient if the legal system provides the right to an administrative act within a reasonable time. An administrative authority is obligated to issue a ruling on submissions of a party without undue delay, within six months at the latest. If the competent administrative authority does not issue a ruling within the term allowed for the decision, the party has the right to file a complaint to the administrative court to claim a breach of the duty to reach a timely decision (*Säumnisbeschwerde*). Only parties of the corresponding administrative procedure who are entitled to get a decision have the right to file a complaint. According to the Federal Administrative Court Procedure Act (FAPA, *Verwaltungsgerichtshofsgesetz*), the court itself has to decide on the case within six months. In case the judgment is not issued within this term, the party can file a motion to set a deadline for violation of the duty to decide by an administrative court of first instance (*Fristsetzungsantrag*) to the Administrative Court. The responding court is instructed to issue the judgment within a maximum term of three months and to submit a copy of the judgment to the Administrative Court or to explain why it did not violate its duty to reach a decision. This term can be extended one more time if the court can submit evidence for reasons regarding the merits of the case which made it impossible to issue a judgment in due time.

The Austrian legal order provides a remedy against unlawful delay, but it is questionable whether the right to an administrative act within a reasonable time is effective. First, it takes a long time to enforce an administrative act, and secondly, if the

63 T. Öhlinger and H. Eberhard, *Verfassungsrecht* (10th edn., Facultas.wuv 2014) para. 661.
64 E.g. citizens´ initiatives.
65 Art. 132 para. 5 Austrian Constitution.

administrative court of first instance does not issue a decision after the Administrative Court has extended the term, the administrative act cannot be enforced.[66] Another problem is the general focus on administrative rulings. Only administrative rulings can be enforced by a complaint to the administrative court of first instance and/or to the Administrative Court. The complaints apply only to an administrative request. If an applicant requests a factual act, such as the submission of information or the conducting of inspections or an ordinance, neither the GAPA nor the Administrative Court Act is applicable and the applicant cannot claim a violation of the duty to decide.[67]

4 Institutional perspective

4.1 Separation of powers

The introduction of the new system of administrative courts of first instance[68] started to make significant changes to the concept of separation of powers between the administration and the judiciary. Before 2014, the constitutional concept provided different instances and possibilities to appeal within the administration and only after the exhausting of the chain of appeals was it possible to apply either to the Constitutional Court or to the Administrative Court. Since 2014, the role of administrative authorities has been significantly limited and all appeals now have to be addressed to the newly introduced administrative courts of first instance.[69] Moreover, from a separation of powers perspective, the link between administrative decisions and judgments by administrative courts became imminent.

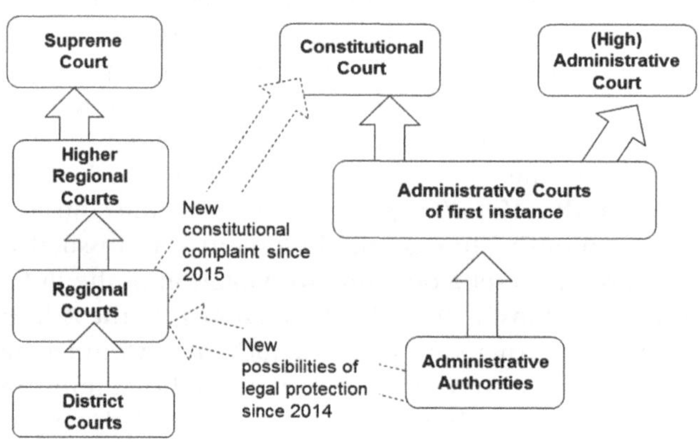

Figure 5.1 Separation of powers and court system

66 Ulrike Giera, *Individualrechte im europäischen Umweltrecht und ihre Durchsetzung im nationalen Recht* (Facultas-Nomos 2015) 228–247.

67 See Raschauer (n. 59) 265; Michael Potacs, 'Subjektives Recht gegen Feinstaubbildung?' (2009) 33 *Zeitschrift für Verwaltung* 874.

68 Most of the Courts were transformed from the existing independent administrative authorities.

69 An exception is a municipality's own sphere of competence where an administrative two-stage appeal still exists that can, however, be excluded by law. See Art. 118 para. 4 Austrian Constitution.

The same constitutional amendment also opened up new possibilities of legal protection from administrative authorities to ordinary courts.[70] Federal or state legislation may provide in specific matters an appeal from the administrative authority to a court of justice instead of an appeal to the administrative court. The quite strict separation of powers between administration and ordinary judiciary[71] was significantly weakened. The legislator can thus change the institutional and procedural concepts of appeal; it will, however, always result in a judicial review of the administrative decision.

4.2 The new system of legal protection in administrative law

In 2014, Austria introduced – as mentioned above – a completely new system of administrative courts of first instance (the so-called 9+2 model): one federal administrative court of first instance, a federal fiscal court of first instance and nine state administrative courts of first instance. With this reform, all stages of administrative appeal were abolished: the appellant can only file a complaint against an administrative ruling before the competent administrative court of first instance and, subsequently, the appellant can appeal against the decision of the administrative court to the Constitutional Court and/or to the Administrative Court. The access to the Administrative Court was limited due to the introduction of the administrative courts of first instance. Revision is only admissible if the solution depends on a legal question of essential importance. This is the case if the decision of the administrative court of first instance deviates from the established case law of the Administrative Court, such established case law does not exist or the legal question to be solved has not been answered in a uniform manner by the previously established case law (Art. 133 para 4 Austrian Constitution). This new system changes the understanding of the Administrative Court, in so far as the control of the administration is primarily the duty of the administrative courts of first instance, and no longer that of the Administrative Court. The function of the Administrative Court is now to ensure the objective legality and a uniform case law of the administrative courts of first instance.[72]

Along with the establishment of administrative courts of first instance, a so-called Administrative Courts Procedure Act (ACPA)[73] was adopted, which regulates the procedure before the administrative courts of first instance. This new procedural statute for the administrative courts of first instance does not provide a solution for the aforementioned problem regarding legal protection.

Another point that has to be regarded critically is the subsidiary application of the General Administrative Procedure Act. The underlying constellation is different in administrative and judicial procedures: While in an administrative procedure, the

70 Art. 94 para. 2 Austrian Constitution.

71 Art. 94 para. 1 Austrian Constitution.

72 See Rudolf Thienel, 'Die Kontrolle der Verwaltungsgerichte erster Instanz durch den Verwaltungsgerichtshof' in Michael Holoubek and Michael Lang (eds.), *Die Verwaltungsgerichtsbarkeit erster Instanz* (Linde Verlag 2013) 331–379.

73 The Administrative Courts Procedure Act (ACPA) (*Verwaltungsgerichtsverfahrensgesetz*) regulates the procedure before the administrative courts of first instance, while the (Federal) Administrative Court Procedure (FAPA, *Verwaltungsgerichtshofsgesetz*) applies to the procedure before the Federal Administrative Court which is, apart from the Constitutional Court, the last instance in administrative law.

relation between administrative authority and applicant[74] is hierarchical, in a judicial procedure, both the administrative authority and the appellant are equal parties to the procedure. Furthermore, administrative and judicial procedures are governed by different principles and standards; a subsidiary application involves the danger of a transfer of administrative standards to the court procedure. Thus, the new enacted ACPA not only solves problems but creates new ones regarding effective legal protection.

4.3 The concept of three supreme courts

Since the enactment of the Austrian Constitution in 1920, the Austrian system of judicial protection has been based on three supreme courts: the Constitutional Court, the Administrative Court and the Supreme Court. There is no formal hierarchy between these three courts and each of them is competent for a different substantive area of law: The Constitutional Court deals with constitutional questions, for example with the infringement of fundamental rights or federal issues;[75] the Administrative Court is competent to decide on violations of administrative law as last instance, if there is no violation of constitutional law at the same time; and finally the Supreme Court has to rule on civil law cases and criminal charges.[76] The relationship between the three courts is characterised by equality, although the position of the Constitutional Court is somehow distinguished because of its exclusive competence to review laws and ordinances and to repeal them in case they violate the constitution.[77]

The Austrian legal system lacks a constitutional complaint to appeal against decisions of civil or criminal courts to the Constitutional Court. Therefore, it is up to the Supreme Court to rule on violations of fundamental rights. While judges argue that there is no need for a constitutional complaint,[78] scholars demand it due to existing deficits in the case law of civil and criminal courts.[79] The Austrian Constitution established the Constitutional Court as a specialised court for constitutional questions. Thus, the Constitutional Court is the 'guardian' of constitutional fundamental rights and not the Supreme Court. The case law differs to some extent from the case law of the Constitutional Court, which involves the danger of having two different standards in the protection of fundamental rights.[80]

74 The accused person in an administrative penal law procedure.

75 See, regarding the Austrian Constitutional Court, Christoph Bezemek 'A Kelsenian Model of Constitutional Adjudication. The Austrian Constitutional Court' (2012) 66 *Zeitschrift für öffentliches Recht* 115; A. Gamper and F. Palermo 'The Constitutional Court of Austria: Modern Profiles of an Archetype of Constitutional Review' (2008) 3 *Journal of Comparative Law* 64.

76 Criminal law must be distinguished from administrative penal law which applies in case of a violation of administrative law. In first instance administrative authorities are competent to decide over breaches of administrative law. An appeal against their decision can be filed before an administrative court of first instance. Another peculiarity of administrative penal law is that administrative bodies are not only competent to impose fines, but also imprisonment.

77 Art. 139, Art. 140 Austrian Constitution.

78 See for example Eckhardt Ratz, 'Grundrechte in der Strafjudikatur des OGH' (2006) 60 *Österreichische Juristenzeitung* 318.

79 See for example A. Stufer and R. Soyer, 'Kritik des Grundrechtsschutzes in der Strafjudikatur des OGH' (2007) 61 *Österreichische Juristenzeitung* 139–148.

80 See Christoph Grabenwarter, 'Die österreichischen Höchstgerichte und deren Verhältnis zueinander' (2008) 16 *Journal für Rechtspolitik* 13.

This problem was addressed by another constitutional amendment of 2013, which came into force in 2015. Although there is still no constitutional complaint against judgments of the Supreme Court, a new appeal was introduced with regard to the judgments of the ordinary (!) courts of first instance. After a judgment of an ordinary court of first instance, the complainant can not only appeal to the ordinary court of second instance, but also file a complaint at the Constitutional Court that the provisions of the statutes, on which the judgment is based in the concrete case, contradict the constitution.[81] The new form of constitutional review enables a certain control of constitutionality in the proceedings of the ordinary courts. It is, however, still not a full constitutional complaint against the judgment of the ordinary court of first instance, and not at all a constitutional complaint against the judgment of the Supreme Court. Thus, the deficits of legal protection regarding a constitutional complaint against ordinary court judgments have not really been solved, although it is fair to say that the structural problems have been reduced.

4.4 Ombudsman board and mediation

From a constitutional perspective, the Austrian Ombudsman system (*Volksanwaltschaft*) is a politically important but legally very weak institution. People can, after exhausting the possibilities of legal protection, file a complaint against maladministration.[82] The Ombudsman board can investigate and make recommendations, but the administrative authorities only have to justify their decisions. In the end, the Ombudsman board cannot effectively protect the rights of individuals. The role of the Ombudsman Board was, however, developed in 2012. The powers of the Ombudsman Board were strengthened with regard to checking human rights in the administration, following a development of ombudsman institutions around the world in the last 20 years.[83] These new competences regarding human rights violation of the administration, however, refer only to parts of law enforcement, including prisons, policing and institutions for handicapped persons.

In certain cases, administrative law also provides possibilities for mediation and alternative dispute resolution, e.g. in the context of energy regulation between consumer and energy companies or in environmental law. The mediation procedures are, however, always provided before a formal legal procedure is started. It might be a possibility for weak legal protection with low access barriers, but legal protection will finally be granted by the courts.

5 Conclusion

An overall evaluation of the principle of effective legal protection would be quite positive. A strong concept of administrative procedures, a new system of administrative court and dynamic case law of the Constitutional Court are constantly improving

81 Thomas Ziniel, 'Strengthening the Judicial Review System in Austria' (2014) 8 *ICL-Journal* 437.

82 See Art. 148a-j Austrian Constitution.

83 See Gabriele Kucsko-Stadlmayer, *Europäische Ombudsmann-Institutionen: Eine rechtsvergleichende Untersuchung zur vielfältigen Umsetzung einer Idee* (Springer 2008).

the legal protection against different administrative acts. The huge impact of ECHR and EU Law is also contributing to an overall stable system.

The positive evaluation does not, however, mask various severe structural problems in the Austrian system of effective legal protection:

- The impact of the European Union not only provides new possibilities for domestic legal protection, but also affects the Austrian concepts of legal protection. The consequence might not only be deficits in legal protection, but also the necessity to reform the whole constitutional structure to create conformity with Union law. The introduction of the administrative courts of first instance can serve as such an example, with it being possible after 20 years to find a proper solution to such problems.
- While the new administrative courts signify a huge improvement to legal protection in Austria, the implementation of the new system goes hand-in-hand with manifold procedural problems in detail. This kind of transitional challenge will hopefully be resolved by the legislative adaption of the new procedural law and by the case law of the administrative courts.
- The concept of individual rights in administrative law remains quite restrictive and limits the possibilities of individuals to participate in administrative procedures. While such concepts help to accelerate administrative proceedings, especially in commercial administrative law, they limit the effectiveness of legal protection.
- The rather strict typology of administrative action also limits the possibilities of legal protection. The constitutional reform created new possibilities on the part of the legislator to open up the system regarding any kind of administrative acts. If the legislation is exploiting this new potential, significant deficits in legal protection could be resolved.

In conclusion, the principle of effective legal protection remains an important project of Austrian constitutional and administrative law. There is still plenty of room for improvement, but it is already based on the strong rule of law in the Austrian legal system.

6 The principle of effective legal protection in Danish administrative law

Søren Højgaard Mørup

1 Historical developments

There is no legally binding principle of effective legal protection in Danish law. It is of course a concern for legislators to take effective legal protection into account when making laws – and the legislation does provide effective legal protection – and it may be of relevance to take into account in judgments where the relevant rules are not clear. But no general legal principle exists regulating the matter – the administration and the courts are only bound by the laws that the legislator has decided should provide legal protection. The Constitution ensures only a minimum level of legal protection.

Danish citizens do however have a high degree of effective legal protection whether speaking of procedural guarantees (e.g. the right to be heard or administrative authorities' duty to give reasons for their decisions) or access to remedies (the courts and the Ombudsman as well as rights to administrative recourse). This is not based on a general principle of effective legal protection, but on specific rules. A great deal of these rules is part of the general administrative law which applies to all administrative decisions unless an exception is made by law. In certain administrative areas (e.g. tax administration) there are rules that give the citizen further specific rights.[1] I shall not go into such special rules. The following thus concerns only the general rules which – normally – are the minimum standards for citizens' rights.

Many of the rules that give citizens procedural guarantees have been developed by either the courts or the Ombudsman. Several of the most important rights have since been codified and expanded in two laws of general administrative law: the Public Information Act (PIA, first adopted in 1964) and the Public Administration Act (PAA, first adopted in 1985).[2] Both acts have been amended since – PIA was generally revised in 2013. It must be said that before 1964 the right of access to information was relatively limited, though the Ombudsman since 1964 has had influence on the application of the law concerning the interpretation, including the application of the principle of 'more publicity', i.e. the duty to consider whether to give citizens access to information that the law does not entitle them to demand.[3]

1 Cf. Consolidation Act No. 175 of 23 February 2011.
2 Act No. 606 of 6 June 2013 and Consolidation Act No. 433 of 22 April 2014 respectively.
3 See s 14 of the Public Information Act and s 10 of the Public Administration Act.

The influence of Danish administrative legal theory should also be considered. Danish administrative law was more or less 'founded' by Poul Andersen in 1924 when he published his doctoral thesis on the invalid administrative acts.[4] Before 1924 there was very little literature, no general laws, and only a few court rulings established the general rules of administrative law. Poul Andersen went on to write Danish administrative law in five editions from 1936 to 1965 and had great influence on the courts and the Ombudsman's (established in 1955) application of administrative law.[5]

2 Constitutional framework

The Danish Constitution '*Grundloven*' sets forth only a few rights for citizens as to effective legal protection. Art. 63 of *Grundloven* grants the right to bring administrative decisions before the courts. A few provisions give further rights in this regard. Thus Art. 73 of the Constitution states, for example, that both the question of the legality of an expropriation as well as the question of what comprises 'complete compensation' can be tried by the courts. The Constitution also declares that it is possible for the legislator to set up administrative courts, but there must be access to appeal to the Supreme Court. The legislator has not set up administrative courts; therefore all administrative matters can be brought before the ordinary courts.

According to Art. 55 of *Grundloven*, the Parliament (*Folketinget*) elects one or two Ombudsmen to scrutinise the state administration. The provision only means that the institution of the Ombudsman once created cannot be abolished. However, it is up to the legislator to establish the extent of control. For instance, the Ombudsman's jurisdiction includes the local municipalities – which comprise a substantial part of the administration – according to the Ombudsman Act but the Constitution does not prevent the legislator from changing this.[6]

The Danish Constitution therefore has relatively little importance when determining rights of citizens in relation to effective legal protection. The constitutional framework is just that: A frame that leaves it open to the legislator to decide what rights to legal protection citizens should have, besides the right to bring matters before the courts.

It is relatively rare that provisions of the Constitution are invoked in cases concerning administrative law apart from the principle of legality which is deduced from *Grundloven* and there are no cases where a violation of *Grundloven* has been found in relation to the general matter of effective legal protection. It may help to understand the lack of rules in the Constitution on effective legal protection that most of the rules were written in 1848–1849, i.e. before there was anything called administrative law in Danish law, and it has only been amended four times, the last time being in 1953. One reason for this is the fact that *Grundloven* is very difficult to change: first,

4 Poul Andersen, *Om Ugyldige Forvaltningsakter* (Arnold Busck, Cph. 1924).

5 Poul Andersen, *Dansk Forvaltningsret* (Nyt Nordisk Forlag – Arnold Busck, Cph. 1936, Gyldendalske Boghandel, Nordisk Forlag, Cph. 1946, Gyldendal, Cph. 1956, Gyldendal, Cph. 1963 and Gyldendal, Cph. 1965).

6 Cf. Helle Bødker Madsen, *Jens Garde et al., Forvaltningsret: Almindelige emner* (5th edn., Jurist- og Økonomforbundets Forlag, Cph. 2009) 449–450, Kaj Larsen, *Hans Gammeltoft-Hansen et al., Forvaltningsret* (2nd edn., Cph. 2002) 866.

a constitutional bill must be passed in Parliament. Then the government must – if it wishes to (it is not obligated) – call for a general election. Then the proposal must be passed once more in the newly elected parliament. Then it must be subjected to a referendum where more than 40% of the all the persons that may vote in parliamentary elections must vote yes in order for the law to pass. Finally, the government must confirm the law.[7] It is also a major concern that there is really no need for provisions in the constitutions securing citizens rights in as much as the ordinary legislation provides such rights.[8]

3 Rights-based perspective

There are a number of possible legal remedies for citizens. As a starting point it must be said that an administrative authority which is aware that it has made an illegal decision is obligated to re-open the case in order to assess whether the decision is invalid.[9] The duty to reassess ends if or when it is or becomes clear that the decision is not invalid (and perhaps also if it is or becomes clear that the illegality is of very little importance). So if it is obvious from the beginning that the decision is legal, the authority does not actually have to re-open the case, but can reply that there aren't sufficient grounds for re-opening the case. Frequently, the problem is that there is a disagreement on whether the decision is illegal, or that there is a disagreement on the use of discretion by the administration rather than the legality of a decision. In that case other remedies become relevant to consider.

As mentioned above, all administrative decisions can be brought before the ordinary courts. The courts can also try claims for damages as well as assess the legality of the use of force. The conditions for bringing a case before the courts will be described below. As also mentioned in chapter 2, *Folketinget* elects an Ombudsman to scrutinise the administration. Besides these two forms of remedies there are in many cases other remedies available.

In many cases administrative recourse is possible, i.e. the citizen has a right to have a case reviewed by another administrative authority. Many administrative authorities are also subject to supervision by another administrative authority. This does not give the citizen a right to review, but the supervising authority may be obligated to review a case (though this is in principle not an obligation towards the citizen).

Since it is a general rule of Danish administrative law it should be noted that even though a remedy is available, it does not mean that the citizen is not obliged to comply with an administrative decision until it is perhaps changed or quashed. However, normally the authority that has made a decision may suspend the effects of that decision until a complaint has been decided.[10] Also both administrative recourse authori-

7 Cf. Jens Peter Christensen, *Jens Peter Christensen et al, Dansk statsret* (Jurist- og Økonomforbundets Forlag, Cph. 2012) 394–396.

8 Cf. Jens Peter Christensen, 'Er grundloven god nok?' *Jyllandsposten* (Viby J 5 June 2013) on the day of the 60th anniversary of the latest revision of the constitution.

9 Cf. Karsten Revsbech, *Jens Garde et al, Forvaltningsret: Almindelige emner* (5th edn., Jurist- og Økonomforbundets Forlag, Cph. 2009) 493–494, Karsten Loiborg, *Hans Gammeltoft-Hansen et al., Forvaltningsret* (2nd edn., Jurist- og Økonomforbundets Forlag, Cph. 2002) 921–927.

10 Cf. Revsbech (n. 9) 323–327, Loiborg (n. 9) 985–987.

ties[11] and the courts may do the same[12] and the Ombudsman – who has no powers to make or change decisions – may ask that the administration does so (and in practice the administration will comply).[13]

It should perhaps be pointed out that there is no requirement of violation of a so-called subjective right for a citizen to be entitled to make a complaint or file a lawsuit against an authority. Instead the citizen must have an interest in the matter – for instance that he is in some way affected by an administrative decision.

In some cases a local authority (a *kommune* or a *region*) is entitled to bring a higher authority's decision before the courts. This situation is in practice the same if the Ombudsman asks that the administration re-evaluate a decision. If the administration chooses not to comply – which does not happen very often – the Ombudsman can recommend that the state pays the cost of bringing the case before the courts if the citizen wishes to do so. Such a recommendation will always be followed. Once the case has been decided by the courts, there is no doubt that the authorities will act in accordance with the verdict by their own accord. There have however been a few cases where it was unclear what the result of a court case actually was (because the verdict was ambiguous) and this can lead to a new court case so that the ambiguity may be resolved.

3.1 Administrative recourse

3.1.1 The administrative recourse system

Administrative decisions are in the first instance for the most part made either by locally elected municipal authorities (*kommuner*) or government (state) authorities. An important exception to the rule that most first instance decisions are made by either *kommuner* or state authorities is hospitals which are governed by elected regional authorities (*regioner*). Other exceptions include independent tribunals or council (*nævn* and *råd* respectively). For example, compensation for expropriation is decided by an independent tribunal when the expropriating authority and the citizen cannot reach an agreement by themselves.[14]

If there is no law stating otherwise the decision made by a *kommune*, a *region*, a *nævn*, a *råd* or by a ministry is not subject to administrative recourse. Decisions made by state authorities other than ministries are normally subject to recourse unless the law states otherwise. For example, a decision made by *Naturstyrelsen* ('the Nature Board') would normally be subject to recourse to the ministry for the environment.[15]

However, in many – probably most – cases the law provides the right to administrative recourse to another authority. Most decisions made by a *kommune* are subject to recourse either to a state authority or an independent tribunal depending on the law. Also in many cases the right to recourse to a ministry from another state authority is

11 Cf. the aforementioned literature.

12 Cf. Ugeskrift for Retsvæsen 1994, pp. 823–827 H, Revsbech (n. 9) 382–385.

13 Cf. Madsen (n. 6) 471, Larsen (n. 6) 885.

14 An overview of the organisation of the Danish administration cf. Jørgen Albæk Jensen, *Jens Garde et al., Forvaltningsret: Almindelige emner* (5th edn., Jurist- og Økonomforbundets Forlag, Cph. 2009) 37–69.

15 Cf. Revsbech (n. 9)303–305, Loiborg (n. 9) 954–963.

replaced by a right to recourse to an independent tribunal (e.g. *Naturstyrelsen*'s decisions can in some cases be appealed to *Natur- og Miljøklagenævnet* (Nature- and Environment Appeal Tribunal) instead of the ministry). And where decisions are made in the first instance by a tribunal there is often recourse to another tribunal (e.g. the decision to limit the owner's use of his fields or to grant access to the public made by a Nature Conservancy Board (*fredningsnævn*) may be appealed to *Natur- og Miljøklagenævnet*). Thus in most cases there will be access to administrative recourse to at least one other administrative authority and in a few cases even two levels of administrative recourse. This goes perhaps some way to explain why there generally has been little support for establishing administrative courts: since there are a large number of specialised and quasi-judicial tribunals, the need for actual administrative courts does not seem very pressing.

3.1.2 Requirement for access to administrative recourse

Administrative recourse is normally only available once an administrative decision has been made. One cannot therefore complain until a case has been decided. If one for instance wishes to make a complaint over the procedure, one must wait till the authority has made its decision before making a complaint. If the authority neglects or refuses to make a decision, this may however in itself be considered a decision and it is thus possible to make a complaint also in that situation.[16] A citizen has the right to a decision within 'reasonable time'. The problem for the citizen is that it is generally a matter or resources and thus a political matter, what a reasonable time is.[17]

Administrative appeal is normally only available to citizens who have a significant and individual interest in a decision.[18] The citizens who are specified subjects to a decision will always be considered to have a significant and individual interest, e.g. the subject of a prohibition according to an individual administrative act or an applicant may, for example, file a complaint. The requirement that the interest must be individual means it is usually not possible to complain about general provisions since no one has an individual interest. However, a citizen will have an individual interest if a decision is made regarding him in accordance with the provisions and the recourse authority may then decide on the legality of the provisions. The requirement that the interest must be both significant and individual means that it is not enough to be individually effected, the citizen must also have a significant interest. This can be determined only case-by-case. Thus, a number of neighbours may be affected by a building permit, but only those that are affected significantly may complain. So a neighbour who loses his perfect view of the sea because of a building permit may be affected significantly, whereas another neighbour who has no special view (e.g. the only view is of some other houses beyond the land where the new building is to be erected) may not be significantly affected. Or, if a great number is affected equally, e.g. 100 people

16 Cf. Revsbech (n. 9) 305–307.

17 Cf. Jens Olsen, *Hans Gammeltoft-Hansen et al, Forvaltningsret* (2nd edn., Jurist- og Økonomforbundets Forlag, Cph. 2002) 923–925. If a decision is not made within reasonable time, the citizen may be entitled to damages cf. Orla Friis, *Jens Garde et al, Forvaltningsret: Almindelige emner* (5th edn., Jurist- og Økonomforbundets Forlag, Cph. 2009) 566.

18 Revsbech (n. 9) 307–313, Loiborg (n. 9) 963–968.

are affected significantly, then no one will be affected individually and none of them may complain. Sometimes the access to recourse is subject to regulation by law. Thus environmental laws often give access to recourse for specific associations. And the law regulating local planning provisions provides access to recourse to anyone with a legal interest.

If a written decision is subject to administrative recourse, it must include information about the relevant recourse authority and how to file a complaint including information about a possible time limit (if this information is not given the time limits are suspended). This does not apply if the decision is entirely in favour of the citizen and the citizen therefore has no reason to complain.

Unless the law states otherwise, there are no formal requirements and no time limits.[19] Thus it is sufficient for a citizen to just phone or send an e-mail to the authority and say that he wishes to file a complaint. It is of course for practical purposes necessary to make clear who is complaining and what the complaint is about – if this is not clear the authority must enquire by itself. If a complaint is made to a wrong authority that authority must forward the complaint to the correct authority. As can be seen it is usually very easy to file a complaint. Only if the law provides must the citizen pay a (usually relatively small) fee, typically 50–100 Euro. On the other hand, if the citizen has expenses in regard to, for example, legal counsel he must normally pay that himself. This must be seen in relation to the recourse authority's obligation to review the case by itself (cf. chapter 4.1).

Often there are in fact time limits and in some cases other requirements, e.g. that a complaint should be written, but as stated the administration must inform about such requirements and must often assist the citizen.

3.2 The courts

Grundloven grants the right to bring administrative decisions before the courts. It must be said that there – in spite of the words of the Constitution – is an exception to this rule. According to a verdict by the Supreme Court the legislator may limit access to courts. Today, two important examples of this remain: the Refugee Tribunal and the Foreigners Tribunal (which resemble a court, e.g. the chairman must be a high or supreme court justice). If a complaint concerns the 'discretionary' decision as to the correct application of the law the case will be thrown out of court. Other matters can be tried, e.g. the correct abstract interpretation of the law, procedural errors and breach of general legal principles. What may at first seem a very problematic exception is in practice not quite so problematic. The reason for the rule is that court cases can take years which would mean foreigners without legal grounds for staying could stay for years.[20]

Unless the law states otherwise there are no time limits (in fact the law very often sets time limits; if so the administration must inform about the time limit) and nor is it a requirement that the means of administrative recourse have been exhausted (in fact the law also in many cases alters this).[21] Only citizens with a legal interest in

19 Cf. Revsbech (n. 9)314–322, Loiborg (n. 9) 968–982.

20 Cf. Revsbech (n. 9) 412–414.

21 Ibid. 365–372.

a decision may challenge it at the courts. This includes anyone with a significant and individual interest in a decision.

The proceedings in most cases follow the general rules of civil court cases. If a criminal case concerns an administrative decision, e.g. the refusal to comply with an order or prohibition, the administrative decision may be challenged during the criminal proceedings.

As a general rule a verdict may be appealed once. So a district court verdict may be brought before a high court. Cases that concern 'matters of principle' may be referred by a district court to a high court and in that case the high court verdict can be appealed to the Supreme Court. Also if a case has been tried at both a district and a high court a party may apply for permission to bring the case before the Supreme Court.

It is possible for other parties to intervene, but it is rather seldom used by private parties. In principle at least a verdict is only binding for the parties to the case. It has been seen that other private parties than the recipient of a permit e.g. neighbours have sued the authority who has issued the permit – without the recipient being party to the case. In my view this can perhaps pose a problem as to the right to a fair trial. In one case the Supreme Court decided that a warehouse was illegally built.[22] The owner was not party to the case. Eventually the warehouse was made legal by way of a new local plan. This too was contested by other private parties, this time without success.[23] If the Supreme Court had decided that the warehouse could not be given a permit it would have had to be demolished. If the owner in such a situation tried to contest such a decision by the administration – one could ask if the owner would have access to a fair trial.

3.3 The Ombudsman

Anyone may make a complaint to the Ombudsman (*Folketingets Ombudsmand*) as long as the complaint is not anonymous. On the other hand, the Ombudsman is not obliged to review the complaint – he may refuse entirely or just review aspects of the complaint.[24]

The Ombudsman's competence does not include all parts of the public administration: certain tribunals fall outside his competence, some because they decide conflicts between citizens (e.g. rent tribunals) or are similar to courts (e.g. tribunals deciding compensation for expropriation). However, the majority of the public administration fall within the Ombudsman's competence.[25] Since the Ombudsman's competence does not include the courts, he will not review cases that are or are about to be brought before the courts. Also since he is a parliamentary Ombudsman he will not review cases where *Folketinget* or a parliamentary committee has expressed an opinion.

The Ombudsman will normally refuse to review a case if the complaint is filed more than a year after the administration made its decision. Also he will refuse cases where the citizen has access to administrative recourse.[26] If a case concerns a commune or

22 Cf. Ugeskrift for Retsvæsen 2004, pp. 1849–1856.
23 Cf. Ugeskrift for Retsvæsen 2011, pp. 1712–1719.
24 Cf. Madsen (n. 6) 468–471, Larsen (n. 6) 879–884.
25 Cf. Madsen (n. 6) 454–464, Larsen (n. 6) 867–879.
26 Cf. Madsen (n. 6) 469–470, Larsen (n. 6) 880–882.

region he will usually send the case to *Statsforvaltningen* before reviewing the case himself.

The Ombudsman cannot make or change decisions. He may express his opinion and can appeal to the administration, e.g. that it reconsiders changing its decision. He may also criticise the administration. Almost always the administration follows an appeal from the Ombudsman. If not he may appeal to the 'free process' authorities to give free process, i.e. the state pays the legal expenses of a court case if the citizen wishes to pursue the matter at the courts. Such an appeal has hitherto always been complied with and it is very hard to imagine this will change.[27]

3.4 Procedural rights – an overview

The citizens' procedural rights are mainly governed by the Public Administration Act (PAA). It is supplemented by unwritten law that in some respects provides further rights especially as to the extent the citizen must be heard on the authorities' initiative.

A citizen has the right to use representatives, but the use of counsel or representatives must be paid for by the citizen himself. In some select areas of the law e.g. concerning taxes and expropriation the law provides for total or partial reimbursement.

The PAA provides a citizen with a significant and individual interest in a decision (cf. para 3.1.2.) and a right to access the documents of the case. The general rule is that a citizen may access all the documents of the case. The most important exception (probably) is that the right to access does not include internal documents i.e. documents that have not been made available to anyone outside the authority (except for certain legal reasons). Also certain external documents are exempted from access. If there is factual information of importance in such documents, this information must however normally be made available. There are also other exceptions to the right to access. For instance, there is generally no access to criminal cases under the PAA (this is governed by the Administration of Justice Act, i.e. the procedural law of the courts). Also information may be exempted due to significant public or private interests but the right to access must be given considerable weight in balancing these interests. A decision whether to give access or not to the documents of a case is a decision in itself meaning that it gives rise to the same rights regarding complaint, reasoning, etc. as any other decision. Even if the citizen does not have an actual legal right to access a certain document or piece of information the authority is obliged – on its own initiative – to consider if it should give access anyway (unless it would be a breach of the rules of confidentiality or the rules on processing of personal data). This includes giving reasons if such voluntary access is refused.

According to the PAA, citizens must be heard before a decision is made in the following situation: if a citizen with a significant and individual interest is unaware of information relating to facts or external professional assessments the authority must make the information or the assessments available to the citizen for comment before a decision is made. This however only applies if the information or the assessments are unfavourable to the citizen and of substantial importance for the decision in question. There are a number of specific exceptions to this rule, for instance if the citizen does not have the right to access to the information. According to unwritten principles of contradiction in some cases the right to be heard is more comprehensive,

27 Cf. Madsen (n. 6) 488–490, Larsen (n. 6) 908–911.

but as a general rule the obligation to take steps to hear the citizen does not include opinions about how a case should be decided or legal matters, e.g. the interpretation of the law, only matters relating to the facts of the case. However, the citizen may at his own initiative make a statement which may relate to facts, the law or just state his opinion. The administration is normally obliged to postpone making a decision until the citizen has had time to make a statement (the administration may set a time limit and in some cases refuse to postpone the decision making, for instance if the law has set a time limit for the administration to make the decision).

The right to access documents and to make a statement should be seen in connection with the right to demand a decision be postponed until access to the documents of the case has been given (decided).

According to the PAA, a written decision must be accompanied by reasons, unless it is entirely in favour of the citizen. If the citizen is informed orally of such a decision, the citizen may within 14 days' demand reasons be given. The reasoning must include the legal grounds for the decision (e.g. the relevant paragraphs and sections of the law according to which the decision is made) and if necessary also a brief account of the facts of the case of substantial importance. If the decision is discretionary the main considerations must also be made clear.

As stated above, information must also in some situations be given about administrative recourse and the access to the courts.

4 Institutional perspective

4.1 Administrative recourse

As it was discussed above, administrative recourse institutions include both governmental (state) administrative authorities and tribunals. This varies from law to law and there is no general rule. There has however been a tendency towards a system where appeals can be made to one level of administrative recourse in the form of an independent tribunal (*nævn*). There are many different *nævn* and thus *nævn* are generally speaking specialised and usually more so than compared to a ministry. Also *nævn* are normally free of political influence (as opposed to a ministry) though there are political members of some *nævn* and the members are appointed by politicians. It must be noted that political motives often are not legal and abuse of power in terms of making decisions based on political views rather than the law is quite rare. In many cases the chairman must be a judge or at least a lawyer in order to ensure the legality of the decisions made by the tribunal, whereas other members provide other kinds of expertise depending on what matters are decided by the board. For example, *Taksationsmyndigheden* (Valuation Board), which has as its sole task to decide on damages claimed by neighbours to windmills, consists of a lawyer who fulfils the conditions for being appointed a judge and a real estate agent, the lawyer acting as chairman. In every *kommune* there is a committee on children and young people *(Børn og unge-udvalg)* which amongst other things decides on the forced removal of children from their home. The committee consists of a municipal judge (as chairman), two members from the council of the *kommune*, and two members who have knowledge of a pedagogical-psychological nature.

Common to all recourse institutions is that they are part of the administration and therefore subject to the rules of general administrative law including the PIA and the PAA. It is a general principle of Danish administrative law that the administrative authority must examine all aspects of a case on its own initiative before making a decision. This means that a recourse authority by itself must examine the law, the facts and the relevant considerations of a case regardless of the issues mentioned in a complaint.[28]

Unless the law states otherwise the review includes discretionary matters. Often the law reduces the review to legal matters (which includes review of the facts of the case). Where application of the law relies on discretion in the sense that the law leaves it open to the administration whether a certain decision should be made only matters of law can be reviewed – if no rule is broken, then the decision must stand, and if a rule is broken, usually the decision can only be quashed and if relevant referred back to the administration, not changed by the recourse authority. However, if the application of the law relies on discretion in the sense that the law uses vague terms, e.g. whether a building project is 'large', this is considered a legal matter and can be reviewed. Sometimes the recourse authority may give the administration a margin of appreciation in such instances, especially if knowledge of the local situation is better determined by the local administration.[29]

Review always includes determining what the facts of a case are.[30] It also includes the interpretation of the law and the application of the law in the specific case (cf. above). The law is not only the written law but also general principles of administrative law: the principles of equality, proportionality, legitimate expectations and the duty to make a decision based on discretion in each case where the law gives the administration discretion to name the most important principles that are not related to procedure. As to procedural rules both the decision's compliance with written and unwritten rules are reviewed.

Generally speaking, the recourse authority can react in the following ways: if the complaint does not meet formal requirements, it may dismiss the complaint. It may uphold the decision. It may quash a decision – and if relevant can refer it back to the administration, if deemed necessary with guidelines. It may also change a decision, but as stated above there may be limitations as to discretionary decisions.[31]

It should be noted, that often the recourse authority may change the decision to what it considers to be the right decision, even if it is unfavourable to the citizen who has complained. Sometimes the law specifies that the citizen should be heard first in such cases – perhaps it is a general rule – and in some cases the citizen can actually revoke his complaint.[32]

4.2 The courts

As stated previously, there are no administrative courts, but only a few specialised courts in Denmark. The Danish Courts include the Supreme Court, two high courts, and 24 district courts as well as courts of the Faroe Islands and Greenland. These

28 Cf. Revsbech (n. 9) 329–331.
29 Ibid. 334–340.
30 Ibid. 341–342.
31 Ibid. 342–350.
32 Ibid. 346–350.

courts handle both criminal cases and civil cases, including both cases where citizens contest administrative decisions and/or claim damages from the administration. Also there is a Maritime and Commercial Court, a Land Registration Court, and the Special Court of Indictment and Revision. The Maritime and Commercial Court has only a few administrative law cases. The Land Registration Court actually is a special form of administration (that traditionally has been performed at the courts). The Special Court of Indictment and Revision has administrative law cases since a judge normally can only be fired by this court, but otherwise it has little to do with administrative law. The Appeals Permission Board has to be also mentioned, which is neither part of the administration, nor is it a court. This board is a special organ to which only some rules of administrative law are not applied. Its chairman is a Supreme Court judge. The board decides mainly on allowing certain types of court appeals which are not available without permission, e.g. the right to appeal to the Supreme Court as a third instance, and as an appeal board regarding decisions concerning legal aid made by The Department of Civil Affairs under the Ministry of Justice.

According to *Grundloven*, 'the courts are entitled to review any question regarding the boundaries of the administration'. What those boundaries are, the Constitution does not say. It was left for the courts to determine this. From 1849 to 1922, review developed from just deciding whether a matter was for the courts or the public administration to decide to examine the legality of administrative acts. However, there was no judicial review of the use of discretion, and only a little case law concerning procedural requirements. From the 1920s the courts developed a new approach that the use of discretion should respect the principles of lawful considerations/interest, equality and proportionality.[33]

Today, judicial review of administrative acts goes as far as to check whether the relevant considerations or interests have been taken into account, but normally not to review the balancing of the lawful considerations or interests as long as the outcome is within the limits of the principle of proportionality and not contrary to the principles of equality and legitimate expectations. For instance, the courts will not decide how to balance the conflicting interest of the environment against the interest of a land owner when the administration has decided to issue or not to issue a permit to build a house outside the city zones. This is a matter for discretion. But the courts will check that all relevant considerations have been made. If a permission is not granted, and this is contrary to previous similar cases, the courts may (and will normally) decide that the owner is entitled to a permit. Also if a permit has been given and the administrative authority wishes to change that decision the courts will decide if the owner has legitimate expectations and if so whether revocation is possible.

Judicial review may possibly extend to the investigation whether the outcome is manifestly unreasonable or unfair. The courts will also review whether there is an obligation to use discretion in each case (as opposed to the administration setting up and following strict rules by its own accord), i.e. whether fettering discretion is prohibited (which

33 Cf. Jørgen Mathiassen, *Jens Garde et al, Forvaltningsret: Almindelige emner* (2nd edn., Jurist- og Økonomforbundets Forlag, Cph. 1989) 321–327.

varies from area to area). Finally, judicial review examines the compliance with procedural rules and the correct determination of the facts of the case.[34]

Of course, the outcome of a judicial case depends on the claims made before the court. A court may always quash an illegal decision and – if relevant and claims to that effect have been made – refer it back to the decision making administrative body. If a case concerns a decision that does not rely on discretion, the courts can change the decision in favour of either party depending on their claim. For instance, in a case concerning the right to a tax deduction that a citizen has been denied, the court may conclude that the relevant administrative organ must acknowledge that the citizen is entitled to the deduction (and it therefore must change its tax decision). If a decision relies on the use of discretion as a general rule the courts will not balance the involved interests – this is left to the discretion of the administrative body. Thus with regard to a discretionary decision where some error has been made – e.g. the citizen was not heard or an illegal interest has been taken into account – or the administrative body has misunderstood the facts of the case – the decision may be quashed and if relevant be referred back to it, but the courts will not change it. However, there are exceptions to this. If the competent administrative body has replaced its discretion with rules of its own (by way of a circular or an administrative practice) whereby it decides cases of the involved type, the courts may decide the case by applying those rules.[35]

4.3 The Ombudsman

As stated in para 3.3 above the Ombudsman is not obliged to review the complaint and may choose just to review aspects of the complaint. The Ombudsman's competence is as a general rule limited to legal matters, see para 4.1 above for an explanation of what this includes. However, he may also as an exception to the general rule – and this is a special ground for review that (normally) is only available to the Ombudsman – review accordance with 'good administrative practise'. This is a special set of norms that includes making decisions within a reasonable time (though in a lawsuit for damages this may also be the basis for a case at the courts), speaking politely to citizens, giving reasons even though it is not required by law, making notes, etc.[36]

In regards to the *kommunerne* (communes), it is stressed in the Ombudsman Act that he should respect the conditions of local government, i.e. refrain from reviewing discretionary decisions, even though he cannot review discretionary decisions anyway. Even though the Ombudsman is not part of the administration, he generally follows rules similar to those that apply to the administrative bodies.[37]

The Ombudsman cannot change a decision, only express his opinion, appeal to the administration, e.g. to reconsider its decision, and criticise the administration. In practise this is just as effective as being able to change a decision.[38] As stated above

34 Cf. Revsbech (n. 9) 385–423, Jon Andersen, *Hans Gammeltoft-Hansen et al, Forvaltningsret* (2nd edn., Jurist- og Økonomforbundets Forlag, Cph. 2002) 819–847.

35 Cf. Revsbech (n. 9) 423–448, Andersen (n. 34) 847–862.

36 Cf. Madsen (n. 6) 475–488, Larsen (n. 6) 892–905.

37 Cf. Madsen (n. 6) 473–475, Larsen (n. 6) 885–892.

38 Cf. Madsen (n. 6) 488–490, Larsen (n. 6) 908–911.

the administration in almost all cases follows the Ombudsman – even if perhaps the administration might not actually agree.

5 European perspectives

European Union law and the European Convention of Human Rights have so far had almost no influence on effective legal protection in administrative law in general. Nevertheless, in specific areas both EU law and international law prescribe specific provisions that influence the rights of citizens but it only pertains to those specific areas.[39] An exception is the Directive 95/46/EC of the European Parliament and of the Council of 24 October 1995 on the protection of individuals with regard to the processing of personal data and on the free movement of such data. This has influenced administrative procedures in general. However as to actually improving the effective legal protection of citizens I think it has mattered relatively little. Mostly it does not hinder authorities from handling data the way they would otherwise be able to, and it does not in most cases give rights to access to information that the citizen was not entitled to according to national rules on access to information. It does however mean that citizens are informed of administrative proceedings that they perhaps otherwise would not be aware of. In many cases citizens are noticed on the proceeding before an unfavourable decision is made, as various rules require their hearing, for instance.

This does not mean that Danish administrative law has not been influenced by foreign or international law. However, owing to the current, high level effective legal protection in Denmark, there is no strong need for borrowing new principles or mechanisms from outside.

6 Conclusion

In my view – as I stated in the opening chapter – citizens are afforded a high degree of effective legal protection in administrative law in Denmark which exceeds the level of protection required by international law. It explains the fact that the general rules of Danish administrative law have not been influenced much by European Union Law and the European Convention of Human Rights.

It is in fact hard to see that there is a great need for further effective legal protection for citizens. I believe that perhaps the biggest problem is related to the time administrative proceedings take. This is however a matter of allocation of resources and thus in the end a political matter: how much taxes should be paid by citizens and how should they be spent. This is of course also the case in relation to (further) financial support of citizens' expenditure on representatives (e.g. lawyers). Other areas where rights might be bettered, e.g. expanding the right to be heard on the authorities' initiative, include hearing a citizen who may be the subject of an administrative

39 The influence of EU-law on Danish Administrative Law was the subject of Niels Fengers doctoral thesis *Forvaltning & Fællesskab* (Jurist- og Økonomforbundets Forlag, Cph. 2004). The thesis spans more than 1000 pages and thoroughly examines the subject. An overview of the current influence of EU law on Danish Administrative Law is found in Niels Fenger, *EU-rettens påvirkning af dansk forvaltningsret* (2nd edn., Jurist- og Økonomforbundets Forlag, Cph. 2013) (which is only about 70 pages).

act about legal opinions and proposals (as opposed to merely the facts of the case) in all cases – this would not only demand more resources but more importantly could prolong administrative proceedings. This would especially cause a problem where there is more than one private party. The same can be said of establishing more levels of appeal bodies.

The level of effective legal protection for citizens must be balanced against other considerations. Rights cost money and the public sector in Denmark is not likely to expand nor is it likely that any government will find it viable to raise the tax level. The demographic development and, e.g., growing healthcare expenses mean that the level of effective legal protection may come under pressure. There is an ongoing discussion of spending on 'cold' vs. 'warm' hands (i.e. administrative employees vs. teachers, day caretakers, doctors and nurses) and it is obvious that cold hands aren't popular when prioritising and budget making in the public sector. There is a lack of understanding that legal protection is generally a prerequisite of getting the citizen the care of the 'warm' hands that the citizen is entitled to. Thus I think the issue today is not if the level of effective legal protection should be raised overall but to maintain the level that has been achieved over the last century.

7 The principle of effective legal protection in French administrative law

Sylvia Calmes-Brunet

Introduction

The principle of the rule of law, which subjects the government to the law 'is intended to protect individuals against arbitrary governmental acts by constraints of substantive law, as well as by the introduction of regulated procedures'.[1] In particular, the principle of legality – that is to say abiding by the law – protects citizens' freedom from the abuse of power of administrative bodies, providing procedural guarantees for this purpose.

The term 'effective legal protection' is part of 'Eurospeak' and its inherent rights are explicitly recognised in European administrative law. Though French law does not explicitly enshrine the principle of 'effective legal protection' as such, it refers to some tenets and mechanisms that obey its logic, most particularly in administrative law. French administrative law – primarily geared towards achieving efficient administration – is traditionally based on objective notions such as 'public interest' (*intérêt général*), 'public service' (*service public*), 'government authorities' (*puissance publique*) or the principle of legality (*principe de légalité*).

However, today it also protects individuals' rights and interests, especially in the context of court proceedings. That means that the 'applicant-citizen' (*administré-requérant*) is better protected than the 'administered-citizen' (*administré-citoyen*).[2] While for a long time the judge was confined to the role of regulating the administration's operations, with power to invalidate decisions taken unlawfully, he became a full judge – who may finally and concretely settle the disputes he is presented for arbitration, in a more subjective sense that trivialises public policy and the law governing it. This is a more egalitarian view of the relationship between government and citizens, which encourages the latter to stand up for their rights and interests.

More generally, the concept of 'legal protection' refers to the subjects and objects of this guarantee and to those who warrant them. On one hand, one has to deal with the protection of the recipients of administrative actions.[3] French law calls them 'administered people' (*administrés*), 'users' (*usagers*) or, during the court proceedings, 'litigants' (*justiciables*). It may also be a matter of protection of third parties of the case. In fact, it embraces the procedural protection of the individual rights and

1 Jürgen Schwarze, *Droit administratif européen* (2nd edn., Bruyland 2009) I–10.

2 Bertrand Faure, 'Les deux conceptions de la démocratie administrative' (2013) 4 *Revue Française de Droit Administratif* (*RFDA*) 709.

3 Cf. more particularly: Rozen Noguellou, 'La décision administrative et son destinataire' (2013) 4 *RFDA* 732.

interests of all affected people. On the other hand, this protection is primarily provided by judges, including administrative judges, since the French judicial system has two branches of the ordinary courts: civil courts (*juridictions judiciaires*, where private law cases are judged)[4] and administrative courts (*juridictions administratives* for administrative law cases).[5] However, legislators remain the guarantors of freedom under the control of the constitutional court (*Conseil constitutionnel*).

French law does not guarantee procedural rights always in an explicit or precise manner. The reason for this is that in the French approach, law is seen as an objective order aiming at effective administration. Due to the conceptual vagueness of individual rights it is not always easy to identify and classify the relevant guarantees in a systemic set of standards. Nonetheless, the principles of effective remedy and fair trial are recognised and they include the following requirements:

- the equal right of access to the administration and administrative documents;
- the principle of sound administration and administrative transparency;
- the right to the reasoning of the judgment and the obligation of administrative bodies to justify their decisions;
- the principle of equality of arms between parties in the adversarial administrative proceeding;
- the right to defence;
- the right to be heard;
- the right to remedy, and the access to courts, where independent and impartial judges decide the case in reasonable time.

1 Historical developments

The intention to remove public acts from courts – called 'parliaments' in the *ancien régime* –[6] dates back to 1641 and 1661 when the Edicts of Saint-Germain and of Fontainebleau were adopted, long before Montesquieu and his theory of the separation of powers. Later, courts opposed any reform at the end of the *ancien régime*, and so the Judicature Act of 1790 (*loi d'organisation judiciaire*) prohibited any intervention by courts in the cases before the public administration. The *Conseil d'État* (Council of State) was created in 1799 as a government advisory body[7] to decide on administrative appeals. The statute of 24 May 1872 and a judgment of 1889[8] established general jurisdiction for administrative judges to annul administrative acts. However, not this ruling of the *Conseil d'État* but a decision of the Court of Disputes (*Tribunal des conflits*)

4 Title VIII of the Constitution uses the expression 'judicial authority' (*autorité judiciaire*), because the 1958 constituent didn't want to give much power to the judges. The *Cour de cassation* is the Supreme Civil Court.

5 The Council of State – *Conseil d'État* (CE) – is the Supreme Administrative Court. The administrative tribunals – *Tribunaux administratifs (TA)* – are the first instance courts and the administrative courts of appeal – *Cours administratives d'appel (CAA)* – the courts of appeal.

6 In France the so-called 'parliaments' (*parlements*) were the superior judicial courts before the 1789 French Revolution.

7 Cf. for example Arlette Lebigre, *La justice du Roi, la vie judiciaire dans l'ancienne France* (Albin Michel 1995) 48 *et seq.*

8 *Cadot* [1889] *CE* n° 66145.

led to the creation of an independent administrative law. This was the *Blanco* case in 1873.[9] The *Tribunal des conflits* stated that the liability of the state must be assessed according to 'special rules that vary according to the needs of the [public] service and the requirement to balance state's rights with private rights', rather than to the principles of the Civil Code (*Code civil*). On this basis, the *Conseil d'État* has developed special rules of administrative law. Most importantly, it has created the 'general principles of law' (*principes généraux du droit*) for protecting citizens' rights, such as the rights of the defense, the right to be heard by the administrative bodies and the courts or the principle of sound administration.

French administrative law is thus essentially based on case law which creates some problems for accessibility to the law. That is why France has just undertaken to legislate and codify for the past 40 years.[10] Concerning citizens' procedural protection, the statutes on the protection of personal data,[11] the right to access to administrative documents,[12] on public and private archives,[13] the law requiring the administrative bodies to duly justify their acts (particularly those that restrict the exercise of freedom, impose a sanction or refuse a permit),[14] the decree concerning relations between the public administration and users,[15] the statute on citizens' rights in their relations with public administration (*droits des citoyens dans leurs relations avec les administrations*),[16] and the statute on the simplification of these relations[17] can be mentioned. Now, even if France is not yet provided with a general statute on administrative procedures, the procedural rights are granted to citizens who are considered as 'users' of the administration. They can enjoy these rights before the courts, particularly the administrative ones. The Code of Administrative Justice (*Code de justice administrative*, CJA), which replaced on 1 January 2001[18] the former regulation,[19] comprises the bulk of written judicial administrative procedure provisions.

2 Constitutional framework

The constitutional court (*Conseil constitutionnel*) was created by the 4 October 1958 Constitution to ensure the smooth functioning of the streamlined parliamentary system, keeping the legislature in its own jurisdiction. But the *Conseil constitutionnel* went beyond this framework in the 1970s. The 1971 decision n° 71–44 DC on freedom of

9 Marceau Long, Prosper Weil, Guy Braibant, Pierre Delvolvé and Bruno Genevois, *Les grands arrêts de la jurisprudence administrative (GAJA)* (19th edn., *Dalloz* 2013) n°1.

10 It is worth mentioning besides the principle of the secret correspondence between lawyers and their clients was instituted by a statute n° 71–1130 of 31 December 1971.

11 N° 78–17 of 1978.

12 N° 78–753 of 1978.

13 N° 79–18 of 1979.

14 N° 79–587 of 1979.

15 N° 83–1025 of 1983.

16 N° 2000–321 of 2000, including the adversarial principle and administrative transparency.

17 N° 2013–1005 of 2013. Particularly, silence kept for two months by the Administration on request meant so far implied rejection of the request. From now on, this silence is worth acceptance decision. From now on as well, for example, an electronic referral to the Administration is possible.

18 Ordinance n° 2000–387 and decree n° 2000–389 of 2000.

19 Code of Administrative Tribunals and Administrative Courts of Appeal (*Code des Tribunaux administratifs et des Cours administratives d'appel*) statute n° 87–1127 of 1987.

association (*liberté d'association*) turned its role as the guardian of the Executive into the defender of individual rights and freedoms, whose scope of reference is now extended to the whole body of constitutional rules (*bloc de constitutionnalité*).[20] For this purpose, it was necessary to open the referral (*saisine*) and allow the political opposition to apply to the *Conseil constitutionnel*, which was achieved by the 29 October 1974 constitutional revision.[21]

The 23 July 2008 constitutional revision marks a decisive new procedural step with the introduction of the '*question prioritaire de constitutionnalité*', which means 'priority ruling on constitutionality'. The traditional constitutionality review established in 1958 in Art. 61 para 2 is an *a priori* control (*déclaration de conformité*) by the *Conseil constitutionnel*, i.e. before the enactment of statutes. However, since the 2008 reform, in force since 1 March 2010, the procedure for the priority ruling on constitutionality (QPC decisions) allows for an already enacted legislative provision to be challenged, whether it 'infringes the rights and freedoms guaranteed by the Constitution' (Art. 61–1). This new procedure is clearly intended to secure citizens' rights and freedoms.

The Constitution of 1958 contains some basic principles like the equality before the law, and states that the civil courts are guardians of individual liberty (Art. 66). The Constitution refers to some other constitutional rules which include the Declaration of human and civil rights (*Déclaration des Droits de l'Homme et du Citoyen*, DDHC) of 1789, the Preamble of the Constitution of 1946 and the 2004 Charter for the Environment. Furthermore, they include the 'fundamental principles recognized by the statutes of the Republic' (*principes fondamentaux reconnus par les lois de la République*) prior to 1946, including the rights to defence,[22] the independence of the administrative court,[23] and the competences (*bloc de compétences*) of administrative courts (namely the control of the legality of administrative decisions).[24] The relevant constitutional rules refer also to the objectives of constitutional value (*objectifs de valeur constitutionnelle*)[25] such as the respect of others' freedom,[26] the accessibility and intelligibility of the law,[27] or the sound administration of justice.[28] In particular, the principles of independence and impartiality of courts, which derive from Art. 16 of the DDHC 1789, are inseparable from the exercise of judicial office. In addition, the right to effective judicial remedy before a court, a corollary of the right of access to a judge, is reinforced as the procedural safeguard of all other rights. 'No substantial violations of the concerned

20 Louis Favoreu, 'Le principe de constitutionnalité, essai de définition d'après la jurisprudence du Conseil constitutionnel' in Marcel Waline (ed.), *Recueil d'études en hommage à Charles Eisenmann* (Cujas 1975) 33.

21 Art. 61 al.2: 'Statutes approved by Parliament may be referred to the *Conseil constitutionnel*, before their promulgation, by the President of the Republic, the Prime Minister, the President of the National Assembly, the President of the Senate, [1974 revision] sixty Members of the National Assembly or sixty Senators.'

22 [1976] *Conseil constitutionnel (CC)* n° 76–70 *DC*.

23 [1980] *CC* n° 80–119 *DC*.

24 [1987] *CC* n° 86–224 *DC*.

25 These 'objectives' are merely guidelines given for constitutional standards.

26 [1989] *CC* n° 88–248 *DC*.

27 [1999] *CC* n° 99–421 *DC*; [2005] *CC* n° 2005–514 *DC*.

28 [2009] *CC* n° 2009–595 *DC*. The requirements of the reasonable time of administrative procedures can be attached to the principle of the sound administration of justice: Jacques Arrighi de Casanova, 'Litigants must be able to easily find a judge who must have, as much as possible, full jurisdiction' (2014) 13 *La Semaine juridique – Édition générale (JCP G)* 599.

person's right to exercise effective remedy before a court' will be allowed:[29] it is unconstitutional to deprive litigants of any opportunity to challenge through effective judicial remedy a measure infringing their rights – for example a decision on the request for extension of a European arrest warrant to other offenses.[30]

While this 'body of constitutional rules' is the main source of rights and freedoms, the other levels of protection should not be overlooked. The *Conseil constitutionnel* states that the substantial protection of rights is provided by legislative actions.[31] The parliamentary legislation as the 'expression of the general will'[32] has long been the main source of law, particularly under the Third and Fourth Republics. Legislative power was understood as the defender of freedom (freedom of the press in 1881, trade union freedom in 1884, freedom of association in 1901). The current Fifth Republic has limited the scope of the statutory law and established the *Conseil constitutionnel*. The development of jurisprudence of the *Conseil constitutionnel* has challenged the omnipotence of the legislative power. Nevertheless, under Art. 34 of the Constitution, the general statutory law still sets the rules regarding 'fundamental guarantees granted to citizens for the exercise of civil liberties'.

3 Rights-based perspective

Interested citizens must be able to make themselves heard by a judge, but also at the stage of the administrative procedure. However, various formal rights that protect private rights and interests are guaranteed more or less effectively, depending on the stages of administrative and judicial proceedings.

3.1 Administrative procedures

While the administrative bodies have 'first privilege' (*privilège du préalable*) which means that they may take binding decisions, and an appeal does not have suspensive effect to the execution of their actions, citizens must be able to defend themselves against them, according to the principle of sound administration including the right to be heard. The *Conseil d'État* has set a general principle of law that all administrative measures of some seriousness (withdrawal of an authorisation for example) must be taken in the context of 'adversarial procedures';[33] that means that the applicants may access their files and can air their opinions prior to decisions. If the administrative body refuses to disclose the file, the applicant may refer to a special commission (*Commission d'accès aux documents administratifs*), which is an independent administrative authority.

The obligation to give reasons for adverse individual administrative acts – and these only – is required by law.[34] Clear and specific reasons must be given in writing and contain the essential grounds relating to the situation of fact and law. The absence

29 [1996] *CC* n° 96–373 *DC*; [2012] *CC* n° 2012–283 *QPC*.

30 [2013] *CC* n° 2013–314 *QPC*.

31 [1969] *CC* n° 69–66 *L*.

32 Art. 6 of the DDHC 1789.

33 *Dame Trompier Gravier [1944] CE Section du contentieux (Sect.)* n° 69751.

34 Statute n° 79–587 of 1979. The obligation to state reasons has been required, since the statute n° 2012–1460 of 2012, also to normative decisions having an impact on the environment.

or lack of motivation may be adjusted. If this is not the case, the administrative act is unlawful and must be annulled.

There are two kinds of administrative appeal (*recours administratif*) to protect rights and freedoms by requesting the public administration to reconsider the case.[35] On the one hand, an internal appeal (*recours administratif gracieux*) may be addressed to the administrative authority that took the decision. On the other hand, a hierarchical appeal (*recours administratif hiérarchique*) may be addressed to a superior body. Internal or hierarchical appeals are possible within two months, provided that there is a preceding administrative decision (*décision préalable*). These appeals are in principle not mandatory before requesting a judge.[36] They provide a two-month time extension for the applicant to apply to the courts.[37] These administrative appeals enable dialogue between public administration and individuals. However, this dialogue is based on the will of the former. If the administrative body refuses to enforce statutes imposing procedural safeguards (access to documents, adversarial principle, etc.), individuals may appeal to the judge (annulment proceeding or state liability proceeding).

3.2 Access to court

'The French administrative trial is primarily used to control the objective legality of the administration, while at the same time it also aims to actually guarantee citizens' individual rights. This justifies that the appeal against an administrative decision does not, in principle, have suspensive effect. This also explains why the conditions of bringing an action are not particularly stringent and why it is possible to address normative regulations that do not affect the individual as such.[38]

According to the jurisprudence of the *Conseil constitutionnel*, the right to access to the court follows from Art. 16 of the DDHC 1789.[39]

The effectiveness of judicial action is largely due to the temporary preservation of the litigants' interests, for as long as it is required to make a decision on the merits of their dispute with an administrative body. For this aim, the administrative court in the so-called 'interim' or 'urgent' (*référé*) proceedings may, since the Statute n° 2000–597 of 2000, take special temporary measures. The major innovation of this reform is the petition for protection of fundamental liberties (*référé-liberté*): the court may order all measures required to safeguard a freedom that has been seriously infringed by the administrative body in a manner that is clearly illegal.

According to the jurisprudence of the *Conseil d'État* and to the CJA, 'annulment proceedings' (*contentieux de l'annulation*) of illegal unilateral administrative acts – whether individual or normative – are to be distinguished from 'full jurisdiction proceedings' (*contentieux de pleine juridiction*).

35 Statute n° 2000–321 of 2000.

36 Except when a 'mandatory preliminary administrative request' (*recours administratif préalable obligatoire:* RAPO) is required (in tax matters for example). Cf. Gweltaz Eveillard, 'Nouvelles précisions sur le recours administratif préalable obligatoire' (2013) 12 *Droit administratif (DA)* 52.

37 *Bansais* [1881] *CE, Rec.* 430 (hierarchical appeal); *Marchelli* [1917] *CE, Rec.* 42 (internal appeal); *M. Ouahrirou* [2009] *CE* n° 322581 (both appeals).

38 Cf. Schwarze (n. 1) 127.

39 [1994] *CC* n° 93–335 *DC*; [1996] *CC* n° 96–373 *DC*.

The judicial review of administrative acts is exercised in a so-called *ultra vires* action (*recours pour excès de pouvoir*, REP),[40] where litigants request the judge to cancel (retroactively and *erga omnes*) a unilateral administrative decision for its illegality. The original administrative decision (*décision préalable*) can be appealed within two months from the 'publication' (of normative acts) or 'notification' (of individual decisions).

The REP is acknowledged as a 'public interest' action. That means that this review is wide open, even in the silence of the statutes, against any administrative decision.[41] But the 'acts of government' (*actes de gouvernement*) on the relationship between public bodies or the international relations of the state and some internal measures of various public authorities are exempt from judicial review.

As experience shows, the principle of legality leads the courts to monitor the compliance of administrative acts with a comprehensive set of standards, including general principles of law that can effectively protect individuals (for example, the right to lead a normal family life).

Furthermore, the *Conseil d'État* admits the possibility of limiting the effects of retroactive cancellation to avoid their 'manifestly excessive consequences', particularly with regard to 'situations that might have occurred'.[42] Henceforth, the courts may decide – and it is a revolution in French public law – the effects of the illegal act[43] will be final or that cancellation will take effect at a later date.

The administrative court may not only annul the objected administrative act, but may, in the 'full jurisdiction' (*plein contentieux*) litigation, substitute it with its own decision. In certain cases this power allows the judges to modify or replace the administrative act, whereas in cases of state's liability or contractual litigation, the court may grant compensation to the applicants, may change its amount, or may restore the contractual situation that the administrative body has improperly terminated.[44] Since the judicial review (REP) cannot be applied against administrative contracts, the *Conseil d'État* established in a judgment of 2007[45] a remedy allowing unsuccessful competitors to obtain cancellation of the contract they have not been awarded and, in a judgment of 2014,[46] the same remedy for third parties to a contract liable to see their interests harmed.

The condition of the applicant's *locus standi* (*intérêt à agir*) is understood in its broadest sense by the judge.[47] The judicial proceedings contain original parties (*parties originaires*), but some other interested natural or legal persons may intervene in the ongoing procedure. Their intervention may be voluntary or induced. Some

40 'A trial against an administrative act' (*un procès fait à un acte*): Edouard Laferrière, *Traité de la juridiction administrative et des recours contentieux* (t. 2, 2nd edn., *Berger-Levrault et Cie* 1896) 560.

41 *Dame Lamotte* [1950] *CE Assemblée (Ass. i.e.* full Court), *GAJA* n° 61.

42 *Association AC! et autres* [2004] *CE Ass, Rec.* 197, *GAJA* n° 112.

43 Regulatory or individual act: *Sire, Vignard* [2007] *CE* (2008) *Actualité Juridique de Droit Administratif (AJDA)* 5 638.

44 *Commune de Béziers* [2011] *CE, Rec.* 117.

45 *Société Tropic Travaux Signalisation* [2007] *CE Ass., Rec.* 360.

46 *Département du Tarn-et-Garonne* [2014] *CE Ass.* n° 358994.

47 Real injury (or at least potential injury), legitimate and sufficiently direct injury. For example, the quality of living in the local community may be deemed sufficient to have interest in bringing proceedings against an act of this community: *Vedel et Jannot* [1995] *CE Ass.* (1996) 3 *RFDA* 313.

third parties involved may be condemned (*mise en cause*) or may be obliged to guarantee the defendant (*appel en garantie*), and others who are likely to be harmed by the upcoming judgment may enforce their rights (*appel en déclaration de jugement commun*).

The court can be seized by a simple letter, whether or not the applicant is represented by a lawyer, and electronic referral to the court is possible.[48] Now, appealing has been subject to a registration fee as of October 2011: €35 in first instance and €150 on appeal.[49] However, this fee may seem to thwart the right to access justice and the right to effective judicial remedy. Yet, the *Conseil constitutionnel*, in a decision n° 2012–231/234 QPC of 2012, has ruled that there was no disproportionate interference with the right to exercise effective remedy before a court or with rights of the defense. For all that, this fee was abolished in 2014, because the Minister of Justice deemed it unfair.[50]

The court leads the judicial inquiry (*instruction*), but the procedure is adversarial, according to a general principle of law.[51] Specifically, this general principle prohibits ruling in a case if parties have been unable to consult the various submitted pleadings and documents that the judge relied on. The ECtHR held that the legal opinions (*conclusions*) by the 'consultant judge' (*commissaire du gouvernement*, called *rapporteur public* since 2009, who is similar to the Advocate General before the ECJ) are to be included in the scope of the adversarial principle.[52] The CJA was thus amended by the decree n° 2009–14 of 2009: 'If the case is to be judged after the consultant judge has delivered his or her legal opinion, the parties or their agents are informed of the importance of this opinion for the case concerned, before the hearing'; according to the same logic, since a decree n° 2011–1950 of 2011, the parties may, after the consultant judge has delivered his or her legal opinion, 'make oral observations in support of their written submissions'.

The parties must adduce evidence of the facts they argue. However, the unequal power relationship between parties to the administrative proceedings leads to some relief, or even a reversal of the burden of proof. In *ultra vires* proceedings, the judge may not require the applicant to provide evidence for the facts: the judge must take all useful measures able to help him or her to form an own opinion, including by requiring the administrative body to produce any documents which allow the verification of the applicant's allegations.[53]

The judgments of the administrative courts are normally made collectively – at least by three judges – but there has been a growing number of exceptions allowing a single judge since 1995[54] for faster treatment of simple or minor cases.

The composition of the court must meet the principle of impartiality, which is a general principle of law.[55] A mere risk of bias is sufficient to consider that the prin-

48 Decree n° 2012–1437 of 2012 and order of 2013.

49 Decree n° 2011–1202 of 2011. Persons enjoying legal aid are exonerated from it (more than a million recipients in 2012).

50 Decree n° 2013–1280 of 2013.

51 *Gate* [1976] *CE*, *Rec.* 40.

52 *Kress v France* (n° 39594/98) (2001), (2001) 32 *Dalloz* 2619.

53 *Cordière* [2012] *CE* n° 354108.

54 Statute n° 95–125 of 1995.

55 *Didier* [1999] *CE Ass.*, *Rec.* 399; *Karsenty* [2005] CE, *Rec.* 151.

ciple has been violated.[56] The *Conseil d'État*'s dualism (both counselor and judge of public administration) has been a problem. The *Conseil d'État*, and the regulatory authority have thus followed the ECtHR:[57] a judge that has given his or her opinion as a counselor must withdraw (that is to say abstain from sitting) at the trial stage.[58] When the impartiality of one member of the court is at issue, parties may request his or her disqualification.

Then, parties must be regularly summoned to the hearing in order to attend and make comments. As a principle, these hearings are open to the public (*audience publique*), although it was not held as a 'general principle of law' for administrative courts.[59]

The secrecy of judicial deliberation is a guarantee of judicial independence. The ECtHR considered that the mere presence, even passive, of the consultant judge (*commissaire du gouvernement*) during deliberations violated the impartiality of the judgment.[60] Consequently, a decree of 2006 excludes the *commissaire du gouvernement* from the deliberations before administrative tribunals and administrative courts of appeal, but the consultant judge is maintained without taking part, before the *Conseil d'État*, unless parties request his or her exclusion, which is in line with European case law.[61]

On one hand, the administrative judges' powers are limited: in principle, they must decide neither *infra* nor *ultra petita*, i.e. they rule upon the totality of the request, but not beyond, except, for example, in all contractual matters where the courts may have general *ultra petita* powers.[62] But, on the other hand, the judge and the legislature have created incentives and coercive measures to strengthen the judgments' binding force, like penalty payments (statute n° 80–539 of 1980) and judicial injunctions (statute n° 95–125 of 1995).

3.3 Judicial appeal

In the *Canal, Robin et Godo* judgment on 1962, the *Conseil d'État* ruled that although exceptional circumstances did justify the creation of a special court (*juridiction d'exception*), they did not allow the exclusion of any judicial remedy against the court's judgments.

3.3.1 Withdrawal

There are remedies against judgments brought before the same court (but other judges) for withdrawal (*rétractation*). Some routes of withdrawal are open to the parties who were present at the proceedings: 'application for review of sentence' (*recours en révision*) and 'request for rectification of factual error' (*recours en rectification d'erreur matérielle*). Other options for withdrawal can be exercised by parties who were not

56 *Syvanise* [2009] *CE* (2010) 1 *Gazette du Palais*.

57 *Sacilor-Lormines v France* (n° 65411/01) (2006), (2007) 3 *RFDA* 342.

58 What the ECtHR Admitted (*UFC 'Que Choisir?' de Côte-d'Or v France* (2009), (2009) 4 *RFDA* 885).

59 *Debout* [1978] *CE Sect, Rec.* 395.

60 *Kress v/ France* (2001), *op. cit.*; *Martinie v/ France* (2006), (2006) 4 *AJDA* 986.

61 *Etienne v France* (2009), (2010) 2 *Droit Administratif (DA)* comment 9.

62 *Commune de Béziers* [2009] *CE Ass.*n° 304802; *Ministre de l'Intérieur* [2011] *CE* n° 348647; *Société Ophrys* [2011] *CE* n° 337349.

present at the proceedings but whose rights are affected by the judgment and who are seen 'third parties' (*tierce opposition*) in the particular case. In the latter, the point is to ensure compliance with the adversarial principle, allowing absent parties to get the case re-judged by the same court.

3.3.2 Appeal and cassation

Appeal is the most classic remedy which allows the interested parties, in principle within two months of receiving notification of the first judgment, to obtain a second trial of the case, in law and in fact, by a higher court. The 'devolutionary effect' (*effet dévolutif*) of appeal allows a complete retrial of the case.[63] The appeal does not have a suspensive effect, but the appellant may obtain a 'stay of execution' (*sursis à exécution*) of the first instance judgment. However, the right to appeal is neither a constitutional principle, nor even a general principle of law. In practice, a number of TA judgments are rendered in the first and last instance and are subject only to appeal in cassation before the *Conseil d'État* (typically in social cases, local taxes, driving licences, pensions).

Cassation is an extraordinary remedy. It is not a complete review of the case but is intended only to check the legal correctness of the decision of the court of first or second instance. This appeal may be filed (within two months) by the parties with an interest before the *Conseil d'État* against any judicial decision of last resort made by a general or special administrative court, even in the silence of the texts,[64] but after filtering. It must in principle be brought by a lawyer who is authorised to appear before the *Conseil d'État* and the *Cour de cassation*. The cassation does not have any suspensive effect, but the appellant may request the court to suspend the execution of the objected judgment. In case of cancellation of the judgment, the *Conseil d'État* may refer the case to the trial court for a retrial, or may itself give final judgment on the merits, 'when the interest of the proper administration of justice requires to do so'.[65]

4 Institutional perspective

4.1 Independent public authorities

Currently, there are 40 public authorities[66] which are independent both from the public administration and the courts and which have different types and names. They can be considered to be quasi-courts.[67] These authorities are relatively close

63 However, the appeal court cannot worsen the appellant's situation, in the absence of application by another party.

64 *D'Aillières* [1947] *CE Ass., GAJA*.

65 Statute n° 87–1127 of 1987.

66 Cf. list of authorities and special statutory law for each authority, available at http://www.legifrance.gouv.fr/Sites/Autorites-independantes, accessed 12 July 2015. Cf. also: Sébastien Martin, 'Les autorités publiques indépendantes: réflexions autour d'une nouvelle personne publique' (2013) 1 *Revue du droit public et de la science politique en France et à l'étranger (RDP)* 53; *Commission des lois du Sénat, Autorités administratives indépendantes – 2006–2014: un bilan* (Patrice Gélard, Rapport d'information n° 616, 2014).

67 Cf. in particular: *Conseil d'État, Réflexions sur les autorités administratives indépendantes* (Rapport public pour 2001, Études et Documents du Conseil d'État n° 52 *La Documentation française* 2002).

to the Executive and may wield great influence in sectors sensitive to the exercise of rights and freedoms, for example the public television and radio, the data protection, or the access to administrative documents. They take individual or even regulatory decisions. But this power is limited by the different statutes and controlled by the *Conseil constitutionnel*,[68] and their decisions are subject to appeal before the *Conseil d'État*. Furthermore, some of these authorities may have sanctioning power, but they also must respect the rights of defense and the right to a fair trial.[69] Indeed, an independent authority can be described as a 'tribunal' within the meaning of Art. 6–1 of the ECHR (but not in the French sense). Therefore, the *Conseil d'État* requires the principle of impartiality.[70] Similarly, the *Conseil constitutionnel* confirms rampant judicialisation of these authorities,[71] by subjecting them to the principles of independence and impartiality of judges arising from Art. 16 of the DDHC 1789.[72]

Independent authorities exist in various fields having different powers. The most recent example is the establishment of the 'High Authority for the transparency of public life' (*Haute Autorité pour la transparence de la vie publique*).[73] Another recently created institution is the 'Defender of Rights' (*Défenseur des droits*), who is the only 'independent constitutional authority' (*autorité constitutionnelle indépendante)*. The 2008 constitutional reform and the statute n° 2011–333 of 2011 have created this new authority, which replaces several previous 'independent administrative authorities'.[74] The Defender of Rights is appointed by the President of the Republic[75] for a six-year, non-renewable term.[76] The Defender shall ensure the due respect of individual's rights and freedoms by the state's administration, territorial communities, public legal entities, and by bodies carrying out a public service mission. Free referral may be made to the Defender by every person who considers any rights to have been infringed by the operation of a public service. But the Defender may also act without referral. He or she may intervene in several fields (public services, children's protection, fight against discrimination, security ethics), and can be assisted by third parties (*collèges*). The Defender has wide-ranging powers (investigation, recommendation, injunction, mediation, referral to the

68 [1986] *CC* n° 86–217 *DC*, [1989] *CC* n° 88–248 *DC*.

69 The full jurisdiction proceeding has applied in administrative sanctions since 2009, under the influence of the ECtHR (*Gradinger v/Austria* (n° 15963/90) (1995), *DA* 1996 n° 116): *Société ATOM* [2009] *CE Ass., Rec. 26*.

70 *Société Profil France* [2008] *CE* Interim order n° 311974.

71 Including the 'Competition Authority' (*Autorité de la concurrence)*, which does not have judicial function, however.

72 [2012] *CC* n° 2012–280 *QPC* (2013) 1 *RFDA* 144.

73 Statutes relating to the transparency of public life n° 2013–906 and 2013–907 of 2013.

74 The 'Ombudsman' (*Médiateur de la République*, created in 1973), the 'Children's Defender' (*Défenseur des enfants)*, the 'High Authority against Discrimination and for Equality' (*Haute Autorité de lutte contre les discriminations et pour l'égalité)* and the 'National Commission on Security Ethics' (*Commission nationale de déontologie de la sécurité)*.

75 After public consultation with the relevant standing committee in each assembly (National Assembly and Senat). The President of the Republic may not make the appointment when the sum of the negative votes in each committee represents at least three fifths of the votes cast by the two committees.

76 Dominique Baudis was the Defender of rights in principle until 2017, but he died on 10 April 2014. He was succeeded by Jacques Toubon on 17 July 2014.

courts), and is accountable for his or her actions to the President of the Republic and to Parliament. The Defender received more than 100,000 applications in 2014.[77]

4.2 National courts

The legal protection of individuals' rights and interests is primarily judicial. Judges are involved in developing standards and make it effective that rights and freedoms, if requested by individual application, are indeed exercised. Progress in the protection of rights is therefore largely due to the growth, expansion and deepening of the judge's controls. There is real 'judicial power', and the principle of 'separation of powers' as well as the 'guarantee of rights' under Art. 16 of the DDHC 1789 prevent the legislator from violating the force of *res judicata* decisions.[78]

4.2.1 The constitutional court (Conseil constitutionnel)

The *Conseil constitutionnel*, which is vested with the power of constitutional review of statutes, uses a number of control techniques for protecting rights and freedoms. For example, the Court may issue 'interpretation reservations' (*réserves d'interprétation*) stating that the examined legislation conforms to the Constitution, but only if it is interpreted in a certain way. In addition, the *Conseil constitutionnel* uses a tool called the 'threshold' or 'floor' effect. This jurisprudence assumes that the legislature does not totally deprive 'legislative protection' of 'constitutional requirements'.[79] Finally, Art. 61-1 of the Constitution allows the repeal (*abrogation*) of any legislative provision, should it violate the rights and freedoms guaranteed by the Constitution. For this reason, litigants may, in all ordinary courts, invoke in their favour the unconstitutionality of a current statute: the matter may be referred by the *Conseil d'État* or by the *Cour de cassation* to the constitutional court.

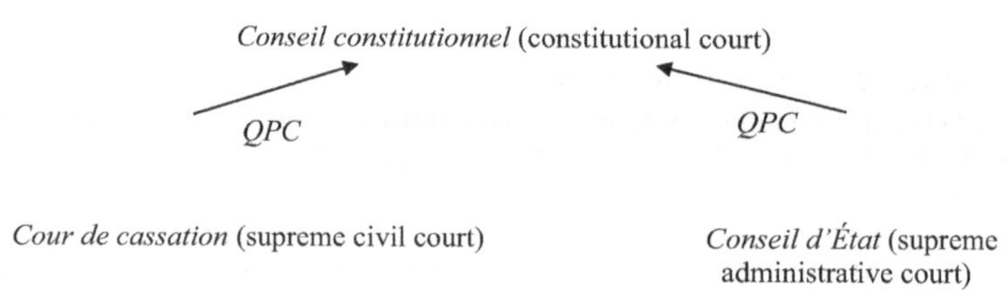

Figure 7.1 The procedure for the priority ruling on constitutionality (*question prioritaire de constitutionnalité: QPC*)

77 Le Défenseur des droits, *Bilan annuel d'activité 2014* (Jacques Toubon 2015).

78 [2005] *CC* n° 2005-531 *DC*. The legislature may, however, adopt a (retrospective) 'validating statute' (*loi de validation*) of administrative acts yet canceled or voidable. The *Conseil constitutionnel* and the *Conseil d'État*, under the pressure of the ECtHR, strengthened the conditions in which this method may be used; in particular, the right to effective judicial remedy must be respected.

79 Cf. [2003] *CC* n° 2003-485 DC and, for example, [2012] *CC* n° 2012-235 *QPC*.

4.2.2 *The court of disputes (Tribunal des conflits)*

The Court of Disputes, created by the 1848 Constitution and an 1872 Statute, is tasked with resolving conflicts of jurisdiction between the two orders of ordinary courts.

In fact, the requirement of an effective guarantee of individual rights can sometimes be met both by the administrative judge and the civil court, as stated by the *Conseil constitutionnel* in its decision n° 89–261 DC of 1989. However, the Court of Disputes tries to rationalise the distribution of powers between the administrative and civil courts. For example, the *SCEA du Chéneau* decision of 2011 extends the jurisdiction of civil courts by reducing the circumstances in which a question must be asked to the administrative judge (*question préjudicielle*). The objective of this and some other recent decisions is to facilitate litigants and their counsel's task by waiving over-subtle jurisdiction distribution and driving through solutions based on the concept of 'scope of competence' (*bloc de competences*), more in line with the need for sound administration of justice and respect for European requirements about the time it took to hand down a judgment.

civil courts → *Tribunal des conflits* (disputes court) ← *administrative courts*

Figure 7.2 The dispute-resolution procedure

4.2.3 *Administrative courts (Juridictions administratives)*

'Resorting to the administrative judge has become common, since citizens no longer feel deference to an administrative body because they require of it impeccable behaviour and respect of fundamental rights, placed at the top of the order of social values'.[80] The number of referrals to the administrative courts is thus steadily increasing, which has justified increasing the number of judges, which is still insufficient to cope with the demand for judgment within a reasonable time. In 2012, 190,000 cases were dealt with by first instance administrative tribunals and 29,000 by administrative courts of appeal (as against 117,500 and 16,000 respectively in 1999). All contentious proceedings increase, on average, by 6% yearly since 40 years.[81] Now, litigants may incur the liability of the state for negligence (*faute simple*) when the duration of the procedure was excessively long.[82] Thus, the average time to judgments became shorter: by

Conseil d'État (supreme administrative court)

↑ *Cassation*

Cours administratives d'appel (administrative courts of appeal)[1]

↑ *Appeal*

Tribunaux administratifs (administrative tribunals)[2]

Figure 7.3 The system of administrative courts

80 David Bailleul, *Le procès administratif* (*LGDJ* 2014) 15.

81 Jean-Marc Sauvé, 'De nouveaux défis pour la Justice administrative de demain' (2015) 1 *Les Annonces De La Seine* 9.

82 *Magiera* [2002] *CE Ass.* n° 239575, *Rec.* 248.

first instance, appeal or cassation, this delay is less than one year since 2011 (nine and a half months for the TA – it was 20 months in 2000).[83]

Besides these administrative courts of general jurisdiction, there are also some 30 'specialised administrative courts' (*juridictions administratives spécialisées*). These are independent and impartial judicial tribunals which are established by various statutes. For example, the last one, the Commission for paid parking's disputes (*Commission du contentieux du stationnement payant*), was created by the ordinance n° 2015–45 of 2015, which reformed the General Local Authorities Code (*Code général des collectivités territoriales*).

These courts are 'special' because their composition is unusual (their members are not only professional judges, but also civil servants, elected representatives and experts) and their jurisdiction is limited to a special field of public sphere. They may have three different types of competence. Some tribunals rule on remedies again administrative decisions, at first and last instance (like the National Court of Asylum). Others may impose disciplinary sanctions (like the Budget and Finance Disciplinary Court), while lastly some of them may have a non-judicial function (for example, the Court of Auditors checks the regularity of all public accountants' accounts).

Even if these are special courts, they are bound by the administrative proceedings' principles and are supervised by the *Conseil d'État*. The number of referrals to these specialised courts is also steadily increasing, even though almost all these courts have remained only little known. For example, the National Court of Asylum took more than 38,500 decisions in 2013,[84] 1,200 more than in 2012.

4.3 Alternative dispute resolution schemes

Mediation is an undeveloped concept in French public law,[85] but the idea is spreading steadily. In the CJA there are only two procedures used in the powers of the administrative judge in terms of mediation: the reconciliation (*conciliation*) and mediation (*médiation*) in the specific case of cross-border disputes. A report prepared in 2007 by the Ministry of Justice on *Arbitration and legal persons of public law*[86] states that, as an exception, several 'public bodies with industrial and commercial functions' like the French post office or railways have the ability to resolve disputes through arbitration. In specific areas (archaeological digs or cross-border contracts for example), the arbitration is also authorised by the statute n° 75–596 of 1975.[87] A mediator and an arbitrator may have similar roles in the amicable resolution of a dispute. However, the difference is that the former cannot impose a solution but only accompany parties to reach a negotiated settlement, while the second is the guarantor of a sentence or a compromise that parties undertake to respect. Moreover, the administrative bodies are now encouraged to make greater use of transactions, for example for public

83 Sauvé (n. 81) 9.

84 *Cour Nationale du droit d'Asile, Rapport d'activité* (2013).

85 The study of the *Conseil d'État* in 2010, entitled *Developing mediation within the framework of the European Union* (*Développer la médiation dans le cadre de l'Union européenne),* following the publication of the 2008 EU Directive, aims to reflect primarily on civil and commercial litigation.

86 *Groupe de travail sur l'arbitrage,* Ministère de la justice (Daniel Labetoulle 2007).

87 Official Journal of 10 July 1975 7076. Cf. Bernard Dreyfus, 'La médiation en droit public – Des textes à la pratique' (2013) *Gazette du Palais* n° 356–358 27.

works or contracts.[88] Many commissions for mediation and reconciliation also exist in tax matters, particularly in the French districts. Or then again, the National Commission for Public Debate (*Commission nationale du débat public*) allows each party to share all of the arguments, and thus helps prevent conflicts. As for the Defender of rights, he or she is also meant to achieve mediation, as do government mediators and their local representatives, where they exist. The development of this spirit of mediation and dialogue can be found in many public or public interest enterprises (like French railways or the subway in Paris).

5 European perspectives

While there are reciprocal influences of European law and French administrative law, some of which have already been mentioned, we cannot really claim rules and principles have been harmonised.

5.1 ECHR law

Procedural rights are best protected by the jurisprudence of the ECtHR, and the ECHR is the largest international source of French administrative litigation law. It guarantees several rights, which individuals may rely on before the French administrative court, even if the former receives those rights rather as, mostly, guarantees for the quality of justice itself. This is particularly the case of the right to a fair trial if punitive measures have been decided (Art. 6–1) and the right to effective remedy before a national authority (Art. 13).

Several examples show that France yielded when it was condemned, by amending its legislation (for example about wiretapping[89] and police custody)[90] or its jurisprudence (for example about transsexuals' rights).[91] Even the *Conseil constitutionnel* operates reversal of jurisprudence, following ECtHR judgments, for example concerning which civil judge is competent to impose a custodial sentence or a pretrial detention.[92]

However, differences remain. Indeed, for the ECtHR, a 'tribunal' is, in the material sense, characterised by its judicial function.[93] But the *Conseil d'État* applies Art.6–1 ECHR to French authorities even if they have no judicial function. For example, the 'Financial Markets Council', which is an independent public authority, is not a 'court' under domestic law, but the principle of impartiality of Art. 6–1 may be a ground for an appeal to the *Conseil d'État* again the disciplinary sanctions adopted by this public authority, because of this authority's 'nature, composition and competences'.[94] In addition, solutions are sometimes contrary to each other. For example, the suspensive

88 Prime Minister circular of 6 April 2011.

89 Statute n° 91–646 of 10 July 1991.

90 Statute n° 2011–392 of 14 April 2011.

91 [1992] *Cour de cassation Ass* n° 91–11.900.

92 Decision n° 2011–135/140 *QPC* of 2011 reversed the n° 93–326 *DC* decision of 1993, considering that only the 'sitting judge' (*juge du siège*), not the judge of the Public Prosecutor's Office (*juge du parquet* or *ministère public*) can bring sufficient guarantees for the protection of individual freedoms.

93 *Demicoli v Malte* (n° 13057/87) (1991).

94 *Didier* [1999] *CE Ass.* n° 207434.

appeal against refusal to accept foreigners' political asylum is only possible within a very short period (48 hours), and this is in practice not compliant with the principle of effective remedy of Art. 13 ECHR. The *Conseil d'État* considers however that this appeal is effective.[95]

5.2 EU law

In some areas, the French administrative law and its objective nature have influenced the procedure of EU law. Indeed, the French *ultra vires* action (REP) is the model for action for annulment under Art. 263 TFEU. Furthermore, the EU Treaty established a European Ombudsman (Art. 228 TFEU), which is close to the model of the French *Médiateur de la République* (now *défenseur des droits*); as a matter of fact, among the six founding members of the European Union, France was the first to establish in 1973 its own Ombudsman. The French consultant judge (*commissaire du gouvernement*, now *rapporteur public)* was also the model for the Advocate General before the ECJ[96].

There has been some resistance on the French side, however, outside the scope of EU law, because of the principle of the primacy of national statutory law, which has long prevailed. It is only from the time of the *Conseil d'État Nicolo* judgment of 1989[97] that one can speak of a Europeanisation movement of French administrative law. Through European influence,[98] the *Conseil d'État Gardedieu* judgment of 2007[99] provides that if a statute infringes international commitment (treaty or agreement), the French State is, by that fact alone, bound to repair all damages arising from the breach. In the same logic, and again under external pressure,[100] the *Conseil d'État* admitted in 2008[101] that, if the content of a judicial decision that has become final is vitiated by a manifest infringement of EU law conferring rights on individuals, then the state's liability is engaged.

It could also be mentioned the *Conseil constitutionnel* decision n° 2013–314P QPC of 2013 about the European arrest warrant, in which the French constitutional judge accepts for the first time to stay proceedings and to refer to the ECJ for a preliminary ruling concerning the transposition by French law of the 2002 Framework Decision. The ECJ considers that the statutory law, which precludes any suspensive remedy against a decision to extend a European arrest warrant to another offence,[102] is not a necessary consequence of the European Framework Decision.[103] Therefore, the statute

95 'Association nationale d'assistance aux frontières pour les étrangers (ANAFE) [2013] *CE* n° 357848' (2013) 29 *AJDA* 1696.

96 Cf. particularly Ami Barav, 'Le commissaire du gouvernement près le Conseil d'État français et l'avocat général près la Cour de justice des Communautés européennes' (1974) 26 no4 *Revue internationale de droit comparé (RIDC)* 811.

97 *Nicolo* [1989] *CE Ass.* n° 108243, *Rec.* 190.

98 Cases C-6/90 and C-9/90 *Francovich v Italie* [1991] ECR I-05357.

99 *Gardedieu* [2007] *CE Ass.* n° 279522 (2007) 3 *AJDA* 585.

100 Case C-224/01 *Köbler v Autriche* [2003] ECR I-10239.

101 *Gestas* [2008] *CE Sect.* n° 295831.

102 It was a case of an English teacher who had come to France with one of his female pupils aged 15 (arrest warrant for 'child abduction'); he was extradited and then accused of 'sexual assault on a minor'.

103 Case C-168/13 PPU *Jeremy F v Premier ministre* [2013].

does not enjoy constitutional coverage of Art. 88–2 of the French Constitution[104] and the *Conseil constitutionnel* considers in the decision n° 2013–314 QPC of 2013 that the statute was an unjustified infringement of the right to effective judicial remedy that derives from Art.16 of the DDHC 1789.

Thus, the French court's and the ECJ's steps and the dialogue between the judges show a common desire to organise a complementary guarantee of rights.

6 Conclusion

On the whole, current French administrative law protects individuals' procedural rights, especially in the context of court proceedings. The courts rely on the case law 'general principles' and on the CJA, which governs general and special administrative law, even if courts and specific statutes may provide some procedural differences for special law (public procurement, urban planning, enter and stay of foreigners, tax law).

Concerning contentious proceedings, several significant developments furthering individual rights' protection can be highlighted, like the clarification of the role of the 'consultant judge' (*rapporteur public*) since 2006, the easy and free access to the courts for *ultra vires* action, the increased concrete powers of the courts in annulment litigation, the interim proceedings (particularly the *référé-liberté)* since 2000, and third-parties' protection (access to the judge, appellation again contracts since 2007).

Concerning the non-contentious administrative procedure, the statute on citizens' rights in their relations with public administration of 2000 changed the nature of relationship between administrative bodies and individuals towards partnership rather than a strict hierarchical relation, and the statute n° 2013–1005 of 2013 intends to simplify this relation and to improve the protection of the rights and interests of the private parties.

However, protections for individual rights should be more increased in non-judicial proceedings, through the adoption of a written general statute on administrative procedures,[105] and through reinforced alternative dispute resolution schemes in administrative law. Moreover, French administrative law basically has remained too complicated, due to the distribution of competences between civil and administrative courts, and to the various 'specialised administrative courts' and 'independent public authorities'. The distinction between the use of annulment proceedings and full jurisdiction proceedings has also become less clear for litigants and their lawyers, so that the question arises if they should not be merged in the future.[106]

104 'Statutes shall determine the rules relating to the European arrest warrant pursuant to acts adopted by the institutions on the European Union.'

105 The statute n°2013–1005 of 2013 authorises the Executive to adopt a 'Code concerning the relations between the public and administrative bodies' (*Code des relations entre le public et les administrations*).

106 Cf. Fabrice Melleray, 'La distinction des contentieux est-elle un archaïsme?' (2005) 30 *La Semaine juridique Administrations et collectivités territoriales (JCP A)* 1296.

8 The principle of effective legal protection in German administrative law

Diana zu Hohenlohe-Oehringen

1 Historical developments

The idea that public power should be limited and that the individual who is subject to that power should have the possibility to defend himself against unjust measures in a procedure before a court had been addressed very early in German history. Already the Imperial Chamber Court (*Reichskammergericht*), founded in 1495, and the Aulic Council (*Reichshofrat*), which was established in 1501, can be regarded as institutions providing for a certain legal protection against the administration.[1] Subjects could sue the ruler by claiming that they were violated in one of their acquired private rights (*jura quaesita*).[2] Particularly, the way to the imperial courts was open in cases of high-handed distraint and imprisonment and in cases of delay or refusal of jurisdiction.[3]

However, the imperial courts came to an end with the fall of the Holy Roman Empire of German Nation in 1806. In the aftermath, the general dynamic to change or at least to modify the existing order in the German territories, which at that time had not yet been unified, led to various attempts regarding the installation of a system to review the administration.[4] These attempts were influenced by two competing concepts. On the one hand, there was the French model of administrative justice according to which the best supervisor of the administration was the administration itself.[5] On the other hand, there was the claim that there should be a clear separation between the administration and the supervision of the administration; the

1 E. Schmidt-Aßmann and W. Schenk in F. Schoch, J.-P. Schneider and W. Bier (eds.), *Verwaltungsgerichtsordnung. Kommentar* (C. H. Beck, loose-leaf book, state Munich April 2013) Einleitung at 71–72, 49–50.

2 S. Schlacke, *Überindividueller Rechtsschutz* (Mohr Siebeck, Tübingen 2008) 30; cf. M. Bullinger, *Vertrag und Verwaltungsakt* (Kohlhammer, Stuttgart 1962) 204–219; W. Rüfner, *Verwaltungsrechtsschutz in Preußen von 1749 bis 1842* (Ludwig Röhrscheid, Bonn 1962) 23–44; idem, 'Verwaltungsrechtsschutz im 19. Jahrhundert vor Einführung der Verwaltungsgerichtsbarkeit' (1963) 16 *Die öffentliche Verwaltung* 719–726, 719.

3 A. Laufs, *Die Reichskammergerichtsordnung von 1555* (Boehlau, Cologne and Vienna 1976); M. Stolleis, *Geschichte des öffentlichen Rechts* (2nd edn., C. H. Beck, Munich 2013) volume 1, 135; T. Würtenberger, *Verwaltungsprozessrecht* (3rd edn., C. H. Beck, Munich 2011) 17–18.

4 See the various contributions in H. R. Külz and R. Naumann (eds.), *Staatsbürger und Staatsgewalt: Verwaltungsrecht und Verwaltungsgerichtsbarkeit in Geschichte und Gegenwart* (C. F. Müller, Karlsruhe 1962) volume 1.

5 H. de Pansey, *De l'autorité judiciaire en France* (Théophile Barrois Père, Paris 1818) 458–460; cf. J. Poppitz, 'Die Anfänge der Verwaltungsgerichtsbarkeit' (1941) N. S. 33 *Archiv des öffentlichen Rechts* 158–221, 159–160 and 192–194; K.-P. Sommermann, *Die deutsche Verwaltungsgerichtsbarkeit*(2nd edn., Forschungsinstitut für öffentliche Verwaltung bei der Hochschule für Verwaltungswissenschaften, Speyer 1991) 2–3.

administration should be controlled by an independent jurisdiction. This view was prominently expressed in Art. X para 182 of the Constitution of St. Paul's Church (*Paulskirchenverfassung*) of 1849, which stated that '[t]he administrative justice stops; the courts decide about all violations of the law'.[6] Although the Constitution of St. Paul's Church never came into effect, this provision was an important stimulus to turn away from exclusive inner-administrative review mechanisms and to take a path leading to an independent administrative jurisdiction.[7]

The first (higher) administrative court (*Verwaltungsgerichtshof*) was established in the Grand Duchy of Baden in 1863,[8] which is commonly regarded as the starting point of administrative jurisdiction in Germany.[9] After the foundation of the German Empire in 1871, further (higher) administrative courts came into being, namely the Prussian Higher Administrative Court (*Preußisches Oberverwaltungsgericht*) in 1875. Besides, institutions for the self-supervision of the administration continued as first instance for the legal protection of the individual, particularly in the form of chambers, advisory boards or committees which were organisationally and often also with regard to their personnel integrated into the administration.[10]

The foundation of the (higher) administrative courts was accompanied by an intensive scholarly discussion about the function the supervision of the administration should have. According to one opinion, the supervision should serve the protection of the objective legal order. In contrast to private law, administrative law was the epitome of normative provisions for the execution of state authority. The correct application of these norms was 'obligation and right of the authorities themselves'. Therefore, administration was 'actually already jurisdiction'.[11]

Administrative law was 'an objective legal order which, even independently of applications of parties, must be applied for the sake of the public law and well-being. Consequently, all kind of supervision over the state administration is directed at the same time at the protection of the general public and of the individual'. It was an error and a civilistic *petitio principii* to think about each jurisdiction primarily as a protection of subjective rights.[12] The 'German basic tendency which always loves and works up enthusiasm for "own rights",[13] misjudges that the person involved particu-

6 Cf. J. Gliss, *Die Entwicklung der deutschen Verwaltungsgerichtsbarkeit bis zur Bundesverwaltungsgerichtsordnung* (PhD thesis University of Frankfurt/Main 1962) 9; Schlacke (n. 2) 32; M. Sellmann, 'Der Weg zur neuzeitlichen Verwaltungsgerichtsbarkeit – ihre Vorstufen und dogmatischen Grundlagen' in Külz and Naumann (n. 4) 25–96, 80; M. Stolleis, *Geschichte des öffentlichen Rechts* (C. H. Beck, Munich 1992) volume 2, 117.

7 F. Hufen, *Verwaltungsprozessrecht* (9th edn., C. H. Beck, Munich 2013) 26; G. Sydow, 'Die Revolution von 1848/49: Ursprung der modernen Verwaltungsgerichtsbarkeit' (2001) 92 *Verwaltungsarchiv* 389–404, 397–404.

8 Cf. M. Montag, *Die Entwicklung der Verwaltungsgerichtsbarkeit in Baden und Württemberg von 1945 bis 1960* (Duncker & Humblot, Berlin 2001) 22.

9 Cf. M. Stolleis, 'Hundertundfünfzig Jahre Verwaltungsgerichtsbarkeit' (2013) 128 *Deutsches Verwaltungsblatt* 1274–1280, 1276.

10 Hufen (n. 7) 28.

11 R. von Gneist, 'Ueber die rechtliche Natur, die Zuständigkeit und die Verhandlungsform der Verwaltungsjurisdiction' in Ständige Deputation des Deutschen Juristentages (ed.), *Verhandlungen des 12: Deutschen Juristentages* (Comissions-Verlag, Berlin 1875) volume 3, 221–241, 232.

12 R. von Gneist, *Der Rechtsstaat und die Verwaltungsgerichte in Deutschland* (2nd edn., Julius Springer, Berlin 1879) 270–271.

13 R. von Gneist (n. 11) 231.

larly supervises the administration in the public interest and was thus 'authorised to an *imploratio officii judicis* or extrajudicial appeal in the canonistic sense'.[14]

In contrast, other scholars argued that the function of administrative jurisdiction should be the protection of subjective public rights.[15] The jurisdiction had the task of determining whether the administrative measures violate a subjective public right of the individual.[16] Public law could be divided into subjective and objective legal norms. The latter contained the order directed to the state organs to look after the public interest as well as provisions concerning the means and ways to reach this target. Conversely, the subjective legal norms were provisions which served the protection of the legal sphere of the individual, which have to be respected 'as absolutely inviolable even *vis-à-vis* conflicting demands of the public interest' and which insofar determined and limited the will of the public authority and of the individuals in the same way as private norms.[17]

The southern German states, like Baden, Württemberg, Bavaria and Thuringia, followed the model of the protection of subjective rights.[18] For instance, Württemberg in 1876 allowed the so-called legal complaint (*Rechtsbeschwerde*) 'against decisions or orders of the administrative authorities', when 'somebody, be it a single person, an association or a cooperation, claims that the decision or order based on considerations of public law was not legally well-founded and that he [she or it] thereby was violated in one of his [her or its] lawful rights or was burdened with an obligation which he [she or it] did not owe'.[19] On the other side, the northern German states under the practical leadership of Prussia as the biggest German state chose a solution which combined elements of an objective supervision of the administration, especially by allowing lawsuits of authorities and popular actions, with such of the protection of subjective public rights.[20] However, some 'milestone decisions'[21] of the Prussian Higher Administrative Court[22] firmly established the function of the administrative jurisdiction to protect the individual.[23] For example, the Court in the so-called *Kreuzberg* judgment of 1882 overruled a police ordinance generously regulating the construction of buildings in the neighbourhood of a certain national monument. It held that the discretion of the police was limited by the right of the property owners to erect buildings on their land and soil. The principle of the inviolability of property had to be respected, and conflicts between the property rights of the individuals and the public interests had to be solved in a considerate manner.[24] The judgment

14 Ibid. 233.

15 O. von Sarwey, *Das öffentliche Recht und die Verwaltungsrechtspflege* (Verlag der H. Laupp'schen Buchhandlung, Tübingen 1880) 73 and 405–419.

16 Ibid. 73.

17 Ibid. 65.

18 Sommermann (n. 5) 4–5.

19 W. Kohl, *Das Reichsverwaltungsgericht* (Mohr Siebeck, Tübingen 1991) 31.

20 Schlacke (n. 2) 39.

21 H.-C. Jasch, 'Das Ringen um die Verwaltungsgerichtsbarkeit. Verwaltungsgerichtsbarkeit als Instrument der Rechtsvereinheitlichung im Dritten Reich' (2005) 38 *Die Verwaltung* 546–576, 546.

22 Cf. L. Frege, 'Der Status des Preußischen Oberverwaltungsgerichtes und die Standhaftigkeit seiner Rechtsprechung auf politischem Gebiet' in Külz and Naumann (n. 4) 140–155.

23 Cf. C. H. Ule, 'Das Preußische Oberverwaltungsgericht in der Weimarer Republik' (1981) 96 *Deutsches Verwaltungsblatt* 709–719.

24 *Entscheidungen des königlichen Oberwaltungsgerichts* (Berlin 1883) volume 9, 353–384, particularly 360–361.

revealed an aspect which moulded the development of administrative jurisdiction in the next decades. That was the linkage between legal protection against the administration and material administrative law. Access to the administrative courts was given when a person could claim that the administration violated one of his subjective rights by a wrong application or non-application of legal norms which also served his or her individual interests.[25]

In the Weimar Republic the system of individual protection by (higher) administrative courts on the basis of state law continued.[26] The Constitution of 1919 in its Art. 107 simply ordered that '[t]here shall be administrative courts in the Reich and in the states, as provided by law, for the protection of individuals against ordinances and decrees of the administrative authorities.' However, due to the traditional enumerative principle governing the competences of the (higher) administrative courts, many fields of administrative action stayed outside their jurisdiction.[27] In such cases, the individual could only claim damages with regard to the violation of an official liability before the civil courts.[28]

In the time of National Socialism, which destroyed the validity of the constitutionally bound rule of law,[29] it was popularly argued in literature that administrative jurisdiction had lost its justification because it was based on a liberalistic ideology and served the protection of subjective rights, which was not compatible with the new state model.[30] Although the administrative courts were not abolished institutionally, they were *de facto* made functionless.[31]

Particularly, the admissibility of the procedure before the administrative courts was subject to the disposition of the administrative authorities. Instead of contesting an ordinance in an administrative court procedure, the affected person had to lodge a complaint with the superior authority or supervisory authority. That authority could then, with regard to the fundamental importance or the special circumstances of the individual case, admit the administrative court procedure instead of the bureaucratic complaint procedure.[32] The decision about the admissibility or inadmissibility itself was a discretionary decision which could not be impugned.[33]

After the end of World War II, the administrative courts provisionally had to stop their activities.[34] However, the creation of administrative courts of first instance

25 Cf. O. Bühler, *Die subjektiven öffentlichen Rechte und ihr Schutz in der deutschen Verwaltungsrechtsprechung* (Kohlhammer, Berlin et al. 1914) 43–47.

26 R. Grawert, 'Verwaltungsrechtsschutz in der Weimarer Republik' in H.-U. Erichsen, W. Hoppe and A. von Mutius (eds.), *Festschrift für Christian Friedrich Menger* (Carl Heymanns, Cologne et al. 1985) 35–55, 46.

27 Grawert (n. 26) 36–37.

28 Montag (n. 8) 26; Schlacke (n. 2) 43.

29 See M. Stolleis, 'Die Verwaltungsgerichtsbarkeit im Nationalsozialismus' in Erichsen, Hoppe and von Mutius (n. 26) 57–80.

30 T. Maunz, 'Das Ende des subjektiven öffentlichen Rechts' (1936) 96 *Zeitschrift für die gesamte Staatswissenschaft* 71–111; R. Höhn, 'Das subjektive öffentliche Recht und der neue Staat' (1936) 1 *Deutsches Recht, Wochenausgabe* 49–72, particularly 57.

31 Cf. J. Muth, 'Die Verwaltungsgerichtsbarkeit und der Krieg' (1939) 9 *Deutsches Recht* 1874–1877, 1874; Jasch (n. 21) 554–556; Kohl (n. 19) 440–450.

32 J. Poppitz, *Die Verwaltungsgerichtsbarkeit im Kriege* (Hanseatische Verlagsanstalt, Hamburg 1941) 12; Gliss (n. 6) 25.

33 Schlacke (n. 2) 47; Schmidt-Aßmann et al. (n. 1) Einleitung at 81, 54.

34 Schmidt-Aßmann et al. (n. 1) Einleitung at 82, 55.

(*Verwaltungsgerichte*), which had not existed before, and the re-establishment of higher administrative courts (*Verwaltungsgerichtshöfe/ Oberverwaltungsgerichte*) in the western occupation zones in 1945 and 1946 were among the first steps to (re)found the liberal order in Germany.[35] At that time, also the enumerative principle governing the competences of the administrative courts was abolished.[36]

To reinstall the rule of law at least in the western parts of Germany, it was regarded as an elementary precondition to grant each citizen rights which he or she could claim before courts in case of a violation.[37] Therefore, with the Basic Law (*Grundgesetz*) of 1949 as the German post-war Constitution, a clear decision was made that there should be an effective legal protection by independent courts even against measures of the administration. The idea was, without forerunner in the Weimar Constitution,[38] particularly formulated as a basic right in Art. 19 para 4 of the Basic Law.[39]

In 1952, the Federal Administrative Court (*Bundesverwaltungsgericht*) was founded.[40] The protection of subjective rights of the individual was laid down in Art. 19 of the Federal Administrative Court Act (*Gesetz über das Bundesverwaltungsgericht*),[41] which stipulated that a lawsuit directed against an administrative act was only admissible if the plaintiff claims to be violated by this act in his (or her) rights.[42] Furthermore, the Federal Administrative Court Act assigned the new Court the function of an appeal court. Besides, the procedural laws of the federal states remained unchanged.[43] These laws, together with judge-made law, continued to rule the legal protection of the individual before the administrative courts and higher administrative courts.[44] However, the various procedural laws of the federal states, which considerably differed from each other, were regarded as an obstacle for the effective legal enforcement of the subjective rights of the citizens *vis-à-vis* the administrative authorities. Thus, the demand was raised that there should be a uniform procedural law for all administrative courts in the Federation.[45] This demand was fulfilled by passing the Administrative Court Code (*Verwaltungsgerichtsordnung*, hereinafter ACC) in 1960.[46] The Code, which is federal law, rules the constitution of the administrative courts, the competences of and procedures before the administrative courts, the means of legal redress,

35 Cf. Montag (n. 8) 40–74; C.-F. Menger, *System des verwaltungsgerichtlichen Rechtsschutzes* (Mohr Siebeck, Tübingen 1954) 3–13.

36 Hufen (n. 7) 33.

37 Cf. Menger (n. 35) 3–13; O. Bühler, 'Altes und Neues über Begriff und Bedeutung der subjektiven öffentlichen Rechte' in O. Bachof, M. Drath, O. Gönnenwein and E. Walz (eds.), *Gedächtnisschrift für Walter Jellinek* (Isar, Munich 1955) 269–286, 269.

38 Montag (n. 8) 25; Schlacke (n. 2) 43.

39 Cf. Schlacke (n. 2) 48; H. Schulze-Fielitz, in H. Dreier (ed.), *Grundgesetz* (3rd edn., Mohr Siebeck, Tübingen 2013) volume 1, Art. 19 IV at 1, 1793.

40 Cf. C. H. Ule, 'Die geschichtliche Entwicklung des verwaltungsgerichtlichen Rechtsschutzes in der Nachkriegszeit' in Erichsen, Hoppe and von Mutius (eds.), (n. 26) 81–103, 92–93.

41 *Bundesgesetzblatt* (Federal Law Gazette) 1952 I, 625.

42 Cf. Bühler (n. 37) 269.

43 Schlacke (n. 2) 48.

44 Cf. Schmidt-Aßmann et al. (n. 1), Einleitung at 84, 55–56.

45 Cf. C. H. Ule, 'Für eine einheitliche Verwaltungsgerichtsordnung!' (1950) 3 *Deutsche Verwaltung* 1–5, 2–5; idem, 'Für eine einheitliche Verwaltungsgerichtsordnung!' (1950) 3 *Deutsche Verwaltung* 41–44.

46 *Bundesgesetzblatt* (Federal Law Gazette) 1960 I, 17; cf. Ule (n. 40) 93–95.

the resumption of procedures, the costs and the enforcement of court decisions. For instance, Art. 42 para 2 of the ACC, similarly to Art. 19 of the Federal Administrative Court Act, stipulates that, unless otherwise provided by law, the action for the rescission of an administrative act (*Anfechtungsklage*) and the action for the issue of an administrative act (*Verpflichtungsklage*) are only admissible if the plaintiff claims that his (or her) rights have been violated by the administrative act or its refusal or omission.[47]

Correspondingly, Art. 113 para 1 of the ACC determines that, insofar as the administrative act is unlawful and the plaintiff's rights have been violated thereby, the court rescinds the administrative act and any ruling on an objection. Art. 113 para 5 of the Code reads that, insofar as the rejection or omission of the administrative act is unlawful and the plaintiff's rights are violated thereby, the court announces the obligation incumbent on the administrative authority to effect the requested act if the case is mature for decision. Otherwise, it hands down the obligation to notify the plaintiff, taking the legal view of the court into consideration. Furthermore, the ACC contains a series of rules concerning the procedure before the administrative courts which guarantee the effective legal protection of the plaintiff's rights. Particularly, there are various provisions dealing with the hearing of the plaintiff in a broader sense. Since 2004, there is even a special legal remedy against the violation of the right to hearing in the administrative court procedure, the so-called hearing reprimand (*Anhörungsrüge*).[48] Finally, it has to be noted that the provisions concerning the administrative procedure before the administrative authorities have been codified in the Administrative Procedure Act (*Verwaltungsverfahrensgesetz*) of the Federation of 1976[49] and in the subsequent administrative procedure acts of the federal states, which followed a model draft and are even today to a large extent identical in their wording. The administrative procedure acts supported the development of the administrative procedure law from an essentially judge-made law and from a basically 'internal law of the administration' to a law having external effects, with subjective procedural rights like the right to hearing, participation of affected persons, inspection of the files or defense against biased officials.[50]

The Administrative Court Code and the administrative procedure acts are linked with each other.[51] For instance, the objection procedure (*Widerspruchsverfahren*), which is an independent administrative procedure, is with its central aspects stipulated as mere preliminary proceedings in the ACC, whereas the legal consequences of procedural defects are only rudimentary ruled in the administrative procedure acts.

After all, the principle of the effective legal protection of the individual against measures of the administrative authorities is in Germany predominantly discussed on

47 See about the drafting history W. Skouris, *Verletztenklagen und Interessenklagen im Verwaltungsprozeß* (Carl Heymanns, Cologne et al. 1979) 28–30.

48 Cf. W. Ewer, 'Aktuelle Neuregelungen im Verwaltungsprozessrecht' (2007) 60 *Neue Juristische Wochenschrift* 3171–3176, 3172–3174; A. Guckelberger, 'Die Anhörungsrüge nach § 152a VwGO n. F.' (2005) 24 *Neue Zeitschrift für Verwaltungsrecht* 11–15; Hufen (n. 7) 36 and 622–624; W.-R. Schenke, 'Außerordentliche Rechtsbehelfe im Verwaltungsprozessrecht nach Erlass des Anhörungsrügengesetzes' (2005) 24 *Neue Zeitschrift für Verwaltungsrecht* 729–739.

49 *Bundesgesetzblatt* (Federal Law Gazette) 1976 I, 1253.

50 Hufen (n. 7) 34.

51 Cf. H. Jochum, *Verwaltungsrecht und Verwaltungsprozessrecht* (Mohr Siebeck, Tübingen 2004).

the level of constitutional law. On the level of statutory law, there exist a set of special rules which concretise this principle. Thus, effective legal protection is generally a question of the correct interpretation and application of the existing legal norms in the ACC and in the administrative procedure acts of the Federation and of the federal states. Problems which might result from any opinion held in jurisprudence or legal literature that certain provisions of statutory law are deficit have to be solved in accordance with the provisions of the Constitution. Furthermore, supranational provisions and jurisprudence can sometimes require amendments in national statutory law.

2 Constitutional framework

Art. 19 para 4 of the Basic Law reads that should any person be violated in his (or her) rights by public authority, he (or she) may have recourse to the courts. This provision does not only mean that the individual has a general right to sue before a court in case of a possible violation of his (or her) subjective rights by administrative measures. Rather, it also contains requirements with regard to the way in which the access to the courts is to be granted.[52]

According to the jurisdiction of the Federal Constitutional Court (*Bundesverfassungsgericht*), this access must be effective (*effektiv*).[53] In other words, the individual has a right to an actually effective (*wirksam*; having considerable effects), quick and comprehensive supervision.[54] However, this stipulation should not be understood as a guarantee for a maximum amount of legal protection.[55] Instead, it predominantly focuses on the target to secure that a violation of subjective rights can be cancelled or at least identified as such on time.[56]

The principle of effective legal protection guarantees that procedural requirements and their practical application do not constitute inadequately high obstacles for the access to the courts.[57] Such obstacles might, for example, be linked with obligatory preliminary proceedings or they might consist in preclusion norms,[58] although the

52 Schlacke (n. 2) 59; Schulze-Fielitz (n. 39), Art. 19 IV at 80, 1831.

53 H. D. Jarass, in H. D. Jarass and B. Pieroth, *Grundgesetz für die Bundesrepublik Deutschland* (13th edn., C. H. Beck, Munich 2014), Art. 19 at 50, 487.

54 See Federal Constitutional Court, *Entscheidungen des Bundesverfassungsgerichts* 35, 263–280, 274; 37, 150–154, 153; 46, 166–185, 178; 49, 329–343, 341; 53, 115,127–128; 65, 1–71, 70; 77, 275–287, 284; 101, 106–132, 122–123; 101, 397–410, 407; 104, 220–238, 231; 107, 299–339, 337; P. Wilfinger, *Das Gebot effektiven Rechtsschutzes in Grundgesetz und Europäischer Menschenrechtskonvention* (Peter Lang, Frankfurt am Main et al. 1995) 8–14. Critical with regard to the notion of effectiveness in this context M. Kaufmann, *Untersuchungsgrundsatz und Verwaltungsgerichtsbarkeit* (Mohr Siebeck, Tübingen 2002) 244–253.

55 Schulze-Fielitz (n. 39), Art. 19 IV at 81, 1831.

56 M. Sachs, in idem (ed.), *Grundgesetz* (7th edn., C. H. Beck, Munich 2014), Art. 19 at 143, 792–793; Schlacke (n. 2) 59; Sommermann (n. 5) 16–17.

57 Federal Constitutional Court, *Entscheidungen des Bundesverfassungsgerichts* 53, 115,127–128; 60, 253–305, 269; 77, 275–287, 284; 85, 337–353, 345–350; 88, 118, 124–125; 118, 1–28, 23; Federal Constitutional Court (Chamber) (2007) 60 *Neue Juristische Wochenschrift* 3117–3118, 3118; (2008) 27 *Neue Zeitschrift für Verwaltungsrecht* 772–775, 773; Sachs (n. 56), Art. 19 at 140, 792 and Art. 20 at 162, 855; E. Schmidt-Jortzig, 'Effektiver Rechtsschutz als Kernstück des Rechtsstaatsprinzips nach dem Grundgesetz' (1994) 47 *Neue Juristische Wochenschrift* 2569–2573, 2572–2573.

58 Schlacke (n. 2) 59; Schulze-Fielitz (n. 39), Art. 19 IV at 99, 1840–1841; cf. H.-J. Papier, 'Einwendungen Dritter in Verwaltungsverfahren' (1980) 33 *Neue Juristische Wochenschrift* 313–321, 318–320; R. Wolfrum, 'Der Ausschluß von Einwendungen im Anhörungsverfahren und sein Einfluß auf den

Federal Constitutional Court and the Federal Administrative Court in several decisions held that it is in principle in accordance with the Constitution when certain objections which could have been made, but had not been made in the administrative procedure, are likewise not taken into consideration in the court procedure.[59] Against this background, the principle of effective legal protection can have advance effects on the administrative procedure which precedes the control by the administrative courts.[60] Besides, it can have advance effects on the administrative procedure with regard to securing the effectiveness of the judicial review. For instance, it can be necessary that reasons are given for the measure which is to be controlled[61] or that the (course of) action of the administrative authority is documented.[62] Furthermore, the principle of effective legal protection orders that there must be a legal protection within reasonable time.[63] The administrative court procedures must not take inappropriately long; a legal protection which comes too late does not adequately take into account the protected interests of the bearer of the subjective rights which are affected by the administrative measure.[64] Correspondingly, the individual has the

---

Verwaltungsrechtsschutz' (1979) 32 *Die öffentliche Verwaltung* 497–502, 499–502; C. H. Ule, 'Zur rechtlichen Bedeutung von Ausschlußfristen im Verwaltungsverfahren für den Verwaltungsprozeß' (1979) 34 *Betriebs-Berater* 1009–1013, 1011–1013; W. Erbguth, 'Zur verfassungsrechtlichen (Un-)Zulässigkeit der materiellen Einwenderpräklusion im Planfeststellungsrecht' in W. Erbguth, F. Müller and V. Neumann (eds.), *Gedächtnisschrift für Bernd Jeand'Heur* (Duncker & Humblot, Berlin 1999) 391–402; M. Niedzwicki, *Präklusionsvorschriften des öffentlichen Rechts im Spannungsfeld zwischen Verfahrensbeschleunigung, Einzelfallgerechtigkeit und Rechtsstaatlichkeit* (Duncker & Humblot, Berlin 2007) 152–166 and 176–211; M. Kaltenborn, *Streitvermeidung und Streitbeilegung im Verwaltungsrecht* (Nomos, Baden-Baden 2007) 306–315.

59 See Federal Constitutional Court, *Entscheidungen des Bundesverfassungsgerichts* 61, 82–118, 109–118; Federal Constitutional Court (Chamber) (2000) *Neue Zeitschrift für Verwaltungsrecht* 546–548, 547; Federal Administrative Court, *Entscheidungen des Bundesverwaltungsgerichts* 104, 337–347, 341.

60 Federal Constitutional Court, *Entscheidungen des Bundesverfassungsgerichts* 61, 82–118, 110; 101, 106–132, 123; 109, 279–382, 364; 116, 135–163, 156; 118, 168–211, 207; 128, 282–322, 313; D. Lorenz, *Der Rechtsschutz des Bürgers und die Rechtsweggarantie* (C. H. Beck, Munich 1973) 178–182; Jarass and Pieroth (n. 53), Art. 19 at 72, 494–495; Kaltenborn (n. 58) 295–315; Schulze-Fielitz (n. 39), Art. 19 IV at 87, 1834.

61 Federal Constitutional Court, *Entscheidungen des Bundesverfassungsgerichts* 6, 32–45, 44–45; 40, 276–286, 286; 103, 142–164, 160–161; 118, 168–211, 208; cf. U. Kischel, *Die Begründung* (Mohr Siebeck, Tübingen 2003) 87–88; Kaltenborn (n. 58) 298–306.

62 Federal Constitutional Court, *Entscheidungen des Bundesverfassungsgerichts* 65, 1–71, 70; 103, 142–164, 159–160; 109, 279–382, 333; 118, 168–211, 208; 128, 282–322, 313–315; Jarass and Pieroth (n. 53), Art. 19 at 74–75, 495–496; Sachs (n. 56), Art. 19 at 143a, 793; Schulze-Fielitz (n. 39), Art. 19 IV at 88, 1834–1835.

63 Federal Constitutional Court, *Entscheidungen des Bundesverfassungsgerichts* 55, 349–370, 369; U. Ramsauer, in E. Denninger, W. Hoffmann-Riem, H.-P. Schneider and E. Stein (eds.), *Kommentar zum Grundgesetz für die Bundesrepublik Deutschland* (3rd edn., Luchterhand, loose-leaf book, Neuwied and Kriftel 2002), Art. 19 Abs. 4 at 76, 46 and 119, 71–72; Schmidt-Aßmann et al. (n. 1), Einleitung at 157, 106; Schulze-Fielitz (n. 39), Art. 19 IV at 111, 1845.

64 Federal Constitutional Court, *Entscheidungen des Bundesverfassungsgerichts* 40, 237–259, 256–257; 93, 1–25, 13–14; Federal Constitutional Court (2014) 33 *Neue Zeitschrift für Verwaltungsrecht* 211–233, 217; Federal Constitutional Court (Chamber) (2004) 23 *Neue Zeitschrift für Verwaltungsrecht* 471–472; (2005) 58 *Neue Juristische Wochenschrift* 3488–3489; Sachs (n. 56), Art. 19 at 144, 793; E. Schmidt-Aßmann, in T. Maunz and G. Dürig, *Grundgesetz* (C. H. Beck, loose-leaf book, state, Munich July 2014), Art. 19 para 4 at 262–263, 195–197; V. Schlette, *Der Anspruch auf gerichtliche Entscheidung in angemessener Frist* (Duncker & Humblot, Berlin 1999); K. Redeker, 'Kann eine Untätigkeitsbeschwerde helfen?' (2003) 56 *Neue Juristische Wochenschrift* 488–489; Sommermann (n. 5) 16–17; G. Britz and D. Pfeifer, 'Rechtsbehelf gegen unangemessene Verfahrensdauer im Verwaltungsprozeß' (2004) 57 *Die öffentliche Verwaltung* 245–250; C. Steinbeiß-Winkelmann, 'Überlange Gerichtsverfahren – der Ruf nach dem Gesetzgeber' (2007) 40 *Zeitschrift für Rechtspolitik* 177–180.

right that he (or she) can so timely take action against possible violations of his (or her) rights that serious and irreparable damages are excluded as far as possible.[65] Thus, the Constitution demands that there must be a provisional legal protection in addition[66] to the legal protection in the main proceedings in cases where without such a protection serious and by other means not avoidable disadvantages would occur which cannot be disposed of any more later by the decision in the main proceedings.[67] However, with regard to the uncertainty about the legal situation which still is to be clarified, decisions about an application for interim measures can be based on a summary examination of the prospects of success in the main proceedings or on a balancing of the consequences of granting or denying the applied measure.[68]

The last explanation leads to a second aspect of the principle of effective legal protection beside the guarantee of effective access to legal protection by the courts. That is the guarantee of an effective judicial supervisory activity with regard to violations of subjective rights by administrative authorities. Thus, the potentially violated person has in principle a right to a comprehensive, which means the grounds for the assessment including examination of the contested measure under legal and factual regards.[69] Conversely, the court, which decides upon its own responsibility,[70] is in principle not bound to the factual ascertainments of the administrative authority.[71] However, the constitutionally guaranteed comprehensive legal protection does not exclude from the outset administrative scopes for arrangement, discretion and assessment which are provided by the law.[72] It is argued in literature that insofar the objective commitment of the public authority to material law and in the consequence also the range of the affected subjective rights of the individual experience a limitation.[73]

65 Federal Constitutional Court, *Entscheidungen des Bundesverfassungsgerichts* 46, 166–185, 179; 79, 69–79, 74; Schlacke (n. 2) 60.

66 Cf. Sachs (n. 56), Art. 19 at 146a, 795; K. Windthorst, *Der verwaltungsgerichtliche einstweilige Rechtsschutz* (Mohr Siebeck, Tübingen 2009) 20.

67 Federal Constitutional Court, *Entscheidungen des Bundesverfassungsgerichts* 35, 263–280, 274–275; 93, 1–25, 13–14; 94, 166–223, 216; Federal Constitutional Court (Chamber) (2001) *Neue Juristische Wochenschrift* 3770–3771; (2002) 3691–3692; (2008) 1369–1371, 1371.

68 Cf. Federal Constitutional Court (Chamber) (2005) *Neue Zeitschrift für Verwaltungsrecht* 927–929, 928; (2004) *Neue Juristische Wochenschrift* 2297–2299, 2298–2299.

69 Federal Constitutional Court, *Entscheidungen des Bundesverfassungsgerichts* 15, 275–283, 282; 54, 277–300, 291; 84, 366–372, 369; 85, 337–353, 345; 101, 106–132, 123; 101, 275–297, 294–295; 101, 397–410, 407; 103, 142–164, 156; Sachs (n. 56), Art. 19 at 145, 794; Schlacke (n. 2) 60.

70 Federal Constitutional Court, *Entscheidungen des Bundesverfassungsgerichts* 96, 44–56, 51; Federal Constitutional Court (Chamber) (2002) *Neue Juristische Wochenschrift* 1333–1334, 1333.

71 Federal Constitutional Court, *Entscheidungen des Bundesverfassungsgerichts* 15, 275–283, 282; 88, 40–63, 56; Sachs (n. 56), Art. 19 at 145, 794.

72 Federal Constitutional Court, *Entscheidungen des Bundesverfassungsgerichts* 61, 82–118, 111; 84, 34–58, 49–50; 88, 40–63, 56; 103, 142–164, 157; 113, 273–319, 310; Federal Administrative Court, *Entscheidungen des Bundesverwaltungsgerichts* 120, 227–239, 231–232; Jarass and Pieroth (n. 53), Art. 19 at 69, 493; W.-R. Schenke, in W. Kahl, C. Waldhoff and C. Walter (eds.), *Bonner Kommentar zum Grundgesetz* (C. F. Müller, loose-leaf book, state, Heidelberg, December 2014), Art. 19 paragraph 4 at 491–590, 353–416.

73 Sachs (n. 56), Art. 19 at 146, 795; cf. Federal Constitutional Court, *Entscheidungen des Bundesverfassungsgerichts* 88, 40–63, 56 and 61; 103, 142–164, 156–157; 113, 273–319, 312–313; Federal Administrative Court, *Entscheidungen des Bundesverwaltungsgerichts* 120, 227–239, 231–232; (2008) *Neue Zeitschrift für Verwaltungsrecht* 220–224, 223; F. Schoch, 'Außerrechtliche Standards des Verwaltungshandelns als gerichtliche Kontrollmaßstäbe' in H.-H. Trute, T. Groß, H. C. Röhl and C. Möllers (eds.), *Allgemeines Verwaltungsrecht – zur Tragfähigkeit eines Konzepts* (Mohr Siebeck, Tübingen 2008) 543–573, 543–553.

In any way, the criterion for judicial control is the law and particularly the subjective rights granted by the law. The dogma of the complete judicial review of the lawful activity of the administrative authorities is restricted by the subjective public right. The examination whether state measures are illegal does not take place in its full range but only to the extent to which the plaintiff is possibly violated in his (or her) rights.[74]

The control of the interpretation and application of objective law in the framework of the legal protection procedure focusing on subjective rights is thus an additional purpose of the controlling task of the courts. It contributes to both the protection of the (objective) legal order and the constitutionality and legality of the administration as such.[75]

Finally, the principle of effective legal protection requires that the courts have sufficient power with regard to their decision. A successful court procedure must in principle be finished with a decision which is able to reach a binding nature by becoming final[76] and which is enforceable so that the material law can be imposed or realised reliably.[77]

It is discussed in jurisdiction and literature whether the principle of effective legal protection includes an obligation of the courts to give reasons for their decisions[78] and to follow maxims like the oral trial and the publicity of the proceedings.[79] Furthermore, the Federal Constitutional Court holds that the Constitution does not guarantee several instances of appeal.[80] But if an appeal is provided for, the access to that legal means must be given consistently, as far as this is possible, and it must not be hindered due to irrelevant considerations.[81]

3 Rights-based perspective

Against the background of these constitutional requirements, the stipulations of the Administrative Court Code are almost necessarily detailed. The basic provision for

74 E. Schmidt-Aßmann, 'Funktionen der Verwaltungsgerichtsbarkeit' in Erichsen, Hoppe and von Mutius (n. 26) 107–123, 109.

75 Schlacke (n. 2) 61; Schmidt-Aßmann (n. 74) 109.

76 Federal Constitutional Court, *Entscheidungen des Bundesverfassungsgerichts* 60, 253–305, 269–270; 113, 273–319, 310; Jarass and Pieroth (n. 53), Art. 19 at 50, 487.

77 Sachs (n. 56), Art. 19 at 147, 795; H. Bauer, *Gerichtsschutz als Verfassungsgarantie* (Duncker & Humblot, Berlin 1973) 102–103; E. Fechner, 'Kostenrisiko und Rechtswegsperre – Steht der Rechtsweg offen?' (1969) 24 *Juristenzeitung* 349–354, 350; Ramsauer (n. 63), Art. 19 Abs. 4 at 76, 47–48.

78 Cf. Federal Constitutional Court, *Entscheidungen des Bundesverfassungsgerichts* 40, 276–286, 286; 71, 122–137, 135–136; Federal Constitutional Court (Chamber) (2/1999) *Neue Zeitschrift für Verwaltungsrecht, Supplement I* 10–12, 11; against an obligation to give reasons in cases of decisions which cannot be challenged in court instances see Federal Constitutional Court, *Entscheidungen des Bundesverfassungsgerichts* 50, 287–290, 289–290; 94, 166–223, 210; Federal Constitutional Court (Chamber) (2004) *Neue Juristische Wochenschrift* 1371–1373, 1372.

79 Cf. Federal Constitutional Court, *Entscheidungen des Bundesverfassungsgerichts* 103, 44–71, 63–71.

80 Federal Constitutional Court, *Entscheidungen des Bundesverfassungsgerichts* 4, 74–96, 74; 49, 329–343, 341; 83, 24–36, 31; 87, 48–68, 61; 89, 381–398, 390; 118, 212–244, 239–240; 122, 248–281, 271; Federal Administrative Court, *Entscheidungen des Bundesverwaltungsgerichts* 94, 279–288, 280; 120, 87–105, 93; 131, 274–315, 285; Sachs (n. 56), Art. 19 at 120, 784; Schulze-Fielitz (n. 39), Art. 19 IV at 94, 1838.

81 Federal Constitutional Court, *Entscheidungen des Bundesverfassungsgerichts* 54, 277–300, 291–293; 74, 228–236, 234; 104, 220–238, 232; 125, 104–141, 137; 122, 248–281, 271; Federal Constitutional Court (Chamber) (2007) *Neue Juristische Wochenschrift* 2241–2242; 3118–3120, 3119.

the opening of recourse to legal action to the administrative courts is formulated as a general clause. According to the ACC, recourse to the administrative courts is available in all public law disputes of a non-constitutional nature insofar as the disputes are not explicitly allocated to another court by a federal statute. Public law disputes in the field of federal state law may also be assigned to another court by a federal state statute. Thus, the competencies of the administrative courts are comprehensive. Consequently, there is no *numerus clausus* of types of lawsuits. Rather, '[f]or any action of the authorities which infringes rights of a citizen there must be an admissible type of lawsuit'.[82] This already indicates that a possible violation of rights is essential for the individual standing before the administrative courts. However, the ACC does not contain a universal provision for the access to the administrative courts but rules requirements concerning admissibility alongside the various types of lawsuits.

3.1 Action for the rescission of an administrative act

The prototype of lawsuit before the administrative courts is the action for the rescission of a burdensome administrative act (*Anfechtungsklage*), ruled in the ACC. This action aims at changing the law by disposing of the legal effects of the contested administrative act which violates the plaintiff in his (or her) rights.[83] It requires the existence of an administrative act.[84]

The administrative act (*Verwaltungsakt*) is legally defined in Art. 35 of the APA as an order, decision or other sovereign measure taken by an authority to regulate an individual case and intended to have direct external legal effect. Moreover, the provision clarifies that an administrative act can also take the form of a general order (*Allgemeinverfügung*) directed at a group of people defined or definable on the basis of general characteristics or relating to the public law aspect of an object or its use by the public at large. A prominent example for the second aspect is the road sign which contains a commandment or prohibition, particularly the no-parking sign.[85]

According to the ACC, the plaintiff is allowed to bring an action for the rescission of the administrative act if he (or she) claims to be violated by the administrative act in his (or her) rights (so-called right or authorisation to sue; *Klagebefugnis*). This provision, which connects the standing with material law, has the function to exclude popular actions with which the plaintiff makes himself (or herself) a representative of public interests or of legally protected interests of third parties.[86] However, the mere assertion of a violation of subjective rights is not sufficient. Instead, the violation must appear to be possible. The plaintiff is primarily authorised to sue when he (or she) is the direct addressee of a burdensome administrative act since such an act at least touches his (or her) general freedom of action, which is guaranteed in Art. 2 para 1 of the Basic Law, if there is no special basic right applicable.[87] When the plaintiff is not the addressee of the contested administrative act but a third party, the situation

82 Hufen (n. 7) 200.

83 Cf. Ibid. 205.

84 Cf. W.-R. Schenke, *Verwaltungsprozessrecht* (13th edn., C. F. Müller, Heidelberg 2012) 62–64.

85 Schenke (n. 84) 70.

86 Hufen (n. 7) 233–234; Schenke (n. 84) 152.

87 N. Achterberg, 'Die Klagebefugnis – eine entbehrliche Sachurteilsvoraussetzung?' (1981) 96 *Deutsches Verwaltungsblatt* 278–283, 278–279; V. Schlette, 'Die Klagebefugnis – § 42 II VwGO' (2004) 26 *Juristische*

is more complicated. The plaintiff must at first be able to claim a right in contrast to mere (in)conveniences, chances for purchase, economic, political or ideological interests or situation-related advantages of geographical or infrastructural nature.[88] Additionally, the right must be attributable as a subjective right to the plaintiff.[89]

The subjectification can take place by means of a statutory protection norm (*Schutznorm*), which does not exclusively serve the public interest but contains rules with regard to a clearly enclosable group of beneficiaries[90] and, thereby, at least also aims at serving the protection of the interests of the plaintiff.[91] For instance, some provisions of building and planning law, emission protection law, nuclear energy law and waste disposal law also protect the interests of neighbours.[92] Furthermore, the subjectification can result from judge-made law, like the rule of consideration (*Rücksichtnahmegebot*),[93] or basic rights.[94] The rule of consideration was developed in planning law before its provisions were interpreted as protection norms[95] and it is in recent times extended to other fields of law, especially water law[96] and historical monument protection law.[97]

Finally, there must be, as in the case of the addressee, the possibility that the subjective right is violated by the contested administrative act.[98] However, the ACC, apart from the general rule, allows to provide by federal law or federal state law that in certain cases an action is admissible although the plaintiff cannot claim that he (or she) himself (herself) is violated in his (or her) own rights. Such statutory exceptions, which provide for an objective supervision procedure, exist, for instance, in favour of recognised nature conservation associations and in favour of chambers of handicraft and of commerce.[99]

Anyway, according to the ACC, a further requirement of the admissibility of the action for the rescission of an administrative act is in principle that the plaintiff has

---

Ausbildung (Jura) 90–98, 92–93; Schenke (n. 84) 167; K. Stern and H.-J. Blanke, *Verwaltungsprozessrecht in der Klausur* (9th edn., C. H. Beck, Munich 2008) 132.

88 Cf. Hufen (n. 7) 237–240.

89 Ibid. 235 and 243.

90 Federal Administrative Court, *Entscheidungen des Bundesverwaltungsgerichts* 52, 122–131, 129.

91 Schenke (n. 84) 155; cf. C. D. Classen, *Die Europäisierung der Verwaltungsgerichtsbarkeit* (Mohr Siebeck, Tübingen 1996) 40–55; J. Pietzcker, 'Die Schutznormlehre' in O. Depenheuer, M. Heintzen, M. Jestaedt and P. Axer (eds.), *Festschrift für Josef Isensee* (C. F. Müller, Heidelberg 2007) 577–595.

92 Cf. Federal Administrative Court, *Entscheidungen des Bundesverwaltungsgerichts* 7, 354–358, 355–356; Hufen (n. 7) 244–249; D. Mampel, *Nachbarschutz im öffentlichen Baurecht* (Verlag für die Rechts- und Anwaltspraxis, Herne and Berlin 1994) 50–55; M. Ruffert, *Subjektive Rechte im Umweltrecht der Europäischen Gemeinschaften* (von Decker, Heidelberg 1996) 90–101; F. Schoch, 'Nachbarschutz im öffentlichen Baurecht' (2004) 26 *Juristische Ausbildung (Jura)* 317–325.

93 See A. Decker, 'Die Grundzüge des (bauplanungsrechtlichen) Gebots der Rücksichtnahme' (2003) 35 *Juristische Arbeitsblätter* 246–252; A. Voßkuhle/A.-K. Kaufhold, 'Das baurechtliche Rücksichtnahmegebot' (2010) 50 *Juristische Schulung* 497–499; U. Ramsauer, 'Die Dogmatik der subjektiven öffentlichen Rechte' (2012) 52 *Juristische Schulung* 769–777, 775–776.

94 Hufen (n. 7) 243.

95 Cf. Ibid. 249–250.

96 Cf. M. Reinhardt, 'Drittschutz im Wasserrecht' (2011) 64 *Die öffentliche Verwaltung* 135–142.

97 Cf. Higher Administrative Court of Hesse (*Hessischer Verwaltungsgerichtshof*) (2010) 63 *Die öffentliche Verwaltung* 661.

98 Hufen (n. 7) 235.

99 Schenke (n. 84) 181; F. O. Kopp and W.-R. Schenke, *Verwaltungsgerichtsordnung: Kommentar* (20th edn., C. H. Beck, Munich 2014), Section 42 at 180–181, 391–393.

unsuccessfully passed an objection procedure before the administrative authority. The provision reads that prior to lodging a rescissory action, the lawfulness and expediency of the administrative act must be reviewed in preliminary proceedings. However, such a review is not necessary if a statute so determines, or if the administrative act has been handed down by a supreme federal authority or by a supreme federal state authority, unless a statute prescribes the review, or the remedial notice or the ruling on the objection contains a grievance for the first time. Thus, the plaintiff must initially have filed an objection against the administrative act. According to the ACC, the objection is to be lodged within one month after the administrative act had been announced to the aggrieved party, in writing or for the record of the authority which has carried out the administrative act.

If the authority considers the objection to be well-founded, it remedies it and rules on the costs. If it does not remedy the objection, a ruling on the objection (*Widerspruchsbescheid*) is to be handed down. That ruling is issued by the next higher authority unless another higher authority is determined by law, if the next higher authority is a federal or supreme federal state authority, the authority which has issued the administrative act, or in matters of self-administration the self-administration authority unless otherwise determined by law.

The rescissory action must be lodged within one month of service of the ruling on the objection. If a ruling on an objection is not required, the action must be lodged within one month of announcement of the administrative act. For a third party which is not the addressee of the administrative act this period only starts running when the ruling on the objection was also served him (or her).[100] However, if he (or she) learns about the ruling on the objection in a different way, the right to sue can be forfeited after one year.[101] If the period has expired, there is the possibility of a *restitutio in integrum* on request if the plaintiff had been unable to adhere to the deadline without fault. The action should be lodged with the administrative court in writing but it can also be lodged at the court for the record of the clerk of the registry.

The action must designate the plaintiff, the defendant and the subject-matter of what is at stake in the action. It should contain a specific motion. The facts and the evidence serving as reasoning should be stated; the original or duplicate of the impugned order and, as far as necessary, the ruling on the objection should be enclosed.

The plaintiff may himself (herself) pursue the dispute before the administrative court. A legal representation is only necessary before the higher administrative court and the Federal Administrative Court, apart from legal aid proceedings.

3.2 Action for the issue of an administrative act

Similarly ruled to the admissibility of the rescissory action is that of the action for the issue of a favourable administrative act (*Verpflichtungsklage*). This action is a special performance action whose target is to condemn the administrative authority to pass a rejected or omitted administrative act. Thus, the court itself with its judgment does not change the law but it orders the administrative authority to do so by issuing the

100 Federal Administrative Court (2010) *Neue Juristische Wochenschrift* 1686–1688, 1687–1688.
101 Hufen (n. 7) 114.

administrative act and thereby influencing the material legal situation, as far as the action is well-founded.[102]

For the admissibility of the action for the issue of an administrative act the plaintiff must claim that the refusal or omission of the administrative act violates his (or her) rights. Thus, the right or authorisation to sue is not linked to the (positive) claim to the administrative act but, as in the case of the rescissory action, to the possibility of the violation of subjective rights.[103] Accordingly, there must be a right attributable to the plaintiff and the possibility of a violation of this right by the refusal or omission of the administrative act. For the stage of admissibility, these requirements must not be interpreted too narrowly and strictly. The attribution of the right to the plaintiff must not obviously and clearly be excluded.[104] The right or authorisation to sue is easily given when the plaintiff can refer to a statutory provision which establishes a claim right and identifies the plaintiff as a possible beneficiary.[105] Furthermore, the right or authorisation to sue can result from a basic right, particularly in its function as an objective duty to protect (for instance life and health in Art. 2 para 2 of the Basic Law).[106] The action for the issue of an administrative act is always admissible if the plaintiff holds a basic right which he (or she) can only make use of when the applied permission is granted (preventive prohibition with the proviso of permission).[107] In the case of the repressive prohibition with the proviso of dispensation the plaintiff has at least a right to an examination whether there are the preconditions for granting an exceptional permission.[108] However, if the action for the issue of an administrative act is not only directed at a release from a statutory prohibition but at an additional performance, the reference to a liberal freedom is not sufficient. Rather, the possibly violated right lies either in a statutory concretisation of such a claim right or in a basic right position in conjunction with the equality clause (derivative participation right).[109] If the plaintiff, by means of the action for the issue of an administrative act, in fact does not want to reach a favouring of himself (or herself) but a burden for a third party, for example the stopping of construction works, the making of protective conditions for activities of this person or the withdrawal of a favouring granted to this person, this is so to speak a mirror image situation of the protection of neighbours. Insofar, the prerequisites of the right or authorisation to sue follow the relevant rules elaborated in the context of the rescissory action, like the protection norm theory and the rule of consideration. Hence, the statutory basis which comes into consideration for the intervention into the rights of the third party must at least also serve the protection of the plaintiff.[110]

102 Ibid. 279.

103 Ibid. 286.

104 Federal Administrative Court, *Entscheidungen des Bundesverwaltungsgerichts* 44, 1–11, 3; (1995) *Neue Zeitschrift für Verwaltungsrecht* 478–481, 478.

105 Hufen (n. 7) 287.

106 Cf. D. Couzinet, 'Die Schutznormtheorie in Zeiten des Feinstaubs' (2008) 123 *Deutsches Verwaltungsblatt* 754–762, 760.

107 Cf. Federal Constitutional Court, *Entscheidungen des Bundesverfassungsgerichts* 20, 150–162, 154–155.

108 Cf. Hufen (n. 7) 287–288; H. Maurer, *Allgemeines Verwaltungsrecht* (18th edn., C. H. Beck, Munich 2011) 227–231.

109 Hufen (n. 7) 288.

110 Cf. Federal Administrative Court (1998) *Neue Zeitschrift für Verwaltungsrecht* 395.

Regarding the possibility of a violation of the plaintiff's rights, there must not be prerequisites which are too demanding since otherwise aspects which belong to the merits would be anticipated. Again at that point the evidence clause finds application saying that the right or authorisation to sue is only excluded when the violation of a right is obviously and clearly impossible according to any way of looking at the legal situation.[111] If the plaintiff has plausibly presented his (or her) subjective claim to the administrative act, its refusal or omission always implies the possibility of a violation of his (or her) rights.[112]

Before lodging the action for the issue of an administrative act, as in the case of the rescissory action, in principle an objection procedure must have been passed according to a provision of the ACC, if the motion to carry out the administrative act has been rejected. Thus, the objection procedure is a precondition for the admissibility of the action directed against the refusal of an administrative act (*Versagungsgegenklage*). This is even true when the administrative authority has only partly complied with the application or has granted a permission whose content is modified *vis-à-vis* the application.[113]

The most important exception of the requirement to having passed an objection procedure is that of the action concerning the inactivity of the administrative authority (*Untätigkeitsklage*). According to the ACC, the action is admissible if, with regard to an objection or an application to carry out an administrative act, it has not been decided on the merits within a suitable period without sufficient reason.

A standard for what is a suitable period is laid down in the ACC reading that the action may not be lodged prior to the expiry of three months after the lodging of the objection or since the filing of the application to carry out the administrative act, unless a shorter period is required because of special circumstances of the case. After the period of three months has expired the action is admissible without preliminary proceedings. The court must decide unless the administrative authority does not itself claim adequate reasons why the objection has not yet been ruled on or the requested administrative act has not yet been carried out. However, if the administrative authority can name an adequate reason for the delay, the action is not inadmissible because of this circumstance. Instead, the court has to suspend the proceedings until the expiry of a deadline set by it, which can be extended. If the objection is admitted within the deadline set by the court or the administrative act carried out within this deadline, there is no further need to legal protection (*Rechtsschutzbedürfnis*). Therefore, the court must declare the main case to have been settled.

If the application is rejected after the action has been lodged, the plaintiff can proceed with his (or her) action by including the negative administrative decision in it and forming the action to a normal action for the issue of an administrative act.[114] Entering into an objection procedure is only necessary if there had been adequate reasons for the delay in the sense of the ACC and if the administrative act was issued

111 Federal Administrative Court, *Entscheidungen des Bundesverwaltungsgerichts* 18, 154–157, 157; 36, 192–218, 199–200; 44, 1–11, 3.

112 Hufen (n. 7) 289.

113 Ibid. 290.

114 P. Weides and R. Bertrams, 'Die nachträgliche Verwaltungsentscheidung im Verfahren der Untätigkeitsklage' (1988) 7 *Neue Zeitschrift für Verwaltungsrecht* 673–679, 676–677; Kopp and Schenke (n. 99), Section 75 at 21, 908–909.

before the expiry of the deadline set by the court.[115] In such a case the court must not decide before the ruling on the objection is issued or the time has expired which the competent authority has at its disposal to decide about the objection. Instead, the court again has to suspend the proceedings.[116]

The period for filing the action directed against the refusal of an administrative act is one month starting with the announcement of the administrative act which rejects carrying out the administrative act applied for or with the service of the ruling on the objection. The action concerning the inactivity of the administrative authority can be lodged after the period of three months has been expired, unless there are special reasons for the decisiveness of a shorter period of time. Before, it is inadmissible because of the missing preliminary procedure, not because of a period for lodging the action had not been kept.[117] There is no fixed time-limit for the action concerning the inactivity of the administrative authority but it is possible that the procedural right to sue becomes forfeited according to the general rules.[118]

As in any case of action, the general need to legal protection is missing if the plaintiff could reach the wished result in an easier way, if the action is a misuse of legal procedures or if the right to sue is forfeited. Particularly, the action concerning the inactivity of the administrative authority requires that the plaintiff has applied at all for the favourable administrative act.[119]

If the plaintiff cannot be successful with his (or her) action for the issue of an administrative act because a favourable good, service or so which exists only uniquely is already irrevocably awarded to someone else, the general need to legal protection is also not accepted.[120] However, the former main case which was the competition complaint concerning a civil servant position is meanwhile decided otherwise. The Federal Administrative Court after an advice given by the Federal Constitutional Court[121] held that also after the appointment of the competitor an action directed to a new administrative act regarding the allocation of the position must be admissible and the selection decision must be open for review.[122]

3.3 General performance action

The third type of action before the administrative courts is the general performance action (*allgemeine Leistungsklage*), which is not explicitly ruled but assumed in the ACC.[123] The general performance action is directed to sentencing the administrative authority, another administrative authority or even a private person, if the plaintiff

115 Federal Administrative Court, *Entscheidungen des Bundesverwaltungsgerichts* 42, 108–115, 112; 66, 342–346, 344; (1992) *Deutsches Verwaltungsblatt* 290–295, 291; Weides and Bertrams (n. 114) 677.

116 Schenke (n. 84) 246; Kopp and Schenke (n. 99), Section 75 at 23, 909–910.

117 Hufen (n. 7) 291–292.

118 Kopp and Schenke (n. 99), Section 76 at 2, 911–912.

119 Federal Administrative Court (1996) *Die öffentliche Verwaltung* 331–333, 331.

120 Hufen (n. 7) 292.

121 See Federal Constitutional Court (Chamber) (2008) *Neue Zeitschrift für Verwaltungsrecht* 70–71.

122 Federal Administrative Court (2011) 64 *Neue Juristische Wochenschrift* 695–700; see also Higher Administrative Court of Lower Saxony (*Niedersächsisches Oberverwaltungsgericht*) (2011) 30 *Neue Zeitschrift für Verwaltungsrecht* 891–893; W.-R. Schenke, 'Neues zur Konkurrentenklage' (2011) 30 *Neue Zeitschrift für Verwaltungsrecht* 321–327.

123 Schenke (n. 84) 113.

is itself an administrative authority, to any behaviour (action, omission or toleration) which does not consist in an administrative act.[124] Against this background, the general performance action has been called a 'kind of "procedural multipurpose weapon"'.[125]

The plaintiff has the right or is authorised to lodge the general performance action if he (or she) can claim that he (or she) is violated in his (or her) rights by the refusal or omission of the behaviour. The relevant rule of the ACC is analogously applicable to the general performance action.[126] However, as in the case of the action for the issue of an administrative act, there must not be placed too strict demands on the existence of a subjective right. Rather, the right or authorisation to sue only has to be denied if, according to any legal view, either the right to the performance obviously and clearly cannot exist or the plaintiff cannot be entitled to that right.[127]

Apart from special cases ruled in civil service law,[128] an objection procedure need not be passed and a period need not be observed. The general need to legal protection in principle follows from the plaintiff claiming to be owner of the material legal position in question.[129] Whether the plaintiff must have filed an application at the administrative authority is disputed. On the one hand, it is pointed to the relationship between court and administration; the latter must have had the chance to act before there could be any judicial review.[130] On the other hand, it is argued that an application is only required for the action for the issue of an administrative act.[131] The provision stipulates that in the case that the defendant has not given rise to the lodging of the action by means of his (or her) conduct, the legal costs shall be imposed on the plaintiff if the defendant immediately acknowledges the claim. This shows that the fact that the defendant has not given rise to the lodging of the action does not exclude the general need to legal protection. Instead, the only disadvantage which occurs is that the plaintiff has to bear the costs if the defendant immediately acknowledges the claim.[132] The general performance action, like the other actions, can be forfeited due to the passing of time[133] or it can qualify as a misuse of legal procedures.

3.4 General action for a declaratory judgment

Another type of action is the general action for a declaratory judgment (*allgemeine Feststellungsklage*). The target of the general action for a declaratory judgment is the establishment of the existence or non-existence of a legal relationship. In this context, a legal relationship is understood as the legal relations of one person toward

124 Federal Administrative Court, *Entscheidungen des Bundesverwaltungsgerichts* 31, 301–307, 303.

125 U. Steiner, 'Die allgemeine Leistungsklage im Verwaltungsprozeß' (1984) 24 *Juristische Schulung* 853–859, 853.

126 Hufen (n. 7) 306.

127 Federal Administrative Court, *Entscheidungen des Bundesverwaltungsgerichts* 36, 192–218, 199–200; 44, 1–11, 3.

128 Cf. Schenke (n. 84) 119.

129 Federal Administrative Court (1989) *Deutsches Verwaltungsblatt* 718–722, 719.

130 Cf. Federal Administrative Court (1978) *Deutsches Verwaltungsblatt* 607–608, 608; Hufen (n. 7) 306; J. Pietzcker, in Schoch, Schneider and Bier (eds.), (n. 1), Section 42 paragraph 1 at 156, 90–91.

131 Cf. Federal Administrative Court (2002) *Neue Zeitschrift für Verwaltungsrecht* 97–99, 98.

132 Schenke (n. 84) 119.

133 Cf. Federal Administrative Court, *Entscheidungen des Bundesverwaltungsgerichts* 44, 294–302, 298.

another person or toward an object, which result from concrete facts on the basis of a legal norm (of public law).[134]

Since this notion is far-reaching and can catch even single claim rights or obligations, it actually includes rights and duties enshrined in an administrative act as well as claims to a performance or omission; in fact, any public-law dispute could be solved by means of a general action for a declaratory judgment. Therefore, the ACC states that the establishment cannot be requested insofar as the plaintiff may pursue or could have pursued his (or her) rights by reformatory action or performance action. Regardless of this subsidiarity, the general action for a declaratory judgment in practice has become a means of an incident, 'secret supervision of statutory law'.[135] The general action for a declaratory judgment can be used for making the claim that no rights and duties arise from a certain legal provision. However, the general action for a declaratory judgment cannot refer to the declaration of the nullity or ineffectiveness of the provision as such but only to that of the existence or non-existence of rights and duties of the plaintiff in the concrete case which result from this provision.[136]

The establishment of the existence or non-existence of a legal relationship can only be requested if the plaintiff has a justified interest in the establishment being made soon (*Feststellungsinteresse*). Thus, the binding declaration of the legal relationship can only be claimed under certain preconditions which have a subjective component and a temporal component. The reason for this stipulation is that the courts should not, against their function, become general information and report offices in legal questions.[137]

The notion of the justified interest appears to be unclear and changeable. On the one hand, it is broader than that of the subjective right in the ACC. On the other hand, any interest is not sufficient. Rather, it must be an interest protected by the legal order. Whether such an interest is given has to be decided with regard to the individual case. It is important to notice that even economic, personal, cultural and ideal interests can be referred to if they are adequately attributable to the plaintiff and protected by the legal order.[138]

The legally protected interest must just exist *vis-à-vis* the defendant[139] and it must be secured or promoted by the declaration of the court. In this context not any uncertainty with regard to the legal good is sufficient. Instead, there must be a concrete need to a clarification, for example because there is a difference of opinion between the plaintiff and the administrative authority concerning a question which is important for the plaintiff because he (or she) has to adjust his (or her) behaviour or his (or her) economic dispositions to the legal situation or because he (or she) wants to avoid

134 F.-J. Peine, *Allgemeines Verwaltungsrecht* (10th edn., C. F. Müller, Heidelberg 2011) 64–65; Schenke (n. 84) 123–124; W. Selb, *Die verwaltungsgerichtliche Feststellungsklage* (Duncker & Humblot, Berlin 1998) 20–45; cf. Federal Administrative Court, *Entscheidungen des Bundesverwaltungsgerichts* 40, 323–331, 325–326.

135 F. Hufen, 'Von der "heimlichen Normenkontrolle" zur umfassenden Gerichtskontrolle exekutiver Normsetzung' in P. Baumeister, W. Roth and J. Ruthig (eds.), *Festschrift für Wolf-Rüdiger Schenke* (Duncker & Humblot, Berlin 2011) 803–811, 803; Hufen (n. 7) 311.

136 Würtenberger (n. 3) 196–197; W. Peters, 'Zur Zulässigkeit der Feststellungsklage (§ 43 VwGO) bei untergesetzlichen Normen' (1999) 18 *Neue Zeitschrift für Verwaltungsrecht* 506–507.

137 Hufen (n. 7) 315.

138 Schenke (n. 84) 191.

139 Federal Administrative Court (1997) *Neue Juristische Wochenschrift* 3257–3259, 3257.

approaching or threatened sanctions, particularly criminal proceedings or a penalty notice. Furthermore, the legitimate interest is given if the administrative authority claims that a certain behaviour was illegal but would be tolerated for a time being.[140]

The temporal component requires that the legitimate interest just exists in the moment of the judgment and that the declaration brooks no delay. If the question is presently open and needs clarification, or if a deterioration or repetition is threatening in the immediate future,[141] there are regularly no problems with regard to time.[142]

When the concreteness of the legal relationship and the qualified need for legal protection with regard to the declaration have been confirmed, there is normally no reason to additionally refer to the right or authorisation to sue.[143] The tendency in jurisdiction to extend the right or authorisation to sue to the general action for a declaratory judgment by an analogous application of Art. 42 para 2 of the ACC[144] is problematic in its generality. There is no loophole in the law which should be closed by analogy, because the popular action can reliably be excluded by a consistent application of the characteristic of the concrete legal situation and by the requirement of the justified interest in the establishment of the existence or non-existence of that situation.[145]

Apart from special cases of civil service law, an objection procedure need not be passed before lodging a general action for a declaratory judgment. Furthermore, there is no period which must be observed. The action can be forfeited if the plaintiff inadequately delays the lodging. However, this aspect should, as a rule, have already been examined in the context of the interest that the establishment is made soon and, if necessary, been denied there.[146]

3.5 Application for a review of statutory law

The last type of action[147] which should be mentioned is the application for a review of statutory law (*Normenkontrolle*). According to the ACC, the Higher Administrative Court adjudicates on application within the bounds of its jurisdiction on the validity of by-laws (*Satzungen*) issued under the provisions of the Federal Building Code (*Baugesetzbuch*) and of statutory instruments (*Rechtsverordnungen*) issued on the basis of the Federal Building Code as well as on that of other legal provisions ranking below the statutes of the federal state (*Landesgesetz[e]*), to the extent that this is provided in federal state law.

The review of statutory law is the only procedure laid down in the ACC which is directed to an objective supervision of state activity, but, nevertheless, it at least equally

140 Hufen (n. 7) 315–316.

141 Cf. Federal Administrative Court, *Entscheidungen des Bundesverwaltungsgerichts* 80, 355–373, 365.

142 Hufen (n. 7) 316.

143 Ibid. 317.

144 Cf. Federal Administrative Court, *Entscheidungen des Bundesverwaltungsgerichts* 99, 64–69, 66.

145 F. Knöpfle, 'Feststellungsinteresse und Klagebefugnis bei verwaltungsprozessualen Feststellungsklagen' in P. Badura and R. Scholz (eds.), *Festschrift für Peter Lerche* (C. H. Beck, Munich 1993) 771–784; H.-W. Laubinger, 'Feststellungsklage und Klagebefugnis (§ 42 Abs. 2 VwGO)' (1991) 82 *Verwaltungsarchiv* 459–495, 491–495; Schenke (n. 84) 131.

146 Hufen (n. 7) 318.

147 Cf. Ibid. 339.

in weight serves the protection of subjective rights of the applicant, if the applicant is not itself a public authority.[148] The subjective element is particularly stressed in the requirement that there must be a right or authorisation to sue. Art. 47 para 2 of the ACC reads that applications can be made by any natural or juristic person claiming to have been violated by the legal provision or its application, or that he (or she/it) will be violated within the foreseeable future, in his (or her/its) rights or by any public authority. This requirement orientates itself toward Art. 42 para 2 of the ACC, although for the application being successful in the merits it is, unlike in the case of the rescissory action or the action for the issue of an administrative act, not decisive whether there is in fact a violation of subjective rights of the applicant.[149] Thus, it is necessary and sufficient that there is a legal position attributable to the applicant and that its violation by the legal provision or its application is possible now or within the foreseeable future.

Particularly, in the case of by-laws issued under the provisions of the Federal Building Code the property owners but also the tenants and leaseholders and, because of their expected restriction as future owners the buyers of plots of land can be considered as applicants.[150] Private concerns which ground subjective rights are any interests of the applicant which are worthy of protection and which are not only insignificantly affected. However, the ACC stipulates that the application by a natural or juristic person relating to a development plan or to statutes according to the Federal Building Code is inadmissible if the person lodging the application only makes objections which he (or she/it) did not make when the plan or the statutes were publicly available for inspection or in the consultation of the interested public or made them too late, but could have made them (in time), and if notice has been drawn to this legal consequence in the consultation. This is an important preclusion norm in the field of planning.[151] Furthermore, the application must be lodged within one year of announcement of the legal provision. This relatively short period is not unproblematic since in the case of legal norms defects often only become obvious a long time after their coming into force.[152] Finally, there must be again a general need for legal protection. This need is missing if there is an easier way to reach the target strived for, if the lawsuit obviously cannot have success or if the application must be regarded as misuse, if it is forfeited or contrary to the previous activities of the applicant.[153] However, the applicant lodging an application according to the ACC cannot be referred to the rescissory action against a building permission which realises the development plan, although the judge in that procedure incidentally examines the plan. This already follows the circumstance that the judgment upon the rescissory action has effects only *inter partes*, whereas the judgment in the procedure to review statutory law has effects *erga omnes*.[154]

148 Cf. Federal Administrative Court, *Entscheidungen des Bundesverwaltungsgerichts* 68, 12–16, 14; 107, 215–223, 217–218.

149 Schenke (n. 84) 306 and 315.

150 Kopp and Schenke (n. 99), Section 47 at 70, 533.

151 Cf. Ibid. Section 47 at 75a, 540.

152 J. Hüttenbrink, 'Das Recht auf fehlerfreie Abwägung als subjektiv-öffentliches Recht i. S. der Antragsbefugnis gemäß § 47 Abs. 2 VwGO n. F.' (1997) 112 *Deutsches Verwaltungsblatt* 1253–1258, 1253.

153 Hufen (n. 7) 355.

154 Cf. Federal Administrative Court, *Entscheidungen des Bundesverwaltungsgerichts* 68, 12–16, 13.

After all, the statutory provisions of administrative court procedure allow access to the administrative courts if the plaintiff or applicant can claim a violation of his (or her) rights by the behaviour of the administration, be it an administrative act, another formal measure or an action, an omission or a toleration, or, in the case of the general action for a declaratory judgment, if the plaintiff has a justified interest in the establishment of the existence or non-existence of a legal relationship. Thus, the procedural law aims at providing a way to the administrative courts, unless special courts have been declared competent, in any situation where there is a possibility that the administration has violated the rights of a person. This corresponds with the constitutional guarantee that any person who is violated in his (or her) rights by public authority can have recourse to a court.

The access to the administrative courts is connected with the procedural or material law which is decisive for the merits. The violation of the plaintiff's or applicant's rights must not appear to be excluded from the outset. Stipulations concerning periods and the necessity of an objection procedure limit the access to the administrative courts under the aspects of time and preliminary supervision by administrative authorities themselves.

The stipulations concerning periods serve the legal security, the legal peace and the efficiency of the public administration.[155] Administrative measures shall become incontestable after a certain period of time so that they can be executed or can form the basis for further measures and that the beneficiaries can trust in their validity and make dispositions accordingly. The objection procedure has the function of a filter. It gives the administration the chance to review and, if it thereby finds some defects regarding lawfulness or expediency, to reverse or amend the decision by itself. This shall lighten the workload of the courts.

The objection procedure is formed to a certain extent parallel to the possible later court procedure. It has no higher requirements regarding admissibility than the latter. When it is not successful, it at least prepares the factual and legal material for the administrative courts. Thus, it in principle supports the effective legal protection of the individual, if it is executed properly and brought to an end within reasonable time, so that the affected person can, if necessary, proceed with his (or her) lawsuit before the courts.

3.6 Appeal and complaint

Judgments of the administrative courts can be controlled by means of an appeal on points of fact and law (*Berufung*), judgments and orders of the higher administrative courts can be revised by means of an appeal on points of law (*Revision*). In individual cases there is the possibility of a direct appeal on points of law from the administrative courts to the Federal Administrative Court. Rulings of the administrative courts or of its members can be controlled by recourse to a complaint (*Beschwerde*).

The two forms of appeal hinder the entering into formal legal force of the impugned court decision (suspending effect). The appeal and the complaint found in principle

155 Cf. Federal Constitutional Court, *Entscheidungen des Bundesverfassungsgerichts* 60, 253–305, 269–270; State Court of Hesse (*Hessischer Staatsgerichtshof*) (1982) *Neue Juristische Wochenschrift* 1381–1385, 1382; Kopp and Schenke (n. 99), Section 74 at 1, 890.

the decision making power of the higher instance (devolutive effect).[156] The appellant or complainant must be authorised to lodge the appeal or complaint (*Rechtsmittelberechtigung*), which is the case if he (or she) took part in the court proceedings on the basis of which the impugned decision was made.

An unwritten requirement for the means of legal redress is the existence of a burden (*Beschwer*). Conversely to Art. 42 para 2 of the ACC, which requires a material burden, for lodging an appeal or complaint a formal burden is sufficient. The formal burden is already given when the appellant or complainant was refused something in the previous instance which he (or she) had applied for.[157] The three means of legal redress must be lodged within a fixed time, which is a month in case of appeals and two weeks in case of complaints against rulings. Furthermore, the appeal on points of fact and law needs to be admitted by the administrative court or by the higher administrative court. According to the ACC, the appeal shall only be admitted under certain, explicitly mentioned preconditions: if serious doubts exist as to the correctness of the judgment; if the case has special factual or legal difficulties; if the case is of fundamental significance; if the judgment derogates from a decision of the higher administrative court, of the Federal Administrative Court, of the Joint Panel of the supreme courts of the Federation or of the Federal Constitutional Court, and is based on this derogation; or if a procedural shortcoming subject to the judgment of the court of appeal on points of fact and law is claimed and applies on which the decision can be based.

The admission requirement was introduced in 1996.[158] Before, the appeal on points of fact and law was generally allowed, except from petty affairs and some special cases ruled in statutory law. With the amendment of the procedural rules, the legislator wanted to relieve the appellate courts.[159] It held that one factual instance was regularly sufficient and that a second factual instance should only be provided for in such procedures where a review of the decision of the first instance was necessary with regard to the matter.[160] As far as the principle of equality is maintained, the limitation of the appeal on points of fact and law is regarded as constitutional since Art. 19 para 4 of the Basic Law, as mentioned,[161] does not guarantee a second instance; even a complete exclusion of an appeal would be in accordance with the Constitution.[162]

The appeal on points of law allows bringing the case before the Federal Administrative Court. Against the judgment of a higher administrative court and against decisions about applications for a review of statutory law according to the ACC the persons who took place in the previous court proceedings can have recourse to an

156 Schenke (n. 84) 386.

157 Cf. Federal Administrative Court, *Entscheidungen des Bundesverwaltungsgerichts* 17, 352–353.

158 Sechstes Gesetz zur Änderung der Verwaltungsgerichtsordnung, *Bundesgesetzblatt* (Federal Law Gazette) 1996 I, 1626.

159 Deutscher Bundestag, Gesetzentwurf des Bundesrates: Entwurf eines Gesetzes zur Änderung der Verwaltungsgerichtsordnung, *Bundestags-Drucksache* 13/1433, 13.

160 Deutscher Bundestag, Gesetzentwurf der Bundesregierung: Entwurf eines Sechsten Gesetzes zur Änderung der Verwaltungsgerichtsordnung und anderer Gesetze, *Bundestags-Drucksache* 13/3993, 13; cf. *Bundestags-Drucksache* 13/1433 (n. 159) 13–14.

161 See above n. 80.

162 Kopp and Schenke (n. 99), Section 124 at 2, 1608.

appeal on points of law to the Federal Administrative Court, if the higher administrative court, or the Federal Administrative Court in response to a complaint against non-admission, has admitted it. Thus, as the appeal on points of fact and law the appeal on points of law requires an admission. The admission-free appeal on points of law in cases of essential procedural defects was abolished in 1990.[163] An appeal on points of law which is lodged without admission is inadmissible. In such a case, the Federal Administrative Court cannot *ex officio* make up leeway for the admission or to ignore the missing of the admission and to deal with the appeal as if it was admissible, when the preconditions for the admission were actually given and the admission was omitted erroneously.[164]

According to the ACC, the appeal on points of law shall only be admitted if the legal case is of fundamental significance, if the judgment deviates from a ruling of the Federal Administrative Court, of the Joint Panel of the supreme courts of the Federation or of the Federal Constitutional Court and is based on this deviation, or if a procedural shortcoming is asserted and applies on which the decision can be based. As the first two aspects reveal, the function of the appeal on points of law is particularly the safeguarding of the unity of jurisdiction and the development of the law.[165] Conversely, the third aspect focuses on the one side on the safeguarding of procedural law, not least with regard to the importance of 'due process' for the protection of the rights of the citizen and the enforcement of public and private interests enshrined in the law,[166] and on the other side on the 'education' of the courts to pay tribute to the procedural rules.[167] Besides, the appeal on points of law can only be based on the impugned judgment resulting from a violation of federal law or of a provision of the administrative procedure act of a federal state the wording of which concurs with the Administrative Procedure Act of the Federation. Thus, federal state law is, apart from the latter exception, not a suitable basis for review. A review of federal state law is only insofar possible as that law must be in accordance with federal law.[168]

A judgment always must be regarded as being based on the violation of federal law if there are absolute reasons for the appeal on points of law. That is the case if the court of decision was not composed according to the regulations, if a judge was involved in the decision who had been excluded from the exercise of judicial office by force of law or had been successfully rejected for concern about partiality, if a party concerned had been refused a legal hearing, if a party concerned in the proceedings was not represented in accordance with the provisions of the law, unless he (or she) explicitly or tacitly consented to the pursuance of the proceedings, if the judgment

163 Gesetz zur Neuregelung des verwaltungsgerichtlichen Verfahrens (Viertes Gesetz zur Änderung der Verwaltungsgerichtsordnung), *Bundesgesetzblatt* (Federal Law Gazette) 1990 I, 2809.

164 Kopp and Schenke (n. 99), Section 132 at 4, 1688.

165 Schenke (n. 84) 391–392; Ibid. Section 132 at 1, 1687.

166 Cf. F. Kopp, 'Individueller Rechtsschutz und öffentliches Interesse in der Verwaltungsgerichtsbarkeit' (1980) 26 *Bayerische Verwaltungsblätter* 263–272.

167 K. A. Bettermann, 'Die Revision wegen wesentlicher Verfahrensmängel insbesondere nach dem BVerwGG' (1954) 7 *Neue Juristische Wochenschrift* 1305–1310, 1308; Kopp and Schenke (n. 99), Section 132 at 1, 1687.

168 Federal Administrative Court, *Entscheidungen des Bundesverwaltungsgerichts* 11, 95–101, 96; 45, 51–65, 55; 51, 104–111, 110; 56, 308–315, 310; 85, 348–368, 353–354; (1987) *Neue Zeitschrift für Verwaltungsrecht* 976; (1991) 69–70, 70.

was handed down on the basis of an oral hearing in which the provisions on the public nature of the proceedings were violated or if the decision is not reasoned.

Finally, the complaint is particularly provided for as a legal means against rulings of the administrative courts which are not passed in the form of a judgment, whereas rulings of the higher administrative courts are regularly not contestable. Furthermore, procedural directions, elucidation orders, orders regarding the postponement of the setting of a deadline, orders for the taking of evidence, orders regarding the rejection of motions for the taking of evidence, on joindering and separation of proceedings and claims and on the rejection of court officials, as well as orders on the rejection of legal aid applications if the court exclusively states that the personal or economic preconditions for legal aid do not apply, cannot be impugned with a complaint.

After all, there is no general right to a means of legal redress against judgments and other kinds of decisions of the administrative courts and higher administrative courts. Instead, appeals against judgments need an admission, and complaints against rulings other than judgments have a limited field of application. However, a second instance and even a third instance for review exist in certain matters and under certain preconditions. Thus, at least cases in which the rights of the appellant or complainant have been violated due to serious ignorance, misapplication or misinterpretation of the law can be filtered out.

3.7 Intervention

The intervention of third parties into the proceedings before the administrative courts in practice takes place only on a small scale. Concentrating on the protection of the individual is from the outset not combined with the matter to give other persons than the plaintiff a share in the proceedings. Particularly, the *amicus curiae* is not known to German procedural law. The contributions of interest groups, NGOs or citizens' groups do not play a settled formal role in the proceedings. At most, in the field of environmental law there are possibilities of influence for recognised nature conservation associations due to the provisions of European law.[169] However, third parties can be included in the proceedings by means of a *subpoena* (*Beiladung*, literally: co-summoning) according to ACC.[170] The *subpoena* serves not least the protection of the interests of the included person, a comprehensive explanation of the facts and, since the *subpoena* leads to an extension of the legal force of the later judgment on the included person, the procedural economy.[171]

The simple or optional *subpoena* is a relatively flexible instrument. As long as the proceedings have not yet been finally concluded or are pending at a higher instance, the court can *subpoena* others *ex officio* or on request whose legal interests are affected by the decision. Thus, the filter criterion are the legal interests which are affected by the decision. The losing of the case by the plaintiff or the defendant must be able to

169 See Schlacke (n. 2) 161–332.

170 See A. Guckelberger, 'Die Beiladung im Verwaltungsprozess' (2007) 47 *Juristische Schulung* 436–441; A. von Mutius, 'Die Beiladung im Verwaltungsprozeß' (1988) 10 *Juristische Ausbildung (Jura)* 273–276; C. Nottbusch, *Die Beiladung im Verwaltungsprozess* (Duncker & Humblot, Berlin 1995); R. Stober, 'Beiladung im Verwaltungsprozeß' in Erichsen, Hoppe and von Mutius (n. 26) 401–421.

171 Schenke (n. 84) 146; Stober (n. 170) 406–408.

improve or to worse the legal situation of the subpoenaed person[172] but he (or she) need not be authorised to sue by himself (or herself) or to be actually or possibly violated in his (or her) rights.[173]

The necessary or obligatory *subpoena* has a different legal quality. If third parties are involved in the contentious legal relationship in such a way that the decision can also only be imposed on them uniformly, they have to be subpoenaed. This means that the *subpoena* is necessary if the court decision the plaintiff has applied for cannot effectively be made without thereby at the same time immediately and inevitably affecting (i.e. forming, confirming or declaring, amending or abolishing) the rights of the subpoenaed person, so that the decision due to legal reasons can only be imposed uniformly on the main parties in the proceedings and the subpoenaed person.[174]

Regarding the consequences of a *subpoena* and of its omission, it must be distinguished between a simple and a necessary *subpoena*. In case of a simple *subpoena* the subpoenaed person can independently assert means of attack and defense and implement procedural acts effectively only within the requests of a person concerned. Conversely, he (or she) can lodge derogating factual motions if a necessary *subpoena* exists. The omission of a necessary *subpoena* is in principle a serious procedural shortcoming which leads to an annulment of the judgment and to a back reference of the lawsuit in the appeal procedure.[175] After all, the *subpoena* is an instrument to prevent the rights of a third party from being violated or at least not sufficiently considered in lawsuits of others.

Finally, the German administrative procedure law knows the institution of the Representative of the Public Interest (*Vertreter des öffentlichen Interesses*) and the Representative of the Interests of the Federation (*Vertreter des Bundesinteresses*). These representatives can be concerned by the proceedings if they avail themselves of their empowerment to participate. They have all rights of a party in the proceedings; particularly they can lodge motions and means of appeal according to the general conditions.[176] The Representative of the Public Interest may be appointed at the administrative court and at the higher administrative court by the federal state government. The Representative of the Interests of the Federation has to be appointed at the Federal Administrative Court by the Federal Government.

The Representative of the Interests of the Federation has the function to support the Federal Administrative Court in finding the law and to collaborate in the interest of the Federation, which is part of the public interest, on its realisation.[177] Thereby, the interest of the Federation has to be understood in a comprehensive and impartial way. It covers the interests of the Federation as a whole, including the concerns of

172 Federal Administrative Court (1999) *Neue Zeitschrift für Verwaltungsrecht – Rechtsprechungsreport* 276–277, 276; Higher Administrative Court (Oberverwaltungsgericht) of North Rhine-Westphalia (1991) *Neue Zeitschrift für Verwaltungsrecht – Rechtsprechungsreport* 486–487.

173 Kopp and Schenke (n. 99), Section 65 at 9, 770.

174 Federal Administrative Court, *Entscheidungen des Bundesverwaltungsgerichts* 51, 268–277, 275; 55, 8–17, 11; 74, 19–28, 23.

175 Federal Administrative Court, *Entscheidungen des Bundesverwaltungsgerichts* 51, 6–15, 11; Schenke (n. 84) 148; Kopp and Schenke (n. 99), Section 65 at 42, 786; von Mutius (n. 170) 276.

176 Cf. Kopp and Schenke (n. 99), Section 63 at 5, 757.

177 Cf. Federal Administrative Court, *Entscheidungen des Bundesverwaltungsgerichts* 18, 205–213, 207.

the federal states and of the municipalities as well as those of the individual citizen.[178] Thus, the Representative of the Interests of the Federation can mediate the interests of private persons.[179]

3.8 Aspects and effects of the inquisition maxim

Beside provisions which directly entitle the affected person to defend his (or her) rights before the administrative courts and to ward off their violation by measures of the administrative authorities, procedural rules should be mentioned which stand in the context of the inquisition maxim and have an immense practical relevance. For instance, a provision of the ACC reads that if the action does not meet the requirements with regard to its content, the presiding judge or the reporting judge shall call on the plaintiff to provide the necessary supplement within a specific period. Thus, the plaintiff is given the opportunity to revise and to complete his (or her) application.

According to the ACC, the court investigates the facts *ex officio*; the parties and the other concerned persons have to be consulted in doing so. The court is not bound to the submissions and to the motions for the taking of evidence of those concerned. It can find out the facts by itself, assess the facts and hear other type of evidence than the concerned persons have presented.[180] That rule follows the idea that there is a public interest in the factual correctness of the decision.[181] Furthermore, the ACC contains a general obligation of the presiding judge to give advice to the parties and to the other concerned persons. The presiding judge shall endeavour to ensure that formal errors are remedied, unclear requests explained, proper motions made, inadequate factual information supplemented, as well as all declarations submitted which are material to the establishment and judgment of the facts. This obligation is valid for the whole procedure, not only for the oral hearing or its preparation. It is an expression of the inquisition maxim and also an aspect of the principle of legal hearing and of procedural justice. It exists *vis-à-vis* any person concerned, but in practice it particularly serves the compensation of the information lead of the administration toward the citizen.[182] Moreover, in the proceedings it has the function to prevent surprising orders and decisions.[183]

Finally, the presiding judge shall discuss the dispute with those concerned in factual and legal terms.[184] This shall secure that no essential factual or legal aspects are

178 Deutscher Bundestag, Beschlussempfehlung und Bericht des Innenausschusses zu dem Gesetzentwurf der Bundesregierung: Entwurf eines Gesetzes zur Neuordnung des Bundesdisziplinarrechts, *Bundestags-Drucksache* 14/5529, 65; cf. W. Rzepka, 'Öffentliches Interesse im Sinne der §§ 35 ff. VwGO' (1992) 38 *Bayerische Verwaltungsblätter* 295–300.

179 Cf. Kopp and Schenke (n. 99), Section 35 at 1, 90.

180 Hufen (n. 7) 551.

181 Ibid. 536; Kopp and Schenke (n. 99), Section 86 at 1, 1080.

182 Hufen (n. 7) 549.

183 Federal Constitutional Court (1991) *Neue Juristische Wochenschrift* 2823–2824; Federal Constitutional Court (Chamber) (1996) *Neue Juristische Wochenschrift* 45–46; Federal Administrative Court (1986) *Neue Juristische Wochenschrift* 445; (2000) *Neue Zeitschrift für Verwaltungsrecht – Rechtsprechungsreport* 396–397; (2008) *Neue Zeitschrift für Verwaltungsrecht* 1025–1027, 1027; (2010) 845–847, 847; (2011) 372–375, 373.

184 Cf. K.-M. Ortloff, 'Rechtspsychologie und Verwaltungsgerichtsbarkeit: Das Rechtsgespräch in der mündlichen Verhandlung' (1995) 14 *Neue Zeitschrift für Verwaltungsrecht* 28–31.

overlooked and that the parties and the other persons concerned get the chance to adjust to the questions which are relevant for the judgment of the case and, if necessary, consider them in their statements and motions.[185]

To conclude, there are a series of provisions in administrative procedure law which prevent the realisation of the formal procedural rights and of the material rights of a party from failing due to his (or her) lack of experience, clumsiness or lack of legal knowledge.[186] At the end, such provisions contribute to a right, law-corresponding, just and, as regards the persons concerned, acceptable decision of the court.[187]

4 Institutional perspective

Pursuant to the Administrative Court Code, administrative jurisdiction shall be exercised by independent courts separated from the administrative authorities. This excludes any administrative jurisdiction by administrative authorities or by committees which do not have the quality of courts.[188]

Among the minimal requirements for an institution to qualify as a court are the decision making by uninvolved third persons,[189] the freedom from instructions and the institutionally guaranteed independence.[190] Hence, the administrative courts are independent and organisationally separated from both the legislation and the executive.[191] Likewise, the administrative judges must be personally and materially independent. The judges are in principle not allowed to exercise at the same time judicial and legislative or executive tasks.[192] Furthermore, the judges are in their judicative activities only bound by the law (Art. 20 paras 3 and 97 of the Basic Law). However, the notion of administrative jurisdiction in the ACC, despite its broad wording, only covers the jurisdiction according to Art. 40 para 1 of the Code. This provision, as already mentioned, reads that recourse to the administrative courts, which are specialised courts, is available in all public-law disputes of a non-constitutional nature insofar as the disputes are not explicitly allocated to another court by a federal statute. Public-law disputes in the field of federal state law may also be assigned to another court by a federal state statute. Therefore, the fiscal courts (*Finanzgerichte*) and the social welfare courts (*Sozialgerichte*), although being special administrative courts, do not fall under the application of the ACC.[193] They are ruled by the Fiscal Court Code (*Finanzgerichtsordnung*)[194] and by the Social Welfare Court Act (*Sozialgerichtsgesetz*).[195]

185 Federal Administrative Court, *Entscheidungen des Bundesverwaltungsgerichts* 51, 111–115, 113; Kopp and Schenke (n. 99), Section 104 at 1, 1258.

186 Cf. Federal Administrative Court (1985) *Neue Zeitschrift für Verwaltungsrecht* 36–37, 37.

187 Kopp and Schenke (n. 99), Section 86 at 22, 1102.

188 Ibid., Section 1 at 1, 5.

189 Federal Constitutional Court, *Entscheidungen des Bundesverfassungsgerichts* 21, 139–148, 145–146; 54, 159–172, 166.

190 Federal Constitutional Court, *Entscheidungen des Bundesverfassungsgerichts* 60, 175–215, 214; 87, 68–90, 85; Federal Administrative Court, *Entscheidungen des Bundesverwaltungsgerichts* 78, 216–223, 219; Kopp and Schenke (n. 99), Section 1 at 4, 6; cf. Kaufmann (n. 54) 203–227.

191 Kopp and Schenke (n. 99), Section 1 at 5, 6.

192 Ibid. Section 1 at 6, 7.

193 Ibid. Section 1 at 3, 5.

194 *Bundesgesetzblatt* (Federal Law Gazette) 2001 I, 442 and 2262.

195 Ibid. 1975 I, 2535.

This concerns disputes in the fields of taxes as well as of national insurance and, according to a recent amendment of the Social Welfare Court Act,[196] also of income support.[197] Furthermore, there exist special disciplinary courts for public servants and professional courts, like the professional courts for the pharmacists.[198]

As regards the relationship between the administrative courts and the ordinary courts, particularly the civil courts, Art. 14 para 3 of the Basic Law stipulates that in the case of dispute concerning the amount of compensation for expropriation, recourse may be had to the ordinary courts. This is an allocation of a matter of public law to the civil courts. The provision has a forerunner in Art. 153 of the Weimar Constitution. That it was maintained under the Basic Law may have to do on the one side with an existing uncertainty about the performance of the administrative courts in 1949. On the other side, aspects of compensation and problems of causality and calculation related thereto belong to the daily work of the civil courts.[199] Moreover, the ACC rules that recourse is available to the ordinary courts for property claims from sacrifice for the public good and from public-law deposit, as well as compensation claims from the violation of public-law obligations which are not based on a public-law contract; this shall not apply to disputes regarding the existence and the amount of a compensation claim in the context of Art. 14 para 1 of the Basic Law, which mentions the regulation of the content and limitations of property. The special provisions of civil service law, as well as those on legal recourse to compensate for property disadvantages for withdrawal of unlawful administrative acts, shall remain unaffected. This stipulation has also partly a constitutional background. Art. 34 of the Basic Law determines in the context of the liability for the violation of official duties that the way to the ordinary courts shall not be closed to claims for compensation or indemnity. The attribution of these claims to the civil courts may be not least explained with their similarity or affinity to typical claims concerning the relationship of one citizen to the other.[200]

Anyway, the governmental draft of the Administrative Court Code had provided for a comprehensive decision making power of the administrative courts in all matters of public law. The realisation of that plan was simply prevented by 'massive lobbying by leading representatives of civil jurisprudence'.[201] The result is a juxtaposition of administrative courts and civil courts in the field of state liability, which bears complications and leads in general to an unclearness of the legal area.[202] This is problematic against the background of the principle of effective legal protection.

The administrative jurisdiction is separated from the constitutional jurisdiction by the competence of the administrative courts to decide in 'all public-law disputes of

196 Siebentes Gesetz zur Änderung des Sozialgerichtsgesetzes, *Bundesgesetzblatt* (Federal Law Gazette) 2004 I, 3302.

197 Hufen (n. 7) 173; critical (and in favour of maintaining the competence of the administrative courts) H. Geiger, 'Verlagerung der Sozialhilfestreitigkeiten auf die Sozialgerichte' (2004) 57 *Neue Juristische Wochenschrift* 1850–1852; A. Decker, 'Ist die Rechtswegänderung für Sozialhilfestreitigkeiten zum 1.1.2005 (formell) verfassungswidrig?' (2004) 23 *Neue Zeitschrift für Verwaltungsrecht* 826–828.

198 Cf. Federal Administrative Court (1992) *Neue Juristische Wochenschrift* 1579–1580.

199 Maurer (n. 108) 691.

200 Cf. Kopp and Schenke (n. 99), Section 40 at 69–73, 209–212.

201 F. Schoch, 'Verwaltungsgerichtsbarkeit, quo vadis?' in Verwaltungsgerichtshof Baden-Württemberg (ed.), *Festschrift 150 Jahre Verwaltungsgerichtsbarkeit* (Boorberg, Stuttgart et al. 2014) 215–240, 217.

202 Maurer (n. 108) 691.

a non-constitutional nature' (Art. 40 para 1 of the ACC). Relevant for the constitutional nature of a dispute is according to the common opinion a twofold constitutional immediateness. This means that the dispute must concern persons who are directly participating in constitutional life and it must additionally relate to rights and duties which are directly ruled in the Constitution.[203]

Besides, the competencies of the Federal Constitutional Court are listed in Art. 93 of the Basic Law. The Federal Constitutional Court in its steady jurisdiction insists that it was no super appeal instance also *vis-à-vis* the administrative courts and that its task was limited to protect specific constitutional law.[204] However, the administrative courts deal to a large amount with constitutional law since they control administrative measures on the basis of legislative acts and of the Constitution. The basic rights and the rule of law play a particularly important role in administrative jurisdiction. Consequently, the Federal Constitutional Court *de facto* has the function of a last instance, when citizens lodge a constitutional complaint according to Art. 93 para 1 point 4a of the Basic Law against the original administrative measure and the administrative court decision(s) which confirm(s) the legality (and constitutionality) of this measure. Therefore, the Federal Constitutional Court in the past made a series of decisions which stressed and clarified aspects of the principle of effective legal protection.

The administrative courts have the power to review an administrative measure under any aspect of statutory and constitutional law, and they are even allowed to incidentally control the constitutionality of the parliamentary act which served as the legal basis for the administrative measure. However, the administrative courts do not have the power to reject the parliamentary act if they hold that it was unconstitutional. Rather, in such a case the administrative courts, like all other courts, are obliged to adjourn the procedure and to present the parliamentary act to the Federal Constitutional Court according to Art. 100 para 1 of the Basic Law (so-called concrete supervision of a norm; *konkrete Normenkontrolle*). The Federal Constitutional Court has the monopoly to declare legislative acts unconstitutional and, thus, invalid.[205] Conversely, the higher administrative courts, as already mentioned, have the competence to review stipulations ranking below the level of legislative acts according to the ACC since such stipulations are not acts of the parliament but abstract and general norms of the executive. However, the existing limitations of the review of material provisions are problematic.

The principle of effective legal protections requires that the citizen has the possibility to go to court in any case where a material provision directly affects his (or her) rights. This is not only true for by-laws issued under the provisions of the Federal Building Code, statutory instruments issued on the basis of the Federal Building Code and other legal provisions ranking below the statutes of the federal state to the extent that this is provided in federal state law. Instead, it can be argued that federal state law has to provide for a review of legal provisions ranking below the statutes of the federal state. Furthermore, there is no argument against the introduction of the possibility of a principal review of federal legal provisions ranking below the statutes

203 Kopp and Schenke (n. 99), Section 40 at 32, 169–170.

204 Federal Constitutional Court, *Entscheidungen des Bundesverfassungsgerichts* 7, 198–230, 207; 18, 85–97, 92–93.

205 Cf. Hufen (n. 7) 337.

of the Federation by the Federal Administrative Court. In any way, the 'secret supervision of statutory law' by means of the general action for a declaratory judgment is not an adequate compensation for the existing deficits of legal protection in this regard.[206]

The administrative courts must refer to the general principles of international law, which are part of federal law according to Art. 25 of the Basic Law. The international treaty law which is implemented in the German legal area has the same rank as legislative acts of the Federation so that must also be considered. Furthermore, the primary and secondary law of the European Union belongs to the standard of review of the administrative courts. From the perspective of European law the national judge has to control, particularly due to a complaint by a private person, whether a state measure is compatible with the applicable Union law, and from the German perspective the national judge is even obliged to determine and apply Union law *ex officio*.[207] Thereby, the primacy of the application of European law can be decisive, when the national law is in contrast with European law. A prominent case of the European Court of Justice which can be mentioned in this context is *Alcan*, where a company against the withdrawal of subventions which were incompatible with European law claimed the protection of legitimate expectations due to the course of time on the basis of the German Administrative Procedure Act, which was from the first sight not congruent with primary European law.[208]

The judicial review is limited to the examination of the legality of the administrative measure, which means that the administrative court's interpretation and application of the law is decisive and prevails over a divergent dealing with the law by the administrative authority. However, there are certain cases where the density of judicial review is limited.

On the side of the factual area of application (*Tatbestand*) of legal provisions, the courts in principle apply a comprehensive supervision of undetermined legal notions (*unbestimmte Rechtsbegriffe*), but there is case law where the administrative courts accept that the administration has a scope of assessment (*Beurteilungsspielraum*) which can only be reviewed under certain aspects. Examples are examinations (in schools and universities), assessments of the performance of public servants, prognostic decisions and risk assessments. In such cases the courts only control whether there are deficits in the assessment, for instance procedural shortcomings, the assumption of wrong facts, violations of recognised principles for the assessment, irrelevant considerations or in other way arbitrary decisions.[209]

As to the legal consequence (*Rechtsfolge*) of legal provisions, the aspect of discretion (*Ermessen*) has to be mentioned. The ACC stipulates that insofar as the administrative authority is empowered to act in its discretion, the court also examines whether the administrative act or the refusal or omission of the administrative act is unlawful because the statutory limits of discretion have been overstepped or the discretion has been used in a manner not corresponding to the purpose of the empowerment.

206 Ibid. 338; cf. M.-E. Geis, 'Die Feststellungsklage als Normenkontrolle zwischen suchender Dialektik und dogmatischer Konsistenz' in Baumeister, Roth and Ruthig (n. 135) 709–719.

207 O. Dörr, 'Grundstrukturen eines europäischen Verwaltungsprozessrechts' (2008) 123 *Deutsches Verwaltungsblatt* 1401–1407, 1405–1506.

208 ECJ, Case 24/95, ECR 1997, I-1607–1625, I-1619.

209 Cf. E. Schmidt-Aßmann and T. Groß, 'Zur verwaltungsgerichtlichen Kontrolldichte nach der Privatschul-Entscheidung des BVerfG' (1993) 12 *Neue Zeitschrift für Verwaltungsrecht* 617–625, 624.

Thus, the administrative court reviews discretionary decisions of the administrative authority only under certain legal aspects; it is not allowed to put its own discretion on the place of that of the administration. Relevant shortcomings with regard to discretion are that the administration did not make use of its discretion (*Ermessensausfall*), that it either considered irrelevant aspects or incorrectly giving the wrong weight to one of the aspects before putting it on Justitia's scales of justice (*Ermessensfehlgebrauch*) or that it chose an alternative to which it was not authorised and thereby overstepped the limits of discretion which were laid down in the authorising norm (*Ermessensüb erschreitung*).[210] However, the administration has the possibility to 'cure' defects concerning discretion according to the ACC. The provision reads that the administrative authority may supplement its discretionary considerations as to the administrative act in the proceedings before the administrative courts.

If the administrative court finds out that there is a discretion defect and if this defect is not 'healed' in the proceedings, the administrative decision is unlawful. In the case of the action for the rescission of an administrative act this leads to the abolition of the act as far as the plaintiff is violated in his (or her) right. It is not decisive whether the administrative authority could have come to the same order or prohibition without discretion defects, because at least the contested administrative act is unlawful and must be abolished under the conditions of the ACC.[211]

After all, the administrative courts have far-reaching powers to control the administrative authorities. There are only few scopes of the administration where the judicial supervision is limited. Furthermore, the administrative courts are the principal actors to control the activities of the administration.

Besides, there are informal legal remedies which the citizen can make use of, like the counter argumentation (*Gegenvorstellung*) directed to the administrative body which has passed or omitted the decision, the complaint to the supervisory official or authority ([*Dienst-*]*Aufsichtsbeschwerde*) or the petition to the parliament or to any other competent authority, which is constitutionally guaranteed in Art. 17 of the Basic Law. A system of citizens' representatives (*Bürgerbeauftragte*) supports the work of the petition committees on the administrative level and helps the citizens with their little and big problems *vis-à-vis* the administration.[212] Special ombudsmen exist in certain fields, for instance the data protection representatives of the Federation and of the federal states and the university ombudsmen to hear reproaches concerning scientific misbehaviour.[213]

Finally, in complex planning procedures sometimes mediation takes place.[214] The federal legislator has passed the Act on the Promotion of Mediation and of Other Procedures of Extrajudicial Dispute-Settlement (*Gesetz zur Förderung der Mediation und*

210 Hufen (n. 7) 420–421; Schenke (n. 84) 253–255.

211 Hufen (n. 7) 421; Kopp and Schenke (n. 99), Section 113 at 20, 1333.

212 Hufen (n. 7) 19–20.

213 Cf. S. Muckel, 'Der Ombudsmann zur Anhörung von Vorwürfen wissenschaftlichen Fehlverhaltens' in P. Hanau, D. Leuze, W. Löwer and H. Schiedermair (eds.), *Gedächtnisschrift für Hartmut Krüger* (Duncker & Humblot, Berlin 2001) 275–297.

214 Cf. H. Pünder, 'Kooperation statt Konfrontation' (2005) 38 *Die Verwaltung* 1–34; T. Mehler, 'Verknüpfung des Ergebnisses einer Mediation mit der fachplanerischen Abwägung' (2012) 31 *Neue Zeitschrift für Verwaltungsrecht* 1288–1291.

anderer Verfahren der außergerichtlichen Konfliktbeilegung) in 2012.[215] This Act contains, among other rules, a legal basis for an intrajudicial mediation also before the administrative courts,[216] the admissibility of which was disputed beforehand.[217] Since the Act is obviously geared to civil procedure, it must be remain to be seen whether the provisions adequately fit the needs of mediation in the administrative court procedure.[218]

5 European perspective

The European law, which comprehensively penetrates the national legal orders, has an important influence on the jurisdiction of the administrative courts in Germany. Moreover, the Europeanisation of material administrative law leads to the Europeanisation of administrative procedure law[219] and in the end also of administrative court procedure law.[220] The change concerns the principle of effective legal protection *vis-à-vis* the administrative authorities particularly in the context of provisional legal protection[221] as well as under aspects of the right or authorisation to sue and the extent of the supervisory powers of the administrative courts.[222]

As regards the constitutional situation, Art. 19 para 4 of the Basic Law guarantees in the framework of European integration that there is an effective legal protection of the individual before German courts to claim subjective rights which are laid down in Community law. At the same time, the provision guarantees an effective legal

215 *Bundesgesetzblatt* (Federal Law Gazette) 2012 I, 1577; see M. Ahrens, 'Mediationsgesetz und Güterichter – Neue gesetzliche Regelungen der gerichtlichen und außergerichtlichen Mediation' (2012) 65 *Neue Juristische Wochenschrift* 2465–2471.

216 See K.-M. Ortloff, 'Vom Gerichtsmediator zum Güterichter im Verwaltungsprozess' (2012) 31 *Neue Zeitschrift für Verwaltungsrecht* 1057–1061; Hufen (n. 7) 44–45.

217 Deutscher Bundestag, Gesetzentwurf der Bundesregierung: Entwurf eines Gesetzes zur Förderung der Mediation und anderer Verfahren der außergerichtlichen Konfliktbeilegung, *Bundestags-Drucksache* 17/5335, 19.

218 Hufen (n. 7) 43–44; sceptical A. Guckelberger, 'Einheitliches Mediationsgesetz auch für verwaltungsrechtliche Konflikte?' (2011) 30 *Neue Zeitschrift für Verwaltungsrecht* 390–396.

219 C. D. Classen, 'Das nationale Verwaltungsverfahren im Kraftfeld des Europäischen Gemeinschaftsrechts' (1998) 31 *Die Verwaltung* 307–334, 333; C. Ohler, 'Europäisches und nationales Verwaltungsrecht' in J. P. Terhechte (ed.), *Verwaltungsrecht der Europäischen Union* (Nomos, Baden-Baden 2011) 331–351, 341; E. Hofmann, 'Das Verwaltungsverfahren unter dem Einfluss des Europarechts' in W. Ewer, U. Ramsauer, M. Reese and R. Rubel (eds.), *Methodik – Ordnung – Umwelt: Festschrift für Hans-Joachim Koch* (Duncker & Humblot, Berlin 2014) 211–228.

220 See D. Ehlers, *Die Europäisierung des Verwaltungsprozeßrechts* (Carl Heymanns, Cologne et al. 1999); M. Burgi, *Verwaltungsprozessrecht und Europarecht: Eine systematische Darstellung* (Franz Vahlen, Munich 1996), particularly 64–73; S. Kadelbach, 'Gemeinschaftsrecht und (vorläufiger) verwaltungsgerichtlicher Rechtsschutz' (1999) 82 *Kritische Vierteljahresschrift* 378–401; J. Kokott, 'Europäisierung des Verwaltungsprozessrechts' (1998) 31 *Die Verwaltung* 335–370; F. Schoch, 'Die Europäisierung des Verwaltungsprozessrechts' in E. Schmidt-Aßmann, D. Sellner, G. Hirsch, G.-H. Kemper and H. Lehmann-Grube (eds.), *Festgabe 50 Jahre Bundesverwaltungsgericht* (Carl Heymanns, Cologne et al. 2003) 507–533.

221 Cf. ECJ, Case C-217/88, ERC 1990, I-2899–I-2909 – *Table Wine*; Joined Cases C-143/88 and C-92/89, ERC 1991, I-534–I-554 – *Zuckerfabrik Süderdithmarschen*; Case C-465/93, ERC 1895, I-3781–I-3797 – *Atlanta Fruchthandelsgesellschaft I*; Burgi (n. 220) 66–70; Kadelbach (n. 220) 396–398; C. Steinbeiß-Winkelmann, 'Europäisierung des Verwaltungsrechtsschutzes' (2010) 63 *Neue Juristische Wochenschrift* 1233–1238, 1234.

222 Cf. Schlacke (n. 2) 505–506.

protection directed at imposing the limits of the claim of European law to find application in the national legal sphere.[223]

Concerning the right or authorisation to sue, the administrative courts dealt with the European demands in the way that they interpreted certain stipulations as protecting third persons. Furthermore, the legislator created new subjective rights in favour of the citizen and construed individual rights required by Community law instead of mere internal administrative regulations (*Verwaltungsvorschriften*) as external legal provisions which obviously authorise the individual to claim them even before the courts.[224]

This development is not without problems for the German administrative court system. This has to do with the functional relationship between the right or authorisation to sue and the density of judicial review.[225] If the individual can claim a violation of his (or her) subjective rights, there is in principle a complete review of the contested measure by the administrative court on points of fact and law. The right or authorisation to sue has the function of a filter to protect the courts against overloading. If more and more persons are allowed to sue, the question arises whether the full program of judicial supervision is still justifiable or at least tenable (in all groups of cases).[226] In addition to this, the influence of European law leads to a revision of the national regime of the legal consequences of shortcomings in the administrative procedure.[227] Currently, for instance, Art. 46 of the APA stipulates that the application for annulment of an administrative act which is not invalid under Art. 44 of this law, listing certain severe violations of formal provisions, cannot be made solely on the ground that the act came into being through the infringement of regulations governing procedure, form or local competence, where it is evident that the infringement has not influenced the decision on the matter.

In the European context, the principle of effective legal protection requires a consideration of the procedure not only in its serving function[228] but also in its legitimising function for the correctness of the material outcome.[229] The European law forces a more intensive judicial review of procedural shortcomings than required by the national rules.[230] Against this background, it can be argued that the European principle of effective legal protection charges or improves its national counterpart.

223 See O. Dörr, *Der europäisierte Schutzauftrag deutscher Gerichte* (Mohr Siebeck, Tübingen 2003) 277–279.

224 See S. Neidhardt, *Nationale Rechtsinstitute als Bausteine europäischen Verwaltungsrechts* (Mohr Siebeck, Tübingen 2008) 76–79; also B. W. Wegener, *Rechte des Einzelnen* (Nomos, Baden-Baden 1998) 274–298.

225 Cf. R. Herzog, 'Verfassung und Verwaltungsgerichte – zurück zu mehr Kontrolldichte?' (1992) 45 *Neue Juristische Wochenschrift* 2601–2605, 2601–2602.

226 Cf. Neidhardt (n. 224) 86–87; Steinbeiß-Winkelmann (n. 221) 1237.

227 Schlacke (n. 2) 506; cf. J. Ziekow, 'Von der Reanimation des Verfahrensrechts' (2005) 24 *Neue Zeitschrift für Verwaltungsrecht* 263–267, 266; R. Wahl, 'Das Verhältnis von Verwaltungsverfahren und Verwaltungsprozessrecht in europäischer Sicht' (2003) 118 *Deutsches Verwaltungsblatt* 1285–1293, 1291.

228 Cf. K.-P. Dolde, 'Verwaltungsverfahren und Deregulierung' (2006) 25 *Neue Zeitschrift für Verwaltungsrecht* 857–865, 858 and 864; Ziekow (n. 227) 264.

229 Cf. W. Erbguth, 'Rechtsschutzfragen und Fragen der §§ 214 und 215 BauGB im neuen Städtebaurecht' (2004) 119 *Deutsches Verwaltungsblatt* 802–810, 802–803; T. von Danwitz, 'Aarhus-Konvention: Umweltinformation, Öffentlichkeitsbeteiligung, Zugang zu den Gerichten' (2004) 23 *Neue Zeitschrift für Verwaltungsrecht* 272–282, 279–282; Wahl (n. 227) 1290–1293.

230 Cf. ECJ, Case C-201/02, ECR 2004, I-748–I-771 – *Wells*; Schlacke (n. 2) 506; Wahl (n. 227) 1290–1291.

A case where this can be demonstrated quite well is *Orfanopoulos*,[231] which concerned the expulsion of aliens having the nationality of other Member States of the European Union on the basis of reasons of the public order, security and health. The European Court of Justice held that there should be a deviation from the national procedural norms on the one side with regard to the point of time which is relevant for considering the individual case and on the other side with regard to the necessity to control not only the lawfulness but also the expediency of an expulsion. The Court stressed that the preconditions for the existence of a present threat must in principle be given at the time at which the expulsion really takes place. The Court explained this view by referring to the standard argument in the context of the European principle of effective protection: while the development of the procedural rules governing actions for safeguarding rights which individuals derive from Community law was an affair of the Member States, 'the fact remains that those rules must not be such as to render virtually impossible or excessively difficult the exercise of rights conferred by Community law'.[232]

The Court's view contradicts the German legal position. With regard to the provisions of the ACC, in case of an action for the rescission of an administrative act, the time of the last administrative decision is decisive, which is regularly the ruling on the objection, irrespective of how much time has passed until the decision of the administrative court.[233]

Against the background of the judgment in *Orfanopoulos*, the Federal Administrative Court modified its jurisdiction. It argued that the Senate followed the interpretation of material Community by the European Court of Justice and 'insofar gives up its previous opposite jurisdiction about the decisive point of time. Thus, for the judicial review of the lawfulness of the expulsions of citizens of the European Union, who bear the freedom of movement, on points of fact and law, now the point of time of the last oral hearing of the court of facts is decisive. [. . .] The courts of facts are [. . .] in the future not only authorised but in the framework of their clarification obligation according to Section 86 paragraph 1 of the Administrative Court Code also obliged to examine whether the official threat prognosis and the discretionary decision with regard to the point of time of the judicial decision are ultimately founded on a correct factual basis [. . .]. If there are new facts which can have effects on the preconditions of the expulsion and the discretionary decision about the expulsion, the court on the basis of an interpretation of Section 114 sentence 2 of the Administrative Court Code in accordance with Community law has to give the aliens' registration service the opportunity to adapt its decision and to particularly also make current discretionary considerations. Insofar, the aliens' registration services have a duty to steadily control, in accompanying the court proceedings, the lawfulness of their expulsion order.'[234]

231 ECJ, Joined Cases C-482/01 and C-493/03, ECR 2004, I-5257–I-5336 – *Orfanopoulos and Oliveri*; see for Turkish nationals in the area of application of Association law ECJ, Case C-467/02, ECR 2004, I-10924–I-10944, I-10943 (at 47) – *Cetinkaya v Baden-Württemberg*.

232 ECJ, ECR 2004, I-5321 (at 80), referring to ECJ, Case 33/76, ECR 1976, 1989–1999, 1997–1998 (at 5) – *Rewe*; Case C-129/00, ECR 2003, I-14672–I-14691, I-14684 (at 25) – *Commission v Italy*.

233 See Federal Administrative Court, *Entscheidungen des Bundesverwaltungsgerichts* 34, 155–159, 158; 60, 133–140, 135; 65, 1–8, 1 and 2–4.

234 Federal Administrative Court, *Entscheidungen des Bundesverwaltungsgerichts* 121, 297–315, 308–310; see with regard to persons having rights on the basis of the Association Agreement between the European

After the European Court of Human Rights had confirmed the position of the European Court of Justice,[235] the Federal Administrative Court expanded its jurisdiction to all foreigners.[236] Furthermore, the European Court of Justice in *Orfanopoulos* limited with regard to certain constellations the scope to decide whether there should be an objection procedure prior to the court procedure. According to the German law, prior to lodging a rescissory action, the lawfulness and expediency of the administrative act must in principle be reviewed in preliminary proceedings. However, the ACC allows making a different ruling by federal state law. In Baden-Württemberg, where *Orfanopoulos* had its starting point, the legislator has made use of this possibility and has excluded the preliminary proceedings in cases of administrative acts passed by the regional authorities (*Regierungspräsidien*).[237]

The European Court of Justice stated that in such a case there was no reliable guarantee for an exhaustive examination of the expediency of the intended expulsion and did not meet the requirements of sufficiently effective protection.[238] It would be likely to deprive Art. 9 para. 1 of Council Directive 64/221/EEC on the coordination of special measures concerning the movement and residence of foreign nationals which are justified on grounds of public policy, public security or public health of its practical effect.[239] Art. 9 para 1 of Directive 64/221/EEC 'precludes a provision of a Member State which provides neither a complaints procedure nor an appeal, comprising also an examination of expediency, against a decision to expel a national of another Member State taken by an administrative authority, where no authority independent of that administration has been put in place. It is for the national court to establish whether courts such as the Verwaltungsgerichte are able to examine the expediency of expulsion orders.'[240] Consequently, the administrative courts in Germany, which due to the concept of the separation of powers and functions cannot examine the expediency of administrative measures, in any case where an objection procedure did not take place, had to sentence the administration at least to carry out an objection procedure with another examination of expediency. Meanwhile, the legal situation has changed since Directive 64/221/EEC was repealed by Art. 31 of the Citizenship Directive 2004/38/EC of the European Parliament and of the Council, which does not prescribe that 'another authority' examines all facts and circumstances including the expediency of the intended measure. Therefore, the legal situation could maintain that there is no objection procedure for citizens of the European Union.[241]

Economic Community and Turkey Federal Administrative Court, *Entscheidungen des Bundesverwaltungsgerichts* 121, 315–324.

235 ECtHR (Grand Chamber), Application No. 1638/03, Judgment of 23 June 2008 – *Maslov v Austria.*

236 Federal Administrative Court, *Entscheidungen des Bundesverwaltungsgerichts* 130, 20–28, 20 and 23–26; cf. I. Kraft, 'Vom Konflikt zur Konvergenz. Zur Rezeption der ausländerrechtlichen Rechtsprechung des EGMR durch die deutschen Verwaltungsgerichte' (2014) 33 *Neue Zeitschrift für Verwaltungsrecht* 969–976, 973.

237 See Art. 15 para 1 of the Act on the Performance of the Administrative Court Code (*Gesetz zur Ausführung zur Verwaltungsgerichtsordnung*) of Baden-Württemberg (*Gesetzblatt für Baden-Württemberg* 2008, 343).

238 Cf. ECJ, Case 222/84, ECR 1986, 1663–1694, 1682 (at 17) – *Johnston*; Case 222/86, ECR 1987, 4112–4119, 4117 (at 14 and 15) – *Heylens and Others.*

239 ECJ, ECR 2004, I-5332 (at 110).

240 ECJ, ECR 2004, I-5333 (at 116).

241 See Bavarian Higher Administrative Court (*Bayerischer Verwaltungsgerichtshof*), Judgment of 17 July 2012–19 B 12.417, particularly at 56.

In sum, the case illustrates not only the entanglement of European Union law, Convention law and national procedural law but also the extent and the ruling density with which the provisions of European law and international law affect the national law of administrative procedure and administrative court procedure. Thus, it can be expected that particularly European law will make changes necessary in the national system of the protection of rights of the individual against measures of the administrative authorities.

6 Conclusion

In Germany, the principle of effective protection of the individual *vis-à-vis* the administrative authorities is primarily regarded as a constitutional principle, which addresses on the one side the legislator and on the other side the courts and the administration itself. In the latter cases it governs the application and interpretation of the procedural norms laid down in the Administrative Court Code and in the Administrative Procedure Act.

In a series of cases, impulses to change existing procedural norms or to introduce new provisions came from the Federal Constitutional Court. Consequently, the fields of activities and the scopes of decision making of the administration which were exempted from judicial review have steadily been reduced. Furthermore, rules had been elaborated to deal with assessments of the factual situation, with prognoses and with discretion of administrative authorities.

The protection of the individual is traditionally connected with the notion of the subjective right. If the plaintiff can claim a violation of his (or her) subjective rights, this opens far-reaching powers of the administrative courts to review the contested administrative measure. Conversely, for persons or associations claiming the violation of rights of others or of objective law the way to the administrative courts is regularly closed completely. There is only a gradual chance due to the influence of European law[242] in favour of nature conservation associations.[243]

Concerning the future development, it can be foreseen that in light of the principle of effective protection the administrative justice will have to face at least four huge challenges: these are the growing complexity of the division of litigations between civil and administrative courts, the legal protection in cases of third persons, the coping with the increasing demands of European law and, finally, the internationalisation of the legal protection against the administration.[244]

242 Cf. ECJ, Case C-115/09, ECR 2011, I-3701–I-3726 – *Trianel Kohlekraftwerk Lünen*; see B. W. Wegener, 'Die europäische Umweltverbandsklage' (2011) 22 *Zeitschrift für Umweltrecht* 363–367.

243 Cf. Ruffert (n. 92) 107–110; W. Porsch, 'Die Zulässigkeit und Begründetheit von Umweltverbandsklagen' (2013) 32 *Neue Zeitschrift für Verwaltungsrecht* 1062–1065, 1063–1064.

244 Schoch (n. 201) 216.

9 The principle of effective legal protection in Hungarian administrative law

Fruzsina Gárdos-Orosz and István Temesi

1 Historical developments

The roots of the principle of legal protection can be traced back to the second half of the nineteenth century in Hungary, during the dual monarchy with Austria. The country has followed various patterns and traditions of Western Europe, like the principle of legality which was borrowed from the German concept of *Rechtsstaat*. The legality became a general requirement in public administration emphasising that public authorities are bound by the law. Another fundamental principle, the separation of powers, inspired the law which separated the Judiciary from the executive power.[1] As a next step, the Hungarian legislature, after the Austrian model, established financial courts which were entitled to change administrative decisions made by administrative authorities in certain financial subjects.[2] Due to the positive experiences of these special courts, the Act No. XXVI of 1896 established specialised administrative courts.[3] These judicial tribunals existed separately from the organisation of ordinary courts and were divided into two sections, one for general administration and another for financial matters.

In the very beginning of the twentieth century, the first elements of administrative procedures emerged also in statutory law, when, for example, the Parliament enacted a law on the legal remedies against administrative decisions. However, as the country had an unwritten, historical constitution, according to the widely shared view of that time, some legal guarantees of personal freedom were guided by legal customs and constitutional conventions.

The establishment of the Communist rule after World War II brought about substantial changes both in theory and practice. The system of administrative courts was abolished arguing that the public authorities in the 'people's democracy' act on behalf of the whole people. Only certain administrative decisions (e.g. in cases of retirement, health insurance, election, nationality) remained subjected to judicial review by ordinary courts. Some decisions in taxation matters could be controlled by a commission belonging to the Ministry of Finances. Disputes of competences between administrative authorities were resolved by the Commission of Competencies before

1 Act No IV of 1869 [stating that 'judges and administrative authorities are not allowed to encroach on the scope of authority of each-other'].

2 Act No XLIII of 1883.

3 Patyi András and Varga ZS. András, '*Általános közigazgatási jog*' (Dialog-Campus 2013) 73.

1954. The adoption of the Act No IV of 1957 on the General Rules of the Administrative Procedure could have been a turning point, as this law allowed the judicial review of administrative decisions in special cases enumerated in legislative acts, statutory decrees or decrees of the Government. But it had only little practical significance, as judicial review has remained exceptional, limited to some special cases, while administrative decisions concerning fundamental rights were excluded from any judicial control.

As a matter of fact, the Constitution of 1949 (the first written basic law in the national history) contained only a short list of rights, focusing on the 'social, economic and cultural rights', while neglecting or minimising the classical rights and liberties. The first administrative code emerged only in 1957 when the National Assembly adopted the Act No. IV of 1957 on the General Rules of the Administrative Procedure. Some other laws established special procedures for taxation, electoral, infraction, etc. procedures, to which the general procedural rules could only be applied in the absence of any specific provisions, or in which they were not used at all. The general administrative code entered into force on 1 October 1957 and was applied until 2005 when a new code became applicable.

Fundamental change arrived only with the democratic transition of 1989, when the system of the protection of fundamental rights was established by a general constitutional revision of that year[4] and the emergence of some new institutions like the Constitutional Court.[5] The new constitutional provisions not only recognised the inviolable and inalienable human rights, but declared also that 'the respect and protection of these rights became a primary obligation of the state'.[6] The judicial review of administrative decisions became also a general rule as the revised Constitution stated that 'legality of administrative decisions are controlled by the court' (Art. 50). However, the judicial review of administrative acts was established only by the Act No. XXVI of 1991 on the extension of judicial review over administrative decision. The new provision was born as a consequence of a Constitutional Court decision which declared that the Parliament had not adopted the appropriate measures to comply with the relevant constitutional provision, and thereby has committed an unconstitutional omission.[7] Subsequently, the legislature empowered the ordinary courts to review the legality of administrative acts. For this purpose, as a result of an internal specialisation, administrative councils (colleges) have been set up in county-level court houses and within the Supreme Court. More recently, the Act No. CLXI of 2011 on the Organisation and Administration of Courts established new courts

4 Act No. XXXI of 1989.

5 For a general description of the Hungarian administrative law after the democratic transition, see Herbert Küpper, 'Hungarian Administrative Law 1985–2005: The Organization of the Administration' in András Jakab, Péter Takács and Allan F. Tatham (eds.), *The Transformation of Hungarian Legal Order 1985–2005: Transition to Rule of Law and Accession to the European Union* (Wolters Kluwer, Budapest 2007) 109–122., and Zoltán Szente, 'Grundzüge des Verwaltungsrechts in gemeineuropäischer Perspektive: Ungarn' in Armin von Bogdandy, Sabino Cassese and Peter M. Huber (eds.), *Handbuch Ius Publicum Europeaum: Band V. Verwaltungsrecht in Europa: Grundzüge* (C. F. Müller, Heidelberg 2014) 803–860.

6 Art. 8 para 2.

7 32/1990. (XII. 22.) CC decision.

for administrative and labour matters in the counties. In fact, these courts are not separated from the county courts in organisational term, but are only remote units of them.[8]

2 Constitutional and legal frameworks

Although the Fundamental Law of 2011 does not refer explicitly to the principle of effective legal protection, it contains its most important guarantees and components. The crucial one is the right to fair procedures assuring that every person has 'the right to have his or her affairs administered by the authorities in an impartial, fair and reasonably timely manner'. This right includes the obligation of public authorities to justify their decisions as determined by law (Art. XXIV para 1). Furthermore, every person has also the right to submit a written application, complaint or proposal, whether individual or joint, to any organ which exercises public power (Art. XXV). Another constitutional provision guarantees everybody's right to seek legal remedy against any court, administrative or other official decision which violates his or her rights or lawful interests. This right to appeal means that the rights and obligations of any person must be 'adjudicated by a legally established independent and impartial court in a fair public trial within a reasonable period of time' (Art. XXVIII para 1). Public authorities are obliged to justify their decisions. This means that administrative authorities and courts have to provide the reasons for their decisions that can serve as basis for legal remedy. Also the lack of a measure that is not to be taken should be reasoned in the decisions (the Art. XXIV para 1). The Fundamental Law comprises also a general entitlement to 'statutory state compensation' for those who suffered 'any unlawful damage caused by the authorities while performing their duties' (Art. XXIV para 2). The legal equality is one of the requirements that serve as a basis for the effective legal protection in law and jurisprudence after the democratic transition of Hungary. According to this legal tenet, all people are equal before the law, and, consequently, 'law binds everyone [in the same way] including individuals and organs of public authority' (Art. XV para 1).

The first commentary on the Fundamental Law published in English claims that Art. XXIV para 1 guaranteeing the right to fair administration 'fills a lacuna' that has been uncovered by the practice of the Constitutional Court.[9] This provision can be regarded as a due process clause specialised in administrative law, while the similar provision of the former constitution was mainly developed only for civil and criminal law procedures. The right to fair trial was not mentioned in the Constitution before 2012, but the Constitutional Court deduced certain elements of it from the concept of the fair and impartial court hearing, and from the procedural guarantees emanating from the principle of rule of law. In a recent ruling the Constitutional Court stated that Art. XXVIII means that '[t]he rule of law requirement of material justice

8 Rozsnyai Krisztina, 'A közigazgatási bíráskodás megteremtésének sarokkövei' in Varga Zs. András and Fröhlich Johanna (eds.), *Közérdekvédelem: A közigazgatási bíráskodás múltja és jövője* (PPKE JÁK-KIM 2011) 95.

9 Loránt Csink, Balázs Schanda and András Zs. Varga (eds.), *The Basic Law of Hungary: A First Commentary* (Clarus Press 2012) 218. 95–101.

can be achieved by respecting the institutions serving legal certainty and guarantees. The Fundamental Law grants a right to a procedure which is necessary and in most cases appropriate to the realisation of material justice'.[10]

In statutory law, beyond the general code of procedural rules, the Act CXL of 2004 on the General Rules of Administrative Procedures and Services (hereinafter: GRAPS), there are some special types of administrative process (for the proceedings of tax authorities, public procurement, nuclear energy, election and referendum procedures etc.) regulated by further legislative acts and government decrees.

Before the enactment of the Fundamental Law of 2011, the Constitutional Court established a robust jurisprudence of the rule of law and determined the exact requirements of the principle of fair trial. Although the fourth amendment of the Fundamental Law in 2013 repealed all Constitutional Court rulings that had been taken prior to the entry into force of the new Fundamental Law, significantly weakening the level of constitutional protection of rights by this way, the former decisions, the standards remained to be points of reference in the jurisprudence of the Constitutional Court.[11] Therefore it is worth invoking the major achievements of the constitutional adjudication in the topic since the democratic transition of 1989–1990.

The concept of legal certainty as a pillar of the principle of rule of law appeared already in the practice of the Court in the early 1990s. In the next years, the Constitutional Court explained step-by-step the basic requirements of these principles which have had implications also in the administrative proceedings. Thus, public authorities must exist in the operational order determined by law, and in a way predictable for the citizens.[12] In another landmark decision, the Court expressed that the principle of legal certainty requires the whole legal system to be clear, unambiguous and predictable.[13] All these have been associated with the requirements that procedural guarantees have to be established for the stability of the existing legal relationships, the full compliance of the procedural rules and that public authorities must operate in a foreseeable and effective way.[14,15]

As to the principle of fair trial used in administrative cases, the Court declared in 1997 that during the judicial disputes, all procedural safeguards ensured by the former Constitution (i.e. every person's right that his or her rights and duties must be judged in a just, public trial by an independent and impartial court established by law) must be realised. Furthermore, all regulations which limit the judicial control of the public administrative bodies' decisions are unconstitutional.[16]

10 9/19992 (I. 30.) CC decision.

11 13/2013 (VI. 17.) CC decision.

12 56/1991. (XI. 8.) CC decision.

13 9/1992. (I.30.) CC decision.

14 See for example the 46/2003. (X. 16.) 62/2003. (XII. 15.), and 2/2007 (I.24.) CC decisions.

15 For an analysis of this practice see Tamás Győrfi and András Jakab, 'Jogállamiság' in Jakab András (ed.), *Az Alkotmány kommentárja* (Századvég Kiadó 2009) 155–170; and Zoltán Szente, 'The Rise and Fall of an Unenumerated Principle. The Protection of Legitimate Expectations in Hungarian Public Law' in Kari Anneken Sperr and Diana zu Hohenlohe-Oehringen (eds.), *The Protection of Legitimate Expectations in Administrative Law: A Comparative Study* (Hart Publishing 2016).

16 39/1997. (VII. 1.) CC decision.

3 Rights-based perspective

3.1 The domestic system of procedural rights in administrative law

The administrative procedure has a prominent role in the effective legal protection of rights. Rights and obligations of individuals, private legal entities as well as public authorities are determined by law. The administrative procedures serve as a general legal framework for the realisation of fundamental rights and duties. They are regulated by acts of Parliament that has the highest rank in the hierarchy of norms, so legislative acts cannot be modified by decrees issued by the Executive.

3.1.1 The right to be a party in administrative procedures

The GRAPS regulates the conditions of standing in administrative procedure. The Hungarian administrative law uses the term 'client' for the persons (or organisations) that have the right to be applicants in these proceedings. According to the GRAPS, clients can be anyone – an individual or an organisation – whose rights or legal interests are affected by a case. In judicial practice, only those can be clients, 'on whom the [administrative] decision has a direct effect'.[17] According to the GRAP, statutes or Government decrees may determine other persons who may be clients in certain matters, without any other condition (like personal involvement). In addition, the client's status may be provided also for civil organisations registered for representing and promoting certain fundamental rights or public interests. Thus, since 1995, a law recognised the right of environment-protection organisations to be parties in the relevant administrative procedures. However, the judicial practice narrowly interprets this empowerment.[18] It is a unique rule of the Code that all those public authorities may also participate in the administrative procedure, whose competences are affected by the case, unless they are themselves the decision making bodies.

The GRAPS obliges administrative authorities to launch a procedure at the client's request. Clients may submit a request to the competent authority verbally or in writing. Exclusive forms of requests are accepted as well, so as to an electronic form or an appropriate software may be defined by law to be used in special cases.

It is worth noting that the GRAPS determines procedural costs for 15 different items (like costs incurred in connection with the client's or witnesses' appearance, experts' fees, translation charges and so on). The most important items are procedural fees and administrative service fees to be paid by clients for the service. In a given procedure – depending on the act or the decree specifying the rules of the given procedure – clients should pay a procedural fee or administrative service fee for the service. Their amounts are determined by the special procedural rules, so they can be different on a case by case basis. These fees do not hinder ordinary citizens in launching administrative procedures, having regard to their low amounts, and the fact that the administrative authority may grant exemption from paying costs to any

17 LB Kf.II.2818/1997.

18 Attila Vincze, 'A közigazgatási jog europaizálódása és a felperesi legitimáció' in Balázs Gerencsér, Lilla Berkes and András Varga Zs (eds.), *A hazai és az uniós közigazgatási eljárásjog aktuális kérdései* (Pázmány Press 2015) 196.

individual who – due to his income and financial situation – is unable to pay for all or for part of the procedural costs.

Once somebody's application has been admitted to be decided, he or she is entitled to fair treatment and has the right for a decision to be adopted within the time limit prescribed by law.

3.1.2 The right to appeal

The Fundamental Law provides the right to appeal in its Art. XXVIII para 7 declaring that everyone has the right 'to seek legal remedy against any court, administrative or other official decision which violates his or her rights or legal interests'. The GRAPS grants the same right in the administrative procedure in its Chapter VIII under the title 'Legal Remedies'. Administrative decisions of the authorities may be appealed independently. GRAPS enables the clients to appeal against 'any decision in the first instance'.

General rules on administrative appeals are regulated by GRAPS. As a general rule the client may appeal against any administrative decision taken in the merits (called resolution) of the first instance. The client may present new facts and evidences in the recourse.

An appeal may be launched based on any kind of reasons why the client's rights or legitimate interests have been adversely affected. In special cases described by legislative acts, the client should present reasons for his or her appeal. Certain injunctions of the administrative body, like rejecting the request without the examination of the merit of the case, suspending or terminating the procedure, or imposing a procedural fine may be appealed by a separate recourse. In certain exceptional cases the possibility of an independent appeal against a first instance ruling may also be encouraged by legislative act if a third party is affected by the ruling.

The GRAPS excludes the right to appeal in cases where it is not permitted by a legislative act or a Government decree. The decision approving the agreement of the clients may not also be appealed as well as those administrative decisions which have been made by the representative body of a local government, or by higher-level administrative authorities like a minister or the head of a central agency. In these cases legal remedy is not excluded, but may be given by a court.

3.1.3 The right to administrative act within a reasonable time

One of the principles of the administrative procedure stated by GRAPS is that clients are entitled to receive fair treatment and have the right to a decision of the competent administrative body within the time limits prescribed by law. While the concept of 'reasonable time' is used as constitutional requirements by the Constitutional Court in certain areas, Hungarian administrative law always sets periods and deadlines for administrative procedures. As a general rule, administrative decisions on the merits of the case must be adopted within 21 days. A shorter time limit may be established by any form of legal regulation, whereas a longer one may be set only by a legislative act or Government decree.

Beside the right to appeal in such cases discussed above, the GRAPS contains several guarantees against the 'silence' of administration. It is a general requirement that the competent administrative body is obliged to settle every case falling within its range of responsibility. If it fails to decide within the period set by law, the client may turn to the superior authority which has to inquire the reason of the 'silence' within eight days, and may instruct the administrative body to conduct the procedure and to make a decision within 15 days. In case of a repeated failure, a disciplinary procedure against the head of the responsible public authority must be launched, and another administrative body must be designated to decide the case. When a local authority fails to decide, the supervisory authority calls it to settle the case within 15 days. Eventually, if all deadlines unsuccessfully expire, the court orders the competent authority to settle the case. In addition, unless law prescribes otherwise, if the client has applied for exercising a right, but the competent body has not decided the case within the legally set time limit, the omission of the administrative body is considered as if it would have approved that right, unless an adverse party is in the administrative procedure.

3.1.4 The right to access to the relevant documents

GRAPS states as a principle that administrative authorities must provide for the right to access to documents to clients and their representatives and other parties involved in the case. This right is subjected to restrictions specified by law. The right to access documents must be also applied if the client has previously not participated in the procedure. In the framework of access, the client is allowed to make copies or extracts of these documents, or may request paid copies. The exceptions are listed by the GRAPS, studying documents by a client is excluded if it comes to drafts of decisions and administrative regulations; documents containing data that make possible the identification of a person if the authority earlier ordered the close treatment of that person's personal data and address; documents containing so-called 'qualified data' – e.g. state secrets – without proper clearance for access or inspection; documents containing information that is protected by law. Providing these data can be denied if the lack of their knowledge will not prevent the client from exercising her rights.

Access to documents can be restricted upon a client's claim also. A client may request the limitation of the adverse party's right of access to the relevant documents with respect to the data expressly specified with a view to the protection of his personal data, business and other interests within reasonable limits. The administrative authority shall approve the request – upon carefully weighing the relevant circumstances of the case – if the lack of knowledge of the data in question will not impair the adverse party in exercising his rights conferred by law.

3.1.5 The right to counsel

The right to legal counsel is also recognised by the GRAPS. This means that the client is either assisted by the authority or by a legal representative. Administrative authorities themselves must give information to the client and other parties about their rights and obligations, in particular the clients without legal representation about the relevant rules pertaining to the case, the rights to which they are entitled to and the obligations to which they are bound, and also on the consequences for any breach of obligation, and on the availability of legal aid in case the client is an individual. In special cases with regard to the complexity of the case clients with legal representation may be required to meet certain obligations prescribed by law.

The notion of the right to legal counsel may be understood in a wide sense that it is possible to take actions in the administrative procedure through legal representative. The general rule is that representation – for example by an advocate – is possible except for cases when personal actions are required by law. GRAPS states that 'if the client is not required by law to proceed in person, the client may be substituted by his legal representative or proxy, and in all cases the client may proceed together with her representative. The same person may not represent the adverse party or parties'.

Contrary to court proceedings, clients usually do not have legal representatives in the administrative procedure. Representation before an administrative authority is not compulsory, it is rather a possibility. There are cases where legal or other type of representation is expressively excluded by law (marriage for example cannot be made through representatives). Legal aid given either by NGOs or by advocates is thus only a possibility for clients in general, but at the same time providing for legal aid is an obligation of administrative bodies. Furthermore, legal assistance is provided by the Legal Aid Service which is run by the Capital and County Government's Offices. The aim of the Legal Aid Service is to ensure the exercise of rights of those who are not capable to do so alone due to their unfavourable situation.

3.1.6 The right to be heard

The client has to be heard without exceptions as the GRAPS requires it declaring that the client has the right to make a statement in writing or verbally, or to refuse to make a statement in administrative procedures. It is quite common in constitutional complaint procedures that the claimant laments that his/her right to adequate hearing was violated in the administrative and also in the following court proceedings, but there are no cases when the Constitutional Court accepted this claim and invalidated an administrative act on this basis.

3.1.7 The right to adequate justification

The duty to give reasons for administrative decisions is laid down in the Fundamental Law of Hungary in its Art. XXIV para 1. One of the principles of the administrative procedures declared in the GRAPS is that 'administrative authorities shall contemplate in their proceedings the facts relevant to the case on hand, shall apply all evidence consistently with its weight, and shall base its decisions on the facts of the case'.

The obligation of giving reasons for a decision in its details is stated by the GRAPS enumerating the essential content of the administrative authority's decision. According to the relevant provision of the law, an administrative decision has to contain the relevant facts of the case and the underlying evidence; evidence presented by the client and found inadmissible, and the reason for this finding; for resolutions adopted under the principle of weighing and deliberation, the criteria and facts employed; reasons for any seizure carried out in the procedures; the statutes upon which the administrative authority has adopted the resolution; reference to the legal regulation conferring the authority's powers and competencies.

On the other hand, it is not necessary to give a statement of reasons in the decision if it approves the request in its entirety and if there is no adverse party in the case or the decision does not affect the rights or legal interests of the adverse party, or if the decision determines exclusively the time and date of a given step of the procedure, or if the content of the decision is exclusively the approval of an agreement of adverse parties.

4 Institutional perspective

By the adoption of the Fundamental Law (the new constitution) of 2011, the institutional system of legal protection of individual rights and legitimate interests has partially changed.[19]

4.1 Internal (administrative) protection of individual rights

The individual rights and legitimate interests are protected by a complex system of legal remedies. Legal protection of individual rights has internal and external mechanisms. In this context, internal protection means the tools of administrative bodies for eliminating unlawful acts and providing devices for clients to stand for their own rights and interests.

4.1.2 Administrative appeals

Unless otherwise prescribed by a legislative act or government decree, an administrative appeal must be lodged within 15 days following the date of delivery of the decision. The person entitled to appeal may resign this right.

The appeal must be submitted to the first instance administrative authority giving the chance to the decision maker to revise its own act. It is also noteworthy that the administrative body may withdraw or change its original decision not only if it finds it unlawful, but also when it agrees with the content of the recourse, unless adverse parties take part in the procedure. Such a decision must be delivered to the party filing the appeal, and to all other persons to whom the contested decision was delivered. It must also be noted that the decision making body, discerning that its decision has been illegal, may withdraw or change it within a year from its notification *ex officio*, if the decision has not been reviewed by any higher authority or court. Legitimate expectations are protected, however, as the decision maker may not do it, if the withdrawal or modification of the original decision would violate rights acquired and exercised in good faith.

The appeal has a suspensory effect in terms of the implementation of the act, except if the GRAPS itself declares it immediately enforceable or if the appellate authority has declared it enforceable abolishing the suspensory effect of the appeal. It is the case when the prompt implementation of the decision is necessary to prevent any life-threatening or potentially devastating situation or to mitigate any detrimental consequences, to maintain public order or for reasons of public security, and when any delay is likely to cause irreparable harm.

If the first instance administrative authority does not agree with the appeal, it has to forward it to the superior body vested with powers to judge the appeal with all

19 For a detailed description of these changes see Krisztina Rozsnyai, 'Änderungen im System des Verwaltungsrechtsschutzes in Ungarn' (2013) 65 *Öffentliche Verwaltung* 335–342.

documents attached within eight days following the deadline for appeal. It attaches also its own opinion about the appeal.

The appellate authority may sustain, reverse or overturn the first instance decision. In some cases defined by law, it may not establish an obligation more severe than what has been adopted in the decision of the first instance under the principle of *reformatio in peius*. Thus, this is not a general, but a special rule, claiming an explicit permission by law. If the available data and information is insufficient to adopt a decision in the second instance or if further evidence is shown up or required for the decision, the appellate body may annul the decision and order the administrative authority of the first instance to reopen the case or proceed to obtain additional evidence on its own accord and make a decision itself. The first instance decision may be annulled and a reconsideration may be ordered by the appellate body, if it thinks that further clients should also be called in the case. In the reopened procedure the first instance authority is bound by the operative part and by the justification of the decision of the second instance.

4.1.3 Complaint of individuals

One of the special procedures in administrative law is the complaint procedure. Legislative Act No CLXV of 2013 on the Complains and Notification of Public Interest gives the possibility for individuals to find a solution for their problems in certain cases. Complaint is a request aiming to cease the violation of an individual's right or interest if the case cannot be subject of an administrative procedure under the effect of GRAPS or of an administrative dispute before court. A complaint may include a suggestion as well. The practice of this new institution raises several questions and so far people are not very active in gaining the full effect of this possibility. The lack of information can be one of the reasons for the deficiencies of this institution, but reasons have also been found in the reserved mentality of the society *vis-à-vis* the State.

4.2 External protection of individual rights

4.2.1 Judicial protection

Administrative decisions are subject to judicial review, based on Art. XVIII para 1 (for judicial protection of individual rights and legal interests), and Art. 25 para 2 point (b) (for judicial review of administrative decisions) of the Fundamental Law of 2011. According to these constitutional provisions, any (natural or legal) person whose rights or legal interests have been directly affected by an administrative act, can bring a case to the court.

In Hungary, since 2013, enforceable administrative acts have been reviewed in the first instance by administrative and labour courts located on the seats of regional (county-level) courts (in the capital city Budapest and in the 19 counties). Thus, these are specialised ordinary, rather than separate administrative courts, as they are integrated into the organisational system of the uniform Judiciary. The competencies of administrative and labour courts cover administrative suits as stated in the legislative act on the civil procedure. Chapter XX (20) of this code under the title Administrative Lawsuits defines that an administrative suit may be filed for the revision of an administrative decision. The notion of administrative decision is defined by the same act with reference to the GRAPS. The lawfulness of administrative contracts are reviewed also by the administrative and labour courts, while state liability cases (claiming compensation for damages caused by an illegal administrative act) are judged by civil law courts.

In fact, administrative decisions only rarely are challenged before a court. Nevertheless, the exhaustion of all available administrative remedies is a precondition of the judicial review. The challenge of the administrative act before a court does not have a suspensory effect, though the plaintiff may ask the court to suspend the execution of the contested decision until the judgment of the court.

As a major rule, the court may annul the administrative decision if the administrative decision is found unlawful and may order the authority to reopen the case if it is necessary (cassatory power).[20] It is necessary then to distinguish the simple annulation of the administrative decision without ordering the administrative authority. In both cases the administrative authority is bound by the judgment of the court.

The court only annuls the administrative act if no further measures have to be taken applying the respective rules. If the administrative authority is not ordered to reopen the case the only consequence of the judgment is that the administrative decision is not enforceable. If it was already enforced, all must be repaired that had been done as a result of the reviewed administrative decision. For example, if the administrative decision was enforceable and the client had to pay to the state budget, this amount is reimbursed. Enforcement of the judgment is the responsibility of the administrative authority involved in the case that had taken actions following the orders of the decision.

If the administrative decision is annulled and the case is reopened, the administrative body begins a new procedure and makes a new decision accordingly to the judgment. This usually happens if the procedural rules were violated, for example relevant facts of the case in the decision making process were not ascertained or evidences were disregarded. Judicial ruling is enforced by the administrative authority of first instance that took the annulled decision. Enforcement is assured by the operation of the hierarchical administrative structure itself because if law is not respected by an administrative authority – including the disregard of the ruling of the court – the superior organ in the hierarchy has to intervene and to order for action. The execution of the judicial decision is encouraged also via disciplinary responsibility of civil servants. It means that disciplinary procedure has to be launched against the defaulter that can be the civil servant or even the leader of the respective administrative authority.

The relevant chapter of the Code of Civil Law Procedure grants full power to the courts in those cases where the competent administrative authority has only a minimal discretionary power (like in tax or social security cases), or if a national-level public authority is the first instance decision maker (without superior authority). The proportion of these judicial cases is estimated as more than a half of all administrative disputes before the courts.[21] The cases where courts are entitled to modify the final

20 The Legislative Act No. III of 1952 on the Civil Procedure defines that 'unless otherwise provided by legislative Act, court annuls the administrative decision and orders the administrative authority that took the resolution to reopen the case if it is necessary'.

21 Péter Darák, 'Administrative justice in Hungary' in András Patyi and Ádám Rixer (eds.), *Hungarian Public Administration and Administrative Law* (Schenk Verlag 2014) 222.

administrative decision in the merits after reviewing the procedure are enumerated by legislative acts.[22] In these cases, the court may change the administrative decision. According to the law, the administrative decisions adopted in discretionary power may be overruled if the decision making administrative body has not established sufficiently the facts of the case, or has not complied with the relevant procedural rules, the criteria of the discretion may not be identified, or the evaluation of evidences has not been reasonable. It is to be noted that not all procedural irregularities may lead to annulment, but only those which affected the final decision on the merit of the case. However, as general experience shows, the courts are usually reluctant to change the reviewable acts.[23]

When the court finds the contested administrative decision lawful, its execution is the responsibility of the respective administrative body in the same way as if the decision would have not been appealed.

Appeals lodged against the judgments of administrative and labour courts are decided in the second instance by regional (ordinary) courts in the country of Hungary and in Budapest.

The judgments of the administrative and labour courts may be appealed only exceptionally, mainly in those cases, in which no administrative appeal was permitted (typically when the administrative decision was made by an authority having national competence). In the latter cases the regional courts have competence (until 2012, the Administrative and Labour Court of the Capital City had an exclusive power in appellate cases. It is worth noting that in regional appeal courts (except for the court in the capital Budapest) there is no specialisation among the judges for administrative matters which is not favourable for effective judicial protection.

The judgments of the appellate courts may also be challenged with an explicit reference to a violation of law, by an extraordinary remedy lodged at the Supreme Court (*Kúria*) within 60 days from their notification. It is a purely legal review, checking the compliance with law; the Supreme Court may not examine the evidence of the case, and may only annul (partially or totally) the contested judicial (and not the administrative!) decision. For this task, a separate administrative-labour law department exists in the Supreme Court.

It is notable that in recent years the dispute about the establishment of the real (separate) administrative courts has intensified,[24] and the Government set up a special commission for codifying a separate code for procedural rules of administrative disputes. The planned reform would significantly transform the system of appeals against administrative decisions.[25] The basic objectives of reform proposals

22 For example: declaration of status of refugee, authorisation of adoption or its rejection, statement of obligation to pay in tax and custom administration, etc. Other examples are enumerated by various legislative acts.

23 Rozsnyai Krisztina, 'Külön, de mégis együtt. A közigazgatási perjog és a közigazgatási eljárásjog.' in Gerencsér Balázs, Berkes Lilla and Varga Zs. András (eds.), *A hazai és az uniós közigazgatási eljárásjog aktuális kérdései* (Pázmány Press 2015) 163.

24 See e.g. Varga Zs. András and Fröhlich Johanna (eds.), *Közérdekvédelem: A közigazgatási bíráskodás múltja és jövője* (PPKE JÁK–KIM 2011); and Herbert Küpper, 'Magyarország átalakuló közigazgatási bíráskodása' (2014) 59 *MTA Law Working Papers*.

25 One of the arguments for simplifying the appellate procedures is that in the jurisprudence of the Constitutional Court the single-stage appeal system satisfies the requirements of the right to appeal.

are to accelerate the whole decision making process, and to settle the administrative cases as soon as possible. For this purpose, one of the recommendations is to make the administrative recourse exceptional, and, instead, to transform the separate administrative courts as general appellate authorities.[26] The idea of abolishment of administrative recourse as a general form of appeal and its replacement with judicial review raises some concerns, especially if the administrative court will have full power to change the administrative acts. In this way, the courts could step into the shoes of administration, as legality control should necessarily extend to a complete reconsideration of the case putting burdens on the courts. So, what is won by the exclusion of administrative appeal, might be lost by the long and complicated judicial process, if the courts have to take over the job of the administrative appeal.[27]

As a very recent development, the standards of administrative justice have significantly been reduced in special cases, mainly in asylum cases, after a new type of state of emergency was introduced by law for the 'mass migration crisis' in order to respond the flow of migrants and refugees entering into the territory of Hungary. The new legislation has introduced extraordinary short deadlines and serious sanctions for judging the requests of asylum-seekers and migrants.[28]

4.2.2 Constitutional complaint

The Hungarian Fundamental Law has significantly modified the competencies of the Constitutional Court and the role of the different constitutional institutions in constitutional adjudication. Among several changes, it introduced three types of constitutional complaints and abolished the former existing *actio popularis*. The system of *actio popularis* meant a legal possibility that anyone could turn to the Constitutional Court claiming that a law, legal provision or regulation is contrary to a constitutional provision and requesting its annulment. Constitutional complaint, under the former jurisdiction, was to be lodged only in case of personal injury caused by the application of an unconstitutional norm.

The aim of the new constitutional complaint mechanisms was to protect against personal injuries caused by ordinary courts or caused in administrative procedures and not cured by courts. Constitutional complaint provides a possibility for constitutional review also in cases where the complainant cannot turn to ordinary courts also in administrative matters. Moreover, the Constitutional Court may supervise the constitutionality of legal provisions when they, applied in certain judicial cases, lead to an unconstitutional court decision. Besides, the new system encourages civil petitioners to turn to the ombudsman in order to initiate the ombudsman's procedure

---

Moreover, the appellate body must be independent to the organ whose act must be reviewed. Certainly, the legislator may determine more appellate forums for certain cases. See 22/1995. (III. 31.) CC decision.

26 *Részletes jelentés az általános közigazgatási rendtartás koncepciójának előkészzítéséről.* [Manuscript]. Source: Ministry of Justice. file:///C:/Users/Szente/Downloads/20150514%20Jelent%C3%A9s%20az%20%C3%A1ltal%C3%A1nos%20k%C3%B6zigazgat%C3%A1si%20rendtart%C3%A1s%20koncepci%C3%B3j%C3%A1r%C3%B3l.pdf.

27 Rozsnyai (n. 23) 160.

28 See the Law No CXLII of 2015 on the modification of the Asylum Act (No LXXX of 2007).

to question the constitutionality of a legal provision before the Constitutional Court. As a result of the introduction of the new types of constitutional complaint, ordinary courts must also show an elevated awareness to questions of constitutionality among the ordinary waves of legal adjudication with regard to the new control mechanism that easily sheds light on the deficiencies of fundamental rights' adjudication. Judicial referral as it existed formerly stayed in force, which means that judges in pending cases turn to the Constitutional Court in case they state that an applicable piece of law is unconstitutional.[29]

In constitutional complaint procedure the Constitutional Court reviews the compliance of the law applied in the given case or of a court decision with the Fundamental Law. So far many appeals have been launched in administrative matters ending with a court procedure, but the case law shows that only few of them gained admission, and were adjudicated in the merits. This means that this legal instrument is not very effective. This phenomenon can be reasoned either with poor petitions or with the very strict admission rules of the constitutional complaint procedure. Furthermore, if the review procedure of the administrative decision by the courts was not violating fundamental rights, it is almost impossible to reach back to the procedure of the administrative authorities and examine it from a constitutionality point of view.

4.2.3 The role of the Commissioner for Fundamental Rights

Although the *actio popularis* ceased to exist in Hungarian law, the Commissioner for Fundamental Rights (parliamentary ombudsman) may initiate a proceeding for an *ex-post facto* review of law before the Constitutional Court.

The ombudsman has wide-ranging powers to investigate the work of administrative authorities, and may initiate various proceedings for redress of infringements of rights or legitimate interests of individuals. In particular, his or her measures and recommendations might have an important role in the protection of rights of vulnerable people.

Proceedings start primarily upon complaints from citizens, but the Commissioner may, when justified, start proceedings *ex officio* as well, or on the proposal of the Deputy Commissioner responsible for the interests of futures generations or on that of the Deputy Commissioner responsible for the protection of the rights of nationalities living in Hungary. The possible methods of inquiry have not changed substantially under the new act on the legal status of Commissioner adopted in 2011. The methods applied are chosen by the Commissioner from among a wide variety of possibilities ranging from simple requests for data to on-site inspections without previous notification. The Commissioner for Fundamental Rights may apply any legal means which are necessary to discover the factual and legal background of a case. Although the recommendations and proposals of the Commissioner are not binding on the executive organs under his or her inquiry, the latters are bound to cooperate, and if they fail to do so, the Commissioner will put it on record in his report. The report is presented to the Parliament and the public will be informed thereof by the annual report of the ombudsman.

29 3033/2013. (II. 12.) CC decision.

4.2.4 The public prosecutor as a defender of public interests

The public prosecutor controls the legality of final or enforceable decisions made by administrative authorities in case the decision was not reviewed by a court. This *ex officio* competence is often initiated by the individuals when it seems to be an effective way to reach legal protection in their case.

If the public prosecutor finds any violation of law that affects the decision of an administrative authority in the merits, he takes an objection against the decision in order to cease the violation of law. The objection can be taken in one year after that the decision became legally binding. The public prosecutor may suggest the suspension of the decision's execution in the objection. In such a case suspension of the execution is compulsory. The objection must be addressed to the superior of the decision making authority and if no response arrives the public prosecutor is entitled to turn to the court against the decision.[30]

However, the relevant competences have apparently been conferred to the public prosecutor for a more effective defence of the objective legal order and for the promotion of public interests, rather than for the protection of individual rights.

4.2.5 Procedure of equal treatment authority

Special form of legal protection in administrative law is the promotion of the equal treatment and the protection of equal opportunities in administrative procedures. It is assured by an administrative authority, the Equal Treatment Authority. Its status is 'autonomous administrative authority' meaning that it is not subordinated to the central government even though it is a part of state administration. One can turn to this authority if one's right to equal treatment is violated by an administrative authority (or any other organisations except for the Parliament, Government, Courts, Constitutional Court, State Audit Office). Violation of the requirement of equal treatment or discrimination is defined by the Legislative Act No CXXV of 2003 on Equal Treatment and the Support of Equal Opportunities.

4.2.6 State liability for the actions of administrative authorities and courts

The responsibility of public administration is one of the most underdeveloped fields of law that may hinder gaining full effect for the principle of effective legal protection. However, the experience shows that it is quite difficult and complicated to justify the claim during a civil law proceeding in practice. The main problem is the underdevelopment of the theory of the responsibility of public administration.[31] One can turn to ordinary courts for compensation of damage caused by an administrative act (or by the lack of a decision). Ordinary courts make their decision applying the Civil Code in a civil procedure if the decision of an administrative authority is illegal, causes damages and all possible legal remedies were utilised in the administrative procedure and before the administrative court without success. So far, there have not been many cases where the responsibility of the state has been acknowledged.[32]

30 See Art. 29 of the Legislative Act No CLXIII of 2011 on the Prosecution Services.

31 Beatrix Borbás, *A bírói hatalom kárfelelőssége* (Hvg-Orac 2014) 23, 210.

32 Ibid., 140.

5 Conclusions

The establishment of administrative courts in 2011 – that started their operation in 2012 – is one of the most important issues in Hungarian administrative law related to the principle of effective legal protection. The other one is the responsibility of administrative bodies and courts.

According to the dominant view in Hungarian administrative law, the general function of judicial review of administrative acts is not only the legal protection of private interests, but also the defence of the 'objective legal order'.[33] This approach is based on Art. 25 para 2 point (b) of the Fundamental Law declaring that the '[courts shall decide on: (. . .) the lawfulness of administrative decisions]'. This Article requires the courts to control the legality of administrative acts in general, not only in case of an infringement of the rights and interests of private parties. Some provisions on administrative trials, like the rules on *ex officio* procedures or the fact that administrative acts can be challenged by the Public Prosecutor's offices, and even by other administrative authorities, enforce the effective legal protection of the 'objective legal order'.

Notwithstanding, it should be noted that in recent times, the claim for the protection of the objective legal order as a basic function of judicial review has been associated with the efforts for establishing special procedural code for administrative disputes, instead of the present situation, when the civil procedural rules are used as supplementary in these proceedings and the administrative court procedure is regulated in the code of civil procedure. The main argument for the change is that because the functions of administrative judges (including the defence of the objective legality) differ from those of the civil courts (adjudicating competing private interests), they need special procedural rules reflecting this difference.[34]

With the ongoing codification of the new procedural rules for administrative judicial review, important issues will be reconsidered in the Hungarian legal system with regard to the effective legal protection in administrative law. It is certainly too early to judge whether the outcome of the codification will be successful, but it is to be emphasised that it will bring important implications for the future settlement of the above discussed issues.

33 Krisztina Rozsnyai, 'A hatékony jogvédelem biztosítása a közigazgatási bíráskodásban' (2013) 1 *Acta Humana* 120–123.

34 Rozsnyai (n. 23) 149–167.

10 The principle of effective legal protection in Italian administrative law

Fulvio Cortese

1 Historical developments

In the Italian legal order, the principle of effective legal protection for the citizens against the public administration could be considered the result of a long and sketchy evolution. In addition, the development of this principle has been following different paths, depending on its twofold nature: the effectiveness of access to justice, on the one hand, and the guarantees connected to procedures in which the public administration exercises its powers, on the other.

First of all, it is worth highlighting that there is no explicit and general definition or formalisation of the principle that can adapt to and sum up both dimensions of these guarantees.

A clear definition of effectiveness in the context of access to justice, for example, might be found in the law regulating the judicial review of administrative action: Art. 1 of the Italian Code of administrative trials and proceedings[1] (*Codice del processo amministrativo*; hereinafter Code) is entitled 'Effectiveness' and it provides that '[t]he administrative jurisdiction grants a complete and effective legal protection in accordance with the principles set out in the Constitution and in European Union law'.[2]

On the other hand, a corresponding definition cannot be found within the context of administrative procedure, even though the Italian law on this matter (no. 241/1990) lists and guarantees the rights of the individual with regard to the exercise of public powers.[3]

Moreover, it is worth noting that, in Italian administrative law, the principle of effective legal protection has always been influenced by the profound and complex legal debate on the nature of so-called 'legitimate interest' (*interesse legittimo*).[4] This is, even now, the definition of the individual legal position before the exercise of public powers. However, the concept was originally created only for the purposes of trials, to ease

1 Legislative decree no. 104/2010.

2 About this legislative provision see Stefano Salvatore Scoca, 'L'effettività della tutela nell'azione di annullamento' (2012) 4 *Diritto processuale amministrativo* 1397.

3 For an overview, see Giandomenico Falcon, *Lezioni di diritto amministrativo* (Cedam 2013) volume 1, 67; Marcello Clarich, *Manuale di diritto amministrativo* (Bologna, ilMulino 2013) 225.

4 Ibid. 78; Mario Nigro, *Giustizia amministrativa* (Bologna, ilMulino 2002) 93. See the theoretical and historical reconstruction of Franco Gaetano Scoca, *Contributo sulla figura dell'interesse legittimo* (Milano, Giuffrè 1990).

access to administrative justice for the individual. It was only in a second instance that the notion of legitimate interest became relevant on this substantial viewpoint as well.

In particular, the concept of legitimate interest – which is enshrined in the Constitution too – is the result of the elaboration by legal scholars and judges, who began to firmly develop the notion since the very origin of the Italian State and, in particular, starting from the difficult enforcement of the relevant provision of law no. 2248/1865.[5] This law provided that civil or political rights were part of ordinary judges' jurisdiction, whereas 'all other legal affairs' (meaning those not included in the notion of civil or political rights) had to be considered as part of administrative jurisdiction. Following the prevailing interpretation at the time, these 'other legal affairs' arose whenever the public administration was acting as a public authority (*iure imperiii*); therefore, the individual could not resort to the common (ordinary) judge, but had the option to start other purely administrative remedies, within the same administration that adopted the act in question.

In this context, the legal position of the citizen was soon defined as legitimate interest and this notion was also used during the debates for the enactment of law no. 5992/1889, on the institution of the IV section of the Council of State (*Consiglio di Stato*).[6] This is the act on the creation of administrative jurisdiction. It has the aim, indeed, of giving administrative courts the power to enforce and protect this kind of individual positions; its jurisdictional function was definitively made clear by a royal decree in 1907.[7] It was this process that created the idea of legitimate interest as an instrumental notion for those cases in which some specific 'legal affairs' could be brought before a special judge. This concept was mixed with the current idea of *locus standi* and was aimed at introducing a trial that, with the rare exception of cases in which the jurisdiction extended also to substantial matters, was limited to the strict evaluation of the legitimacy of the public administration's acts, which could be challenged just for violation of the law (*violazione di legge*), lack of competence (*incompetenza*) and 'abuse of power' (*eccesso di potere*, i.e. *ultra vires*).

This framework was maintained even after the entry into force of the Constitution (1948), which, apart from taking into account the present status of this evolution, forced interpreters to reconsider, in the light of constitutional principles, the entire system and to adopt, especially from the 1970s onwards, a new understanding of the notion of legitimate interest, in more 'substantial' terms. This new viewpoint, in its multifaceted variations, gave rise to two trends, which developed in parallel, but at different speeds, and were only completed in the last 20 years.

The first one concerns the progressive understanding of the concept of legitimate interest as a subjective situation that could play an important function of legal protection for the citizen not only in trial terms, but also from the perspective of the definition of the individual's rights and means towards the public administration. This trend found normative enforcement in abovementioned law no. 241/1990, which, dealing with the discipline of the procedures that any public administration should

5 Aldo Travi, *Lezioni di giustizia amministrativa* (Torino, Giappichelli 2014) 18. A deeper analysis is offered by Salvatore Sambataro, *L'abolizione del contenzioso amministrativo nel sistema di giustizia amministrativa* (Milano, Giuffrè 1977).

6 Travi (n. 4) 29. Originally the Council of State (with its three sections) had only consultative functions.

7 Ibid. 34.

follow while exercising its powers, affirmed the existence of specific rights for the citizen in the relationship with public administration. This assumption gave rise, on the one hand, to the idea that these procedural rights represent the core (the substance) of legitimate interest and, on the other hand, to the idea that the guarantees thereby provided by law give shape to a very general principle of 'due process' (specifically aimed at establishing the need for the effectiveness of these guarantees and for the unrenounceable nature of some essential prerogatives, such as participation and the right to express one's opinions and defences).[8]

The second trend developed through the progressive enlargement of concretely accessible remedies for the individual, as the owner of the legitimate interest within the administrative trial. In fact, the administrative trial has gradually faced a process of transformation, offering the citizen not only the traditional level of guarantee – based on the option of challenging administrative acts and decisions on the grounds of legitimacy – but also the option of obtaining compensation for damages[9] and, lately, of sentencing (in some circumstances, but not only in the case of 'silence' of public bodies) the administration to adopt the act required. As a consequence, it is often stated that the administrative trial has undergone an evolution, from a 'trial on the act' (i.e. on the legitimacy of administrative action) to a 'trial on the relationship between administration and citizens' (i.e. a trial aimed at verifying what is in the citizen's responsibility and what is within the administration's powers).[10]

This complex evolution is the product of the influence of the principles of effectiveness and completeness of legal protection as expressed in EU directives on public procurements and of the synergy between the need to enforce these principles and the interpretation given by case law and legal scholars.[11] Most of them had actually affirmed that within the administrative trial the citizen should be granted legal protection not only with regards to his (legal and patrimonial) position against administrative acts, but also with reference to the existence of an interest in obtaining a concretely useful act, that could properly respond to his needs.[12]

2 Constitutional framework

Keeping in mind the historical evolution of effective legal protection as expressed above, from the constitutional viewpoint, the relevant framework concerning the

8 The principle of due process in administrative law gradually took a constitutional relevance. See Laura Buffoni, 'Il rango costituzionale del giusto procedimento e l'archetipo del processo' (2009) 2 *Quaderni costituzionali* 277.

9 The generalisation of the liability rule in the Italian administrative law took place from a famous decision of the Court of Cassation (*Corte di Cassazione*): 22 July 1999, n. 500. For a comment, see Luisa Torchia, 'La risarcibilità degli interessi legittimi: dalla foresta pietrificata al bosco di Birnam' (1999) 9 *Giornale di diritto amministrativo* 843. In general, see Falcon (n. 2) 246; Clarich (n. 2) 287.

10 Bruno Sassani, *Dal controllo del potere all'attuazione del rapporto: ottemperanza amministrativa e sentenza civile* (Milano, Giuffrè 1997); Diego Vaiano, *Pretesa di provvedimento e processo amministrativo* (Milano, Giuffrè 2002). For a general reconstruction see Mariano Protto, *Il rapporto amministrativo* (Milano, Giuffrè 2008).

11 E.g. Mariano Protto, *L'effettività della tutela giurisdizionale nelle procedure di aggiudicazione di appalti pubblici: Studio sull'influsso dell'integrazione europea sulla tutela giurisdizionale degli operatori economici nei confronti delle amministrazioni nazionali* (Milano, Giuffrè 1997); Stefano Tarullo, *Il giusto processo amministrativo: Studio sull'effettività della tutela giurisdizionale nella prospettiva europea* (Milano, Giuffrè 2004).

12 E.g. Leonardo Ferrara, 'Domanda giudiziale e potere amministrativo. L'azione di condanna al facere' (2013) 3 *Diritto processuale amministrativo* 617.

principle of effectiveness of legal protection for the individual against public administration can be considered in two different perspectives.

With regard to the effectiveness of jurisdictional protection for administrative action, the core of the guarantee is set by Art. 24.1 of the Constitution: '[e]veryone can take judicial action to protect individual rights and legitimate interests'. This means, first of all, complete access to justice and, as provided also by law, also includes the principle of concentration of all legal protections before a specific judge.[13]

In this regard, Art. 103.1, has enshrined into the Constitution the distinction between ordinary and administrative court. Therefore, the ordinary is the one responsible for the protection of individual rights, whereas the other (a special court) is the guardian of legitimate interests. This provision goes further, affirming that, with regard to some specific subjects, the law could devolve upon administrative courts the protection of individual rights as well. This is the so-called principle of 'exclusive jurisdiction' (*giurisdizione esclusiva*) devolved to the administrative courts; subject matters included in this definition are now enumerated by the Code.[14] Nevertheless, as stated by the Italian Constitutional Court in its decision no. 204/2004, this possibility is limited to those cases in which it is concretely difficult to distinguish between individual rights and legitimate interests and in which the public administration can intervene exercising its authoritative power.

The guarantee provided by Art. 24.1 of the Constitution, moreover, has always been interpreted as a limit to the possibility, for the law-maker, to entertain a hypothesis of 'conditioned jurisdiction' (*giurisdizione condizionata*), meaning those cases in which the law requires a compulsory preliminary activation of proceedings or remedies of any nature, that could make access to justice for the individual more difficult or even impossible. This limit could only be overtaken, in the opinion of the Constitutional Court, through very precise dispositions, which are very unlikely to be widely interpreted, except in the case of particular general interests to be protected, or in the case of risks of abuse, or for specific social interests or, finally, for higher reasons of justice.[15]

The principle of full access to justice is also connected, in the field of administrative justice, to Art. 113.2 of the Constitution which states that '[s]uch judicial protection may not be excluded or limited in particular kinds of appeal or for particular categories of acts'. Based on this article, legal scholars are still very strict towards those provisions that exclude jurisdictional action for so-called 'political acts'.[16]

The principle of the effectiveness of legal protection for administrative acts is also enforced, at a constitutional level, by those provisions regarding individual judges. These are, in particular, in Art. 24.2[17] and in Art. 111, paragraphs 1, 2 and 6[18] of the Constitution.

13 This profile has been clarified by the Constitutional Court (06 July 2004, no. 204).

14 See Art. 133.

15 See Francesco Paolo Luiso, *Diritto processuale civile* (Milano, Giuffrè 2009) volume 1, 27–30.

16 For a wide and recent review of this topic see Giuseppe Tropea, 'Genealogia, comparazione e decostruzione di un problema ancora aperto: l'atto politico' (2012) *Diritto processuale amministrativo* 329; Luca Buscema, 'Atti politici e principio di giustiziabilità dei diritti e degli interessi' (2014) 1(1) *Rivista AIC* (available at http://www.rivistaaic.it/atti-politici-e-principio-di-giustiziabilit-dei-diritti-e-degli-interessi.html) accessed 19 October 2014.

17 'The right to defence is inviolable at every stage and moment of the proceedings.'

18 '1. The law shall be administered by means of a fair trial governed by Act of Parliament. 2. The parties to all trials may speak in their own defence in the presence of the other parties, with an equal status,

The latter provisions are the results of a profound constitutional reform, enacted by constitutional law no. 1/1999, which, following the influence of the case law of the European Court of Human Rights, was aimed at expressly acknowledging some general principles which were already (even though implicitly) contained in Art. 24.1–2 of the Constitution.[19]

The effectiveness of legal protection for administrative acts, moreover, is granted, at a constitutional level, by all of those general provisions from which interpreters have derived a correspondence between those constitutional contents which were originally envisaged for the ordinary jurisdiction, but that are applicable even in the case of administrative jurisdiction. For example, reading together Art. 28 and. 24.1 of the Constitution, a solid basis for the constitutional guarantee of a compensatory remedy also for breach of legitimate interests can be postulated which was first acknowledged by the case law and the law maker.

Besides, it is worth mentioning that Art. 117.1 Const. states that '[l]egislative powers shall be vested in the State and the Regions in compliance with the Constitution and with the constraints deriving from EU legislation and international obligations'. This means that legal protection of individual rights and legitimate interests, as provided for by law (not only in the field of trial proceedings), must be pursued in accordance not only with constitutional principles, but also with the standards of the EU and the ECtHR.[20] Art. 1 of the Code represents the legislative statement of this principle. Differently, the Constitution does not contain any express rule concerning the effectiveness of the substantial guarantees provided for by the law for the citizen against the administrative power. Nevertheless, the Italian Constitutional Court has qualified those general principles (and the principle of due process too) expressed by law no. 241/1990 as materially constitutional principles,[21] that is as a specific enforcement by law of those more general principles provided by the Constitution.[22] Law no. 241/1990, in fact, provides that the law itself shall single out 'the guarantees for the citizens towards the public administration' and that 'these guarantees are defined by the general principles established by law'. More precisely, these are all of those guarantees that could be set forth just by the law maker at a state level and that could not find a different discipline at a regional level, because they are an expression of the essential level of benefits that, according to the Constitution, must be uniformly protected throughout the country. Among these guarantees, the following provisions of law no. 241/1990 are included: those on the 'duty of the public administration to ensure the participation of stakeholders to the whole path of the administrative procedure, identify a person responsible for the procedure, to conclude the procedure within the given time limit and to ensure access to all

---

before an independent and impartial court. An Act of Parliament shall lay down provisions to ensure that trials are of a reasonable length. 6. All judicial decisions must be motivated'.

19 Marta Mengozzi, *Giusto processo e processo amministrativo: Profili costituzionali* (Milano, Giuffrè 2009) 3.

20 Silvia Mirate, *Giustizia amministrativa e Convenzione europea dei diritti dell'uomo: l'"altro" diritto europeo in Italia, Francia e Inghilterra* (Napoli, Jovene 2007); Miriam Allena, *Art. 6 CEDU: procedimento e processo amministrativo* (Napoli, Editoriale Scientifica 2012).

21 E.g. Constitutional Court, 23.03.2007, no. 104.

22 Art. 97. See Buffoni (n. 8), especially for the traditional arguments of scholars in this perspective; Franco Gaetano Scoca, 'Amministrazione pubblica e diritto amministrativo nella giurisprudenza costituzionale' (2012) 1-2 *Diritto amministrativo* 21.

administrative documents, and those provisions regarding the maximum length of administrative procedure'.[23]

At the same time, since the law maker is obligated to respect the limits deriving from the EU legal order, the law no. 241/1990 might also be considered part of this duty. This provision in fact recalls, among the general principles of administrative action, those also related to the EU order and leaves for the interpreter the option of identifying them specifically.

3 Rights-based perspective

3.1 The parties' rights in the administrative proceedings

As for the administrative procedure, the law no. 241/1990 contains specific rules and principles guaranteeing individual rights and privileges for the effectiveness of legal protection.

One of them is the right to obtain a decision within a due time limit.[24] The law no. 241 provides that the individual may – in case when the competent administrative body does not pursue its duties – launch a surrogate procedure before the same body or access to judicial remedies. Moreover, in certain sorts of procedures, the law provides for the right to obtain, in the case of undue delay of the decision making administrative body, a €30 forfeiture compensation for every day of delay.[25]

The law provides also the right to receive a notification about any administrative procedure.[26] All those who are affected by the administrative act to be adopted should get such a notification. This communication must contain the information about the competent administration, the object of the procedure, the due time for its conclusion, the person responsible for the procedure and the office to contact for more information, to view or register relevant documents, acts or testimonials. Another right is the entitlement to intervene into a particular administrative procedure and to register and deposit acts or documents. All stakeholders are entitled to do so. The law recognises also the right to have access to every administrative document useful to protect one's legal interest or position. In case of denial or silence, the law provides for the option of making an action before the administrative court or before the local Ombudsman or before the National Commission for access to administrative acts.[27]

23 Giuseppe Morbidelli, 'Regioni e principi generali del diritto amministrativo' (2010) 1 *Diritto e società* 81.

24 Art. 2. The deadline for the decision is usually 30 days since the citizen's request.

25 See the Decree no. 69/2013.

26 See the Law no. 241/1990.

27 There is another form of right of access in the Italian administrative law, especially in the context of the rules on transparency of public administration. It was provided by legislative decree no. 33/2013 (Art. 5) and is called 'civic access'. In particular, the law provides that anyone has *per se* a right to have access to a wide range of information and documents. See Mario Savino, 'La nuova disciplina della trasparenza amministrativa' 8-9 (2013) *Giornale di diritto amministrativo* 795; Anna Simonati, 'La trasparenza amministrativa e il legislatore: un caso di entropia normativa?' (2013) 4 *Diritto amministrativo* 749; Enrico Carloni, *L'amministrazione aperta: Regole, strumenti, limiti dell'open government* (Rimini, Maggioli 2014) 231.

The duty of the decision making body to give reasons of its act (with the exception of normative and general acts) is also provided as well as the right to the notification of the denial of the request as a condition of the validity of the act.

All of these rights – aimed at ensuring citizens' participation, the right to express one's opinion and defences during the procedure, efficiency, transparency, publicity and the economy of public actions – must be granted both for every administrative procedure whatever their nature (revocation, *ex officio* annulment or validation) is.

Nevertheless, the omission of some of these guarantees (for example, the omission of the guarantee on the right to communication) does not entail *per se* the voidness of the final act: the court may concretely evaluate if the result of the final decision of the administration would have been different if full participation were ensured to all stakeholders. Just in this hypothesis, the court could declare the act void.[28]

3.2 Access to courts

With reference to access to justice, the principle of effectiveness is realised through the recognition of a set of rights for the citizen:

(a) The right to a judge pre-established by law:[29] the judge called to decide the litigation has to be the one established by law in general and preventive terms; in other words, it is only for the law to determine, in the abstract, the relevant jurisdictional body and judges' competences; this could be done only before the litigation arises. The pre-establishment of the judge is functional to the realisation of the principle of impartiality of the jurisdictional function.

(b) The right to claim: this could be intended as the faculty for the individual owner of a legitimate interest to make an action before the administrative court, in order (1) to challenge, within a 60-day time limit, an illegitimate act of the administration (on the grounds of breach of law, lack of competences or 'abuse of power') and to obtain its *ex tunc* (retrospective) annulment;[30] (2) to obtain, within the prescribed 180-day time limit, the declaration of invalidity (*nullità*) of an administrative act (in the cases provided by the law); (3) to be able to sentence, within one year from the expiration of the deadline given to the administration by the legislation for the adoption of a specific act, the public administration to give an answer (or to adopt a certain act in all of those cases in which the use of a discretionary power is not required); (4) to be able to sentence, within a 120-day time limit, the administration to pay compensatory damages deriving from the adoption of an illegitimate act (or deriving from the administration's 'silence'). This remedy could be activated even without a previous challenge of the detrimental administrative act;[31] (5) sentencing, within the 60-day time limit that the law provides for the challenge of a denial, the administration to adopt a specific

28 Art. 21 octies. See Falcon (n. 2) 149.

29 Art. 25.1 of the Constitution.

30 See the relevant provisions of the Law no. 241/1990 and the Code.

31 However, the law provides that the judge could even decide not to compensate damages, if it is proved that the damage could have been avoided if the citizen would have promptly challenged the detrimental administrative act.

measure (with the exception of those cases in which the public administration has to use its discretionary power – see (3) above); (6) to obtain a precautionary measure, which normally goes together with the complaint indicated sub no. 1 above, but which could also be granted by the judge *ante causam*, if necessary; (7) to obtain the implementation of the decision of an administrative or ordinary judge, even before it becomes final (this is known as 'compliance judgment', *giudizio d'ottemperanza*).

(c) The right to defence: for the citizen, this includes the option of giving a personal account to the judge, but also access (at the same conditions as the administration) to evidence, as provided by law, and to further remedies, such as the 'additional reasons claim' (*ricorso per motivi aggiunti*)[32] or 'incidental claim' (*ricorso incidentale*), which is accessible both to the administration and to the subjects that have an interest in the preservation of the challenged act (it's a sort of 'counterclaim').

(d) The right to appeal: it is the right to claim before the Council of State (*Consiglio di Stato*) the decisions of first instance administrative tribunals, which have been instituted by the main administrative centre of each Region since 1971; first instance decisions could be challenged within 60 days from the official communication of the decision to the parties. The decisions of the Council of State can be challenged before the Court of Cassation (*Corte di cassazione*). This possibility is limited to jurisdictional reasons (see Art. 111.9 of the Constitution); in other words, the Court of Cassation could decide just on the correct identification of the jurisdiction (that is, to decide whether it was legally correct that the decision was undertaken by the administrative judge instead of by the ordinary one).

(e) The right to access extraordinary means of appeal (in some specific circumstances), against final decisions: these are *ricorso per revocazione* and *opposizione di terzo*; the first one is aimed to challenge judiciary decisions that, for example, have been pronounced on the grounds of grave mistake of fact, on the basis of evidences which have been later declared to be false or mistakes caused by the malice of the parties or of the judge; differently, the second remedy is accessible for those that could not participate to the legal proceeding in which a detrimental decision has been adopted and become final.

Moreover, it is worth noting that, in order to ensure the effectiveness of legal protection for the citizen against the public administration, the law provides that an error in identifying the correct (ordinary or administrative) jurisdiction does not jeopardise the effects of the issues presented before the judge, except for the decadence of the effects intervened in the meantime.

In addition, the provision of several 'special trials' (i.e. in case of 'silence' of the administration, or for the protection of the right to have access to administrative documents, for the challenge of some specific acts, such as those regarding public procurements, or for electoral litigations, etc.) and the possibility that the trial could come to an end already after a precautionary decision or after a 'brief decision' (that

32 By this remedy, the citizen that has already filed a complaint could challenge, in the same complaint, other administrative acts that have been at a later stage adopted by the administration (or that were not already known to the claimant) and that are connected to the challenged acts.

means a decision adopted in eased terms) are not *per se* a factor that alters the principle of the effectiveness of legal protection in administrative proceedings. These provisions have the same ratio, which is to speed proceedings and to make, this way, more effective the protection that the legal order could grant to the individual in case of interests that deserve quick decisions or – in other words – to grant more time and more space to those litigations that need more complex judicial evaluations.

The main factors that influence the above-described framework could be identified as follows.

(a) A first factor concerns the multifaceted and 'classical' theme of the division of jurisdiction between ordinary and administrative courts, on the basis of the distinction between individual rights and legitimate interests. As mentioned above, this distinction is the result of legal scholars' and case law interpretations, that tends to detect a legitimate interest every time the public administration is using its authoritative power and when the citizen has an interest which is not completely and directly granted by the law. Nevertheless, there are still some areas of conflict between the interpretation given by the Court of Cassation and the Council of State as to the substantial boundaries of these hypotheses.[33] For the Court of Cassation, the presence of a legitimate interest is excluded if the power of the administration is bound or if there is an inviolable or fundamental right or when the act adopted by the administration is void. The Council of State tends to reiterate its traditional perspective, even when the administration is adopting merely unfair behaviours or when the existence of requirements provided by law needs to be ascertained.

(b) A second factor is the absence of specific and direct remedies for the protection of individual legal positions of constitutional rank or for the guarantee of general interests that could undergo a prejudice at the moment of the adoption of normative acts (regulations).

In the Italian legal order, direct access to constitutional adjudication for the protection of fundamental rights and freedoms is not given to the individual. At the same time, the individual does not have the right to challenge before the administrative court a normative act *per se* either: normative acts (regulations) can, in fact, be challenged only if they contain specific provisions that are directly detrimental to the individual or to a particular category of subjects (in this latter case, the law provides for a particular kind of power to make an action for those associations, such as environmental or consumers ones, that pursue a general interest). Except for these cases, to challenge the legitimacy of normative (or general) administrative acts, the individual should wait for an administrative act that gives concrete application to what is provided by the normative (or general) act and challenge the second act. This act has to be addressed to the individual. This way, he/she can make an action before the administrative court, challenging the administrative act and, through it, bringing the normative act before a court.

Nevertheless, it must be mentioned that the so-called 'complaint for the efficiency of public administrations and authorities' (regulated by legislative decree no. 198/2009)

33 Travi (n. 4) 75.

allows persons who have a direct interest in the adoption of an administrative act, but also some categories of subjects identified in the law, to initiate a trial before the administrative courts in order to complain about a failure in fulfilling the rules for the correct implementation of a public service and also about the failure to adopt a 'compulsory general administrative act that does not have a normative content' and that was supposed to be adopted within a due date. This is a sort of 'class action' that has not been used very often until now and whose concrete significance is still controversial among legal scholars.[34]

(c) A third factor is the absence of a significant space for alternative dispute resolution remedies (i.e. different from jurisdictional ones), even in the case of administrative acts characterised by wide guarantees or by the highly technical nature of the evaluations to be made by the administration. As mentioned above, the principle of full access to justice does not permit the law maker to provide for different ways of dispute resolutions in the cases in which individual rights and legitimate interests are at stake. The Constitutional Court has stated that the law can provide previous administrative complaints or preliminary and conciliatory stages, but affirmed also that these could not completely block access to jurisdiction. At the same time, it should be excluded that the administrative court should restrain from granting legal protection to those cases in which the public authority is acting on the basis of a specific (technical) expertise or through special procedures provided by law (for example, with independent authorities); in fact, the administrative court has progressively recognised the option of varying his control over administrative acts and adopting even a strict control over technical administrative acts, even recurring to the advice of technical experts.[35]

(d) A fourth factor regards the circumstance that the administrative adjudication of the courts has always had a leading role to define the effectiveness of jurisdictional legal protection.

In the Italian law on judicial review of administrative action, several principles and instruments have been defined through judicial interpretation. More precisely, through case law judges have recognised the option of claiming compensation in the case of damages arising from unlawful acts; they clarified judicial powers in the case of 'silence' of the administration and recognised a particular condemnation for the administration, aimed at obtaining a particular act. Moreover, apart from the requirements set by the institutions of the European Union, the administrative court has always emphasised its powers in the definition of boundaries and limits of parties' prerogatives. This happened, in particular, with regard to the hypothesis of 'abuse of process' (*abuso del processo*), which has been connected to the principles of solidarity and effectiveness of legal protection before the judge.[36] This way, the letter of the

34 For a first and general comment see Umberto G. Zingales, 'Una singolare forma di tutela del cittadino nei confronti della p.a.: la class action' (2010) 3 *Giornale di diritto amministrativo* 246.

35 About this topic see Gian Claudio Spattini, 'Le decisioni tecniche dell'amministrazione e il sindacato giurisdizionale' (2011) 1 *Diritto processuale amministrativo* 133.

36 Fulvio Cortese, 'Il giudice amministrativo e l'abuso del diritto' (2012) 10 *Giornale di diritto amministrativo* 959. The leading case – in which it has been stated the existence of a general principle of prohibition of abuse of trials – was decided by the Plenary Session of Council of State, 23 March 2011, no. 3.

Italian Code of administrative trials and proceedings has sometimes been interpreted as a real general interest in a fair trial, which is able to prevail even against the private interest of the parties.

4 Institutional perspectives

As mentioned above, in Italy, judicial remedies against the action of public administration could be activated by citizens before a specialised judge, the administrative jurisdiction. This happens, in particular, when citizens are willing to defend their legitimate interest. Differently, if the issue concerns a subjective right, the jurisdiction belongs to the ordinary judge.[37]

Based on the above mentioned 1971 reform,[38] regional administrative tribunals (for the first instance proceeding) and the Council of State (for appellate decisions) are the judges in charge for administrative jurisdiction.[39]

The first ones (regional administrative tribunals: *tribunali amministrativi regionali* – TAR) are located in the chief town of the Region, even if in some Regions there might be secondary seats. They have a territorial competence, which cannot be derogated. Their competence is established on the basis of an alternative criterion: either the competence is identified looking at the seat of the administration that adopted the act to be challenged or that adopted the behaviour considered to be detrimental (in this case the competent tribunal will be the one located in the same Regions of the administration), or relevance is given to the effects of that act or of that behaviour (in this case, the competent tribunal will be the one in the regional district in which those effects arise; if they have a national range, the competent tribunal will be the one seating in Rome, for Lazio Region – TAR Lazio).

The Council of State seats in Rome. It should be noted that, with regards to Sicily, the functions of the Council of State are performed by the Council of Administrative Justice for Sicily, which works as a 'section' of the Council of State.

Regional administrative tribunals normally function by boards composed of three judges; at every regional administrative tribunal are normally instituted one or more sections. The Council of State is also organised into sections. Nevertheless, not all of them are deputed to work as appellate judges: three of them have a consultative function and issue opinions for the Government. These consultative sections are also called to decide on extraordinary claims presented before the President of the Republic.[40]

About this topic see: Piera Maria Vipiana, 'Il Consiglio di Stato e l'abuso del processo amministrativo per contraddittorietà dei comportamenti processuali' (2012) 6 *Giurisprudenza italiana* 1429; Federico Dinelli, 'La questione di giurisdizione fra il divieto di abuso del diritto e il principio di parità delle parti nel processo' (2012) 7-8 *Foro amministrativo CDS* 1998; Annalisa Giusti, 'Principio di sinteticità e abuso del processo' (2014) 1 *Giurisprudenza italiana* 149; Giuseppe Tropea, *L'abuso del processo amministrativo: Studio critico* (Napoli, Edizioni Scientifiche Italiane 2015).

37 See above, chapter 1.

38 See above, para 3.2.

39 On a general basis, administrative judges are employed through a public competitive exam, which is open just to some specified categories of individuals. However, one-fourth of the members of the Council of State are nominated by the Government.

40 The extraordinary claim before the President of the Republic (*ricorso straordinario al Capo dello Stato*) is a non-jurisdictional remedy, which is not challengeable. It could be activated by any citizen in alternative to a jurisdictional administrative remedy (*electa una via non datur recursus ad alteram*). The reclaim

The other sections are jurisdictional in nature; their decisions are issued by a board composed of at least five judges.

A specific commitment, in the Council of States, belong to the Plenary Assembly (*Adunanza Plenaria*): it is a particular board that authoritatively represents all jurisdictional sections. These latter can or have to (depending on the cases) submit to the Plenary Assembly particularly relevant issues and this board is called to guarantee a uniform interpretation and application of the law. Even if a *stare decisis* rule is not properly existing in Italy, the Plenary Assembly's decisions are generally binding the other sections of the Council of State to defer to the Plenary Assembly all litigations that are reasonably considered to end up with a decision that moves away from the official and funded jurisdictional interpretation.

In general, administrative judges should restrain to the evaluation of the legitimacy of the administrative action, by verifying the subsistence of the grounds provided by law (law violation, lack of competence, abuse of power). This means that they could not substitute themselves to the administration, unless the law expressly gives them the power to intervene in the merits of the litigation (this happens, for example, in the hypothesis in which the public administration does not respect a final decision pronounced by an administrative or ordinary judge).[41] As mentioned above, however, the law provides that in some circumstances the administrative judge could indicate to the administration the correct behaviour: this happens, for example, in the case of 'silence' of the administration, when it does not have a discretionary power; nevertheless, the same could also happen, sometimes, also in cases in which the judge is called to verify administrative evaluation which are technical in nature.

Administrative trials are grounded on the principle of demand, as happens for ordinary trials. In some cases, though, the administrative judge could also decide to get evidence *ex officio*, in consideration of the traditional 'superiority' of the administration and of the difficulties that the citizen has in getting all relevant documents and evidences before the beginning of the trial.

Legal protection of citizens against the public administration does not exclusively belong to courts, even if extra-jurisdictional or alternative remedies are very few (according to the constitutional principles on the prohibition of cases of 'conditioned jurisdiction'),[42] except for administrative claims and, in particular, the extraordinary claim before the President of the Republic (cited above).

Some functions for the protection of rights and legitimate interests of citizens could also be played by the Ombudsman, seating in every Region. This particular organism, however, does not have the power to void or to declare unlawful the acts of the public administration; his commitments are limited to persuasion and solicitation, except for some specific hypothesis in which the Ombudsman could give a non-binding opinion on the correctness of the administrative action (this happens

---

could be presented within 120 days from the communication of a detrimental administrative act. This claim is addressed to the competent Ministry, even if it has to be decided by the Council of State, by an *ad hoc* opinion. The discipline of this remedy is provided by Art. 8 of the decree of the President of the Republic n. 1199/1971. This decree sets also the law regulating two other types of general administrative remedies: a 'hierarchical claim' (*ricorso gerarchico*) and an 'opposition remedy' (*ricorso in opposizione*) before the same body that adopted the detrimental administrative act.

41 This is the so-called 'compliance judgment', see *supra*, at para 3.2.

42 See *supra*, chapter 2.

in the already mentioned hypothesis of the protection of the right to have access to administrative documents).[43]

Finally, there are some specific remedies (in the form of arbitration or alternative dispute resolution) provided by the discipline on public procurements, especially for some sorts of litigations that might arise during the execution of contracts in this area.[44] There are other similar remedies foreseen by the discipline of some independent authorities.

5 European perspectives

As mentioned above, the influence of the obligations deriving from European Union law constitutes a structural element, both from the viewpoint of judicial protection and under the perspective of the principles that the administration shall respect during procedures.

First, most recent developments in the area of judicial legal protection in administrative law received a critical impulse from the national implementation of the European directives on public procurements.

Some of the most significant examples of this influence are:

(a) The official recognition of new rights for the individuals. Is the case, for example, of the acknowledgement of compensatory damages for the breach of legitimate interests or for the admissibility of cautionary remedies even *ante causam* (before the formal claim). These extensions (originally admitted only in the field of public procurements)[45] became compulsory for all types of litigations, in compliance with the principle of equality.
(b) The official recognition of new judicial powers. A similar path has been followed with regards to the admissibility of a very special claim, with very strict time limits, in which the judge can decide – depending on the concrete case – either for the inefficacy of the contract on public procurement stipulated as a result of an unlawful procurement race (giving the victory to the claimant), or deciding on mere compensation for the damage.[46]
(c) The provision of new kinds of stronger legal protection. This is the case of the new wording of the law no. 287/1990, which gives the Italian Antitrust Authority the prerogative to access to administrative courts against all the general administrative acts, regulations and any other act issued by a public administration in violation of the rules on fair competition and market.[47]
(d) The recent evolution of the national judicial opinions about some relevant remedies. It is the case of the concrete rules on the 'incidental claim' (mentioned above) in the field of public procurements. The ECJ, in particular, ruled that the Council Directive 89/665/EEC of 21 December 1989 on the coordination of the laws, regulations and administrative provisions relating to the application

43 See *supra*, at para 3.1.
44 See legislative decree no. 163/2006, Art. 239–243.
45 See legislative decree no. 80/1998, Art. 35.
46 See legislative decree no. 163/2006, Art. 245–245 ter.
47 Travi (n. 4) 196.

of review procedures to the award of public supply and public works contracts 'must be interpreted to the effect that, if, in review proceedings, the successful tenderer – having won the contract and filed a counterclaim – raises a preliminary plea of inadmissibility on the grounds that the tenderer seeking review lacks standing to challenge the award because its bid should have been rejected by the contracting authority by reason of its non-conformity with the technical requirements under the tender specifications, that provision precludes that action for review from being declared inadmissible as a consequence of the examination of that preliminary plea in the absence of a finding as to whether those technical requirements are met both by the bid submitted by the successful tenderer, which won the contract, and by the bid submitted by the tenderer which brought the main action for review'.[48] Before that judgment the Council of State ruled that 'the counterclaim contesting the *locus standi* of the party which has brought that action must always be examined first, even in cases where there were only two tenderers, namely the unsuccessful tenderer (the applicant in the main action) and the successful tenderer (the counterclaimant)'.[49]

More generally, it is important to note that the need to guarantee principles set at the EU level has widened, also from the procedural perspective, the spectrum of remedies actionable by the individual. Among these, it is worth mentioning the remedies that could be activated to protect legitimate expectations. This principle is, actually, one of the cornerstones of the system of guarantees concerning the fair administrative procedure, which has sometimes been expressly stated by the law-maker;[50] it also constitutes a parameter for the possibility of compensating damages that are somehow independent from those that arise in specific acts. Therefore, if the acts or behaviour of administrative bodies generate legitimate expectations, the private parties may claim for damages caused by subsequent acts or behaviour that breach those expectations.[51]

There is another relevant example that deserves mention: the principle of collaboration between citizens and public administration during the preparatory phase of a procedure.[52] This principle has been affirmed especially in those procedures that find their main source in EU law (i.e. antitrust), but administrative courts generally tend to extend it.

The case law of the ECtHR has played a seminal role as well, especially with regard to the guarantees offered in administrative procedures or before administrative courts. Its most relevant effect could be found in the legislative interventions, following the jurisprudence of the Strasbourg court that attempted to make trials quicker (either by providing for special trials, or providing that persons that suffered a damage caused by unreasonable delays of the judicial proceeding could activate an *ad hoc* reparatory remedy)[53].

48 See Case C-100/12 Fastweb SpA ECLI:EU:C:2013:448.

49 See Plenary Session of Council of State, 7 April 2011, no. 4.

50 See, for example Law no. 241/1990 and no 311/2004.

51 Fulvio Cortese, 'La revoca negli appalti pubblici tra danno precontrattuale e indennizzo' (2013) 2 *Giornale di diritto amministrativo* 169.

52 Anna Simonati, *Procedimento amministrativo comunitario e principi a tutela del privato* (Padova, Cedam 2009) 66.

53 See law no. 89/2001.

Some other relevant effects derived from the need to respect ECtHR's case law. In particular, a very significant example in the Italian legal order is represented by a highly controversial case, regarding a particular way for the public administration to have access to property through occupation (without a formal taking procedure).[54] In this particular case, the Italian law maker, as a consequence of ECtHR decisions, has been forced by the Constitutional Court to address the issue and, therefore, to change the law: as a result, the rules concerning the compensation payment has been changed and adapted to the Conventional principles, by making them more adherent to the value of the damage suffered by the private subject who endured the occupation.[55]

6 Conclusion

From this general framework, some conclusive remarks could be drawn on the evolution of the principle of effectiveness of legal protection in the Italian legal system, from the administrative law viewpoint.

Historically, the principle of effectiveness (both in procedure and in trials) represented a goal to pursue and implement. For example, the emergence of the notion of legitimate interest was functional in recognising the possibility of having access to subjective situations that, otherwise, would not find legal protection. The constitutional recognition of this principle, moreover, has boosted the importance of this target, highlighting the substantial dimension of legitimate interest and driving the law-maker to the adoption of a dedicated law (the legislative decree no. 104/2010), that enumerates rights and principles that are instrumental to the effectiveness of legitimate interests before the concrete exercise of public powers. These outcomes, though, were mainly characterised by a specific attention to the subjective profile of legal protection: that is the set of prerogatives and benefits that the citizen can take advantage of in his relationship with the public administration. The result to be pursued for legal scholars and for courts was to transform the legitimate interest into a subjective legal position having the same value as a subjective right.

The most recent reforms of the Italian administrative system, on the one hand, are characterised by the acceleration of this process of assimilation between legitimate interests and subjective rights, especially with regard to the need to improve the standards of legal protection of legitimate interests in the field of EU law. On the other hand, they show the emersion of a new kind of objective impulse, in which legal protection and its effectiveness are to be considered a value of the legal order as a whole, to be protected even beyond 'egoistic' interests of private or public parties. From this perspective, another viewpoint that deserves due consideration is the attitude that can be observed in the last reforms, for example in those concerning the taxes that the citizens have to pay to have access to justice, which have been considerably increased. In the last few years, the rules on taxes to be payed to have

54 Antonio Gambaro, 'Giurisprudenza della Corte europea dei diritti dell'uomo e influenza sul diritto interno in tema di diritto di proprietà' (2010) 2 *Rivista di diritto civile* 115.

55 Constitutional Court, 24 October 2007, no. 349; Constitutional Court, 08 October 2010, no. 293.

access to justice have undergone profound changes, especially due to budgetary reasons. The trend – which has been deeply criticised –[56] is for a progressive increase of these expenses, with the general goal of discouraging specious claims and to reduce litigations before the administrative courts. In this new scenario, the role of the courts has become more and more relevant. But also the role of the law maker has strengthened.

56 The issue regarding the compatibility of the italian legislation and the principle of access to justice (as stated in the European public procurement law) was raised recently before the ECJ: Tribunale Regionale di Giustizia Amministrativa, Trento, 29 January 2014 (for a comment of this decision, see Luca Presutti, 'L'incompatibilità del contributo unificato negli appalti pubblici con la direttiva ricorsi' (2014) 6 *Urbanistica e appalti* 709). However the ECJ rejected the question: see Case C-61/14 Orizzonte salute ECLI:EU:C:2015:655.

11 The principle of effective legal protection in administrative law in Lithuania

Jurgita Paužaitė-Kulvinskienė

Introduction

The principle of effective legal protection is one of the general principles of European legal order. In Lithuania this principle is a constituent part of the constitutional principle of the rule of law. This topic is extensively discussed in Lithuanian legal scholarship. Various aspects of the right to effective judicial protection have been addressed by Lithuanian scholars, like the correlation of the principle of effective judicial protection with other constitutional principles,[1] the right to judicial protection in criminal procedure,[2] the implementation of the right to judicial protection in administrative procedure,[3] and the implementation of the right in civil procedure.[4] One should also note respective comparative researches on the implementation of the principle in administrative law. Lithuania's case is usually analysed in a comparative perspective with some EU Member States – Germany,[5] or France.[6]

1 E. Kūris, 'Konstitucinių principų plėtojimas konstitucinėje jurisprudencijoje' in *Konstitucinių principų plėtojimas konstitucinėje jurisprudencijoje: Lietuvos Respublikos Konstitucinio Teismo ir Lenkijos Respublikos Konstitucinio Tribunolo konferencijos medžiaga* (Vilnius, Lietuvos Respublikos Konstitucinis Teismas 2002) 208–334.

2 A. Abramavičius, 'Teisė į teisminę gynybą Lietuvos Respublikos Konstitucinio Teismo jurisprudencijoje' (2009) 3 *Jurisprudencija* 21–40.,G. Goda, 'Konstitucinė justicija ir baudžiamojo proceso teisės mokslas' (2011) 78 *Teisė* 68–92.

3 Dainius Raižis, 'Žmogaus teisių ir pagrindinių laisvių apsaugos konvencijos įtaka administracinių teismų praktikai teisės į teisingą teismą kontekste' (2010) 4 *Visuomenės saugumas ir viešoji tvarka* 161–174; Dainius Raižis, *Procesas pirmosios instancijos administraciniame teisme: daktaro disertacija* (Mykolo Romerio universitetas 2008) 170; Virgilius Valančius, 'Žmogaus teisių užtikrinimas administraciniuose teismuose taikant Europos žmogaus teisių ir pagrindinių laisvių apsaugos konvenciją' in *Teisė besikeičiančioje Europoje* (Mykolo Romerio universitetas 2008) 497–524; Virgilius Valančius and Rimvydas Norkus, 'Nacionalinis teisinis diskursas dėl administracinio proceso' (2006) 3 *Jurisprudencija* 91–98; Dainius Pelenis and Jurgita Paužaité-Kulvinskiené, 'Effektiver gerichtlicher Schutz' in Albrecht Weber (ed.), *Fundamental Rights in Europe and North America* (Martinus Nijoff Publishers 2008) 137–149; Jurgita Paužaité-Kulvinskiené, *Administracinė justicija: teorija ir praktika* (Justitia 2005) 245.

4 Egidius Laužikas, Valentinas Mikelénas and Vytautas Nekrošius, *Civilinio proceso teisė: II tomas* (Justitia 2004) 640; Vytautas Nekrošius, 'Kai kurie civilinio proceso teisės klausimai Lietuvos Respublikos Konstitucinio teismo doktrinoje' (2007) 63 *Teisė* 76–87.

5 Jurgita Paužaité-Kulvinskiené, 'Der Aufbau der deutschen und litauischen Verwaltungsgerichtsbarkeit' (2000) 36 *Teisė* 75–84.

6 Ligita Ramanauskaité, 'Lithuanian administrative procedure by contrasting it with French administrative procedure' (2004) 50 *Lithuanus* 45–53.

1 The principle of effective legal protection and the constitutional framework in Lithuania

The principle of effective judicial protection (*teisė į teisingą teismą*) is a constituent part of the system of constitutional principles[7] and takes part in developing the aspects of the constitutional principle of rule of law. The principle of rule of law (*teisinės valstybės principas*) which encompasses many interrelated imperatives, the content of the principle of effective judicial protection shall be revealed in the context of other constitutional principles, for example good administration, limitation of powers of the state authority, service of state institutions to the people and other principles.

In the jurisprudence of the Constitutional Court (*Lietuvos Respublikos konstitucinis teismas*) the principle of effective legal protection is first of all related to the right of effective judicial protection.[8] This was determined by the active stand taken by the Constitutional Court while developing the catalogue of constitutional rights where the priority was given to the interpretation of the right to access the court. Art. 30(1) of the Constitution, which sets forth the right to access to court expressly, does not establish the principle of effective judicial protection. Its features and content are defined by systematic interpretation of other provisions of the Constitution in the constitutional jurisprudence and at present may be regarded as the principle of effective judicial protection. Constitutional jurisprudence employs similar terms: 'due legal process' and[9] 'due legal procedure'.[10] At present it is not clear whether the content of effective legal protection will be interpreted as a unit encompassing the rights of effective judicial protection together with the rights to proper procedures of public administration and whether it will be referred to the interrelation of judicial procedure with procedures of public administration and their influence on each other. In the context of the aforementioned constitutional cases the Constitutional Court has noted that executive authorities in their activities are bound by the requirements of due legal procedure deriving from the Constitution. The requirements of proper legal procedure that are applied to the procedures of public administration are implemented in a more concrete way within the principle of good administration[11] rather than the principle of effective judicial protection.

7 Ruling of 13 December 2004 of the Constitutional Court, *Valstybės žinios*, 2004, No 181–6708; Ruling of 2 June 2005 of the Constitutional Court, *Valstybės žinios*, 2005, No 71–2561.

8 Lietuvos Respublikos konstitucinio teismo 2002 m. liepos 2 d. nutarimas 'Dėl karių galimybės kreiptis į teismą' Valstybės žinios. 2002, Nr. 69–2832; Lietuvos Respublikos konstitucinio teismo 2004 m. rugpjūčio 17 d. nutarimas 'Dėl teisės kreiptis į teismą', Valstybės žinios. 2004, Nr. 146–5311; Lietuvos Respublikos Konstitucinio Teismo 2006 m. rugsėjo 21 d. nutarimas 'Dėl teismų sprendimų motyvų surašymo ir skelbimo, sprendimo už akių, taip pat dėl apeliacijos', Valstybės žinios. 2006, Nr. 102–3957; 2008 05 28 dėl ATPK tyrimo principo apimties; 2010 05 13 dėl ABTĮ 16 str. 2 d.

9 Ruling of 31 May 2006 of the Constitutional Court [on quota of the white sugar export] Valstybės žinios, 2006, No 62–2283.

10 Ruling of 30 June 2008 on the Constitutional Court [on recovery of a state loan] Valstybės žinios, 2008, No 75–2965.

11 Jurgita Paužaitė-Kulvinskienė, 'Das Recht auf eine gute Verwaltung in der Rechtsprechung des litauischen Verfassungsgerichts' (2009) 10 *Osteuropa-Recht* 350–366.

The principle of effective legal protection in administrative justice from the procedural point of view is related to other procedures – constitutional, civil, and criminal procedure. Thus, this principle cannot be interpreted 'autonomously', that is only in the sphere of administrative procedure. The constitutional framework creates a universal system for judicial protection and joins judicial procedures, which are different by their essence and nature. The universality of judicial protection was first recognised by the Constitutional Court of the Republic of Lithuania as early as 1996.[12] Subsequent rulings in 2002[13] and 2004[14] referred to the principle of judicial protection as a value category, that is as dynamic and one of the most important constitutional objectives.

Secondly, the principle of effective legal protection at the jurisprudence of the Constitutional Court is discussed in relationship with the right to a fair trial. So, the legal protection means at the first step the judicial protection or the right to a fair trial. Art. 30(1) of the Constitution provides that 'the person whose constitutional rights or freedoms are violated shall have the right to apply to court'. In the constitutional jurisprudence[15] and legal theory[16] this right is regarded as an absolute constitutional right. This means that every individual shall have the possibility to defend their rights and freedoms in a court against both illegal actions of other people and public authorities and their officials. Pursuant to the Constitution (*Konstitucija*) the legislator is bound by the positive duty to establish legal regulation that allows for the resolution of all disputes concerning the violations of rights and freedoms of individuals, as well as acquired rights, before courts. Since the right to access a court is an absolute one it shall not be unnecessarily restricted and there shall be no unjustified burden to be put on the implementation of the right. Otherwise, this regulation would be just an inactive declaration.

In the jurisprudence of the Constitutional Court the principle of the effective judicial protection consists of three elements:

(a) right to access the administrative court;
(b) right to a fair trial; and
(c) rights to defence.

This grouping is based on the classification provided by the digest of official constitutional doctrine in Lithuania and the legal regulation laid down in Art. 47 of the

12 Ruling of 18 April 1996 of the Constitutional Court [on the Law on Commercial Banks] *Valstybės žinios*, 1996, No 36–915.

13 Ruling of 2 July 2002 of the Constitutional Court [on the opportunity for soldiers to apply to court] *Valstybės žinios*, 2002, No 69–2832; Ruling of 23 October 2002 of the Constitutional Court [on the protection of the private life of a public person and the right of a journalist not to disclose the source of information] *Valstybės žinios*, 2002, No 104–4675.

14 Ruling of 17 August 2004 of the Constitutional Court [on the right to apply to court] *Valstybės žinios*, 2004, Nr. 146–5311; Ruling of 29 December 2004 of the Constitutional Court [on the restraint of organzsed crime] *Valstybės žinios*, 2005, No 1–7.

15 Ruling of 30 June 2000 of the Constitutional Court [on the right to compensation for damage inflicted by unlawful actions of interrogatory and investigatory bodies, the prosecutor's office and court] *Valstybės žinios*, 2000, No 54–1588.

16 Armanas Abramavičius, 'Teisė į teisminę gynybą Lietuvos Respublikos Konstitucinio Teismo jurisprudencijoje'(2009) 3 *Jurisprudencija* 23.

Charter of Fundamental Rights of the European Union taken as a source and which provides insight into the universal system of judicial protection. The imperatives developed by the Constitutional Court have an impact on all branches of procedural law and are peculiar not only to administrative but also to civil and criminal procedure. These imperatives may be divided into two groups.

The first group of constitutional imperatives concerns the institutional ones. These requirements are significant for establishing fundamental and the most important principles that must be applied to the organisation and activities of the judicial system. In this regard, one should note the approach of the Constitutional Court of the Republic of Lithuania on the establishment of the specialised system of administrative courts. Having interpreted the Constitution, the Constitutional Court provided respective provisions that were highly relevant to administrative procedure law and administrative law.

The second group of constitutional imperatives, which can be conditionally titled procedural imperatives, are relevant for laying down the constitutional foundations of trial (administration of justice) to different stages of the proceedings; however, these procedural imperatives may have certain peculiarities depending on the category of the case under consideration.

2 Rights-based perspective

2.1 Participation

Procedural rights of legal protection during the procedure at the entities of public administration and during the court procedure are mainly supplemented by both the provisions of the Law on Public Administration (LPA, *Viešojo administravimo įstatymas*) and legal norms laid down in the specialised legal regulation or by the provisions of the Law on Administrative Procedure (LAP, *Administracinių bylų teisenos įstatymas*). The administrative procedure is regulated by the LPA for all matters of administrative law. Other laws and legislative acts regulating the specific protection in different fields of public administration (tax law, municipality law, environmental law, social security law, asylum law) are adopted on the basis of the general provisions of this law. The LPA foresees the main principle for the handling of the entities of public administration – the administrative decision. There are two of kinds of administrative decisions: individual administrative decision (e.g. construction permit, license for business etc.) and normative administrative decision (legislative acts of the minister, acts of the government, acts of the local authorities etc.). The procedure of administrative decisions in different sectors of administration are regulated in special laws and other legislative acts. In these acts are written the requirements for administrative decisions, the institutions who are responsible for that and sometimes specific rules concerning the procedure.

The LPA implicitly establishes that administrative decisions cannot, in the absence of statutory provision, be revoked. Under general rule, administrative decisions communicated to the person concerned become final. This naturally leads the individual concerned to reasonably expect that the initial legal decision will not be amended by the subsequent decision. In Lithuania neither the legislator nor administrative courts have ever recognised the position that the public authorities have an inherent power to amend or withdraw a formal decision. In the LPA the Lithuanian legislator implicitly has established that the public authorities do not hold the power to revoke formal a administrative decision they adopt. This general rule applies to all types of decisions immaterial of their legal consequences, i.e. lawful and unlawful, favourable, declarative and other formal decisions are all irrevocable in the absence of express statutory power. The single exception to the rule set out in the LPA provides that a formal decision may be amended only to the extent necessary to correct clerical errors.

In this context one should note that until 2007 Lithuanian law did recognise the power of the public authorities to alter or withdraw the formal decision subject to the consent of the individuals affected. In the absence of the consent of the individuals concerned, the errors were remedied by the quasi-judicial bodies or courts. In addition to this, the legal regulation in effect until 2007 provided that the public authorities *ex officio* were entitled to correct legal errors as long as it was not regarded as an interference with respective rights and interests of the individuals concerned. The rationale for the amended legal regulation may be linked to the loyalty to normativism or the reluctance to give more powers to the public authorities. One may argue that this approach will slow down the rate of administrative change and introduce unwelcome conservative decision making. Nevertheless, Lithuanian administrative courts have accepted these changes in legal regulation rather easily and coherently. Faced with the choice between legality and individual justice the Lithuanian courts tend to find for the principle of legality on this point. The courts have stated on more than one occasion that the public authorities shall act in accordance with the principle that they are allowed to do only what is expressly set out in the laws. Thus, under these circumstances one may rightly assume that the priority is given to the principles of legality and primacy of law. In this regard, the Supreme Administrative Court of Lithuania has stated that the principle of legality shall mean that the formal decision is valid until it is annulled by the superior body of public authorities or the court.[17] The same approach is evident in another case wherein the Supreme Administrative Court has emphasised that when the public authority decides the matter by adopting a formal decision it creates certain rights and duties to the individuals concerned. The Court went on to state that the practice where the public authority kept changing its mind was compatible neither with the principle of good administration nor with the principle of legal certainty or legality. Thus, the administrative decision adopted by the public authority shall be binding and legal, that is it shall not be altered or withdrawn *ex officio* by the public authority which had adopted it.[18]

The exceptions to the aforementioned rule of irrevocability are only found in the special legal regulation which expressly provides that respective public authorities are entitled to amend or revoke their final decisions. One should note that Lithuanian administrative law precludes the secondary legislation which introduces the power of the public authorities to revoke formal administrative decision. The right to revoke the adopted decision which confers rights to individuals shall be regulated by the law and cannot be set out in the secondary legislation.[19] The statutory intervention into the final administrative decision can be initiated by both the parties concerned

17 Case No. A-602–2104/2012, 27 April 2012.
18 Case No. A-602–227/2012, 12 March 2012.
19 Case No. I-502–6/2012, 16 March 2012.

and the public authorities themselves. In most of the cases the provisions of the special legal regulation entitle the administration to amend the final decision if it was obtained in bad will (by fraud, false information etc.), or the factual circumstances which were the ground to adopt the respective decision change.

Nevertheless, the absence of general rules on the revocation of administrative decisions and the tendency to be against the ability to revoke the initial decision immaterial of the type of the act and its legal consequences create the tension between legality, legal expectations, and public interest. This is readily apparent in the case law of administrative courts and can be exemplified by the jurisprudence of the Supreme Administrative Court of Lithuania.[20]

2.2 *Right to appeal*

The appeal to a superior administrative authority against an administrative decision can be an obligation (only in the cases foreseen in special law and only after this stage is possible to appeal to the administrative court) or an alternative (the person can choose between the appeal to an authority or direct to the court). There is a possibility to apply to an administrative dispute commission prior to bringing the case to an administrative court. Application to administrative dispute commissions prior to bringing a case to an administrative court is not compulsory, save for the matters provided by laws. In the absence of specific rules provided by law about the necessity of an administrative claim prior to bringing a case to an administrative court, administrative decisions can be brought to an administrative court directly.

The court shall not offer assessment of the disputed administrative acts and acts (or omission) from the point of view of political or economic expediency and shall only establish whether or not there has been in a particular case a violation of a law or any other legal act. Art. 89 of the LAP describes grounds for annulment of contested acts (e.g. illegality in essence, i.e., conflicting by its contents with legal acts of superior power, illegality, as it was adopted in violation of the basic procedures, etc.). The contested act (or a part thereof) may also be annulled on other grounds recognised as material by the administrative court.

The scope of control by administrative courts depends on the nature of the case. There is no clear provision in Lithuania, whether administrative courts are entitled to examine advantages and drawbacks of the administrative decision. However, Lithuanian administrative courts carry out control of compatibility of administrative acts with the principles of subsidiarity, proportionality, objectivity and other principles of public administration, as they are set down in the LPA and developed in the jurisprudence of the ECJ. In this respect administrative acts may also be annulled, if, for example, other possible acts to a lesser degree of influence on a person's rights were possible.[21] Lithuanian administrative courts recognise areas which are reserved to the exercise of discretionary powers by administrative authorities (e.g. discretionary power of the head of state authority to decide whether a specific need exists to move a state servant from one post to another;[22] discretionary power of the municipal authority

20 Case No. A-756–35/2010, 1 February 2010.

21 Case No. A 1–362–2004.

22 Case No. A 7–433–2005.

to set an expiry date of the licence to provide transport services;[23] discretionary power of the Communications Regulatory Authority to impose obligations on an operator having significant market power on the relevant market[24] etc.). Judicial control in these areas is limited to objectivity, impartiality and criteria, which had been taken into consideration by an administrative authority while exercising discretionary powers.

2.3 Right to access to administrative court

2.3.1 The range of judicial review

The requirements of the right to legal protection in Art. 30, para 1 and Art. 33, para 2 of the Constitution are detailed in the Court Law and the LPA but they do not contain a clearly established universal principle for the jurisdiction of public disputes (except constitutional) as regards the administrative courts although this duty should be raised for the legislature by the aforementioned provisions of the Constitution. The competency of the administrative court is restricted on the basis of the LPA to only disputes concerning rights in the areas of public or internal administration. In addition, the principle for the establishment of the competency of the administrative courts by lists is established in the LPA. It duplicates the norm of the LPA establishing the general competency of the administrative courts. In the practice of Lithuania's administrative justice, the LPA should be interpreted as an auxiliary (representative) list of disputes helping courts decide the problem of the jurisdiction of a dispute. The LPA indicates that other cases can also be assigned to the competency of the administrative courts; from a practical position this should be construed as a mechanism helping to avoid disputes in practice concerning the jurisdiction between general competency and administrative courts.

The LPA foresees a positive restriction according to the LPA and a negative restriction of the competency of an administrative court. The so-called supra-judicial acts, i.e. the examination of the activities of the President, Seimas, Seimas Members, Prime Minister, Government *in corpore*, and the judges of the Constitutional Court, Supreme Court of Lithuania, and Appeal Court of Lithuania, as well as the procedural activities of the judges of other courts, public prosecutors, pre-hearing investigation officials and bailiffs are not ascribed to the competency of the administrative courts. The legislature in 2000 revoked the exception in this list concerning the activities of the Seimas ombudsmen, recognising that there are no grounds, neither according to their nature nor according to the legal status of the entity, to include the activities of the Seimas ombudsmen on the list of exceptions. On the basis of the LPA, the legality of the procedural actions of judges, public prosecutors, and bailiffs has been given on the basis of special laws to general competency courts to hear. However, when these entities are not performing their procedural activities but performing public administration functions, both the legality of their activities and the reimbursement of damages should be within the jurisdiction of the administrative courts. The administrative courts do not decide cases, which are ascribed to the competency of the

23 Case No. A 5–913–2004.
24 Case No. A 1–362–2004.

Constitutional Court, general courts, or other specialised courts. It is thereby sought in advance to avoid problematic cases where a dispute concerning a right in the area of public or internal administration has the features of both an administrative and a constitutional or civil dispute.

2.3.2 Objectives of the legal protection

There is no limitation for natural or legal persons to bring a case before an administrative court. There is a possibility to bring a complaint in order to protect state or another public interest laid down for the prosecutor, entities of administration, state control officers, other state institutions, agencies, organisations or natural persons, but only in the cases prescribed by law. Administrative courts can also decide cases relating to disputes between public administrations, which are not subordinated to one another, concerning competence or breaches of laws, except for civil litigation cases assigned to the courts of general jurisdiction. Public entities are not entitled to challenge their own administrative acts before administrative courts. If an unlawfulness of an administrative act violates public interest, only the prosecutor or other persons, in the cases prescribed by law, may bring this case before a court. Normally judges do not have the right to initiate a case. But if a judge has information about a criminal action, he has the obligation to inform the prosecutor. Once the case is ongoing, the court can 'actively' participate in the proceeding by asking for evidence, appointing witnesses, experts, etc.

Every interested person can apply to a court for the protection of his/her infringed or contested right or interest protected under law. Every applicant who challenges an administrative act has to demonstrate a particular interest in the annulment of this act. Only an application to an administrative court as an individual in order to protect his/her own infringed or contested right or interest is admissible. The Supreme Administrative Court of Lithuania has ruled numerous times that there are no grounds for the annulment of the disputed administrative act if it is determined that this administrative act has not violated the rights and/or legal interests of the claimant.[25] It is possible to bring a complaint to protect the State or other public interest laid down for the prosecutor, entities of administration, state control officers, other state institutions, agencies, organisations or natural persons, but only in the cases prescribed by law. The participation of a public prosecutor in administrative procedure when defending a public interest is presented as one of the most important exceptions to the interest of a party. The conception of an administrative disputes concerning a right in the area of public administration are distinguished: (a) a dispute concerning the use of a right; (b) a dispute concerning the use of a subjective right; (c) a dispute concerning the legality and validity of an act; and (d) a dispute in the area of public or internal administration. Attention should be paid to the fact that in the area of Lithuanian positive law two concepts are distinguished: 'public administration' and 'internal administration' but there are no clear criteria for the delimitation of these concepts. The conception of public and internal administration should be interpreted in the sense of the provisions of the LPA, which defines public or internal administration by two criteria: subjective, that is an obligatory entity of a

25 See e.g. Case No. A 2 1049–2004; Case No. A 2 108–2005.

public/internal administration, and material, that is the activities of a public/internal administration. However, positive law today does not provide an unambiguous answer of whether both criteria are necessary in the case of each dispute or what the relationship between them is.

Cases concerning violations of administrative law are today one of the most relevant problems because they are still being heard according to the Soviet-style Code of Violations of Administrative Law of 1985. From January 2017 the new modern Code of Administrative Violations must come into force. Until 2011 a temporary compromise was in force that cases concerning violations of administrative law ware heard in the first instance by both general competency district courts and administrative courts. In both cases, decisions were heard by appeal procedure in the Supreme Administrative Court of Lithuania, which was the last resort. This question was essentially decided and from 2011 only the general courts deal with the cases on administrative violations in first and appeal instances.

Cases concerning the legality of normative administrative legal acts are distributed, depending on the type of act in dispute, between the Constitutional Court of Lithuania and the administrative courts. In addition, general competency courts can also perform the incidental control of legality. The conformity of Parlament resolutions, Presidential decrees, and Government acts to the Constitution and the laws and the conformity of laws to the Constitution are within the competency of the Constitutional Court. The control of the conformity of all the remaining normative administrative acts, which are enacted by both state (territorial or central) and municipal public administration entities, to the laws is within the competency of an administrative court. The normative act is defined by the LPA: (a) the area of enacting the act is in performing public or internal administration functions; (b) the non-individualisation of entities; and (c) an act is not applied only once. The question of the legality of normative administrative acts in an individual case can also be decided by general competency courts, that is a person is entitled but not obligated to petition an administrative court. The practice of the administrative courts broadly explains the extent of the judicial control and verifies not only the statutory legality of administrative normative acts but also their constitutionality. The principled and the incidental forms control are examined separately. The right of incidental control is granted to persons when a specific case concerning the violation of their rights is being heard. In the case of principled control, there is a finite group of specific entities, which can file a petition concerning the legality of a normative administrative act. Such entities include *Seimas* (Parlaments) members, *Seimas* (Parlaments) ombudsmen, state ombudsmen, government representatives, public prosecutors, and courts (i.e. not necessarily entities of the public administration).

2.3.3 Content of protection

Following the given classification, administrative courts in Lithuania carry out a full review of administrative acts. According to the LAP, upon hearing the case, the administrative court can: (1) revoke the contested administrative act (part thereof) or obligate the appropriate entity of administration to remedy the committed violation or carry out other orders of the court; (2) oblige the appropriate entity of municipal administration to implement the law, a Government resolution or another legal act; (3) settle the dispute in any other manner provided for by law. So the decision of the court may contain this new administrative act; (4) award damages or redress of a moral wrong caused to a natural person or an organisation by the unlawful acts or omission in the sphere of public administration performed by state or municipal institutions, agencies, services and their employees in the discharge of their official functions (extra-contractual liability).

In the cases relating to omission by an entity of administration, that is failure to perform official duties or in the cases regarding the delay in settling the matters, the administrative court may adopt a decision obligating the appropriate entity of administration to make a relevant decision or comply with any other court order within the prescribed time limits.

It should be noted, however, that administrative courts do not offer assessment of the disputed administrative acts (or omission) from the point of view of political or economic expediency and only establish, whether or not there has been, in a particular case, a violation of a law or any other legal act, whether or not the entity of administration has acted within the limits of its competence, also whether or not the act (action) complies with the objectives and tasks for the purpose whereof the institution has been set up and vested with appropriate powers.

As there is no concept of administrative contract in Lithuania and all the disputes arising from contracts (including contracts with administrative authorities) fall under the jurisdiction of courts of general jurisdiction, administrative courts do not deal with contractual liability of administrative authorities.

The LPA determines the limits of the control by an administrative court: the control of the formal legality of the actions of a public entity is restricted to the verification of whether an incompetent entity passed the act being appealed or in passing it the principle procedures were violated; and during the control of the material legality, an administrative court analyses whether the act being appealed is in essence wrongful because by its substance it conflicts with legal acts already in force. The factual and legal grounds for passing discretionary administrative decisions are not controllable because in frequent cases the legal acts are lacking, pursuant to which the discretionary authorisations in the specific area are being implemented. In addition, the LPA prohibits the control of the legality of the activities of the public administration from the standpoint of economic and political expediency. However, it does not thereby prevent the possibility of the verification of the acts of the public administration from the standpoint of expediency in respect to human rights. It should be noted that the LPA does not contain a finite list of the grounds for the revocation of acts being appealed just like no finite list has been established for the kinds of demands which can be filed with an administrative court (or kinds of administrative claims).

In the procedure of cases concerning the legality of normative administrative acts, it is verified as to whether the specific normative administrative act conforms to a law or a Government normative act. These grounds are general for an administrative and general competency court but the practice of the administrative courts explains the extent of judicial control broadly and verifies not only the statutory legality but also constitutionality of normative administrative acts.

2.3.4 Procedural rules for administrative litigation

The Law on Administrative Proceedings expressis verbis covers only some principles of procedure before the administrative courts: the right to judicial protection, judicial independence, public hearing, public pronouncement of the judgment, equality of arms between the parties, binding effect of the judgment. However, other important principles of judicial proceedings follow from the European Convention on Human Rights, Lithuanian Constitution, jurisprudence of the European Court of Human Rights and Lithuanian Constitutional Court, and are applied in Lithuanian administrative courts as well: access to legal aid, adversarial hearing, secrecy of judicial deliberation, obligation to motivate judgments, etc. The Supreme Administrative Court of Lithuania often uses procedural principles as a source of law and refers to them in its judgments.

A complaint/petition may be filed with the administrative court, within one month from the day of publication of the contested act, the day of delivery of the individual act to the party concerned, the notification of the party concerned of the act (or omission), within two months from the day of expiry of the time limit set by a law, or any other legal act for the compliance with the demand. If the public or internal administration entity delays the consideration of a certain issue and fails to resolve it within the due date, a complaint about the failure to act (in such delay) may be lodged within two months from the day of expiry of the time limit set by a law or any other legal act for the settlement of the issue. No time limits shall be set for the filing of petitions for the review of the lawfulness of administrative legal acts by the administrative courts. The decision taken by an administrative disputes commission or any other institution for preliminary extrajudicial investigation of disputes, adopted after investigating an administrative dispute in accordance with the extrajudicial procedure, may be appealed to an administrative court within 20 days after the receipt of the decision.

If it is recognised that the time limit for filing a complaint has not been observed for a good reason, at the claimant's request, the administrative court may grant restoration of the *status quo ante*. The petition for the restoration of the *status quo ante* shall indicate the reasons for failure to observe the time limit and present the evidence confirming the reasons for failure to observe the time limit. There are no special screening procedures before administrative courts. Only the compliance of the complaint with the formal requirements and the time limits for lodging a complaint are verified in order to decide whether a complaint is acceptable. The LAP sets minimal standards of the complaint to administrative courts. Except for cases provided for by law, complaints/petitions shall be received and heard by the administrative courts only after the payment of the stamp duty. The assistance of a lawyer is not compulsory in administrative courts. The parties to the proceedings can defend their interests in court themselves or through their representatives.

Complaints shall be made in writing. The LAP sets prerequisites of the complaint to administrative courts. The complaint needs to include some information about the parties of the administrative dispute (the claimant's and respondent's name, surname (name of the institution), personal code number, place of residence (seat) etc.), the particular contested action (omission) or act, date of its performance (adoption), the circumstances upon which the claimant's claim is based, supporting evidence and the claimant's claim. There is no need to give legal grounds of the complaint, only factual circumstances have to be presented. There are no specific templates of the complaint at hand and the claimant is free to choose one him- or herself.

There is a possibility of bringing proceedings via information technologies. Whilst lodging a complaint, the applicant is required to identify him- or herself by using a specific code issued by the court or by using the so-called 'e-government gateway', which is accessible via online banking data, e-signature, personal identity or civil servant cards. Making an effective use of this procedural right to institute proceedings via information technologies leads to significant concessions, such as exemption from the duty to provide the court with additional copies of one's complaint or a requirement to pay only 75% of respective stamp duty. Moreover, in the cases prescribed by LAP the subpoena may be also received by electronic means.

Cases in regional administrative courts relating to the compensation for material and moral damage inflicted in the sphere of public administration, tax disputes, office-related disputes or disputes related to the execution of settlement agreements reached by the parties shall be heard by one judge, whereas other cases shall be heard by a chamber of three judges. In certain cases a chamber of judges may also be formed for the hearing of cases where the hearing by a single judge is provided. At the Supreme Administrative Court of Lithuania cases shall be heard before a chamber of three judges. An expanded chamber of five or seven judges may be formed for hearing complex cases or such a case may be referred to the plenary session of the court.

The judge whose opinion in the case differs from that of the majority of the judges may write his dissenting opinion. The dissenting opinion shall not be announced publicly, but shall be attached to the case file. There is no difference between lower and higher jurisdictions in this respect. The LAP also provides that if the case in which the judge has presented his separate opinion has not been heard on appeal or where a dissenting opinion has been expressed by a judge of the court of appeal, after the decision becomes effective the case with the judge's separate opinion attached shall be referred to the Supreme Administrative Court of Lithuania and the President of the Court shall decide whether to make a recommendation to resume the proceedings.

The injunction relief is available in administrative cases in all matters. The court or the judge may, upon a motivated petition of the participants in the proceedings or upon his/its own initiative, take measures with a view to securing a claim. The claim may be secured at any stage of the proceedings if failure to take provisional measures to secure a claim may impede the enforcement of the court decision or render the decision unenforceable.

The right to access to a court also concerns the procedural rules, including procedural rules of non-judicial level. This matter has been dealt with by the Constitutional Court of Lithuania. The Court held that non-judicial systems for settling disputes are constitutionally justified[26] where certain public authorities and officials have authority to settle respective disputes in out of court procedures. However, judicial protection shall remain the priority form for protection.[27] Non-judicial administrative procedure

26 For the cases where granting respective jurisdictional authority to public authorities and officials is expedient and justified see the Ruling of 2 July 2002 of the Constitutional Court [on an opportunity of soldiers to apply to court] Valstybės žinios, 2002, No 69–2832; Ruling of 4 March 2003 [on restoration of the rights of ownership] *Valstybės žinios*, 2003, No 24–1004; Ruling of 7 February [on social insurance indemnities for occupational diseases] *Valstybės žinios*, 2005, No 19–623; Ruling of 13 December 2004 [on Civil Service] *Valstybės žinios*, 2004, No 181–6708, 2004.12.29, No 186.

27 Ruling of 4 March 2003 of the Constitutional Court [on restoration of the rights of ownership] *Valstybės žinios*, 2003, No 24–1004.

cannot replace nor can it become an alternative to judicial procedures for settling disputes.[28] The establishment of non-judicial procedures is possible where respective preconditions are met: (1) the authority to settle the disputes granted to respective institutions shall be established by the law and cannot be derived from any other form of legal acts; and (2) there shall be a right to appeal against the decision adopted by the institutions before a court; and (3) the pre-litigation procedure shall not unnecessarily restrict or put a burden on the implementation of the right to access to court.

It is clear from the case law of administrative courts in Lithuania that the pre-litigation procedure is regarded as a jurisdictional procedure that compliments the judicial procedure. Judicial and non-judicial procedures are two forms for settling the dispute[29] and both of them are constitutionally justified[30] and do not compete with each other. The choice between the desirable forms belongs to the individual concerned – judicial or non-judicial protection. The functions of the pre-litigation system may vary depending on the type of category. However, the pre-litigation procedure cannot replace the judicial procedure and shall be employed as a compulsory or chosen stage before applying to a court.

The jurisprudence of the Constitutional Court on the pre-litigation procedure in the sphere of administrative law is not particularly rich. It was recognised in a Constitutional Court ruling[31] that when the service contract with the professional soldier or that with the volunteer soldier had to be terminated, an appeal may be lodged with the court regarding not only the violation of the dismissal procedure established by legal acts but also the reasonableness of his dismissal from military service.

Meanwhile, the ruling of 15 May 2007 of the Constitutional Court[32] reviewed respective provisions on the Law on State Secrets and Official Secrets. The challenged legal regulation laid down that the Commission for Secrets Protection Co-ordination was a special administrative pre-judicial institution; however, its decisions were not final and could be directly appealed before an administrative court under the rules of the Law on Administrative Proceedings. The imperatives on the right to access to a court and pre-litigation procedure, which were developed in the constitutional jurisprudence, were further developed by the case law of administrative courts.

The case law of administrative courts provides that the rules on pre-litigation procedure shall be clearly established, i.e. it shall set the institution (institutions) and the principal activities of the respective institution shall be jurisdictional (settling of disputes) rather than activities related to public administration.[33] In Lithuania there are cases where the pre-litigation procedure is identified with the activities of public administration. The ambiguity in legal regulation is interpreted to the advantage of the individual concerned. Nevertheless, even though the objective of the pre-litigation procedure is not to make the protection of infringed rights or interests more

28 Friedrich Schoch, Eberhard Schmidt-Assmann and Rainer Pietzneer, *Kommentar VwGO, I Band* (C. H. Beck 2003) Rn. 16–17.

29 Activities for settling disputes are called jurisdictional activities.

30 *Jurgita Paužaitė-Kulvinskienė*, 'Administracinė justicija: teorija ir praktika' 38.

31 Ruling 2 July 2002 of the Constitutional Court [on an opportunity of soldiers to apply to court] *Valstybės žinios*, 2002, No 69–2832.

32 Ruling of 15 May 2007 of the Constitutional Court [on state secrets and official secrets] *Valstybės žinios*, 2007, No 54–2097.

33 See the Case No AS442–609/2009.

complex but on the contrary, to establish an additional mechanism in pursuit of settling legal issues,[34] the case law of administrative courts allows to carry out the judicial and non-judicial procedures at the same time.[35] It is clear from the case law that the courts do not accept administrative complaints if the individual has initiated a non-compulsory pre-litigation procedure and still has not exhausted it.[36] Meanwhile, non-compulsory pre-litigation procedure may be initiated in parallel with judicial civil procedure in civil matters.[37]

One more issue on access to court concerns the accessibility of judicial protection. The accessibility means that a non-compulsory pre-litigation procedure shall not render impossible in practice or excessively difficult the exercise of the right of judicial protection. A compulsory single-stage out of court procedure for settling disputes could satisfy this condition. On this point, it should be observed that there might be problems with compulsory multi-stage non-judicial procedures. One should note the peculiarities of administrative dispute (Ruling of 2 July 2002 of the Constitutional Court). In Lithuania multi-stage non-judicial procedure in administrative cases is prescribed by several laws. Not all of these cases where compulsory multi-stage pre-litigation procedure (i.e. where more than one subsequent decision adopted by different authorities of public administration is required) is established can be constitutionally justified. No constitutional doubts arise regarding the disputes related to public order and security. For example, the actions (decisions) of institutions and their officials which enforce criminal penalties may be appealed before the head of institution of penalties' enforcement.[38] The decisions adopted by the head of the institution and their actions may be appealed before the Director General of the Prison Department. Meanwhile, the actions and decisions of the Director General of the Prison Department may be appealed within 20 days before the regional administrative court. It appears that the multi-stage compulsory non-judicial procedure laid down in the Code of Enforcement of Penalties is in compliance with the criterion of constitutional objectivity to guarantee public order and security. However, the recognition of expert qualification or registration of weapons and ammunition is a rather

34 Case No A143–191/2010.

35 It should be noted that the Law on Administrative Proceedings does not provide an explicit ground for the court to refuse to accept an administrative complaint submitted to it if it is established that the non-compulsory pre-litigation institution has received a complaint filed by the same parties regarding the same subject-matter and background. There are also no restrictions on the right to access to a court where the dispute is settled at the non-compulsory pre-litigation institution in civil matters. Pursuant to the Law on Administrative Proceedings, the complaint may be inadmissible where the complaint concerning the dispute between the same parties and identical subject matter and background is heard at the compulsory pre-litigation institution and the applicant has not exhausted it.

36 Case No AS438–502/2008.

37 For example, pursuant to the Law on Consumer Protection, the parties to the dispute shall be entitled to appeal to the court of general jurisdiction requesting to settle the dispute in essence during the process of settlement of the dispute in the authority for the settlement of disputes as well as after this institution takes a decision.

38 Pursuant to the Code of Enforcement of Penalties of the Republic of Lithuania, the actions and decisions of institutions and their officials who enforce penalties of community service, deprivation of individual freedom, detention, custodial sentence, and life imprisonment may be appealed before the head of institution of penalties' enforcement.

regular procedure of public administration and no specific or extraordinary objectives regarding public order and security are attained in the sphere.

2.3.5 Appeal against the first court decision

As a general rule, the decisions of the court of first instance which have not been appealed against become effective after the time limit for appeal has elapsed (decisions of regional administrative courts may be appealed against within 14 days of the pronouncement of the decision). A court decision adopted after a case had been heard on appeal becomes effective from the day of the adoption of the new decision. A regulatory administrative act (or a part thereof) is considered to be annulled and, as a rule, may not be applied from the day of the official announcement of the effective decision of the administrative court declaring it as illegal. However, having regard to the specific circumstances of the case and having assessed the possibility of the negative legal consequences, the administrative court may establish in its decision annulling a regulatory administrative act (or a part thereof) that it may not be applicable from the day of its adoption or may suspend the validity of the regulatory administrative act (or a part thereof) recognised illegal until the coming into effect of the court decision.

The Supreme Administrative Court of Lithuania acts as an appellate instance for most of the cases heard by regional administrative courts (in certain cases – by district courts), as well as the single and last instance for the cases relating to the lawfulness of regulatory administrative acts adopted by the central entities of state administration as well as for the lawfulness of acts of general character passed by public organisations, communities, political parties, political organisations or associations. It is also the last instance for deciding the issues concerning the assignment of cases to the relevant administrative courts. The Court was formed and started its activities from 1 January 2001. The Supreme Administrative Court of Lithuania is the appellate instance for cases from decisions, rulings and orders of regional administrative courts as the courts of the first instance. Rulings of the Supreme Administrative Court of Lithuania are final and not subject to appeal. It is also the first and final instance for certain categories of administrative cases assigned to its jurisdiction by law. For example, members of the Parliament of the Republic of Lithuania (the Seimas), courts, the Seimas ombudsmen, the Children's Rights Ombudsman, national audit officers and prosecutors are entitled to challenge the lawfulness of normative administrative acts by applying directly to the Supreme Administrative Court of Lithuania. Furthermore, the resolution of disputes concerning violations of the laws on election or referendum is also assigned to the jurisdiction of administrative courts. Individuals specified in the Law on Presidential Election, the Law on Election to the Seimas, the Law on Referendum and the Law on Election to Municipal Councils are entitled to file petitions concerning decisions of the Central Electoral Commission directly to the Supreme Administrative Court of Lithuania. In such cases the Court adopts decisions as a court of sole and final instance.

Upon appeal, the Supreme Administrative Court will review the contested ruling in full. It is also not bound by the arguments raised by the parties in the appeal. The Court is responsible for the developing of uniform practice of administrative courts in interpretation and application of statutes and other legal acts. For that purpose it periodically issues its bulletin under the title 'Practice of Administrative Courts'.

2.3.6 *Suprajudicial acts*

The right to access to court embodies not only an absolute but also universal feature of procedural subjective right. This feature was emphasised by the Constitutional Court in its jurisprudence. The Court held that infringed rights of an individual, *inter alia* acquired rights and legitimate interests, must be protected without prejudice to the fact of whether they are directly established in the Constitution. Effective protection of rights does not limit itself to the protection of rights and freedoms laid down in the Constitution. The same effective protection must be granted to the rights and freedoms of an individual which are not directly conferred by the Constitution as the rights and freedoms which are established in the Constitution. Moreover, in accordance with the Constitution the protection shall be granted to rights and freedoms laid down in international legal acts, the European Convention for the Protection of Human Rights and Fundamental Freedoms, European Union law and international bilateral treaties which are a constituent part of Lithuanian legal order.

In 2010 the Constitutional Court addressed the issues concerning jurisdiction within different legal systems and the peculiarities of suprajudicial acts. This matter was also discussed by one of the most prominent interwar legal scholars in Lithuania Mykolas Roemeris.[39] This is the so-called problem concerning the general or attributive jurisdiction of the administrative court. It is clear from the dynamics in European administrative law that there are two principles on the jurisdiction of administrative court: the principle of universal competence over public disputes (except constitutional ones) (so-called universal clause, *Generalklausel*) and principle of enumeration. Different countries nowadays combine both principles, however one of them is given priority. The choice of which principle on the jurisdiction of administrative court is established in the law on administrative procedure also depends on constitutional jurisprudence. Art. 111(2) of the Constitution of the Republic of Lithuania does not specify the jurisdiction of administrative courts. There are no provisions on the distribution of jurisdiction between administrative courts and courts of general jurisdiction.

The Law on Administrative Proceedings establishes the principle of universal competence over administrative disputes, that is every individual is entitled to access to a court where their rights are infringed in public administration matters. Meanwhile, the Law establishes the enumeration principle and sets cases of negative and positive restrictions on the jurisdiction of administrative courts.[40] The combination of both principles in one legal act indeed brings certain confusion into legal regulation. In legal theory the definition of jurisdiction of the administrative court is mostly dealt with in the perspective of distribution of jurisdiction between courts of general jurisdiction and administrative courts.[41] In practice disputes on the distribution of

39 Mykolas Roemeris, *Konstitucinės ir teismo teisės pasieniuose* (Pozicija 1994) 63. The author also formulated the definitions of both terms: 'body of general jurisdiction is a body entitled to perform all actions, except those which the law clearly takes out of the jurisdiction; meanwhile, the body of attributive jurisdiction is a body which only is entitled to perform actions that the law clearly assigns to it, it cannot engage in other activities'.

40 *Jurgita Paužaitė-Kulvinskienė*, 'Administracinė justicija: teorija ir praktika' 76.

41 See e.g. Deividas Poška, 'Bendrųjų ir administracinių teismų kompetencijos atskyrimas. Probleminiai aspektai' (2006) 59 *Teisė* 88–106 and Janina Stripeikienė in *Administraciniai teismai Lietuvoje: nūdienos iššūkiai Ambrasaitė-Balynienė, G. et.* (Lietuvos vyriausiasis administracinis teismas 2010) 302–332.

jurisdiction between courts of general jurisdiction and administrative courts are heard by a specially designated body – the Board on Jurisdiction. In establishing the scope of the jurisdiction of administrative courts it is equally important to address the question of suprajudicial acts, i.e. acts which are allocated neither to administrative courts nor courts of general jurisdiction. The activities of the Parliament, members of the Parliament, the President of the Republic, the Prime Minister, the Government (as a collegial body) and judges of supreme courts (the Constitutional Court, the Supreme Court, and the Court of Appeal) do not fall into the jurisdiction of administrative courts.

The special Board on Jurisdiction interprets this provision as a rule delimiting the jurisdiction between administrative courts and the Constitutional Court; however it basically has no prejudice to the right to access to court. The fact that the dispute is related to the activities of the Parliament or the President of the Republic of Lithuania does not affect the jurisdiction of courts. It is necessary to establish whether the activities of those subjects are regulated by the norms of public law and if so, the case will be resolved by administrative court. It is appropriate to point out that in its previous practice[42] the Board on Jurisdiction was assigning the disputes to the courts of general jurisdiction even where the cases concerned the activities of respective authorities regulated by norms of public law. The dispute concerning a decree of the President by which an individual was removed from the list to receive a state award was assigned to the court of general jurisdiction. One should also note the case[43] where a dispute concerning an application filed by a public education organisation asking to annul a resolution adopted by the Government of the Republic of Lithuania (as a collegial body) by which the permit to engage in the organisation of studies, was assigned to the court of general jurisdiction. Even though the Board on Jurisdiction recognised that by adopting the disputed resolution the Government as a collegial body exercised the functions assigned to it by legal acts, it ruled that the dispute cannot be assigned to the administrative court and thus should be heard by the court of general jurisdiction.

The principle of legal clarity presupposes that legal regulation on administrative procedure shall be clear and unambiguous; however, it is not easy to establish whether the right to access to administrative court encompasses the possibility to appeal against the activities of the President of the Republic and the Government. On the one hand, infringed rights, including administrative ones, may be defended before a court despite the fact of whether the constitutional right to access to a court is established by the law or other legal act.[44] Moreover, the rights of an individual

42 Applicant asked the court to rule on the decree adopted by the President of the Republic of Lithuania which was adopted in implementing the provisions of the Law on State Awards. Thus, pursuant to the LAP, the dispute cannot be assigned to the jurisdiction of administrative court. Having regard to the fact that the applicant was challenging an individual act which directly concerned his rights and legitimate interests and having referred to the Code of Civil Procedure which establishes a broader jurisdiction to the court of general jurisdiction rather than administrative courts, the Board on Jurisdiction ruled that the legal dispute shall be heard in courts of general jurisdiction. The Board on Jurisdiction. Decision of 16 April 2007 in case *public body Tarptautinė Baltijos akademija v the Government of the Republic of Lithuania.*

43 The Board on Jurisdiction. Decision of 7 July 2005 of in the case *public body Tarptautinė Baltijos akademija v the Government of the Republic of Lithuania.*

44 Ruling of 23 June 1999 of the Constitutional Court [on transfer of premises to societies of many-flat houses] Valstybės žinios, 1999, No 56-1813. Meanwhile, in another decision, the Constitutional Court

shall not be defended in a perfunctory manner, but in reality and effectively, *inter alia* against unlawful actions of state institutions.[45] In the decision adopted in 2006[46] the Constitutional Court expressed its position on the review of the legality of acts (omission) issued by the Government *in corpore*. It held that where there is no legal regulation due to the inaction of the Government and thus the rights of individuals are infringed, courts of general jurisdiction and administrative courts shall ensure the protection of infringed rights against the omission of public authorities by applying the provisions of the Constitution directly. The right to access to administrative court concerning the activities of the Government was addressed by the Constitutional Court also in 2010.[47] In this case the Court directly reviewed the constitutionality of the LAP. Applicants – Vilnius regional administrative court and the Supreme Administrative Court of Lithuania – referred to the Constitutional Court asking to rule whether the provision setting forth that the activities of the President of the Republic and the Government (as collegial body) do not fall within the jurisdiction of administrative courts as laid down in this law, is in compliance with the Constitution.

Three important aspects were emphasised in this constitutional case. First of all, the tendency to concentrate the constitutional review within the Constitutional Court was verified, that is administrative courts are not entitled to review matters that are assigned to the jurisdiction of the Constitutional Court. However, the administrative court is allowed to preliminarily assess the activities of the President of the Republic and the Government in as much as it is necessary for submitting the reference to the Constitutional Court where it should justify the doubts concerning the compliance of the act with the Constitution and statutes. Secondly, according to the Constitutional Court, the LAP must be interpreted as *inter alia* meaning that the activities of the President of the Republic and the Government in exercising state power cannot be the subject matter of an administrative dispute heard before the administrative court. However, it is possible that besides the discharge of state functions assigned to them, the institutions implementing state power also perform other activities. Thus, the exercise of state power may not be equated with activities embraced by the notion 'public administration' which is employed in the LAP. In cases where the aforementioned subjects are not participants in constitutional but administrative legal relations the legality of their activities may be assessed in administrative court and these activities are not regarded as suprajudicial. In this regard, the Constitutional Court even defines the categories where cases of this kind are possible, that is cases on the omission (delay) and actions for damages and civil service disputes. Thirdly, the

ruled that the judicial protection of infringed rights shall be guaranteed despite the fact of whether the rights are directly established in the Constitution. Ruling of 8 May 2000 of the Constitutional Court [on operational activities] Valstybės žinios, 2000, No 39–1105.

45 Ruling of 8 May 2000 of the Constitutional Court [on operational activities] Valstybės žinios, 2000, No 39–1105.

46 Ruling of 8 August 2006 of the Constitutional Court [on dismissing the legal proceedings on the compatibility of certain provisions of the Law on Courts, the Law on Remuneration for Work of State Politicians, Judges and State Officials and the Resolution of 28 December 2003 adopted by the Government with the Constitution] Valstybės žinios, 2006, No 88–3475, amendment – 2006.12.16, No: 137.

47 Ruling of 13 May 2010 of the Constitutional Court [on investigation into activities of the President of the Republic and those of the Government in administrative courts and on the dismissal of a member of the State Gaming Control Commission] Valstybės žinios, 2010, No 56–2766.

constitutional case under consideration also provides the decision on the jurisdiction of courts. It was ruled that cases concerning the result or consequence of the activities (failure to act) of the President of the Republic or the Government whereby the rights or freedoms of a person have been (could be) violated, *inter alia* concerning compensation for damage may be considered by the administrative court but not by courts of general jurisdiction.

2.3.7 Judicial fees

In administrative courts, the applicant should pay a court fee. There are exemptions, however, in cases about complaints in order to protect the State or other public interests, in cases concerning compensation for material and moral damages inflicted by unlawful acts or omission in the sphere of public administration, for example. Other litigation-related costs include: costs paid to witnesses, experts, and expert organisations; costs relating to the publication of hearing time and place in the press; transport costs; costs for the rental accommodation in the place of the court; other necessary and reasonable expenses. Under the LAP, each complaint (application) in administrative court is subject to a stamp duty in the amount of EUR 28 (excluding the exceptions). An appeal for the review of a court judgment must be subject to a stamp duty at the 50% rate payable upon the lodging of the complaint (application) with the first instance court. No fees in the cases on normative administrative acts.

An estimation of expert fees and other litigation-related fees, except from lawyer fees and costs, associated with the application for interim relief are regulated by a Government Resolution in 2002. There is a recommendation from the Minister of Justice and the Chairman of Bar concerning lawyer fees. The general rule is that the losing party has to bear all costs, including stamp duties and costs related to initial court proceedings. The party is also obliged to reward the costs of the winning party. The stamp-duty, expenses for correspondence, expert costs, and other costs usually are paid in full. But the legal costs for legal representation during the court proceeding are reduced as recommended by the Minister of Justice and the Chairman of Bar. However, these amounts are only recommended and depend on the complexity of the court proceeding, case material, and other factors. Nevertheless, in the absolute majority of administrative cases, state courts reduce parties' requested legal expenses for their legal assistance according to the recommended amounts and reasonableness

3 Right to be heard

In the LAP the Lithuanian legislator has established that an individual whose rights and interests are challenged has the right to be heard. This expressly establishes the obligation on the administration to start consultations on the adoption of respective administrative decision. The obligation on the institution to consult with the applicant is also laid down by the legal regulation passed in the special fields of administrative law, e.g. in the Law on Electronic Communications, or in the Law on Provision of Information to the Public etc. It is clear from the regulation in respective spheres of administrative law that the obligation to start consultations is expressed mostly in the areas where the administration faces the challenge of balancing the public interest with private interests, e.g. in the spheres of land planning or environmental protection. The due implementation of the obligation to hear the person concerned is a central point in any administrative procedure. The right to provide clarification, to submit comments and to give opinion on the matters in question is one of the main ones in entire administrative procedure. However, the obligation to hear the person concerned is not absolute and has certain exceptions allowing the adoption of the decision without consultations. Under general rule, the decision is adopted without consultations if the application is decided at once and this decision does not infringe the rights or interests of third parties.

The hearing of cases before administrative courts must be held in public. The presence in the courtroom of persons who are under the age of 16 is not allowed, unless they are parties to the proceedings or witnesses. The principle of public hearing is not applicable where the law prescribes written proceedings for the hearing of complaints and cases. To hold oral proceedings is a default obligation for courts of first instance, whereas the Supreme Administrative Court holds written proceedings, unless the chamber of judges decides otherwise. Parties to the proceedings have a right to ask the court of appellate instance to hold oral proceedings instead of written ones, yet the court is not bound by such a motion.

4 Right to legal counsel

The assistance of a lawyer is not compulsory in Lithuanian administrative procedure or administrative courts. The parties to the proceedings can defend their interests themselves or through their representatives. In this regard, there is no difference between the procedure before regional administrative courts and the Supreme Administrative Court. According to the LAP, the parties can be represented not only by a lawyer, but also by an another capable person, irrespective of his/her background. However, in practice, as a rule, parties are represented by lawyers.

5 Duty to give reasons

The obligation to state reasons in writing for all decisions is required by the LPA, so it is a general principle. But LPA contains an exception to it in cases when 'the application of the addressee of the administrative act is satisfied and the rights and freedoms of third parties are not restricted'. The reasoning does not have to set out the factual basis for issue of an administrative act. In general, administrative decisions are issued in writing. However, in some situations the law allows the oral issuing of administrative acts in urgent situations, when the case is objectively insignificant and the issuing of an administrative act in writing is impossible or insignificant.

The LPA dos not provides any specification for the reasons, if they must be adequate, clear and sufficient. In Art. 8(1) LPA regardless of the form in which 'reasons' is specified, there is definitely, what could be called a 'core definition'. Basically, stating reasons requires giving the factual and legal basis for the issue and also the considerations made when taking the decision. Administrative acts must consist of established facts, their evaluation and the provision of legal acts on which the decision is based.

6 Right of access to information

An applicant who considers that his request for information has been ignored, wrongfully refused or inadequately answered has access to a review procedure before an administrative disputes commission. The commission may be appealed within a month after the receipt of the information or within a month from the date of the information has been made available. The decision of the commission may be appealed to the administrative court within 20 days after the day of the receipt of the decision. In the case of refusal, the public administration entity must adopt an individual administrative act, which must contain, clearly formulated, all rights and duties and the specific appeal procedure. The reasons for a refusal should be provided to the applicant within 14 days after the receipt of this demand by the public authority. The request can be written or oral. The information can be given orally if the applicant does not ask for a written answer.

The applicant does not have to state an interest. When an applicant requests to make information available in a specific form (including in the form of copies), the public authority have to make it available (with certain exceptions). As a major rule, the requested information must be made available to an applicant within 14 calendar days after the receipt by the public authority. An application to an administrative dispute commission prior to applying to an administrative court is compulsory in this case. All information must be provided to the court if the court requests it. This information can influence the court decision. One of the types of judgments in administrative courts is to meet the complaint (grant the application) and rescind the contested act (or a part thereof), or to obligate the appropriate entity of administration to rectify the committed violation or to comply with any other order of the court. Courts can order information to be disclosed.

7 Legal aid

There is legal aid available in administrative legal protection. The current legal aid scheme is governed by the law on legal aid. Legal aid is divided into primary and secondary legal aid. Primary legal aid includes legal information and legal consultations outside the judicial procedure and is accessible to all citizens, EU citizens, and foreigners, irrespective of their financial resources. Secondary legal aid includes preparation of procedural documents, representation in courts, waiver of the stamp duty and other procedural costs. Access to secondary legal aid depends on the level of estate and income and covers 50 or 100% of all procedural costs. Some groups of persons (i.e. recipients of social allowance) can receive legal aid independent of their income. Legal aid is granted through special services, which are accountable to the Ministry of Justice. The refusal to grant legal aid is subject to appeal before administrative courts. Legal aid is subject to requirements as to resources, nationality, residence and admissibility. Everybody is entitled to primary or secondary legal aid if he/she is a Lithuanian national, a citizen of the EU, or a foreigner who is lawfully residing in Lithuania or in another EU state. Legal aid is given if the action is not manifestly inadmissible or devoid of substance.

Legal aid for NGOs is not foreseen. Law firms do not provide *pro bono* legal assistance in Lithuania. The legal clinics are responsible for primary legal aid. The primary legal aid is also given by the municipalities and by Ministry of Justice Information Bureaus in several cities (Kaunas, Klaipėda, Šiauliai, Druskininkai and other). The secondary legal aid is granted through five special services (in Vilnius, Kaunas, Klaipėda, Panevėžys and Šiauliai), which are accountable to the Ministry of Justice.

8 Reasonable time for procedure

Meanwhile, the administration is obliged to adopt a well-motivated decision within a reasonable time frame. Provisions of the LPA establish the time limits on the adoption of the respective administrative decision. Legal regulation laid down in particular fields of administrative law may establish different time frames (usually from two to six months subject to the complexity of the matter). Nevertheless, the administration is obliged to adopt a decision within a reasonable time frame irrespective of the particular sphere of administrative law. The general rule is the public administration shall complete the administrative procedure and adopt the decision of the administrative procedure within 20 working days from the beginning of the procedure. The public entity initiating the administrative procedure may extend the period up to ten extra working days where, due to objective reasons, the administrative procedure cannot be completed within the set time limit. A person shall be notified about the extension of the time limit for the administrative procedure in writing or by e-mail (where the complaint has been received by e-mail) and the reasons for the extension. An administrative court may initiate responsibility of a public authority when the administrative organ does not adopt the decision during the time limit and it has resulted in damage to the claimant. In several fields, the law established a regime of tacit acceptance. The silence of the administration causes the appearance of a tacit acceptance within the period fixed by law. There are some special time limits set by law for administrative procedures in different matters (e.g. social security and asylium cases).

According to the LAP the preparation of administrative cases before the court must be completed no later than one month after the date of the complaint (application). The proceedings before the administrative court must be completed and a decision made in the first instance no later than two months after the order for the case to the court hearing date, if the law does not provide shorter duration.

Where appropriate, the trial period may be extended up to one month. In cases concerning the legality of normative acts of the administration the time period may be extended up to three months. The judgment shall be drawn up and communicated to the public generally on the same day after hearing the case. Judgments relating to the legality of administrative acts and other complex cases may be passed and announced later than but not more than ten days upon the completion of the hearing of the case (in practice, it's used in almost all cases). When the right to a judicial decision within a reasonable time has caused damage, the person can obtain compensation for the damage. This possibility is foreseen in the Law on Compensation of Damage caused by Public Authorities.

In 2013–2014, the average length of proceedings in the Supreme Administrative Court of Lithuania lasted 6,53 months. According to the 'The 2014 EU Justice Scoreboard' data, Lithuania has one of the shortest length of court proceedings in Europe, as well as very little pending cases in courts. Since 2009, the hearing of appeals duration was also reduced 1.6 times.

9 Alternative dispute resolution

Arbitration in administrative matters is not yet a possible alternative. The settlement of an administrative dispute without referring the matter to the court is possible only in concrete cases, where it is explicitly provided for by law. In certain spheres the possibility of reaching a friendly agreement exists. For example, according to the Law on Tax Administration, the taxpayer and the tax administrator may sign an agreement concerning the sum of the tax due and the tax rate when neither of the parties has enough proof to base its separate estimates upon. After such an agreement is signed, the taxpayer gives up the right to contest the correctness of the calculation of the tax, and the tax administrator – to set a higher rate than had been agreed.

The LAP foresees a possibility for the parties to end the dispute (or a part thereof) by reaching a settlement agreement. Such a settlement agreement should not contravene the law and results in 50% concession of a stamp duty, once successfully accepted by the court.

3 Institutional system of legal protection

The principle of effective legal protection (*efektyvios teisminės gynybos principas*) presupposes an institutional system of legal protection. Starting in 1990 the approach towards legal protection in administrative law in Lithuania changed significantly. The development of the model of legal protection under administrative law in Lithuania concerns Art. 111(2) of the Constitution which provides the possibility for founding specialised courts to hear administrative cases. This constitutional norm was sufficient foundation for starting the reforms but it took seven years to implement these provisions in practice. One of the reasons is the lengthy political and scientific discussions concerning the need and financial possibilities of founding specialised administrative courts. After 1999 judicial control of the legality of the activities of the executive branch was operated within the quasi-judicial and judicial (administrative courts) system.

The principal legal acts – the LAP, the LPA, the Law on the Establishment of Administrative Courts (*Administracinių teismų įsteigimo įstatymas*), and the Law on Administrative Tribunals (*Administracinių ginčų komisijų įstatymas*) – have requested a new quality for legal protection in the sphere of public administration. It is also necessitated by Lithuania's membership of the European Union which requires taking into consideration the specific features of the European Union's *acquis communitaire* in the sphere of public administration and applying the principles developed during several decades of jurisprudence by European institutions of justice, that is the European Court of Justice and the European Court of Human Rights. In addition, one may reasonably question whether uniform administrative legal protection is possible in all the Member States and what possibilities Lithuania's administrative justice system has in this process. Attention should be paid to the fact that not only new members of the European Union such as Lithuania or the new comers such as Croatia and Bulgaria with a new system of administrative court, but also the older members such as Austria, France, Italy, Spain, and Portugal have reformed their administrative justice systems. Expanding discussions concerning the monitoring of the justice systems of the EU Member States and the initiatives such as the EU-Justice-barometer are also helping to implement and achieve the same level of effective legal protection in administrative law.

The dual institutional mechanism of legal protection under the current administrative law in Lithuania includes a judicial system (administrative courts) (*administraciniai teismai*) and a quasi-judicial system (administrative dispute commissions) (*ne teisminio nagrinėjimo administracinės institucijos*). The protection has some common features in quasi-judicial and judicial systems. The differences are: in a formal sense – according to the status of the administrative tribunals and administrative court; in a material sense – according to the scope of the dispute to be resolved; in a procedural sense – according to the law of procedures being employed; and in a functional sense – according to the aims in resolving the dispute.

3.1 The decision making administrative bodies

According to the LPA, the term 'entities of public administration' (*viešojo administravimo subjektas*) means institutions, agencies, services and civil servants (officials) having public administration rights granted to them under laws and implementing in practice the executive power or separate functions thereof. The entities of the public administration are acting on two levels: on the state administration level and on the local public administration level. The main legal form of acting is an administrative act (decision). Administrative decisions (acts) are classified into: individual administrative acts (*individualus administracinis aktas*) and normative administrative acts (*norminis administracinis aktas*). In most cases, the term of individual administrative act means an act of single application of law directed to a specific person or a definite group of persons. Normative administrative act is a legal act establishing the rules of conduct and intended for an individually unidentifiable group of persons.

In Lithuania, there is no legal concept of an administrative contract. All contracts, regardless of which institution is the party thereto, are regarded as civil contracts (this also includes public procurement). Administrative acts can also be classified into the groups of administrative acts adopted by central entities of state administration, and acts adopted by territorial entities of state administration. The distinction between these acts has a jurisdictional significance. Individual administrative acts adopted by central entities of state administration are usually reviewed by Vilnius Regional Administrative Court (as part of its so-called Additional Competence), whereas administrative regulatory enactments adopted by the same central entities of state administration are within purview of the Supreme Administrative Court of Lithuania.

3.2 Quasi-judicial administrative system

Pre-litigation procedure shall be regarded as a jurisdictional procedure supplementing the judicial procedure or as an alternative procedure. Judicial and non-judicial procedures are two forms of dispute settlement. They are both constitutionally justified[48] and do not compete with each other. It is for the individual concerned to choose the desirable form of judicial or pre-litigation protection. The pre-litigation system is not part of the judiciary; however, from a functional point of view it contributes to the administration of justice.[49]

48 *Jurgita Paužaitė-Kulvinskienė*, 'Administracinė justicija: teorija ir praktika' 38.

49 *Birutė Pranevičienė*, *Kvaziteismai* administracijos veiksmų teisėtumo kontrolės ir administracinių ginčų nagrinėjimo sistemoje: daktaro disertacijos santrauka (Lietuvos teisės universitetas 2002) 16.

The European Court of Justice has noted that the concept of court set forth in Art. 267 of the TFEU is a concept of Community law[50] and it may encompass not only judicial but also pre-litigation authorities. In the case *Nidera Handelscompagne BV v Valstybinė mokesčių inspekcija prie Lietuvos Respublikos finansų ministerijos*[51] the Tax Disputes Commission under the Government of the Republic of Lithuania was regarded as a 'court'. In assessing whether the pre-litigation authority may be recognised to be a court within the meaning of Art. 234 EC one should note the following aspects: whether the authority was established in accordance with law, whether its jurisdiction is compulsory, whether the procedure at the institution is adversary, whether the institution applies legal acts, and whether it is independent.[52]

In order to establish the pre-litigation procedure, from 1990 Lithuania implemented two directions of reform on pre-litigation institutions: first, already functioning authorities of public administration were vested with the right to resolve administrative disputes (e.g. the Competition Council, the Public Procurement Office); secondly, new institutions were established for settling administrative disputes.

The general pre-litigation system for administrative disputes was established in 1999 together with the establishment of the system of administrative court after the Parliament adopted the Law on Administrative Disputes Commissions and the Law on Administrative Proceedings. The Administrative Disputes Commissions are pre-litigation authorities of general jurisdiction. They are entitled to hear disputes only where the law does not provide for any other pre-litigation procedure. Priority is given to specialised pre-litigation institutions. If there is no specialised institution for settling the dispute out of court, then the administrative dispute is heard by administrative dispute commissions. The rules on the establishment of administrative disputes commissions and the principles of its activities are laid down in the Law on Administrative Dispute Commissions (LADC). Meanwhile, the rules on activities of the commissions are provided by the Resolution adopted by the Government of the Republic of Lithuania. At present there are the Chief Administrative Disputes Commission and several administrative dispute commissions of municipalities (even though these commissions should function in 60 municipalities).

Specialised institutions for resolution of administrative disputes out of court were established by adopting specialised laws: the Tax Disputes Commission under the Government of the Republic of Lithuania, the Contention Commission at the Ministry of Social Security and Labour, the Central Commission of Labour Experts, the State Social Insurance Fund Board etc. The rather broad system of pre-litigation institutions may be divided on the basis of different criteria. According to the place taken by the institution in the system of public authorities the institutions may be grouped into: institutions related to the authorities of executive branch (e.g. the Tax Disputes Commission, the State Consumer Rights Protection Authority) and institutions related to the legislator (the Seimas Ombudsmen's Office, the Office of Equal Opportunities Ombudsperson).

50 European Court of Justice, *Judgment of 30 March 1993, C-24/92 Corbiau v Administration des Contributions [1993] ECR 1–1277; Judgment of 17 September 1997, C-54/96 Dorsch Consult Ingenieurgesellschaft mbH v Bundesbaugesellschaft Berlin mbH [1997] ECR I-04961.*

51 European Court of Justice, *Judgment of 21 October 2010, C-385/09 Nidera Handelscompagnie BV v Valstybinė mokesčių inspekcija prie Lietuvos Respublikos finansų ministerijos [2010] ECR I-10385.*

52 European Court of Justice, *Judgement of 30 June 1966, Case 61/65 Vaassen-Göbbels [1966] ECR 261.*

As to the nature of their decisions, one can differentiate the institutions whether they make compulsory decisions or issue only recommendations. They have different composition as there are institutions composed of professional lawyers, others employ specialists of different fields. According to the functions one may distinguish between institutions having only a jurisdictional (dispute solving) function and others with administrative functions.

3.3 Judicial system – system of administrative courts

Creation of the judicial system in Lithuania had respective periods. The period from 1992 until 1999 concerned the preparation of the legal framework on the establishment of administrative courts in Lithuania. During this period no legal acts contained a clear institutional and procedural conception of Lithuania's administrative justice; the implementation of Art. 111(2) of the 1992 Constitution of the Republic of Lithuania had a good reason to be extended. The first stage of reform in 1999–2001 did not achieve the formation of an independent specialised administrative court system in an institutional sense. Instead, an intermediate model was selected, which partially depended on the courts of general jurisdiction in both an institutional and a procedural sense. At this stage a packet of legal acts (the Law on Administrative Proceedings, the Law on Establishment of Administrative Courts, and Amendments to the Law on Courts), which was enacted on 14 January 1999, established the following system of administrative courts: five regional administrative courts; the Superior Administrative Court; and the Administrative Case Division of the Court of Appeal of Lithuania. Administrative courts began to operate on 3 May 1999. During this period, the function of the supreme administrative court belonged to the Administrative Case Division of the Court of Appeal of general jurisdiction.

In the second stage of the reform, a new, two-level administrative court system was established. Five regional administrative courts were retained and the Supreme Administrative Court of Lithuania, which operates throughout the state's territory, was established. The Administrative Case Division of the Court of Appeal were abolished. Thus, after the new versions of the Law on Administrative Proceedings and the Law on Establishment of Administrative Courts came into force on 1 January 2001, the administrative court system that had existed for only a year and a half was reorganised and a model of independent administrative justice where administrative courts are independent from the courts of general jurisdiction was implemented. The essential aspect of this reform was the establishment of the Supreme Administrative Court of Lithuania.

Currently, five regional administrative courts are the courts of special jurisdiction established for hearing complaints in respect of administrative acts and acts of commission or omission (failure to perform duties) by entities of public and internal administration. Regional administrative courts hear disputes in the field of public administration and deal with issues relating to the lawfulness of regulatory administrative acts, tax disputes, etc. The Supreme Administrative Court is the first and final appeal instance for administrative cases assigned to its jurisdiction by law – cases on normative administrative acts with the central public state administration. It is the only appeal court for hearing administrative cases that have been examined by regional administrative courts. The Supreme Administrative Court develops a uniform practice of administrative courts in the interpretation and application of laws and other legal acts. There are 65 judges assigned to the review of administrative acts. Out of this number 48 serve in regional administrative courts and the remaining 17 are tenured in the Supreme Administrative Court of Lithuania. This number amounts to approximately 8% of all judicial positions.

3.4 Ombudsman

The *Seimas* Ombudsman Office (*Seimo kontrolierių įstaiga*) is one of the institutions protecting human rights and providing the legal protection in Lithuania. The Law of the Republic of Lithuania on the *Seimas* Ombudsman from 1994 enhanced the possibilities of the ombudsman to solve citizens' complaints regarding the abuse of office and bureaucracy of state and municipal officers or other violations of human rights and freedoms in the field of administration. The Parlaments Ombudsman's Office was established in 1994 by law. The *Seimas* Ombudsman's Office has a special place within the system of state institutions: it is neither the legislative, nor the executive, nor the judicial branch of power.[53] One of the main non-judicial remedies in the sphere of public administration is the petition for the Ombudsman concerning the abuse of office and bureaucracy of officers of the state government and municipal institutions. A number of the complaints that the *Seimas* Ombudsman's Office receives speak about the citizens' trust in the institution as well as the advantage of such a means to defend one's rights over another – it is cheap, accessible to everybody and it is also efficient enough. The task of the ombudsman is not to impose penalties on officers for violations but to prevent them from abuse of office and bureaucracy, and in this way improving the work of the public administration system and protecting human rights.

It may be observed that during the 20 years of activities of the *Seimas* Ombudsman's Office that the number of grounded and ungrounded complaints has been equal. Thus, it may be concluded that the quality of the officers' work is gradually improving. However, the situation in state institutions and municipal and county administrations is totally different: even if there is a distinct tendency towards the improvement of public administration in state institutions, the situation in county and local government is much worse. Every year the ombudsman investigates about 2,000 complaints. The complaints, which were found grounded, amounted to 30–40 per year%.

The complaints received by the Seimas Ombudsmen's Office have revealed the following key problems so far: inappropriate examination of requests from members of the public and inappropriate provision of services to them, refusal to provide requested information, non-fulfilment of the functions assigned to institutions and unreasoned decision making. After complaints were found to be grounded, the ombudsman brought the established violations to the officers' attention and the officers were asked to resolve these issues during the set period under the procedure provided by the law and other legal acts. Having established the contradictions or loopholes in the legal acts, the Ombudsman informed the *Seimas* and the Government and drafted 32 proposals to amend, and supplement legal acts or pass new ones. Having investigated the complaints and established a violation the Office made a decision to refer the material to investigative bodies or bring a court action in 10–20 cases per year.

53 *Birutė Pranevičienė*, 'Ombudsmenas ir viešasis administravimas' (2002) 32 *Jurisprudencija* 95–103.

The ombudsman uses mediation as an effective tool. Using this method, he/she turns to the institution concerned presenting the issues related to the contents of the complaint and asking to resolve the problem in good will. In many cases, following such mediation, problems raised in the complaint are resolved. Certainly, in some cases this method does not help, therefore, a thorough investigation of the complaint is conducted. The most important advantage of complaint investigation by mediation is that the complaint is examined and the problem is resolved particularly rapidly – within one month on average. This enables more efficient and speedier protection of a person's violated rights by focusing on systematic human rights problems, which are relevant to the major part of the society.

4 Conclusions

The current institutional model of effective judicial protection in Lithuania will presumably be improved. The reforms on the system of administrative courts have been completed by establishing a two-stage model of administrative justice. However, the complex system of pre-litigation institutions in respective spheres (tax disputes, social insurance disputes etc.) is not capable of ensuring equal and effective standards of legal protection in all categories of administrative cases.[54] Today no institutional structure for Lithuania's administrative justice exists but the material and procedural aspects of its functioning are causing the most problems.

There are dynamic changes to the procedural element of effective legal protection, which are determined not by the compliance of Lithuanian ordinary law on administrative procedure with supranational law but by the creativity of constitutional and administrative jurisprudence. Despite the fact that the scope of the relationships regulated by the LPA is very broad, the law does not address some questions at all. It also fails to address the need to improve its individual norms that have arisen in order to ensure effective legal protection and access to administrative court. One of the solutions has been discussed during the preparation of a modern Code of Administrative Procedure and this would be the basis for hearing disputes in both administrative courts and administrative quasi-judicial commissions.

54 Daniel A. Bilak, *Administrative Justice in Lithuania* (UNDP 2003) 31–33; *Birutė Pranevičienė*, 'Kvaziteismai administracijos kontrolės sistemoje' 76.

12 Dilemmas and challenges of legal protection against administrative actions in the Republic Macedonia

Gordana Siljanovska-Davkova and Renata Treneska-Deskoska

1 Historical developments

After World War II, in Macedonia and generally in Yugoslavia, in which Macedonia was one of the six republics, basic ideas in administrative law demonstrated two specific elements: first, the citizen's relationship to the administration was not characterised in terms of rights; and secondly, the means of recourse from a primary decision were to superior, internal administrative bodies rather than to independent external bodies such as courts.[1]

For the first time in communism, in 1952 general administrative-judicial control of public administration was introduced in Yugoslavia, with the Law on Administrative Disputes. Before that period, as in other communist countries, there was a resistance to submitting administrative acts to the control of the courts.[2] In administrative-judicial procedure, protection of rights and legal interests of individuals and legal persons was established, with providing a right to submitting a lawsuit, if they were not satisfied with the final outcome of the two-tier administrative procedure. Administrative-judicial first instance was installed within the Supreme Court of Macedonia and Federal Supreme Court, in which specialised Administrative Division was organised. The procedure that was applied by the Supreme Courts (both federal and Macedonian) in deciding administrative disputes was not judicial and was different from the procedure followed in other cases. Other external forms of control, such as ombudsmen, were non-existent.

The second Law on Administrative Disputes in Yugoslavia was adopted in 1977, three years after the adoption of the Constitution of the Republic of Macedonia of 1974. It was in force in Macedonia even after 1991, till 2007. The Constitution contained several guarantees for legal protection in administrative law. It provided that administration could decide in individual cases for rights and obligations only in a procedure prescribed by law in which everyone would have an opportunity to defend his rights and interests and could submit a lawsuit or other legal remedy provided by law against the adopted act (Art. 265 para. 1 of the Constitution). Right to complaint against the decisions and other individual acts of judicial, administrative and other state bodies was also guaranteed. But the Constitution also enabled legal ground for

1 *Administrative Procedures and the Supervision of Administration in Hungary, Poland, Bulgaria, Estonia and Albania.* SIGMA Papers, No. 17, OECD Publishing. 16.

2 Ivan Koprić, *Administrative Justice on the Territory of Former Yugoslavia* (SIGMA) 2 (available at http://www.sigmaweb.org/publicationsdocuments/36365948.pdf).

exception of the right to complaint if there was another way of protection of rights and of the legality (Art. 266 of the Constitution). Administrative dispute was provided for deciding on the legality of final individual acts (Art. 267).

The administrative act in ex-Yugoslav legal doctrine was defined as a legal (normative), individual, unilateral, binding act of administrative authority, deciding on administrative matters.[3] Administrative acts are individual in the sense that they refer to a particular case or cases and their application is limited to that case(s).[4]

Although, despite the constitutional basis of the administrative-judicial protection of rights, important guarantees for effective legal protection were missing in the practice, like right to trial within reasonable time, right to trial by independent court, right to be heard etc.

2 Current constitutional framework

The contemporary Macedonian Constitution was adopted in 1991 and changed several times. The right to effective legal remedy is not explicitly mentioned in the Constitution, but its certain aspects are guaranteed. Effectiveness of legal remedies is part of the principle of the rule of law, which is guaranteed in Art.8 of the Constitution as a basic value of the constitutional order. The administrative procedure is a fundamental instrument of the rule of law, particularly in relation to a protection of the constitutional rights of individuals against possible abuse of power by administrative bodies.[5] Effectiveness of legal remedies is also directly related to equality before the law, protection of personality and human dignity, the equal protection of rights, the right to judicial protection, and legality and finality.

The right of appeal is a constitutionally recognised right. Art. 15 of the Constitution guarantees the right to appeal against individual legal acts issued in a first instance proceedings by a court, administrative body, organisation or other institution carrying out public mandate. One of the fundamental principles of administrative procedures is the principle of two-tier proceeding (principle of deciding in two instances). This principle was general till 2005, when Art. 15 of the Constitution was changed. Now, the principle of two-tier proceeding is not a general one. Amendment XXI of 2005 guarantees the right to appeal against verdicts in first instance proceedings by a court. But it also provides that the right to appeal or any other legal protection against individual legal acts must be determined by law. So, current constitutional provision allows for the exclusion of the administrative appeal in certain administrative matters, if it is prescribed by a law. Therefore, the possibility to file an administrative appeal is a rule, but both Law on General Administrative Procedure and special laws can and do contain exceptions.

The right to a trial within a reasonable time is not mentioned explicitly in the Macedonian Constitution. Instead, the principle of priority and urgency for protection of constitutional rights and freedoms is mentioned. Art. 50 of the Constitution

3 Ivo Krbek, *Upravni akt* (Jugoslavenska akademija znanosti i umetnosti, Zagreb 1957) 16.

4 Vuk Cucić, 'Administrative Appeal in Serbian Law' (2011) 32 *Transylvanian Review of Administrative Sciences* 52.

5 H P Nehl, *Principles of Administrative Procedure in EC Law* (Hart Publishing 1999) 70–100 and Polona Kovač, 'Effective Adjudication through Administrative Appeals in Slovenia' (2013) 9 *Utrecht Law Review* 3.

guarantees that every citizen may invoke the protection of freedoms and rights determined by the Constitution before the regular courts, as well as before the Constitutional Court of Macedonia, through a procedure based upon the principles of priority and urgency. In addition, the relevant requirement of ECHR is indirectly recognised by the Macedonian legal system, as Art. 118 of the Constitution declares the supremacy of international treaties over conflicting national laws.

Amendment XXV of 2005 has created a basis for introduction of administrative courts in Macedonia. This constitutional amendment states that judicial power is exercised by courts, which are autonomous and independent. The Constitution does not specify the types of courts, their spheres of competence, their organisation and procedure, and these issues are left to a law adopted by a two-thirds majority vote of the members of Parliament.

The constitutional guarantees of legal protection in administrative law are further developed in the General Administrative Procedure Law, adopted in 2005, several sector-specific laws and the Law on Administrative Disputes (hereinafter LAD), adopted in 2006, but entered into force in 2007. The main orientation of the new legal regulation in administrative and administrative-judicial procedures was towards an optimal extent of codification, legality and substantive correctness in decision making and towards reliable bases of solutions.

Some provisions of LAD gave an opportunity for the Constitutional Court to interpret the meaning of the right to appeal as one of the elements of the principle of effective legal protection. The LAD did not regulate this right, but allowed only a limited possibility to submit the appeal against administrative acts which meant limitation of this right and a substantial procedural guarantee for effective legal protection in administrative law. The Law contained a provision that right to appeal was guaranteed only against court decisions adopted on oral hearings, called and held on the proposal of the parties in the proceedings. The Constitutional Court, taking into consideration that the courts usually decide on closed sessions, and oral hearings are only exceptions, concluded that the LAD made the appeal exceptional legal means which could be used very selectively and restrictively, and it is contrary to the constitutional provision guaranteeing right to appeal.[6] The Constitutional Court also noted that the LAD did not contain a systematic approach to the right to appeal and the precise term for submitting it. Further, it pointed that the right to appeal cannot be exercised restrictively, through norms that did not completely regulate this right, or they regulated it selectively.[7] After that decision of the Constitutional Court, the Supreme Court adopted a General Legal Opinion in 2009 in which it concluded that it is competent to decide on the complaints against the judgments of the Administrative Court following the procedure of the Law on Civil Litigation. One year later the Parliament amended the relevant provisions of the LAD extending the right to appeal and introducing the High Administrative Court to decide on them.

6 Decision of the Constitutional Court No. 231/2008 of 16 September 2009.

7 The Constitutional court also adopted another Decision on the issue of right to appeal, abolishing the part of the provision of the Law on Administrative Disputes regulating conditional possibility for use of this legal means, with the same argumentation as in its previous decision. See Decision No. 51/2010 from 15 December 2010.

3 Rights-based perspective

3.1 Rights of the parties in the administrative procedure

3.1.1 The right to be a party/right to intervention

Every natural or legal person upon whose request the proceedings is started or against whom the proceedings is leaded, or who has right to participate in the proceedings in order to protect his/her rights and interests, is considered as a party in the administrative procedure. State bodies, branches of the companies, associations, municipalities, groups of people, which do not have status of legal persons, are also considered as a party, if they are holders of rights and duties which are decided in the administrative proceedings. Trade unions can also be party, if the right of legal interest of some of their members is decided in such procedures. NGOs, foundations and political parties, which have an aim of protecting of a certain rights and interest of their own members, may upon request or with a consent of their member, initiate or intervene in an ongoing administrative proceedings concerning such rights or interests. Finally, the Public Prosecutor, the Public Attorney or other state organs with competence to protect public interest have the rights and duties of a party in the administrative procedures.

3.1.2 Ex officio reparation

The administrative body can *ex officio* repair its own decision in a procedure of repeating the administrative procedure and in a procedure for annulment of the decision. The repeating of the administrative proceeding can be initiated by the party or can be started *ex officio* by the administrative body that adopted the decision. Also, the Public Prosecutor can demand repeating of the procedure under the same conditions as a party. The procedure can be repeated if there are new evidences; the decision was issued on the basis of fake document or statement or was a consequence of a criminal act; the decision was based on the judgment in criminal procedure, which was abolished after that; the decision was reached upon a previous issue, which was later decided differently in its essential points etc. If the decision was subject to administrative dispute, the procedure can be repeated only for the facts which were established by the administrative body, but not for those which were established by the court in its proceeding.

The decision can be repaired *ex officio* in the period of five years after its delivery to the party. The exceptions to this term are possible if the decision is rendered on the basis of a criminal act or a substantially different solution on the previous issue in the case. The administrative body can repeal its own decision or replace it with a new one.

The procedure for annulment of the decision is started *ex officio* if:

(a) the decision, which was adopted was in court jurisdiction, or the issue that was solved in the decision could not be solved in administrative procedure;
(b) the enforcement of the decision can lead to the crime or other offence;
(c) the execution of the decision is not possible;
(d) the decision was adopted in *ex officio* started procedure, which was not allowed for such issues etc. The decision can be annulled as a whole or partially.

3.1.3 Right to appeal

The administrative procedure is two-tier. Under certain conditions the party has a right to appeal also in the case when the body has not adopted a decision in the determined term. Besides the parties, the Public Prosecutor, Public Attorney and other state bodies are entitled to appeal against administrative decisions of first instance, when the law was violated in favour of individual or legal persons against the public interest. However, there are cases in which the parties cannot file an appeal, because there is no higher administrative body. This is the case when the Government issued the original decision. Notably, the interested parties may bring these decisions before the Administrative Court.

The administrative appeal has suspensive effect and the decision cannot be enforced until the decision of the body in second instance is not delivered to the party. Of course, there are exemptions of the suspensive effect of the appeal if the emergency measures should be taken or to avoid the appearance of irrecoverable damage.

The appeal is submitted to the first instance body that issued the decision. If this body finds that the appeal is justifiable it can solve the issue differently and replace its own decision with a new one. If the first instance body finds that the proceeding was not completed and that could have effect on the decision, it can carry on the procedure and issue a new decision. Of course, the party has also the right to appeal against the new decisions in both cases.

If the first instance body does not replace its decision, it should send the appeal to the higher body, which can reject the appeal, annul the decision in total or partially, or modify it. If the second instance body determines that a non-competent body adopted the decision, it would annul the decision and would send the issue to the competent body. If the higher body finds that a competent body issued the decision, but the evidences are not properly established, or the disposition in the decision is unclear or inconsistent with the reasoning, it can solve the issue and adopt the decision. If the higher body considers that the first instance body can solve the irregularities of the procedure faster and more efficiently, it will annul the decision and return the case to it. The party has a right to appeal against the decision that will be issued by the first instance body. If the new appeal is submitted against, the higher body will solve the issue.

The parties can also submit an appeal when the administrative body does not solve the issue and adopt the decision. If the higher body finds that the decision is not adopted because of justifiable reasons, it will determine the term in which the first instance body must solve the issue. That term should not be longer than 30 days. If the reasons for delay are not justifiable, the higher body will demand from the first instance body to send it all documents from the case and will solve the case by itself.

3.1.4 Right to be heard

The General Administrative Procedure Act of 1999 (GAPA) guarantees the procedural rights to the parties, like the right to be heard and to participate in the administrative procedure. For example, oral hearing is obligatory if two or more parties with conflicting interests participate in the procedure and if there is a need for hearing of the witness or expert witness. In the cases in which the oral hearing is not obligatory, the parties can propose it. The law allows exceptions to the hearing in the cases of the so-called 'short procedures', when there is a need for emergency measures in public interest.

3.1.5 Duty to give reasons

In general, the administrative body is obliged to give reasons in its decisions. In simple cases in which only one party participates, as well as in simple cases in which two or more parties participate, but none of them objects to the raised demand which is accepted by the administrative body, the reasoning in the decision can contain short explanation of the demand of the party and citation of the legal acts on the basis of which the case was solved. In such cases the decision can be written in a form prescribed by the law.

In other cases the reasoning of the decision should contain: a short explanation of the demands of the parties; the established facts; the reasons that were decisive upon evaluation of the evidence; the reasons because of which some of the demands of the parties were not accepted; the legal acts and reasons on which the decision was made. If the appeal does not postpone the decision, the reasoning contains reference to the legal act providing that. The reasoning should also contain explanation on the conclusions against which the appeal is not allowed. If the administrative body has discretionary power in decision making, it should give the reference to the legal act that provides such competence and to give the reasons on which it based the decision.

The legal provisions prescribing the duty to give reasons in the decision are applied also to the decisions issued in the appellate procedure. The reasoning in the second instance decision should contain the evaluation of all statements in the appeal.

3.1.6 Decision within reasonable time

In order for efficiency, the law regulates the duration of administrative procedures, which can take 15 or 30 days depending on the difficulty of the case. In 2008, a new legislation introduced the institution of the 'silence of administration'. According to the new regulation, if the competent administrative body does not decide the case, it has to be regarded as the request of the party has been accepted. Since the law had set strict conditions for this outcome, it was criticised as declaratory, frivolous, unrealistic and inoperative. As a consequence, the relevant law was modified in 2011 again, deleting the provision that silence is acceptance and providing procedure that follows after the silence of administration and enabling the interested parties to turn to the State Administrative Inspectorate for demanding oversight over the 'silent' administrative body. If the oversight does not result in adoption of a decision in an additional period of time, the party has the right to start an administrative dispute. Nevertheless, the critiques have not ceased even after the amended regulation, because, 'under the current legal framework, the principle of tacit administrative approval was applied inconsistently, causing uncertainty and delays for citizens'.[8]

3.1.7 Other fair process rights in administrative procedure

In Macedonian administrative procedure, the parties have the right to access to the file and to make a copy of it, bearing the costs for that. This access is provided in the

8 2013 Progress report, European commission, Brussels, 16 October 2013 SWD(2013) 413 final, 9.

presence and oversight of the official person. Right to access to the file has also every person who has legitimate interest for that.

In addition, the GAPA prescribes obligation for the administrative body to take care that the ignorance of the parties and other persons participating in the procedure does not damage their legal rights. The administrative body is also obliged to inform the parties for the course of the proceeding.

3.2 Rights of the parties before the court

If an administrative act violates the rights or legitimate interests of the parties, or the objective legal order, its judicial review can be launched by a special form of action, administrative suit. The object of the judicial proceeding is the final (legally enforceable) administrative act. The administrative act can be disputed if the law is applied incorrectly; the act was adopted by an incompetent body; the procedure for adoption of the law was incorrect (the facts are not established correctly; or an incorrect conclusion was derived from the facts).

Everyone who can be a party in administrative procedure can also be a plaintiff in the administrative dispute before the Administrative Court. So, every natural or legal person whose right or legal interest is violated by an administrative act can submit the administrative suit. State bodies, branch of companies, municipal bodies, or groups of people who do not have legal personality can start an administrative dispute if they can be holders of rights and obligations, which were decided in administrative procedure. Municipal bodies can also be party of administrative dispute if the right to local self-government was violated. The trade unions, political parties and NGOs under the same conditions as in administrative procedures, can be party in the administrative dispute. Besides these, if the law or public interest is violated with administrative act or administrative contract, the State Attorney can submit administrative suit.

The administrative suit does not have suspensive effect. Exceptions to this rule are provided in the law.

Before 2008, the Administrative Court had the power to control the legality of all government acts (individual and general) regulating individual relations. However, the Constitutional Court abolished this competence, arguing that the power to control legality of general legal act falls within its own competence.[9]

It is to be noted that in some cases private interests might remain unprotected. The Government, for example, often issues decrees on *inter partes* relations imposing obligations on citizens which may not be reviewed by any court.[10] The problem arises from the restrictive definition and interpretation of the general act by the Constitutional Court. Some acts are considered by the Constitutional Court as individual ones and it refuses to decide on their legality. On the other side, the Administrative Court does not consider itself as competent to decide on the legality of these acts. That leaves 'empty spaces' in which no judicial protection is provided in certain cases.

9 Decision of the Constitutional Court No. 75/2007.

10 Borce Davitkovski and AnaPavlovska-Daneva, 'Realizing Citizens' Rights Through the Administrative Procedure and Administrative Dispute in the Republic of Macedonia' (2009) 1 *Hrvatska javna uprava* 134.

The administrative disputes are decided before the Administrative Court in special proceeding, regulated by the LAD. Generally, the Court decides in administrative cases in closed sitting on the basis of the record, petition and the response to the petition. The Court will hold oral hearings in certain cases.[11] The parties of administrative disputes have the right to get a judicial decision within a reasonable time on the basis of LAD.

An important measure for greater effectiveness of the legal protection is the right of the Administrative Court to decide in full jurisdiction. According to the LAD, these cases are, for example, in case of error in law, in legal disputes about administrative contracts; in legal disputes about acts passed in a misdemeanour procedure, in the situation of silence of administration, etc.

The Court is obliged to give reasons for its decision. The statement of reasons should include the facts and evidence, and the relevant law that has been applied. The Administrative Court has also to show why particular arguments or evidence submitted by a party have not been accepted.

The right to appeal against the first instance judicial decision has been regulated in details since 2010. The appeal can be submitted to the Higher Administrative Court within 15 days from the delivery of the decision. The appeal is allowed in case of the essential violations of the procedure, if the facts were wrongly and only partially established, or in the case of alleged error in law.

The law also provides extraordinary legal remedies: a party may demand the repetition of the proceedings if:

- new facts and evidence have been raised and they can contribute to a different decision;
- an interested person was not given a chance to participate in the administrative dispute;
- it is needed after the concerning judgment of the ECtHR; or

when the objected decision:

- was adopted as a result of criminal offence;
- is based on an abrogated judgment;
- has been grounded on false documents.

4 Institutional perspective

4.1 Judicial protection in administrative law

In 2007, the Administrative Court, as a special judicial tribunal for adjudicating administrative disputes was established. Before, the Supreme Court had the power to control the lawfulness of administrative acts. In June 2011 the High Administrative Court started working as an appellat court in administrative disputes.

11 In those cases in which (a) it is needed because of the complexity of the administrative dispute; (b) it is necessary for better clarification of the administrative matter or for establishing factual situation; (c) when the court takes evidence; (d) when there is a silence of the second instance administrative body; (e) when the court cannot take decision on the basis of the facts determined in the administrative procedure (because there is contradiction between them, they are not fully established etc.); or (f) when the court decides on the merits of the case (decides in full discretion).

The reason for changing the model of the administrative adjudication in the Republic of Macedonia was systematic delay in the resolution of administrative appeals, which lead to expensive, protracted and exhausting administrative-judicial procedures.[12] The time from the beginning of the lawsuit until the final judgment in administrative disputes before the Supreme Court ranged from six months to several years.[13] Each year in the administrative department, from around 3000 cases only about 2000 were decided, or about 67%.[14]

When the Administrative Court came into existence, it 'inherited' 5,804 cases from the Supreme Court that had been competent in administrative disputes beforehand. The Law establishing the Administrative Court entered into force in May 2006, but the Court started working on December 2007. In the meantime the administrative cases were pending, enhancing the case load of the new court. In fact, the Administrative Court cannot solve even the number of new cases that it receives each year. The number of cases that remain undecided was progressing till 2011. While the Supreme Court decided an average of 45% of its cases before 2007, the Administrative Court decides only 37% of its pending cases.

If we take the high number of unresolved cases as an indicator of inefficiency, one of the reasons for the shortage is the technical and personal deficiencies of the Administrative Court. The insufficiency of the assistants as well as the inexperience of the judges of the Court has contributed to its inability to cope with its increasing case load. Another obstacle for efficient administrative judiciary is lack of cooperation between Administrative Court and state bodies, which did not deliver to the Court the acts that were needed for deciding the lawsuits.[15]

The High Administrative Court was introduced by law in 2010, but started working with delay (on 30 June 2011). Nevertheless, its efficiency is better than the first-degree court, as Table 12.2 shows.

Table 12.1 The case load of the Administrative Court 2008–2013

Year	*New cases*	*Total number of cases*	*Decided cases*	*Unresolved cases*
2008	8497	14301	5147	9154
2009	9043	18197	7857	10340
2010	9792	20132	6322	13810
2011	11867	25726	9746	15980
2012	14675	30591	16363	14228
2013	12754	27005	14544	12461

Source – *The Reports for the work of the Administrative Court 2008–2013*

12 Strategy for Reform of Judicial System, 2004, 15–16 and Draft Law on Administrative Disputes, April 2006.

13 Natasa Pelivanova and BrankoDimeski, 'Efficiency of the Judicial System in Protecting Citizens against Administrative Judicial Acts: The Case of Macedonia' (2011) 1 *International Journal for Court Administration*, 45–53.

14 Strategy for Reform of Judicial System, 2004. The inefficiency of the Supreme Court in deciding administrative matters was also noted in the reports of the Ombudsman. Report for the work of the Ombudsman for 2000, 14.

15 Report for the work of the Ombudsman for 2012, 49.

Table 12.2 Complaints submitted to High Administrative Court from 2011–2013

	2011	*2012*	*2013*
Cases from previous year		5	40
New cases	55	1750	1982
Resolved cases	50	1715	1935
Unresolved cases	5	40	87

The inefficiency of the administrative judiciary is criticised in the reports of the Ombudsman. In 2009, the Ombudsman received 79 complaints for violation of the right to trial in reasonable time in administrative matters (10.62% of all complaints for trial in reasonable time); in 2010 from all complaints for trial in reasonable time, 10.04% were about administrative disputes, and 9.56% in 2011. The Ombudsman noted that the duration of the 'judicial procedures in administrative matters lasts two or three years, beside the fact that the Administrative court does not decide in adversarial procedure'.[16]

The Supreme Court of the Republic of Macedonia according to current law is competent for extraordinary legal remedies in administrative law as well as to decide on the demands for protection of the right to trial in reasonable time in all types of court proceedings, including administrative ones. It means that parties whose right to trial within the reasonable time in criminal, civil or administrative procedure is violated, can initiate procedure before the Supreme Court for its protection. That is a new competence given to the Supreme Court under the influence of the judgments of the European Court of Human Rights against Macedonia on the basis of Art.6 of the European Convention of Human Rights.

According to the Constitution, the parties of administrative disputes, after exhausting all available judicial remedies, in defence of certain basic rights like freedom of conscience, freedom of expression or right to association, may submit a constitutional complaint to the Constitutional Court. The Constitution uses the term 'claim for protection of freedom and rights' for this special procedure, and entitles only citizens to launch it. Such a complaint may be submitted against an administrative act or activity within two months from the day of the final legally valid individual act, or from the day when the citizen got information about the activity, but not later than five years. In these cases, 'the Constitutional Court may provide direct protection for the mentioned freedoms and rights only if they are violated by a final individual act of an ordinary court'.[17]

4.2 The role of the Ombudsman in the rights protection in administrative law

Although the institution of Ombudsman (People's Defender) was introduced by the Constitution of 1991, the Law on Ombudsman was adopted in 1997. In accordance with the law, the Ombudsman is competent for protection of the constitutional and legal rights of citizens when violated by state and public administration, and other

16 Report for the work of Ombudsman for 2011.

17 Svetomir Skarich, 'Constitutional Courts of the Republic of Macedonia' in Giussepe deVergottini (ed.), *Giustizia constitutionale e sviluppo democraticone i paesi dell Evropa Centr-orientale* (Torino 2000) 143.

bodies performing state functions and organisations with public mandates. The Ombudsman cannot interfere in the cases, which are in court procedure.

The procedure before the Ombudsman can be initiated by a person whose rights are violated, or by the Ombudsman himself/herself. But, if the Ombudsman is to institute the proceedings, either on his own initiative, or upon a petition, which has been lodged on behalf of the aggrieved person by a third party, the consent by the aggrieved person shall be required to start the proceedings. The proceedings before the Ombudsman are not formal and free-of charge for the petitioners. That makes the Ombudsman more accessible to the individuals. The Ombudsman will not institute the proceedings if more than one year has elapsed from the wrong-doing or the last decision of the body, except when he assesses that the petitioner has been late for justifiable reasons.

The administrative bodies are obliged to furnish the Ombudsman with all the information and data, within their competencies, irrespective of the level of secrecy, and shall enable him/her to carry out the investigation. All officials and other employees of the body must respond to the Ombudsman's call to co-operate in an investigation and provide all necessary explanations. The Ombudsman may summon any witness or expert to an interview about the case he/she is dealing with.

When the Ombudsman considers that the right of complainant is infringed by the administrative bodies, he/she may give recommendations, proposals, opinions and indications on the manner of the removal of the determined infringements. Ombudsman can also raise an initiative for commencing disciplinary proceedings against an official or even submit a request to the competent Public Prosecutor for initiation of a criminal procedure. The Ombudsman may also request temporarily postponement of the implementation of the administrative act until the decision by the second instance body or competent court is adopted if he/she estimates that infringements of rights and execution of the administrative act may cause irreparable damage to the right of some of interested persons in the proceeding.

The administrative organs and other organisations have the obligation to act upon the proposals, opinions, and recommendations of the Ombudsman, and within a time framework, not longer than 30 days, inform the Ombudsman about the undertaken measures and actions initiated by his requests. If they fail to comply and do not inform the Ombudsman about the implementation of his proposals and recommendations, or only partially adopt said activities, the Ombudsman can inform the next higher organ about it, an authorised ministry, the Government of the Republic of Macedonia, and, with a special report, the Assembly of the Republic of Macedonia, or publicise the case. After the procedure is completed, the Ombudsman notifies the petitioner.

The Ombudsman in Macedonia is not always satisfied by the attitude of the bodies of state and public administration and other organisations towards him. He has declared many times that the responsible officials did not respond to invitations for conversation. Sometimes they sent lower administrative officials, and often their responses were not on the satisfactory level. Also, there is a remarkable percentage of recommendations and suggestions of the Ombudsman, which were not fulfilled by the respective bodies. For example, in 1998, in 42.20% of the cases, the bodies did not respect the recommendations of the Ombudsman, in 1999 it was 37.65%,[18] in 2000 it was 39.03%.[19]

18 Report for the work of the Ombudsman for 1999, 18.

19 Report for the work of the Ombudsman for 2000, 21.

5 European perspectives

The case law of the European Court of Human Rights has influenced the Macedonian legal frame in the field of respect and protection of the right of trial within reasonable time.

ECtHR practice had contributed to the already mentioned improvements in the Law on Administrative Disputes with the changes guaranteeing the right to appeal and increasing the transparency and possibility for oral hearings in the administrative dispute procedure, too. At the beginning, LAD did not regulate the right to appeal, but introduced a very limited possibility to submit it. Actually, LAD was missing a systematic approach to the right to appeal and there was no precise term for submitting it. But, following the ECtHR case law, the legal changes were introduced guaranteeing the right to appeal in administrative court procedure. Also, firstly, Macedonian LAD stipulated oral hearings as an exception, only as a possibility, not as an obligation for the Administrative Court. This provision was criticised as not complying with the right of fair trial as it is regulated in ECHR and was changed in 2010. After Macedonia was condemned for violation of Art. 6 and Art.13 of ECHR in many cases, including those on administrative disputes,[20] in order to improve the effectiveness of judicial proceedings, the Law on Courts was changed in 2006, introducing a special procedure for complaints on violation of the right to trial in reasonable time. An interested party could apply to the immediately higher court if he/she considered that the court deciding his/her case breached the right to a hearing within a reasonable time. The immediately higher court was to deal with the length complaint within six months after the application had been lodged and to decide whether the court below had breached the right in question. It would award just satisfaction to the claimant if it found a violation of the right to a hearing within a reasonable time. The just satisfaction was payable from the court's budget.

The ECtHR criticised these provisions of the 2006 Act, because they contained terms that were open to various interpretations and it was not clear which court was competent to decide upon the length of remedy.[21] The criticism was useful and resulted in changes to the Law in 2008, according to which the Supreme Court had exclusive competence to decide upon the length of remedy. A special department was created within the court to deal with length-of-proceedings cases. An interested party can seek protection of his or her right to a hearing within a reasonable time while proceedings are pending, but not later than six months after the decision becomes final. The Supreme Court decides, at two levels of jurisdiction, within six months after the complaint is lodged. In doing so, the court applies the rules and principles of the European Convention and the criteria established in the Court's case law, namely the complexity of the case, the applicant's conduct and the conduct of the competent authorities. If it finds a violation, the Supreme Court awards compensation and, where appropriate, sets a time-limit for the court in question to determine the case on the merits. Decisions at first level may be appealed against before the Supreme Court's second instance panel. The compensation is paid to the successful claimant within three months after the Supreme Court's decision becomes final.

20 *Dumonovski v Macedonia* App no 13898/02 (ECHR, 8 December 2005); *Docevski v Macedonia* App no 66907/01 (ECHR 1 March 2007).

21 *Parizov v Macedonia,* App no. 14258/03 (ECHR 7 February 2008) §§ 44 and 46.

The Government of Macedonia in 2012 adopted a Strategy for adoption of a new Law on the General Administrative Procedure. The Strategy points that provisions which regulate the silence of the administration should be carefully reviewed and also envisages a review of legal remedies in order: to introduce an effective, convenient and economical way to protect the legal rights of the parties before filing an appeal to the administrative courts; to provide the opportunity and duty to effective self-control of administrative authorities; and to reduce the administrative burden on the courts by resolving cases within the internal procedures for legal remedies. It also points to the need for increasing control over the legality of administrative acts and actions within the administrative procedure in order to reduce the number of initiation of administrative disputes.

6 Conclusion

We have many dilemmas about the level of effectiveness and efficiency of the Macedonian system of legal protection in administrative matters, led by detected shortcomings. First, besides the legal changes, there are still legal gaps in the competence regulation of the Administrative and other courts that leave certain rights without judicial protection. Secondly, rights of the parties to be heard in the administrative dispute procedure are still not properly and strongly guaranteed, in the absence of strict and precise obligation for oral hearings. Thirdly, we are lacking complaint as a regular legal remedy for procedural or administrative actions towards acts which are not administrative. This is very important, knowing that the administrative activities are not limited only to administrative acts. Fourthly, the practice shows that our administrative justice is slow and delayed. Fifthly, ECtHR practice is still not given deserved attention and implementation. Sixthly, there is no permanent and adequate cooperation among courts, state and public administration and other relevant organs.

To those legal problems, we can add political ones, such as: problems with independence and impartiality of our judicial system as well as lack of professional, competent and depoliticised administration, recruited by merit system; absence of developed legal culture, as a result of authoritarian heritage, weak institutions and *partitocrazia*; fragile civil society, that is often object of instrumentalisation; weak public opinion, created by media under state, oligarchic and party pressure; unheard scientific community. All these factors are obstacles to effectiveness of legal protection in administrative matters in Macedonia.

Macedonia became a candidate for EU membership in 2005 and since then has achieved many times positive reports by the Commission, but has not been given a date for negotiations by the Council. EU itself has defined the terms under which accession could occur (the Copenhagen criteria). Membership criteria are also related to a democratic political system and system of public administration. Knowing that the EU–prospective is the key force and a powerful motive for positive democratic developments, Macedonia has to work on the ability to take on the obligations of membership. Independent and efficient judiciary, including the administrative one that protects citizens against administrative acts and activities is both an obligation and challenge for us.

13 The principle of effective legal protection in administrative law in The Netherlands

Karianne Albers, Lise Kjellevold and Raymond Schlössels[1]

Introduction

Towards the end of the nineteenth century, discussions on the administrative judicial system in the Netherlands gained momentum. Under the influence of developments in France (e.g. *recours pour exces de pouvoir*) and Germany (*Verwaltungsrechtsschutz*) an extensive debate took place about the desirability of an independent administrative judiciary with a general jurisdiction. However, the discussions did, to put it mildly, not go smoothly. Not everyone shared the opinion that a State under the rule of law (*Rechtsstaat*)[2] required independent judicial control of (decisions of) the administration.

This started to change in the beginning of the twentieth century. The Netherlands legislator finally established specialised administrative courts. The first major administrative court became the Central Appeals Tribunal (*Centrale Raad van Beroep*, 1902), which, for example, adjudicates social security disputes. Nevertheless, it took a long time before the final settlement of disputes by the administration itself came completely to an end. Only in 1985 did the European Court of Human Rights in *Benthem v The Netherlands*[3] put an end to the appeal to *de Kroon* (The Crown). The Crown (from a constitutional viewpoint: the Government) was, for a long time, the body that decided in the highest instance regarding many administrative disputes.

The present system of administrative justice came into being at the beginning of the 1990s. The enactment of the General Administrative Law Act (hereafter GALA) was especially important. This law strengthened the position of private persons with regard to the administration. It emphasises sound administration and the procedural rights of private persons (for example, the principle of hearing both sides of the argument). Under the influence of the GALA, effective and timely legal protection has become increasingly important. In 2013, new reforms of administrative procedural law took place.[4] These are intended to lead to a less time-consuming and more effective administrative justice.

1 Raymond Schlössels is professor of Constitutional and Administrative law at Nijmegen University. Lise Kjellevold-Hoegee is a staff lawyer at the Dutch Bar Association and Karianne Albers is associate professor of Constitutional and Administrative law at Open University Netherlands (Heerlen).

2 During the nineteenth century the German concept of *Rechtsstaat* dominated the discussion of administrative justice in the Netherlands. J. van der Hoeven, *De drie dimensies van het bestuursrecht* (Alphen aan den Rijn, Samsom H. D. Tjeenk Willink 1989) gives an analysis of the history of Netherlands administrative justice.

3 *Benthem v The Netherlands* App no 1/1984/73/111 (ECHR, 23 October 1986).

4 The changes with respect to digital litigation will not be dealt with here.

In this contribution we will explore the general principle – or the basic assumptions – of effective legal protection in Netherlands administrative law.[5] We will discuss the history of administrative justice and its constitutional framework (II). We then go on to discuss the present-day system of administrative legal protection (III). Thereafter we focus on the characteristics of Netherlands administrative procedure and the specific rights of parties (IV). We also pay attention to some European aspects (V) and specific problems of the Dutch system of administrative justice (VI). This contribution is drawn together by a conclusion (VII).

1 Netherlands administrative justice and the constitutional framework

1.1 Rule of law and administrative justice

The principle of the rule of law and democracy are closely connected. The administration has to act in accordance with democratically granted and clearly regulated powers. It goes without saying that the government must respect the fundamental rights of its citizens. Judicial control of the administration and legal protection against the infringement of civil rights are essential building blocks in a careful system of checks and balances.

At present, we can speak of constitutional cooperation[6] between legislator, judiciary and administration. This is crucial for the legal protection of the rights of private persons with respect to the administration. Principles of sound administration and many procedural rights protect private persons' interests. In many countries, the situation was different a century ago. Unwritten administrative law hardly existed. The administration could act freely within the limits of its powers (*pouvoir discretionaire, freies Ermessen*). There was little room for judicial intervention and control, except, for example, where the administration had infringed property rights. The situation in the Netherlands fit into this image. This explains why proposals made in 1905 for the introduction of general administrative courts in the Netherlands still met with fierce opposition.[7] The conviction that administrative courts were unnecessary fit the legal culture of that period. In the Netherlands there was great faith in the integrity of the administration. So, the necessity of administrative legal protection by courts was not felt.

However, in the twentieth century, a 'rights-based perspective' made considerable headway. The position of private persons with respect to the administration became stronger. Legal protection against (decisions of) the government (and administrative bodies) developed in the Netherlands along different lines:

(a) specialised administrative courts were set up in certain fields (among other areas, civil servants law, social security law and economic administrative law);
(b) various administrative legal disputes were decided by the administration itself and in particular by 'the Crown' (for example, environmental disputes);

5 We do not deal with the specific legal protection with respect to administrative decisions involving a 'criminal charge' (for example, administrative penalties).
6 B. W. N. de Waard, *Samenwerkende machten: Wetgeving en rechtspraak in dienst van het bestuur* (Zwolle, W. E. J. Tjeenk Willink 1994).
7 Van der Hoeven (n. 2) 124–142.

(c) since 1976 the Council of State (Law Department) provided, more or less, as a general administrative court (appeal against single case-decisions);
(d) the civil courts were given an important task in providing general and additional legal protection (among which, the granting of compensation for damages).

The result was a complex system of legal protection in which the Crown's position was striking. For many years this instance – the highest Dutch administrative body – functioned as 'pseudo court'. It was only in the 1980s that efforts were made to fundamentally reform this system. We will describe the present system below (in para 3 of this chapter).

1.2 The constitution

Since 1887, the Netherlands Constitution (*de Grondwet*) has contained a legal basis for the legislator to design an administrative judicial system.[8] However, there is no constitutional requirement to actually set up (separate) administrative courts. Even the present-day Constitution regulates amazingly little with respect to legal protection against the government. For example, unlike the German *Grundgesetz*, the Netherlands Constitution does not provide for an explicit right of access to court and fair trial.[9] This is remarkable. However, the Constitution does contain provisions on the organisation of the judiciary. The Constitution also provides, for example, for the right to a public hearing and the requirement of giving a reasoned judgment.

The Constitution even contains one provision that plainly seems to be in conflict with effective legal protection. Netherlands courts may not review national legislation for its conformity with the Constitution (constitutional review), or with general legal principles.[10] Moreover, the Netherlands does not have a (separate) constitutional court. This is a controversial point and may even be incomprehensible to non-Dutch lawyers. Nevertheless, in practice it does not lead to a less effective legal protection. Netherlands law stands in an open relationship with international law (monist system). All Netherlands courts may review whether national legislation is in accordance with provisions in treaties that are self-executing ('are universally binding').[11] Most basic rights, as they are codified in the international human rights treaties fall within this category. From this perspective, there is in fact an effective constitutional review. By reviewing whether Dutch administrative law provisions are compatible with the relevant treaties the administrative courts have, for example, held that many discriminatory provisions in social security laws are in conflict with the principle of equality.

2 The present system of legal protection in administrative law

The Dutch system of legal protection against administrative decisions generally has three phases. First, there is a mandatory preliminary procedure (usually an objection procedure), subsequently appeal is open to the administrative department of the district

8 C. A. J. M. Kortmann, P. P. T. Bovend'Eert, J.L.W. Broeksteeg, C.N.J. Kortmann, B.P. Vermeulen *Constitutioneel recht* (7th edn., Deventer, Kluwer 2012) 62–267.

9 However, there is a draft law in consultation to amend the Constitution on this point.

10 Binding regulations of the Government and ministers, as well as regulations of provinces and municipalities *may* be examined for compatibility with the Constitution.

11 Kortmann et al. (n. 8) 173–175.

court (*Rechtbank*) and finally appeal (in second instance) is open to the Administrative Law Division of the Council of State (*Afdeling bestuursrechtspraak van de Raad van State*). Yet, there exist a lot of exceptions and procedural abnormalities. For example, in several administrative cases no preliminary procedure is required. In other cases there is no appeal in second instance. Besides, specialised administrative courts are competent in tax disputes, social security matters and in economic administrative law (see below).

2.1 The mandatory preliminary procedure

A preliminary administrative procedure generally precedes appeal to the administrative court. Key functions of this procedure are reconsideration and correction of (legal) errors. The GALA contains two preliminary administrative procedures: the objection procedure and the administrative appeal.

The objection procedure is the usual preliminary procedure. In this phase the administrative body which originally gave the (disputed) decision examines its own decision's lawfulness. The objection procedure contains a number of guarantees, such as, the duty to hear the arguments of the interested parties. The objection procedure has to be initiated by an interested party which has also the right to appeal to the administrative court (after the reconsideration is completed). There are no costs for the objection procedure.

In the Netherlands it is thought that such a mandatory preliminary (objection) procedure offers a number of advantages. First, the influx of cases at the administrative court can be limited. A second advantage is that if appeal is nevertheless lodged with the administrative court following the decision on the objection, the dispute will have been to a certain extent delimited during the objection procedure. As a result, the administrative court can more easily get to the core of the case. The objection procedure can also be used to clarify the facts and to remedy legal errors. Thirdly, the objection procedure offers the possibility to resolve the dispute informally (for example, through mediation). In the Netherlands the interest of informal dispute resolution between the administrative bodies and private persons has grown significantly in the recent years. For example, by means of a simple phone conversation the administration will often try to settle a dispute without the objection procedure having to be used.

Administrative appeal is another mandatory preliminary procedure. This procedure is only applicable where this has been provided for in a special statutory regulation. Administrative appeal excludes the objection procedure. Administrative appeal means a review of the original decision by a different administrative body (generally one higher in the hierarchy). An example is the lodging of administrative appeal with the provincial administration against a decision of the Municipal Executive (made up of mayor and aldermen).

2.2 The organisation of the Dutch administrative justice

The objection procedure results in a new decision (the reconsidered decision). Administrative appeal results also in a (new) decision of the (higher) administrative body. An interested party may lodge an appeal with the competent administrative court against those (new) decisions. An administrative court may only examine the lawfulness of a decision and not its effectiveness.

The district court (*Rechtbank*) is the general administrative court in first instance (since 1 April 2013 there are eleven district courts on 16.8 million inhabitants).

Parties and administration may thereafter (so in second instance) appeal against the judgment of the district court. The nature of the case determines which high administrative court is competent. At present (2016), there are (still)[12] five highest administrative courts that hear administrative appeals:

(a) the Supreme Court (*Hoge Raad*, HR),[13] competent in tax law cases;
(b) the Administrative Law Division of the Council of State (*Afdeling bestuursrechtspraak van de Raad van State*, ABRvS), the highest administrative court with general jurisdiction; e.g. competent in cases involving planning law, environmental law and immigration law;
(c) the Central Appeals Tribunal (*Centrale Raad van Beroep*, CRvB), which, for example, adjudicates social security disputes;
(d) the Trade and Industry Appeals Tribunal (*College van Beroep voor het bedrijfsleven*, CBB), which rules on disputes in the field of economic administrative law; and
(e) the Appeals Court Arnhem-Leeuwarden (*Gerechtshof* in Arnhem-Leeuwarden), competent in cases of administrative penalties for traffic violations.

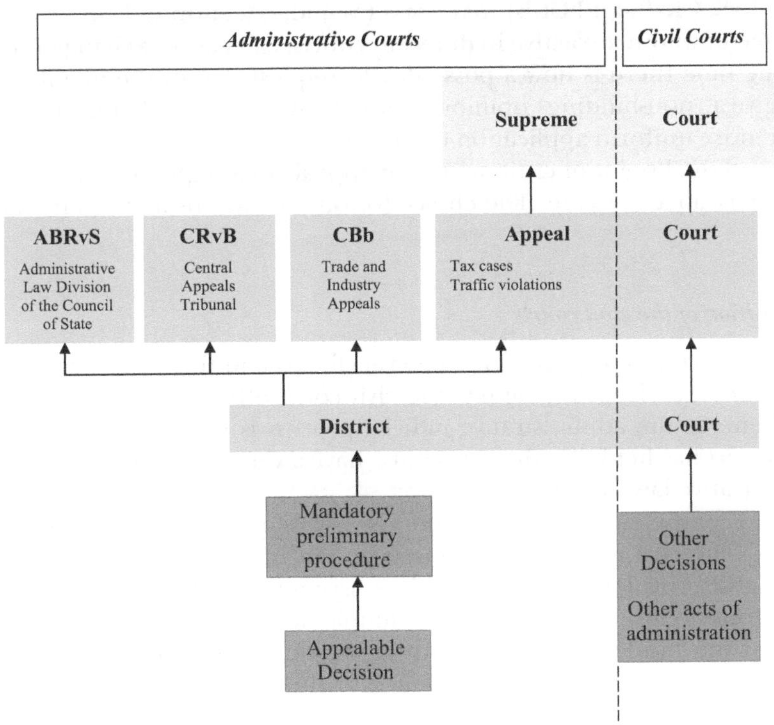

Figure 13.1 Administrative and civil courts in the Netherlands

12 There are plans to reform the organisation of the high administrative courts by limiting the number of them. The continued existence of the Central Appeals Tribunal (CRvB) and the Trade and Industry Appeals Tribunal (CBB) are uncertain.

13 The Supreme Court is not an appeals but a cassation court. In tax cases, after appeal with the district court, appeal may be lodged with a court of appeal. Thereafter, cassation before the Supreme Court is possible. As a rule, cassation is not possible in other kinds of administrative cases.

2.3 Bottlenecks in the organisation of administrative justice

There are a number of bottlenecks in the Dutch system of administrative justice. Some of these are important with regard to effective legal protection.

First, the limited jurisdiction of the administrative courts is a subject that comes up repeatedly in the Dutch legal literature.[14] The jurisdiction of the Netherlands administrative court is linked to the concept of decision. If a dispute between a private person and the administration does not involve an appealable decision, the civil court is generally competent. Disputes which come within the jurisdiction of the civil court concern e.g. acts with no intended legal effect (factual acts), civil law acts, or decisions which are *ex lege* excluded from appeal. This system has the disadvantage that private persons sometimes have to bring the dispute with both the administrative court and the civil court in order to get a full settlement.

A second point of criticism is that, in a system with various highest administrative courts (see above), the unity of the law is insufficiently guaranteed (e.g. the interpretation of the GALA). The involved courts try to reach agreements on the interpretation of the law through consultation. However, such informal discussions and agreements are not very transparent. Since 2013, three of the highest administrative courts (ABRvS, CRvB, and CBB) may use a five-judge section in leading cases. These judges, some of whom are active in different courts, can easily exchange information. At the same time there is now a possibility to request one of the members of these courts to give a (non-binding) opinion in administrative cases. These facilities should improve a more uniform application of the law.

A third and final point of criticism is that appeal (to a higher court) is not open in every administrative law case. The choice for one or two instances is not always well grounded.

2.4 The position of the civil courts

The Dutch civil courts play an odd – but crucial – role in the legal protection against the administration. To put it simply: the civil court offers supplementary legal protection whenever the administrative judicial process is inadequate. Since 1915, the Supreme Court has held that the civil courts have a very broad competence,[15] including administrative law disputes.

The broad competence of the civil court is very valuable but it does have less attractive aspects. The civil court is not allowed to 'get in the way' of the administrative court. The civil court has to ensure that inconsistent case law does not arise and that private persons do not try to by-pass the administrative court. In order to prevent the civil courts from hindering the administrative ones, the Supreme Court has developed a number of rules giving precedence to the administrative courts. Thus, for example, the civil court must refer a private person to an administrative procedure that offers sufficient guarantees. A claim may also be inadmissible if there was an administrative procedure available (which was not used).

14 See, for example, R. J. N. Schlössels, *Het besluitbegrip en de draad van Ariadne* (inaugural lecture Nijmegen, Boom Juridische uitgevers 2003); F. J. van Ommeren, P.J. Huisman, G.A. van der Veen, K.J. de Graaf *Het besluit voorbij* (Den Haag, Boom Juridische uitgevers 2013).

15 Hoge Raad, 31 December 1915, NJ 1916/407.

Further, there are rules on the basis of which the civil court has to follow the judgments of the administrative court. We will only mention two of the most important ones here. If the administrative court has quashed a decision, the civil court will assume that the decision was indeed unlawful (assume a tort).[16] On the other hand, if the administrative court has held that an appeal against a decision is unfounded, the civil court will assume that the decision was lawful. Moreover, lawfulness is assumed – apart from some exceptions – if the private person has not appealed the decision even though it was possible to do so.[17]

2.5 The position of the national Ombudsman

The office of National Ombudsman has existed in the Netherlands since 1 January 1982. The control by the Ombudsman covers – in brief – all acts by the (civil servants of the) central administration and the police. Acts of the local and regional authorities may be covered as well. The legislator allows the municipalities and provinces to set up their own independent ombudsman or committee by way of alternative. An ombudsman examines whether an administrative act is an act of sound administration. The National Ombudsman cannot make legally binding decisions. Nevertheless, his decisions have a great deal of authority. His recommendations are generally followed by the administrative body.

3 The Dutch administrative procedure in more detail

3.1 Access to the administrative courts

Access to the Netherlands administrative courts is to a large extent based on the concepts of 'administrative body' (*bestuursorgaan*), 'decision' (*besluit*) and 'interested party' (*belanghebbende*).

3.1.1 The administrative body

The definition of administrative body is provided for by the GALA. Under the definition fall, first of all, the bodies of the central, local and regional authorities, such as the Government, the ministers, the Municipal Executive (made up of mayor and aldermen) and the mayor. In addition, there are many special administrative bodies that have been set up under specific laws. A well-known example is the 'Administration Agency for Employed Persons Insurance', which deals with the implementation of various social security laws. Legal persons under private law are sometimes administrative bodies as well. This is the case to the extent public law powers are granted to a private law legal person. The private law legal person is considered to be an 'administrative body' when it exercises those public law powers, but only then. An example is the Authority for the Financial Markets, which, among other things, supervises securities transactions. This authority is a foundation under private law.

16 Hoge Raad, 31 May 1991, AB 1992/290.
17 Hoge Raad, 16 May 1986, AB 1986/573.

3.1.2 The decision

The concept of decision is defined by the GALA in a way that it is a written decision of an administrative body containing a legal act that has the character of public law. The competence of the administrative court is linked to the concept of decision. As the GALA declares, '[a]n interested party may appeal a decision with the administrative court.'

Only a written decision by an administrative body is a decision within the meaning of the law. As a result, there is no possibility of appealing an oral decision with the administrative courts. The fact that a decision must entail a legal act means that the decision must be aimed at having legal effect. A negative decision, such as the refusal to grant a permit, has no legal effect. However, the GALA has provided for several 'corrections' in such cases. As a negative decision has far-reaching consequences for the applicant, the legislator has provided that the denial of a request for a single-case decision[18] is equated with a decision. In addition, in the interest of effective legal protection, the non-timely grant (or denial) of a decision has been equated with the taking of a decision.

An administrative decision has a public law character. Hence, private law legal acts by the administration (for example, the buying and selling of land) are not decisions. It must generally be based on the powers given to the administration by the legislator. Both single-case decisions and decisions with general implications (such as the decision to make a street one way) fall under the concept of administrative decision.

The main rule is that appeal may be lodged with an administrative court against a decision within the meaning of the GALA by a natural or legal person who is an 'interested party' (see below). Nevertheless, there are several important exceptions to this rule.

The most controversial one is that appeal is not permitted against generally binding provisions, such as municipal regulations. Nor is appeal possible against national laws. This, however, is because the national legislator is not an administrative body.

The prohibition of appeal against generally binding provisions has its origin, among other things, in the principle of separation of powers. The Netherlands legislator was of the opinion that, for example, the administrative court may not quash by-laws enacted by democratically chosen municipal councils. This legislator's 'antique' standpoint is no longer valid. In practice, there is actually no real limitation to the review of generally binding provisions. After all, a private person (with sufficient interest) can generally challenge a by-law in the civil courts. These courts provide supplementary legal protection (see above).

There is also a possibility to challenge a generally binding provision before the administrative courts 'by way of exception'. This works as follows: an interested party lodges an appeal against another decision which is based on a generally binding provision. He then argues that this decision is unlawful because the generally binding provision on which it is based is unlawful. The administrative court will then (also) review the generally binding provision.

18 Compare: P. Craig, D. Curtin, G. della Canea, H.C.H. Hofmann, O. Mir, J.P. Schneider, M. Wierzbowski, J. Ziller 'Single Case Decision-Making' (*Book III of the Research Network on EU Administrative Law* 2014) (available at www.ReNEUAL.eu) accessed 10 June 2015.

3.1.3 The interested parties

In the Netherlands only interested parties may appeal with the administrative court (and follow the objection procedure that precedes appeal). The GALA defines 'interested party' as: 'that person whose interest is directly affected by a decision'. The administrative court sets five requirements when applying the concept of interested party:

(1) The party must have its own interest. A (written) authorisation is required if one contests a decision on behalf of someone else.
(2) The interest must be capable of being objectively determined. Interests involving matters of principle or of a purely emotional, psychological, or instinctive nature are not sufficient.
(3) A current interest must be at stake. A future interest is not sufficient.
(4) The interest has to be personal. It must be sufficiently differentiated from that of a random person. Hence, for environmental, construction and planning decisions the distance to, and the view from, the property dealt with in the decision is relevant: a person who lives 150 metres from a new wind turbine may contest the permit, but a person who lives 1000 meters away may not.
(5) A direct interest must be at stake. A derived interest is, in principle, not sufficient. There can often be said to be a derived interest if a person is indirectly affected by a decision, via a contractual relationship with an interested party. Thus, a supplier of a supermarket will generally not have an interest in the permit to build that supermarket.

Netherlands administrative law broadens the concept 'interested party' for legal persons that promote general and collective interests. That these interests are being promoted has to be evident from the statutory aims of the legal person (for example, a foundation) and from its actual activities. The statutory aim must also be sufficiently defined. In particular in environmental law, the right of appeal of interest groups (for example, organisations that are involved in natural and environmental conservation) can contribute to an effective legal protection.

3.2 Time periods for objection and appeal

Objection and appeal are admissible only if the objection and appeal notice is filed in a timely fashion. Netherlands administrative law generally uses a relatively short objection and appeal period of six weeks. In many cases a pro forma objection or appeal is made. The applicant then has the opportunity to provide grounds for the appeal during a given period (often four weeks).

3.3 Financial thresholds

There are no costs for filing an objection. A financial contribution (court fee) for the administrative court procedure[19] has to be paid by the parties. In 2016, this is EUR 46-EUR 168 for natural persons in district court procedures. For legal persons and

19 In civil cases the court fees are higher.

administrative bodies the fee is EUR 334. The court fees are higher for appeal. In most cases natural persons have to pay EUR 251 and legal persons and administrative bodies, EUR 503. Court fees are intended to act as a threshold for the lodging of an appeal. Although the financial threshold has been kept relatively low, the threshold should not be so high that private persons are denied access to a court (cf. Art. 6 ECHR).

3.4 The 'reformed' Netherlands administrative procedure

Netherlands administrative procedure has undergone a major metamorphosis in the past 20 years. In the past ten years in particular the court-culture has changed. The most recent legislative reforms took place in 2013. The buzz words nowadays are: speed, effectiveness and efficiency. Digitalisation (electronic proceedings) is also receiving much attention.

The new approach aims at dealing with cases more 'expeditiously' during the proceedings. Long pleadings by the parties are no longer welcomed. The administrative judge will try to get to the core of the case as quickly as possible.

3.5 Scope of the proceedings

A first, important step toward present-day administrative legal procedure was taken in 1994. At that time the legislator abandoned what is known as the classical control and examination model. This model assumes that an administrative judge will examine *ex officio* whether a decision is compatible with the law (legality control). *Ex officio* review of decisions for their conformity with the law can have serious disadvantages for private persons. For example, their legal position may be worse than it was before the appeal (*reformatio in peius*). Furthermore, a judge may go beyond what the private person has requested (*ultra petita*). These weaknesses have been acknowledged in the Netherlands and have led to a revision of the administrative procedure.

Since 1994, the main rule is that the administrative court will give a judgment on the grounds of the notice of appeal. Only in exceptional cases is examination *ex officio* permitted.[20] Naturally, the court must check whether it is competent and whether the appeal is admissible. However, the appellant himself may determine which issues he wants to put before the court and which not. In other words, he must bring the dispute regarding a decision before the court. In Dutch administrative procedure private persons do not have to be represented by an attorney (although it is often wise to have legal representation because cases and administrative procedure law are complex). The appellant may formulate the appeal in his own words. The administrative judge can ask questions and may 'delimit' the scope of the appeal. Simply stated: the judge must examine closely why the decision is challenged. The judge then applies the law: *iura curia novit* ('the court knows the law').

The end of *ex officio* legality control since 1994 has not led to a conflict with the European requirements of an effective and non-discriminatory legal protection and the principle of effective legal protection (requirements of equivalence and effectiveness;

20 D. Brugman, *Hoe komt de bestuursrechter tot zijn recht?* (dissertation Nijmegen) (Den Haag, Boom Juridische uitgevers 2010).

the principle of effective judicial protection).[21] In the *Van der Weerd* case[22] the Court of Justice of the European Union made it clear that EU law does not require that the national court make an examination ex officio if the rights of one of the parties protected by Union law are at stake. Of great importance, however, is that during the procedure a party is in fact given the real opportunity to put forward appeal grounds that are based on Union law. The Netherlands administrative procedure meets this requirement.

3.6 Individual legal protection

The Dutch legislator has also emphasised the principle of individual legal protection. This is in fact one of the fundamental goals of administrative justice. Unlawful actions of the administration become relevant only if the private persons are prejudiced in their interests. Hence, nowadays the administrative courts do not 'simply' quash decisions in case of violation of the law. The administrative court may even 'ignore' violations of the law on the strict condition that it is plausible that interested parties did not suffer damages because of the infringement. Annulation requires that a violated rule or principle protects the interests of the involved party in an evident way. After quashing the administrative courts must attempt to settle the dispute in a final way, if possible by deciding the case themselves (instead of the competent administrative body).

3.7 The judgment of the administrative court; effectiveness

The Dutch administrative courts may give a final judgment in a dispute if the appeal succeeds. Thus, after quashing a decision, it may confirm the legal effects of the quashed decision. Further, after quashing a decision, it may give a decision itself (instead of the administration). However, the administrative courts for a long time did not often make use of this possibility.

The reason for this restraint is because under the separation of powers doctrine the administrative court is not allowed to step into the shoes of the administration. Consequently, the administrative courts usually use this power only if the administration reasonably could have taken only one decision.

In the period 2008–2010, the administrative courts have moved away from this 'reserved' approach. From 2008, the judgments handed down by the highest administrative courts put more emphasis on the fact that an effective and definitive legal protection is of great importance. Both the Administrative Law Division of the Council of State and the Central Appeals Tribunal take the position in their judgments that when an administrative court quashes a decision it must consider whether it is possible to settle the dispute definitively. On the basis of the new case law[23] the

21 In relation to Netherlands law, see J. H. Jans, R. de Lange, S. Prechal and R. J. G. M. Widdershoven, *Europeanisation of Public Law* (Groningen, Europa Law Publishing 2007), chapter II.

22 Joined cases C-222/05 to C-222/05 *J. van der Weerd and Others v Minister van Landbouw, Natuur en Voedselkwaliteit-* [2007] ECR 1–04233.

23 ABRvS 17 March 2010, ECLI:NL:RVS:2010:BL7777, *JB* 2010/109; ABRvS 17 March 2010, ECLI:NL:RVS:2010:7778, *JB* 2010/110; ABRvS 23 June 2010, ECLI:NL:RVS:2010:BM8841, *JB* 2010/179; CRvB 3 November 2010, ECLI:NL:CRVB:2010:BO4110, *JB* 2011/11 and CRvB 14 March 2011, ECLI:NL:CRVB:2011:BP6843, *JB* 2011/110.

administrative court must investigate if it can give a new decision to replace the decision being quashed.

This approach was given a legal basis in the 2013 revision of the GALA.[24] It follows from the GALA that if an administrative court quashes a decision, it must assess *ex officio* whether it can settle the dispute definitively within the limits of the law. Of course, the views of the parties need to be heard before the dispute is settled in a final way.

If a final settlement of the dispute is not possible, the administrative court has the authority to give an interim ruling. In this ruling it can ask the administration to remedy the defect. In appeal (higher court) the administrative court can also give an order for it to do so. The interim ruling with feedback to the administration is known in the Netherlands by the somewhat odd name 'administrative loop' (*bestuurlijke lus*). This concept is interesting because the administrative court can give the administration the 'opportunity' to remedy or revise its own decision. This can speed things up a lot. Moreover, the law provides that other parties' interests may not be disproportionately prejudiced. If (even) an interim ruling does not lead to settlement of the dispute, the court will then decide that the administration must take a new decision on the basis of its judgment.

3.7.1 Confirming the legal effects of a quashed decision

In a number of situations the administrative court may confirm the legal effects of the quashed decision. First, this may be done for reasons of efficiency (procedural economy). One example of this is where a new decision is of no help to an interested party because the decision was quashed for procedural irregularity. Accordingly, the administration will likely take a new decision with the same substance as the one that was quashed. If the new decision will not deviate from the original one, it may be more efficient to confirm the legal effects of the quashed decision.[25]

Secondly, it may be efficient to confirm the legal effects if the quashed decision has had factual consequences that cannot be changed. In such a case the administrative court may conclude that it is better to confirm the legal effects of the quashed decision. Before arriving at this assessment, the court will have to weigh all the interests at stake. A well-known example is that of a house that has already been built. If the building permit is quashed *ex post*, it does not mean that the house will be demolished. Demolition would often be a very far-reaching measure. This is certainly the case if the defect in the permit is a minor one. In this case it is better for the administrative court to confirm the legal effects of the permit. Damages may be granted for other interested parties (if they so request) if the conditions for liability have been met.

Lastly, the administrative court may confirm the legal effects of a quashed decision to avoid *reformatio in peius*. An example is found in the law on subsidies: during the proceedings in appeal, the administrative court may conclude that the administrative body has incorrectly interpreted the regulations on the granting of a subsidy;

24 *Staatsblad* 2012, 684. See C. L. G. F. H. Albers, 'Het wetsvoorstel aanpassing bestuursprocesrecht. Knippen en plakken in plaats van een fundamentele herbezinning' (2011) 50 *De Gemeentestem*.

25 See also ABRvS 31 July 2013, ECLI:NL:RVS:2013:529, *JB* 2013/183.

nevertheless, a correct application of the regulation would lead to a lower amount of subsidy.

3.7.2 The power of the administrative court to settle the dispute itself

If the administrative court cannot confirm the legal effects of a quashed decision, it must investigate whether, after the quashing of the decision, it is possible to decide the case itself. The court's authority to give a decision itself (in other words, instead of the administration) is laid down by the GALA. If, following the quashing of the decision, the administrative court does give a judgment itself, the court's judgment will replace the quashed decision. The administrative court will thus determine what the administration's decision should be.

In any case, the administrative court may give a decision itself if it is clear that there is only one lawful decision that the administration can take.[26] If, after the annulment of the administrative decision a number of lawful actions can be taken, the situation is different.[27] In order to prevent the administrative court from taking over the constitutional role of the administration, it may not, for example, step into the administration's shoes and weigh the relevant interests. Nevertheless, under certain circumstances the administrative court may decide itself, even though the administration does have some discretionary powers. Nowadays the administrative court is allowed to decide itself if the court is certain that the new (lawful) decision that would be taken by the administration will not be any different than the decision it is going to take.[28] This approach attempts to build a bridge between the requirement of the separation of powers and effective and timely dispute settlement.

Where the administrative court itself takes a decision the case must either involve a decision where the administration has no discretion (whereby on legal grounds only one correct decision is possible) or a case in which it is clear to the court what the (new) decision must be. The court can take into consideration standard policy and the standpoints taken by the parties during the proceedings. In any case, the parties (administration and private persons) may, if they so agree, request the administrative court to decide the dispute itself.

3.7.3 Administrative 'loop' and the instruction to the administration

Since 2010, the Netherlands administrative courts have another interesting competence: they have the power to give an interim ruling, as has been mentioned above. In this interim ruling the court can give the administration the opportunity to remedy a defect in the decision (or to have it remedied). This power (which, as noted above, is given the rather odd name 'administrative loop') offers the administration the possibility to repair the decision before the final judgment is handed down.

The 'administrative loop' is also part of the contemporary practice of effective dispute settlement. If the administration had the opportunity to remedy the defect, the administrative court may continue to hear the case. Parties then have the chance to

26 CRvB 3 January 2003, ECLI:NL:RVS:2003:AF3991, *AB* 2003/99.

27 ABRvS 31 July 2013, ECLI: NL:RVS:2013:529, *JB* 2013/183.

28 ABRvS 21 March 2012, ECLI:NL:RVS:2012:BV9463, AB 2012/233, JB 2012/112.

comment on the changes made and the way the defect was remedied. The improvements in the decision can then be taken into consideration by the court in its final judgment.

In the first instance (district court), the administration is not required to follow the court's request to remedy the decision. This is not the case in an appealing proceeding. The appellate court, by means of an interim ruling can order the decision to be repaired. If the administrative body does not remedy the defect, the administrative court (on its own) will review the original (disputed) decision. It will likely to be quashed. For an effective and final dispute settlement it seems obvious that the court then will order the administrative body to take a new decision, taking into consideration the court's judgment. The court is not, however, required to do this.

If the court chooses to order the administration to give a new decision, it can give instructions with respect to that new decision. The court can also require the administration to take a different action on the basis of the court's judgment. Even if the court does not give (after quashing) an explicit order that a new decision is to be given, it is obvious that the administration will use the judgment as basis for its new decision.

3.7.4 The competence of the administrative court to award damages

The competence of the Dutch administrative court to award damages is limited. At the request of an interested party damages may be awarded for, among other things, an unlawful decision, an illegal action in the course of administrative procedure and a non-timely decision. The request can be made during the proceedings concerning the decision or in a separate procedure.

However, even in these cases the administrative court does not always have competence. Since 2013, the competence to award damages has been regulated as follows. In certain cases the administrative court has exclusive competence: roughly speaking, in tax, social security and civil servants cases. The civil court has competence in all other disputes above a threshold of EUR 25,000 (larger and more complex claims). Below this threshold, the interested party can choose between the administrative court and the civil court. The background to this distinction is that in the Netherlands the civil court has traditionally been viewed as the court with the most expertise in the area of liability and damages. This can easily be explained because in the Netherlands the liability of the government is based on the (civil-law) doctrine of tort. The civil courts have considerable experience with this doctrine.

3.8 Duration of the procedure

The (lengthy) duration of administrative decision making and legal procedures is a recurring theme in the Netherlands literature and legal practice. Administrative bodies are bound to legal decision periods. If statute law does not provide a specific period, single case decisions should be taken within eight weeks of receiving the application. The problem is that these decision periods are not always met.

In the Netherlands a private person has various possibilities to seek relief if the duration of the decision making process exceeds the period set by law. He can, for example, complain to the National Ombudsman. However, the National Ombudsman cannot compel the administrative body to finalise a decision within a certain time period. But the Ombudsman may express that the administrative body acts in an improper way. Administrative bodies will take this 'hint' very seriously.

Appeal to the administrative court is also possible if no decision is given at all. In that case the court will not look at the substance of the case. It will only determine that the decision was not taken within a reasonable time and that the decision still has to be given. As a rule, the administrative court will set a term of two weeks and will also impose a default penalty.

As to the delay during the administrative legal procedure, on the basis of the jurisprudence of the European Court of Human Rights (ECtHR), the highest Netherlands administrative courts have embraced the right to compensation of damages when a 'reasonable period of time' is exceeded.[29] It is important to note that under the principle of legal certainty they have extended this right to cases that formally do not fall under Art. 6 ECHR. The administrative case law assumes that if a 'reasonable period of time' has been exceeded, this will cause stress and frustration. This forms the grounds for compensation for immaterial damages. This period starts at the moment when an objection or appeal is brought against a decision. For the Dutch administrative law this means that the period usually starts at the same point in time as the day on which the notice of objection is filed. The end of a 'reasonable period of time' is at the moment at which a dispute is definitively settled. If the administrative court quashes a decision with an order to the administration to take a new decision, the period needed in which to take a new decision and the length of any possible procedures count as well. There can only be said to be a definitive settlement of the dispute if the decision is no longer challenged or – when it is still being challenged – if the highest national court has given a final judgment.

Since the beginning of 2014, a reasonable period of time for regular procedures in administrative law (objection, first instance and appeal) is considered to be four years. Of this, there is a period of a half year for the objection procedure, for the procedure at the district court a period of a year and a half[30] and for appeal (second instance) a period of two years. If these periods are exceeded, the responsible governmental body[31] must pay, as a major rule, EUR 500 in immaterial damages for each extra half year. The complexity of the case, the way in which administration and administrative court have dealt with the case and the actions of the litigating parties are circumstances that may lead to a different outcome.

4 European aspects

4.1 Access to an independent tribunal: The case of appeal to the 'Crown'

For a long time the Dutch system of legal protection against administrative decisions leaned firmly on the system of appeal to the Crown (see Introduction). In *Benthem v The Netherlands*, however, it was held by the European Court of Human Rights that

29 *Kudla v Poland* App no 30210/96 (ECHR, 26 October 2000). See also *Pizzati v Italy* App no. 62361/00 (ECHR, 29 March 2006).

30 In 2012, approximately 80% of the cases in first instance were decided within one year.

31 This can be the administrative body that was responsible for the non-timely judicial process or the State to the extent there can be said to be a non-timely judicial process.

appeal to the Crown was not access to an independent tribunal. This did not come as a surprise. Because many administrative disputes fall under the protection of Art. 6 ECHR, the conclusion was inevitable: the Crown's function in settling administrative disputes had to be replaced with an independent tribunal (or court).

The present system of administrative justice came into existence in 1994. It provides for a broad range of independent administrative justice, often in two instances (first instance and appeal). In general, the system works well. A fundamental criticism can be made with respect to the position of the Council of State as it is involved not only in the judicial process but also in giving advice on the quality of legislative proposals. As a result, its (objective) impartiality is questionable.[32] However, important legal measures have been taken to prevent conflicts with Art. 6 ECHR. Thus, the various functions of the Council of State (advice on legislation and administrative justice) have been (more) strictly separated. The situation is nevertheless considered by some to not (yet) be ideal. The present Government has plans to further reform the administrative judicial system but at the moment it is not clear what the result will be. It is unlikely that the Council of State will lose its judicial function. Discussions are going on (2016).[33]

Access to the court is guaranteed in the Netherlands by Art. 6 ECHR. Where the fundamental rights and freedoms protected by European Union (hereafter EU) law are at stake the right to access to the court is also given strong protection by Art. 47 of the Charter of Fundamental Rights of the European Union. Further, specific treaties provide for access to the courts. We note the well-known Treaty of Aarhus with respect to environmental law.[34]

Although access to the courts is thus not explicitly anchored in the Netherlands Constitution (see above), this right is sufficiently guaranteed under treaties and EU law. Factors that might limit access to the administrative courts, or make access difficult (for example, court fees, short periods for appeal, and the mandatory administrative preliminary procedure) are not particularly egregious. If access to the administrative courts is nevertheless restricted too severely, the (civil) courts offer supplementary legal protection.

4.2 Fair trial and requirements of a proper administration of justice

Art. 6 ECHR and EU law are extremely important with regard to the substantive requirements for effective legal protection. It goes without saying that the requirements of a 'fair trial' and 'full jurisdiction' find their expression in the GALA.[35] There the rights of parties are provided for. Clear examples are the principle of hearing both sides of the argument, the requirement that all documents must be made available (adversarial proceeding; equality of arms), the right to a public trial and the right to

32 *Procola v Luxemburg* App no. 48/1993 (ECHR, 28 September 1995). See also *Kleyn e.o. v The Netherlands* App nos. 39343/98, 39651/98, 43147/98, 46664/99 (ECHR, 6 May 2003).

33 See R. J. N. Schlössels and L. J. M. Timmermans, 'Baron von Münchhausen aan het werk in de polder: de hoogste bestuursrechtspraak als (Never) Ending Story?' (2015) 2 *Tijdschrift voor Constitutioneel Recht* 124–149.

34 *Tractatenblad* 2001, 73.

35 See in depth R. J. N. Schlössels and S. E. Zijlstra, *Bestuursrecht in de sociale rechtsstaat* (6th edn., Deventer, Kluwer 2014) 60–78.

a reasoned judgment. In the Dutch system of legal protection in administrative cases an administrative judge is in charge of the proceedings and has many powers which can be exercised *ex officio* (for example, appointing an expert witness). Even so, the court will nevertheless still have to hear testimony and to provide information. In this respect, Netherlands law has a tradition of following the principles of sound administration of justice. According to a widely shared approach in the Dutch administrative law, there are four basic principles: (1) the right to access to court and to a final decision within a reasonable time, (2) equality of arms and the adversarial principle, (3) the principle of impartiality, and (4) the right to a reasoned judgment.[36] These principles are also enshrined and elaborated[37] in the GALA, or based on Netherlands case law.

5 Some problems of the Dutch administrative justice

The above does not mean that there is no criticism of administrative justice in the Netherlands. On the contrary, a lively debate is going on. We would like to mention some of the points that have led to discussion. A point of criticism has to do with the effectiveness and timeliness of administrative justice. For many years there were complaints about the administrative courts' inability to reach a final settlement of disputes between the administration and private persons. One major problem was that decisions were too often quashed by the administrative courts on grounds of technicalities (inadequate reasoning, a lack of due care in the preparation of the case). After the decision was quashed, the administration had to take a new decision and the whole procedure often started all over again. Many viewed this as 'viscous'. It weakened the fundamental right to a final decision as well. After all, legal certainty means that persons must be cognizant of their situation. Measures (new legislation, new case law) have since been taken to solve this problem. The administrative courts nowadays try, as seen above, to settle disputes in a final way.[38] Determining the extent to which the administrative judicial system is effective is difficult as a theoretical exercise. For this reason empirical research on administrative justice – often commissioned by the Ministry of Justice – is conducted on a regular basis.[39] It can be seen from this research that in the majority of cases the administrative court decides in favour of the administration.[40] Accordingly, taking a case to the administrative courts seems to be not particularly 'effective' for a private person. This may be because often appeals are lodged that have no chance of succeeding (the threshold for lodging an appeal in the Netherlands is namely not very high). That in most cases the administration is the successful party may also mean that the quality of its decision making is high. It could also indicate that the administrative courts are too passive or reserved. Some critics

36 B. W. N. de Waard, *Beginselen van behoorlijke rechtspleging* (dissertation Utrecht, Zwolle, W. E. J. Tjeenk Willink 1987).

37 E.g. the right to be heard, the right to access to relevant documents and the right tot respond to advice.

38 Between 2007 and 2012 the percentage of cases in which the administrative courts have *attempted* to give a final judgment has risen enormously, to above 60% at the very least.

39 See, for example, A. T. Marseille, *Effectiviteit van bestuursrechtspraak* (Den Haag, Boom Juridische uitgevers 2004).

40 In 2004, this occurred in 70% of the cases.

even claim that the administrative courts are too 'administration-friendly'. However, in our view, this criticism cannot be substantiated.

Much attention has been paid to the substantive judgment of the court. The principle of 'full jurisdiction'[41] (as one aspect of the requirement of effectiveness) leads to questions when the administrative court reviews the discretionary powers of the administration. Traditionally, administrative law in the Netherlands uses a 'test of reasonableness'. The court respects the weighing of interests made by the administration. This is all the more so where the court is examining generally binding regulations (e.g. municipal regulations). It will make a 'correction' only where the administration has not exercised its powers reasonably.

The court's review is becoming intensified under the influence of EU law and the proportionality principle.[42] Efforts to achieve effective and final dispute settlement also affect the intensity of review. Hence, it appears that, in practice, the Netherlands administrative courts nowadays are not overly reserved in their review of the administration's discretionary power.

6 Conclusion

The administrative law – in particular the establishment of administrative courts – has had a turbulent history in the Netherlands. The Dutch system (influenced by French and German administrative law) developed in the twentieth century by trial and error. During the twentieth century more or less specialised administrative courts had been established. Moreover, from 1915 onwards, the civil courts had offered systematic 'supplementary' legal protection in administrative disputes. And since 1976 the Council of State (Law Department) provided legal protection against single case-decisions. Consequently, an effective (but not very tidy) system of legal protection with respect to the administration had come into being.

The present system of administrative courts was substantially established in 1994. If we ignore all the exceptions, one can say that in the Netherlands appeal with an administrative court is possible against decisions taken by the administrative bodies. An important exception is formed by generally binding provisions. In principle, private persons must seek relief regarding such provisions in the civil courts. The administrative legal procedure generally begins with an objection procedure. Thereafter, it is possible to appeal to the district court (in first instance) and then appeal to the highest administrative courts (second instance).

The traditional appeal for annulment has been transformed into a more 'modern' administrative procedure. The administrative procedure is aimed at speed and an effective dispute settlement. Moreover, digital litigation is becoming increasingly important. The administrative court will attempt to get to the bottom of the case quickly. On grounds of the instructions in the law it has to try to settle the dispute – while respecting the procedural rights of the parties – definitively (final

41 P. van Dijk, F. van Hoof, A. van Rijn, L. Zwaak *Theory and Practice of the European Convention on Human Rights* (4th edn., Intersentia, Antwerpen/Oxford 2006) 561–562.

42 See Paul Craig, *EU Administrative Law* (2nd edn., University Press 2012), chapters 19 & 20; J. H. Jans, S. Prechal and R. J. G. M. Widdershoven, *Europeanisation of Public Law* (Groningen, Europa Law Publishing 2015), 183–206.

dispute settlement). An annulment is preferably combined with the confirmation of legal effects or a final judgment by the court. Much attention is paid to deciding cases within a reasonable period of time. There is also new case law on compensation for a non-timely judicial process. These are positive developments. The reforms of the Netherlands administrative legal procedure appear to have strengthened the principle of effective legal protection.

14 The principle of effective legal protection in Polish administrative law

Joanna Lemańska

1 Historical development

Poland regained its independence only in 1918. Earlier, its territory was part of three neighbouring countries, as the Kingdom of Prussia, Russia and Austria partitioned the land of the Polish State between 1772 and 1795. When Poland's regained statehood was being formed, the theory of administrative law was already developed and abundant in other European states. Therefore, some administrative law doctrines of other countries inescapably influenced the Polish theory of this field of law. It explains many similarities to the German or Austrian legal doctrines.

In the interwar period, the administrative court system in Poland had the form of a single-instance court, modelled after the Austrian system. It was not reactivated in the socialist Polish People's Republic after World War II for political reasons. The former system was nevertheless re-established in 1980 with the creation of the Supreme Administrative Court. In 2004, it was reformed to introduce a two-level system of administrative courts. As a principle, the activities of administration bodies were subjected to scrutiny by the courts.[1] The right to access to court has a centuries-old tradition in Polish legislation. Its modern sources can be traced back to the Constitution of 3 May 1791, the first Polish Constitution, which guaranteed that 'the courts of first instance shall always be ready and vigilant to render justice to those who need it'.[2]

With the political changes which occurred in Poland in 1989, the approach to human rights and their observance has changed fundamentally. Poland became a member of the Council of Europe on 26 November 1991, and it ratified the Convention for the Protection of Human Rights and Fundamental Freedoms signed in Rome on 4 November 1950, which came into effect on 19 September 1993.[3] In accordance with Art. 91 para 1 of the Polish Constitution, a ratified international agreement (and this is the legal status of the Convention in the Polish system of sources of law) once published in the Official Gazette of the Republic of Poland, becomes part of the national legal order and is applied directly, unless its application requires an act to be passed. Such a document may constitute the direct basis for the decisions of national authorities and, moreover, in accordance with Art. 91 para 2 of the Polish

1 Special provisions may entrust administrative matters to the jurisdiction of courts of law, for example, issues related to the social security system, or concerning the delimitation of the property.

2 Karolina Wojszkun, 'Prawo do sądu jako podstawowa zasada prawa administracyjnego' (2012) 1 (14) *Krajowa Rada Sądownictwa Kwartalnik* 24.

3 Dz. U. 1993 No. 61 item. 284.

Constitution, it has precedence over national acts, if those cannot be reconciled with it. Nevertheless, it should be noted that although formally the Convention did not apply in Poland until 1993, its provisions were respected in practice.

2 Constitutional framework

The concept of a fair trial in the Polish Constitution is not one-dimensional, but rather composed of different elements in the form of procedural rights.[4] Until the entry into force of the new Constitution, the Polish Constitutional Tribunal (*Trybunał Konstytucyjny*) derived the right to trial from Art. 1 of the Constitution of the Polish People's Republic, amended in 1989, which defined Poland as a democratic state of law and implementing the principles of social justice.

In its judgment of 7 January 1992, the Polish Constitutional Tribunal stated that one of the fundamental principles of a democratic state of law (*demokratyczne państwo prawne*) is the principle of public access for the citizens to court in order to enable them to defend their interests before an independent body guided solely by the law in force in the country. According to the Tribunal, an individual's right to a fair and public trial in which his or her administrative, civil rights are decided upon, as well as the proceedings in which he or she is presented with criminal charges, followed from the principle included in Art. 1 of the Constitution, stating that Poland is a state of law.[5] The current Constitution of 1997 expressly provides in its content the right to trial, and Art. 45[6] is the key in this matter. According to its content, everyone shall have the right to a fair and public hearing of his case, without undue delay, before a competent, impartial and independent court. Exceptions to the public nature of hearings may be made for reasons of morality, state security, public order or protection of the private life of a party, or other important private interest. In shaping this regulation, premises specifying the subject of judgment were excluded. In fact, Art. 45 of the Constitution uses the general term 'case' (*sprawa*). This concept covers all situations in which there has been a violation of freedoms or rights. On the other hand, its creators used the concepts defining all the basic components of the right to trial (fair trial).

As it has been pointed out, the right to court has been regulated in the provisions of the Polish Constitution in a manner different from that specified in Art. 6 of the ECHR. The main difference consists in the fact that the right to trial is referred to in two provisions of the Constitution: the above-mentioned Art. 45 and Art. 77 para 2.[7] While the former Article defines the right to trial in positive terms, the latter concerns the prohibition of barring the judicial settlement of the infringement of freedoms and rights. This approach complements the constitutional guarantee of the right to

4 Tomasz Tadeusz Koncewicz, 'Prawo do rzetelnego postępowania w europejskiej przestrzeni prawnej Jaka procedura? Jakie prawo?' (2013) 1(11–12) *Palestra* 69

5 The Constitutional Court's judgment of 7 January 1992, K 8/91, OTK 1992/1, Item. 5.

6 Art. 45 of the Constitution says '[e]veryone shall have the right to a fair and public hearing of his case, without undue delay, before a competent, impartial and independent court. Exceptions to the public nature of hearings may be made for reasons of morality, State security, public order or protection of the private life of a party, or other important private interest. Judgments shall be announced publicly.'

7 According to Art. 77 of the Constitution '[s]tatutes shall not bar the recourse by any person to the courts in pursuit of claims alleging infringement of freedoms or rights'.

court. This regulation is supplemented by constitutional provisions concerning the issue of the access to the courts and the structural requirements for court proceedings. According to Art. 176, court proceedings must have at least two stages.

It is worth noting that the provisions of the Constitution of the Republic of Poland provide a standard of protection higher than that indicated in the Convention stipulations.[8]

It should also be noted it was not intended that the disputes in the field of public administration be permanently excluded from the scope of Art. 6 para 1 of ECHR.[9]

In one of the key decisions in this field, *Ringeisen v Austria*,[10] the European Court of Human Rights clearly stated that Art. 6 para 1 of the ECHR concerns any procedure the result of which has a decisive impact on the civil rights and obligations. The character of the legislation which governs how the matter is to be determined (civil, commercial, administrative law, etc.) and that of the authority which is invested with jurisdiction in the matter (ordinary court, administrative body, etc.) are therefore of little consequence. This allowed to take include typical administrative matters in the right to trial. As it is pointed out, the ECtHR considers procedures which fall within the scope of public law under national law, but the outcome of which determines the rights and obligations of a private nature.[11]

The existence of adequate review of judgment in the due administrative course of instance understood as one of the types of internal review is not classified as a mandatory European standard.[12] But today, the role of the administrative review in the due course of the proceedings is largely to act as a 'filter' (prior to judicial procedure) to prevent the flooding of the courts with complaints, and allowing substantive settlement of at least a portion of cases without the need to involve the courts.[13] So, the obligation to initiate a specific verification administrative procedure before bringing the case to court is justified by the need to prevent the excessive load on the courts, and in the long term to ensure adequate efficiency of judicial review.[14] That is why it would be considered desirable to introduce administrative appeals, prior to the court review.

In Art. 78 of the Polish Constitution of 1997,[15] all citizens are guaranteed the right to appeal against decisions, including administrative ones, issued in the first instance. This provision is general in nature and it is included in the second chapter of the Constitution devoted to the human and citizen freedoms, rights and obligations, in

8 Adam Zieliński, 'Wokół reformy polskiego sądownictwa' (2009) 1(2) *Państwo i Prawo* 20.

9 Zbigniew Kmieciak, *Postępowanie administracyjne i sądowoadministracyjne a prawo europejskie* (Oficyna Wolters Kluwer SA, Warszawa 2010) 99.

10 *Ringeisen v Austria* (1971) Series A no 13, thesis 94.

11 Council of Europe/European Court of Human Rights (Guide to Art. 6 RIGHT TO A FAIR TRIAL (civil limb) (available at http://www.echr.coe.int/Documents/Guide_Art_6_ENG.pdf) accessed 8 July 2015.

12 See Art. 22.2, section III, Recommendation CM/Rec(2007)7 of the Committee of Ministers to Member States on good administration/The committee of ministers (Recommendation CM/Rec(2007)7 of the Committee of Ministers to Member States on good administration) (available at https://wcd.coe.int/ViewDoc.jsp?id=1155877) accessed 8 July 2015.

13 Kmieciak (n. 9) 82.

14 Ibid. 115.

15 Art. 78 of the Constitution: 'Each party shall have the right to appeal against judgments and decisions made at first stage. Exceptions to this principle and the procedure for such appeals shall be specified by statute.'

the section which regulates the measures of protecting freedoms and rights. This is a provision which guarantees the right to a second instance trail, regardless of Art. 45 of the Polish Constitution, which regulates the appropriate right to trial. Any deviation from the principle of two instances can only be introduced by an act, and as an exception to the rule, it must be clear and unambiguous, and at the same time, it should be dictated by particular circumstances and comply with the principle of proportionality.[16]

3 The rights-based perspective

3.1 Administrative procedure

3.1.1 Principle of two instance

The Polish Code of Administrative Procedure (*Kodeks Postepowania Administracyjnego*, Act of 14 June 1960, hereinafter CAP) provides the principle of two instance in Art. 15. The principle of two-instance proceedings means the right to have the same administrative case examined and settled by two different public administration bodies. In the Polish legal system, those include remedies such as an appeal, complaint[17] or application for re-examination of the case, and in the case of acts and actions which are non-actionable in one of these forms – a written request to remedy the infringement. A party or entities enjoying the rights of a party, may appeal against the decision issued in the first instance to a higher level body. In the case of a decision issued in the first instance by a government minister or the Local Government Court of Appeal (*Samorządowe Kolegium Odwoławcze*), which do not have a higher level body of similar nature, another appeal measure is possible: an application for re-examination of the case (by this body) to which the provisions on appeals apply. An administrative appeal is a regular appeal measure, submitted against non-final decisions, unlike in the case of extraordinary measures, which may be submitted against final decisions.

3.1.2 Administrative appeal

Administrative procedure – as a necessary condition prior to the submission of a complaint to an administrative court – should not be excessive, and the applicant must be guaranteed a reasonable period of time to lodge a judicial complaint. The duration of such preliminary procedure should be taken into account when conducting it is required before lodging a complaint with the court. A reasonable period of time for hearing the case, as it is imposed by Art. 6 para 1 of the ECHR, starts from the date of lodging a complaint on the decision of the administration authority and not later than the date of lodging the appeal (complaint) with the administrative court.[18]

16 Andrzej Wróbel (Komentarz aktualizowany do art.15 Kodeksu postępowania administracyjnego) (available at http://lex.online.wolterskluwer.pl/WKPLOnline/index.rpc?#content.rpc—ASK—nro=587633099&wersja=-1&localNroPart=0&reqId=1436361715383_283328973&class=CONTENT&loc=4&full=1&hId=3) accessed 11 May 2014.

17 Complaints relate to the principle of procedural cases.

18 *König v Germany* (1978) Series A no 27, thesis 85.

An administrative appeal is submitted to the second instance body by the agency of the first instance body in the period of 14 days from the date of delivery or announcement of the decision, unless an act provides otherwise. In the period of seven days from the date on which the appeal was submitted, the first instance body should decide, by way of the so-called self-control, if the appeal should be allowed in full. If the appeal has been submitted by all the parties and the administrative organ finds that such appeal should be allowed in full, it may issue a new decision in which it may repeal or amend the decision appealed against, with reservation that it is not possible to allow the party's request in the new decision only partially; the parties are also entitled to appeal against the new decision. Meanwhile, should the first instance body find that the appeal should not been allowed in full, in the prescribed period of seven days, the body should send the appeal together with the files of the case to the second instance body and should notify the parties to the proceedings of this fact.

3.1.3 Duration of administrative procedure

The CAP includes the principle of fast proceedings. According to this law, administrative bodies should act penetratingly and fast, using the simplest measures possible which aim to settle the case. The CAP sets specific periods for certain procedures,[19] which means that administrative bodies are obliged to settle cases without undue delay. As a general rule, appeal proceedings should be settled within one month from the date of receipt of the appeal.

A party has the right to complaint to a higher instance administrative body in the case of a body's failure to settle a case in the period specified by law. The complaint is, therefore, a specific remedy against the public authority's actions (or failure to act). If the higher instance administrative body finds the complaint justified, it sets an additional period for settlement of the case and orders explanation of the reasons and determination of persons responsible for failure to settle the case in time, and, if necessary, also adoption of measures which prevent further failures to settle cases within the prescribed periods in the future. This provision is not perfect, because it does not remove at all the body's inaction state.

Somewhat in anticipation of the presentation concerning administrative courts, one may add that according to the act on proceedings before administrative courts, an administrative court is competent to examine a complaint against inaction in issuing an administrative decision. Nevertheless, if such complaint is allowed, the court may only establish another date for settlement of the case by the body. Also this regulation does not fully prevent inaction of administrative bodies. However, the determination of an additional period for the settlement of the case may be important from the perspective of potential civil law claims for compensation due to delay in administration's activity.

19 Art. 35 of the CAP: '§ 1 Public administration bodies are obliged to settle cases without undue delay. (. . .) § 3. A case which requires explanatory proceedings should be settled within one month at the latest, and a particularly complex case not later than within two months from the date of institution of the proceedings, while in appeal proceedings – within one month from the date of receipt of the appeal.'

Polish jurisprudence, especially in the scope of appeals against the decisions of public authorities, provides numerous examples of violating the analysed requirement, combined with exceeding the specified statutory time for the settlement of the case in the appeal procedure. To make a complaint to the administrative court, the applicant must – in the case of the authority's failure to act – first initiate measures aimed to remedy the situation (in extreme cases, including a complaint on the administrative court's failure to act), which inevitably prolongs the duration of proceedings classified as pre-trial (preliminary) procedures. The interests of the applicants are better protected when lodging a complaint to the administrative court must be preceded by a written request to remedy the infringement. In the absence of response to this request, the complaint must be lodged within 60 days from the date of referral to the competent public authority.[20]

3.2 *Judicial procedure*

3.2.1 *Object of review*

Administrative courts in Poland control public administration activities. This control is exercised on the basis of the legality criterion, that is, compliance of the activities of an administrative body with generally binding law.

This review should be carried out in three areas: the compliance of the settlement (decision or another act) or the action with the substantive law; the observance of procedures required by law; and also complying with the rules of competence.[21]

Control of public administration activities by administrative courts covers judgments in cases where complaints have been filed against:

(a) administrative decisions (building permit, etc.);
(b) orders issued in administrative proceedings, or ending proceedings, and also orders resolving cases on their essence (e.g. decision to suspend construction work);
(c) orders issued in enforcement and injunction proceedings;
(d) acts or activities other than those specified in points 1–3 as regards public administration concerning rights or obligations stemming from provisions of law;
(e) written interpretations of tax law issued in individual cases by fiscal chamber directors;
(f) local and government legislation (communal, district, provincial);
(g) decisions of local and state authorities and their associations, other than specified in point 6 above,
(h) acts of supervision over local authority bodies' activities,
(i) inactivity of administrative authorities in cases specified in points 1–5 above.

Some issues were expressly excluded from the jurisdiction of the administrative courts, for example those relating to matters arising from the organisational hierarchical

20 Kmieciak (n. 9) 116.

21 Kabat A., Komentarz do art.3 ustawy – Prawo o postępowaniu przed sądami administracyjnymi, Lex as of 2013.04.30/Andrzej Kabat, *Komentarz do art. 3 ustawy – Prawo o postępowaniu przed sądami administracyjnymi* (LEX Wolters Kluwer SA 2013).

relations between public administration bodies; visas issued by the consuls. These cases are, however, of marginal importance for the public administration.

3.2.2 The right to lodge a complaint – formal and fiscal requirements

Prohibitive legal fees may be a factor impeding access to the court. The level of fees applicable in administrative court proceedings in Poland can be considered as moderate.

A provincial administrative court first examines the propriety of a complaint from a formal legal standpoint. If no legal defects are established, it is accepted for substantive review.

The right to lodge a complaint with the administrative court is combined with the concept of legal interest. It is permissible for a complaint to be lodged also by other entities than those having a legal interest, namely, the prosecutor, the Ombudsman and a social organisation in the scope of its statutory activities, in matters concerning the legal interests of other persons, if it participated in the administrative proceedings. Parties to the proceedings before administrative courts are the appellant, whose rights or obligations are alleged to have been infringed by unlawful acts or omissions of state authorities (natural persons or organisational units, even though they do not possess a legal personality) and the public administration authority issuing an appeal the decision (resolution, etc.) or other entity exercising public tasks.

3.2.3 The right of all sides to be heard in the proceedings

Proceedings before the administrative court are held on the basis of an adversarial procedure, and the parties have equal rights and the possibility to present all arguments, without any forms of preference or discrimination.

3.2.4 Duration of court procedure

The deadline provided the Act on proceedings before administrative courts (*Prawo o postępowaniu przed sądami administracyjnymi*) corresponds to the standard reasonable period of time necessary to lodge a complaint.

Complaints against decisions and orders (administrative acts) are filed at the provincial administrative court within 30 days via the administrative authority that issued the decision or order at last instance. The period of 30 days for lodging a complaint is counted from the date of delivery to the applicant of the decision on the case. After receiving a complaint, an administrative authority is obligated to send the complaint together with the reply thereto to the provincial administrative court within 30 days. Failure to meet this obligation may be punishable by a fine.

A court should issue a judgment within a reasonable time. In the Polish legal system, means of disciplining the course of administrative court proceedings are provided by regulations determining, for certain categories of cases, deadlines for setting the date for a trial or hearing of the case by the court. For the majority of cases, however, no such deadlines exist. The principle prevails that a case before an administrative court should conclude as swiftly as possible, generally at initial proceedings.

In practice, the deadlines for issuing administrative courts decisions in Poland are considerable, especially before the Supreme Administrative Court. This is clearly a violation of the right to a fair trial, especially as in light of the case law of the ECHR, the Member States are responsible for organising their legal systems in a manner guaranteeing the right to obtain a judicial decision within a reasonable deadline, and therefore the excessive work load of the courts cannot be taken into account.[22] The inefficiency of the Polish legal system has, unfortunately, led to frequent violations of Art. 6 para 1 of the Convention. Poland has constantly been among the countries from which the greatest number of complaints concerning the excessive length of judicial proceedings were filed.[23] In response to the ECtHR's criticism of the Polish justice system (especially on the basis of precedent-setting case *Kudla v Poland*)[24] the Act of 17 June 2007 on the complaint against infringement of the right of a party to have the case examined in legal proceedings performed or supervised by a prosecutor and court proceedings without undue delay was adopted,[25] which covers the proceedings before the administrative courts. As a result, there has been some improvement in the speed of operation of the Polish courts;[26] however – as demonstrated by statistical data –[27] this measure is not very effective in practice.

3.2.5 Other aspects

In principle, unless a specific provision states otherwise, court hearings are public and the administrative court rules at the hearing.

The simplified procedure for settling certain categories of cases is rarely used in practice. When a party submits a request for a case to be heard in this mode, its use is only possible in the absence of requests for a hearing by the other parties within 14 days of the notification of the request.

Challenging an act of the administrative authority before the administrative court does not suspend its execution. Therefore, the court can grant appropriate interim protection, but it is necessary to lodge a request in this regard. Provisions concerning the stay of execution of the act or action, including those issued by an administration authority, may be modified or revoked by the court at any time should circumstances change.

As a rule, if the complaint is upheld, the administrative court prepares a justification of the decision *ex officio*. This is not the case if the applicant's claim is dismissed, when the grounds for judgment issued by the county administrative court shall be drawn up at the request of the parties, filed within seven days from the date of the judgment. This solution is a regression in relation to the former state of affairs, which provided for the obligation of preparing a justification of the decision *ex officio* in any

22 Guide to Art. 6. RIGHT TO A FAIR TRIAL. (civil limb). Council of Europe/European Court of Human Rights, 2013 p. 66 (available at www.echr.coe.int).

23 See the justification for the bill of the Act of 17 June 2007 on the complaint against infringement of the right of a party to have the case examined in legal proceedings performed or supervised by a prosecutor and court proceedings without undue delay, fourth-term Polish Parliament, no printing: 2256

24 *Kudła v Poland* ECHR 2000-XI.

25 Dz. U..U. No. 179, item.1843.

26 Adam Zieliński, 'Wokół reformy polskiego sądownictwa' (2009) 1(2) *Państwo i Prawo* 19.

27 Hanna Knysiak-Molczyk, 'Skarga na przewlekłość postępowania sądowoadministracyjnego w orzecznictwie Naczelnego Sądu Administracyjnego' in Janusz Sługocki (ed.), *Dziesięć lat polskich doświadczeń w Unii Europejskiej Problemy prawnoadministracyjne* (PRESSCOM 2014) 399–401.

case. The absence of a written justification for a judgment dismissing the complaint limits or even rules out the possibility of establishing the scope of *res judicata* designated by the decision made for the purposes of any subsequent verification of any act in one of the extraordinary modes of administrative proceedings.[28]

4 Institutional perspective

The use of the right to trial is to be made use of not before any court, but only before a court with jurisdiction over the subject matter (matter of dispute). The entry into force of the Polish Constitution in 1997 resulted in the formal separation of the two divisions of the judicial system – ordinary courts and administrative courts.

Importantly, the above-mentioned list of matters excluded before administrative courts does not include the cases 'within the jurisdiction of other courts', an exemption which appeared in the prior regulations. At the same time, rules were introduced, according to which a court of law (ordinary court) may not reject a claim on the grounds that the case is in the jurisdiction of a competent public authority or an administrative court if the public authority or the administrative court is recognised as having no jurisdiction in this case.[29] In turn, the regulations concerning proceedings before administrative courts stipulate that the administrative court cannot reject the complaint on the ground that it has no jurisdiction in the case if a court of law found to have no jurisdiction in this case.[30] As we can see, the legislators provided a solution in the case of a negative conflict of competence.

The solutions do not define the rules and procedure in cases where both a public administration authority or an administrative court and an ordinary court of law consider themselves to have jurisdiction to conduct proceedings in a particular case (positive conflicts of jurisdiction) and, consequently, in each of these procedures 'competitive' decisions are taken,[31] which in turn can lead in extreme cases to the proceeding being null if it is conducted by a court with no jurisdiction for the matter.

4.1 Structure of polish administrative courts

The organisational structure and jurisdiction as well as procedure of the courts are specified by the law. Administrative judiciary in Poland is a system of two instances. It comprises provincial administrative courts (*wojewódzkie sądy administracyjne,*) and the Supreme Administrative Court (*Naczelny Sąd Administracyjny,* hereinafter SAC). A case pending before an administrative court can therefore be generally heard twice (first before a provincial administrative court, whose judgment may then be reviewed by the SAC).

In a separate constitutional provision, the tasks of the administrative court system are specified. According to Art. 184, the Supreme Administrative Court and other administrative courts shall exercise, to the extent specified by statute, control over the performance of public administration. Such control shall also extend to judgments

28 Kmieciak (n. 9) 145.
29 Art. 199^1 of the Civil Procedure Code.
30 Art. 58 para 4 of the Administrative Court Procedure.
31 Kmieciak (n. 9) 128.

on the conformity to statute of resolutions of organs of local government and normative acts of territorial organs of government administration.

As we know, we can create models of the jurisdiction of administrative courts: (1) so-called full judgment; (2) verification judgment, as a rule, cassation. In accordance with Art. 133, para 1 of the Act on proceedings before administrative courts, the court issues a judgment after the close of the hearing, on the basis of the case file. The factual state of the case is determined by the administration itself.[32] Administrative court conducts only supplementary evidence – on the basis of a document and only in exceptional cases. Therefore, it does not seek to re-establish the facts of the case, but to make the assessment whether the authorities with jurisdiction for the case have done so in accordance with the rules applicable in the administrative procedure, and then – if they have correctly applied the provisions of the substantive law to the findings.[33] The court examines the full range of the legality of the contested act, action or inaction of the administration authority. An administrative court is not bound by the allegations and conclusions cited in the complaint and the legal basis referred to therein.

We should notice the use of cassation-type remedies by the court. If the contested act or action is found to violate the law, the court removes the act from the legal system with *ex nunc* or *ex tunc* effect (recognition of the action as legally ineffective). Determining that an action of an administrative body violates the law may also result in obliging it to take some action, such as issuing an act or performing an action by a specified date. In special situations, the court is obliged to make use of a given measure in order to remedy the infringement in respect to acts issued or actions taken 'in all proceedings conducted within the limits of the matter which the complaint concerns if it is necessary for settling it in a final manner'.[34] A certain kind of derogation towards the reformatory type of judgment is constituted by the possibility for the judgment of the administrative court to recognise the right or the obligation arising from the law in the event the complaint regarding an act or an action is upheld.

A judgment eliminates the contested act from the legal transactions and transfers the cases back to an administrative body to decide upon, usually with instructions concerning making a new settlement. This approach diverges from the concept of the right to trial presented in the jurisprudence of the Polish Constitutional Tribunal, which requires the right to obtain a binding settlement of the case by the court. As emphasised by the Polish Constitutional Tribunal, the right to trial is one of the fundamental rights of the individuals and one of the fundamental guarantees of the rule of law, which are composed in particular of: the right of access to a court, that is the right to initiate a procedure before the court – a body with specific characteristics (independent, impartial and objective); the right to shape the judicial procedure in accordance with the requirements of fairness and openness; and the

32 In the course of work on judicial reform, the issue posed a problem, as opinions were voiced indicating that the principle of fair trial means that the administrative court should not only examine the application of the law, but also establish the facts (see Sieniawska K. and Skonieczny P., *Pojęcie 'sądu administracyjnego' w europejskiej konwencji o ochronie praw człowieka i podstawowych wolności* [Casus, Summer 1999] 20).

33 The Supreme Administrative Court's judgment of 7 February 2006, II GSK 359/05, ONSAiWSA 2006/5/145.

34 Kmieciak (n. 9) 155.

right to trial judgment, that is the right to obtain a binding settlement of the case by the court.[35] As we can see, the latter condition is not satisfied in full; however, as indicated in the doctrine, this does not rule out the possibility of obtaining legal protection and can be easily explained by the particular nature of the judicial system expressed through the exercise of the review of the legality of the actions of public administration.[36]

These doubts were resolved by the decision in *Potocka and others v Poland*.[37] The applicants put forward the complaint that they had no access to the court within the meaning of Art. 6 para 1 of the ECHR. They argued that the Polish Supreme Administrative Court did not have full jurisdiction as to the facts and the law, because it was only able to examine the lawfulness of the decision under appeal and could not consider any other aspects of the case, such as questions of facts and of expediency. The Polish government, in turn, argued that the Court meets the requirements of the court in the sense of Art. 6 para 1 of the ECHR. The SAC is competent to examine whether there had been a breach of substantive law in the proceedings giving rise to the contested decisions and is required, in doing so, to review the merits of the applicant's case as well. The ECtHR upheld the government's view that the Polish Supreme Administrative Court – to the extent to which its jurisdiction has been determined – meets the standards required of a 'court'. It admitted that although the court has been established to analyse the legality of administrative decisions, it has been provided with the authority to waive in whole or in part the contested act if it finds a breach of the procedural requirements of fairness.[38]

It should be born in mind that what is necessary is not only an effective access to the court, but also access to an effective court.[39] As a result of the decision of the administrative court, a certain state of transition is created and it is the responsibility of the public administration authorities to stabilise it.[40] Even a judgment which implies a freedom of choice between several options for new decisions accompanied by proper justification often leaves a certain freedom in the choice of a variety of settlement options. The fact that so understood a decision margin exists is sometimes abused, which may result in another complaint being made to the administrative court.[41] There is no sanction in the event that, after the cassation judgment of the administrative court, the administration fails to comply with the opinion expressed in the judgment or re-issues identical decisions based on these motives or even fails to issue any decision or at least not in the deadlines specified by law. The only exception to this is a situation in which in the event of failure to execute a judgment upholding a complaint on the failure to act or an excessive time of proceeding, and in the case of the inactivity of the authority or an excessive time of proceeding following the judgment repealing the act or action or declaring them void, the party, after prior written

35 The Constitutional Court's judgment of 18 December 2007, SK 54/05, *OTK-A 2007/11/158*, 158/11/A/2007.

36 Kmieciak (n. 9) 112.

37 *Potocka and others v Poland* ECHR 2001-X 62–66.

38 Guide to Art. 6. RIGHT TO A FAIR TRIAL. (civil limb). Council of Europe/European Court of Human Rights, 2013 pp. 26 and 28 (available at www.echr.coe.int).

39 Kmieciak (n. 9) 192.

40 Ibid. 110.

41 Ibid. 108.

summons to the competent authority to execute the judgment or settle the case, may lodge a complaint in this regard, demanding that fines be imposed on that authority.

This is undoubtedly a weakness of the Polish system. In practice, the administrative courts have repeatedly repealed successive decisions issued within the same administrative cases, which causes considerable delay in the final settlement of those. Apart from repeatedly repealing the incorrect decision, the courts do not have at its disposal any measures to discipline administrative authorities.

For this reason, we can observe the desire to supplement the traditional system of judicial protection, derived from the Austro-Hungarian tradition (cassation type of jurisdiction) with solutions typical for the full appeal model. It is justified mainly by the difficulties in ensuring the proper execution (fast and consistent with legal analyses and directions of the court) taking into account the appeal to judgment. But this is still under discussion.[42]

4.2 Second instance of judicial procedure

The right to trial does not cover guaranteeing the instance model of the judiciary system. Art. 6 does not in itself require that Member States organise appellate and cassation courts. However, if such a system exists, this Article is applicable, given that the applicant has a formal opportunity to appeal to a higher national court.[43] Nevertheless, as emphasised by the Polish Constitutional Tribunal, the right to trial is strengthened by the guarantee of the instance structure as the principle of court and administrative proceedings.[44] The Constitution of the Republic of Poland does not determine on what assumptions the principle of two instances of administrative court proceedings should be based, leaving the legislature to regulate this issue. The court of first instance examines the full range of the legality of the contested act, action or inaction of the administration authority. The procedure is different in the case of instance review of a judgment made.

A cassation appeal is a statement bound by specific formal requirements, among others, the need to appropriately formulate and justify charges as well as indicate the laws violated. The cassation appeal should be drawn up by an advocate or legal adviser. The Supreme Administrative Court examines the case within the limits of a cassation appeal. This means that the parties filing a cassation appeal must point out a violation of a specific law by the judgment issued and the case will be reviewed from this standpoint. However, the SAC *ex officio* takes into account the invalidity of the proceedings (which arises in the case of very serious errors in proceedings). Parties may cite the new justification for the grounds for cassation, but are bound by its scope.

The system of remedies adopted for the proceedings before the administrative courts in Poland is a mixed model. The predominant element in the cassation-type model of an appeal is naturally constituted by cassation.[45] An exception is observed in

42 As pointed by Z. Kmieciak, this issue was already discussed in the 1920s. (Ibid. 107).

43 Dovydas vitkauskas and Grigoriy Dikov, *Protecting the right to a fair trial under the European Convention on Human Rights* (Council of Europe 2012) 22.

44 The Constitutional Court's judgment of 20 September 2006, SK 63/05, *OTK-A 2006/8/108, Dz.U.2006 / 170/1224.*

45 Michał Kania, *Zwyczajne środki zaskarżenia w postępowaniu przed sądami administracyjnymi* (Oficyna Wolters Kluwer SA 2009) 73 & 90.

the form of the possibility of the SAC issuing a reformatory ruling in a situation where there are no violations of the rules of procedure that may have a significant impact on the outcome of the case, and there is only a violation of substantial law. The solution is a compromise between the 'weakened' cassation model and the review model. Therefore, the submission of a cassation appeal does not always lead to cassation. As a result, the cassation appeal is a conventional name of the remedy used in administrative court proceedings.[46] A cassation appeal in administrative court proceedings is an ordinary remedy: it is lodged concerning a judgment or the order terminating the proceedings issued in the proceedings before the regional administrative court. A cassation appeal is a devolutive.

A cassation appeal can be based on the grounds of[47] the violation of substantive law through its erroneous interpretation or improper application, or based on the infringement of proceeding rules, if the infringement could have a significant impact on the outcome of the case. As a result, the SAC does not review all the decisions of the regional administrative court, which one of the parties contest, but only those containing the above-mentioned infringements. The question of so-defined bases for cassation raised doubts concerning the guarantee of the right to a fair trial. The solution was criticised on the grounds that the construction of cassation appeal in administrative court proceedings proposed by the legislators does not lead to resolving the cases pending before the court of first instance, but only to the SAC control of proceedings of the lower court. Therefore, the cassation appeal does not act as an appeal measure, allowing the SAC to examine a second time of case of administrative court second, that is a case related to the control of the activities of public administration. The compatibility of the rules governing the cassation bases was ruled upon by the Constitutional Tribunal, which, in the judgment of 20 September 2006,[48] pointed out that so-defined cassation bases are in compliance with Art. 45 of the Polish Constitution. The Tribunal, stressing that it treats the right to trial as one of the fundamental rights of the individual and one of the fundamental guarantees of the rule of law, pointed out that while the claim based on the stipulations of Art. 45 para 1 of the Constitution concerns the 'consideration of the matter', the principle of instances applies to the decision making process, and therefore the first decision in this case. Therefore, in essence, it concerns a certain stage of settling the case. The role of the judicial review of instance, raised to the rank of a constitutional right, is to prevent confusion and arbitrariness in the first instance. At the same time, the Tribunal pointed out that the legislators' freedom in shaping appropriate procedures does not extend to the right to introduce arbitrary solutions that limit beyond measure, and thus without an important reason, the procedural rights of the parties, the implementation of which is a prerequisite for the proper and fair settlement of the case. Therefore, if limiting the parties' procedural rights is unnecessary from the point of view of the purposes intended by the legislators, such as ensuring greater effectiveness and speed of proceedings, and at the same time distorts the position of the parties, it prevents ensuring the proper balance between their positions in the process, and thus violates the

46 Kania (n. 45) 190.

47 Art. 174 of the Administrative Court Procedure.

48 The Constitutional Court's judgment of 20 September 2000, SK 63/05, *OTK-A 2006/8/108, Dz.U. 2006 / 170/1224.*

basic postulate of procedural fairness or finally leads to the arbitrary resolution of the 'case'.[49] According to the Constitutional Tribunal, the regulation, contained in the Polish administrative court procedure, does not establish any subjective or objective restrictions of the right to lodge a cassation appeal. This is due to the fact that it does not limit the possibility of initiating second instance proceedings or exclude obtaining a judgment of the court of second instance.

The adopted solution was also criticised for simply transferring to the administrative court proceedings the stipulations of the Civil Procedure Code, which – as pointed out by the Constitutional Tribunal itself – is not an option that can be considered as ideal. In fact, cassation appeals in the two types of proceedings are quite different. In proceedings before the civil courts, a cassation appeal is a remedy filed in the course of the proceedings to the Supreme Court (*Sąd Najwyższy*) for final review of the legality of decisions by courts of second instance. In the proceedings before the administrative courts, on the other hand, it constitutes an appeal to first instance decisions. Also the role of the administrative courts is different than those of courts in civil proceedings: they only control the activities of public administration, and exercise this control most of all in terms of compliance with the law. They do not apply the substantive law in the same manner as the courts of law. All these fundamental differences lead to the conclusion that the transfer of the civil code solutions directly to the domain of administrative court procedures is not an appropriate solution, and it may lead to certain restrictions in the full examination of the case.

5 European impacts

As mentioned above, the guarantee of the right to trial has had a long tradition in the Polish legal system. After the turmoil associated with the events following World War II, after 1989, the Polish state faced the difficult task of restoring democracy. There is no doubt that in making legislative changes, legislators based on the content of the European Charter of Human Rights, even before it was formally ratified. The painful experience of previous years resulted in the fact that the newly adopted solutions not only mirrored European standards (and in that scope, their impact must be seen as very significant), but in many cases developed those even further, which is also reflected in the provisions of the Polish Constitution. As a result, complaints to the ECtHR against Poland concerning violations of the right to trial are few in number and predominantly related to the excessive length of proceedings rather than the basic assumptions of the judicial system. It should also be noted that the Polish legislature respects and complies with ECtHR and ECJ rulings, and any finding of misconduct results in a corresponding change in Polish regulations (for example, introducing into administrative and administrative court procedures measures that allow eliminating the excessive length of proceedings).

6 Conclusions

In principle, the implementation and protection of the right to trial in the context of administrative procedures and administrative court proceedings in Poland needs

49 The Constitutional Court's judgment of 28 July 2004, P 2/04, *OTK-A 2004/7/72, Dz.U.2004 / 175/1825.*

to be evaluated as positive. As emphasised by some scholars, much has been done to ensure that the course of court proceedings in Poland corresponds to the standards of fair trial.[50]

The subjective scope of the right to trial is presented in the Polish Constitution quite extensively: Art. 45 para 1 of the Constitution defines the right to trial in positive terms. On the other hand, Art. 77 para 2 includes the prohibition of barring the judicial settlement of the infringement of freedoms and rights. Such a formulation complements the constitutional guarantee of the right to trial. 'Everyone's right to trial means that 'no one' (with the restriction of seeking freedoms or rights) can be barred from judicial settlement.[51] It can also be argued that this protection is generally effective. This is confirmed by the fact that only a small number of complaints are filed against Poland at the European Court of Human Rights, especially in the field that is the subject of the present report. Cases are heard by an independent and impartial judicial authority. The control in itself is a two-instance procedure, and judicial control is additionally preceded by the examination of the case in the second instance by the administrative authorities. Certain doubts of the manner of shaping the jurisdiction of the administrative courts, which is close to the traditional model of verification judgment, and as a rule, based on cassation, are certainly not a hindrance to the effective protection of individual rights through the courts.[52] The cassation model of the remedies is rare in judicial systems based on the principle of two instances. It is necessary to regulate a new institution of remedy in our administrative court proceedings,[53] for example a two-instance system of administrative courts with reformatory–cassatory jurisdiction. Increasingly, it is postulated that administrative courts be granted the power to rule on the merits of the case, or to create, instead of a second instance of the administrative system or an additional, lowest rung of it, specialised tribunals, modelled after the English system, and entitled to rule on the merits of the case. However, such opinions are merely a reaction to some of the shortcomings pointed out above and remain simply debating points.

Basically, the biggest problem consists of the excessive length of proceedings,[54] especially the decisions of the Supreme Administrative Court, which in a certain perspective can lead to the need to reform the system of administrative courts in Poland (for example, through the creation of local branches of the Supreme Administrative Court). It is also pointed out that efficiency of enforcement of court judgments is still too small.[55] Therefore, although, as indicated above, the Polish legal system provides a standard of requirements to ensure a fair trial higher than that provided for in the European standards, everyday practice would indicate the need for further changes aimed at a more complete implementation of this right. If we assume, after Tomasz

50 Adam Zieliński, 'Wokół reformy polskiego sądownictwa' (2009) 1(2) *Państwo i Prawo* 18.

51 The Constitutional Court's judgment of 10 May 2000, K 21/99, OTK ZU No. 4/2000, pos. 109.

52 Kmieciak (n. 9) 167.

53 Ibid. 99.

54 Hanna Knysiak-Molczyk even speaks of the 'Achilles heel' of Polish justice, see: Hanna Knysiak-Molczyk, 'Skarga na przewlekłość postępowania sądowoadministracyjnego w orzecznictwie Naczelnego Sądu Administracyjnego' in Janusz Sługocki (ed.), *Dziesięć lat polskich doświadczeń w Unii Europejskiej* Problemy prawnoadministracyjne (PRESSCOM 2014) 398.

55 Adam Zieliński, 'Wokół reformy polskiego sądownictwa' (2009) 1(2) *Państwo i Prawo* 19.

T. Koncewicz, that the right to a fair procedure consists of two components: the right to judicial protection (understood as the access to the court) and the right to effective judicial review (appropriately shaped procedures),[56] it should be pointed out that in the Polish system, we observe actual availability of judicial protection, and despite a slight doubt as to the quality of the procedure, overall, judicial protection may be deemed effective.

56 Tomasz Tadeusz Koncewicz, 'Prawo do rzetelnego postępowania w europejskiej przestrzeni prawnej Jaka procedura? Jakie prawo?' (2013) 1(11–12) *Palestra* 70.

15 The principle of effective legal protection in administrative law in Slovenia

Erik Kerševan

1 Historical developments

History has shown a continuous development of different administrative procedural regulations valid in the territory of Slovenia already in States preceding its independence in 1991. If we start with some facts and figures, the first regulation dates back to the General Administrative Procedure Act of Kingdom of Yugoslavia in 1930, based on an example of the Austrian regulation from 1925. Similarly, a system of judicial review of administrative acts was introduced by unification of countries in the Kingdom of Yugoslavia with the Act on Council of State and Administrative Courts of 1921, based on the French model of administrative justice, since such was already in place in Serbia.

Even in the time of the communist regime, the general principles of administrative procedure were introduced already in 1946 followed by the codification of judicial review of administration introduced by the Administrative Disputes Act in 1952 and (re)introduction of the codified federal General Administrative Procedure Act (GAPA) in 1956, which was later changed and modernised continuously. This act served as a basis of regulation in force in the independent Republic of Slovenia, which was adopted in 1999 under the same name as a part of new legislation of the independent state. This act has seen a number of revisions and modifications, but its core structure remained basically the same. After independence a new Administrative Dispute Act was also adopted in 1997, which brought new development on the regulatory level, but its role in the democratic legal order, based on the respect for the rule of law, changed dramatically, since the courts were quite overwhelmed by the number of cases that had to be resolved. Therefore a completely new Administrative Dispute Act was passed in 2006 and came into force in 2007.

This regulation has shown a division of two levels of administrative decision making and control: first is the very strict and detailed regulation of administrative procedure, which has given a very strong importance to the intra-administrative review of legality: the administrative appeal is a very powerful remedy and there are a number of extraordinary legal remedies that can be used against final acts of administration. This is probably a result of historic approach that was aimed at ensuring the resolution of all questions of both law and fact before administrative bodies, since the judicial dispute between an individual and the state was in the 50 years of communist regime very rare and also frowned upon.[1] In other words, whereas the detailed

1 Even in legal books, e.g. the legal commentaries to Administrative Disputes Act, a very detailed argumentation why the 'bourgeois' institution of administrative dispute as judicial control of administration

regulation aimed at efficient functioning of administration was in conceptual accordance with communist regime paradigms, the effective independent judicial control in a system, which did not recognise the separation of powers, was not. This gave the individual quite powerful protection of his legally guaranteed rights and obligations within administrative decision making, but very limited (in theory and practice) protection in judicial administrative dispute procedure. Together with these remarks, two other important aspects have to be stressed. First, there were wide administrative areas, where the administrative bodies had discretionary powers, which could not be effectively challenged by the individual, either by appeal or by other legal remedies. And secondly, available legal remedies, although effective, were also widely used for the protection of public interest: state bodies (e.g. state prosecutor, state attorney) had – and still have – the right to appeal administrative decisions and even start judicial review proceedings to protect the objective legality as a recognised aspect of public interest.[2] Following this reasoning also many extraordinary legal remedies could – and still can – be used *ex officio* by administrative bodies themselves to annul or change an (allegedly) unlawful administrative act.

The approach to legal remedies in the Slovenian legal system is derived from this tradition and was – and remains – ambiguous, since the effectiveness of legal remedies was not aimed solely at ensuring the protection of individuals' rights and legitimate interests but also at ensuring a very strong intra-administrative control with the aim of protecting public interest. Still, the most obvious development in recent years has shown a growing understanding of the importance of effective, impartial and independent judicial review and more and more energy has been aimed at ensuring its modernisation and effectiveness.

2 Constitutional framework

The Constitution of the Republic of Slovenia has several provisions determining not just the principle, but also the right to effective legal remedy and judicial protection.

First, based on the model of Art. 13 of the European Convention on Human Rights (ECHR), there is Art. 25 in the Slovenian Constitution that determined that there has to be a right to an (effective) legal remedy: 'Everyone shall be guaranteed the right to appeal or to any other legal remedy against the decisions of courts and other state authorities, local community authorities, and bearers of public authority by which his rights, duties, or legal interests are determined.'

This legal remedy not only has to exist in law, but it also has to be effective in practice, as has been repeatedly stressed by the Constitutional Court: it has to be available against all administrative acts, affecting the legal position of an individual, it has to be able to suspend the implementation of the challenged administrative act and the decision on appeal has to be adopted by a higher-level administrative

is not contrary to 'socialist society' and the 'general theory of Marxism-Leninism of the State dying out on the way to developing consistent socialist democracy in transitional period' was presented. See e.g. Mirko Perović, *Komentar Zakona o upravnim sporovima* (Savremena Administracija, Beograd 1972) 5–11.

2 Both are a widely reflected concept of acceptable form of administrative dispute in a socialist society, see Branko Majstorović, *Komentar Zakona o upravnim sporovima* (Izdanje Službenog lista SFRJ, Beograd 1965) 5–11, 40–46.

authority.[3] Therefore it can be interpreted that a two-level decision making structure of administration is a constitutional requirement, since there has to be a body, deciding on appeal within the administration itself, unless there are clear reasons in public interests why there has to be a final level administrative decision taken by the body responsible in the first instance.[4] The appeal in administrative procedure was – and still is – seen by many scholars and recognised by jurisprudence for many years as the most important implementation of the constitutional right to an effective remedy in the area of administrative law.[5] This has of course led to detailed regulation of appeal procedure in the GAPA and in many cases courts have examined various aspects of this regulation, including its conformity with constitutional requirements.

Interesting legal debates have found ground in the combination of this constitutional right with another, also enshrined in the Constitution as one of the most important guarantees of the rule of law: the right to judicial protection. The right of any person to have judicial protection is determined by Art. 23 of the Constitution, which has in substance copied Art. 6 of the European Convention of Human Rights, but is not limited in its scope to civil matters and criminal charges, but has extended its validity also to administrative matters, which was confirmed by the interpretation of the Constitutional Court.[6] Art. 23 states that: 'Everyone has the right to have any decision regarding his rights, duties, and any charges brought against him made without undue delay by an independent, impartial court constituted by law. Only a judge duly appointed pursuant to rules previously established by law and by judicial regulations may judge such an individual.' In this regard every statutory provision that limits the powers of the courts (Administrative Court included) can be challenged before the Constitutional Court and is examined in extensive scrutiny of the so called 'strict proportionality test': whether the limitation of the constitutional right to effective judicial protection is aimed at achieving a constitutionally acceptable goal, whether it is necessary and appropriate for achieving this goal and whether the values protected by this measure are in proportion with the limits set on the right of judicial protection.[7]

The combination of the right to an effective legal remedy and the right to judicial protection – and its possible limits in administrative matters – have been (and still are) a challenge for both the parliament and the Constitutional Court. After the new Constitution of the independent state was adopted in 1992, these two rights were interpreted as being separate constitutional guarantees, aimed at effective legal protection of individuals and therefore both of them had to be implemented in relevant legislative provisions. This in civil and criminal matters was not so difficult, as it meant that after the first instance of judicial protection a right to appeal to a second-level has to be granted to all parties of the proceedings. But in administrative matters, where the procedure of administrative bodies was followed by the judicial review procedure, these demands of an effective legal protection led to an overburdening of the system

3 Constitutional Court Decision No. U-I-219/03 of 1 December 2005.

4 Constitutional Court Decision No. U-I-313/96 of 8 April 1999.

5 See especially Tone Jerovšek, 'Pravica do pritožbe (25. člen)', Lovro Šturm (ed.), *Komentar Ustave Republike Slovenije* (Fakulteta za podiplomske državne in evropske študije, Kranj 2002) 274–294.

6 The scope of protection is therefore similar to the new Art. 47 (Right to an effective remedy and to a fair trial) of the Charter of Fundamental Rights of the European Union.

7 See Constitutional Court Decision No. U-I-18/02 of 24 October 2003.

and in consequence to lower effectiveness of legal remedies. The question of guaranteeing both the right to an effective legal remedy and the right to judicial protection has also had its impact on the organisation of legal remedies and structure of administrative bodies and courts, having jurisdiction in judicial review. In the early 1990s it was thus interpreted as a constitutional requirement to form three levels of legal protection in all administrative matters, after the administrative act has been issued in the first instance. There is no need to stress that four levels of decision making in the same administrative matter has hindered efficiency of both administrative appeal procedures and judicial protection. These organisational and procedural requirements have been abandoned following a decision of the Constitutional Court, which confirmed that the right to judicial protection in administrative matters is equivalent to the right to an effective legal remedy and that provisions of Arts. 23 and 25 of the Constitution should be interpreted in combination, meaning that there is no constitutional right to have either an administrative appeal against the administrative act or a judicial appeal against the first instance decision of the administrative court, if there is an effective judicial review of an administrative act established by law.[8] The result is therefore now similar to the sense of Art. 47 of the Charter of EU Fundamental Rights.

To summarise, all the constitutional rules and principles require that in administrative matters there has to be effective legal protection of persons' rights and legitimate interests, at least in the form of an effective judicial review of all administrative decisions and actions, by which these rights or interests are (or can be) affected.

3 Rights-based perspective

The legal protection of individuals in administrative matters is regulated by two different laws.

The GAPA regulates in considerable detail the administrative decision making in the first instance, appeal procedure and extraordinary legal remedies that can be used against a final administrative act, and the Administrative Dispute Act of 2006 (ADA) regulates specialised judicial review procedure that can follow the exhaustion of administrative appeals. As presented above, the appeal procedure and the access to administrative courts together form an implementation of the constitutional requirement of effective legal protection in administrative law.

In both procedural laws – although different in concept and characteristics – all fundamental principles of fair procedure are guaranteed: in all cases all parties to the proceedings have the right to access to all the relevant documents, the right to counsel and the right to be heard. Every formal administrative act has to give reasons, with only some exceptions expressly regulated by law (e.g. urgent matters, matters of minor importance). The Administrative Court has to give reasons for its judgments both in regard to facts and law, but can in parts refer to the reasoning of disputed administrative act, if the court agrees with it, without repeating it expressly in the judgment in its entirety.

There are however, some widely used fundamental concepts that have to be briefly explained to understand the functioning of legal remedies in administrative matters.

8 See Constitutional Court Decision No. U-I-219/03 of 1 December 2005.

Legal protection in Slovenian legal order is given in administrative matters both to rights and legitimate interests of legal persons or individuals affected by certain administrative decision making. Whereas the concept of rights under public administrative law is relatively less problematic, the role of 'legitimate interest' in administrative law is harder to explain. It is of course clear that the 'legal right' is in its substance a legally protected interest, meaning a private interest recognised by the legislator and given its legal basis in appropriate form of the law. But in Slovenian administrative law tradition, a weaker form of protection of private interests is also recognised, meaning that also in cases where the legislator has not given to a certain private interest the legal recognition and protection in the form of a 'right', there can be some legal empowerment of such an interest to be pertinent (relevant) also in administrative decision making. If a certain interest is individual (as opposed to general), directly linked to the administrative matter in question and based on a legal provision, granting it legal protection, the administrative bodies and courts in administrative dispute are bound to give it appropriate protection. Examples of this legitimate interest are found in cases where a certain party desires a favourable administrative act based on discretionary powers of administration (e.g. citizenship), meaning that there is no legally enforceable right to attain it. Legitimate interests also have to be respected in cases where there is a decision to be taken about rights or obligations of a certain party, if there is a person is participating *ex parte* in these proceedings, (e.g. neighbour to an investor seeking a building permit) and his interest fulfils the abovementioned criteria.[9] The legal remedies are in principle the same for the protection of both rights and legitimate interests under administrative law, but the recognition of a certain private interest as a legitimate interest (and not just a plain economic, moral or general interest) can be more widely left to the interpretation of administrative bodies and – above all – courts exercising judicial review of administration.[10] It also has to be stressed that the protection of legitimate interest is in legal remedies limited in its scope to the issues directly affecting and/or violating the interest in question and cannot be extended to other aspects of legality.[11]

3.1 Legal protection in administrative procedures

The right to appeal is in the GAPA regulated as one of the fundamental principles. It guarantees both the protection of rights of parties to the proceedings, as well as the protection of public interests and the fundamental principle of legality. In

9 Regarding these issues extensively in Vilko Androjna, Erik Kerševan, *Upravno procesno pravo* (GV Založba, Ljubljana 2006) 45–62.

10 In practice, a very important criterion is the question of teleological interpretation of the provision of a law: the private interest can be found to be legitimate, if there was an intention of the legislator to protect this specific interest, which differentiates it from other potential or present interests and can be found to protect only a determined (or determinable) number of persons. This goes well with the concept of German 'Schutznormntheorie', see, Hans-Joachim Driehaus and Rainer Pietzner, *Einführung in das Allgemeine Verwaltungsrecht* (C. H. Beck, München 1996) 49, and Klaus Stern, *Verwaltungsprozessuale Probleme in der öffentlich-rechtlichen Arbeit* (Beck, München 2000) 200, quoted also in Constitutional Court decision No. Up-1850/08 of 5 May 2010.

11 Procedurally it is of course a challenge if the *ex parte* participant points out questions of fact and/or law, which have to be examined *ex officio* by the administrative body.

administrative procedure appeal is an ordinary legal remedy, available to all persons affected by the decision, which was issued at first instance.[12]

The right to appeal in the administrative procedure is allowed against any administrative decision, which was issued at the first instance. The persons entitled to appeal are those, who had a formal legal status of parties to the first instance proceedings. It has to be mentioned that any person who shows legitimate interest can formally take part in the administrative procedure initiated by a party or *ex officio*, before the administrative act is issued. Right to appeal is also granted to those, who were not taking part in administrative procedure, if their rights or legitimate interests under public law are affected by the administrative act and they can show that an appeal could remedy that situation. The law regulates, however, that if the person was already invited to take part in first instance procedure, but did not respond to this invitation, his right to appeal is limited, both in the time limit to appeal as well as in substance.

The appeal has in principle a suspensive effect and is decided by a superior administrative body. This is only a principle, however, since in cases regulated by law, the appeal does not stay the execution of the challenged administrative act, so that whole fields or areas of administrative law have such exceptions regulated: no appeal in e.g. tax law, decisions of inspections, etc. has suspensive effect. The Constitutional Court held in several cases that this does not violate the provisions of the Constitution.[13]

An appeal can be used against a first instance decision based on questions of both fact and law. The points of law that can be used in an appeal are both the questions of procedural and substantive (material) rights and legitimate interests under public law, that have been violated. Discretionary decisions can also be appealed based on the grounds that the discretionary powers were not used within the limits of the law or not following the legal aim, because of which these powers were granted to the administration. A violation of discretionary powers can also occur if the discretion was not used in accordance with the principle of proportionality or could have been used in a more appropriate manner to satisfy public interests.

The 'silence of administration' can also be a ground to appeal, on the basis of a legal fiction that the party's application was rejected or that the procedural outcome in *ex officio* proceedings was unfavourable. This fiction appears after expiry of a time limit, given to administrative bodies by law to reach a decision, which is one month in simple and two months in complex matters, which can be extended for another 30 days, if the circumstances justify it.

While the appeal procedure cannot be started by administrative bodies on their own motion, there are strong elements of protection of public interest and 'objective legality' of administrative action. The act can be appealed also by state prosecutors or state attorneys even if they were not parties to the proceedings if they claim that the administrative act is illegal and violating public interest. According to the principle of protecting objective legality of the act, the appellate administrative body

12 The exception to the right to an administrative appeal has to be expressly regulated by an act of parliament and is present e.g. in cases of decisions of independent regulatory authorities (Agency for protection of competition, Bank of Slovenia, etc.), where these decisions can be directly subjected to judicial review.

13 See Constitutional Court Decision No. U-I-297/95 of 28 October 1998.

has extensive powers (and duty) to examine *ex officio* possible violations of both substantive and procedural law, even if they were not disputed by the appellant. When deciding on appeal it can annul the act even against the interests of the person who started the appeal procedure, meaning *ultra petitum*, in cases defined by the GAPA. Depending on the case, these powers can contribute to effective legal remedy of the persons affected by the administrative act, but can be hardly interpreted as such in cases where the end result of administrative appeal procedure is contrary to the interests of these persons and in effect protecting only the public interest.

The powers of a superior body when deciding on appeal are very wide, since it can annul a decision (*ab initio*) and refer it back to the administrative body in first instance, but it can also change the challenged decision itself in any way it deems is required by law to reach a correct and just result of the proceedings. Since the appellant's interest is in acquiring a final substantive solution (*in merito*) to his claims, the question of effectiveness in this regard has been concentrating on the issue of delimiting these procedural powers: when in the case of a well-founded appeal a final decision has to be taken in second instance and when can the case be referred back to first instance, prolonging the procedure. It is quite clear that in principle the resolution of the appeal case in second instance gives a finality to the decision taken, so that the referral back to the first instance should be an exception, when circumstances justify such a decision (i.e. when the procedure would be more expediently resolved by the capacity of the first instance administrative body). The GAPA has been trying to resolve this in such a way, but due to the need (or desire) of superior administrative bodies to lower their burden, a high number of cases of successful appeals still end as a repeated first instance procedure, which of course can end in a new appeal by the aggrieved party.

To counter this ineffectiveness new provisions have recently been included in GAPA, which allow the superior administrative body to refer the case back to the first instance body only once. Following these provisions, the superior administrative body is on (possible) second, consecutive appeal bound to resolve the matter itself with a final decision, but the question still remains, how (and if) that will contribute to the overall effectiveness of appeal as a legal remedy. There is no legal remedy if this administrative obligation is violated and the overburdening of second level administration could cause the legal protection to become less, not more effective.

After an administrative decision is final, there are several extraordinary legal remedies regulated by GAPA or in certain fields of administration other laws (e.g. Act on Taxation Procedure) that can (and are) effectively used to remedy a violation of law and/or rights and legitimate interests of persons affected by this decision. These can be used to remedy both the errors in established facts, based on new evidence, as well as grave procedural violations, (e.g. when a person affected by the decision was not taking part in the proceedings, reopening of the administrative procedure) and grave violations of substantive law. There are extraordinary legal remedies that can be used both by persons affected as well as certain authorities charged with protecting the public interest (state prosecutor, state attorney, inspector) or even *ex officio* by administrative bodies themselves. In these cases, the responsible (supervisory) administrative body adopts its decision in the form of a new administrative act, which can subsequently be subjected to judicial review in administrative disputes in accordance with ADA.

3.2 Judicial review

A final administrative act can be subjected to judicial review before the Administrative Court. Any final administrative act that is in substance a decision on rights or obligations of persons can be challenged by an appropriate claim in a specialised judicial procedure. The Constitution does not require a special administrative court to be established, but it does provide for a special procedure that has to be regulated for the judicial review of administrative actions. There is an explicit provision in the Constitution stating that there is a special judicial review procedure (administrative dispute, *upravni spor*)[14] of the legality of 'final individual acts with which state authorities, local community authorities, and bearers of public authority decide the rights or obligations and legal interests of individuals and organisations, if other judicial protection is not provided by law for a particular matter.'

This means that there has to be a judicial procedure for the review of final individual acts and that this procedure has to be specially regulated by law in the form of administrative dispute or another form of specialised judicial procedure (e.g. social dispute against administrative acts regarding pensions, public health and other social rights). The possibility to bring actions against the public authorities in courts of general jurisdiction does not satisfy this constitutional requirement, since these courts do not have necessary powers to ensure effective protection of legally guaranteed position of individuals and organisations under administrative law. This constitutional provision is interpreted as a rule that the courts of general competence do not have powers to decide upon the legality and validity of administrative acts[15] and cannot order the administration to perform actions under statutes to satisfy the rights of individuals under public law.

In relation to the scope of judicial review in administrative dispute procedure the focus of the abovementioned Art. 157 of the Constitution is on the review of 'administrative act'[16] and does not mention other forms of administrative action or relevant remedies of judicial protection. This can be regarded as a constitutionally recognised significance of the judicial protection against the administrative acts as the (probably still) most important and widespread form of administrative action. It would be wrong to interpret this provision as a limit to judicial power and the scope of judicial review, necessary to guarantee effective judicial protection. The ADA follows the same legal structure and the definition of the administrative act tries to encompass all forms of administrative decision making based on powers under public law. It has to be

14 The term 'administrative dispute' in this case determines the judicial review process in which a (private or legal) person as a plaintiff brings an action against the administration in relation to its decisions or actions brought under *iure imperii*, exercising public authority (*processo amministrativo, Verwaltungsprozess, contentieux amministratif*). Disputes in relation to public procurement are in Slovenia not a part of administrative dispute, since it is deemed to be a dispute related to *iure negotii*, since the public body isn't acting in its authoritative capacity, but forming contracts of private law. The disputes are resolved by a special tribunal, National Review Commission for Reviewing Public Procurement Procedures.

15 An interesting and recent example can be found in Constitutional Court Decision No. Up-457/09 of 28 September 2011.

16 The definition is very similar on the traditional meaning of German 'Verwaltungsakt' that serves as the basis of judicial review in Federal Republic of Germany, see Harmut Maurer, *Allgemeines Verwaltungsrecht* (Beck, München 2002) 187 ff, also in Austria, Ludwig Adamovich and Bernd-Christian Funk, *Allgemeines Verwaltungsrecht* (3., neubearbeitete Aufl., Springer, Wien 1998) 262 ff.

stressed that the term 'administrative act' is defined by law: 'Pursuant to this Act, an administrative act shall be an administrative decision and other public law, unilateral, authoritative individual act, issued within the framework of implementing administrative function, in which a body makes a decision on a right, obligation or legal benefit of an individual or legal entity, or of any other person who may be party to the proceeding of issuing the act'. As an important aspect of trying to guarantee extensive scope of effective judicial protection the Constitutional Court stressed in a recent case that the state has to act through administrative acts for its decisions *ex iure imperii* to have a legally valid effect. If the State uses another form of action contrary to the law, there can be no change in rights and obligations of individuals and legal entities.[17]

This definition itself has however limited the competence of the Administrative Court to review administrative acts that are final not just in a formal, but also in a material sense, meaning that in principle the decision making in administrative procedure has to be concluded with a final decision, based on the merits of the case, before the judicial review procedure can be initiated. This gives primacy to appeal administrative procedure, which has to be resolved with a final decision, before the claim in administrative dispute can be filed with the court. If, as a result of successful administrative appeal, the matter is referred back to first instance for further consideration, no party can start the administrative dispute procedure in court, since there is no substantially final administrative act yet that can be challenged. This is in effect a major contribution to effectiveness of legal remedies in administrative law, since it has enabled a coherent approach and relation between two separate procedures. In this way, the administrative bodies are not waiting for any courts' judgments before continuing to reach a final decision in administrative procedure and the courts are not burdened with cases and questions, which could only be preliminary in the sense that no substantially final decision would have been reached by the administration in the time of the court's judgment.

According to this concept of judicial review of administrative acts, there has to be an authentic dispute between two sides of the case, so that it would be unconstitutional to change it into something incompatible with its basic nature. Thus, it would be unacceptable to grant the Administrative Court the power to launch an *ex officio* judicial process before the final decision in an administrative case. However, there are some competences and powers that the court deciding in administrative dispute procedure does not have and that represent an important limitation to effectiveness of legal protection in judicial review. Foremost, although of limited importance because of reasons given above, the Administrative Court has no competence to rule on actions of the administrative bodies that do not correspond to the definition of an administrative act. Some of these are less problematic, since they do not affect the rights and obligations of individuals (e.g. governmental acts of political discretion)[18] and would therefore not give standing to any plaintiff to challenge them. The other

17 See Constitutional Court Decision No. Up-626/12 of 12 July 2012: 'The authoritative deciding of bearers of public authority on the rights, obligations, or legal benefits of individuals is consistent with the principle of a state governed by the rule of law (Art. 2 of the Constitution) and possible only on the basis of an issued administrative decision that takes into consideration Art. 22 of the Constitution, which determines the right to the equal protection of rights in proceedings.'

18 Similar as in Germany '*Regierungsakte*', see Harmut Maurer, *Allgemeines Verwaltungsrecht* (Beck, München 2002) 192–197.

forms of action (or omission) could on the other hand represent violations or rights of persons who would require judicial protection, but – since there is no formal obligation to issue an administrative act – the possibilities are very limited.[19] The Administrative Court can review the legality of such an action only if it violates the constitutional rights of the plaintiff and there is no other (primary) effective judicial protection available to him.

The person entitled to start the administrative dispute as a plaintiff can only be the person, who was a party or an accessory participant in the proceedings of issuing an administrative act. This formal status is a necessary requirement, so that no person can use this legal remedy if he has not tried to protect his interests in the administrative procedure, or used appeal or extraordinary legal remedies to try to rectify the violation of his procedural rights to participate in administrative decision making process.[20] However, this status is not enough to act as a plaintiff, since he has to show that he has legitimate interest in starting these proceedings in court, that is that the administrative act is affecting his rights and legally protected interests under public law and that success in administrative dispute could remedy this situation, the infringement of his rights has to be shown as at least possible and not just of negligible consequences, etc. On the other hand, there are less clear cases of subjects having standing in administrative dispute that protect public interest and not individual rights. For instance, there is a possibility that a public attorney challenges an administrative act if it is contrary to the law and violates public interest in favour of an individual, so that both the plaintiff and the defendant in this case are bodies of state administration.[21] Besides the plaintiff and the defendant a position to intervene in an administrative dispute is given to persons who would be affected by the decision of the court (e.g. losing the rights, granted by the disputed administrative act), but is also limited to persons who had standing in the concluded administrative procedure.

The ADA tries to guarantee effective judicial protection of plaintiff's rights by giving him several different claims (actions): claim to annulment of the administrative act, issuing or service of administrative act (action due to silence), change of administrative act (action in dispute of full jurisdiction) and action to determine the unlawfulness of an administrative act. There is a risk that enumerating the fixed forms of actions and available remedies can prevent plaintiffs from achieving constitutionally

19 An example occurred in a publicly reported case, where the police has put up roadblocks aimed to prevent a Roma family to return to their settlement, citing rules and powers regarding protection of public order, but no administrative acts were addressed to individuals and therefore no appeal or judicial review under general rules of GAPA or ADA was possible.

20 Against the final decision by which a person was refused the right to participate in the procedure of issuing the administrative act, the action may be brought by the person to whom the right to participate in the procedure was refused by this decision.

21 Similar to that is the granting of formal status as a plaintiff to associations, registered as protecting the environment in public interest, that can challenge any administrative act, that would violate the rules of law, aimed at environmental protection (Art. 64 of Environment Protection Act), since these groups are protecting public interest against the decision of an administrative body, also charged with protection of public interest. The reasoning behind these solutions is to give standing to someone in cases where otherwise would be no (obvious) plaintiff, but the question remains whether the judicial review process is the right forum to do so.

guaranteed effective protection,[22] so that a general clause in addition to the present forms of action, enabling the administrative court to grant 'any necessary relief or take any necessary measure' to secure the effective protection of persons' rights and legal interests under administrative law would be appropriate.[23]

The administrative act can be challenged both on questions of fact and of law, so that the court is not limited in any way to examine its legality. There can even be new evidence (but existent in the time when the disputed act was adopted) presented to the court, if the party can justify why it has not been used in administrative procedure. There is an important provision in the ADA, which to raise the effectiveness of protection of rights of the plaintiff, provides for the court the obligation that it has to remedy the violations of procedural rights, which occurred in administrative procedure, by granting the plaintiff these rights or enabling him to exercise his rights in the court's proceedings instead. Based on these procedural measures, the lawsuit can be rejected even if the court realises that the procedure before the administrative body was unlawful, but it has by its own actions eliminated such violation in its procedure. The violations of substantial (material) law can of course also be claimed, but in relation to discretionary powers the court is limited in its possibility to make a ruling on the legality of a discretionary decision, except if these powers exceed the limits set by law or are used contrary to the aim, determined in the law itself, of granting these powers to the administration (misuse of discretion).

The court can respond to these actions with corresponding sentences, where in case of a successful lawsuit in the vast majority of cases the judgment annuls the disputed administrative act and refers the case back to the responsible administrative body. The court decides in dispute of full jurisdiction only in very exceptional cases, so that the court decides in the matter itself, granting the plaintiff his right or determines his obligation in lieu of administration. The principle of separation of powers is much quoted in this regard, interestingly lately more by the theory than the practice of the Constitutional Court and other responsible courts. There has been some pointing out to the specifics of procedure of judicial review, especially regarding the power of full jurisdiction in administrative dispute and the constitutionality of the limitations of the Administrative Courts' powers to change the challenged act and thereby decide on the administrative matter with its own judgment.[24] The regulation of ADA is deemed to be in accordance with constitutional requirements, since in relation to the administrative acts the possibility of their annulment has found to be a basic and effective remedy of plaintiffs in judicial review of administrative action. The Administrative Court shall (and should) therefore use its powers of full jurisdiction, when it is necessary to ensure effective protection of the rights and legal interests of persons affected.[25]

22 As in the case of Constitutional Court Decision No. U-I-181/09, Up-860/09, Up-222/10 of 10 November 2011.

23 Interestingly, a similar form is already used in Administrative dispute act in relation to a special procedure for subsidiary protection of constitutional rights of individuals that can be used before the Administrative Court.

24 See Constitutional Court Decision No. U-I-181/09, Up-860/09, Up-222/10 of 10 November 2011, para 12: the role of the courts in administrative dispute is based foremost on the judgment on legality of acts of administration and not on decision making about rights or obligations and consequential duplication of actions of the executive or infringement of its area of competence.

25 'In conformity with the principle of separation of powers, in administrative lawsuit judicial control is exercised over administrative decisions, which, however, does not constitute the assuming of the

The judgment that annuls the unlawful administrative act is according to ADA in itself just a decision that causes formal cessation of the disputed act, without resolving the question on merits. The consequence is a referral of the case back to a responsible administrative body, that has to decide again and issue a new administrative act, that can again be subjected to appeal (if delivered in first instance) and judicial review (if final both in formal and substantial meaning). This does not give a high level of legal protection, so to raise the effectiveness of this type of judgment the ADA has introduced a legal obligation for administrative bodies to follow the reasoning of the court in their subsequent proceedings. According to express provision of the law the competent administrative body must issue a new administrative act within 30 days of the day it received the judgment, or within the period set by the court. The law also states that all other administrative bodies deciding on ordinary or extraordinary legal remedies against the new administrative act, issued on the basis of the court's ruling, are also bound by the legal opinion of the court, expressed in this ruling.

This means that in principle the administrative bodies have to follow the legal reasoning of the court and in case they violate this obligation, the Administrative Court in the subsequent administrative dispute can use its powers to decide in full jurisdiction, changing the disputed act and giving a final decision on administrative matter. However, since – because of the reasons given above – the Administrative Court is reluctant to use these powers and in practice only annuls the disputed act again with a new referral to the administrative body, the question remains, whether the Administrative Courts' judicial protection is in practice effective enough. If the administration in a given case does not respect a court's decision that can in itself be a violation of the rule of law, and if there is no remedy to ensure that in the end the court's judgment is respected, that problem should be treated very seriously. So far, unfortunately, no new mechanisms have been developed to ensure the stricter implementation of Administrative Courts' rulings and this remains an open challenge to the effectiveness of legal protection, since there has been a quite low, but still significant number of cases observed in judicial practice, where the administration did not act accordingly.

The question of granting the affected plaintiff damages in cases that the administration has acted unlawfully is a very complex one in the Slovenian legal system. The Constitution guarantees that everyone has the right to compensation for damage caused through unlawful actions in connection with the performance of any function or other activity by a person or authority performing such function or activity within a state or local community authority or as a bearer of public authority. The competence for deciding on this responsibility lies with the courts of general competence, which base their decisions on general provisions of the Civil code, and the question whether they have the competence to decide on the legality of an administrative act in these proceedings is still a disputed one.[26] The Administrative Court also has the power to

function of State administration. The court will in the framework of administrative lawsuit only decide concerning a particular right itself (lawsuit within full jurisdiction) where any other action would constitute inadmissible interference with the right to due process of law, for example, where because of failure of administration to act or for any other justified reasons the individual could in fact not exercise his rights or protect his legal entitlements.' See Constitutional Court Decision No. U-I-146/98 of 24 June 1998.

26 Both in theory as well as in judicial practice there have been several different views, whether the competence of Administrative Court to review the legality of administrative acts should be exclusive or

award damages to the plaintiff seeking them, if it finds the administrative act to be unlawful and violating the rights or legitimate interests of the plaintiff. In practice the Administrative Court almost never uses these powers, mainly as a measure to limit its overburdening, so the plaintiff is directed to lodge his claim with the court of general competence.

4 Institutional perspective

There are several institutions that have competences to ensure effective legal protection in administrative law in Slovenia. First, the appeal procedure in administrative institutional framework is handled by superior administrative bodies, mostly central government ministries (or mayors of municipalities at the local level) that have strong powers to annul or change the appealed administrative act and also several possibilities to use extraordinary legal remedies to the same effect.

After the administrative procedure is concluded by issuing a final administrative act, the lawsuit against it in administrative dispute is decided by the Administrative Court, which is a specialised court that is a part of judiciary,[27] composed of higher court judges. Since the Constitution states that there is a (one) Supreme Court, which is the highest court in the country, there can be no Supreme Administrative Court as in several other European states, so that all legal remedies against the decisions taken by the specialised Administrative Court are decided by the Administrative Chamber of the Supreme Court of the Republic of Slovenia. Following these fundamental constitutional rules, it can be stated that the Parliament is free to decide whether to form specialised courts or not, but it cannot alter the status of judges sitting in these courts and it cannot exclude the final jurisdiction of the Supreme Court in all matters of law.

The role of the Supreme Court in administrative dispute is to ensure a uniform application of the law and decide in principle mostly on extraordinary legal remedies, although an appeal against the judgment of Administrative Court is possible in a limited number of cases (e.g. in cases where the judgment would change the administrative act in dispute of full jurisdiction, based on new factual basis, established by the Court). In principle this means that judgments of Administrative Court are final and are to be implemented by the administration. Based on jurisprudence of the Court, only in cases where the lawsuit is rejected, there can be an extraordinary legal remedy (revision) addressed to the Supreme Court, but only based on questions of law. The revision is only allowed on a limited number of grounds, which justify its acceptance to consideration by the Supreme Court, i.e. the importance of question of law to be resolved, resolving the problem of diverging jurisprudence of Administrative Court and prevention of grave consequences, caused to the party by the disputed administrative act. In practice, only a very limited number of cases are accepted for extraordinary revision by the Supreme Court.

shared with courts of general competence in cases of claiming damages against the State. The respect for finality administrative acts and judgments of Administrative Court, the omission to challenge the administrative act in administrative dispute, etc., are complex issues that are to be further developed in Slovenian legal practice. See also Martina Bukovec, 'Odškodninska odgovornost države' (2004) 30 *Podjetje in delo* 7.

27 As already mentioned above, regular courts cannot rule on validity of administrative acts, but can award damages if a party has suffered them because of unlawful administrative action.

The relation between the courts deciding in administrative dispute and the Constitutional Court is regulated in Art. 156 of the Constitution: 'If a court deciding some matter deems a law which it should apply to be unconstitutional, it must stay the proceedings and initiate proceedings before the Constitutional Court. The proceedings in the court may be continued after the Constitutional Court has issued its decision.' This means that if the court examining the legality of an administrative act finds that a Government Decree (or other forms of secondary legislation), that were used as a legal basis for the challenged administrative act is contrary to constitutional requirements, it can set it aside (*exceptio illegalis*) and does not apply it as a basis for its ruling. If the constitutionality is questioned in relation to an act of Parliament, the court can stay its proceedings and demand the Constitutional court to decide on this question. After the Act has been abrogated by the Constitutional Court, the administrative dispute continues and the court can decide its case without basing its ruling on the abrogated act. This gives in practice very effective legal protection against regulations of both Government and Parliament in administrative matters.

It is important also to stress that the effective protection in administrative dispute is also supervised by the Constitutional Court in cases of constitutional complaint (Art. 160 of the Constitution). This appeal enables the unsuccessful plaintiff to claim that in the given administrative matter the decisions of administrative bodies and/or courts have violated his human rights and fundamental freedoms. The appellant can also claim that the violation of his constitutional rights by the individual act is a direct result of unconstitutionality of the legal basis (normative acts, laws, statutes or regulations) of the act in question. If the Constitutional Court finds any such laws and by-laws to be unconstitutional it can abrogate them with *erga omnes* effect, as well as annul the disputed administrative act or judgment, issued on their basis to the appellant.

It is quite fascinating that there are no alternative dispute resolution mechanisms, tribunals[28] or other bodies that have competence to resolve the issues and disputes in administrative law in Slovenia. This is probably also reflected in the GAPA which does not provide any legal basis for contractual resolution (settlements) of administrative matters in the form of public law contracts between administrative bodies and parties to the proceedings. The possibilities of the Ombudsman to influence these procedures is therefore also limited to his opinions as to appropriate decision making in cases of formal procedures and legal remedies.

5 The European perspective

In this part also some questions of European influence and European Union Law, together with the European Convention of Human Rights, can be addressed, since together with some other facts they do form an important insight into the development of effective legal protection in Slovenia.

28 National Review Commission for Reviewing Public Procurement Award Procedures (shortened: National Review Commission) is a specific, independent, professional and expert state institution providing legal protection to tenderers at all procedural levels of the award of public contracts. There is no competence of Administrative Court in these matters, but the position of this Commission equals a status of a tribunal in the sense of EU Law.

It has to be said, that after the independence of Slovenia in 1991 and through the whole of the process of acceding to the European Union, serious efforts have been made to improve our procedures and relevant legislation has been adopted to ensure effective legal protection, also in administrative law. At lot has been achieved also through other methods (informatisation, e-govt, etc.) and the situation in ensuring expedience in judicial review has been vastly improved after ADA was adopted in 2006 (cases are resolved by Administrative Court on average in six months). But – and there is always that – since then, almost no real progress has been made on improving the system of legal protection. European influence in this regard is virtually nonexistent, since there have been very few questions for preliminary rulings made to the European Court of Justice (ECJ) and Slovenia has been found to be in breach of European law obligations in a very limited number of cases, both by the ECJ as the ECtHR – and in those not related to procedural issues of administrative law. The legislation has been in different areas of administration harmonised following specific EU Directives, so that there has been effort made to ensure compliance with these demands, but because of procedural autonomy of EU Member States, not much has been changed in general rules or principles of legal protection.

6 Conclusion

The debate of whether the Slovenian system of administrative law guarantees effective legal protection is – and will probably always be – ongoing. It can definitely be stated that there is no challenge to the question, whether there is an adequate minimum level of effectiveness of legal remedies in administrative law, which corresponds to constitutional requirements and demands of both EU law and ECHR standards, where applicable. However, there is further ground for improvement in the debate how to strengthen the legal protection of rights of individuals and legal entities to guarantee a final and timely resolution of administrative cases. The adoption of ADA and its implementation in 2006 has proven to be a success, since the burden of administrative justice has been lowered and the time to resolve administrative disputes is in all surveys of Slovenia's judicial system shown to represent the best score in comparison with other areas of law, being also more than comparable to other EU Member States. On the other hand, the handling of administrative appeals has remained a challenge to be resolved, since there has been a considerable backlog in several administrative areas and there really has been a disputable practice of constant referral of difficult cases back and forth between different levels of administration. The development in several European countries (e.g. Austria, Germany) has been directed at reducing the administrative appeals as a predominant legal remedy and Slovenia should study the results of these efforts. Of course, the balance between intra-administrative legal protection mechanisms and subsequent judicial review should be carefully examined and established in an optimal scale, so that for a small country as Slovenia the future model could be different from bigger legal systems. And finally, even though the cases of non-observance of judicial decisions by the administration is low, there has to be some further development of enforcement mechanisms to ensure also that the effectiveness of legal protection is not dependent solely on the (good)will of administration but guaranteed to anyone protecting his rights under administrative law.

16 The principle of effective legal protection in Spanish administrative law

Angel Manuel Moreno

1 Historical developments

In Spain, the Principle of Effective Legal Protection (hereinafter, PELP) in administrative law is the result of a long historical process, of which the roots may be traced back to the beginning of the nineteenth century, when the rule of law and the process of 'constitutionalisation' of Public Administration began to develop in the country.

From the outset, though, an important preliminary remark should be made: in Spain, the 'principle of effective legal protection' has not been traditionally recognised under that precise wording or terminology. Rather, the PELP is the result and the cumulative effect of different subjective rights (procedural rights, right to access to court, judicial review, etc.) and institutional-procedural arrangements. The closest terminology in Spanish would be that of '*protección judicial efectiva*' or '*tutela judicial efectiva*' (effective judicial protection), which is an important part of the PELP but does not convey the whole meaning of such a principle.[1]

Thus, from 1812 (enactment of the very first Constitution in the kingdom) until 1978 (promulgation of the current constitution), there was a complex and somehow erratic development of the principle, the understanding and depth of which depended on the changing political momentum and the prevailing political ideology (conservative-liberal). Specifically, the institutional system for controlling the activity of Public Administration underwent several changes, due to the convulsive political moves and phases of that period. Different statutes were passed during the nineteenth century (in 1845 and 1888).[2]

In 1956 the first modern system of control of administrative action, performed by 'pure' and authentic judicial organs was established (*Ley de la Jurisdicción Contencioso-Administrativa*, Administrative Courts Act). From a historical perspective, the paradox of this statute is that it was enacted just in the middle of General Franco's regime, which, after the Spanish War (1936–39), instituted an authoritarian and non-democratic political system that lasted for almost 40 years. The legal protection

1 The terminology used in domestic Public Law is linked to the English version of Art. 47 of the EU Charter of Fundamental Rights. Although effective protection of the courts stands at the core of the PELP, we understand that this principle encompasses a broader notion, and includes principles such as those of 'publicity of the legal norms', 'non-retroactivity of criminal or sanctioning rules', 'legal certainty', etc.

2 On the historical evolution of the Spanish system, see: Juan Alfonso Santamaría Pastor, *Sobre la génesis del Derecho Administrativo español en el Siglo XIX (1812.1845)* (Madrid 2006); Juan Ramón Fernández Torres, *Historia legal de la jurisdicción contencioso-admnistrativa (1845–1998)* (Madrid 2007).

mechanism introduced by this law was in general assessed as a good and advanced system of protection of subjective rights, at least from the technical point of view. It therefore constituted a guarantee for the PELP, although many political rights and civil liberties continued to be ignored by the political regime, and thus remained out of the reach of that Act.[3]

As far as the PELP in administrative procedures is concerned, during the nineteenth century every central government department had their own special or specialised procedures, thereby establishing a plethora of *ad hoc* individual procedural rights. However, a key legal development took place in 1958: the enactment of the Administrative Procedure Act (*Ley de Procedimiento Administrativo*). This law unified the administrative procedures; established a general and multi-purpose procedure (*procedimiento administrativo general*); abrogated dozens of special administrative procedural regulations and established several procedural rights. This key piece of legislation has also been evaluated as a good law, providing for the effective legal protection of many individual rights *vis-à-vis* administrative agencies.

Therefore, the situation of the PELP in the period 1936–78 may be characterised as paradoxical since a comprehensive, technically good system of individual rights protection was attained by the two abovementioned key statutes (together with the Expropriations Act of 1954), but this was achieved: (a) within a political and constitutional context that did not recognise fundamental rights as we understand them today; and (b) in the absence of a written Constitution.

The reintroduction of democracy in the kingdom in 1975–78 opened the door for the framing of a new, modern Constitution. This *Magna Carta*, the Constitution of 6 December 1978,[4] would eventually recognise fundamental rights and political freedoms that were largely ignored during the previous regime. This is now the fundamental framework for the PELP in Spain. The Spanish Constitution of 1978 recognises the basic material and procedural grounding principle of the entire legal system (Art. 9). On the other hand, it proclaims an ample list of fundamental rights (Arts. 14–29) and establishes a comprehensive system of protection for such rights (Art. 53).

The approval of the new Constitution required a comprehensive revision of most of the administrative statutes and regulations passed during the preceding political system. For the interest of the contribution, it must be emphasised that the Administrative Procedure Act of 1956 was replaced by a new, general statute on Administrative Procedure: *Ley 30/1992, de 26 de noviembre, de régimen jurídico de las Administraciones públicas y del Procedimiento Administrativo Común* (hereinafter, L30/92). For its part, the Administrative Courts Act 1956 was replaced by a new statute (bearing the same name) in 1998: *Ley de la Jurisdicción contencioso-administrativa* (hereinafter, LJCA). The 1998 Act regulates the system of administrative courts; standing and access to judicial review of administrative decisions and regulations; judicial proceedings; appeals;

3 Furthermore, this Statute was preceded in 1954 by the Expropriations Act (*Ley de Expropiación Forzosa*) which established clear limitations and safeguards of private property against the eminent domain of Public Administration and, even more importantly, comprehensively regulated the cases and conditions for governmental liability towards the individual. This statute is partly in force today.

4 Passed by both Houses of the Parliament (*Cortes Generales*) on 31 October 1978; ratified by referendum on 7 December 1878; sanctioned by His Majesty the King of Spain on 27 December 1978.

enforcement of judgments, etc. These two statutes (as amended) are currently the most important pieces of 'regular' domestic legislation in the field of effective legal protection and they have a cross-cutting application in any form of administrative action: adjudication, planning and regulation.

2 Constitutional framework

In Spain, the PELP is not established in the domestic Constitution under such exact wording. Currently, the said principle cannot be characterised as a uniform or precisely delineated principle, but rather as the result of several sub-principles and fundamental rights that are recognised in the Constitution, in regular legislation and in case law. Since the right-based perspective is addressed *infra*, we should identify here those architectural principles. They constitute the backbone of the PELP, and they are proclaimed as the very foundations of the state and of the legal order:

(a) The principle of the rule of Law (Art. 1.1 of the Constitution).[5]
(b) Public authorities are bound by the Constitution and by all other legal provisions (Art. 9.1).
(c) The paramount legal principles of the domestic legal system are: the principle of legality, the principle of hierarchy and publicity of legal rules, that of legal certainty, the non-retroactive character of punitive provisions (including administrative ones), and the principle of accountability of public authorities (Art. 9.3).[6]
(d) Effective judicial protection of the individual by the courts (Art. 24.1).[7]

It is important to note that this group of constitutional principles has been supplemented by several statutes, which may be classified in two categories. On the one hand, special statutes regulating the basic content of the fundamental rights enshrined in the Constitution in Arts. 14–29. These statutes must be passed by an absolute majority of the Lower House of Parliament (*Congreso de los Diputados*) and are called in Spanish '*Leyes Orgánicas*'.[8] On the other hand, laws and decrees regulating the different forms of governmental action (sectoral legislation): expropriations, law and order, telecommunications, business regulation, government intervention in individual freedoms, etc.

Furthermore, the precise content of those constitutional principles have been interpreted and clarified by the Constitutional Court. Since its establishment in 1979, the said court has issued hundreds of rulings dealing with fundamental rights, access to judicial remedies, effective protection of courts, etc. Consequently, the Constitutional Court (and, to a lesser extent, the administrative chamber of the Supreme Court) is

5 'Spain is hereby established as a social and democratic State, subject to the rule of law, which advocates as the highest values of its legal order, liberty, justice, equality and political pluralism.'

6 'The Constitution guarantees the principle of legality, the hierarchy of legal provisions, the publicity of legal enactments, the non-retroactivity of punitive measures that are unfavourable to or restrict individual rights, the certainty that the rule of law will prevail, the accountability of the public authorities, and the prohibition against arbitrary action on the part of the latter.'

7 'Every person has the right to obtain the effective protection of the Judges and the Courts in the exercise of his or her legitimate rights and interests, and in no case may he go undefended.'

8 'Organic acts' would be a literal, though unsatisfactory translation into English.

the supreme interpreter of the Constitution, and logically the highest defender of the PELP in Spain.

The number and variety of rights and sub-principles constituting the PELP and the huge number of rulings issued by the Constitutional Court (and by the Supreme Court, administrative chamber) does prevent the identification of 'landmark cases' defining or circumscribing the scope and limits of the PELP in administrative law, as there are literally hundreds of rulings. However, the following ones (restricted to Art. 24, effective protection from courts) should be mentioned:

- Ruling 197/1988, of 24 October 1988 (access to justice and the appeals system).
- Ruling 129/1995, of 11 September 1995 (access to courts).
- Ruling 58/1990, of 29 March 1990 (lawsuits in administrative courts affecting third parties).
- Ruling 39/1983, of 20 October 1983 (certain statutory limitations on access to justice in administrative courts held as unconstitutional).
- Ruling 149/2000, of 3 June 2000 (exclusion of judicial review of some decisions of the electoral administration held as unconstitutional).
- Ruling 32/1982, of 7 June 1982 (doctrine on the enforcement of administrative courts' judgments).
- Ruling 78/1996, of 20 May 1996 (constitutional doctrine on injunctive relief in administrative jurisdiction).[9]

3 Rights-based perspective

3.1 The domestic system of subjective rights for legal protection

The very first title of the Constitution is devoted to 'rights and liberties' and covers Arts. 14 to 55. However, all of these provisions do not recognise a 'right' in the sense of 'fundamental' or 'subjective right'. On the contrary, within this title one should distinguish between different kinds of rights and protected goods. Since there is a noticeable terminology maze in this field,[10] we will try to circumvent this nominal problem by using a literal translation of the domestic typologies. Thus, the Constitution includes different types of protected goods:

On the one hand, '*Derechos fundamentales*', that is, fundamental rights fall within this category. In this sense Arts. 14–29 of the Constitution do enumerate a list of fundamental rights, which enjoy a threefold system of protection and guarantees. Most of these rights have a clear impact on the PELP. From this narrow perspective, the most important ones are:

- principle of non-discrimination, equality under the law (Art. 14);
- personal freedom and security (Art. 17);
- right to privacy, secrecy of communications (Art. 18);
- citizen participation in public affairs (Art. 22);

9 This doctrine eventually became enshrined in an amendment to the 'LJCA' of 1998.

10 Civil rights, civil liberties, human rights, fundamental rights, basic rights, public subjective rights, simple statutory rights, etc.

- right to access to justice, effective protection from courts, prohibition of lack of defence, judicial guarantees such as the right to a lawyer, to be informed of the charges brought against the citizen, right to judicial proceedings without undue delays, to the use of evidence, not to make self-incrimination and the presumption of innocence (Art. 24);
- legal certainty and prior definition of offences and penalties (including administrative ones) (Art. 25);
- right to petition (Art. 29).

These rights enjoy the strongest level of legal protection. They can only be regulated by special Parliament Acts (called 'organic statutes' see, *supra*), and those acts may be found unconstitutional by the Constitutional Court if they ignore the essential meaning or content (*contenido esencial*) of the corresponding fundamental right. Moreover, these rights are protected by a complete set of specific legal remedies: (1) any citizen can claim judicial protection through a special, summary judicial proceeding in administrative courts,[11] and (2) any citizen can eventually have access to the Constitutional Court by means of a specific judicial proceeding of 'constitutional protection' (*recurso de amparo*), after exhausting the appropriate judicial proceedings before ordinary courts.

On the other hand, the Constitution recognises 'simple' or 'weak' constitutional rights and duties (Arts. 30–38): for instance, the right to private property, to free economic initiative, to form professional associations, to collective bargaining, etc. These items are construed as true rights in the technical sense of the word, but they have a weaker constitutional protection: they cannot be protected either through the above mentioned special judicial proceeding in administrative courts or by the *recurso de amparo* appeal in the Constitutional Court. However, these rights must be regulated by ordinary Parliamentary Acts (requiring no special majority).

Finally, the Constitution establishes several 'guiding principles of social and economic policies' (*principios rectores de la política social y económica*), in Arts. 39–52. This group includes a heterogeneous list of elements. On the one hand, some of those items may be construed as 'social' or 'welfare' rights, such as the right to an adequate system of social security, the right to health and to a public system of health protection, the right to adequate housing, or the right to a decent environment. On the other hand, the Constitution includes also vague or general mandates to the public authorities, which are essentially aspirations and social goals to be achieved. Art. 48[12] and Art. 44[13] are good examples of such items.

11 A special type of judicial proceedings in administrative courts is devised for the case that an administrative agency clearly violates one of the 'fundamental' rights enshrined in Arts. 14–29 of the Constitution: *recurso especial en protección de derechos fundamentales*. This proceeding is a fast-track and expeditious procedure, but it is severely restricted to checking whether the agency committed a clear violation of a given fundamental right. The consideration of infringements of 'regular' legislation falls outside the scope of this proceeding.

12 'The public authorities shall promote conditions directed towards the free and effective participation of young people in political, social, economic and cultural development.'

13 '1. The public authorities shall promote and watch over access to cultural opportunities, to which all are entitled. 2. The public authorities shall promote science and scientific and technical research for the benefit of the general interest.'

The very legal nature of these principles enshrined in Arts. 30–52 of the Constitution has been the source of much controversy among scholars and courts. In any case, these 'rights' do not enjoy any specific legal protection or procedural remedy, contrary to what happens with the rights analysed above. The sole support accorded by the Constitution to those 'guiding principles' is that: (1) 'the recognition, respect and protection' of those principles 'will shape positive legislation, judicial practice and the activities of the public powers', and: (2) they can only be invoked in courts in the way provided for by the statutes and regulations that regulate them (Art. 53).

3.2 Procedural rights

In administrative law, the PELP includes certain rights that may be characterised as 'procedural', that is, rights that may be exercised in the context of a given administrative procedure in which the individual is an 'affected party'. The Constitution recognises some of these rights in Art. 104 and foresees a subsequent statutory regulation thereof:[14]

- the right to be heard;
- the right to have one's affairs and applications handled through the appropriate administrative procedure established by the Law;
- the right to access to the administrative file.

Beyond these constitutional provisions, the majority of the procedural rights of the citizens are at present extensively codified in the Administrative Procedure Act (Act 30/1992) of 1992, as amended. These rights include the following ones:

- The right to initiate a procedure by filing appropriate applications (not to be confused with 'petitions'). Any legal or physical person may initiate an administrative procedure by asking something that is connected with his 'rights' (in the true sense) or legitimate interests: a licence, a permit, a grant, admission at a public university, etc. If no genuine 'rights' are at stake, citizens may file mere 'petitions', where the duty of the agency to form a complete file and to adjudicate on the merits is lighter (for instance, a petition to the city council, asking for a change in the name of a street). Administrative agencies may also initiate *ex officio* administrative proceedings (for instance in the case of expropriations or administrative sanctions). As a rule, only those who have initiated an administrative procedure, or whose rights (in the true sense) may be affected by the administrative decision have the right to intervene in an ongoing procedure, although some pieces of sectoral legislation (for instance, in the domain of environmental protection) do recognise extended participation rights to the members of the public at large and to NGOs.[15]

14 'The law shall regulate: (a) the hearing of citizens directly, or through the organisations and associations recognised by law, in the process of drawing up the administrative provisions which affect them; (b) the access of citizens to administrative files and records, except as they may concern the security and defence of the State, the investigation of crimes and the privacy of individuals: (c) the procedures for the taking of administrative action, guaranteeing the hearing of interested parties when appropriate'.

15 A good example is the Act 27/2006, on access to information, participation in decision making and access to justice in environmental matters.

- The right to counsel and to the use of advisors.
- The right to be heard (also explicitly recognised by the Constitution in Art. 105(a).
- The duty of the agency to give reasons (for administrative decisions): the reasoning of the decision should be at least briefly explained, stating the reasons or legal and factual considerations applicable to the case.
- The right to access to the file and to all the relevant documents used for the adoption of the decision.
- The right to have access to administrative archives and registers.
- The right to have access to 'administrative' information (that is, information in any format held by administrative agencies and bodies). Recently a new statute has expanded the procedural rights of the citizen, in the domain of transparency and access to administrative documents.[16]
- The right to file administrative appeals.
- The right to intervene and the right to obtain an administrative decision within a reasonable time (as a guarantee against the silence of the administrative body).
- The right to identify the public officials and the civil servants that manage the citizen's files and procedures.
- The right to obtain information and guidance on the legal and technical requirements laid down by the applicable laws and regulations.
- The right to file complaints and suggestions.
- In some regions, the right to use other 'co-official' languages in administrative procedures, different from Spanish (Catalan, Basque, Galician).
- The right to formulate claims and to produce arguments in his own defence, within the administrative file.
- The right not to present documents which are already held by the administrative authority.
- The right to use electronic communications and technologies in their relations with Public Administration.[17]

4 Institutional perspective

4.1 Available institutions and procedures for legal remedy

The sub-principles and the substantive and procedural rights presented in the preceding points are protected by a complex system of legal remedies, which are summarily presented infra: (a) first, by the system of administrative appeals, that is, appeals before the same or another agency or body; (b) secondly, by the system of judicial control of administrative activity (basically ensured by administrative courts); (c) thirdly, by filing an appeal in the constitutional court (*recurso de amparo*). These are described more extensively in the following headings.

On the other hand, Spanish administrative law does recognise the possibility for administrative agencies to withdraw or modify a previous decision (*revision de oficio*). In

16 Ley 19/2013, de transparencia, acceso a la información pública y buen gobierno.

17 A specific statute regulates this aspect of administrative procedures and recognises specific rights in this domain: Act 11/2007, of 22 June 2007.

reality, this is not a genuine legal remedy at the disposal of the citizen, since the agency decides unilaterally such withdraw or modification. Therefore, this power is subject to strict limits in the Administrative Procedure Act 1992: it may be exercised at any time after the adoption of the decision, if the said decision is considered by the agency to be null and void (due to serious violations of the substantive legislation or of procedure). In other cases, different from absolute nullity, the agency must go to the judicial branch (as a regular citizen) and ask the court to set aside its own decision. To do so, the agency has a four-year deadline from the adoption of the decision. Special rules apply in those cases when the administrative decision at stake imposes a restriction on the juridical sphere of the citizen (a monetary sanction, an order to close a business, etc.).

4.1.1 Administrative appeals

Administrative appeals (*recursos administrativos*) constitute the first and easiest legal remedy at the disposal of the citizen in order to protect his rights and legitimate interests against administrative decisions (either explicit or tacit).[18] As a rule, there is always the possibility to file an appeal within each of the different levels of Government (inter-governmental appeal is not feasible, as this will be contrary to the principle of territorial autonomy). In general, only those persons who have been a 'party' (*interesado*) in the appropriate administrative proceeding may file administrative appeals. Appeals must be grounded on an infringement of the law, or on the violation of a right. Through the institution of an administrative appeal, the citizen may ask the competent agency (see infra) to perform a far reaching review of the administrative decision, be it explicit or 'tacit': to have it annulled, modified, etc. However, administrative appeals may not be used against administrative regulations, or against administrative decisions that have become 'firm' (*actos firmes*)[19].

In general, administrative appeals do not have suspensive effects, but the citizen may ask for the suspension of the contested decision in some exceptional cases: (a) if the enforcement of the decision will produce irreversible harm on him; or (b) if the decision is allegedly 'null and void' (*nulo de pleno derecho*).

The different types of general administrative appeals are regulated by the Act on Administrative procedure 1992:

(a) There is an appeal to be lodged before a higher administrative authority: *Recurso de alzada*. For instance, the General Director for Industry refuses to grant a licence to a company. Then, the applicant can file a '*recurso de alzada*' before the Minister for Industry, who is the 'boss' of the General Director.
(b) When the contested administrative decision is directly adopted by the highest governmental official or organ within an agency (for instance a Minister, within a Ministry), then the affected person may lodge an appeal called '*Recurso de reposición*', that has to be adjudicated by the same body. This appeal, though, is optional.

18 On administrative appeals, see: Luciano Parejo Alfonso, *Lecciones de Derecho Administrativo* (7th edn., Valencia, 2015) 637–645.

19 A decision becomes 'firm' at administrative level if (for instance) the citizen did not file the applicable appeal within the strict time-limits established by the law.

Apart from this, there are other types of administrative appeals which are regulated by sectoral legislation: for instance, there is a 'special' appeal on public procurement (*recurso especial en material de contratación pública*) or in the field of taxes (*reclamaciones económico-administrativas*). These complaints are lodged in specialised administrative or independent bodies/tribunals (not true 'courts').

Concerning other independent or administrative organs/bodies that might contribute to the PELP as complementary systems, the Ombudsmen (the national one or the several regional or local ones) play a minor role in the matter, because the Ombudsman cannot repeal or amend any decision or administrative regulation. Consequently, these bodies are not regarded as effective and genuine legal remedies to guarantee the PELP in Administrative Law.

Since this book deals with the principle of effective legal protection, we should not avoid the question whether the system of administrative appeals constitutes an effective mechanism or legal remedy to ensure the principle of legal protection in Spain. Unfortunately, I would not subscribe a positive answer to that question, or at least not in general terms. Several aspects justify this assessment:

(a) First, most administrative appeals are adjudicated by the same administrative organisation that reached the decision to be challenged. In the case of the *recurso de alzada*, a higher authority will adjudicate the appeal, but it still belongs to the same department, division or body. In the case of the *recurso de reposición*, the effectiveness of this remedy is even more reduced, since the authority that adjudicates that appeal is the same that took the challenged decision (for instance, the deputy minister). The possibilities that a given governmental or political official will change his mind in the 'second instance' are very limited, from a realistic point of view. In general, the Spanish administrative tradition has not incepted true 'independent' boards of appeal, as it happens in other countries or organisations (the USA, the UK, the EU, etc.). There are, though, some exceptions: in the field of tax collection, the individual may file an appeal in an independent reviewing body; and in the field of public procurement, the transposition of EU directives on the matter triggered the inception of appeals boards (*tribunal administrativo de recursos contractuales*) that are independent from the body or authority that took the contested public procurement decision.

(b) Secondly, and for complex historical reasons, public administration enjoys several privileges in the handling of administrative procedures and by taking decisions. For instance, all administrative adjudications are considered, *iuris tantum*, to be rightful and correct, and sometimes it is hard for the citizen to destroy those legal presumptions. In the case of administrative procedures aimed at imposing fines or monetary sanctions on individuals and firms, the facts that are noticed or seen by public authority agents (for instance, a police officer) are under the law presumed to be true. Therefore, the citizen is confronted with the challenge to prove things which sometimes are hard to prove, or 'negative facts'. Once the fine is finally imposed by the agency, the citizen may certainly file administrative appeals, but the administrative bodies usually reject most of them on the ground that 'the citizen did not destroy the presumption of certainty enjoyed by the claim of the agent'. Once the final decision is taken, the citizen has to pay the fine within a strict limit, and if he does not so the agency may seize his monies (in bank accounts) or other properties, without the need to going to court. That is, public authorities may enforce their own decisions, unilaterally and without the assistance, permission or approval of an independent law court. Of course the citizen may file lawsuits against that governmental action, but: (1) from the outset, it has to constitute a deposit or a bank guarantee, otherwise his lawsuit will not be admitted; (2) litigating is costly and (3) at the end of the day, he may lose the case and, on top of that, he might face the payment of all the litigation costs produced by both parties.

Since the exhaustion of the appropriate administrative appeals is a common precondition to sue a governmental agency in the administrative courts we may assume that, in too many cases, administrative appeals are not only a waste of time and money for the citizen, but also a procedural hurdle: for instance, if a citizen forgot about filing a '*recurso de alzada*' in due time, then the administrative decision will become 'untouchable' (*firme*) and the possibility to go to courts will be closed.

4.1.2 Administrative courts

As noted above, Art. 24 of the Constitution is the paramount provision in the field of citizens' access to justice. It states that everyone has the right to obtain effective protection from the courts in the exercise of their rights and legitimate interests, and that no situation involving a lack of defence will be allowed. The Constitutional Court case law on this provision (which is huge and generous) is binding on all Spanish courts.

For historical reasons, in Spain the judicial power is structured along five different jurisdictional tracks or court systems (*jurisdicciones)*, according to the subject-matter of the lawsuit:

- civil and commercial courts;
- criminal courts;
- administrative courts (*jurisdicción contencioso-administrativa*);
- labour and employment courts;
- military courts.

Each jurisdiction culminates in one chamber (*Sala*) of the Supreme Court, but each one is regulated by a different statute on procedure, coming with a specific case law on standing and access to that specific jurisdiction. This five-pronged decisional structure of the Judiciary is supposed to be harmonised by the case law of the Constitutional Court on Art. 24 of the Constitution. From the perspective of this contribution, the most important courts are the administrative ones (*jurisdicción contencioso-administrativa).* Public Administration may also be brought to civil or labour courts, but these cases are of minor importance here.

Administrative courts handle administrative law claims following a specific procedural legislation: the 29/1998 Act, of 18 July 1998 (LJCA).[20] Administrative courts may control the legality of different forms of administrative action, namely: (a) the

20 For instance, the Act 27/2006, of 18 July, on the right of access to information, participation in environmental decision making and access to justice in environmental matters, is a 'special rule' on standing.

administrative decisions (either 'explicit' or 'tacit'); (b) the administrative regulations, issued by local, regional or state bodies; (c) the administrative inactivity; (d) and the simple administrative activity lacking procedural grounding or *de facto* activity (*vía de hecho*). Administrative courts also control the legality of the administrative or managerial activity of the other branches of government (the Parliament, the Judiciary Governing Board, the constitutional court, the electoral administration, etc.).[21]

The system of administrative courts (*Jurisdicción contencioso-administrativa*) is composed of different judicial bodies, whose competence is defined by a complex set of rules or criteria relating to territorial competence, the subject-matter, and the monetary value of the decision. This means that each court deals with separate types of decisions but some (higher) courts, on top of their 'natural' competences, work also as appeal courts of other (see infra). The names and main competences of such bodies may be described as follows:

(1) Administrative judges (*juzgados de lo contencioso*) either having a national or a provincial jurisdiction. These are one-person judicial bodies and may be identified as lower or first instance courts. Among other matters, they control the decisions of local authorities (land use plans and regulations are outside their competence).
(2) The administrative chamber of the Regional High Courts. There is one such higher court in each of the 17 autonomous communities ('regions') of the Kingdom. Among other matters, they control regional agencies and departments. They also adjudicate judicial appeals filed against the rulings of the administrative judges (*recurso de apelación*).
(3) *Audiencia Nacional*: this is a central, high administrative chamber that has territorial jurisdiction over the whole country and controls, among others, the decisions of Ministers and Secretaries of State.
(4) Supreme Court, Administrative Chamber (*Tribunal Supremo, Sala de lo contencioso administrativo*). Among other powers, this court controls the decisions and regulations adopted by the Council of Ministers (or 'central Cabinet'). The Supreme Court has also jurisdiction to revise the rulings of the *Audiencia Nacional* and of the Regional High Courts, on cassation appeal (*recurso de casación*, see infra).

The scope of review exercised by administrative courts is large, and judicial powers are great: administrative courts can not only declare illegal an administrative decision and annul (quash) it, but they also have the power: (a) to recognise an individual situation or right; (b) to order the agency to do or to cease to do something; (c) to order the agency to compensate the applicant for the damages suffered. That is, a citizen might seek monetary compensation for damages resulting from governmental activity, for instance, when she or her property is damaged or impaired as a direct consequence of that activity.[22]

21 On the Spanish system of judicial control of administrative action, see, in general: Luciano Alfonso (n. 17) 655–756; J. González Pérez, *Comentarios a la Ley de la Jurisdicción Contencioso-Administrativa* (Ley 29/1998, de 13 de julio) (Madrid 2008); Alberto Palomar Olmeda (ed.), *Tratado de la Jurisdicción Contencioso-Administrativa* (Cizur Menor 2008); Jesús Leguina Villa and Miguel Sánchez Morón (eds.), *Comentarios a la Ley de la Jurisdicción Contencioso-administrativa* (Valladolid 2001).

22 The criteria that must be met in order to obtain damages from governmental action result from a long standing case law, originating in the Expropriations Act 1956 (see, fn 3) and now codified in the

Administrative courts can not only control the legality of 'individual' decisions (a licence, a permit, a sanction) but also that of plans (land use plans, waste management plans, water plans, etc.). Moreover, they can annul administrative regulations approved by local or regional councils, or by the Council of Ministers, that is, rules that do not have the nature of parliamentary legislation, and which are a very important source of administrative law in Spain. However, administrative courts have no powers to modify the wording or the text of unlawful regulations or plans (they can only declare them illegal). Neither do they have powers in the cases of mere or simple governmental 'passivity' (for instance, bad or weak enforcement of environmental rules) which does not meet the criteria established by the LJCA for governmental 'inactivity'.

As in other countries, in Spain the actual scope of review of judicial control depends largely on whether the governmental decision consists of a 'law-bound' decision (*acto reglado*) or a discretionary one. In the first case, administrative courts have no limits in analysing, quashing or modifying the actual content of the decision. However, when the administrative decision is a discretionary one *(acto discrecional*), administrative courts restrain themselves to checking 'legality' issues (procedure, participation, competence of the decision maker, etc.), while courts tend to defer to administrative discretion as to the actual content of the decision. Thus, whenever there is a case of complex balancing of conflicting interests, the administrative agency enjoys a large remit of discretion. As a rule, the court will only quash (annul) a discretionary decision when the plaintiff can demonstrate that the agency ignored clear statutory or procedural rights; or when the administrative decision cannot clearly be grounded in the facts and materials produced within the procedure; or when the decision is arbitrary or clearly not sound, etc.

Judicial proceedings in administrative courts are closely related to the administrative appeals, described above. As a rule, the available administrative appeals must be exhausted before going to court, except when the decision has been taken by the highest body of the relevant agency (for instance, a decision adopted by the Minister, or by the Council of Ministers, which have no hierarchical higher body). In that case, though, an optional administrative appeal is still at the disposal of the individual (*recurso de reposición*). Therefore, the different means of review (administrative and judicial) cannot be employed concurrently and the first one must always precede the judicial challenge.

Alternative dispute resolution mechanisms (like arbitration, conciliation or mediation) have little importance in providing legal protection against damages to the rights and interests of private parties produced by governmental action. Petitions and non-formal procedures also have little significance with respect to the PELP.

4.1.3 Constitutional complaint

When an administrative agency adopts a decision that clearly violates one of the 'fundamental' rights enshrined in Arts. 14–29 of the Constitution, then the citizen may

Administrative Procedure Act 1992. These basic criteria are: (a) an actual impairment of damage, that the citizen is not supposed or obliged to support; (b) a governmental activity involved in the public services; (c) a causal link between the governmental activity and the private damage produced. This is an 'objective' type of liability, indeed.

lodge an appeal in the constitutional court (*recurso de amparo*). This special appeal is regulated by the Organic Act of the Constitutional Court of 1979. The access to the constitutional court, though, is far from being automatic. First of all, the citizen must exhaust previously all the judicial remedies available in the administrative jurisdiction, something that may take years of litigation. On the other hand, the plaintiff must have his appeal admitted by the court. In this sense, the criteria for admission of this special constitutional complaint have been made more and more restrictive over the last years by means of different amendments of the Act on the Constitutional Court and by the case law of the said Court. In practice, admissibility works almost as a discretionary system.

4.2 The effectiveness of judicial review of administrative action

There is no doubt that the effectiveness of any jurisdictional system is a key element in the field of the PELP. In this sense, the situation in Spain deserves to be carefully analysed, in terms of the following aspects:

4.2.1 Standing

The rules on standing in the administrative jurisdiction are enshrined in the 1998 Administrative Courts Act (LJCA), precisely in Art. 19. These provisions must be applied and interpreted in the light of the dense case law of the Administrative Chamber of the Supreme Court and that of the Constitutional Court dealing with Art. 24 of the Constitution. Another interpretative instrument that has to be taken into consideration by courts when deciding about standing problems is Art. 53.3 of the Constitution, which states that judicial practice should be inspired by the 'guiding principles' of the social and economic policies (Arts. 39–52 of the Constitution). Therefore, the administrative courts must interpret in a 'progressive' and extensive way the wording of the LJCA.

These rules on standing are general and applicable throughout the whole area of administrative law. The requirements for standing do not change according to the type of remedy requested (e.g. actions for annulment/damages) although sectoral legislation may establish complementary rules in a given field of governmental activity.

The LJCA follows a generous approach to standing. There are several standing situations. Among these, we should focus on the following:

- Any legal or physical person may have access to administrative courts, as long as they have a right (in the technical meaning) or a legitimate interest that is affected or damaged by an administrative decision or regulation. The wording legitimate interest has been interpreted by administrative courts in an increasingly progressive way.
- Associations, trade unions and groups of affected parties also have standing for the protection of their collective rights and legitimate interests.
- And finally, '*actio popularis*' is also recognised in several cases. Thus, the LJCA establishes this possibility as '*acción popular*', where standing is recognised to anyone, without the need to prove a personal damage or interest. This special action

has to be recognised by sectoral legislation.[23] The paramount example is the standing recognised to NGOs and associations to defend environmental interests.[24]

Therefore, although the Spanish system does not grant a universal standing in administrative courts (no domestic system does so), it is fairly generous. For the sake of this contribution, we might support the conclusion that standing issues do not represent a real problem in the field of the PELP.

4.2.2 Timely justice

A widely shared negative aspect of Spanish administrative justice is that it is very slow. This seems to be an uncontroversial, well-documented conclusion, supported by the regular statistics and data offered by legal professionals, organisations and bodies. As a rule, the proceedings are protracted and take too long. Several reasons explain this structural situation: the number of cases is very high, there are not enough courts and many of these are understaffed. In some higher regional courts, the number of pending cases may be counted in the dozens of thousands. The delays in the Spanish court system are sometimes scandalous. For instance, the Constitutional Court took twelve years to adjudicate a claim of unconstitutionality formulated against a 1988 State Act on local finances. In another decision, rendered in December 2000, the Constitutional Court declared unconstitutional a 1991 Statute of the Balearic Islands that had established an environmental tax. The central government challenged that legislation in 1992 and the Court accepted this claim – eight years later. A case originating in a lower court and arriving at the Supreme Court through the route of subsequent appeals can easily take up more than five years. At present (2015), the lower administrative courts of Madrid are giving appointments for preliminary trials of cases in 2016. And this is just the first procedural step in the so-called 'shortened procedure', etc.

As a consequence of this unsatisfactory situation, challenging administrative decisions does not make sense for many people, especially if the economic value of the lawsuit is small (for instance, traffic fines). In other cases, the judicial process is so slow that, when the ruling is finally released, it may have lost its significance. Therefore, administrative justice is often ineffective. Art. 24 of the Constitution proclaims that everyone has the right to have a judicial proceeding without undue delays (*un proceso sin dilaciones indebidas*). However, the different procedural laws do not establish deadlines for handling a case, nor are there precise standards to ascertain when justice has been 'timely'.

4.2.3 Injunctive relief

The Constitution enshrines the right of everyone to an effective judicial protection. In the Administrative Law arena, this certainly includes the right to injunctive relief, that is, the possibility to suspend or paralyse the enforcement or application of a

23 Several legal provisions do grant this 'open' standing, like the law on coastal management (Act of 28 July 1988); or the Decree 833/1975, on atmospheric pollution; the laws on natural parks, the legislation on Urban Planning and development, etc.

24 See the 27/2006 Act, on access to information, participation and access to justice in environmental affairs grants a very generous standing to environmental NGOs.

challenged administrative adjudication or regulation during the handling of the lawsuit, until the controversy is adjudicated on the merits (something that may happen several years after lodging the lawsuit). Therefore, injunctions are very important in the Administrative Law scenario, because they are too frequently the only means to avoid serious and irreversible damage to citizens or to diffuse, societal interests.

To understand the system, it is worth clarifying that, in the Spanish system of administrative litigation, a plaintiff may produce five different types of claims or petitions (*pretensiones*) in the administrative courts. Namely, the plaintiff may ask the court:

(a) to declare illegal, and therefore annul an administrative decision or rule, in total or in part;
(b) to recognise that the plaintiff has a concrete right that was disregarded by the agency;
(c) to order the agency to pay compensation for damages caused or produced on the plaintiff by the public services;
(d) to stop an illegal governmental activity;
(e) to order an administrative body to act in a certain 'positive' way, to which it was obliged *vis-à-vis* the plaintiff on the basis of a pre-existent contract, covenant or another form of engagement (administrative inactivity).

This differentiation among the possible claims is very important from a technical point of view, since judicial review of administrative decisions and regulations is very formal. Therefore, each type of plea may claim a specific form of injunctive relief.

In the Spanish system of judicial control of administrative action, interim relief (for instance, in the form of stopping the execution of a public infrastructure project) is not granted automatically. The plaintiff, though, may obtain injunctive relief under certain conditions, but these criteria are not clearly defined in the legislation. The 1998 LJCA is, once more, the decisive legislative arrangement in this field. This Act regulates interim relief, but it does so in a laconic and broad way. First, the Act states that the plaintiff may ask, at any time in the proceedings, the adoption of interim measures 'that will ensure the effectiveness of the final ruling'. Interim measures are not adopted *ex officio* by the court.

Those measures may be adopted by the court 'only when the implementation of the contested decision or administrative regulation could prevent the lawsuit from attaining its legitimate objective'. On the other hand, interim relief may be refused when such measures might produce a 'serious disturbance of the general interest or of a third party', something that the court 'will weight in a reasoned manner'. Therefore, the plaintiff has the burden to identify clearly a workable line of reasoning in order to convince the judge that, if the decision is not suspended, his rights or interests will suffer a serious and irreversible impairment. The other side of the coin is that the court has to find a balance between the possible public costs and the benefits of issuing a motion to stop the administrative decision or plan. The granting of interim measures must be preceded by a contradictory hearing. In addition, when the interim measure could produce 'damages of any sort' (for instance, to the public or general interest), the court may decide to impose on the plaintiff the duty to present any kind of sufficient insurance or warranty to cover those potential damages. For instance, to get the suspension of a major public infrastructure project, the plaintiff may be obliged to constitute a guarantee, something which is often dissuasive.

As can be appreciated, the key instrument of interim relief is not regulated in a precise way by the controlling statute. Therefore, the legal regime of interim measures in Spain is largely controlled by the case law of the Supreme Court (administrative chamber) and that of the Constitutional Court. A high level of discretion is left to the administrative judge or court: whether to grant injunctive relief or not; whether to impose a warranty on the plaintiff or not; if yes, in which amount, and so on. Consequently, injunctive relief is a complex area formed by hundreds of judicial decisions, which do not actually form a clear line of reasoning. It is therefore difficult to provide a clear assessment or actual figures or percentages about the frequency of the grant of injunctive relief in administrative litigation in Spain. However, the two extreme positions should be discarded: it is not true that courts always refuse to grant relief, and the opposite view is also certainly false. The granting of injunctive relief depends also on factual, case-by-case circumstances: the quality of the plaintiff's written arguments, the existence of a *fumus boni iuris* (the appearance of a good right) on the part of the citizen, the seriousness and clarity of the alleged violation of controlling rules, etc. The result is a complex matrix of dialectical variables, whose result is hard to predict beforehand. On the other hand, the slowness of the judicial process ends up affecting the effectiveness of the injunctive relief mechanism itself. Due to the heavy workload of the judiciary, when the court has the opportunity to consider the application for interim measures (not the merits of the case), it is sometimes too late. In an attempt to fix this anomaly, the Supreme Court (inspired by the law on civil procedure) has developed since 1993 a judicial practice consisting in considering the application for interim measures through a fast-track procedure, without waiting until the regular schedule of the case. These are 'urgent and speedy interim measures' (*medidas cautelarísimas*).[25] This fast-track procedure can only be followed on petition of the plaintiff, when there are circumstances of extraordinary urgency, which would not allow the court to consider carefully the granting of the interim measures in due time.

This judicial practice eventually became enacted by LJCA of 1998 which was modified by Act 37/2011. The most important feature of this 'urgent and speedy' interim measures mechanism is that no contradictory hearing is required, so the court may decide to grant injunctive relief within a very short deadline, without even listening to the government attorney. The court order cannot be appealed. In this order, the court may find either: (a) that there is a case of urgency and that interim measures are needed; or (b) that there is no urgency; in this case, the question of the interim measures will be adjudicated following the general rules.

4.2.4 The right to appeal judicial decisions

The right to appeal judicial decisions is a part of the fundamental right to judicial protection. However, this is not an absolute right, and the law may establish cases when a first instance court ruling will not be appealable in a higher court. In the

25 Orders of the Supreme Court (Administrative Chamber) of 2 and 11 November 1993.

administrative jurisdictional track, most court decisions and orders are appealable at least once, by lodging different types of appeals either in the same court (*recurso de súplica*)[26] or in a higher court (*recurso de apelación, recurso de casación*). As a consequence of an appeal, the revising court enjoys full authority to annul or revise in any way the lower court ruling. Even the refusal to grant injunctive relief can be appealed. However, some administrative court rulings cannot be appealed if they adjudicate minor cases[27] or the appeal is not convenient on expediency reasons.[28]

The *apelación* appeal may be filed to challenge the rulings issued by the administrative judges (*Juzgados de lo contencioso*), and it is lodged in the Higher Regional Court (*Tribunal Superior de Justicia*). However, and from a legal point of view, the most important appeal is the 'cassation' one (*recurso de casación*). This appeal is lodged in the Supreme Court against rulings issued by the Higher Regional Courts or by the *Audiencia Nacional* (national court). This special appeal gives the Supreme Court the possibility to establish legal principles or doctrines, or to establish the right interpretation of a controversial legal provision. Since many laws and regulations incorporate broad or imprecise wordings, the case law of the Supreme Court (*jurisprudencia*) is of paramount importance and it may be depicted as a true and genuine source of law, although Spain is not by tradition a common law country.

The cassation appeal, however, is far from being a universal and open legal remedy. On the contrary, this appeal may only be filed on certain limited legal grounds (breach of statutory or case law) and provided that the appealed ruling meets certain criteria. Furthermore, the heavy workload of the Supreme Court prompted the enactment of new legal rules in 2011, which in fact do restrict the possibility to file '*casación*' appeals in the Supreme Court. Thus, the Act 37/2011, of 19 October 2011, introduced new procedural rules in the administrative jurisdiction. Allegedly, the goal of this statute was to combat judicial slowness and to reduce the duration of lawsuits in the administrative courts. To this end, this Act raised the minimum value of a case in order to be heard by the Supreme Court (in a '*casación*' appeal). In the current version of the LJCA, the case should involve a litigious affair with a monetary value of at least €600,000 (the previous figure was €150,000) to be admissible under a cassation appeal. The idea is to prevent unimportant cases from reaching the Supreme Court. However, these new procedural rules may have a clear negative impact in the PELP, since the new rules do restrict *de facto* the access to Supreme Court appeals. A high number of cases are no longer eligible to be appealed in the Supreme Court, then enlarging the number of cases that will be heard only once by the judiciary. The same Act 37/2011 raised the threshold (monetary value of a case) required to file an *apelación* appeal: from 18.000 to €30.000. This involves an additional, negative impact on the effectiveness of the principle of legal protection. Not to forget that 'cheap' cases may very well be important cases, indeed.

26 As a rule, the *súplica* appeal applies not to final rulings, but to interim or other types of judicial orders or provisions (in Spanish, *providencias* and *autos*).

27 Thus, administrative judge rulings that adjudicate lawsuits whose monetary value is under 30.000 euros are not appealable to the Higher Regional Courts.

28 Some administrative judge rulings that adjudicate electoral lawsuits are not appealable to the Higher Regional Courts (for instance, proclamation of candidates) because that would conflict with the timely development of the electoral process.

4.2.5 The enforcement of judicial rulings

The enforcement of judicial decisions in administrative law cases does also present an unsatisfactory situation in Spain. Not only is the judicial process slow in general terms, but judicial decisions, once released, may be ineffective because they are not enforced or implemented, and, if they are, this is done with undue delays.

There are different reasons for this. Although the law states that courts are empowered to enforce their own rulings, the enforcement of judicial rulings that condemn administrative agencies does correspond *de facto* to the governmental body that lost the lawsuit, due to the very nature of the administrative process. In most cases, and after a reasonable time, the enforcement of the ruling has to be demanded explicitly by the citizen who won the case. Here, another problem of slowness may appear, as the agency may take its time to enforce the judgment. Undue delays in the execution of court rulings may therefore be another cause of ineffectiveness of the PELP. In case of open unwillingness to apply a judicial decision on the part of the agency, the court may impose penalty payments on the official running the administrative body (director general, mayor, etc.), and even trigger criminal proceedings, but this option is rarely implemented. The courts can also use compulsory powers to have its ruling enforced, but this has to be asked for by the original plaintiff. Moreover, the law establishes that public-domain goods and assets of administrative agencies cannot be seized by courts. Sometimes, the judgment is simply not implemented by the public administration, for reasons of bad faith, political considerations or defiance, high costs involved in the enforcement of the ruling, the claim that the enforcement corresponds to another agency, etc. This situation is not unusual, unfortunately, and can only be solved by means of a radical change of mentality and legal culture among politicians and governmental officials.

4.2.6 Costs of administrative litigation

The costs of litigating in the administrative courts may be an additional, deterrent factor for citizens, thus hindering *de facto* the effectiveness of the PELP. Therefore, the situation in Spain should be here presented summarily.

4.2.6.1 GENERAL FEATURES

To better clarify the following points, it is important to note that the expenses generated by any legal proceeding (*costas*) are governed by different statutes, depending on the 'jurisdictional track' (*orden jurisdiccional*) that is involved in the proceedings. Therefore, attention must be paid to how the issue of expenses is governed in the administrative judicial track by the LJCA of 1998. The costs of the cases handled by civil or criminal courts are regulated by the procedural regulation of those courts.

In administrative litigation, the regular costs (*costas procesales*) include:

(a) The lawyers' fees. In the administrative jurisdiction, the plaintiff must be defended by an attorney (*abogado*) incorporated in a bar association and he must also be represented by another legal professional, called *procurador* or 'legal representative', who is also incorporated in a different professional association. Therefore, the plaintiff must pay the services of two legal professionals. This rule applies always when the proceedings take place in a collegiate court (Higher regional court, *Audiencia nacional* or the Supreme Court). However, when the proceeding takes place in a one-person court (*juzgados de lo contencioso*) the plaintiff may decide to be defended and represented by the same attorney (*abogado*), who in those cases plays both roles simultaneously.

The incidence of this dual regime on litigation costs should not be misunderstood. This regime does not make a given case expensive *per se*. A 'single' system of representation could be more expensive (for instance, in the case of protracted or complex litigation) than double or dual representation: the number of intervening lawyers is not what makes a case expensive, but the very nature, complexity and duration of the lawsuit. Therefore, the question whether lawyers' fees are *per se* a deterrent factor in administrative litigation deserves a nuanced appraisal and must be answered on a case-by-case basis.

(b) Cost of evidence: the plaintiff must bear the cost of evidence and proof proposed to the court and admitted by the said court. In administrative litigation, the usual evidence consists of reports or opinions by technical experts, empirical tests or laboratory analysis (*prueba pericial*).

(c) Court fees: as in other countries, citizens have to pay court fees or charges (*tasas judiciales*). These fees have different amounts, depending on the jurisdictional track, the proceedings (first instance lawsuit, appeal, etc.), and they do vary according to the monetary value of the case. Theoretically, this is a payment for the enjoyment of the public service, but the amount of these charges has traditionally been modest and did not cover the real cost of the service.[29] In the administrative courts, until 2012, the fees amounted to €120 for an abbreviated procedure (*procedimiento abreviado*), €210 for an ordinary procedure (*procedimiento ordinario*), €300 for an appellate proceeding (*recurso de apelación*) and €600 for a cassation appeal (*recurso de casación*). The situation changed dramatically in 2012, when the Spanish Parliament passed a law which increased sharply these amounts.[30] In the administrative jurisdictional track, the fees have two parts or components, the fixed part and the variable one. The fixed-part amounts are as follows: €200 for a 'shortened procedure' (previously, 120) €350 for an ordinary procedure (previously, €210), €800 for an appellate proceeding (previously, 300) and €1,200 for a cassation appeal (previously €600, meaning a 100% increase). The variable part consists of the 0.5% of the monetary value of the lawsuit, with a maximum of €10,000.

This piece of legislation was strongly criticised by many groups, parties and lawyers' associations, because the new fees might have a deterrent impact on citizens willing to challenge an administrative decision or activity. The Cabinet, though, justified this initiative on the need to get funding for the appropriate running of the judiciary and for financing the free litigation scheme for those citizens under a certain income level. In this sense, persons eligible to benefit from the Free Legal Assistance Program (*Justicia gratuita*, see below) were exempted from

29 According to official sources, the government collected €173 million in 2010 (source: Ministry of Justice).

30 Act 10/2012, of 20 November 2012.

paying those court fees. In 2015, and in the light of much social rejection, the Cabinet further decided to eliminate the fees when the litigant is natural person.[31]

(d) Other regular costs: administrative litigation involves other regular costs: for instance, when a lawsuit has been filed and admitted by the court, an announcement or notice thereof must be published in the corresponding official gazette. Such publication has a cost, which must be borne by the plaintiff. If the plaintiff has asked for injunctive relief, he may be required by the court to pay a security or bond to avoid the production of irreversible damages. This might also be very costly and even hard to get (the usual form is a bank guarantee, *aval bancario*).

Summing up, as for the actual costs in administrative litigation, those procedures entail uncertainty about the monetary amount for which the losing party may be liable, because the actual costs are hard to predict from the beginning. The expenses of an administrative court case cannot be predicted in advance because they are the result of a number of factors, such as the complexity of the case, the number and nature of expert witnesses, the evidence produced, the eventual appeals that could be lodged, etc. On the other hand, there is no clear legal mandate that the costs related to administrative procedures should not be prohibitively expensive. In any case, the sharp increase in court fees did had a real deterrent factor for many potential litigants, especially in minor cases (traffic fines, for instance).

4.2.6.2 THE 'LOSER-PAYS' PRINCIPLE

As in other legal systems, the Spanish one follows the loser-pays principle. That is, it shifts litigation costs to the loser of the lawsuit in some circumstances. The LJCA of 1998 also regulates this issue but recent amendments resulted in a more restrictive regulation for the citizen. Until 2011, that statute established a different regime for first instance proceedings (*proceso en primera instancia*) and for appeal proceedings (*recursos contra sentencias y autos*).[32] Thus, in first instance proceedings, the general rule was that each party had to bear its own costs (lawyers, evidence, etc.), but the court could declare that the loser had to pay all the costs involved in the proceedings, that is, the costs of both parties.[33] In the second instance (an appeal against the lower court decision), the rule was different: the losing party had to pay for the total costs of the appellate proceedings.

The precedent legal framework changed dramatically in November 2011, when a new law on litigation costs was approved: the Act 37/2011 of 19 October[34]

31 Royal Decree 1/2015, of 27 February 2015.

32 In the administrative, jurisdictional track, an appeal instance or '*segunda instancia*' implies that a lower administrative court has already adjudicated a legal challenge (*recurso contencioso-administrativo*) against an administrative decision.

33 This possibility would apply when one party acted in bad faith, or with procedural recklessness (for instance, he supported a clearly unsustainable position). Furthermore, the court could also impose the payment of the total cost on the loser when the court found it appropriate for a higher effectiveness of the judicial protection.

34 *Ley de medidas de agilización procesal.* This Act was published in the State Official Gazette of 11 October, 2011 (see: www.boe.es).

introduced new procedural rules in, among other domains, the Administrative jurisdiction. This statute amended the LJCA of 1998 and the traditional regime governing the loser-pays principle. Namely, the Act establishes that, in the administrative courts, the general rule is now that the litigation costs will be borne by the party that loses the case entirely, also in first instance proceedings. The situation in appeals proceedings remains unchanged: the loser-pays principle is still the rule. The court, however, may decide otherwise and split the costs when it finds circumstances that would justify not applying the loser-pays principle, for instance, when the case 'presented serious doubts about the facts or the applicable law', as the LJCA now states.

In those cases where none of the parties wins the case entirely (the legal challenge to the administrative decision has only been accepted or rejected in part), then each party must bear his own costs, and the common litigation costs will be split in half. But here again, the court may decide otherwise, then applying the 'loser-pays' principle to the loser if it finds that the said party filed the challenge or sustained the action in bad faith or recklessly.

Prima facie, the goal of the new law is to combat judicial slowness, to prevent unreasonable challenges to administrative action and to reduce the duration of lawsuits in the administrative courts. In this sense, this new provision is supposed to discourage frivolous appeals. However, these new procedural rules may have a clear negative impact in the domain of access to justice and the PELP since it may deter potential litigants from defending their rights and legitimate interests in courts, for fear to face the payment of the total costs of the lawsuit.[35] Unfortunately, this is really happening now in many cases.

4.2.6.3 PUBLIC PROGRAMS ON LEGAL AID

In Spain, there is a scheme in place to provide legal aid to those wishing to take legal action and lacking enough financial resources: *asistencia jurídica gratuita*. This is a direct consequence of Art. 119 of the Constitution, under which '[j]ustice will be free when the laws will so say and, in any case, for those who provide evidence of lack of resource for litigating'.

The system consists of a program which assists financially the litigants, and which applies in all jurisdictions (civil, administrative), regardless of the type of the case.[36] The cost of this program of legal assistance is entirely supported by the government, and is run by special bodies. The legal scheme on Free Legal Assistance is currently governed by Act 1/1996, of 10 January 1996, on free legal assistance (*Ley de asistencia jurídica gratuita)*. This statute has a general application in any kind of legal proceedings, so it also applies to administrative litigation.

Under this statute, any physical person (or an NGO) lacking financial or monetary resources may be granted free legal assistance, as long as he meets the statutory

35 Even if a citizen is right and the agency behaves unlawfully, there are many situations where he may lose a case against the Public Administration (failure to solve procedural intricacies, not meeting a deadline, etc.). In this case, the loser-pays principle may be a very painful and harsh rule for the citizen. Not to forget that the decision of the court might not be appealable, and then there will be no room for rectifications.

36 Techniques such as *pro bono* practice, 'legal clinics', etc. are rare and are not a part of this mechanism.

requirements in terms of maximum annual income. Free Legal Assistance is granted (on demand of the plaintiff) by different Commissions on Free Legal Assistance (*comisiones de asistencia juridical gratuita*), which are specialised governmental bodies acting in each province and in each autonomous community. When a citizen or an NGO is denied the right to free legal assistance, the applicant has the right to appeal in the administrative courts.

5 European perspectives

In general, European administrative law has had a limited influence on the actual implementation of the PELP in Spain. Several reasons explain this situation. On the one hand, the standards of protection of individual rights (as a result of domestic Law) are already high in comparison with European standards. When Spain joined the European Communities in 1986, the Constitution had already been passed some years earlier, and regular domestic legislation already ensured a fair protection of individual rights. Furthermore, and until the Lisbon treaty, the sectoral EU legal rules (and the corresponding ECJ case law) had little to do with fundamental rights. EU secondary law has had, however, some impacts that may be mentioned here: (a) the enlargement of standing and access-to-justice in environmental matters, due to several EU directives on the matter (for example, Directive 2003/35); (b) the establishment of a special type of administrative appeal in the domain of public procurement, due to the transposition of the EU directives on the matter. However, there is no significant impact on the material or substantive aspects of the PELP.

On the other hand, substantial improvements could be made in the knowledge and use in domestic courts of EU Law principles, doctrines and case law. As a matter of fact, EU law courses do not have the weight they deserve in the regular curricula of most Spanish law schools. In addition, law graduates become judges by succeeding in recruitment procedures that are long and difficult to prepare, but where EU Law subjects have a minor importance. This is probably one of the reasons why Spanish administrative courts have formulated so far few preliminary rulings to the ECJ, as compared with the courts of other Member States.

As far as the ECtHR is concerned, the case law of the Strasbourg court is certainly impressive, and the Constitution provides for the adequate connection between domestic practice and that European body of law. The ECtHR case law has certainly had a relevant impact on the PELP, but mainly in connection with criminal law. There have not been relevant cases having an impact on the domestic understanding or implementation of the PELP in administrative law. Some judgments of that European court are, however, noticeable in the sense that they have expanded the understanding of some fundamental rights guaranteed by the Constitution.

Therefore, one cannot support the view that EU Law or the ECHR changed the domestic understandings of the PELP in administrative law.

6 Conclusion

In the light of the preceding pages, some conclusions may be drawn about the reception and implementation of the PELP in Spain. The most important one is that the principle is well-established in domestic public law, although not under that precise wording. Moreover, and from a formal point of view, it is protected by a system of institutional arrangements providing for adequate legal remedies. The system may be evaluated as comprehensive, fair and reasonable. Administrative courts have ample powers to revise and control administrative action, and they are independent and professional.

However, there are also negative aspects, which might have a negative impact in terms of the very effectiveness of the said principle. These aspects include the following:

(a) The lengthy proceedings in administrative courts. Lawsuits usually take several years to be adjudicated. When the judicial decision is rendered, it is sometimes too late.
(b) Litigation costs: challenging administrative action is in most cases costly. The plaintiff must pay court fees which sometimes may deter potential ligitants; as a rule, the citizen has to pay for not only one, but two lawyers; evidence may be expensive or hard to get; moreover, if the plaintiff loses the case, he must pay his own litigation costs, plus those of the agency (loser-pays principle); there is a Free Legal Assistance program but it does not cover individual citizens earning a regular salary.
(c) There is also an unsatisfactory situation in the field of granting interim relief in the form of suspension of administrative decisions, regulations and plans.
(d) The system of administrative appeals is in most cases ineffective.
(e) Administrative bodies enjoy several procedural and substantive privileges, which are hard to combat by the individual.
(f) The system of court rulings enforcement (which is *de facto* left in the hands of the defendant administrative authority) could certainly be improved.
(g) There are too many restrictions for lodging cassation appeals in the Supreme Court, or even for a regular appeal in the higher regional courts; 'petty' or minor cases (in terms of monetary value) are only adjudicated once.
(h) There is little possibility to sue governmental agencies in the case of simple inactivity or 'passivity'.

As a result of these reasons, it is not unusual that citizens, groups or firms would decline to defend their rights against administrative bodies and agencies because of the shortcomings of the judicial system described previously. This situation has been worsened since 2011, when some procedural reforms were adopted, with the result of making it more difficult, hard or expensive to go to courts.

Consequently, the situation is far from being satisfactory and there is still plenty of room for improvement, if we want the Principle of Legal Protection to be really effective in practice.

17 The principle of effective legal protection in Swiss administrative law

Felix Uhlmann

1 Historical developments

The Swiss Constitution of 1874 guaranteed only few procedural rights (such as the right to be sued at one's home court). This applies also for many substantive fundamental rights. Over a century, the Swiss Supreme Court has developed many procedural guarantees, such as the right to be heard and other principles of effective legal protection.[1] The legal basis of these rights was the equal protection clause.[2]

Shortcomings of the procedure typically involved a deficit in independent judicial control. Many Swiss cantons as well as federal rules only granted limited access to courts in administrative matters. The typical legal recourse involved an appeal to the hierarchal higher administrative body, including the Federal Council or the executive of the cantons.[3] Appeals to the Swiss Supreme Court were possible in some cases, excluded or reduced to a review with very limited scrutiny in others.

The Swiss system was incompatible with the ECHR as far as 'civil rights' were concerned. These civil rights included matters that were considered 'administrative' under Swiss law. Switzerland therefore had to extend judicial control on such matters as the bar exams which lead – among other factors – to the framework of the current Swiss constitution and to a reform of the judicial process.[4]

2 Constitutional framework

The Swiss Constitution of 1999 dedicates three Articles to procedural rights. Art. 29, 29a and 30 are the cornerstones of legal protection, and they form part of the fundamental rights of the Constitution.

Art. 29 of the Swiss Constitution stipulates general procedural guarantees: '[e]very person has the right to equal and fair treatment in judicial and administrative proceedings and to have their case decided within a reasonable time.' These guarantees

1 Regina Kiener, Bernhard Rütsche and Mathias Kuhn, *Öffentliches Verfahrensrecht* (Dike, Zurich/St. Gallen 2015), 35.

2 Ulrich Häfelin, Georg Müller and Felix Uhlmann, *Allgemeines Verwaltungsrecht* (7th edn., Dike, Zurich/St. Gallen 2016), 576; BGE [Bundesgerichtsentscheid/Decision of the Federal Supreme Court] 134 I 23, 42.

3 René Rhinow, Heinrich Koller, Christina Kiss, Daniela Turnherr and Denise Brühl-Moser, *Öffentliches Prozessrecht: Grundlagen und Bundesrechtspflege* (3rd edn., Helbling Lichtenhahn, Basel 2014), 412.

4 Ibid. 419.

apply in any proceeding, may they be administrative or court proceedings, irrespective also of whether they concern civil, criminal, constitutional or administrative matters. These guarantees encompass fundamental rights such as the right to be heard or the right to legal aid, as explicitly stipulated in Art. 29 paras 2 and 3.[5]

Art. 30 of the Swiss Constitution provides for additional guarantees in judicial proceedings. A court must be legally constituted, competent, independent and impartial. Its hearings and its judgments shall be in public.[6]

Art. 29a of the Swiss Constitution, which has been in force since 1 January 2007, sets out the conditions to access to courts: '[i]n a legal dispute, every person has the right to have their case determined by a judicial authority. The Confederation and the Cantons may by law preclude the determination by the courts of certain exceptional categories of case.' Applicable procedural law and constitutional practice must specify the term 'legal dispute'. Only the law may restrict access to courts, and as the Constitution points out explicitly, only exceptionally. Art. 29a was clearly inspired by Art. 19 para 4 of the German *Grundgesetz* (*Rechtsweggarantie*).

The Constitution remains silent to the question of the scope of judicial review. Art. 29a is generally understood to guarantee a onetime review of facts and law by a court. A right to appeal, especially an appeal to the Swiss Supreme Court cannot be deduced from Art. 29a;[7] it is part of more specific provisions of the Constitution such as the right to appeal in penal matters (Art. 32) or on the Swiss Supreme Court (Art. 191). It is also undisputed that an (administrative) court may not review questions of administrative discretion.[8] The right stipulated in Art. 29a only guarantees review of facts and law but not of administrative discretion.

3 Procedural rights in Swiss administrative law

3.1 Administrative acts (rulings) as cornerstones of legal protection

Legal protection in Switzerland is traditionally linked to the nature of administrative action. Administrative action carried out in the form of administrative acts, also called rulings (*Verfügungen, décisions, decisioni*), typically triggers legal protection, either within the administration, to courts, or both.[9] In federal law, an administrative decision must be notified to the parties in writing. It 'must state the grounds on which [it is] based and contain instructions on legal remedies' (Art. 35 para. 1 APA).

This leads to the question what kind of administrative action must be clothed in the form of administrative act. According to the definition of the Federal Act on Administrative Procedure, Administrative Procedure Act (APA) '[r]ulings are decisions of the

5 See, for an overview, Jean-François Aubert and Pascal Mahon, *Petit commentaire de la Constitution fédérale de la Confédération suisse* (Schulthess, Zurich/Basel/Geneva 2003), § 29 5 f.

6 See for further details Berhard Ehrenzeller, Benjamin Schindler, Rainer J. Schweizer and Klaus A. Vallender (eds.), *Die schweizerische Bundesverfassung: St. Galler Kommentar* (3rd edn., Schulthess, Zurich/St. Gallen 2014), Art. 30 BV, 7 ff.

7 Pierre Tschannen, *Staatsrecht der Schweizerischen Eidgenossenschaft* (3rd edn., Stämfpli, Berne 2011), § 6 3.

8 Rhinow et al. (n. 3) 1120.

9 Kiener et al. (n. 1) 1245.

authorities in individual cases that are based on the public law of the Confederation and have as their subject matter the following:

(a) the establishment, amendment or withdrawal of rights or obligations;
(b) a finding of the existence, non-existence or extent of rights or obligations;
(c) the rejection of applications for the establishment, amendment, withdrawal or finding of rights or obligations, or the dismissal of such applications without entering into the substance of the case' (Art. 5).

The law specifies that also enforcement measures, interim orders, decisions on objections, appeal decisions etc. fall under the scope of this clause but not declarations made by authorities on the rejection or raising of claims. It may be that an administrative act is simply declaratory, clarifying the existence, the non-existence or the extent of public law rights or obligations. Such a declaratory ruling must be given if the applicant has an interest that is worthy of protection.

The Swiss Cantons have codes of administrative procedure of their own. These codes are applicable not only for cantonal acts based on cantonal law but also for cantonal acts applying federal law (or both cantonal and federal law). Many federal laws are implemented by the cantons. Although the cantons must not adhere to the federal definition of an administrative act (and the consequences on legal protection that follow from that approach), there are no noticeable differences in cantonal law. Hence, the definition of administrative acts is common both in federal and cantonal procedures.[10]

Administrative acts concretise rights and duties derived from primary and secondary legislation. The law applies to a specific case through administrative acts. They clarify and stabilise the legal situation for individuals.[11] Administrative acts may still rule the individual situation even if they were originally defective or became defective from subsequent developments such as an amendment to the applicable law.[12] These acts are the predominant form of action for administrative bodies. Again, the cantons, although not obliged by law in most cases, more or less follow the federal example set out in APA.

The critical element of Art. 5 – and hence the often critical point whether legal protection can be sought – is the question whether certain administrative actions infringe individual rights. The Swiss Courts repeatedly had to deal with this question. For example, they answered in the affirmative that an administrative act is needed in cases of a building permit, allowing neighbours to challenge that act in court.[13] An insurance company requested an administrative act in order to challenge administrative burdens of the supervisory body. The request was granted by the Federal Administrative Court.[14] A police officer in Geneva challenged the decision of the authorities to transfer him to another post. The canton of Geneva considered the relocation of the employee as an internal act not triggering any form of legal protection. The Swiss

10 Hafelin et al. (n. 2) 851; Felix Uhlmann, in Bernhard Waldmann and Philippe Weissenberger (eds.), VwVG, *Praxiskommentar zum Bundesgesetz uber das Verwaltungsverfahren* (Schulthess, Zurich/Basel/Geneva 2009) Art. 5 16.

11 Christoph Auer, Markus Müller and Benjamin Schindler (eds.), *VwVG Kommentar zum Bundesgesetz über das Verwaltungsverfahren* (Dike, Zurich/Basel/Geneva 2008) Art. 5 20.

12 Häfelin et al. (n. 2) 1087.

13 BGE 133 II 249.

14 BGVE 2007/50.

Supreme Court disagreed and requested an administrative act.[15] The cases illustrate the practical importance of administrative acts. Courts have typically tried to draw the line between administrative acts and other forms of administrative action by looking at the rights and interests of the private parties involved.[16]

The link between administrative acts and legal protection illustrates why private parties are looking for – or in the words of one scholar, 'hunting for'[17] – this form of administrative action. Indeed, until recently, legal protection outside the scope of administrative acts was typically less attractive for private individuals. If there was no administrative act to challenge, the only possible legal remedy was a claim on state liability. It was typically targeted against real acts (*Realakte, actes matériels, atti materiali*) such as governmental accidents, police action, public information etc.[18] A notable case involved a governmental warning on the consumption of Swiss cheese (*Vacherin Mont d'Or*) for fear of *listeriosis*, hence not legally prohibiting the selling and distribution of that cheese (administrative act), but obviously heavily affecting market demand. The producers of that cheese only had the possibility of a claim for state liability based on the allegedly disproportionate warning. They were not successful.[19] The disadvantage of state liability claims is both procedural and in substance. In state liability cases, claimants must prove various prerequisites such as damage, illegality of state behaviour, causality etc. Especially in cantonal proceedings, the procedure involves principles of civil procedure and burdens claimants with costs much higher than in a typical administrative case.[20] Unlike an administrative act that usually may only be enforced after its legality has been reviewed in court, state liability cases take place after the detrimental action of the state. Financial compensation is usually the only legal remedy which may prove unsatisfactory. Finally, state responsibility typically requires malpractice by the state whereas administrative acts are subject to full scrutiny.[21]

When reforming federal procedure the legislator tried to fill that gap of legal protection by introducing a new article in the Administrative Procedure Act (Art. 25a). It stipulates that any person who has an interest worthy of protection may request from the authority to decide on the legality of its own acts. The decision resulting thereof must be given in the form of an administrative act, hence triggering administrative protection. It is clear that the new provision tries to overcome some shortcomings that are to be found in state liability. It tries to prevent or to stop unlawful real acts.[22] Its procedure follows the logic of legal protection through administrative acts: If the applicant possesses an interest 'worthy of protection',[23] she or he may request an administrative

15 BGE 136 I 323, 328 ff., E. 4.3.–4.5..

16 Hafelin et al. (n. 2) 851, 874 and 881; Waldmann Bernhard, *Vom Umgang mit organisatorischen, innerdienstlichen und anderen Anordnungen ohne Verfügungscharakter*, ZSR 133/I (2014) 489 ff., 507f.; Felix Uhlmann, in Waldmann and Weissenberger (n. 12) Art. 5 96 f.

17 Sergio Giacomini, 'Vom Jagdmachen auf Verfügungen' (1993) 94 *Zentralblatt* 237.

18 Häfelin et al. (n. 2).

19 BGE 118 Ib 473.

20 Alfred Kölz, Isabelle Häner and Martin Bertschi, *Verwaltungsverfahren und Verwaltungsrechtspflege des Bundes* (3rd edn., Schulthess, Zurich/Basel/Geneva 2013) 1957.

21 Hans Rudolf Schwarzenbach-Hanhart, *Staatshaftungsrecht bei verfügungsfreiem Verwaltungshandeln: Mit praktischer Anleitung zum Vermeiden/Vermindern dieser wachsenden Risiken (Risikomanagement)* (Stämpfli, Berne 2006) 21.

22 Isabelle Häner, in Waldmann and Weissenberger (n. 12) Art. 25a 37.

23 BGE 121 I 87, 91 f., E. [Consideration/Erwägung] 1b.

act, hence opening the procedural path. Again, legal protection follows the logic of administrative action through administrative acts. The scope of legal protection in these cases is largely defined by the term 'interest worthy of protection'.[24] It is the same term that is used by the APA to draw a line between appellants having standing and those that have not. This subject will be referred to below.

The new provision is highly relevant for legal protection. In a recent case the Swiss Supreme Court upheld a decision by the Federal Administrative Court that private parties can refer to Art. 25a APA when challenging the supervision of the federal authorities on nuclear plants (BGE II 315, 322 ff. E. 3, 4 and 5). Such supervisory acts are informal in most cases hence excluding third party intervention. Under the new provision, if private parties are sufficiently affected by supervisory acts (or the neglect thereof), they may request an administrative act on the effectiveness of supervision.

The Swiss cantons are not bound by the new Article of the APA in their own domain. In some cases they have copied the provision, in others they have opted for independent solutions (such as a direct appeal against real acts) or refrained from doing anything. It is disputed whether the latter is still permissible under Art. 29a of the Swiss Constitution as this provision guarantees judicial protection in any legal dispute. The Swiss Supreme Court has not yet decided upon this issue.

3.2 Procedural rights and administrative acts

As explained above, the duty of the administrative bodies to act through administrative acts triggers a number of procedural rights.[25]

The most important guarantee is the right to be heard.[26] It encompasses access to relevant documents, the possibility to propose witnesses and other means of evidence, to be informed of the possible administrative act beforehand etc. It is the cornerstone of procedural fairness, open enough to cover new grounds (e.g. right to reply) and to be adapted in the concrete situation of the case. As mentioned before, it is granted already by the Swiss Constitution. Procedural law and court practice concretise the right in specific situations, such as restrictions in cases of relevant third party interests (e.g. business secrets) or state interests (e.g. state security). Such restrictions often necessitate a fair balance of interests. Courts are typically reluctant to restrict access to relevant documents. If a restriction is necessary, they will try to summarise the content of the document in order to allow a fair discussion on the relevant facts of the case. The court itself has access to all documents of the administration – cases of documents not released to the courts are extremely rare.[27]

While access to documents is probably the most relevant aspect of the right to be heard, it should be noted that the scope of this right goes much further: the right may also be violated if relevant evidence is rejected by the court, such as witness hearings (rare in administrative cases) or the appointment of a court expert. The court must

24 Isabelle Häner, in Waldmann and Weissenberger (n. 12) Art. 25a 34.

25 For simplicity, the following quotations only contain constitutional and federal law. The legal situation in the cantons is very similar, partly because of the compulsory nature of constitutional law, partly because of the example set out by federal law.

26 Kölz et al. (n. 19), 487 ff.; Rhinow et al. (n. 3) 309 ff.

27 One notorious example involved constructions plans on nuclear weapons, see the investigation of the Swiss Parliament (Fall Tinner, *Rechtmässigkeit der Beschlüsse des Bundesrats und Zweckmässigkeit seiner Führung, Bericht der Geschäftsprüfungsdelegation der Eidgenössischen Räte vom 19. Januar 2009* [BBl 2009] 5007).

also effectively deal with the private parties' arguments. If a decision is already taken irrespective of the arguments, the right to be heard is clearly violated. The obligation to consider all arguments manifests in the duty of the authority to state the grounds for its decision. In the decision, it must also contend – if only briefly – with the private parties' arguments.

The right to be heard also requests that the administrative process is sufficiently transparent. The authority must clearly designate an administrative act as such. This means that the private parties know when the process has ended – but also that the process is still ongoing as long as no administrative act has been issued. This obligation goes hand in hand with the duty of the authority to be transparent on the process and on the possible measures intended. The authority may neither be unduly vague about its actions nor may it 'surprise' the private parties by its procedure. The latter is instructively illustrated by a recent decision of the Swiss Supreme Court: the local authorities have invited applicants for naturalisation to a first 'get-to-know'. They had not made clear that they plan to test the applicants on their knowledge on Swiss culture, history etc. While it is admissible to expect applicants to have a basic knowledge on Switzerland, it is not correct to test that knowledge without proper notice (BGE 140 I 99, 101 ff. E. 2 and 3). The case also shows that the right to be heard is a flexible instrument of courts to intervene against any form of administrative process that does not seem fair.

A fair process also includes the right to a decision within a reasonable time (Art. 29 of the Constitution).[28] If the authority does not act within a reasonable time, an appeal may be launched at any time. The reasonableness must be determined in the light of all circumstances of the case. The authority may consider the complexity of the case, the urgency of the matter and the behaviour of the parties. No grounds for a delay are internal matters of the authority such as the lack of sufficient personnel.

A last important aspect of the overall fairness of the procedure is the right to legal aid.[29] The right to legal aid and to a counsel if necessary is clearly guaranteed by Art. 29 para 3 of the Swiss Constitution: 'Any person who does not have sufficient means has the right to free legal advice and assistance unless their case appears to have no prospect of success. If it is necessary in order to safeguard their rights, they also have the right to free legal representation in court.' The aid can only be granted if a reasonable person would deem sufficient the chances of success. The need for legal counsel depends on the complexity of the matter and the abilities of the private party: if that person may represent him or herself without greater difficulties before the authority, a right to free legal representation will be denied. If the parties are covering the costs themselves, legal representation is possible in most administrative and court matters. However, there is no obligation to mandate a lawyer or another specialist. There are no procedures in Swiss administrative law that require legal representation. Even before the Swiss Supreme Court, cases in administrative and constitutional law may be brought and are brought by anybody capable of acting.

As discussed before, the form of an administrative act implies *per se* that there is a legal remedy against that act. Administrative acts are subject to an appeal. The administrative act must contain instructions on legal remedies. Depending on the relevant administrative procedure, the appeal may go directly to a court or first to a higher

28 Markus Müller, in Auer et al. (n. 10) Art. 46a 2 f. and 6 ff.
29 Martin Kayser, in Auer et al. (n. 10) Art. 65 1 ff.

administrative authority and then to a court.[30] Exceptions must be clearly stated by law and are restricted to exceptional cases.[31] In practice, these exceptions involve highly political matters such as issuing a permit to build a nuclear power station or matters on national security (Art. 32 para. 1 lit. a and e ACA). Some exceptions concern technical or subjective matters such as bonuses for civil servants (Art. 32 para. 1 lit. c ACA). In total, the exceptions are narrowly drawn by the legislator – as requested by the Swiss Constitution.

The right to an appeal may not be so obvious for third parties. It depends on the term 'party'. Any party of the procedure may launch an appeal (and has the right to intervene earlier in the procedure). The Administrative Procedure Act defines parties, i.e. the holders of the procedural rights, by their material interest to participate: 'Parties are persons whose rights or obligations are intended to be affected by the ruling.'[32] A similar wording is used for the definition of *locus standi* in an appeal. A right to an appeal is accorded to anyone that is 'specifically affected by the contested ruling' and 'has an interest that is worthy of protection in the revocation or amendment of the ruling' (Art. 48 para. 1 APA). Participation in the proceedings of the first instance is generally required for an appeal.

3.3 Legal protection against normative acts

Most normative acts can be challenged in a concrete case before a court (or before an administrative body). A court will then proceed to a two-tier review. First, it investigates whether the normative basis is legal (*vorfrageweise, inzidente, konkrete Normenkontrolle*) and then, if the normative basis proves to be legal, whether the norm was applied correctly in the case before the court.[33] Art. 190 of the Swiss Constitution sensibly restricts judicial review of statutory acts, as federal laws must be applied even in the case that the court finds it unconstitutional.[34] A direct challenge of normative acts (*abstrakte, direkte Normenkontrolle*) is possible regarding cantonal laws and ordinances. The latter includes internal normative acts (*Verwaltungsverordnungen*) if these affect private parties and their review proves impossible or impractical in a concrete case.[35] The cases that are challenging cantonal normative acts are decided directly by the Swiss Supreme Court if there is no legal remedy on the cantonal level – which is typically the case for cantonal laws. The Swiss Supreme Court may quash cantonal laws and render them fully or partly invalid.[36] Cantonal constitutions escape this control as they must be approved in a legal procedure by the Swiss Parliament (Art. 51 para. 2 and 172 para. 2 of the Swiss Constitution).[37]

The standing is far more generously admitted than in individual cases. A person may challenge a normative act if she or he can claim that there is a – even remote – possibility that she or he will be affected by the act (*virtuelles Betroffensein*).[38] An appeal

30 See infra Chapter 4.
31 See supra Chapter 2.
32 Art. 6 APA, also that 'other persons, organizations or authorities who have a legal remedy against the ruling' as parties.
33 Rhinow et al. (n. 3) 707 f.
34 See infra Chapter 4.2.
35 BGer [Bundesgericht/Federal Supreme Court], October 18, 2002, 1P.240/2002.
36 Kölz et al. (n. 19) 1675 ff.
37 Kiener et al. (n. 1) 1780.
38 Ibid. 1724.

against a normative act does not preclude a later legal remedy against an individual administrative act applying the mentioned normative act. In this respect, a normative act may be challenged twice, first in abstract terms how the act could be applied and later on how the act was actually applied.

4 Institutional framework

4.1 Administrative authorities

Administrative authorities play a vital role in effective legal protection in administrative law. As shortly explained in the historical context, only hierarchical higher administrative bodies were competent to grant legal protection.[39] Although these bodies were not institutionally independent – as they supervised the administrative acts of their subordinate bodies – the level of protection should not be underestimated for the following reasons. First, these bodies, often affiliated to the office of Justice of the Canton or at least staffed with qualified lawyers, developed high standards of judicial protection. Secondly, the superior administrative bodies usually know the daily work of the lower units well, hence strengthening administrative oversight. Thirdly, administrative control within the public administration has the practical advantage of full scrutiny: Whereas courts typically do not review questions of administrative discretion, the appellant or supervisory administrative bodies show less or no restraint.[40]

In the Swiss cantons – it is to be noted that the cantons as federated states also execute a substantial amount of federal law – the typical legal recourse goes first to the hierarchical higher administrative bodies, possibly involving up to three instances including the cantonal executive.[41] The recourse then turns to the cantonal administrative courts. These courts have to guarantee Art. 29a of the Swiss Constitution which means that they must at least fully review questions of law and questions of fact. From the cantonal administrative courts, most cases can be taken to the Swiss Supreme Court (*Bundesgericht, Tribunal fédéral, Tribunale federale*). The Swiss Supreme Court typically reviews only questions of law.[42]

Administrative acts of the federal administration can be taken to the Swiss Federal Administrative Court (*Bundesverwaltungsgericht, Tribunal administratif fédéral, Tribunale administrativo federale*). Judicial control by a higher administrative body is the exception in the federal system. It has some practical significance in areas that are excluded from judicial protection and may involve the Swiss Federal Council.[43] According to the existing legislation, the Federal Administrative Court reviews questions of law, fact, and administrative discretion. However, judicial practice has developed some restraint in the latter area; such cases often require specialised technical understanding, knowledge of the local circumstances or subjective factors (exams, administrative decisions on personnel etc.).[44] Decisions from the Swiss Federal Administrative Court may be challenged before the Swiss Supreme Court. Some subject matter areas such as cases on immigration and

39 Rhinow et al. (n. 3) 412.
40 Kiener et al. (n. 1) 13.
41 Ibid. 42.
42 Ibid. 40.
43 Tschannen (n. 7) § 38 20.
44 Häfelin et al. (n. 2) 444.

asylum, on exams, and on subsidies are fully or partly excluded from review of the Swiss Supreme Court (Art. 83 lit. c, d, k and t SCA), hence rendering the Federal Administrative Court the last national instance.

4.2 Courts

As explained above, judicial control by courts is a constitutional requirement. Hence, most administrative acts may be challenged directly (like the acts of the federal administration) or indirectly via higher administrative bodies (e.g. acts of the cantonal administration) before an administrative court. The law may only 'preclude the determination by the courts of certain exceptional categories of case' (Art. 29a of the Swiss constitution). The rare cases of excluded matters before the Swiss Federal Court involve sovereign acts and highly political administrative acts (e.g. on nuclear energy) (Art. 32 para. 1 ACA). Judicial protection is also excluded in areas that are difficult to assess for courts from a practical viewpoint such as bonuses for civil servants.[45] The cantons may exclude administrative acts of political nature.

The most important restriction on judicial control is not based on these exceptions but on Art. 190 of the Swiss Constitution. According to that provision, the 'Federal Supreme Court and the other judicial authorities apply the federal acts and international law'. As a consequence of this provision, there is no constitutional review of federal laws, or more precisely, Swiss courts must apply federal laws even if they are considered unconstitutional.[46] Judicial practice has carved some exceptions out of this rule, such as federal laws which violate the ECHR. Still a substantial part of federal legislation is not subject to court sanctions in case of a violation of the Constitution. The rationale of this provision is that the last word on questions of constitutionality should not be given to a court but to the legislator itself, being the organ with the highest democratic legitimation. The federal legislator is not beyond the Constitution but beyond constitutional control; it is bound by the Constitution and has to respect it. It means that the federal Parliament itself must decide upon questions of constitutionality of federal laws – which it does regularly, supported with expert opinion of the Federal Department of Justice. Several attempts of the Swiss government to abolish Art. 190 of the Swiss Constitution have failed as Parliament objected to a shift in power to the Courts.[47]

It is to be noted that Switzerland does not have a special constitutional court. Constitutional questions may be decided by every Swiss court including cantonal courts as well as courts in civil or penal matters, and in concrete cases even by administrative bodies.[48] Switzerland, hence, has opted for a so called 'diffuse' system of constitutional review, closer to the US court system than to the German model of concentrated constitutional review.

According to the APA, '[t]he appellate authority shall itself make the decision in the case or in exceptional cases shall refer the case back to the lower instance and issue binding instructions' (Art. 61 para. 1 APA). Referral to the lower instance is typically made if further fact finding has to be done by the lower instance or if the lower instance may exert discretion to decide the case.

45 Rhinow et al. (n. 3) 444.

46 Kiener et al. (n. 1) 1763.

47 Astrid Epiney, Art. 190 BV paras. 8 ff. in Bernhard Waldmann, Eva Maria and Astrid Epiney (eds.), Basler Kommentar, Bundesverfassung, Helbling Lichtenhahn, Basel 2015.

48 Ibid. 1719.

Both the appellate administrative authorities and the courts may grant interim relief. Typically, an appeal by itself has a suspensive effect.[49] As the APA declares, a court may also take 'other precautionary measures [. . .] to preserve the current situation or to temporarily safeguard interests that are at risk' (Art. 56 APA). Swiss courts approach the question of suspensive effect and of precautionary measures typically with a balancing test between the interest of the state and of private parties. If they believe that the result of the case is evident, they also may take into account the probable outcome of the case.[50]

A simplified version of the institutional framework may be depicted as follows:

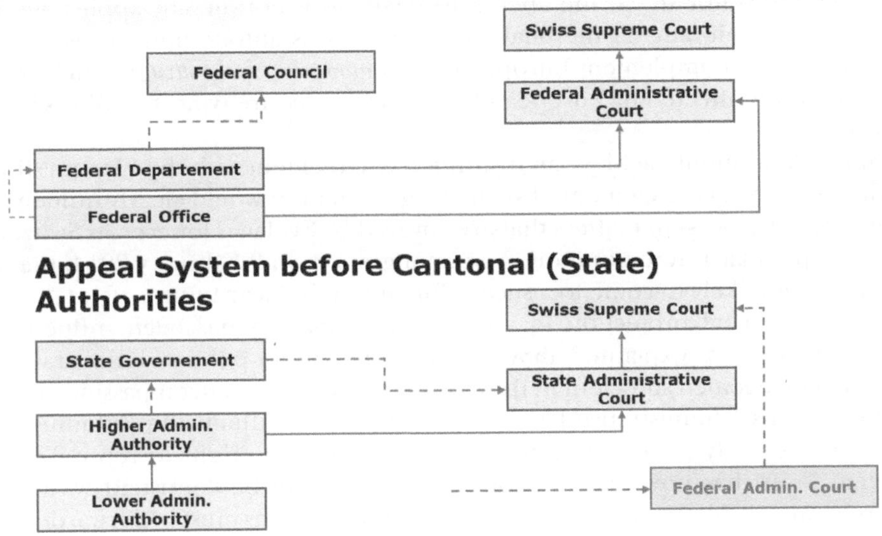

Figure 17.1 Appeal system before federal authorities

4.3 Other bodies and procedures

In the federal system, special committees serving as courts have been abolished, with the exception of the Independent Complaints Authority for Radio and Television. The committees have been replaced by the Federal Administrative Court, being competent in all matters decided by the federal administration.[51] In the cantons, special committees still exist, most notably in the areas of construction, taxes, culture and education. From there, the cases go to the cantonal administrative court and eventually further to the Swiss Supreme Court.[52]

Some Swiss cantons know the institution of the Ombudsman that has some practical significance.[53] On the federal level, an initiative to introduce the Ombudsman failed. There are however two independent, personalised functions of control of state set administrated prices (*Eidgenössischer Preisüberwacher*) and of data protection and publicity of the public administration (*Eidgenössischer Datenschutzbeauftragter*). Both

49 For details see Rhinow et al. (n. 3) 680 ff.
50 Kiener et al. (n. 1) 1327 ff.
51 Rhinow et al. (n. 3) 783 ff.
52 Kiener et al. (n. 1) 1404.
53 Häfelin et al. (n. 2) 1768 ff.

may resort to legal remedies but their most efficient tools are negotiations with the administration and public information.

Alternative Dispute Resolution (ADR) has been recently introduced into the APA which says that the court 'may suspend the proceedings with the consent of the parties in order that the parties may agree on the content of the ruling' (Art. 33b para. 1 APA). It may encourage the agreement by appointment of a neutral mediator. It is too early to comment on the practical consequences of this provision.

5 European perspective

As Switzerland is not an EU member, European law is not directly applicable. However, it may be relevant via the bilateral treaties or as autonomous decision of the Swiss authorities to implement European law (*autonomer Nachvollzug*). Still, legal protection is hardly affected by European law as the procedure typically follows internal Swiss law.

If Switzerland should achieve an institutional agreement with the EU, questions of jurisdiction were a core element of such an agreement. It would clearly influence the administrative process in matters that are covered by EU law. However, as Switzerland adopted a popular referendum on mass immigration on 9 February 2014, the negotiations are not likely to come to a successful end in the near future.

In contrast, legal protection in administrative matters has been influenced by ECtHR decisions. As explained above, legal protection in public administration has not only been deemed sufficient in the case of 'civil matters', encompassing areas that fall under Swiss administrative law. The ECtHR is still influencing (administrative) procedure, recently for example in cases concerning the right to reply. The Swiss Supreme Court has now shaped a practice that should be consistent with ECtHR requirements: all documents submitted in court procedures must be forwarded to the parties, in administrative procedures all relevant documents.

6 Conclusions

The principle of effective legal protection in administrative law is to a large extent honoured by Switzerland. The main principles are strongly routed in the constitution. Deficits of legal protection that are a consequence of the (relatively narrow) concept and nature of the administrative act have been overcome (or should be overcome) by the amendment of the APA on real acts. The extent of procedural rights seems sensitive; there are neither apparent gaps nor are these rights overly restricted by law or court practice.

The most problematic provision – in my view – is Art. 190 of the Swiss Constitution. There is no (or only a limited) protection under the ECHR against infringements based on Swiss federal law. The Swiss Supreme Court must apply these laws even if deemed unconstitutional. A similar problem arises for more and more radical popular initiatives on the Swiss Constitution: these propositions may only be 'softened' by the Swiss Supreme Court, but the core of these initiatives typically targeting migrants, criminals and religious minorities are untouched by judicial control. They may well undermine effective legal protection of these groups.

18 The principle of effective legal protection in administrative law in the United Kingdom

Robert Thomas

1 Introduction: Historical developments

Effective legal protection and access to justice are fundamental principles in the UK: it is essential that everyone be able to secure access to justice irrespective of their social status, race, sex, or financial power. However, it is equally true that the task of securing access to justice is often problematic. As a nineteenth century Irish judge, James Matthew, once noted, '[i]n England, justice is open to all – like the Ritz Hotel' – in theory, everyone can access justice, but in practice only a few people may actually succeed in doing so. While effective legal protection is a fundamental principle, in practice it is hedged around with various practical difficulties. The challenge for the legal system is the extent to which it can actually secure its vision of effective legal protection in practice.

This country report describes and analyses the institutions and procedures for securing effective legal protection in the UK. This raises a number of themes. One theme concerns the constitutional framework and basis for effective legal protection. Unlike other countries, the UK has no written constitution. The basis for effective legal protection is not therefore contained with an overarching higher-ranking constitutional norm. Instead, it is to be found in accumulation of practice, precedent, case law and legislation.

A second theme concerns the powerful position of the executive and its attitude toward effective legal protection. In a formal sense, the UK constitution is based upon a hierarchy of institutions as ordered by constitutional principles. Parliament is sovereign. To ensure that the executive acts in accordance with legislation and the common law, the courts check and review the legality of executive decisions. However, in practice, this formal construct does not reflect the reality of how political and administrative power is exercised. In practice, Parliament is largely controlled by the executive. The courts have no power of constitutional review and must apply primary legislation. The executive, therefore, occupies a particularly powerful place within the UK's constitutional system, which, in turn, requires an effective system of accountability. Yet, the executive possesses an ability to influence the design and operation of legal protection. The courts have a residual ability, through techniques such as statutory interpretation and common law principles, to ensure legal accountability of government. There is an inherent – and sometimes acute – tension between the institutions involved and the underlying political and legal forces in play (executive power and policy considerations versus effective legal protection), especially when the executive seeks to constrain access to effective legal protection.

A third major theme over recent years has been the effects of financial austerity. Since 2010, the UK Government has significantly reduced public spending. This programme has affected most areas of government including the legal system. Effective legal protection costs money in terms of the resourcing of courts and tribunals and publicly funded legal representation. An important area of debate is whether such cuts are permissible or whether they unduly restrict access to justice and legal protection.

Legal protection in the UK has a long history. For many centuries, the courts supervised and checked the decisions of inferior public bodies by ensuring that they acted within the limits of their jurisdiction. The courts also applied ordinary principles of private law to protect individuals. For instance, in a famous case, where a publisher's house and papers had been ransacked by the king's messengers sent by the Home Secretary, the remedy was an ordinary action for trespass for which damages were awarded.[1] However, there was no developed system of administrative law with special administrative courts. Instead, what developed was a piecemeal system of tribunals, which determined appeals against administrative decisions, and individual judicial decisions. During the twentieth century, concerns over the lack of effective legal protection of individuals against government increased substantially. The courts often adopted a deferential approach toward government decisions. As the nature and role of the modern state changed, concerns were raised that the individual no longer had any effective legal protection against government. Yet, in the second half of the twentieth century, a number of reforms were introduced to meet such concerns.[2] The courts developed principles of judicial review to impose the rule of law on government.

The UK now has a developed system of administrative law comprising courts, tribunals, and ombudsmen. This system differs in important respects from continental systems. First, it is the ordinary courts – not specialised administrative courts – that review the legality of administrative decisions. At the same time, there is a degree of specialisation: judicial review challenges are channelled into the Administrative Court, that division of the High Court that deals with judicial review. Secondly, while the Administrative Court sits at the apex of the whole system, tribunals determine the majority of the challenges against government decisions. A third point is that the principles and norms governing legal protection are not codified anywhere, though there are various non-binding codes of good administration.[3] The procedures used in any particular administrative context will be an amalgam of statute, common law, and administrative guidance.

2 Constitutional framework

As is well-known, the UK does not have an over-arching formal constitutional text or framework. The constitution is a product of historical developments, political and governmental practice, and judicial decisions. There is plenty of debate amongst academic lawyers as to the nature of the UK's constitution, whether it is an essentially political or

1 *Entick v Carrington* (1765) St Tr 1030.

2 See Jeffrey Jowell, 'Administrative Law' in Vernon Bogdanor (ed.), *The British Constitution in the Twentieth Century* (Oxford University Press, Oxford 2003).

3 Parliamentary and Health Service Ombudsman, *Principles of Good Administration* (2007); Administrative Justice and Tribunals Council, *Principles of Administrative Justice* (2010).

legal constitution. For some scholars, the UK constitution does possess a legal foundation which is based upon the rule of law and the ability of the courts to expound upon fundamental legal principles.[4] From this perspective, there is an underlying normative basis for the constitution. By contrast, other scholars start from a far more descriptive standpoint: the constitution is what happens.[5] There are two fundamental constitutional principles: parliamentary sovereignty and the rule of law. Parliamentary sovereignty means that Parliament can make any law if it wishes; there are no higher-order constitutional principles or norms against which the constitutionality of legislation can be assessed. The rule of law means that governmental decisions must be in accordance with legislation and common law principles as developed by the courts.

The principle of effective legal protection is an important component of the rule of law. As a former senior judge, Sir Thomas Bingham has stated the core principle of the rule of law is that all persons and authorities within the state, whether public or private, should be bound by and entitled to the benefit of law publicly made, taking effect in the future and publicly administered in the courts.[6] The courts interpret legislation and review the exercise of administrative powers against procedural and substantive safeguards of legality. They presume that Parliament legislates against a wider backdrop of such safeguards which the courts will apply. The courts will only allow such principles and standards to be overridden by explicit statutory language. As Lord Steyn has noted, '[u]nless there is the clearest provision to the contrary, Parliament must be presumed not to legislate contrary to the rule of law. And the rule of law enforces minimum standards of fairness, both substantive and procedural.'[7]

As a general principle, every governmental decision should be susceptible to review before the courts. The notion that the courts are the ultimate defenders of the individual and the providers of effective legal protection is deeply embedded in the common law. Judicial review is one of the most important means by which the Government and other public bodies are held legally accountable for the lawfulness of their decisions and actions, including their compatibility with the requirements of human rights law. According to the President of the Supreme Court, Lord Neuberger, 'the courts have no more important function than protecting citizens from the abuses and excesses of the executive'.[8]

The courts review administrative decisions under three general principles: legality; procedural fairness; and irrationality. The expansion of judicial review over the last half century has been justified by the courts on account of the deficiencies of, and weak protection provided by, the doctrine of ministerial responsibility, that is, the political accountability of government ministers to Parliament, in which those ministers themselves necessarily have a majority of MPs. In 1911, a judge robustly stated that '[i]f ministerial responsibility were more than the mere shadow of a name, the matter would be less important, but as it is the Courts are the only defence of the liberty of the subject against departmental aggression'.[9] In 1995, Lord Mustill noted that the employment

4 See, eg, T. R. S. Allan, *Constitutional Justice: A Liberal Theory of the Rule of Law* (Oxford University Press, Oxford 2001).

5 J. A. G. Griffith, 'The Political Constitution' (1979) 42 *Modern Law Review* 1.

6 Tom Bingham, *The Rule of Law* (London: Allen Lane 2010) 8.

7 *R v Secretary of State for the Home Department, ex parte Pierson* [1998] AC 539, 591 (Lord Steyn).

8 Lord Neuberger, 'Justice in an Age of Austerity' Tom Sargant Memorial Lecture 2013, 15 October 2013 (available at http://supremecourt.uk/docs/speech-131015.pdf) accessed 15 June 2015.

9 *Dyson v Attorney-General* [1911] 1 KB 410, 424 (Farwell LJ).

of Parliamentary remedies against the abuse of executive power had 'on occasion been perceived as falling short, and sometimes well short, of what was needed to bring the performance of the executive into line with the law, and with the minimum standards of fairness implicit in every Parliamentary delegation of a decision making function.'[10] To avoid a vacuum in which the citizen would be left without protection against a misuse of executive powers, the courts had no option but to occupy the dead ground by developing judicial review to an unprecedented extent. In addition to domestic common law of judicial review, there is also judicial review under the Human Rights Act (HRA) 1998. This involves judicial scrutiny of administrative decisions to protect Convention rights under the ECHR. Human rights challenges require the courts to adopt a more intensive scrutiny by using the doctrine of proportionality.[11]

A good illustration of the approach of the courts and their changing approach is provided by the issue of ouster clauses – statutory provisions that seek to exclude government decisions immune from judicial review. Such provisions present an inevitable tension between Parliamentary sovereignty and the rule of law: should the court respect Parliament's right to say what the law is and exclude judicial review? Or should the court interpret the relevant legislation in a manner that undermines Parliament's intention?

The classic case is *Anisminic* decided in 1969, in which a statutory provision that the determination of a particular government body 'shall not be called in question in any court of law' was construed by the House of Lords as meaning that only a lawful – not purported – determination could be excluded from judicial scrutiny.[12] As the final word on whether or not a determination was lawful lay with the courts, the practical effect of the ouster clause in excluding judicial review was reduced to nil. *Anisminic* was a direct challenge to Parliament; despite Parliament stating that the relevant decisions should not be challengeable, the courts insisted that they had the right to review. The case illustrates the court's inherent jurisdiction to supervise and correct all inferior decision makers to ensure that they do not exceed their jurisdiction. *Anisminic* also provided a deft way in which courts can get around statutory attempts to exclude their jurisdiction, an approach applied in subsequent cases.[13] However, the reasoning in *Anisminic* was rather tortuous and arcane: there was no explicit discussion of the principle of legal protection or access to the courts.

By the 2000s, things had moved on and the courts had become bolder. The immediate background was the Government's failed attempt, in 2004, to exclude all immigration and asylum decisions from judicial scrutiny. In the event, that attempt failed because of parliamentary opposition – a good illustration of Parliament's role in maintaining effective legal protection. However, the episode deeply troubled the judges. If the executive exerts considerable power over Parliament and there is no constitutional guarantee of legal protection, what then is to prevent the executive from abolishing judicial review? If matters came to a head, what would the courts do? One view is that the tradition of parliamentary sovereignty is too deeply embedded to be qualified by the courts alone. For Lord Neuberger, the courts must be vigilant to protect

10 *R v Secretary of State for the Home Department, ex parte Fire Brigades Union* [1996] 2 AC 513, 567 (Lord Mustill).
11 See *Kennedy v Charity Commission* [2014] UKSC 20, [2014] 2 WLR 808.
12 *Anisminic v Foreign Compensation Commission* [1969] 2 AC 147.
13 *R v Secretary of State for the Home Department ex parte Fayed* [1998] 1 WLR 763.

individuals against the abuse of power, but they cannot go against Parliament's will as expressed in statute.[14] By contrast, Lord Steyn has noted that if Parliament were to assert an extravagant power by removing judicial review, then the courts 'may have to consider whether this is a constitutional fundamental which even a sovereign Parliament . . . cannot abolish'.[15] Lord Hope expressed similar views, opining that 'parliamentary sovereignty is no longer, if it ever was, absolute',[16] and that 'the rule of law enforced by the courts is the ultimate controlling factor on which our constitution is based'.[17] The courts have therefore become more explicit in defending legal protection, but, given the wider constitutional position, they are in a relatively vulnerable position: excessive judicial activism will lay them open to criticism of unelected judges interfering with political matters.

Effective legal protection is provided not just by courts, but also by tribunals. Whenever Parliament establishes a scheme of government administration that involves making individualised decisions concerning whether or not an individual qualifies for a certain benefit or status or their financial liability, it often, though not always, establishes a right of appeal against negative decisions to tribunals. Tribunals have full jurisdiction in that they can determine appeals on issues of both law and fact. Other remedies, such as ombudsmen, are also statutory creations. Furthermore, perhaps the most important expansion of legal protection for individuals – the Human Rights Act 1998 – was enacted by Parliament to give further effect to the European Convention on Human Rights into domestic law.

3 Rights-based perspective

Traditionally, English law has not tended to use the language of rights; English law typically fastens, not on principles, but on remedies.[18] Nonetheless, such remedies prioritise effective legal protection and access to justice. However, over recent years, the courts have become more explicit in defining justiciable errors in terms of principles or rights of which there are a number, including: the right of access to the courts; the principle of legality; and the general principles of judicial review (legality, procedural fairness, and unreasonableness). The courts adopt a variable intensity of review: a low intensity of review is applied to cases involving issues that depend involve political judgment, such as matters of national economic policy or those issues which are outside the normal expertise of the judges.[19] In cases where fundamental rights are concerned, the courts adopt a more intensive scrutiny. These principles also inform how the courts interpret legislation. Furthermore, the courts have emphasised that the principle of legality requires clear statutory language before interfering with fundamental rights, such as access to justice and effective legal protection. The courts will, therefore, interpret such legislation as narrowly as possible so as to uphold effective legal protection.

14 Lord Neuberger, 'Who Are the Masters Now?' (2011) *The second Lord Alexander of Weedon lecture* 72–73.

15 *Jackson v Her Majesty's Attorney General* [2005] UKHL 56, [102].

16 Ibid. [104].

17 Ibid. [107].

18 *Davy v Spelthorne Borough Council* [1984] AC 262, 276 (Lord Wilberforce).

19 *Nottinghamshire County Council v Secretary of State for the Environment* [1986] AC 240, and *R v Secretary of State for the Environment, ex parte Hammersmith and Fulham London Borough Council* [1991] 1 AC 521.

The most important right is the right of access to the courts. 'It is a principle of our law that every citizen has a right of unimpeded access to a court. . . . Even in our unwritten constitution it must rank as a constitutional right.'[20] The courts are acutely conscious of the importance of the right of access to the courts and will go to some lengths in order to protect this right. To illustrate the point, consider the many cases concerning the right of access to justice by prisoners. A number of cases have concerned the confidentiality of communications between a prisoner and his lawyer and whether or not the prison authorities can examine such communications. In *Leech* the Court of Appeal held that a prison governor did not have the right to examine and stop a prisoner's letters to his lawyer.[21] In *Daly* the House of Lords held that a blanket policy requiring prisoners to be absent from their cells during a search of legal correspondence was unlawful because the materials being searched were protected by legal professional privilege; the possibility that a prison officer might improperly read the correspondence and the inhibiting effect upon the prisoner's willingness to communicate freely with his legal adviser, amounted to an infringement of the prisoner's right to legal professional privilege and therefore access to justice.[22] Cases such as these illustrate the courts' ability to prevent indirect inhibitions on judicial protection.

In many instances, individuals can appeal against administrative decisions (for instance, social security decisions) to tribunals. Tribunals are quicker, cheaper, more informal, and more expert than the courts.[23] As tribunals are less adversarial and formal than the courts, the need for the parties to be legally represented, and so the need for legal aid funding, is reduced. They are not bound by the formal procedures and rules of evidence that the higher courts must follow; they can therefore deal with appeals in a more informal, user-friendly way. Tribunals are a relatively efficient way of dealing with the very high volume of cases generated by the modern administrate state. The relevant concept here is 'proportionate dispute resolution' – there must be a proportionate relationship between the issues at stake in a dispute and the costs of the procedures used to resolve it.[24] For example, it would be out of proportion for disputes over entitlement to welfare benefits, although of immense significance to individuals, to be resolved through a judicial process akin to that used by the higher courts, which might cost more than the amount of money at stake – especially when the volume of such disputes is substantial. Parliament decides whether or not cases should be handled by the courts or tribunals. The Leggatt Report on tribunals suggested three tests to inform such decisions: (i) the desirability of direct participation by tribunal users; (ii) the need for special expertise in the particular subject-matter; and (iii) expertise in administrative law.[25]

Individuals can participate in the administrative process through the doctrine of procedural fairness. This is an especially important area protected by the common law. As Lord Sumption recently noted, '[t]he duty to give advance notice and an opportunity to be heard to a person against whom a draconian statutory power is to

20 *R v Secretary of State for the Home Department, ex parte Leech* [1994] QB 198, 210 (Steyn LJ).

21 Ibid.

22 *R (Daly) v Secretary of State for the Home Department* [2001] 2 AC 532.

23 *Report of the Committee on Administrative Tribunals and Enquiries* (Cmnd 218, 1957), [38].

24 Department for Constitutional Affairs, *Transforming Public Services: Complaints, Redress and Tribunals* (White Paper, Cm 6243 2004) ch 2.

25 Report of the Review of Tribunals by Sir Andrew Leggatt: *Tribunals for Users: One System, One Service* (London: August, 2001) [1.11]–[1.13].

be exercised is one of the oldest principles of what would now be called public law.'[26] When a statute has conferred on any public body the power to make decisions affecting individuals, then the courts will often impose additional procedural safeguards to ensure that the procedure followed is fair.[27] As one judge once said, 'the justice of the common law will supply the omission of the legislature'.[28]

The basic principles of procedural fairness are as follows: (1) Where an Act of Parliament confers an administrative power there is a presumption that it will be exercised in a manner which is fair in all the circumstances. (2) The standards of fairness are not immutable. They may change with the passage of time, both in the general and in their application to decisions of a particular type. (3) The principles of fairness are not to be applied by rote identically in every situation. What fairness demands is dependent on the context of the decision, and this is to be taken into account in all its aspects. (4) An essential feature of the context is the statute which creates the discretion, as regards both its language and the shape of the legal and administrative system within which the decision is taken. (5) Fairness will very often require that a person who may be adversely affected by the decision will have an opportunity to make representations on his own behalf either before the decision is taken with a view to producing a favourable result; or after it is taken, with a view to procuring its modification; or both. (6) Since the person affected usually cannot make worthwhile representations without knowing what factors may weigh against his interests, fairness will very often require that he is informed of the gist of the case which he has to answer.[29]

The application of these principles will depend upon the nature of the individual decision making process. Procedural fairness is 'essentially an intuitive judgment'.[30] The courts have laid down the requirements of procedural fairness in many cases. These include the following: the need for government to notify an individual of adverse concerns before making a decision; the ability of that individual to respond and comment upon such concerns, whether by way of an oral hearing or on the papers; and, if there is to be an oral hearing, whether there should be cross-examination of witnesses. The position as regards the making of secondary legislation is that government may be obliged by statute to consult affected parties or it may do so as a matter of practice. There is no common law duty to consult before making regulations.[31]

Closely linked to the procedure before a decision is the issue of whether reasons should be given for a decision. There is no general duty to give reasons, but legislation often requires reasons to be given in particular contexts. If not, then the courts will often impose a duty to give reasons at common law if the refusal to do so would be unfair by adversely affecting an individual's rights or the lack of reasons would render the decision aberrant.[32] If reasons are given, then they must be proper, adequate and intelligible and deal with the substantial points raised.[33]

26 *Bank Mellat v Her Majesty's Treasury (Respondent) (No. 2)* [2013] UKSC 39, [29] (Lord Sumption).

27 *Lloyd v McMahon* [1987] 1 AC 625, 702–703 (Lord Bridge of Harwich).

28 *Cooper v Board of Works for the Wandsworth District* (1863) 14 CB(NS) 190, 194 (Byles J).

29 *R v Secretary of State for the Home Department, ex parte Doody* [1994] 1 AC 531, 560 (Lord Mustill).

30 Ibid.

31 *R (BAPIO Action Limited) v Secretary of State for the Home Department* [2007] EWCA Civ 1139.

32 *R v Higher Education Funding Council, ex parte Institute of Dental Surgery* [1994] 1 WLR 242.

33 *Re Poyser and Mills' Arbitration* [1964] 2 QB 467, 478 (Megaw J); *South Bucks District Council v Porter* [2004] 1 WLR 1953.

The importance of timely decisions is widely recognised; the phrase 'justice delayed is justice denied' derives from Magna Carta (1215). Yet, in general terms, there is no legal requirement for an administrative decision within a reasonable time. Timeliness is often viewed more as a matter of quality service standards. Government departments often have specific targets, for instance, that a certain percentage of decisions will be taken within a certain timeframe. But, such targets are not legally binding. There are specific legal provisions concerning the timeliness of decisions in some contexts. For instance, if the Home Office cannot decide an asylum application within six months, then it must either inform the applicant of the delay or notify the applicant of the anticipated timeframe for a decision, but this does not oblige the Home Office to take a decision within the stipulated time-frame.[34] However, government departments are reluctant to be legally bound by time-limits. For instance, when the Department for Work and Pensions (DWP) introduced a mandatory reconsideration process to review initial negative decisions, it refused to introduce a time limit. At the same time, following concerns about the absence of a time limit for DWP decision makers to respond to social security appeals, a time limit of 28 days was introduced in 2014.[35]

The courts have, in general, been reluctant to tie down public bodies to make decisions within specific timeframes. Many challenges against delay have arisen in the immigration context and the cases tend to be fact-specific. The courts have held that if someone has established the right to some benefit of significance, such as refugee status, and all that is required is its formal grant, then the public body must confer that benefit without unreasonable delay.[36] The resources available to the authority will be part of the circumstances which can be taken into account when determining whether the delay is reasonable. On the other hand, in the context of the Home Office's legacy programme of clearing an enormous backlog of undecided asylum cases, the courts have ruled that claims based on delay are unlikely, save in very exceptional circumstances, to succeed. Unreasonable administrative delay is unlawful.[37] The courts have also held that delay may be a factor when assessing whether the removal of a foreign national would breach the right to family life.[38] The general position is that administrative delay does not by itself comprise illegality, but it will be maladministration (and therefore amenable to the jurisdiction of ombudsmen). The court's proper sphere is illegality, not maladministration.

4 Institutional perspective

We now consider the institutional framework for the effective legal protection. This comprises: courts; tribunals; and ombudsmen (see Table 18.1).

34 Immigration Rules, r.333A.

35 Administrative Justice and Tribunals Council, *Time For Action* (2011).

36 *R v Secretary of State for the Home Department, ex parte Mersin* [2000] INLR 511.

37 *R (FH; K; A; V; H; SW; HH; AM; SI & ZW) v Secretary of State for the Home Department* [2007] EWHC 1571 (Admin).

38 *EB (Kosovo) v Secretary of State for the Home Department* [2008] UKHL 41.

Table 18.1 Administrative Law processes for challenging administrative decisions

Administrative Law Mechanism	*Institution*	*Legal basis*	*Function*	*Procedure*	*Technique*	*Remedy*
Judicial Review	Administrative Court and the Upper Tribunal	Inherent common law jurisdiction	To review the legality of administrative decisions	JR procedure in Part 54 Civil Procedure Rules	Adversarial	Discretionary public law remedy
Appeals	Tribunals	Statute	To determine merits appeals on issues of both fact and law	Appeal directly to Tribunal or via public authority; specialised procedural rules	Adversarial/ Inquisitorial/ Enabling	Allow or dismiss appeal
Complaints and investigations	Ombudsmen and other complaint-handling bodies	Statute	To investigate complaints of maladministration against public authorities	Complain either via a Member of Parliament or directly to the ombudsman	Investigative	Recommendation and compensation

Judicial review claims are heard by the Administrative Court to determine the legality of administrative decisions. The court has an inherent common law jurisdiction (meaning that it is not provided by statute) which is limited to reviewing the legality of administrative decisions, not primary legislation. Broadly speaking, the courts can review government decisions on the following grounds: legality; irrationality; and procedural fairness. The general principles of judicial review also encompass many other principles such as: legitimate expectations; proportionality; taking account of relevant considerations and excluding irrelevant considerations; the principle that public power must not be exercised for an improper purpose; and the principle against the fettering of administrative discretion. The courts also have a jurisdiction to review the legality of regulations and secondary legislation. The courts often adopt a pragmatic approach. As one judge once explained, 'the ultimate question would, as always, be whether something had gone wrong of a nature and degree which required the intervention of the court and, if so, what form that intervention should take'.[39] If something appears to have gone wrong, then the judge searches for a legal hook to hang it on.[40]

Claimants for judicial review must first apply to the court for permission to proceed, that is, they must show that they have an arguable case. Many judicial review claims are filtered out at this stage (see Figure 18.1). Those challenges given permission can then proceed to a substantive hearing to determine whether the impugned decision was unlawful. An important recent development has been the regionalisation of the Administrative Court. The Administrative Court has long been based centrally in London, but in 2009 regional centres were established to improve access to public

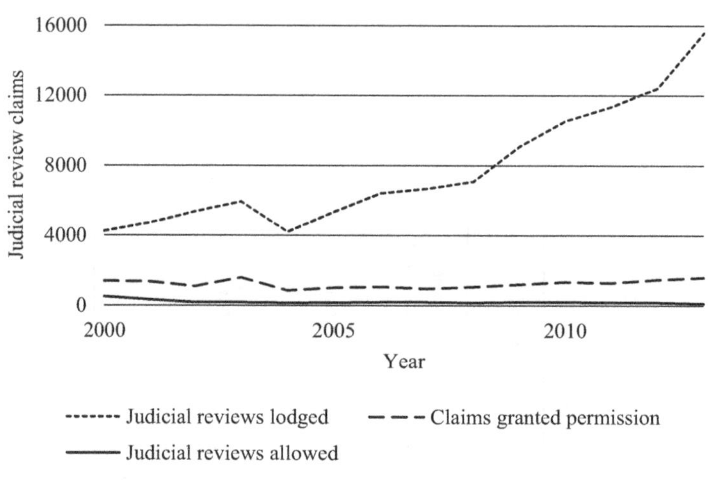

Figure 18.1 Judicial review claims

39 *R v Take-over Panel, ex parte Guinness plc* [1990] 1 QB 146, 160C (Lord Donaldson MR).

40 Lord Carnwath, 'From Judicial Outrage to Sliding Scales – Where Next For Wednesbury?' (ALBA Annual Lecture, 12 November 2013) (available at http://supremecourt.uk/docs/speech-131112-lord-carnwath.pdf) accessed 15 June 2015.

law redress by enabling people to bring their cases locally.[41] The Upper Tribunal also decides judicial review claims in certain areas, such as immigration.

Secondly, there are tribunals. Whereas judicial review focuses upon the legality of decisions, tribunals determine substantive appeals. An individual who has made an application to a public body, for instance, for a welfare benefit or immigration status, can appeal against a decision to the relevant tribunal.[42] Tribunals operate in many areas of government, such as: social security; immigration; tax; mental health; education; transport; and information rights. First instance tribunals are concerned with fact-finding. They are more informal and less legalistic than the courts. For instance, tribunals tend to adopt an inquisitorial procedure – unlike the more adversarial procedure adopted by the higher courts. This increases the ability of tribunals to provide effective legal protection. Appeal rights are statutory and can therefore be created or withdrawn in accordance with government policy. For instance, the current UK government wishes to save money by reducing immigration appeal rights. In the absence of an appeal right, an individual may seek judicial review. Nonetheless, the courts have repeatedly emphasised the importance of tribunals: 'In this day and age a right of access to a Tribunal or other adjudicative mechanism established by the state is just as important and fundamental as a right of access to the courts.'[43]

Tribunals have become increasingly important for a number of reasons. They now comprise the principal means for challenging governmental decisions. The number of appeals determined by tribunals far exceeds that of the courts (Figures 18.2 and 18.3). The previously disparate and unsystematic tribunals 'system' was reformed in 2007: existing tribunals were brought together into two generic tribunals: the First-tier Tribunal (which determines first instance fact-based appeals) and the Upper Tribunal (which determine onward challenges from decisions of the First-tier Tribunal)

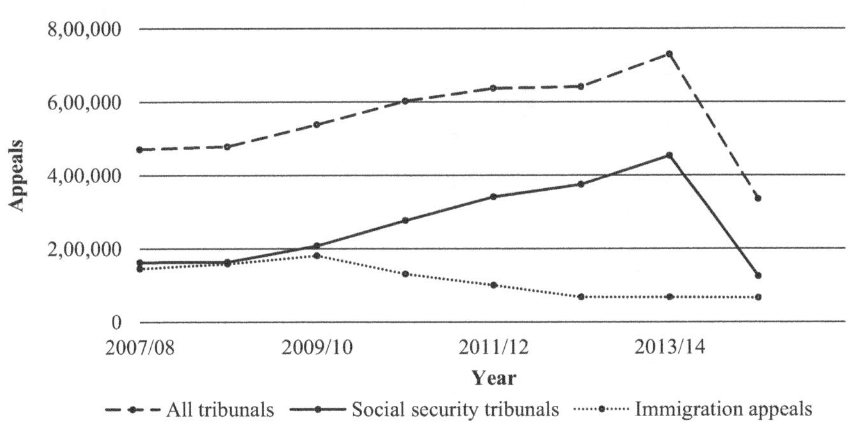

Figure 18.2 Appeals disposed by tribunals

41 S. Nason and M. Sunkin, 'The Regionalisation of Judicial Review: Constitutional Authority, Access to Justice and Specialisation of Legal Services in Public Law' (2013) 76 *Modern Law Review* 223.

42 R. Thomas, *Administrative Justice and Asylum Appeals: A Study of Tribunal Adjudication* (Oxford: Hart Publishing 2011).

43 *Saleem v Secretary of State for the Home Department* [2000] Imm AR 529, 544 (Hale LJ).

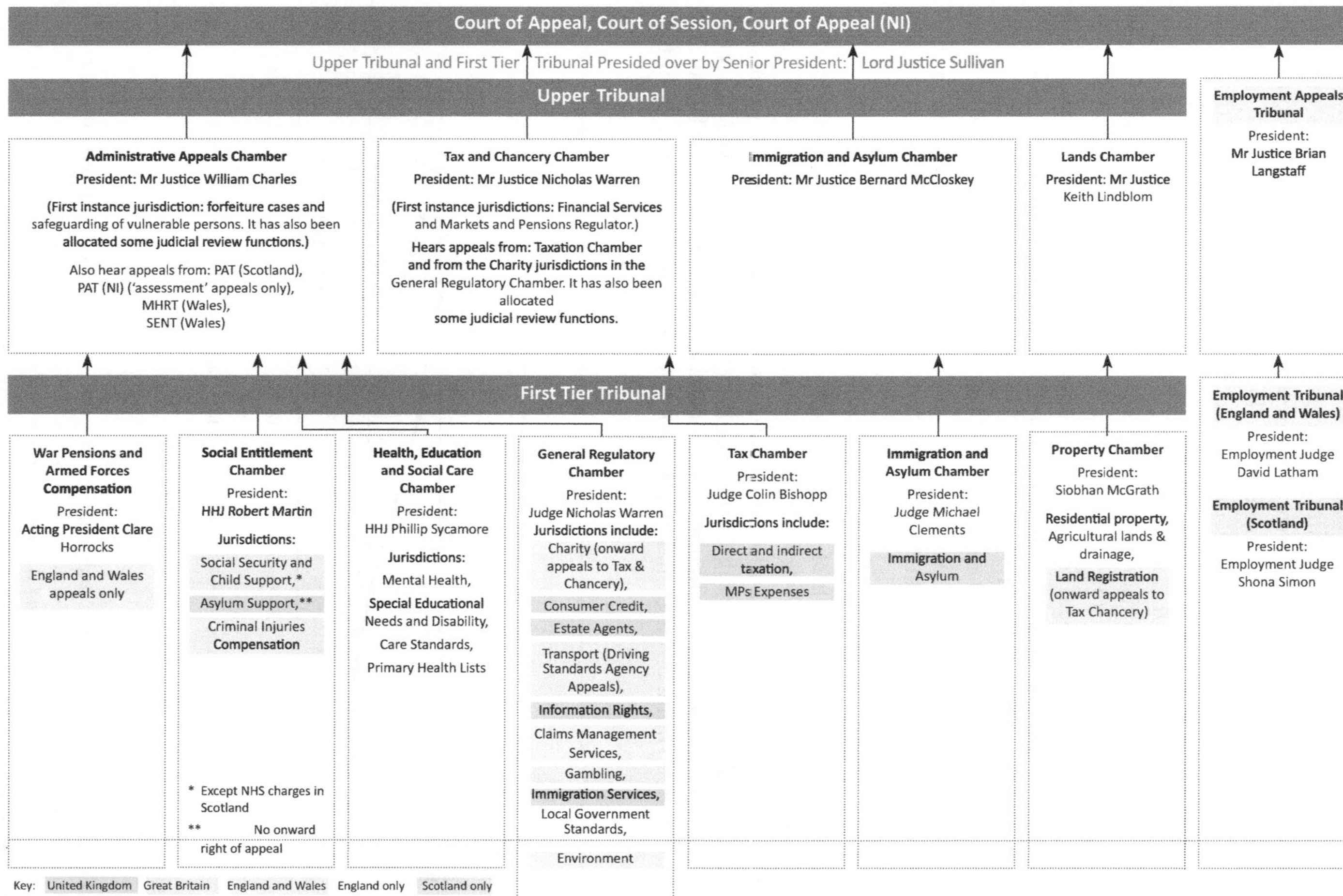

Figure 18.3 The tribunal structure in the United Kingdom

on a point of law.[44] Both of these tribunals are divided into chambers, such as the Immigration and Asylum Chamber. The Upper Tribunal is a specialist and expert body of equivalent standing to the High Court. It is expected that the Upper Tribunal will take a lead by producing guidance on key important issues and the higher courts will, in general, respect its decisions. Also, responsibility for some types of judicial reviews has been transferred from the Administrative Court to the Upper Tribunal. In 2013, most immigration and asylum judicial review cases were transferred to the Upper Tribunal (Immigration and Asylum Chamber) to relieve the pressure on the Administrative Court.

Thirdly, there are complaint systems and ombudsmen. All public authorities will have some complaints processes. Complaints can also be made to Members of Parliament who will then take the matter up with the relevant government department. In some contexts, a complaint dissatisfied with the response from the public authority, can then pursue the matter to an independent complaint handling body. For instance, the Adjudicator's Office investigates complaints from individuals and businesses unhappy about the handling of their complaints by HM Revenue & Customs. A number of ombudsmen schemes have also been created to investigate complaints. The principal ombudsman schemes in the UK are: the Parliamentary and Health Service Ombudsman (PHSO), which investigates complaints against central government; the Local Government Ombudsman; and the public services ombudsmen for Wales, Scotland, and Northern Ireland. Ombudsmen have proliferated over recent years and there are now a considerable number of such schemes.

The jurisdiction of ombudsmen is one of maladministration not legality. The Ombudsman's *Principles of Good Administration* indicate the standards expected of public bodies: getting it right; being customer focused; being open and accountable; acting fairly and proportionately; putting things right; and seeking continuous improvement. Ombudsmen can intervene if there is injustice to an individual in consequence by maladministration. Remedies will normally include recommendations to improve for the future and learn lessons as well as compensation to an individual who has sustained injustice. Ombudsmen recommendations are not legally enforceable, but they are almost always followed by government.

5 The limits on effective legal protection

Each of these institutions faces challenges in seeking to provide effective protection to individuals against the state. These challenges arise from a number of issues, including: resources; political reasons; the inherent design of the legal institutions; and the relationships between different institutions. We will consider each institution in turn.

Judicial review has expanded since the 1960s in response to the growth of administrative power and the judicial recognition that political forms of accountability were largely ineffective in terms of providing legal protection. The courts have also expanded their jurisdiction over areas of government that were previously 'no-go' areas. For instance, before the 1970s areas of government activity, such as prisons, immigration and asylum, and the armed forces were largely exempt from any judicial

44 Tribunals, Courts and Enforcement Act 2007. See further M. Elliott and R. Thomas, *Public Law* (Oxford: Oxford University Press, 2nd edn., 2014), 330–9.

scrutiny at all, yet gradually, the courts have opened up such areas to scrutiny. This has had the effect of exposing such areas of government to legal control.

At the same time, the expansion of judicial review has been accompanied by the need to limit access to the Administrative Court. The court itself has various mechanisms for regulating its own jurisdiction. An individual can only pursue judicial review if given permission to proceed by the court itself. Furthermore, before seeking judicial review, claimants must have exhausted other reasonably available means of seeking redress. The principle of exhausting alternative remedies is justified on two grounds: if Parliament has provided a statutory appellate scheme, then the courts should not usurp its functions; and, secondly, it is normally in the public interest that the judicial review jurisdiction should be exercised speedily and, given the constraints imposed by limited judicial resources, this necessarily involves limiting the number of cases given permission to proceed to judicial review.[45]

The need to use limited judicial resources effectively also underlies the relationship between the High Court and the Upper Tribunal. For many years, tribunals were seen as inferior jurisdictions to be closely supervised by the High Court. In operation since 2008, the Upper Tribunal, a superior court of record, has a status at least as equivalent to that of the High Court. The question has, then, arisen whether the Upper Tribunal (more precisely, the Upper Tribunal's refusal of permission to appeal) is itself subject to judicial review. The Supreme Court's answer in *Cart* was that the Upper Tribunal could be subject to judicial review, but only if the case raised an important point of principle or practice or there were other compelling reasons.[46] Unrestricted judicial review of non-appealable decisions of the Upper Tribunal was neither proportionate nor necessary for maintaining the rule of law given the Upper Tribunal's status and limited judicial resources.[47] The use of resources must be proportionate to the significance of the case and the previous opportunities for challenge. The courts are, therefore, willing to recognise the importance of limited resources upon effective legal protection, but they prefer to retain ownership of such decisions.

Over recent years, the Government has sought to limit access to judicial review.[48] The Government's case was that judicial review has been used too much as a political campaigning tool by pressure groups and by lawyers seeking to exploit the legal aid system.[49] Furthermore, judicial review has been used to delay major infrastructure projects. Although the Government's case was couched in the language of seeking to manage judicial review and to limit the court's jurisdiction to its proper role, it is apparent that it was a thinly-veiled attempt to constrain judicial review.

45 *R v Panel on Takovers and Mergers, ex parte Guinness plc* [1990] 1 QB 146, 177 (Lord Donaldson MR).

46 *R (Cart) v Upper Tribunal* [2001] UKSC 28.

47 See *R (Cart) v Upper Tribunal* [2001] UKSC 28, [100] (Lord Simon Brown).

48 Ministry of Justice, *Judicial Review: Proposals for Further Reform* (Cm 8703, 2013); Criminal Justice and Courts Bill 2014.

49 Chris Grayling, 'The Judicial Review System is Not a Promotional Tool for Countless Left-wing Campaigners' *The Daily Mail*, 6 September 2013 (available at http://www.dailymail.co.uk/news/article-2413135/CHRIS-GRAYLING-Judicial-review-promotional-tool-Left-wing-campaigners.html) accessed 15 June 2015 and Chris Grayling, 'We Must Stop the Legal Aid Abusers Tarnishing Britain's Justice System' *The Daily Telegraph* 20 April 2014 (available at http://www.telegraph.co.uk/news/uknews/law-and-order/10777503/Chris-Grayling-We-must-stop-the-legal-aid-abusers-tarnishing-Britains-justice-system.html) accessed 15 June 2015.

The Government's proposals to limit judicial review included the following: (1) introducing a 'no difference' principle: the courts would have to refuse judicial review where it would be 'highly likely' the outcome of the decision would not have been substantially different if the public authority's conduct complained of had not occurred; (2) restricting legal aid for judicial review claims, so that judicial review challenges would not normally receive legal aid funding unless the case was sufficiently meritorious to justify payment; (3) making third parties who intervene in judicial review cases pay their own costs; and (4) capping protective cost orders, which limit the costs exposure of a party where the legal issues raised are of general public importance. The Government's initial proposals would have restricted the rules governing standing to bring judicial review claims, so that challenges by non-governmental organisations would have been prohibited. The Government's concern was that the courts' wide approach to standing has tipped the balance too far, allowing judicial review to be used to seek publicity or otherwise to hinder the process of proper decision making, but this proposal was abandoned following criticism from the judiciary.[50]

These proposals prompted vigorous opposition and criticism from the legal profession, the judiciary and Parliament. Parliament's Joint Committee on Human Rights recognised that the Government has a legitimate interest in ensuring judicial review is not abused, but was highly critical of all of the Government's proposed reforms.[51] The Committee concluded that there was a poor evidence basis for the reforms and that they would limit effective legal protection. The Committee's view was that a 'no difference' principle would give rise to the risk of unlawful administrative action going unremedied and therefore risks incompatibility with the right of practical and effective access to court. The Committee also expressed concern that the reforms would significantly deter interventions in judicial review and that restricting the availability of costs capping orders to cases in which permission to proceed has already been granted by the court would be too great a restriction that would undermine effective access to justice. However, most of the Government's proposals were enacted into legislation in 2015.[52]

Another recent reform that has generated considerable concern was the withdrawal of legal aid for judicial review cases unless either the case has been given permission to proceed by the court or if the Lord Chancellor considers the case to qualify for legal aid.[53] Concerns have been raised that the likely substantial reduction in the number of providers willing to provide public law assistance in legally aided cases will have a substantially detrimental effect on access to justice, legal protection, and legal accountability of government.[54] The courts have though struck down part of this policy as unlawful.[55]

50 See Lady Hale, 'Who Guards the Guardians?' Speech given at the Public Law Project Conference 2013 (available at http://supremecourt.uk/docs/speech-131014.pdf) accessed 15 June 2015.

51 Joint Committee on Human Rights, *The implications for access to justice of the Government's proposals to reform judicial review* (HL 174 HC 868 2013–14).

52 Criminal Justice and Courts Act 2015, ss 84–90.

53 The Civil Legal Aid (Remuneration) (Amendment) (No. 3) Regulations SI 2014/607.

54 Justice, *Briefing note on the Civil Legal Aid (Remuneration) (Amendment) (No 3) Regulations* (2014) (available at http://www.justice.org.uk/data/files/resources/370/JUSTICE-Judicial-Review-Legal-Aid-Regulations-Briefing-March-2014.pdf) accessed 15 June 2015.

55 *R (Ben Hoare Bell) v Lord Chancellor* [2015] EWHC Admin 523.

Similar themes arise in relation to tribunals. The courts have emphasised that access to tribunals is as fundamental as access to the courts themselves and have acted to protect access to tribunals. For instance, in *FP (Iran)*, the Court of Appeal struck down a procedural rule which stated that the immigration tribunal had to hear an appeal in a party's absence.[56] The applicant had not been informed of the date of the appeal hearing by his representative and so had, not through his own fault, lost out on the opportunity to be heard in his appeal; the court therefore held that the rule was productive of irremediable unfairness.

There are, though, a number of ways through which the effective legal protection provided by tribunals has been weakened. Appeal rights are statutory and therefore it is always open to Parliament, at the behest of the government, to amend or withdraw appeal rights. In practice, government that exerts considerable influence in this regard. While some appeal rights, such as those in the social security context, are well-established, appeal rights in other areas have been repeatedly reformed and amended. For instance, appeals against a child's exclusion from school have been downgraded to a review process applying the principles of judicial review to be operated by non-legally trained panel members. Concerns have been raised about the ability of non-legal members to apply the principles of judicial review. Furthermore, the review panels cannot order a child's reinstatement at school, but only direct the school to reconsider the exclusion.[57] Similarly, immigration appeals have recently been significantly reduced.[58] This was opposed by a Parliamentary committee on the basis that the significant limitation of appeal rights is incompatible with the common law right of access to a court or tribunal in relation to unlawful decisions, and the right to an effective remedy. Nonetheless, the Government largely controls the legislative process. Individuals who could previously appeal will now have to seek judicial review.

Another concern has been that the trend toward internal administrative reconsideration of initial decisions in high-volume jurisdictions (such as social security and immigration) either before tribunal appeals or as a substitute may operate to the disadvantage of individuals seeking to challenge decisions. In the social security context, mandatory reconsideration has been interposed between initial decision making and access to tribunals. Benefit claimants refused initially can no longer access the tribunal directly; they must first apply for mandatory reconsideration. This is not necessarily objectionable: internally reviewing disputed decisions can be quicker and cheaper than going direct to a tribunal. At the same time, there is a risk that a system of mandatory reconsideration may operate as a barrier – especially for vulnerable people who may find the system difficult to navigate. The concern is that claimants with winnable cases may be deterred by mandatory reconsideration from reaching the tribunal that might overturn initial decision. Similarly, in the immigration context, the disparity in success rates between tribunal appeals (44%) and administrative review (20%) casts doubt upon the latter as a means of effective legal protection.

56 *FP (Iran) v Secretary of State for the Home Department* [2007] EWCA Civ 13.

57 Education Act 2011.

58 Immigration Act 2014.

Reductions in publicly funded legal advice and representation (legal aid) have also weakened effective legal protection provided by tribunals. Legal aid has, to some extent, been available for different tribunals for many years. For instance, advice and assistance was available for social security appellants whereas users of immigration appeals could access legal aid depending on a financial means test. It was often argued that legal representation significantly enhanced an individual's ability to succeed in their appeal, but the Government has always resisted any extension of the limited legal aid available. That was the position until 2012. However, determined to cut public spending, the Government withdrew almost all legal provision for challenges against administrative decisions.[59] Publicly funded advice and assistance for social security appellants was cut altogether – as was legal aid for immigration appeals (except bail and asylum cases). These measures were introduced amongst much opposition from the legal profession and campaigning groups on the basis that it would significantly reduce the ability of people to secure justice before tribunals. It remains to be seen what effect the legal aid changes have on tribunals. The risk is that people with unmeritorious cases may proceed nonetheless and people with arguable cases may not proceed (good advice can filter out hopeless cases and encourage people with strong cases to appeal).

Ombudsmen are generally considered to be a useful mechanism of investigating complaints, promoting the principles of good administration, and identifying deficiencies in government and doing so in a way that avoids the cost, formality, and legalism of the courts. Nonetheless, despite their positive aspects, ombudsmen face challenges in providing effective protection. In 2014, the House of Commons Public Administration Select Committee (PASC) highlighted the concern that there is a 'toxic cocktail' in respect of complaints handling – a combination of a reluctance on the part of citizens 'to express their concerns or complaints' and a defensiveness on the part of services 'to hear and address concerns' – which can undermine efforts to deliver excellent public services.[60] An effective ombudsman service can help to address this, but change is urgently needed if ombudsmen are to deliver a more effective service that is responsive and proactive. A range of concerns relate to their accessibility; for instance, the requirement for a complaint to be referred by an individual's Member of Parliament to the Parliamentary Ombudsman has been a longstanding issue. The Ombudsman can only investigate if there is a specific complaint; it lacks the ability to seize the initiative for itself by undertaking 'own-initiative' investigations. The Ombudsman could also be a more high profile body and its accountability and oversight should be enhanced. More generally, the PASC concluded that the Parliamentary Ombudsman, established in 1967, is impeded by out-of-date legislation so it fails to meet the expectations of today's citizens; it is in danger of become 'stuck in time'. New legislation is required for a modernised ombudsman service. The goal is that of simplifying the complaints maze and the fragmented ombudsmen system by creating a unified public services ombudsman. The current Government has pledged to reform the Parliamentary Ombudsman.

59 Legal Aid, Sentencing and Punishment of Offenders Act 2012.

60 House of Commons Public Administration Select Committee, *Time for a People's Ombudsman Service* (HC 655 2013–14).

6 European perspectives

European law – both EU and ECHR – are part of UK law and a major influence. Before the Human Rights Act (HRA) 1998, the UK courts recognised the need to interpret domestic law in line with the ECHR. The HRA was enacted to give further effect to Convention rights in domestic law and there is an immense body of case law and literature on the impact of the HRA. At the same time, both the terms of EU membership and the place of the ECHR in domestic law can be highly politically contentious issues. There are particular historical and geographical reasons why the British people can be sceptical of pan-European bodies, such as the European Court of Human Rights. Political opinion ranges from those who support the status quo to those who would like to withdraw from both the EU and the ECHR.

On the impact of EU membership on effective legal protection, a few key points can be highlighted. First, the UK courts have long accepted that the supremacy of EU law qualifies the constitutional doctrine of parliamentary sovereignty. In other words, when Parliament enacted the European Communities Act 1972, it achieved what had previously been considered impossible: Parliament bound its successors.[61] This important qualification of the fundamental constitutional doctrine has been cited as a precedent which shows that the general doctrine of parliamentary sovereignty is being qualified and that it may have other qualifications unrelated to the EU membership.[62] To the extent that EU membership entails judicially enforceable limits on Parliament's freedom to make law, it also contributes to the wider shift of questioning the appropriateness of an absolute doctrine of sovereignty. Secondly, with EU membership all of the legal doctrines and rights are enforceable in the UK courts. Furthermore, EU membership has exerted a 'spillover' effect whereby European concepts of legal protection – such as legitimate expectations and proportionality – have been increasingly developed and assimilated into domestic law.[63]

The Human Rights Act 1998 was enacted to give further effect to the ECHR in domestic law and to 'bring rights home' by making them enforceable in the domestic courts. A key provision states that public authorities cannot act in a way that is incompatible with Convention rights.[64] Another important provision requires the courts, so far as it is possible to do so, to read and give effect to primary and subordinate legislation in a way which is compatible with the Convention rights.[65] If the courts cannot interpret legislation in accordance with the ECHR, then it may issue a declaration of incompatibility against the relevant Act.[66] Such a declaration does not invalidate the legislation, but it highlights the incompatibility and the Government will virtually always amend the relevant Act to bring it into line with the ECHR. The courts and tribunals must now therefore give effect to Convention rights under the Human Rights Act 1998 and there have been many cases involving human rights challenges. A prominent case involved the terrorism legislation enacted after 9/11, which allowed the government to define suspected foreign terrorists without trial. The House of Lords

61 *R v Secretary of State for Transport, ex parte Factortame (No 2)* [1991] 1 AC 603.

62 Elliott and Thomas (n. 44) 330–339.

63 R. Thomas, *Legitimate Expectations and Proportionality in Administrative Law* (Oxford: Hart Publishing 2000).

64 Human Rights Act 1998, s 6(1).

65 Ibid. s 3(1).

66 Ibid. s 4.

declared the legislation incompatible with human rights law on the basis that it discriminated between foreign and UK nationals and disproportionately infringed the right to liberty (Art. 5, ECHR). Despite the intensely political nature of the law, the Government accepted the judgment and amended the law accordingly.[67]

The HRA has had a major impact as regards judicial enforcement. The courts have had to take a far more intensive scrutiny of public decisions that has previously been the case. The domestic standard of substantive review – *Wednesbury* unreasonableness – requires the courts to inquire whether or not an administrative decision is completely unreasonable or outrageously defies logic or accepted moral standards. Before the HRA, the courts did adopt a slightly more intensive scrutiny to public decisions affecting human rights; they recognised the need to engage in anxious or heightened scrutiny.[68] However, even this approach is inapplicable in human rights challenges. Instead, the courts must apply the doctrine of proportionality to provide an effective remedy for protecting Convention rights. The European Court of Human Rights in *Smith and Grady* made it clear that the domestic test of unreasonableness effectively excluded any consideration of whether the interference with the applicants' rights answered a pressing social need or was proportionate to the aims being pursued.[69] The House of Lords subsequently accepted that proportionality was the applicable test in human rights cases.[70]

This has resulted in a bifurcated judicial review jurisdiction. The principle of proportionality is, technically at least, not recognised under ordinary domestic judicial review; the traditional ground of review, *Wednesbury* unreasonableness, requires the court to adopt a less intensive scrutiny by asking whether the decision was so unreasonable that no reasonable decision maker could ever have arrived at it.[71] Yet, proportionality must be applied in the context of human rights challenges to ensure that the applicant is afforded an effective remedy.[72] Under the Human Rights Act 1998, the court's role is one of merits review by deciding for itself whether the decision was in accordance with Convention rights.[73] By contrast, the role of the courts at common law is 'often more about process than merits'.[74] There are some underlying similarities.[75] However, the courts have stressed that in the context of fundamental rights, the scrutiny is likely to be more intense than where other interests are involved. Furthermore, the advantage of proportionality is that it introduces an

67 *A v Secretary of State for the Home Department* [2005] 2 AC 68; Prevention of Terrorism Act 2005.

68 *R v Secretary of State for the Home Department, ex parte Bugdaycay* [1987] AC 514, 531 (Lord Bridge). See also *R v Ministry of Defence, Ex p Smith* [1996] QB 517, 554 (Lord Bingham MR): 'The more substantial the interference with human rights, the more the court will require by way of justification before it is satisfied that the decision is reasonable.'

69 *Smith and Grady v United Kingdom* (1999) 29 EHRR 493.

70 *R (Daly) v Secretary of State for the Home Department* [2001] 1 AC 532.

71 *Associated Provincial Pictures Houses Ltd v Wednesbury Corporation* [1948] 1 KB 223.

72 *Smith and Grady v United Kingdom* (1999) 29 EHRR 493; *R (Daly) v Secretary of State for the Home Department* [2001] 1 AC 532.

73 *Huang v Secretary of State for Home Department* [2007] UKHL 11; [2007] 2 AC 167 [11] (Lord Bingham).

74 *Kennedy v Charity Commission* [2014] UKSC 20 [245] (Lord Carnwath).

75 In *R v Ministry of Agriculture, Fisheries and Food, ex parte First City Trading* [1997] 1 CMLR 250, 278–279 Laws J noted that '*Wednesbury* and European review are two different models – one looser, one tighter – of the same juridical concept, which is the imposition of compulsory standards on decision makers so as to secure the repudiation of arbitrary power.'

element of structure into the exercise, by directing attention to factors such as suitability or appropriateness, necessity and the balance or imbalance of benefits and disadvantages.[76]

Standing back from the case law for a moment, the wider political picture is that the place of the ECHR in UK law is a highly controversial issue. The ECHR and human rights have often received inappropriately unfavourable media coverage, much of which is ill-informed. It is ironic that government ministers in the Labour Government which introduced the HRA (1997–2010) also occasionally criticised the courts for their decisions applying the HRA. Some would like to abolish the Human Rights Act altogether. In 2013, two senior Conservative Ministers (the Home Secretary and the Secretary of State for Justice) pledged to repeal the HRA.[77] In response, the president of the European Court of Human Rights (ECtHR) has warned that it would be a 'political disaster' for the UK to withdraw from the ECHR.[78] Another view, expressed by the former Lord Chief Justice, is that the ECtHR has exceeded its limits as an unelected court. While supporting the European Convention on Human Rights, Lord Judge's view is that the court, as an unelected body, has over-reached itself in attempting to dictate rather than influence the social legislation of Member States and that this raises serious questions of sovereignty.[79] The prevalent attitude in the UK is that no court – however distinguished its judges may be – should arrogate to itself the power to overrule the decisions of an elected legislature. The Conservative Government elected in 2015 pledged to replace the Human Rights Act with a British Bill of Rights and to limit the role of the European Court of Human Rights.

Whatever happens, the courts have, in the meantime, been preparing the ground for a possible post-HRA scenario by emphasising the importance and vigour of common law protections for fundamental rights and by viewing the common law as the primary springboard in human rights cases rather than the ECHR. A number of recent cases from the UK Supreme Court over the last year have placed particular and renewed emphasis on the common law as a source of fundamental constitutional values and rights. The courts have noted that while the Human Rights Act 1998 is of unquestionable importance, it does not supersede the protection of human rights under the common law or statute law. Human rights continue to be protected under domestic law. The values underlying both the Convention and the domestic constitution should be protected by a detailed body of domestic law.[80] For instance, in *Daly* a policy that prisoners be excluded from their cells during searches was unlawful when applied to a prisoner who had legal correspondence in his cell because of the prisoner's common law right of legal confidentiality: the same result was required by both Art. 8 ECHR and the common law. According to a Court of Appeal judge,

76 *Kennedy v Charity Commission* [2014] UKSC 20, [54] (Lord Reed).

77 May, Theresa, Speech at the Conservative Party Conference September 2013 (available at http://www.conservativepartyconference.org.uk/Speeches/2013_Theresa_May.aspx) accessed 15 June 2015. See also 'Theresa May: Tories to Consider Leaving European Convention on Human Rights' BBC News 9 March 2013 (available at http://www.bbc.co.uk/news/uk-politics-21726612) accessed 15 June 2015.

78 'Human Rights Row: UK Quitting Would Be Disaster – ECHR Head' BBC News 14 January 2014 (available at http://www.bbc.co.uk/news/uk-politics-25726319) accessed 15 June 2015.

79 'European Court of Human Rights "risk to UK sovereignty"' BBC News 28 December 2013 (available at http://www.bbc.co.uk/news/uk-politics-25535327) accessed 15 June 2015.

80 *Osborn v Parole Board* [2013] UKSC 61 [56]–[57] (Lord Reed).

'[t]he development of the common law did not come to an end on the passing of the Human Rights Act 1998. It is in vigorous health and flourishing in many parts of the world which share a common legal tradition.'[81]

Such decisions are clearly part of a concerted judicial policy to limit the possible adverse consequence of any attempt to repeal the Human Rights Act 1998. If the Act were repealed, then the effects may be much less than anticipated by the proponents of such reforms. This is because the common law – including rights derived from the ECHR but absorbed into the common law – would remain even in the event of HRA repeal/ECHR withdrawal and the common law remains a vigorous source of law capable of being developed incrementally by the courts in accordance with the needs of society and to enable them to perform their constitutional function of maintaining the rule of law.

7 Conclusion

Legal protection is a long-established principle in the UK. Traditionally, the foremost purpose of the courts has been the need to protect the liberty of individuals against the state. Over the last century or so, the scope of modern government has increased the range of ways in which individuals interact with government. This has prompted the development of a range of remedies to ensure legal protection of the individual. Given the absence of a civilian tradition of administrative law and the domestic constitutional doctrines of parliamentary sovereignty and the rule of law, the UK has developed its own system of administrative law on an incremental and *ad hoc* basis based upon the three principal mechanisms: judicial review; tribunal appeals; and ombudsmen investigations. This has been a collective endeavour with the judiciary, legislature, and executive all recognising the importance of legal protection. Over recent years, this overall system has been enhanced: the tribunal system has been brought together into a coherent system; judicial review has expanded and the courts have emphasised the right of access to the courts as a fundamental constitutional principle; and the profile of ombudsmen has been raised. Despite the strengths of this system, there are weaknesses and shortcomings, some of which arise from poor institutional design, others from the current fiscal climate, and others would appear to be politically motivated attempts by the executive to reduce legal protection. So, the administrative justice still seems to be fragmented and incoherent in part; the ombudsmen system is 'stuck in time' and its effectiveness could be enhanced; legal aid provision has been restricted and tribunal appeal rights have been reduced. In 2015, the Government has sought to reduce the role of judicial review and plans to repeal the Human Rights Act 1998. This indicates that the idea of the political constitution, with its emphasis upon political rather than legal accountability, has deep roots in the UK. On the other hand, it is unlikely that there can be a return to the past. Judicial review has grown and human rights have become embedded in the common law. The need for effective legal protection will remain. A government can introduce limits to effective legal protection, but cannot abolish it altogether.

81 *R (Guardian News and Media Ltd) v City of Westminster Magistrates' Courts (Article 19 intervening)* [2013] QB 618, [88] (Toulson LJ).

Part III

Comparative studies

19 The principle of effective legal protection in international and European law – comparative report

Konrad Lachmayer

1 Effective legal protection as a European principle

1.2 The two faces of the principle of effective legal protection in Europe

While national constitutions do not explicitly refer to the principle of effective legal protection, European Law mentions it in their core documents: Art. 19 TEU, Art. 47 CFR and Art. 13 ECHR refer to 'effective legal protection' or 'effective remedy' as a principle to be guaranteed by the Member States. Both the Union and the European human rights system request the Member States to guarantee effective legal protection with regard to their European legal obligations. It is necessary to distinguish these European parameters with regard to the Member States from the determination of the European institutions itself. It is common knowledge that the adequate duration of a judicial procedure is part of effective legal protection.

Although the Member States are obliged to provide such procedural guarantees, the ECtHR is struggling to significantly fulfil the requirement of effective legal protection itself. The ECJ is concerned about access to courts in the Member States, but the Court itself is quite difficult to access for individuals and it is also due to the case law of the ECJ that this situation has not changed.[1] There seems to be a discrepancy between the European and domestic levels when it comes to the required standards of effective legal protection. On the one hand, it is necessary to stress that the proper application of effective legal protection on a national level would relieve the transnational level from the need to provide the same intensity of legal protection. The principle of subsidiarity also supports stronger application of effective legal protection on the domestic level. On the other hand, the European Union also directly enforces EU law and is therefore in need of effective legal protection on a European level. It does not serve the principle of effective legal protection to create dual standards.

When it comes to applying effective legal protection principles of the EU and the ECHR, one has to consider the different levels of application. The ECHR is responsible on the domestic level as well as, according to Art. 52 para 3 CFR, in the EU.[2] Arts. 6 and 13 ECHR do not, however, apply to the ECtHR itself. In contrast to this, the

1 See Görisch in this book.

2 See Paul Craig, *The Lisbon Treaty – Law, Politics and Treaty Reform* (Oxford University Press, Oxford 2010) 232–234; David Anderson and Cian C Murphy, 'The Charter of Fundamental Rights' in Andrea Biondi, Piet Eeckhout and Stefanie Ripley (eds.), *EU Law after Lisbon* (Oxford University Press, Oxford 2012) 155, 162–163.

EU principle of effective legal protection in Art. 47 CFR does not only address the Member States but also the institutions of the Union itself.[3] Thus, while the EU and its Member States are bound by the principle of effective legal protection, the ECtHR is itself not bound by this principle. The following matrix applies:

Table 19.1 Interrelations of different European principles of effective legal protection

	ECHR Principle (Art. 6, 13 ECHR)	*EU Principle (Art. 47 CFR)*
Domestic Level	x	x
EU	x	x
ECtHR	–	–

The ECtHR, however, has to consider questions of its own effective legal protection in its case law to ensure its own credibility. The ambivalence of the extreme increase in court cases and the duration of court procedures on the one hand and effective legal protection on the other hand is challenging the possibilities of the ECtHR. Court procedures like the pilot judgment procedure help to find solutions to this dilemma. Moreover, the effectiveness of the ECtHR also depends on the enforcement of the judgments, which is facing problems of the effectiveness of international law in general. The ECtHR has to be understood as a Court between the international law system and the system of the EU. It, remains, however, a court of international law and ultimately depends on the willingness of the Member States to comply with the case law of the court.

1.2 A European principle regarding domestic procedures

The Union and the ECHR system have created a complex system to strengthen effective legal protection in the Member States. Both supra-/international orders have developed procedural standards of legal protection: first and primarily by the dynamics of the case law of the courts and second by additional amendments of and additions to the relevant treaties. The examples of the latter are relevant, though not as important to the overall developments.[4] Protocol No. 7 of the ECHR, for example, introduced further procedural rights, especially the right to appeal in criminal matters, which might also affect criminal procedures in administrative law. The Lisbon Treaty did declare the CFR as obligatory, thus reforming the fundamental rights system of the EU.[5] Art. 47 CFR dispensed with all the restrictions of Art. 6 ECHR and its different scope and concept to Art. 13 ECHR. The result is an impressively comprehensive concept of effective legal protection in Art. 47 ECHR, which applies in the scope of EU law in the Member States.[6]

3 See also Art. 41 CFR; Klara Kanska, 'Towards Administrative Human Rights in the EU: Impact of the Charter of Fundamental Rights' (2004) 10(3) *European Law Journal* 296–326.

4 See Breuer in this book.

5 Paul Craig, *The Lisbon Treaty – Law, Politics and Treaty Reform* (Oxford UniversityPress 2010) 193–245.

6 See Pekka Aalto et al., 'Art. 47 – Right to an Effective Remedy and to a Fair Trial' in Steve Peers, Tamara Hervey, Jeff Kenner and Angela Ward (eds.), *The EU Charter of Fundamental Rights: A Commentary* (Hart Publishing 2014) 1197, 1209–1210.

The case law of the courts, however, has created crucial dynamics to establish important elements of the principle of effective legal protection. Over the decades, the ECJ and the ECtHR have developed – within their own legal framework and regarding their role and function as supra-/international courts in a transnational legal system – a particular approach towards legal protection.[7]

Görisch analyses in his paper how the ECJ developed the principle of effective legal protection in its case law.[8] Starting with the Johnson case,[9] the Court developed several substantive elements of the principle, including the right to access to a court, especially on a domestic level, as well as basic standards of court procedures, including binding effects of judgments, the duration of court procedures, liability claims, etc.[10] The Court granted not only the rights of individuals to gain access to legal protection (by the principle of equivalence and effectiveness),[11] but affected and shaped procedural and institutional settings of certain Member States.

The ECtHR followed a two-fold strategy regarding Art. 6 and Art. 13 ECHR. While Art. 6 ECHR is dominant in the case law of the EctHR,[12] Art. 13 ECHR has also contributed to the overall understanding of effective legal protection in the context of the ECHR.[13] Both Articles, however, include significant restrictions, especially when it comes to administrative law. The ECtHR, however, has tried to overcome certain limitations (e.g regarding the right to an administrative act within a reasonable time). The case law of the Court, moreover, includes the right of access to a court, right to intervention, suspensive effects, execution of national judgments, and locus standi of persons no longer affected or state liability.

In a comparison of the legal starting points of two different courts in Europe (ECJ and ECtHR), the case law shows different characteristics due to the divergent legal basis and reasoning of the courts. While the ECtHR follows a rights-based perspective, the ECJ primarily follows a rule of law-based argumentation with regard to the concept of a 'general principle of EU law'.[14] At least some convergent developments can be identified when it comes to certain procedural standards. As Breuer points out, the ECJ referred explicitly to the ECHR regarding the principle of effective legal protection.[15]

In conclusion, the emerging and increasing scope, intensity and details of the principle of effective legal protection can be traced in the jurisprudence of the European Courts. It had different effects on the domestic developments of legal protection, though these effects were significant, at least in certain jurisdictions.[16] It can

7 See Chapter 3.

8 See Görisch in this book; see also Deok Joo Rhee, 'The Principle of Effective Protection. Reaching Those Parts Other [Principles] Cannot Reach' (2011) 16 *Judicial Review (JR)* 440–457.

9 ECJ, Case 222/84 – *Johnston* [1986] ECR 1651.

10 Anthony Arnull, 'The Principle of Effective Judicial Protection in EU Law: An Unruly Horse?' (2011) 36 *EL Rev* 51–70.

11 See Takis Tridimas, *The General Principles of EU Law* (2nd edn., Oxford University Press, Oxford 2006) 424–427.

12 See B Rainey, E Wicks and C Ovey, *Jacobs, White & Ovey The European Convention on Human Rights* (6th edn., Oxford University Press, Oxford 2014) 278.

13 Ibid. 141.

14 See Tridimas (n. 11).

15 See Breuer in this book; Case 50/00 P *Unión de Pequeños Agricultores v Council* [2002] ECR I-6677, para 39.

16 See Chapter 3.

be assumed that the case law of the two courts will remain dynamic, when upcoming challenges have to be resolved by an adaption of the principle of effective legal protection.[17]

1.3 A European principle regarding European procedures

Besides the relevance of the European principle of effective legal protection for the Member States of the European Union, the other dimension of the principle is directed at the European institutions themselves. While the principle of effective legal protection is not binding for the ECtHR, the Union's institutions are bound by the case law of the ECJ regarding effective legal protection, as well as by the ECHR and the CFR, which again refers back to the ECHR, but also accedes it in its scope of effective legal protection. The ECtHR itself, however, restricted itself with the *Bosphorus* jurisdiction to the further review of EU law. It is thus up to the ECJ to guarantee the principle of effective legal protection according to its own case law, the CFR and the ECHR in the Union.

The discussion of the accessibility of the ECJ itself is also part of the debate of the principle of effective legal protection, as Görisch points out.[18] The significant restrictions – also imposed by the ECJ itself – might be legitimate to a certain extent, as domestic courts primarily guarantee the effectiveness of legal protection in EU law. The limited possibilities to gain legal protection against administrative action of EU agencies or institutions remain relevant.[19] Moreover, the EU Treaties limit the scope of jurisdiction of the ECJ to a certain extent.[20] The application of the principle of effective legal protection, therefore, does not seem to reach the same intensity at the Union level in comparison to the requirements of the ECJ regarding the Member States.[21]

Finally, the ECJ is not entirely opposed to other concepts or principles of EU law to establish effective legal protection when the Court is reviewing EU legislation. In the context of the European Arrest Warrant, the ECJ has limited the possibilities of legal protection due to the principle of mutual recognition.[22] The Court does not only strengthen effective legal protection, therefore. While the Court lays great emphasis on effective legal protection to promote EU legislation in the Member States,[23] it is more reluctant to strengthen effective legal protection, especially in cases in which effective legal protection would interfere with other interests or concepts in the EU legislation.[24]

17 See Chapter 4.

18 See Görisch in this book.

19 But see the possibilities of Art. 277 TFEU.

20 See e.g. Art. 275, 276 TFEU.

21 See in legal comparison to the US in the context of administrative rulemaking, especially regarding the European Commission Alexander H Türk, 'Oversight of Administrative Rulemaking: Judicial Review' (2013) 19(1) *European Law Journal* 126, 142.

22 Anneli Albi, 'Erosion of Constitutional Rights in EU Law: A Call for "Substantive Co-operative Constitutionalism"' (2015) 9 *Vienna Journal on Constitutional Law* 151, 175–176

23 See Alec Stone Sweet, 'The European Court of Justice' in Paul Craig and Gráinne de Búrca (eds.), *The Evolution of EU Law* (2nd edn., Oxford University Press, Oxford 2011) 121, 149–151.

24 Craig, however, characterises the ECJ – in comparison to US and Canadian courts – as a court which is influenced by civil law tradition, which tends to reduce the independence of administration or administrative agencies. See Paul Craig, 'Judicial Review of Questions of Law: A Comparative Perspective'

2 International perspectives on effective legal protection

2.1 Effective legal protection and the international rule of law

Unlike in European Law, the role of the principle of effective legal protection is neither crucial nor central in international law. The traditional paradigm, which is not based on the involvement of individuals, gives states other possibilities for managing conflicts, for example in the context of state responsibility.[25] This does not mean that there are no institutional and procedural possibilities available to claim rights. On the contrary, the ICJ as a starting point shows the possibilities to resolve conflicts in international law using legal procedures. Before approaching questions of effectiveness, the challenges of legal protection have to be addressed. Legal protection in international law is deeply linked to the development of an international rule of law.[26] While it is an ongoing process to strengthen the rule of law in international law and to expand different approaches, these developments are confronted with several setbacks and loopholes.[27]

The dynamics towards an international rule of law, therefore, are not so much linked to the uniform structures of international law[28] as to the decentralised and fragmented[29] character of international law. Different international treaty regimes and international organisations have established, especially in the last 25 years, manifold concepts of legal protection or quasi-court structures. Obviously these developments primarily address inter-state situations. International Economic Law[30] and the role of the WTO dispute settlement bodies can serve as an example.[31]

The role of legal protection in international law can and also must be seen in the context of the increasing role of the individual in international law. Different areas of international law not only address the individual but also integrate individuals formally – at least to a certain extent – in international law.[32]

Two kinds of international involvement of individuals shall be distinguished here: the first group refers to forms of international law which promote rights of individuals against states; the second group includes the cases in which international law

in Susan Rose-Ackerman and Peter L. Lindseth (eds.), *Comparative Administrative Law* (Edward Elgar 2010) 461–462.

25 See Anthony Aust, *Handbook of International Law* (2nd edn., Cambridge University Press, Cambridge 2010) 386–395.

26 See e.g. Jeremy Waldron, 'The Rule of International Law' (2006) 30 *Harvard Journal of Law & Public Policy* 15–30; Simon Chesterman, An International Rule of Law? (2008) 56 *American Journal of Comparative Law* 331–361.

27 See a critical approach in Ugo Mattei and Laura Nader, *Plunder – When the Rule of Law Is Illegal* (Blackwell Publishing 2008).

28 See e.g. the UN Charter or the Vienna Convention of the Law of the Treaties.

29 See Martii Koskenniemi, Fragmentation of International Law: Difficulties Arising from the Diversification and Expansion of International Law, Report of the Study Group of the International Law Commission, 13 April 2006 (available at http://legal.un.org/ilc/documentation/english/a_cn4_l682.pdf).

30 See regarding the interrelation between European courts and the WTO Francis Snyder, *The EU, the WTO and China – Legal Pluralism and International Trade Regulation* (Hart Publishing 2010) 152–208.

31 See Andreas Paulus, 'International Adjunction' in Samantha Besson and John Tasioulas (eds.), *The Philosophy of International Law* (Oxford University Press, Oxford 2010) 207, 214.

32 See Kate Parlett, *The Individual in the International Legal System: Continuity and Change in International Law* (Cambridge Universit Press 2013).

addresses the individual as a threat or at least as a person affected by international law enforcement.

The first field of reference is obviously international human rights protection and all forms of courts which give individuals the possibility to file a complaint against human rights violations by states. The European human rights system is not only the most relevant one,[33] but also a model for other human rights bodies in international law.[34] As it is discussed in this article, the principle of effective legal protection is promoted by the ECtHR regarding proceedings in the Member States; it is, however, only of limited relevance when it comes to the European human rights system itself. Although the European standards of international human rights protection are significant – in comparison to other regional human rights systems – it still remains a challenge to strengthen effective legal protection on a European level.[35] The situation becomes even more problematic with regard to other regional human rights systems and finally ends at the point where other human rights systems do not provide any legal protection for individuals at all. At that point, human rights protection remains within traditional concepts of international law and does not includes individuals. Thus, the legal protection is not guaranteed.

Another example of this first group are bilateral investment treaties (BITs).[36] The protection of transnational investments in international law has developed significantly in the last 30 years and created a new field of legal protection for international corporations to protect their investments. The protection of the right to property in the context of BITs might be the most effective legal protection of individuals in international law. It does not grant protection to the whole population, but usually only to wealthy and powerful transnational corporations. It features some characteristics of international law, which still depends on the power of states and other actors in international law. Legal protection in general and the effectiveness of legal protection in particular are best guaranteed in cases in which the persons concerned have significant influence themselves or come from powerful states which support the effectiveness of legal protection. In this context, the dual standards of effective legal protection as a principle of international law become obvious.

The second aspect of involving individuals in international law treats them as a potential threat to international law, addressing them in a negative sense. One example – as illustrated by Stephan Wittich[37] – in this book refers to international counter-terrorism by the UN Security Council's Sanctions Committees.[38] The opportunities of the individuals to get any form of legal protection in the context of international counter-terrorism measures are quite limited. It is remarkable that the UN Security Council has reacted at all and that it has at least improved the overall

33 See regarding the interrelation between the ECtHR and public international law in general C. Binder and K. Lachmayer (eds.), *The European Court of Human Rights and Public international Law: Fragmentation or Unity?* (Facultas 2014).

34 See e.g. the Inter-American Court of Human Rights.

35 Pal Wenneras, *The Enforcement of EC Environmental Law* (Oxford University Press, Oxford 2007).

36 See Anthony Aust, *Handbook of International Law* (2nd edn., Cambridge University Press, Cambridge 2010) 344–353.

37 See Wittich in this book.

38 See https://www.un.org/sc/suborg/.

situation with the establishment of the Office of the Ombudsperson.[39] Although it is not possible to speak of legal protection in a narrow sense, the first steps in the direction of legal protection have been taken.

Another example in which proper legal protection in a narrow sense is missing are so called peace-keeping or police missions in post-conflict situations. Individuals in these examples are not treated as terrorists or criminals, but are affected by international law enforcement as regular citizens. Their possibilities to gain legal protection are quite limited, if at all existent. Usually, international forces or police officers have certain forms of immunities and legal protection is only guaranteed transnationally in the country where the international soldier or officer comes from or internationally, for example, by the ECtHR. In a similar way to the establishment of the UN Ombudsperson in the context of the sanction committee, the EU Police Mission in Kosovo established a Human Rights Review Panel[40] as a quasi- or pseudo-court system, which does not grant legal protection, but does at least create some sort of accountability and transparency.

Finally, the concept of International criminal law, especially the establishment of the ICC and other *ad hoc* courts, shall be mentioned.[41] In the context of accusing influential and powerful political figures of crimes, for example against humanity, a highly elaborate procedure has been established. The legal protection of powerful persons – although accused of terrible crimes – is very effective[42] by international standards.

In conclusion, the first and biggest challenge in international law is the establishment of any legal protection for individuals at all under an international rule of law. Only if this first major step is accomplished in a particular part of the fragmented system of international law can the second step regarding the effectiveness of legal protection come into consideration. The effectiveness is often limited due to the overall concept of international law[43] and is usually only improved in cases in which the international power of states and the interests of legal protection converge.[44]

2.2 *Effective legal protection in global administrative law and global legal pluralism*

The Global Administrative Law (GAL) approach[45] is one of several different paradigms to address the developments in international law. An interesting element of the GAL approach is the attempt to develop an administrative law understanding in international law, which includes analysis of international law based on rule of law. Insights from GAL provide new structures and concepts of international law and include the institutional and procedural perspective of international law. The whole approach as such is promoting an

39 See https://www.un.org/sc/suborg/en/ombudsperson.

40 See http://www.hrrp.eu/.

41 Ian Brownlie, *Principles of Public International Law* (7th edn., Oxford University Press, Oxford 2008) 587, 604.

42 Which is necessary to provide the legitimacy of these procedures.

43 See Tom Bingham, *The Rule of Law* (Penguin Books 2010) 110–119.

44 See Brian Z. Tamanaha, *On the Rule of Law: History, Politics, Theory* (Cambridge University Press, Cambridge 2004) 127–136.

45 See B. Kingsbury, N. Krisch and R. B. Stewart, 'The Emergence of Global Administrative Law' (2005) 68 *Law and Contemporary Problems* 15–61.

understanding of international law, resulting in the promotion of legal protection. It is part of the logic of its 'administrative' understanding of international law, which provides the necessary institutional and procedural preconditions for effective legal protection. Based on a GAL approach, a rights-based perspective of effective legal protection can be set up to identify existing elements of legal protection and to develop new concepts of legal protection to promote its effectiveness in international law.

Another important approach towards international developments of law is Global Legal Pluralism,[46] which not only focusses on international law, but also on the different layers of law between public and private law, as well as domestic, transnational and international law. The insight from Global Legal Pluralism into the principle of effective legal protection does not have a one-dimensional perspective of the possibilities of legal protection. Legal protection might be guaranteed not only on different levels in a legal multi-level system, but also in different legal procedures. Moreover, Global Legal Pluralism clarifies that new challenges for the effective legal protection of domestic administrative law might arise from different actors or legal concepts, including international standard-setting bodies, transnational corporations or subnational autonomous regions.[47]

In conclusion, both approaches promote the increasing, methodological approach of comparative international law,[48] which is not only integrating international law in comparative legal efforts, but also using comparative legal methods to address the interrelation between the different legal regimes of international law established by different international treaties or international organisations. This comparative report also follows this strategy to create a more comprehensive understanding of the principle of effective legal protection.

2.3 The interrelation between European law and international law

A specific perspective of the principle of effective legal protection can be analysed due to the interrelation between international law and European Union law. The ECJ has increasingly defended its own rule of law regarding international law. It is worth evaluating two examples in this regard: first, the *Kadi* case; secondly, the EU's accession to the ECHR.

In the *Kadi* case, the ECJ[49] argued for the independent evaluation of EU legislation with regard to international law in a dualistic approach. Kokott/Sobotta[50] summarised

46 See Paul Schiff Berman, *Global Legal Pluralism: A Jurisprudence of Law Beyond Borders* (Cambridge University Press, Cambridge 2014).

47 See Peer Zumbansen, 'Transnational Legal Pluralism' (2010) 6 *Comparative Research in Law & Political Economy Research Paper* 01/2010 (available at http://papers.ssrn.com/sol3/papers.cfm?abstract_id=1542907).

48 Ugo Mattei and Boris N. Mamlyuk, 'Comparative International Law' (2011) 36 *Brooklyn Journal of International Law* 385–452. Martii Koskenniemi, 'The Case for Comparative International Law' (2009) 20 *Finnish Yearbook of International Law* 1–8; Anthea Roberts, 'Comparative International Law? The Role of National Courts in Creating and Enforcing International Law' (2011) 60 *International and Comparative Law Quarterly* 57–92.

49 Case C–402/05 P and C–415/05, *P. Kadi and Al Barakaat International Foundation v Council and Commission* [2008] ECR I–6351.

50 Juliane Kokott and Christoph Sobotta, 'The Kadi Case – Constitutional Core Values and International Law – Finding the Balance?' (2012) 23 *European Journal of International Law* 1015–1024.

the crucial argument as follows: 'Its central argument was that the protection of fundamental rights forms part of the very foundations of the Union legal order. Accordingly, all Union measures must be compatible with fundamental rights. The Court reasoned that this does not amount to a review of the lawfulness of the Security Council measures. The review of lawfulness would apply only to the Union act that gives effect to the international agreement at issue and not to the latter as such.'[51] The Court relates to the core of the principle of effective legal protection as the *Kadi* was not granted the guarantees of judicial protection. The EU defended its autonomy to enable the rule of law in general and the principle of effective legal protection in particular. The EU/international law relationship shows that effective legal protection cannot be understood in a one-dimensional way by looking at only one level in a multi-level network of legal systems, but must be established by the specific interrelation of systems. While international law might not be able to grant effective legal protection, other legal orders might provide – at least regionally – a certain amount of legal protection.

In an overall evaluation of the EU/international law relationship, the complete opposite to the previous example is also possible. When the EU fails to provide effective legal protection in a EU police mission outside the territory of the European Union, it might be an international court, like the ECtHR, which could provide effective legal protection to the individuals concerned. This insight into the strengths of a multi-level system also refers to the interrelation between the ECHR and its Member States. It is necessary to create an international mechanism for legal protection to contribute to effective legal protection in the domestic legal order. It 'did not suffice to leave protection of fundamental rights to national constitutions'.[52] It is, however, also necessary to understand that the opposite argument is also valid. It is not possible to fully rely on the effective legal protection of international human rights mechanisms like the ECtHR, for example, due to the length of procedures, but it is primarily necessary to strengthen effective legal protection by national constitutions and domestic courts.

The second example regarding the interrelation between the EU and international law refers to the accession of the Union to the ECHR.[53] The ECJ defended in its Opinion 2/13[54] the autonomy of EU law, like in the *Kadi* case but under different circumstances regarding the rule of law and the principle of effective legal protection.[55] While in the *Kadi* case, the rule of law was under threat, the accession of the EU to the ECHR can be understood as strengthening the rule of law and the principle of effective legal protection. The ECJ was much more defending its own European (judicial) rule of law, which would have been significantly changed by the accession to the ECHR. The general insights of the example are from a pro-EU perspective that it might sometimes be necessary to avoid too close interrelations in the multi-level system to uphold the internal concept of the rule of law. From a more sceptical

51 Ibid. 1016.

52 See Breuer, in this book.

53 See Piet Eeckhout, 'Opinion 2/13 on EU Accession to the ECHR and Judicial Dialogue – Autonomy or Autarky?' (2015) *Jean Monnet Working Paper* 01/15 (available at www.JeanMonnetProgram.org).

54 Opinion 2/13 of the Court delivered on 18 December 2014.

55 See Daniel Halberstam, '"It's the Autonomy, Stupid!" A Modest Defense of Opinion 2/13 on EU Accession to the European Convention on Human Rights' (2015) 16 *German Law Journal* 105.

perspective, one might argue that the strengthening of effective legal protection on a European level was prevented by prohibiting an accession to the ECHR.

3 The influence from an international/European level on the Member States

3.1 The relevance of the European Union

The relevance of EU law to the principle of effective legal protection in the Member States is highly divergent.[56] While some Member States like Germany, Austria or Italy are highly influenced in their administrative (procedural) law, other states are only affected by certain EU secondary laws, for example public procurement law, environmental law,[57] data protection or antitrust law (e.g. the Netherlands, Denmark or Spain).[58] Finally, in some Member States, the EU's principle of effective legal protection does not seem to have any significance at all. The reasons for this non-relevance of the EU in the context of administrative procedural law differ greatly. In the context of Spanish administrative law, the low level of legal education regarding EU law and the overall problematic situation of administrative procedural law also lead to a lack of application of or an ignorance towards EU law's principle of effective legal protection. In contrast to this, the relevance of EU law in the Danish case seems to be very small due to the fact that the Danish system of legal protection is highly developed and EU law has not created the necessity to change the overall system.

This short analysis can be furthered by looking at the different parts of effective legal protection presented in this book. The principle of effective legal protection relates to different perspectives, including the institutional and procedural perspective as well as a rights-based perspective. The influence of EU law can be distinguished as illustrated in the following matrix:

Table 19.2 Influence of EU law on the domestic principle of effective legal protection

	High influence	*Specific influence*	*Minor/No Influence*
Institutional Design	Austria, Lithuania		Hungary, France
Procedure	Germany, The Netherlands, Poland	Denmark (Data Protection); Spain (Public Procurement); Slovenia (Public Procurement); France (Data Protection)	Hungary
Rights-based	Italy, United Kingdom	France (Legal certainty; Foreigners' rights)	Denmark, Hungary

56 John S. Bell, 'Comparative Administrative Law' in Mathias Reimann and Reinhard Zimmermann (eds.), *The Oxford Handbook of Comparative Law* (Oxford University Press, Oxford 2006) 1259, 1281.

57 Pal Wenneras, *The Enforcement of EC Environmental Law* (Oxford University Press, Oxford 2007); see also Ulrike Giera, *Individualrechte im europäischen Umweltrecht* (facultas 2015).

58 Arnull (n. 10) 51, 63–68.

Moreover, it is interesting to observe the relevance of the principle of effective legal protection in European states that are not EU members, like Switzerland or Macedonia. On the one hand, Swiss law is highly affected by EU law, because of the independent decision to adopt EU law in Switzerland *(autonomer Nachvollzug)*;[59] on the other hand, Switzerland is not committed to an accession to the Union.[60] On the contrary, recent political developments have tended to widen the distance between Switzerland and the Union. It is interesting that, in the context of effective legal protection, the case law of the ECJ seems not to affect Swiss administrative procedural law. In contrast to this ambivalent situation in Switzerland, the role of EU law in Macedonia, as a state which aims to accede the Union (candidate country), is different. In comparison to Switzerland, however, the level of effective legal protection in Macedonia is much lower and still requires a lot of improvement to comply with European standards.[61]

3.2 The relevance of the European Convention of Human Rights

The ECHR introduced a rights-based approach in contrast to the broad and different conceptual legal approaches of EU law. However, the ECHR cannot be limited to its impact on individual rights in domestic law, and also affects institutional design and procedural law, which also affects administrative law.[62] In comparison to the impact of EU law, it can be observed that the role of the ECHR varies in the different Member States. The focus on human rights is strengthening the system; the ECHR, however, is part of international law and is not automatically part of the domestic legal system like certain legislation of the Union. Thus, the legal significance also depends on the role of the ECHR in the particular legal system. The Austrian integration of the ECHR as national constitutional law is an exemption; other countries, like Switzerland or the UK, also give the ECHR a particular role in their legal systems. Usually, the ECHR is applied in a similar way to statutory law. The role of the ECHR, however, not only depends on its legal status, but also on the specific domestic culture and attitude towards the European human rights system.[63]

The ECHR has created different constitutional effects. There has been broader influence in Austria or the UK on a constitutional level. In other countries, the ECHR has shaped specific provisions of the Constitution, such as in our context regarding the principle of effective legal protection (Art. 111 Italian Constitution, Art 45 Polish Constitution or Art 25 Slovenian Constitution). In other countries, like Germany, the impact cannot be observed in a textual dimension of the constitution, but in a substantive perspective of reasoning by the court.

59 See Uhlmann in this book.

60 See e.g. Melissa Eddy, 'Swiss Voters Narrowly Approve Curbs on Immigration', 9 February 2014 *The New York Times* (available at http://www.nytimes.com/2014/02/10/world/europe/swiss-voters-narrowly-approve-curbs-on-immigration.html?hp&_r=0).

61 See Gordana Siljanovska-Davkova and Renata Treneska-Deskoska in this book.

62 See Niels Fenger, 'New Challenges for Administrative Law Theory' in Anna-Sara Lind and Jane Reichel (eds.), *Administrative Law Beyond the State – Nordic Perspectives* (Martinus Nijhoff Publishers 2013) 120, 128–133.

63 See Dean Spielmann, 'Jurisprudence of the European Court of Human Rights and the Constitutional Systems of Europe' in Michel Rosenfeld and András Sajó (eds.), *The Oxford Handbook of Comparative Constitutional Law* (Oxford University Press, Oxford 2012) 1232–1252.

The following matrix illustrates the substantive influence of the ECtHR's case law towards the principle of effective legal protection:

Table 19.3 Influence of the ECtHR on the domestic principle of effective legal protection

	High influence	*Certain influence*	*Minor/No Influence*
Institutional Design	Austria, The Netherlands	Macedonia, France (Position of the 'general counsel'; Only the 'sitting' judge can bring effective guarantees for the protection of individual freedoms)	Denmark, Hungary, Switzerland
Procedure	Poland, The Netherlands, United Kingdom	Germany, Macedonia, France (Judgments within a reasonable time)	Denmark
Rights-based	Austria, France (Art. 6–1 and 13 ECHR + case law of the ECtHR), United Kingdom, Slovenia, Lithuania	Switzerland	Denmark, Spain

Art. 6 ECHR can be understood as a core complex of rights within the system of the ECHR and is very important when it comes to the principle of effective legal protection. The provision stands out in its importance in the case law of the Court.[64] Although Art. 6 ECHR is relevant for domestic administrative law, it is, however, limited in its scope with regard to 'civil rights and criminal charges'. On the one hand, the different scope and concepts regarding Art. 6 and Art. 13 ECHR[65] have broadened the significance of the ECHR regarding effective legal protection; on the other hand, the limits concerning the principle of effective legal protection have become clear and show the potential of further developments, which are fulfilled almost completely by Art. 47 CFR. The effects of the CFR on the application of the ECHR in the Member States of the EU will show how the CFR can contribute to further developments of the principle of effective legal protection.[66]

3.3 Conclusion

The influence of supra-/international legal orders on domestic law does not follow a coherent structure. On the contrary different forms of influences on European states

64 See Breuer in this book.

65 See Tanja Vospernik, 'Das Verhältnis zwischen Art 13 und Art 6 EMRK – Absorption oder "Apfel und Birne"?' (2001) 56 *Österreichische Juristenzeitung* 361.

66 The scope of the CFR, however, is limited to the scope of application of EU law. Thus, a certain field remains which will neither be covered by the principle of effective legal protection in EU law nor by the case law of the ECtHR according to the ECHR.

can be identified with regard to different European legal orders (EU law, ECHR). It might seem to be worth applying Vicki Jackson's concept of the role of the transnational in Supreme or Constitutional Courts in the context of the impact of different administrative legal orders too. Jackson differentiates between three modes: 'engagement, convergence, resistance'.[67] When it comes to the impact of the case law of the ECJ or the ECtHR regarding effective legal protection, European states tend to develop differently.

It is, moreover, necessary to mention that the attitude towards EU law and the ECHR might differ for different reasons; but in most cases the overall approach of each Member State will not differ as much as expected. If one takes the German example into consideration, for instance, one might identify a general acceptance of EU law as well as ECtHR case law, but in both cases it is possible to observe the German approach to uphold its own constitutional identity and not to accept all developments, but rather establish and consider certain limits due to the domestic constitutional system.[68] Another example might be the Hungarian approach, which is characterised by general scepticism towards European developments and tries to reject judgments of the ECtHR or legal requirements of EU law.[69] In this case, EU law might be relatively more able to achieve compliance and such convergence of developments.

The first group of states usually accept the developments on a European level. They change their constitutions, apply case law – even if they have not been directly affected by the concrete case – and implement new structures in their procedures due to European requirements. Moreover, and maybe most important, they also grant at least a certain level of effectiveness to legal protection. Effective legal protection cannot be achieved by statutory provisions alone but also have to be reflected in court judgments as well as by the administration's whole legal culture of applying the law. Effective legal protection has to show not only legal but also real implications. The reasons for engaging in European developments of effective legal protection might be different, but will often reflect an open attitude towards European legal orders. Engaging in the process does not exclude a strong domestic constitutional identity. Although the UK legal system can be understood as engaging in the European legal order and applies the principle of effective legal protection domestically, political resistance there against the European Union (and its law) as well as against the ECHR and the case law of the ECtHR is increasing. The overall situation might change rapidly if new political developments lead to a new approach within the UK legal system.

The second group of states might accept convergence with European developments of effective legal protection. This group includes different countries: some states might have constitutional provisions, but cannot provide full effective legal protection due to the legal culture or legal education of practitioners in the country (Italy might be an example); other countries, like Denmark, apply effective legal

67 Vicki C Jackson, *Constitutional Engagement in a Transnational Era* (Oxford University Press, Oxford 2010) 17–102.

68 See Diana zu Hohenlohe-Oehringen in this book.

69 Gábor Halmai, 'An Illiberal Constitutional System in the Middle of Europe' in W. Benedek, F. Benoit-Rohmer, W. Karl, M. C. Kettemann and M. Nowak (eds.), *European Yearbook on Human Rights* (NWV Verlag 2014) 497–514.

protection to a significant extent, but do not refer to European principles or change their own legal system, while still fulfilling European requirements. In both cases, a certain form of convergence can be observed.

Finally, a small, third group of states resist European standards of effective legal protection. Again, different possibilities exist: one is the Hungarian example, which is step by step developing away from effective legal protection in a European sense, though an end to participation in the system of European rule of law cannot be observed. The relevance of the European principle of effective legal protection is certainly on the decline.[70] Another example might be states which cannot live up to the institutional, procedural or rights-based standards of the European principle of effective legal protection. They might not be explicitly resisting the European system, but they still fail to comply significantly, which also creates a major lack of compliance. One example might be Macedonia, which is not part of the Union; certain elements in the Spanish legal system also point in the direction of resistance instead of convergence.

In conclusion, it is possible to distinguish different intensities of influence of the European principle of effective legal protection in domestic jurisdictions around Europe. Political developments in the Member States of the Union (e.g. UK or Hungary) clearly show the fragile political situation around Europe. The overall level of effective legal protection reached in Europe does not seem to be guaranteed in the next years or decades. On the contrary, it will be up to the relevant persons and institutions in each legal system to maintain the standards of effective legal protection already reached. From a pessimistic perspective, a decline of the standards seems more probable than an improvement over the coming years;[71] from an optimistic perspective, it will be necessary to increase efforts to keep certain standards of effective legal protection at the same level.

4 Effective legal protection in a multi-level system

4.1 Complexity and heterogeneity

As effective legal protection depends on so many different elements, like institutional design, for example, of courts, procedural concepts and guarantees, as well as individual rights, the scope of effective legal protection is already complex within one legal system. If one tries to identify the principle of effective legal protection in the multi-level system of global, European and (comparative) domestic governance,[72] two characteristics arise: complexity and heterogeneity. It would be an overly simple picture of the situation to claim a uniform concept of effective legal protection throughout the different legal orders. On the contrary, one can identify complex structures and interrelations.[73] The interplay of international, European and domestic law again

70 Ibid.

71 See e.g. the refugee crisis and the reduced number of countries which can still be considered as secure states.

72 See regarding the multi-level network in administrative law Henrik Wenander, 'A Toolbox for Administrative Law Cooperation Beyond the State' in Anna-Sara Lind and Jane Reichel (eds.), *Administrative Law Beyond the State – Nordic Perspectives* (Martinus Nijhoff Publishers 2013) 47–75.

73 S Boyron and W Lacey, 'Procedural Fairness Generally' in Mark Tushnet, Thomas Fleiner and Cheryl Saunders (eds.), *Routledge Handbook of Constitutional Law* (Routledge 2013) 259, 272.

cannot be characterised by a uniform concept, but has to be studied and analysed individually. This task is a crucial purpose of this book project in general. The interrelation between for example Hungarian administrative law and Art. 6 ECHR has to be viewed completely differently from the correlation between UK administrative law and the very same provision of the ECHR. The link between the ECHR and EU law in general and the CFR in particular is another example of this complex network. The complexity of the interrelation becomes even more demanding when one takes into account that the interrelations are not static but dynamic, thus always changing due to new case law and statutory law. It does not seem to be possible to grasp the full picture at one moment, while legal dynamics are already continuously shifting the interrelations.

It is, however, possible to make some conclusions on the principle of effective legal protection within these complex and heterogeneous interrelations. First, the overall rising importance of effective legal protection shall be mentioned. Although in different states (like in Spain, Macedonia or Hungary) there is still a long way to go to establish legal protection, the overall importance is on the rise. Secondly, European legal concepts are shaping and affecting legal orders in the context of effective legal protection, although not all European states are doing so in the same way. Thirdly, effective legal protection is becoming a more differentiated and sophisticated concept, systematically including more and different kinds of elements with regard to its institutional, procedural and rights perspectives. Fourthly, when it comes to European law itself and even more so with international law, the level of effective legal protection (although exceptions exist) cannot usually be compared to effective legal protection within most European states, which provides a much more complex, broader and deeper concept of effective legal protection. This situation seems legitimate in the context of a multi-level system because the complexity and intensity of legal protection increases as the concept comes closer to the individuals concerned. As international and European law increasingly affect individuals themselves, it becomes necessary to deepen the concepts of effective legal protection on an international and European level. Fifthly, the example of the ECtHR gives an interesting insight into effective legal protection in general. If legal protection becomes effective, the applications of individuals will rise (in the case of the ECtHR dramatically); this effect, however, has the potential (as the example of the ECtHR illustrates) to endanger the effectiveness of legal protection once again. Thus, there is a major attempt to open up the possibilities of legal protection as widely and as effectively as possible, but this optimising of legal protection will lead to a huge number of proceedings, which cannot be dealt with in the end. The challenge thus remains to ensure that a legal system which provides effective legal protection remains efficient.

4.2 Effectiveness and flexibility

If one tries to identify the relevant parameter for successful effective legal protection, it is necessary to understand that the principle of effective legal protection cannot remain identical – despite the differences in the particular legal systems.[74] If legal protection is to remain effective, it has to change. As legal orders are highly dynamic

74 See critical in this regard Arnull (n. 10) 51.

for different reasons, for example political developments, technological progress or legal globalisation, the principle of effective legal protection has to adapt to be able to guarantee the same level of legal protection.

The history of the development of effective legal protection clearly shows the adaptation to different challenges. First, the effectiveness has to be observed as a particular element. It is not enough to grant legal protection, which was already a historic achievement over the centuries, and it is necessary to create effectiveness within the institutional and procedural design. The case law of the ECtHR, as well as the case law of the ECJ, illustrates how the courts have developed step by step the principle of effective legal protection. Effective legal protection in the EU also means to deal legally with development in international law. The ECJ has shown in the *Kadi* case that it is necessary to clarify the interrelation between international law and European law to uphold a European rule of law. The same applies on a national level. If domestic courts are challenged with international or European law, they have to create new legal techniques within national law to grant effective legal protection.

This challenge to effective legal protection will remain in the future. The principle of effective legal protection has to be like a chameleon, adjusting and changing to stay relevant. It is first of all the task of the courts to interpret the principle of effective legal protection in a dynamic way to address the upcoming challenges of effectiveness of legal protection. The challenges for the concept of effective legal protection also depend on the position of the court within the multi-level system. Thus, the principle of effective legal protection cannot and shall not have the same contents when it is addressing different courts and different procedures on different levels in the multi-level system. Finally, it is also a responsibility of the legislator to consider reforms of the institutional and procedural design to make effective legal protection possible.

4.3 Permanent performance of legal protection as a basis of the rule of law

One might identify different foundations of the rule of law: for example the principle of legality (as an expression of legal certainty),[75] law and order (as an expression of legitimacy)[76] or the principle of proportionality (as an expression of human rights).[77] Obviously, it is possible to develop different perspectives on the rule of law; all the perspectives mentioned have certain elements of relevance, which can be identified in each legal system (to a greater or lesser extent depending on the legal culture). It seems within the territorial scope of Europe[78] that in our times[79] effective legal protection forms the core of a rule of law.

75 This could be described as a typically Austrian approach. See e.g. H. Mayer, G. Kucsko-Stadlmayer and K. Stöger, *Grundriss des österreichischen Verfassungsrechts* (11th edn., Manz 2015) para. 165, 569–574.

76 See regarding the law and order aspect of the rule of law, e.g. A. W. Bradley and K. D. Ewing and C J S Knight, *Constitutional and Administrative Law* (16 edn., London, Pearson 2014) 95–96.

77 David M. Beatty, *The Ultimate Rule of Law* (Oxford University Press, Oxford 2005) 159–188.

78 In other parts of the world, the establishment of the independence of the judiciary or the guarantee of the principle of legality or the foundation of social justice might be a core element of the rule of law debate.

79 If one looks back in legal history, it becomes obvious that other principles like the overall establishment of a human rights system have formed the focus of the dynamics of the rule of law.

Effective legal protection as a fundamental perspective of the rule of law unifies questions of independence of courts, individual access to courts, fair trial and further functions of legal protection, such as ensuring the objective monitoring of the compliance of the administration regarding statutory law. The principle includes perspectives regarding the institutional and the procedural design as well as a rights-based perspective. If one tries to identify how the rule of law principle is doing in the legal order, it seems necessary to look at the principle of effective legal protection to see if the courts are working.

Only a permanent performance of legal protection creates the necessary fundament for the rule of law in the multi-level system in Europe today. Although we have seen that the principle of effective legal protection is characterised by complexity and heterogeneity in the different legal orders, it is the flexibility of the principle of effective legal protection which makes it possible for the rule of law to remain relevant in changing legal systems in global governance.

20 The principle of effective legal protection in administrative law – a comparison

Zoltán Szente

1 Comparing rights, institutions and procedures

If we look at the real and alleged difficulties in comparing the situation of effective legal protection in the administrative jurisdiction of 14 countries and the implications for international and European law, our task appears to be almost hopeless. The problems and obstacles have been carefully analysed many times by legal comparatists. It is said that 'while constitutional law is becoming ever more comparative (. . .), administrative law remains bound to the nation state'.[1] The extent to which administrative law can be compared is sometimes questioned because of its strong national character.[2] Another problem is the absence of a generally accepted method for comparison.[3] Moreover, it is a common feature of public law that its rules are largely influenced by non-legal factors.[4] Consequently, the comparison must extend not only to the relevant legal principles and rules, but also to the historical, political and constitutional context. Another difficulty is that, sometimes, different concepts are used for the same phenomenon, or the same concepts describe different phenomena.[5]

Despite all of these difficulties, there are some other circumstances which facilitate our undertaking. First, it is held that, while the institutional arrangements of public administration show some specific features in various countries, the standards of administrative procedures often have more in common.[6] Secondly, our topic is specialised enough for a fully-fledged comparison, as it focuses on the tools of legal protection of individual rights in administrative law. In spite of the national differences

1 Tom Ginsburg, 'Written Constitutions and the Administrative State: On the Constitutional Character of Administrative Law' in Susan Rose-Ackerman and Peter L. Lindseth (eds.), *Comparative Administrative Law* (Edward Elgar, Cheltenham, Northampton 2013) 117.

2 Martina Künnecke, *Tradition and Change in Administrative Law: An Anglo-German Comparison* (Springer-Verlag, Berlin, Heidelberg 2007) 4, 7.

3 Matthias Ruffert, 'The Transformation of Administrative Law as a Transnational Methodological Project' in Matthis Ruffert (ed.), *The Transformation of Administrative Law in Europe: La mutation du droit administratif en Europe* (Sellier. European Law Publishers, Munich 2007) 4–5.

4 Jürgen Schwarze, *Europäisches Verwaltungsrecht: Entstehung und Entwicklung in Rahmen der Europäischen Gemeinschaft* (Nomos Verlagsgesellschaft, Baden-Baden 2005) 83.

5 With regard to this problem, see Pierre Legrand, 'The Impossibility of "Legal Transplants"' (1997) 4 *Maastricht Journal of European and Comparative Law* 111–124.

6 John S. Bell, 'Comparative Administrative Law' in Mathias Reimann and Reinhard Zimmermann (eds.), *The Oxford Handbook of Comparative Law* (Oxford University Press, Oxford 2006) 1262, 1278.

in terms of the methods used and the established institutions, the basic forms and processes of rights-protection are fairly similar. Although all modern legal systems are based on their own specific understanding of the rule of law, and have special legal institutions and approaches, the essential components of legal protection can be found in all of them. It is true that their systems of judicial review of administrative acts, for example, differ from one another, but almost all the same rights of procedural fairness can be found in each of them. In other words, there are sufficient common traits in this field in European administrative systems to provide a proper basis for a wide-ranging comparison.

National administrative traditions that have had a major influence on other administrative systems are identified at different levels of abstraction by postulating three decisive national pathways (the diverse traditions of English administrative law, French *droit administratif* and German *Verwaltungsrecht*) to a systemic grouping of countries sharing a common administrative inheritance (from the Anglo-American to the Islamic model of public administration, for instance).[7] It is certain that the most influential of the above-mentioned administrative cultures, or more precisely, their institutions, customs or techniques, have left their mark on the systems of rights-protection in national administrative laws.

Moreover, the various administrative law regimes are deeply rooted in legal cultures, and so their rules and principles are closely linked to the values of the civil or common law systems.[8] This classification of legal systems can also provide a well-established analytical framework that can be used for the body of law relating to administrative matters that evolved from the first half of the nineteenth century onwards.[9]

Finally, the different institutional settings and administrative machineries of legal protection could be examined within the context of Europeanisation or under the scheme of global administrative law.

All the special administrative law traditions, the legal families or the convergence/divergence dichotomy could probably offer an adequate analytical framework for our comparative study. Presumably, the major characteristics and trends of legal protection in the sphere of administrative law are influenced by various factors from the national traditions, the major features of the different legal systems or the harmonising effects of European or global administrative law. When we chose another conceptual and analytical framework for this study, we did not do so because we wanted to deny the impact of all these factors. However, when we explore and compare the existing systems of legal protection in administrative law, and the major trends of development, all these elements of the wider context are potential independent variables explaining the similarities and differences for which the explanation can be the subject of further research.

7 Martin Painter and B. Guy Peters, 'Administrative Traditions in Comparative Perspective: Families, Groups and Hybrids' in Linda Pearson, Carol Harlow and Michael Taggart (eds.), *Administrative Law in a Changing State: Essays in Honour of Mark Aronson* (Hart Publishing, Oxford 2008) 19–30.

8 Sabine Kuhlmann and Hellmut Wollmann, *Verwaltung und Verwaltungsreformen in Europa: Einführung in die vergleichende Verwaltungswissenschaft* (VS Verlag für Sozialwissenschaften, Wiesbaden 2013) 20.

9 Bernardo Sordi, '*Révolution*, *Rechtsstaat*, and the Rule of Law: Historical Reflections on the Emergence of Administrative Law in Europe' in Susan Rose-Ackerman and Peter L. Lindseth (eds.), *Comparative Administrative Law* (Edward Elgar, Cheltenham, Northampton 2010) 28.

Our comparison does not aim to give a general assessment of the quality of the various systems of legal protection, nor does it attempt to compare the achievements of the different forms of rights-protection. However, if we can identify common standards of legal protection in administrative law, each jurisdiction can be examined in the sense of how far they reflect certain fundamental values, and maybe we can gain a better understanding of the nature and mechanisms of legal protection in this special field of law.

2 The constitutional and legal fundaments of the principle of legal protection in administrative law

If we look at the constitutional texts of the European countries, we cannot find the principle of effective legal protection in them. This term does not appear in a single constitution. Yet it would be a nonsense to conclude that its guarantees are not recognised by the present-day national basic laws. However, as most authors of this book show, not only are the crucial components of the legal protection of individual rights embedded in the constitutions, but also the requirement of 'effectiveness' of rights-protection is indeed present in them, albeit indirectly. So even if this abstract principle does not appear at constitutional level in this special form, its composite parts and sub-principles are well-established in most countries. As Professor Moreno puts it in his contribution, the principle of effective legal protection is the result or cumulative effect of different subjective rights.[10]

In general, it can be said that since there is a great diversity of constitutional traditions in the countries explored in our book, the level and specific features of the relevant constitutional regulations also differ. However, it can be observed that, while the more recent constitutions usually comprise the principles of due process rights (sometimes extending them explicitly to administrative law), the older constitutions, which used to be only rarely amended, like the Danish *Grundloven*, paid little attention to these things. Nevertheless, this does not mean that the procedural safeguards are unknown in the latter countries; in fact, the statutory law or the judicial practice may have successfully replaced them.

Effective legal protection is recognised by most national legal systems, specified by national legislation, and explained and extended frequently by jurisprudence of the constitutional or ordinary courts, even if the national constitutions do not contain any reference to the exact concept. As a matter of fact, constitutional provisions do not stand in themselves, but are strongly linked to constitutional practice, conventions and customs – not only in Britain, where an unwritten constitution exists, but in other countries as well. Thus, a number of legal protection requirements have been fleshed out by courts in many countries, recognising such significant principles as the right to claim compensation for damages caused by unlawful acts or extending the scope of judicial review to the cases of 'silence' of public administration (like in Italy). It is also true that statutory law has a much greater role in establishing procedural rights in some countries with civil law systems; in Denmark, for example, judicial practice has had only minor relevance in this aspect. However, even in some countries where the legal system is based on Roman law traditions, the constitutional court has

10 Moreno in this book.

played a decisive role in elaborating and expanding procedural fairness. As Diana zu Hohenlohe-Oehringen reports, the German Federal Constitutional Court has explicitly declared that the judicial protection of individuals must be effective,[11] but besides that, the *Bundesverfassungsgericht* had a significant role in the development of standards for rights-protection. In this way, the effectiveness of legal protection is a constitutional requirement in Germany, as it directly follows from the interpretation of the *Grundgesetz* which guarantees legal remedies against restrictions of basic rights.[12] The constitutional courts had achieved a great deal in Central and Eastern European countries in particular after their transition to democracy. Everything points to the fact that these bodies contributed significantly to the establishment of the system of tools and instruments of rights-protection in the area of administrative justice. The extension and content of judicial review of administrative acts in these countries was shaped by constitutional controversies, and the constitutional courts had a prominent role in this process, as was the case in Hungary, Macedonia, Poland and Slovenia. In Slovenia, although the right to judicial protection is not specified by the Constitution with regard to administrative law cases, the Constitutional Court (*Ustavno sodišče*) has recognised it for acts of public administration, and the Court applies a strict scrutiny test in those cases where legislation restrains the relevant powers of the courts.

As for the basic components of the effective protection of rights, even the dichotomy of the rights-based and the institutional approaches, used in this book as the basic conceptual and analytical framework, conspicuously emerges in most national constitutions in a way that certain fundamental rights are explicitly recognised, while other constitutional provisions add institutional guarantees to them.

In fact, there is no constitution in the administrative law systems investigated here which would completely ignore the claim for procedural fairness. Even those basic law systems which pay little attention to these issues contain some sporadic guarantees, like the Dutch constitution, which does not explicitly state the right of access to court, nor the fair trial principle; however, some other guarantees emerge in the constitutional text, like the public authorities' duty to give reasons for their judgments or the institutional independence of the judiciary.[13] The principle of rule of law is generally recognised by the constitutional texts, which usually comprise some of its constituent parts or sub-principles in various forms, for instance the principle of legality and legal certainty, or the protection of legitimate expectations. Although there is a great variety in national constitutions in terms of which procedural guarantees are embedded in them and in what form, most basic law systems encompass the right to fair trial which often emerges as a sort of 'mother-right' for a lot of more specific rights and legal entitlements, like the right to be heard or the right to appeal. The right to access to court or judicial review, or the right to remedy are also widely recognised by constitutions.

As for institutional guarantees, almost all constitutions examined in this book include the principle of judicial independence and impartiality. Where ombudsman-type institutions exist, their legal status and functions also have constitutional grounds.

11 Hohenlohe-Oehringen in this book.

12 Eberhard Schmidt-Aßmann, *Das allgemeine Verwaltungsrecht als Ordnungsidee: Grundlagen und Aufgaben der verwaltungsrechtlichen Systembildung* (Springer-Verlag, Berlin, Heidelberg 2006) 228.

13 See Albers–Kjellevold–Schlössels in this book.

Normally, constitutional texts encompass broad principles and guarantees. Fundamental rights have a universal character, so the procedural safeguards of legal protection are not usually specified for administrative law. Likewise, the courts have a general scope of responsibility, like other public bodies which have any protective or controlling function. But this also implies that the application of all relevant constitutional provisions, for the same reason, is not excluded in the area of administrative law. So the principle of rule of law, or the explicit standards of fair trial, must naturally prevail in administrative court procedures too.

Notwithstanding this, the constitution in some countries also contains explicit rules and safeguards for administrative matters. In those countries where specialised courts are in charge of administrative review, they are explicitly recognised. The ordinary and administrative courts are expressly distinguished by the Italian Constitution specifying that the former are the guardians of individual rights, while the latter are responsible for the protection of legitimate interests. The Danish Constitution grants the right to citizens to bring administrative decisions before the courts. There is a special situation in Slovenia where the constitution does not require the establishment of special administrative courts, but prescribes specific proceedings for the judicial review of administrative decisions. On this basis, the prevailing interpretation is that the ordinary courts with general competence do not have the power to adjudicate administrative disputes – these must be settled by special administrative courts.

As is usual with other legal guarantees, the scope and limits of the relevant rights and safeguards, as well as their components and institutions, are specified by statutory law and/or, depending on the national legal culture and tradition, by the judicial case law. The general frames and abstract phrases of constitutions provide enough scope for the lower-level regulation and the courts to improve the level of protection and its effectiveness.

In a number of countries with civil law traditions, the body of law guiding the administrative procedures is gathered and systemised in a general code. In the countries examined in our book, there is a code of administrative procedures in Austria (1925), Denmark (1985), Germany (1976), Hungary (2004), Italy (1990), Lithuania (1999), Macedonia (2005), the Netherlands (1994), Poland (1960), Slovenia (1999) and Spain (1992). In Switzerland, not only is there a general administrative procedural code at federal level (1968), but the federated states also have their own codes. Certainly, administrative codes cannot embrace all details of administrative procedures, so it is quite usual for a number of other legislative acts to regulate the special or extraordinary proceedings. Although the range of these special procedures varies in the different countries, the proceedings of tax authorities, the nuclear supervisory bodies or electoral commissions usually have specific rules. Only in Britain and France does no general code of administrative procedures exist. In the United Kingdom, the legal protection of individual rights is, as Robert Thomas notes in his study, 'an amalgam of statute, common law, and administrative guidance'.[14] In France the relevant regulation can be found in different legal acts and in the practice of the *Conseil d'Etat*, and a number of procedural rights have been crystallised by the *Conseil constitutionnel* in the last four decades.

14 See Thomas in this book.

In those countries where the legality of administrative acts is reviewed by special administrative courts, these judicial proceedings have special rules compared to the procedural rules of ordinary courts. There is a special code for administrative disputes before the courts in all post-communist countries, except for Hungary and Slovakia.[15] Among the Western European countries featured in this book, there are specific rules for administrative litigation in France, Germany, Italy, the Netherlands and Spain. Certainly, there are some differences in the competences of administrative courts in these countries, and other (criminal or civil) procedural rules might also be followed, mainly for state liability cases, if these disputes are settled by civil courts, for example.

Where there is no separate code for the judicial review of administrative acts, the procedural rules of civil law courts are used, like in Denmark or Hungary, with some modifications specified for administrative disputes.

3 Rights-based perspective

In all likelihood, owing to the different constitutional traditions and legal cultures, the principle of effective legal protection does not have a uniform doctrine in the various jurisdictions. In Britain, for example, the doctrine of procedural fairness has a core importance in administrative justice, which has different standards that can only be determined by courts after the consideration of all circumstances of the particular situation. In Italy, the concept of the 'legitimate interest' of citizens has a prominent role and, as Fulvio Cortese shows in his chapter, the procedural rights represent the substance of this value in the new understanding of legal protection. In Germany, the tradition of 'subjective public-law rights' plays a decisive role in guaranteeing enforceable rights for individuals against public authorities.

However, in-depth analysis of procedural fairness is far beyond the scope of this book. The positive law governing the organisation and procedures of administrative bodies, of course, does not give any justification for the particular rights, as they do not follow any theoretical classification of procedural rights. Usually, the administrative codes or other statutory instruments simply enumerate the relevant rights without distinguishing the 'procedural' rights as defined above. Rather, they define the core content and limits of these rights.

3.1 Participatory rights

3.1.1 Right to be a party/right to intervene (standing rules)

As a rule, the function of the right of citizens to launch an administrative procedure, or to be a party to such a process in other ways (i.e. in *ex officio* processes, or by intervention) is to protect, recognise or grant their legal rights or legitimate interests. The original parties may participate in administrative appellate procedures.

While the duality of 'legal rights' and 'legitimate interests' (or in some countries: 'legal interests') features in all administrative jurisdictions, whatever the legal source of this recognition, there are some differences both in regulations and practices

15 Herbert Küpper, 'Der Stand des allgemeinen Verwaltungsrechts in Ostmitteleuropa' (2011) 52 *Jahrbuch für Ostrecht* 299.

concerning their scope and limits. German administrative law seems to request a legally acknowledged 'interest' for being a client, while in other countries (such as Switzerland), the public authorities have a wider margin of appreciation to examine whether an interest in question is worth protection or not.

In most countries, administrative law allows some other people or organisations to intervene in the ongoing procedure, despite the fact that their – or their members' – rights are not directly affected by the expected administrative decision. In particular, civil organisations representing general or public interests (e.g. environmental protection or public health) are empowered to initiate an administrative procedure, or to get involved in an existing process. If their intervention has been permitted, they enjoy the same rights as the original parties of the case. By special arrangement, in certain carefully defined cases in Spain, everybody may file an application (*acción popular*) on the basis of *actio popularis.*

In the post-communist countries, the public prosecutors, as general guardians of the legality or public interest, may also be parties in administrative procedures, and they may intervene in the ongoing disputes, enjoying all rights of the parties, so they may initiate a reconsideration of the first instance decision of the competent administrative agency, and they have the right to appeal against the decisions (even if the prosecutor was not a party in the relevant procedure, like in Slovenia). Sometimes they have special supervisory powers as well, like in Hungary, being able to warn an administrative body for its illegal practice, or initiate supervisory control by a higher-level administrative agency. In addition, people whose rights or legitimate interests are affected and violated by the upcoming administrative act are also allowed to intervene.

3.1.2 Right to be heard (right to make statements)

The rights of the clients of an administrative procedure to express their views both on facts and law of their own case, to present evidence or to react to the positions of other participants are an inherent element of the participation of the parties. These rights are generally known and recognised by administrative law in the reviewed countries.

In most cases, the lack of the claimant's statement does not usually prevent the administrative body from making a decision in the case, unless the procedure has been launched by the party and the act may not be brought without his or her statement. However, if the applicant refuses to participate during the procedure, he/she must face all possible consequences of this refusal.

Whether obliged to or not, administrative authorities may often hold public hearings, usually when there are opposing parties in the case, in order to establish the relevant facts, to clarify the various claims, or just to hear the competing opinions. Notwithstanding this, there might be special sorts of procedures (e.g. 'shortened' or 'emergency'), in which no public hearing must be held, even if the conditions for this are met.

3.1.3 Right to access to the documents of the case

The right of the parties to access to the relevant information and documents of the case together with the right to be heard are often considered as indispensable parts of the right to defence. It is difficult to imagine there being any fair procedure if a party does not have the opportunity to know the relevant circumstances or the positions of the opposing parties. This right usually involves all affected persons having the right to receive a notification about the administrative procedure or act. Another well-known measure to counterbalance the informational advantages of the public authorities is that the administrative agencies cannot require the client to provide information and data they have stored.

Although the right to access to the relevant documents is a generally accepted element of the due process in administrative law, it is not an unconditional instrument in the hands of the private parties. Statutory law usually makes exceptions to this rule, or, like in Britain or Switzerland, the judicial case law has specified its conditions in specific situations. In spite of diverse regulations in the various countries in this field, third-party interests, personal data, business secrets or public interests (from the protection of the documents of *travail préparatoire* to state security information) provide acceptable reasons for restrictions. In most cases, the courts are endowed with the power to balance the competing interests and can decide in each particular case which information can be made accessible to the affected parties. There is some evidence that the courts (in Switzerland, for example) are reluctant to restrict access to the relevant documents, and even if they have to do so, they try to keep the adversarial parties on an equal footing (e.g. by briefly summarising the relevant content of the confidential documents).

In addition, reasonable limitations can also be imposed on exercising the right to access to files of the case, such as requiring those demanding access to bear the costs of making copies.

There are a variety of remedies employed when the competent administrative organ denies access to information of the case. In Denmark, such a refusal is considered as a separate act which itself may be appealed against. In France, the parties may turn to a special commission for remedy, as is also the case in Italy, where, eventually, the complainants may bring the refusal before the court. The prevailing rule is that, if the administrative authority fails to provide access to the documents, the parties should have some sort of legal remedy, even if the refusal does not necessarily lead to the repetition of the procedure, or to the annulment of its outcome or the administrative act.

3.1.4 The right to get an act within a reasonable time

Normally, legal protection provides instruments and tools against administrative acts. Thus, it is a general rule that administrative bodies may impose any obligation or right for private parties only in formalised acts. In all countries explored in this book, administrative law provides guarantees against the 'silence' of public administration, that is to say, tools for citizens to stand up for their rights and interests even if the competent administrative authority fails to make a formal act in their individual case within a reasonable time. It means that the absence of the relevant administrative act does not leave the affected persons without legal defence; if the administrative authority gives any action (only) in an informal way, or it omits to issue an act, such behaviour itself becomes the subject of legal protection.

Certainly, the meaning of 'reasonableness' is a crucial aspect of this procedural right. The question is: when is the duration of the respective administrative procedure 'reasonable'? In a group of countries, there is a standard period of time both for the first and the appellate bodies to settle the case, and this is set by law. It is quite usual for the administrative procedural codes to determine a general deadline for the normal decision making processes. In some countries, mainly in Central and Eastern Europe, the competent public authority has to make a decision within 30 days from the beginning of the proceeding. Of course, this is only the general rule, and the various statutes determine other deadlines for administrative bodies for certain specific procedures. Taking into account the complexity or other difficulties of the case, these rules often allow the decision making body to extend the deadline (usually only once) when simultaneously notifying the parties and presentations of the reasons for prolongation.

In other countries, there is no such general period, but the duration of the reasonable time can be fixed only after due consideration of all relevant circumstances of the case. This is the case in the UK, where no such general requirement exists, because the timeliness, as Robert Thomas notes in this book, is often viewed as a matter of quality service standards.[16] However, as Angel Moreno points out in his chapter, if no deadlines are set for handling a case (which is, as a general rule, three months in Spain), it is difficult to enforce the right to a decision within a reasonable time,[17] in particular when deference is the prevailing judicial attitude towards administrative decision making.

There is an intermediate rule in the Netherlands, where, if the statute does not specify a different period, the administrative bodies have to settle the case within eight weeks.

In this regard, there are also several different types of redress. One of the options of the legal protection is to turn to the superior authority to oblige the silent administrative body to make a decision in the case. Alternatively, where the ombudsman institution is known, it may also be asked to contact the body authorised for settling the case, and to request it to adopt the desired act.

Other tools of legal protection against an administrative body's silence might also be available. In Italy, if the competent administrative body fails to perform its duty, the parties of the original procedures may launch a surrogate proceeding (trying to force the administrative organ to make a decision), or may turn to the court to oblige it to do so. In Hungary, in cases launched by private parties for granting or declaring a right or a legal entitlement, if the competent body is silent until the end of the legally set procedural time, the claim is regarded as approved by the administrative body. This kind of *praesumptio legis* can be a good incentive to the competent administrative agency to complete the procedure with an act, otherwise it might be challenged by its own superior authority for its negligence. A similar solution was also used in Macedonia until 2011; since then, however, the parties have to turn to a special organ instead to examine the reasons of silence, and if no redress is provided, the parties may then turn to the court.

This latter way, that is the judicial one, is the most usual – and ultimate – remedy open for parties whose application has remained unaddressed. Citizens may turn to the court to oblige the administrative body to make an act in their particular case. The courts always have to examine whether the rights and interests of private parties involved make it really necessary to issue a formal decision. The rules of standing in

16 Thomas in this book.
17 Moreno in this book.

these special disputes require the plaintiffs to prove that the silence of the competent administrative body is harmful to their legal rights or legitimate interests. Once such an action has been admitted, the court must consider the urgency of the case, the behaviour of the parties and other aspects, such as the complexity of the administrative dispute or the possible consequences of delay. If the plaintiff's claim is justified, the courts may instruct the appropriate administrative body to conduct the procedure and to settle the case. In some countries, an additional incentive for the particular agency involves the law sanctioning its undue delay by a pecuniary compensation for every day until the decision has been taken. This is the case in the Netherlands, for example.

The failure of the public administration to settle the case within the time set by law can also lead to a civil law claim for compensation due to the unlawful and unjustified delay of the competent body. However, the delay in itself only rarely causes material damage for which compensation could be demanded before a court.

The same instruments, more or less, are in the hands of the parties for enforcing the implementation of the final (non-reviewable) administrative act. Due to the legal nature of the decision (i.e. it is now legally enforceable), the complainants are most likely to turn to the court at this stage. In many countries, there is therefore a special action for legal claims to enforce the execution of the decision that was taken beforehand (like the request of the parties for 'compliance judgment' (*giudizio d'ottemperanza*) in Italian administrative law).

3.1.5 Duty to give reasons

Today, the obligation of the public authorities to give reasons for their actions has become a general requirement in national administrative law jurisdictions. In some countries, it is a relatively new duty for administrative organs, being established only in 1979 in France, for example, and all indications show that in some areas it was encouraged by EU law. Interestingly, there is no such general duty in Britain, only in specific procedures or areas, as the legislation often requires it from the decision making bodies. In addition, if a relevant statute is lacking, the courts, under common law, may impose this duty if its refusal could lead to unfair consequences.

Although there is some diversity in the various national systems of administrative law concerning what are the essential and indispensable elements of the compulsory reasoning of an act, it is a more or less accepted principle that, once the administrative organ gives reasons, its statement must be proper and adequate, and the major points of the decision must be mentioned. In terms of form, the relevant statement must be given in writing, specifying the major reasons of the decision in a clear and easily comprehensible style.

In some countries, the decision does not have to include reasons, if it is favourable to the party who initiated the procedure.

3.1.6 The right to appeal to a higher administrative body/tribunal

The administrative appeal is a common device of legal protection, available in all countries examined in this book (except Austria since 2014). In some countries, it is considered as a constitutional requirement (like in Poland or Slovenia), but this kind of remedy plays an important role in other jurisdictions as well.

Usually, an administrative appeal may be submitted only against the merit of the first instance decision; this recourse may only rarely be based exclusively on procedural faults, except those errors which are considered so serious by law that they can lead to the annulment of the administrative act. Most formal irregularities may be objected to during the administrative procedure, and are reviewable by the decision making authority itself or by other bodies or commissions, without interrupting the whole process.

It is a commonly shared feature that an administrative appeal is possible only once. Otherwise, the administrative stage of the whole procedure could be extremely long, also delaying the closure of the dispute, as the administrative recourse may not be a substitute for the judicial review of the same decision. Nevertheless, in Denmark, even if only exceptionally, an administrative appeal may be lodged twice to different administrative organs.[18]

In certain procedures, no administrative appeal exists, but this is the exception and there must be some special reason based on the nature of the ground case or of the respective administrative body (usually having an exclusive power). Thus, when there is no higher or superior administrative body (e.g. when a ministry, an independent tribunal or a local authority was the decision maker), or if there is a particularly strong public interest in the speed of the procedure, the administrative appeal may be excluded. But the basic principle is that these cases may be brought before the court, so the absence of the administrative recourse does not mean the lack of judicial appeal; it is just that, conversely, if no right to appeal exists within the organisational system of public administration, the judicial protection is even more important.

The effectiveness of legal protection of individual rights is often promoted by certain formal provisions. Thus, the appeals are addressed to the appellate authority, but technically they usually have to be submitted to the first instance body. The rationale of this solution is to give the decision making body the opportunity to check and possibly revise its own act. If the organ is aware of the parties' objections, there might be a chance to convince it to change its decision, not necessarily to provide more effective legal protection, but to make sure whether the act was really lawful and correct. After all, the first-tier administrative authority has the power to change its preceding act, or to make a new one. In any case, the parties do not lose their right to appeal against the new act, if they are still not satisfied with it.

Moreover, statutory rules usually prescribe the decision maker's duty to give information in its decision about the relevant recourse authority and how to complain against it, except if the decision is in favour of the client. Or, if a complaint has been submitted to the wrong authority, it must forward it to the competent one.

Generally, an administrative recourse may only be submitted within a period of time set by law. As in usual, it is requested by legal certainty. However, in Denmark, unless the law orders otherwise, there are no formal requirements and time limits for appeal.

It is also a widespread legal practice that the administrative appeal has a suspensive effect (however, there are some exceptions, like French administrative law), which means that the decision cannot be executed until the end of the appellate procedure. It is assumed that, till the final and enforceable act has been adopted, the administration has not settled the merit of the case. However, when a delay in implementation would cause irrecoverable damage (e.g. in case of emergency measures), the first

18 Mørup in this book.

instance decision may be executed immediately. Besides, the legislator may define other exceptions to the suspensive effect of the administrative appeal as well, like in tax cases (e.g. in Slovenia), or the administrative authority that has made the original decision may suspend its execution until the complaint against it has been decided, though it is not obliged to do so (in Denmark).

The appellate administrative body usually has full jurisdiction in administrative review cases: it may reject the appeal, or change or invalidate the decision of the first instance agency. In the latter case, the normal form of remedy is to return the case to the first-tier administrative body to repeat the original procedure and to make a new act.

The silence of the administration can already be redressed in the administrative phase of the case, when not only the disputed act, but also the failure or inability of the competent body to act, may be appealed against to a higher-level administrative agency. The appellate administrative authority is in a position to examine the reasons of the silence of the competent body, and may instruct it to perform its duty to act, or may take over this responsibility, and substitute the missing decision with its own act.

3.2 Right to access to court

3.2.1 Participatory rights in judicial proceedings

Although the procedural rules of the judicial proceedings usually show significant differences from those of the administrative procedure, the participatory rights of the parties in judicial disputes are roughly the same as in the process of administrative decision making. Accordingly, those whose rights or legitimate interests have been adversely affected by a decision are entitled to appeal against an administrative act. In this regard, there are also differences in the related national regulations. According to German administrative law, for example, a presumed violation of a subjective right is needed, but nowhere can the applicant's claim be based on mere economic, political or other interests, even if the courts may have greater freedom to acknowledge a specific personal interest worthy of protection than in Germany.

The procedural codes enable social organisations that promote general and collective interests to launch an appeal just like in administrative processes, while the ombudsman and public prosecutor also have the right to appeal. In Macedonia, local governments can also be plaintiffs of administrative lawsuits, if an administrative act violates the autonomy provided for them by law. At first sight, this seems to be an exception, but actually, it is not (or should not be): the European Charter of Local Self-Government requires the signatory countries to provide legal protection for local authorities.[19]

The right to make a statement, the right to access to the documents of the lawsuit and the duty of the court to make a judgment within a reasonable period, and to give reasons for its judgment, are also provided during the judicial review. However, different conditions are sometimes set for exercising procedural rights before the court. Thus, in certain cases, if the plaintiff refuses to make formal statements or to

19 Art. 11 of the Charter reads as '[l]ocal authorities shall have the right of recourse to a judicial remedy in order to secure free exercise of their powers and respect for such principles of local self-government as are enshrined in the constitution or domestic legislation.'

give information as requested by the court, this behaviour might lead to the cessation of the proceeding. In France, for example, if applicants have merely filed a summary request announcing an explanatory statement and if they do not produce this statement within three months, the *Conseil d'État* automatically and without prior notice abolishes the procedure.

In an administrative lawsuit, the right to legal counsel is of enhanced importance compared to the administrative process, where the parties make only exceptional use of the assistance of legal representatives. Judicial disputes take place according to stricter procedural rules and often require special legal expertise. In most administrative law regimes, legal representation is not obligatory in administrative litigation, but neither is it prohibited, if the plaintiff covers the costs. Nevertheless, the participation of legal counsel is sometimes legally required, during proceedings before the higher courts, for example, or in extraordinary appellate proceedings.

Normally, the parties must pay for their counsel themselves, but legal aid provided by the state is an important element of legal protection in administrative disputes in all countries. It means that the state provides help for those who lack sufficient financial resources to get legal assistance in representing their interests before the court. Legal aid (or partial state support) is granted on a conditional basis everywhere. Most frequently, it is not granted in petty cases, or if the complainant, according to the judgment of a reasonable person, does not have a real chance of winning the case.

3.2.2 The scope and limits of judicial review

In theory, all administrative acts may be challenged based on both questions of facts and law of the case. The plaintiff has to refer to the infringement of his or her substantive and procedural rights. In reality, however, administrative law often features exceptions to the right to access to court in connection with the special character of certain cases. The range of non-justiciable acts varies in the different countries. In Denmark, for example, judicial control is partially excluded in refugee matters and in certain other affairs affecting foreigners, where tribunals have adjudicated the dispute. In France, acts of government and the internal measures of administrative agencies are removed from the scope of judicial review. The latter is a normal exception, in any case, as internal organisational matters and governmental decisions of a political nature are exempt from judicial review in other places, too. In most cases, the application has to meet some formal requirements that mean procedural limitations of judicial protection.

Of course, the crucial issue of judicial review is the extent of the courts' intervention. As a consequence of the principle of separation of powers, the judiciary may not take over the functions and powers of the executive agencies – its mandate may not go beyond legality control. However, this postulate does not offer clear criteria to separate the area of administrative activity from the legitimate scope of judicial power. It is certain that the degree of judicial intervention is in connection with the dichotomy of substantive and procedural rights, as judicial deference is more probable with substantive (policy) issues of administration, while it is usually much more intensive in judging the formal legality of administrative acts.[20]

20 Hanns Peter Nehl, 'Administrative Law' in Jan M. Smits (ed.), *Elgar Encyclopedia of Comparative Law* (Edward Elgar, Cheltenham, Northampton 2006) 26.

Besides this, in some countries, several different types of judicial review proceedings may be launched depending on the legal claim of the plaintiff, like in Germany, where they may not only file suit for the annulment of an administrative act, but may also request the court to oblige the competent public authority to make an administrative act or to recognise a legal relationship (making a 'declaratory judgment'), with each claim having to be adjudicated in different proceedings.

Normally, the judicial review extends to the questions of facts and law which means that the court examines all the relevant facts and legal issues of the case. As the country reports of this book show, the intensity of judicial review varies not only depending on the nature or subject of the particular administrative action, but also in the various administrative jurisdictions. Although it is hard to classify clearly the possible degrees of judicial scrutiny, it is a general fact that the review of administrative cases involving political judgment or when administrative agencies are conferred with wide-ranging discretionary power can be characterised by judicial deference. The Polish administrative courts, for instance, do not seek to re-establish the facts of the case, but only check whether the relevant law has been correctly applied to the situation as stated by the administrative body in its own procedure. In Switzerland, the judicial practice has developed a deferential approach, in particular when the administrative decision requires special expertise or knowledge of local circumstances. In Italy, the role of administrative judges is also limited to checking the legality of the administrative acts. Notwithstanding this, in some circumstances, the Italian courts can indicate the legally correct behaviour to administrative bodies, particularly in case of the silence of the administration, or when there is only one proper response to the legal question disputed in the case. The administrative judge might have the widest powers in France and Spain, where in most cases the courts can not only annul, but also change the administrative decision.

The idea of judicial deference is probably behind the restrictive legal provisions which set conditions for the annulment of the enforceable administrative acts. In general, the courts must take account of the possible consequences of the repeal, and statutes often exactly circumscribe the procedural irregularities which can lead to the voiding of an act. One of the commonly used standards for such procedural errors is that a faulty act must be invalidated if it has influenced the outcome of the procedure, that is to say, a different result would have been achieved without the error. On the other hand, if a repeated procedure, without the error, would probably produce the same result, then repealing the act and reconsidering the case would be unreasonable. Notwithstanding this, the law may specify concrete procedural faults which cause the decision to be declared void. In France, for example, the lack of reasoning leads to the annulment of the act.

As a result of the recent reforms of administrative law in the Netherlands, the judges have some very special tools at their disposal. For instance, the court may call up the decision making body to remedy the error in the administrative procedure or act. If the administrative agency can (or is willing to) do this, the annulment of the contested act, or possibly the repetition of the administrative procedure, can be avoided. Furthermore, the court, under certain conditions, may confirm the legal effect of the repealed administrative decision. This serves to simplify the whole proceeding, as the court may overlook the procedural errors, if these did not influence the merit of the case, instead of referring the case back to the first instance administrative body for a repeated procedure. Moreover, the court may do the same if the original decision has already been effectuated, or the previously existing situation cannot be restored. To put it bluntly, the court's power to resolve the case, instead of returning it to the decision making administrative body, and thus to confirm the legal effect of a rejected act seems to be an unprecedented extension of judicial competence in reviewing administrative acts. Nevertheless, as Albers, Kjellevold-Hoegee and Schlössels point out in their chapter, the courts use these mandates carefully and undertake to replace the decision of the administrative authority only if there is only one legally proper solution in the case before them. Still, these are unusual extensions of the judicial intervention in favor of the simplification and acceleration of the whole process of administrative problem-solving.

In contrast to these cases, the courts have a wider power when the administrative act is legally bound, excluding any margin of appreciation of the competent agency. On such occasions, the court may quash or change the act. Of course, the cases in which administrative courts exercise full power in the judicial review process are always specified by law.

The most sensitive issue of judicial review is, however, the adjudication of the administrative acts that have been released by exercising discretionary power. In general, these acts are also appealable on several possible grounds. This is true when the decision has been issued *ultra vires*, which means that the administrative authority went beyond the legal limits of the margin of appreciation, or if the competent body fails to follow legal criteria determined by law for exerting discretionary power. Furthermore, if the use of discretionary power has not been kept to the legal aim for which it was granted, the act may also be annulled. And finally, even if the decision making authority has not overstepped its limits of discretion, and this power has been used for a legitimate purpose, the act might be erroneous if it is not in accordance with certain substantive principles, such as proportionality or equality. Traditionally, it is believed that the courts exercise the most intense scrutiny of administrative discretion in German administrative law,[21] but even if this is so, it can hardly be generalised or typified as a systemic feature of administrative jurisdictions.

A special form of legal protection is the tool of injunctive (or interim) relief granted by the court for avoiding serious and irreversible damage in the litigants' interests. These are interim injunctions which do not interrupt the ongoing judicial proceeding. It can be noted that such warrants may also be issued to protect public interest, at the request or proposal of the public prosecutor, for instance.

When the court only has the power to annul the illegal act, but the dispute must be settled by a valid administrative decision, it refers the case back to the administration for a new procedure. In this case, the competent administrative body is bound to the judicial ruling. The courts frequently indicate in their judgments the proper application of law in the particular case, or give information about how the relevant statutes should be implemented or interpreted by the executive authorities. As mentioned above, in the Netherlands, if the court repeals the decision of the administrative authority, it examines *ex officio* whether the case can be resolved immediately by making a new decision, or if it has to be sent back to the original administrative body. Certainly, the court can make a decision within the limits of the law, while respecting the scope of responsibility of the competent administrative agency.

Under special circumstances, the judicial proceeding may end without a substantive decision by the court. This is the case if the plaintiff withdraws his/her claim, or

21 Ibid. 26–27.

refuses to give a formal statement needed for the continuation of the proceeding. The court also abandons the case when the parties, under the relevant rule, conclude an agreement with each other, or choose a form of alternative dispute resolution. In such cases, the dispute no longer needs to be adjudicated by a court, but it is not problematic for legal protection, as all these reasons for extrajudicial solution are based, at least partly, on the will of the claimant.

In most countries, the power of judicial review extends to state liability cases as well, and the courts may grant compensation for damage caused by unreasonable delay or other acts of omission on the part of the administrative authority, or may intervene in the contractual relationship of the parties (e.g. modifying their contracts).

Usually, the right to access to court embraces the parties' right to appeal against the first instance judgment. The extraordinary appeal to the highest-level court, however, does not fall within this category, as it is not an established right of the plaintiff, but is subject to strict procedural conditions.

4 Institutional approach

As we have seen, individual rights are the foundations of procedural fairness in administrative law. In this regard, three types of institution must be discussed: the administrative authorities, the administrative courts (or ordinary courts having the appropriate power to review administrative acts) and the extrajudicial bodies.

4.1 Administrative protection

4.1.1 Ex officio withdrawal or modification of illegal actions

In some countries, under certain circumstances, administrative law allows the decision making executive authority to revise, modify or even withdraw its own earlier act. This enables the decision making body, if it discovers itself that its action was illegal, to repair the injurious act. (This may also be requested by the parties.) This kind of *ex officio* reparation is widely known in Europe, being used by the Danish, Hungarian, Macedonian or Spanish administrative law systems, among others.

As in the case of all other special mechanisms, this procedure also has some prerequisites, so it must be put into action within a time-limit, and the decision may be changed or withdrawn only if it has not been adjudicated by a higher body (or a court).

In a strict sense, the *ex officio* change or withdrawal of the act is not a real appeal, as private parties who object against the decision of the administrative organ do not have the right to oblige the competent body to do so. The primary function of these procedures is not to guarantee the legal rights and legitimate interests of the parties, but to preserve legality. These are really corrective mechanisms for maintaining lawful operation. This is true even if such a procedure is initiated by the parties of the respective administrative procedure.

However, in certain countries (it is true of Dutch or French administrative law, for example), this form of revision, together with the formal administrative appeal, is classified as two types of 'preliminary' or 'pre-trial' recourse, that is to say, compulsory procedural stages that come before opening the judicial route, based on the logic that the *ex officio* modification or withdrawal of the original act might also redress the infringements of the client's rights.

4.1.2 Administrative recourse

As has been described above, administrative appeals may be submitted to a higher authority which has the power to reconsider and override the first instance administrative act. Most frequently, executive bodies having a specialised range of responsibilities are organised into a hierarchical system of administration, though in certain countries (such as Hungary), integrated administrative authorities exist at various territorial (provincial, regional) levels and examine the appeals submitted against the lower-level administrative units. Where administrative tribunals exist, like in Britain, France or Denmark, an appeal against the first instance administrative act may be lodged with an independent tribunal. As a special rule, if the first decision was made by a tribunal, the recourse authority is normally another tribunal (see Danish administrative law). In some countries (in particular in Britain and Denmark), it tends to be the case that the administrative appeal must be addressed to an independent tribunal which combines the special expertise necessary in the particular case and some elements (e.g. independence) of judicial bodies. Nevertheless, as they can be regarded as parts of the executive, rather than the judicial power, these channels may be considered special sorts of administrative recourse. Possibly, the place of tribunals can be determined more precisely at a half-way between administration and courts. They are surely not courts,[22] but they are not administrative bodies either. It is certain that they exercise a different kind of administrative adjudication compared to the courts' role in judicial review, as they may examine the merit of the case as well (merits review).[23] In Austria, the institution of administrative appeal was abolished in 2014 in parallel with the establishment of the first instance administrative courts.

It has also been mentioned that, when no higher authority exists, as in the case of government ministries, autonomous authorities (e.g. regulatory agencies) or local governments, the first instance administrative decision cannot be appealed against.

As a standard rule, the appellate authority has full power to reconsider the merit of the case. Their jurisdiction is wider than the judicial review power of the courts, as they may legitimately take account of policy aims and considerations, and they are never bound by the outcome of the discretion of the lower administrative authority. Full jurisdiction also means that the appellate body is not bound to the request submitted in the appeal (e.g. the recourse authority may change the decision, even if it is unfavourable to the appellant).

The administrative appellate procedures can keep the petty and unfounded claims away from the courts. Thus any legal claim for repealing an administrative act should first go through all administrative forums. However, French administrative law is an exception to this general rule, as the exhaustion of all possible administrative remedies is not a prerequisite for the judicial route in this country, except for some special (e.g. tax) cases. Furthermore, as Jurgita Paužaité-Kulvinskiené writes in his chapter, in the Lithuanian administrative procedural law, the claimants can choose whether they appeal to a higher administrative body, or turn directly to the administrative court.

22 Peter Cane, *Administrative Tribunals and Adjudication* (Hart Publishing, Oxford 2010) 3.

23 Peter Cane and Leighton Macdonald, *Principles of Administrativ Law* (2nd edn., Oxford University Press, Oxford 2012) 209–237; Peter Cane, 'Judicial Review and Merits Review: Comparing Administrative Adjudication by Courts and Tirbunals' in Susan Rose-Ackerman and Peter L. Lindseth (eds.), *Comparative Administrative Law* (Edward Elgar, Cheltenham, Northampton 2013) 426–448.

4.1.3 Supervision

In some countries, such as Denmark, administrative supervision is seen as a special form of legal protection. However, under certain circumstances, the supervisory act itself can become the subject of judicial proceedings. In Switzerland, at least, if such an act affects somebody's legitimate interests, he or she may request a formal administrative act regarding the supervisory measure which can be challenged before the court.

4.2 Legal protection by quasi-judicial bodies

In certain countries, special bodies adjudicate the first instance decisions of administrative organs. Their usual name (they are called 'administrative' or 'independent' 'tribunals') indicates their special legal status: they are intermediate bodies between the administrative authorities and the courts, combining some structural and operational features of the latter institutions, with not only professional judges, but also often civil servants sitting on the bench, for example.

The procedures of administrative tribunals are usually cheaper, quicker and more flexible than those of the courts. Since they are specialised for a particular area of administration or public service, they have the necessary expertise for proper judgment of the facts of the case before them. They can be efficient and effective enough to manage a high volume of similar cases and can thereby disencumber the courts.

Administrative tribunals operate in many areas of administration, such as social security, education, taxation, transport or immigration. These bodies are used most widely in Britain, where a whole system of administrative tribunals has developed, and they rule in most appellate cases. They decide on issues of both law and fact with full authority. Uniquely in the UK, the higher level tribunal, called the Upper Tribunal, completely replaces the courts in certain matters, such as immigration and asylum cases, which means that its decisions cannot be appealed against to the court. There is a great specialisation (or, from another point of view, a fragmentation) of the tribunals in France as well, where the decisions of these independent bodies can be appealed against to the *Conseil d'État*. Tribunals or 'commissions' have different areas of competence; some of them rule on remedies against administrative acts making final or appealable decisions, others are in charge of non-judicial – even regulatory – functions, and so on.[24] Such committees also exist in some other countries, like in Denmark or the Netherlands. In Italy or Switzerland, administrative tribunals operate at a regional level and are in charge of adjudicating in certain areas like construction, taxes, culture or education.

The rationale of the administrative tribunals is that they may filter out more effectively the cases which should not go to the courts. Moreover, since they have special expertise in their range of responsibility and, at the same time, have certain attributes of judicial impartiality and independence, they have a better chance of checking the merit of the cases, or resolving them to the satisfaction of all parties.

24 For an in-depth analysis of the differences and similarities of the British and French systems of tribunals, see Peter Cane, 'Administrative Tribunals and Adjudication'.

4.3 Judicial protection

4.3.1 Institutional arrangements of administrative litigation

According to the conventional classification, there are three major types of judicial review of administrative decisions. In the tradition of the French *droit administratif*, the judicial control of administration is exercised by specialised courts, distinct *corps* of judges, and special procedural rules. The administrative courts, headed by the *Conseil d'État*, adjudicate in disputes on the legality of administrative acts, but they also have jurisdiction over public contracts, state liability and civil service cases. In the British system, based on common law, all matters and judicial cases concerning public and private persons belong to the same (common law) courts, as the Diceyan concept of rule of law requires this on the grounds of the principle of equality before the law. And finally, in the countries following the traditions of the German *Verwaltungsrecht*, there is a separate branch of courts within the ordinary (and uniform) system of judiciary.[25] In a sense, this is an intermediate structural arrangement between the former two institutional settings.

It is worth noting that the new generation of administrative courts created in the post-communist countries after their democratic transitions[26] have been set up mostly based on the various existing models of administrative justice.

Other classifications differentiate between 'objective', 'subjective' and 'mixed' forms of judicial protection according to the allegedly preferred functions of the courts, whether they protect the objective legal order, the subjective rights or both.[27] According to this categorisation, France, Italy, Greece, Poland and Spain belong to the first group, Germany and Austria to the second and Portugal and United Kingdom to the third.[28] Certainly, not only this kind of grouping, but also the classification of the various national systems can be questionable.

In reality, there are no 'pure' models, in the sense that the differences consist perhaps only in degree of judicial specialisation. In Britain, which has long been considered as a separate model of administrative justice, as Robert Thomas reports, a separate division of the High Court was set up in 2000, named the Administrative Court and with regional centres since 2009. However, judicial review is based exclusively on common law, and this main remedy for unlawful administrative decisions has developed largely via judicial case law. Moreover, the Administrative Court consists of judges who also adjudicate in criminal and civil law cases. Consequently, it cannot be regarded as a continental-style specialised administrative court. There are no specialised administrative courts in Switzerland, the Netherlands, Denmark and Hungary,[29] either. In Denmark and the Netherlands, as a major rule, the ordinary courts review

25 Bell (n. 6) 1280.

26 Before 1989/1990, there were separate administrative courts with limited jurisdictions only in Yugoslavia and Poland. Küpper (n. 15) 298–299.

27 Martin Kayser, 'Rechtsschutz und Kontrolle' in Armin von Bogdandy, Sabino Cassese and Peter M. Huber (eds.), *Handbuch Ius Publicum Europaeum: Band V. Verwaltungsrecht in Europa: Grundzüge* (C. F. Müller, Heidelberg 2014) 1070–1071.

28 Ibid. 1071.

29 However, in Hungary, administrative disputes are settled at first instance by so-called 'labour and administrative courts', which work within the organisational system of the (uniform) judiciary.

the administrative decisions, but there are also some specialised courts for specific areas (e.g. for land registry in Denmark, or for tax or social security matters in the Dutch system).

Administrative courts in France, Italy and Poland are clearly separate from the other parts of the judiciary. It means that administrative disputes are not channelled into the ordinary judiciary at any level, but are kept within a separate and autonomous system of administrative litigation (even if in both countries the lowest level administrative tribunals, on account of their composition and competence, are only quasi-judicial bodies). As Sylvia Calmes-Brunet shows in her chapter, the independence and special competences of administrative courts are considered constitutional values,[30] although they only indirectly follow from the constitutional text.

In most countries, some sort of 'mixed' system exists, which means that even if administrative disputes are settled (mainly at first instance) by a specialised court, one of the appellate courts is a high-level ordinary court having general competence. So, although 'real' administrative courts work in Germany, Spain, and in all post-communist countries (except Hungary) addressed in this book, they form a branch of the judiciary instead of there being complete separation from the organisational system of ordinary courts. They consist of administrative judges having special expertise in administrative law. This institutional arrangement does not exclude the existence of further specialisation, as separate courts adjudicate in certain areas (for example in fiscal and social welfare matters) in Germany, using specific procedural rules.

Certainly, whatever institutional arrangement is used for administrative litigation, the independence of the courts is a primary rule of law requirement.

Where specialised administrative courts exist, apart from their structural settings, they and the civil courts have separate areas of competence in the field of state liability cases, that is to say, the adjudication of compensation claims. There is more or less a separation of the jurisdictions between administrative courts and constitutional courts, where the intrinsic logic of this division is that, while administrative courts review the legality of individual administrative acts, constitutional courts adjudicate in legal controversies of a constitutional nature (like in cases of individual constitutional complaints or jurisdictional disputes of public authorities). In certain cases, however, administrative regulations may be reviewed by other high courts, as is true in Hungary, where the legality of local government decrees is controlled by a special chamber of the *Kúria* (supreme court) with cassatory power.

With the exception of Slovenia, administrative disputes in all countries are settled by courts at two levels, in whatever structural arrangement they exist. But even in Slovenia, where there is only one administrative court, an extraordinary appeal can be lodged at the Supreme Court. The judicial appeal against the judgment of the first instance administrative court is not a general right of the plaintiff in Germany either, but in certain matters and under certain conditions, as they are defined by law, a second or even a third instance of review exists in that country. In the countries where administrative tribunals adjudicate in disputes about the legality of administrative

30 See Calmes-Brunet's contribution in this book.

acts, their rulings, generally speaking,[31] may be appealed against to a higher-level administrative court.

In most countries, an extraordinary legal remedy is available against the enforceable judicial rulings, which may usually be lodged at the highest (supreme) court of the land. These mechanisms give the opportunity for the highest courts to establish general principles or doctrines for law application by the lower courts, or to give the right interpretation of controversial legal rules in order to promote uniform adjudication; sometimes, these emerge in a special type of appeal (e.g. as cassation appeals), but these cases can be selected by the highest courts on the basis of their legal significance or the financial value that is disputed in the case. As a rule, the extraordinary remedy is not appropriate for reconsidering the merit of the case; instead, its purpose is only to check the legality of the challenged judicial decision, which can only be annulled if the respective court has failed to comply with the law. In addition, as its name shows, this route is open when extraordinary conditions are met (such as grave and manifest error in law, or providing new evidence), so it cannot be considered a very effective tool of legal protection of individual rights.

4.3.2 Major characteristics of judicial proceedings

In most countries, administrative litigation is conducted by special procedural rules. In fact, in all CEE countries, except for Hungary and Slovakia,[32] and in all other jurisdictions examined in this book, where specialised administrative courts exist, there is a special set of rules for administrative judicial proceedings. Alternatively, where no such courts operate, the procedural rules of civil law courts are applied to administrative trials, often with minor modifications or specific supplements.

While administrative procedures are inherently inquisitorial, the nature of judicial proceedings depends on the legal cultures and traditions of the different countries. Accordingly, there is some diversity in this regard. Whereas the judicial disputes are more or less adversarial (where the parties have an active role in submitting evidence to the judge, who ensures compliance with the procedural rules) in Dutch, French or Polish administrative law, the judicial proceeding in Germany is rather inquisitorial (which means that the court investigates and establishes the facts of the case *ex officio*). However, it would be wrong to suppose sharp distinctions between the national administrative jurisdictions in this respect.

What is certain is that the position of the administrative agency is essentially different in judicial proceedings, where it is equal to that of the claimant with regards to all guarantees of a fair trial, from equality of arms to the right to legal representation. It sheds light on the distinctive character of the judicial process compared to that of the administrative procedure. While in the latter, the administrative authority, as an agent of public power and interest, is usually (but not always) in an unequal position (as an arbiter of the parties' claims, for instance), during the administrative dispute before a court, both the decision maker and the addressee of the decision are equal parties

31 However, there are some exceptions to this practice. See, for example the competence of the Upper Tribunal in Britain. See Professor Robert Thomas' chapter in this book.

32 Küpper (n. 15) 300–301.

of the process, which has important implications for their rights and capabilities (e.g. the burden of proof is often reversed). As a consequence, equality of arms between the parties is a general principle of administrative trials, so all parties have to be given the same opportunities to present their evidence and standpoints.

The availability of judicial control in administrative disputes is often limited on a formal basis for the sake of legal certainty and the effective working of the courts. To a degree, these formal requirements are similar to those used in administrative appeals. For example, it is a common feature of the administrative law in the countries examined here that they set a deadline for judicial appeal; where such a period is defined, it varies from 15 to 90 days from the notification of the enforceable administrative act. There is also the example of setting manifold periods for the different types of disputes, like in Italy or Germany, where a number of different judicial disputes are specified by law in administrative matters.[33] Moreover, the complaint has to be lodged with the administrative body whose act is disputed, but it has to be addressed to the court. In contrast to the administrative appeal, however, the procedure cannot be interrupted here, as the administrative body concerned may not change or withdraw its own decision in this phase; the judicial application is bypassed only in order to inform the competent public authority about the upcoming judicial dispute, and to receive its reply to the complaint. The requirement of the written form of the application gives the courts the opportunity to carry out a preliminary filtering of the requests and to ask the applicant to submit the missing documents or correct the obvious formal mistakes, if necessary.

The object of the judicial dispute is the final (legally enforceable) administrative decision (apart from rare exceptions where the lack of administrative decisions is objected against). Only the final acts are reviewable, after the exhaustion of all available administrative remedies, and where the merit of the case has been resolved. So the unsuccessful administrative appeal (in a preliminary or objection procedure) is usually needed for judicial review.

The duration of the judicial process is usually not set by law; however, the citizens' right to get a decision in their case within a reasonable time is just as important in the court proceedings as in administrative procedures. So the unusual or unnecessary length of a judicial process might be the subject of special remedy (e.g. in a constitutional complaint where this is possible, or before the European Court of Human Rights).

4.3.3 The effects of the judgments of the administrative courts

The judgment of the courts has an *inter partes* effect in individual administrative disputes. This means that it resolves concrete cases and is valid only for the parties of the judicial proceeding. It is also true in the case of constitutional complaints, despite these being decided by constitutional courts. *Erga omnes* rulings may be issued only in those rare situations where the administrative courts are empowered to review the legality of normative acts (administrative regulations, statutory instruments, government ordinances, local government decrees, etc.).

33 From this point of view, Danish administrative law is fairly special, as it generally does not determine any time limit for the claimants to turn to the court.

In some countries, special judicial processes can be launched for specific aims of legal protection, in order to redress certain procedural mistakes or an omission by the competent administrative body, such as obliging it to act or to provide the right to access to the relevant documents, if the public authority fails to do it. The reason for these proceedings is to speed up the pending administrative dispute, eliminating possible obstacles or anticipating certain procedural mistakes at the administrative stage of the case. Therefore, these special actions are actually corrective measures taken by courts.

There are some other widely-used guiding principles of the judicial process in administrative disputes affecting its outcomes. The principle of *non ultra petita* is frequently recognised and respected by national administrative laws. It means that the administrative judge cannot go beyond the limits of the application of the claimant. Again, there can be some exceptions to this general rule. Thus, the French administrative courts are not tied to the request of the claimant in matters of administrative contracts.

The national regulations vary in terms of whether the lawsuit has a suspensive effect on the execution of the challenged act or not. Generally, the judicial review proceeding does not suspend the implementation of the contested decision, but the parties may ask the court to issue an injunctive relief granting provisional protection for the interests of the parties. So the court may order the suspension to avoid serious and irreversible damage to citizens or to the public interest, or if the implementation could make the lawsuit impossible or pointless. Nevertheless, the reverse situation may occur, when the prohibition of the enforcement of the challenged administrative act would trigger similar effects. Thus, the national systems of administrative law differ from each other in terms of which presumption they consider as the major rule to which exceptions can be made: where the rebuttable presumption of the legality of the contested administrative acts prevails, for instance, it may indicate a judicial deference towards administrative actions. It can be added that the interim relief of the court on the suspension can usually also be appealable.

In most administrative jurisdictions, special judicial actions are laid down by law for the execution of the enforceable judgments. Unfortunately, the failure of the administration to implement the judicial decisions can be remedied only by a new lawsuit wasting more and more time. Therefore, administrative reforms have tried to make progress in this area, introducing penalties or disciplinary rules against the administrative body or officials who are accountable for such kinds of failure.

4.4 Legal protection against illegal normative acts; constitutional complaints

Whatever blurred borders there are between constitutional and administrative law, the review of statutory rules (in general terms: normative acts) is conventionally classified as a public power of a constitutional nature. The same is true even for the adjudication of individual decisions, when they are challenged on constitutional grounds, in particular in the case of infringements of fundamental rights.

Among the countries studied in this book, the constitutional court reviews the constitutionality of parliamentary statutes and lower level regulations in Austria, France, Germany, Hungary, Italy, Lithuania, Macedonia, Poland, Slovenia and Spain, empowered to invalidate the unconstitutional normative acts. Although the power to initiate constitutional review is strictly limited,[34] the ordinary or administrative judge can usually turn to the constitutional court if he or she finds that legislation which is to be applied is unconstitutional, and should be overturned.

No such courts exist in Denmark, the Netherlands, Switzerland and the United Kingdom. However, in some of them (like in Denmark) the constitutionality of statutes and administrative rules may be reviewed by the ordinary courts. In these countries, as a major rule, there is a *praesumptio legis* for the constitutionality of the statutes. However, it cannot be said that even in these countries the courts would be powerless if they were to encounter unconstitutional (administrative) rules. In Switzerland, for example, the Supreme Court, apart from the federal laws, may repeal the statutory instruments and cantonal laws, while in the other countries the ordinary courts often set aside or ignore the basic constitutional principles. In addition to this, as Felix Uhlmann indicates in his chapter, the judicial practice seems to question the applicability of federal laws which violate the ECHR.

In some countries the high courts also have some power to check the legality of normative administrative acts. In Germany, the High Administrative Court has a limited power to review the validity of by-laws and other statutory instruments, while the Federal Constitutional Court has an exclusionary power of constitutional review of parliamentary laws. In Hungary, as described above, a specialised council of the supreme court exercises legality control over local government decrees.

Besides constitutional review, some constitutional courts have other tools for rights-protection. Adapting the doctrine of *verfassungskonforme Auslegung* developed by the German Federal Constitutional Court, they may state that the reviewed statute conforms with the constitutional provision, only if it is interpreted in a certain way (determined by the Court), without repealing it. This technique can be found in the practice of the French *Conseil constitutionnel* and the Hungarian *Alkotmánybíróság*, too.

In addition, effective tools for the legal protection of individual rights are provided by those procedures in which certain executive acts may be challenged by citizens before the constitutional court. In fact, in this way, administrative disputes may become constitutional controversies in which it is more likely to refer to fundamental rights and general constitutional principles. In Austria, Germany, Hungary, Macedonia, Slovenia and Spain, individuals may submit constitutional complaints against individual administrative or judicial acts, and the adjudication of these cases by constitutional courts might lead to the annulment of the underlying norm if it violates the constitution. Certainly, there are differences between the relevant regulation of the German *Verfassungsbeschwerde*, and the Spanish *recurso de amparo* and other forms of individual complaints, but these are transcended by the similarities (like the general condition that the citizen must first exhaust all the judicial remedies available in the administrative jurisdiction) and by the inherent goal of these procedures (i.e. to provide an ultimate remedy based on constitutional rights).

34 In France, for example, since the constitutional amendment of 2008, litigants may invoke the unconstitutionality of the statute applied to their case before the court; only the court may initiate the constitutional review through the *Conseil d'État* or *Cour de Cassation* at the Constitutional Council. However, in Hungary, until 2011, through *actio popularis*, anyone was able to lodge an application to the Constitutional Court to review the constitutionality of any laws without any personal interests.

4.5 Ombudsman-type and other special forms of institutional protection

The institution of the ombudsman is present in all the 14 countries examined in this book. As a matter of fact, several different models are used or followed by the various countries in respect of legal status, competences and organisational and procedural issues. There are ombudsmen with general jurisdiction, and (less often) commissioners specialising in certain types of cases. They enjoy everywhere far-reaching independence, and they are usually only accountable to the national legislature (though in Italy and Switzerland they exist only at a regional level).

But their common features and potential to offer legal protection in administrative decision making is now more important. It is a decisive feature of the ombudsman-type protection that the commissioners may only give recommendations or non-binding opinions for the respective executive agencies, but their actions cannot be enforced. Instead, they have to rely on their own professional prestige and moral authority to achieve real and effective results. In most cases, ombudsmen have wide-ranging investigative power, and they may launch several different procedures about other bodies. But most of all, they may exert influence through their recommendations, aiming to eliminate maladministration, improve the quality of administration and promote redress of individual infringements of the clients' rights.

As a major rule, the competence of ombudsmen does not cover all administrative agencies, and tribunals, and does not extend to courts at all. Moreover, their procedure or action is not a precondition for applying for 'normal' (administrative or judicial) remedies.

Some other public bodies might have a limited role in legal protection as far as administrative decision making is concerned. Thus, in particular in the CEE countries, the public prosecutor also has wide-ranging investigative powers. In contrast to the consultative nature of the ombudsman, he or she may bring legally binding actions. However, the prosecutor's contribution aims primarily at promoting and protecting the public interest, and he or she is available only indirectly for legal protection of individual rights.

4.6 Alternative dispute resolution

Surprisingly, despite the fact that the tools of alternative dispute resolution (ADR) are aimed at making a compromise between administrative authorities and the citizens as their clients, these instruments and processes are hardly used in the administrative systems explored here. Certainly, the comparative evaluation of the application of these devices is a matter of subjective judgment. However, even when all well-known ADR techniques (i.e. mediation, reconciliation and arbitration) are used, as in France, they exist only in an undeveloped form. Many national reporters have said that these mechanisms have limited significance in the system of legal protection (though in Germany, there is a federal law on these procedures), and there is also an example for the lack of them (in Slovenia). In many countries, only one or two forms of ADR are recognised by law or used in practice, or their application is limited to some specific procedures (like in public procurement in Italy). There is no general recognition of the courts' power to suspend the ongoing procedure, with the consent of the parties, giving them the opportunity for an amicable (out-of-court) agreement, either. Experience shows that, even when some methods of ADR were recently included in the statutory rules (like mediation in 2004 in the Hungarian general administrative code), their use has remained sporadic and rare.

What is important, as the Italian Constitutional Court has explicitly declared in a ruling, is that the various tools of ADR cannot replace the judicial protection of individual rights and legitimate interests, so cannot, for example, deny citizens access to the courts.

Although some authors have reported the growing use of these routes to settle the case, in the Netherlands and France, the main experience is the reluctance of the administration to employ them. One of the reasons for this can be the lack of relevant traditions and customs, while in certain jurisdictions (in particular in the post-communist countries) the old attitudes of public administration, mainly the deeply-rooted approach of the hierarchical relation between the public authorities and their clients, can also contribute to the administrative feeling of dislike or antipathy towards the use of these odd and unaccustomed tools and instruments.

5 Challenges and problems of effective legal protection

As country studies show, institutional deficiencies, inappropriate procedures or certain attitudes of administrative bodies may cause problems for the effectiveness of the system of legal protection. These challenges may be classified in various ways depending on whether we concentrate on their reasons, concrete forms or consequences. However, I want herewith just to gather the most important problems to which most national administrative law systems have to face.

5.1 Length of procedure

It is a general problem that the access to administrative justice, or, in other words, to get redress for the infringements of personal rights or legitimate interests frequently takes too much time; the lengthiness of the remidial procedures sometimes is intolerably long. The administrative decision making process might be complicated or even inextricable and need not only time but also money and patience. There can be more reasons behind this phenomenon: the large number of ongoing cases (or, otherwise, not enough courts); the insufficient personnel and financial resources of courts; or the institutional arrangements or regulation (e.g. if laws do not set deadlines for the judicial processes, and no standard practice of what makes procedure 'in due time'), etc. Under such circumstances, many may think that the challenge of the administrative acts, even if they have had adversarial effects on them, does not make sense. The subject or value of the lawsuit can be too small, or the personal interest for remedy may lose its significance until when the final decision will be taken. Some national authors reported about such problems, like Joanna Lemańska arguing that her country, Poland is among those countries from where a lot of complaints have been filed to the ECtHR for years. Sometimes, paradoxically, the length of procedure of the court or the tribunal, which are intended to protect individual rights, causes some delay. In France, for example, the average length of judicial proceedings in administrative cases is about nine and a half months.

The instruments of legal protection can be misused, if they are not applied to their original function. Thus, for example, the unlimited submission of the same claim to repeat an administrative procedure, or the demand of large amount document to be accessed that are unnecessary for the proper protection of legal interests, the use of the judicial way to delay an investment project, the exercise certain rights only for seeking publicity or hindering the normal operation of public administration, are all abuses of the procedural rights. It is clear that the use of financial, personnel and other resources of public administration must be proportionate to the significance of the case in both the administrative and the judicial proceedings. But the simple reference to the potential danger of misusing procedural rights or protective tools cannot justify the unreasonable restriction of these instruments.

Some countries have made efforts to cope with the problem of the slowness of the judicial proceedings, like Spain, where a new law was introduced in 2011 in order to reduce the duration of administrative litigation through raising the minimum value of a case to be heard by the Supreme Court, while other countries have introduced administratice reforms with the purpose of accelerating administrative and judicial processes.

5.2 The scope of judicial review

Judicial review does not cover all administrative acts. In particular, administrative regulations, or higher-level laws often may not be challenged before a court. In Switzerland, for instance, the federal laws are exempt from judicial review. The problem is that if a law of the Federal Parliament causes a bulk of infringments of individual rights or legitimate interests, there is no any institutional tool to redress them. In some other countries, where no constitutional review is recognised, government ordinances may also be immune from judicial oversight. Sometimes exemptions originate in national traditions or peculiarities. In Macedonia, the Government can issue special *inter partes* decrees that may impose obligations on citizens, but no judicial way is provided for reviewing these acts. As this example shows, sometimes the problem is that individual decisions come into sights in the form of normative acts, and the administrative courts are not mandated to review them. Consequently, there might be gaps in the sphere of judicial control. In Switzerland, where the direct democracy is a basic pillar of the political system, more and more radical popular initiatives are proposed on socially vulnerable groups, targeting the legal standing of migrants, religious or other minorities, and the judicial control of these political actions have only limited opportunities.

Another unbeneficial tendency is the restriction of the appeal rights which can be observed in some countries (e.g. in Britain or Hungary), in particular under special conditions or in special situations, like in times of the mass migration or terror dangers. Under such circumstances, political motivations may also limit the access to courts, in order to accelerate the ongoing decision making processes, or to avoid political inconveniences or loss of popularity. As the governments have in all countries considerable influence on the law-making process, they have plenty opportunities to reduce the level of rights-protection, or to disrupt the balance for the benefit of the effectiveness of the administrative decision making at the expense of individual rights.

5.3 Costly litigation

The costs of administrative litigation (which may be imposed as registration fee, legal aid, or just charge for the judicial service) can have a deterrent effect on the citizens to seek administrative justice from courts. When the litigation needs high costs or excessive burdens, to challenge administrative acts does not make sense for many people, especially if the economic or other kinds of interests affected by the administrative procedure are small; or, if the judicial process is slow, the importance of the final court decision might lose its significance for the parties. So the costs of judicial procedure might have negative effects on the rights-protection, as the payment requirement, whatever its legal title is, might be a too rigid condition for the citizens, and might hold back them from litigation, in particular if they are uncertain in the final outcome of the judicial procedure.

While more countries have tried to overcome these obstacles, introducing the-loser-pays principle or extending the legal aid programs, these attempts often have obvious limits; in most countries, for example, these charges do not cover the real costs of the administrative justice.

Finally, it is worth noting that higher costs can have also beneficial effects on the effectiveness of the administrative disputes, as they keep the petty and unfounded cases far from the bench.

5.4 Non-compliance of judicial decisions

It is an undisputable case of the ineffectiveness of legal protection when the final judgment of the administrative judge is not implemented, or it is enforced only with undue delay, or only partially or falsely. The reason for non-compliance is often that the judicial decision should be implemented by the administrative body which just has lost the lawsuit. The execution can be costly, when, for instance, it needs the contribution of other bodies, or the restoration of an earlier legal situation. Needless to say, political considerations can also hinder or delay the implementation. In such cases, the court may, in a special ('enforcement') proceeding impose penalty on the recalcitrant administrative organ, or even may trigger criminal proceeding, as in the Spanish administrative law (it is not a widespread practice in Europe, however). But even if the judgment of the court can be enforced against the reluctant public authority, the new compliance procedure takes time again reducing the effectiveness of the rights-protection.

5.5 Poor institutional arrangements

As we have seen, the tools of legal protection make a whole system in each country discussed here. However, the elements and institutions of these systems have developed gradually, and their establishment connected frequently to general and multipurpose administrative reforms. Even when the very specific instruments of rights-protection used to be designed, other considerations and interests were apparently taken into consideration. For this reason, the system of protection of rights is not always complete or without flaws. Furthermore, diverging institutional interests or the lack of cooperative organisational culture can also make the protection of rights difficult. But as there are no universally good institutional arrangements, there are no structural 'evils' either, so institutional setting must always be evaluated in its own (national) context. Still, some authors have reported on poor institutional arrangements.

In certain countries, that makes some problems that civil courts have some overlapping powers in state liability cases with specialised administrative courts. In such cases, it is frequently complicated and difficult to draw the line between the competences of these courts. Another time the lack of cooperation between the administrative courts and other state bodies causes conflicts, as the Macedonian report says. In the Netherlands, there is some problem with the division of competences between the various courts. Under such circumstances, when five different (and special) appeal courts exist in administrative matters, it can be difficult to ensure the uniform adjudication which is a basic requirement of legal certainty.

5.6 Low quality regulation

Out-of-date or poor legislation can also reduce the level of legal protection, for example when public authorities are given special privileges to delay the decision making or to initiate specific procedures (like withdrawal or a reconsideration of the case for public interest) which is in contrast with the principle of legal certainty. Another trend that can also be observed, at least in some countries, is the proliferation of special administrative actions. As a consequence of the growing sectoral law-making, the actors of various fields and branches of administration often strive for special procedural rules for their activities. The sectoral interests, especially when they are underpinned by special procedural rules might go against the established system of rights-protection, as the distinct features of these special rules may claim special treatment. The level of protection of individual rights can be endangered also by the popular efforts to simplify and speed up the administrative dispute resolution. Secondary importance can be attributed to the procedural rules claiming that the procedural fairness would not have led to a different outcome of the procedure; consequently, it would be a waste of time and energy to repeat the whole procedure just for correcting an insignificant irregularity.

5.7 Financial austerity policies

The worldwide financial crisis has had some indirect negative effects not only on the effectiveness, but also on the availability of the instruments of the rights-protection, as many governments, for budgetary reasons, have made efforts to narrow or limit the ways of legal remedies. No doubt, the institutions and procedures of effective legal protection, from maintaining court-houses to financing legal aid, needs appropriate resources. The financial austerity programs, which were introduced in most countries after 2008 aimed at reducing these costs. It is a real risk to limit the scope or availability of judicial review for budgetary reasons or in order to accelerate or simplify the administrative process. The new Hungarian Fundamental Law, for instance, declares that '[i]n performing their duties, the Constitutional Court, courts, (. . .) and other state organs shall be obliged to respect' 'the principle of balanced, transparent and sustainable budget management' (Art. N paras 1, 3), whatever it means. As we could see in the British report, the Government proposed the introduction of a 'no difference' principle which means that the judicial review should be denied if the court's ruling would not have probably been substantially different than that of the administrative body's decision. Some efforts are made from time to time to restrict the legal aid for judicial review in many countries.

While the efficiency of the administrative and judicial bodies, including the mechanisms of legal protection, is a legitimate objective of the government, the principle of procedural fairness must not be destroyed by financial considerations.

6 Major trends of effective legal protection in administrative law

The national reports give a good opportunity to identify general trends of the development of the principle of effective legal protection. In fact, we must be careful to generalise certain phenomena, even if they have been occurred in a number of countries examined here. Similar measures can have different reasons or motivations depending on the peculiar context or traditions. They can be answers to different challenges, inspired by diverse motivations, and they can have disparate implications. Still, it is worth drawing attention to certain tendencies or similarities that can be found in the various administrative jurisdictions in relation to the system of legal protection of individual rights and legitimate interests. All these need further research exploring the national context and special reasons of (the same) changes.

6.1 Constitutionalisation of administrative law and the rise of human rights approach

The constitutionalisation of administrative law is a general tendency.[35] It is not surprising: administrative authorities exercise public power under constitutional limitations; constitutional principles permeate the whole legal system; and respect for human rights at all levels of government has become a general principle of constitutional law, affecting *per se* the terrain of administrative law. As we have seen in conceptualisation chapter, the procedural rights of the private parties in both the administrative procedures and judicial processes are seen more and more as basic human rights; or, they may protect or promote the enforcement of (other) human rights.[36] However, administrative law has preserved many of its distinctive characteristics from those of the constitutional law.[37] Procedural principles and rights have various levels and importance – not all of them can be regarded fundamental rights, as certain irregularities that have not influenced the outcome of the decision making process, do not lead to the annulment of the administrative act. In fact, a delicate balance must be between the respect for procedural rights and the general interest for an effective administration.

The rise of human rights approach manifests in the growing use of judicial constructions and doctrines, from the proportionality test to the *verfassungskonforme Auslegung* in administrative procedures and judicial review processes that have been developed for human rights adjudication. These arguments can be invoked also in administrative appeals not only in specialised constitutional procedures (like constitutional complaint), but in the usual proceedings of legal remedy too.

There might be similar reasons for the tendency that the classical function of legality control, that is the defence of the objective legal order has gradually been completed with the protection of rights and legitimate interests of the parties. While the traditional model allowed, for example, that the appellant party's position become worse than before the appeal, and the court could go far beyond what has been

35 Carol Harlow, 'Global Administrative Law: The Quest for Principles and Values' (2006) 17 *The European Journal of International Law* 205, 208; Ruffert (n. 3) 38–41.

36 See e.g. for the common law systems Janina Boughey. 'The Use of Administrative Law to Enforce Human Rights' (2009) 17 *Australian Journal of Administrative Law* 25–38.

37 Ginsburg (n. 1) 117–127.

requested by the recourse, the legislation and the judicial practice increasingly in more and more countries bypassed the principle of *reformatio in peius*, and *ultra petita*, once a judicial appeal was put in motion by a private party.

6.2 Expansion of judicial review

In historical perspective, the direction of progress of judicial review of the acts of the Executive goes towards the establishment of the specialised administrative courts. Even today, there are certain examples of such a trend (e.g. in Austria with the establishment of the first instance administrative courts in 2014, or in Macedonia, where a High Administrative Court was set up in 2011 as an appellate court). However, while the specialisation of the judiciary can prevail also in the unified organisational system of the courts, as many examples show, the experiences of the very recent trends to establish specialised administrative courts do not lead to unequivocal conclusions. In Macedonia, where the reason for changing the former model of administrative adjudication based on the ordinary courts was to speed up the relevant procedures, the records of the Supreme Court in administrative appellate cases have been better than those of the newly established Supreme Administrative Courts so far. In Hungary, according to some reform conceptions, the price of the establishment of the independent administrative courts would be the abolishment of administrative appeals. If such a transformation would be combined with the mandate of full power for the administrative courts, it was an obvious risk that the courts takes over the function of public administration. In fact, the full independence of the administrative courts of the organisation system of the whole judiciary is not a principal issue; the essence is the independence of these courts from the executive power, and the accessibility of judicial way for every interested parties of administrative procedures.

The scope of legality control has spread out in the recent decades; today, courts do control not only the regularity of the decision making process that is the formal compliance with the rules on the competence and procedure, but also the respect of general constitutional values and requirements and international law from the principle of proportionality to legitimate expectations. The judicial review of administrative acts has expanded to such areas of administrative decision making where it was for a long time unprecedented and unthinkable. As a matter of fact, for today, the legal control of these decisions became the major rule, to which only narrowly tailored exceptions are accepted. Even in those countries, which were traditionally mistrustful of judicial review of legislative acts, this expansion is observable. In Britain, for example, since the approval of the Human Rights Act in 1998, the courts may scrutinise the administrative acts in order to protect the individual rights entrenched in the ECHR. In France, the *Conseil d'État* extended the scope of judicial protection to the administrative contracts, as the statutes do not refer them to judicial review.

The extension of judicial review to new and new areas of administrative actions, or the principle of governmental liability for damages caused by administrative acts are frequently posited as achievements or innovations of EU law.[38] The effects of the ECJ jurisprudence or the Europeanisation (i.e. standardisation of certain procedural forms and guarantees) cannot be denied. However, it is easy to accept that both the

38 Künnecke (n. 2) 2.

ideas of judicial review of administrative decisions and the state liability originate from and deeply rooted in the national administrative jurisdictions and were found or even elaborated far before the emergence of the European administrative space, whatever it means.

Another dimension of the expansion of judicial control is the strengthening of the judicial intervention. While the traditional deference of the courts to the public administration is strong in cases where the administrative authority exercises discretionary power, the judicial supervision seems to tend to shift away from a cassatory review towards full jurisdiction. Such trends (or upcoming reforms, at least) can be observed in Poland and Hungary. It is true, however, that we do not know much about the real motivations of these plans – they can indicate certain distrust to public administration, or they can follow only the international trends of judicialisation of administrative governance.[39] Whatever reasons motivate the extension of judicial review, the principle of separation of powers should prevail, leaving administrative organs to make policy choices and to exercise discretion conferred on them by law, and enabling courts to check whether these decisions have been taken within the limits of the legal mandate.

Today, the judicial review of administrative acts is regarded as a constitutional cornerstone of legal protection, and its scope is still widening. This expansion has reached on many countries the normative acts of the executive too. Another direction of the development was the recognition of the fact that the unlawful administrative acts can do harms, and the damages, even if it is caused by exercising public power, must be compensated. The state liability thereby exceeds the terrain of the traditional civil law, as the claim of citizens whose rights or legitimate interests have been adversarial affected by an illegal act of administration, can derive not only from a contractual relationship with public authorities, but from the normal operation of the executive agencies.

6.3 Administrative reforms for simplifying and accelerating administrative procedures

In recent years, legislative reforms have been started in some countries for making the administrative procedures quicker, more effective and efficient. Such kind of rationalisation has several different ways and means: for example, the application to be submitted to the administrative body is less and less bound to formal requirements (in a way that if law does not require otherwise, the process can be set in motion by an e-mail, phone call or oral announcement); or, administrative organs must examine the merit of the requests of the individuals, rather than their forms in order to avoid the waste of time.

Another trend is to find effective ways to prevent unreasonable challenges of administrative acts before a court. Seemingly, these efforts can make obstacles to

39 From the huge literature of this phenomenon, see Alec Stone Sweet, *Governing with Judges: Constitutional Politics in Europe* (Oxford University Press, Oxford 2000); Martin Shapiro and Alec Stone Sweet, *On Law, Politics, and Judicialization* (Oxford University Press, Oxford 2002); Ran Hirschl, *Towards Juristocracy: The Origins and Consequences of the New Constitutionalism* (Harvard University Press, Cambridge and London 2004).

administrative justice. However, keeping petty and unfounded claims remove from judicial way can enhance the capacity of the courts to provide more effective protection against the significant and serious violation of individual rights and legitimate interests.

At the same time, the exaggerated procedural simplification itself might weaken or even destroy the effective legal protection. Legal representation for instance, is not mandatory, but the rights and interests of private persons can be infringed if they do not have access to legal counsel who can help them to stand for their personal interests before a well-equipped and powerful administrative authority. Some formal requirements can also slow down the decision making process, still, they appear to be indispensable, like the right of the parties to present statements or to access the relevant documents of the case. The referral of the case by the court back to the first instance administrative body can be seen as a waste of time for many, but in a number of cases the merit of the case may be resolved more expediently and in a fair way by the original decision maker. Therefore, the most that can be said in this regard is that a balance must be struck down in each country between the diverge interests and considerations stipulating that the effectiveness of the legal protection of the rights of the parties have to be guaranteed whatever methods are used for promoting the simple and rapid proceedings.

6.4 The rise of global administrative law and the Europeanisation of national administrative jurisdictions

It is quite surprising how rich is the academic literature discussing the EU administration or the 'global administrative law', compared to the investigation of the 'grassroot' administration, that is the administrative systems of the nation states. Although the protection of the rights and interests of private parties in administrative procedures is one of the fashionable and favourite topics of administrative science, the mainstream literature has focused on the European and/or global level of administrative activity so far, rather than on the national level where far the most individual cases and disputes are decided. It is a real puzzle if we know that the primary and most important sphere of rights-protection in administrative procedures is the day-by-day administration of the nation states.

The widely shared approach behind this phenomenon is that we live today in the era of 'global governance' which can be 'characterised by a shift away from State-centric conceptions of power towards one in which international and supranational institutions, as well as informal networks and private actors, exert an increasing influence on policy preferences and outcomes'.[40] According to this approach, today, in the 'post-Westphalien order' of the European states, many institutions and procedures of administrative law are more and more associated with international and supranational organisations and communities which have their own institutions, rules or even identities. 'There are shifts from state-centered administrative law to global administrative law' which does not mean only the transfer of certain traditional powers of

40 Gordon Anthony, Jean-Bernard Auby, John Morison and Tom Zwart, 'Values in Global Administrative Law: Introduction to the Collection' in Gordon Anthony, Jean-Bernard Auby, John Morison and Tom Zwart (eds.), *Values in Global Administrative Law* (Hart Publishing, Oxford 2011) 1.

the nation states to European or other international organisations, but is allegedly a qualitative change 'from an autarchical and hierarchical administration to collaborative administrative action'.[41] The rise of global administrative law can be illustrated by the emergence of certain kinds of composite procedures (where both the national and international authorities have special roles and they must co-operate with each other), the growing administrative practice of international organisations, and the strengthening of mutual relationships between public authorities and citizens (or their organisations). However, even though the 'administration is becoming increasingly international',[42] the vast majority of individual administrative actions are proceeded by national administrative authorities under the procedural rules of domestic law. In fact, the transfer of administrative competences means mainly the shift of regulatory functions, and, to a much lesser extent, adjudicatory powers from government agencies to non-state actors.[43]

The most important area of the globalisation is the rise of the European administrative law. According to the conventional wisdom, there is an intensive interaction between the national administrative law regimes and the growing EU law. The influence of the administrative law of the European Union is not limited to the areas of EU policies, but also on those fields which have remained in national competence.[44] Though the European impacts can be discovered primarily in constitutional law, through the European requirements of the protection of basic rights, the administrative law is also concerned.[45] Besides the law-making of the European institutions, the jurisprudence of the European courts, and reception of the general public law principles belong also to the channels of the European influence.[46] The adaptation to the European norms takes place also in a multifaceted way. Thus, while the primary and secondary legislation of the EU set legal harmonisation requirements, the practice of the European courts provides interpretive tools for the national authorities.[47] Many scholars expect that the impacts of European administrative law on the national jurisdictions will strengthen if the growing needs for a uniform EU administrative procedural code[48] will be satisfied.

41 Javier Barnes, 'Towards a Third Generation of Administrative Procedure' in Susan Rose-Ackerman and Peter L. Lindseth (eds.), *Comparative Constitutional Law* (Edward Elgar, Cheltenham, Northampton 2013) 336.

42 Sabino Cassese, 'A Global Due Process of Law?' in Gordon Anthony, Jean-Bernard Auby, John Morison and Tom Zwart (eds.), *Values in Global Administrative Law* (Hart Publishing, Oxford 2011) 17.

43 'Rights and obligations are more loosely defined in adjudication procedures, while they tend to be better structured in rule-making procedures'. Ibid. 51.

44 Jürgen Schwartze (Hrsg.), *Das Verwaltungsrecht unter europäischem Einfluß: Zur Konvergenz der mitgliedstaatlichen Verwaltungsrechtsordnungen in der Europaischen Union* (Nomos Verlagsgesellschaft, Baden-Baden 1996) CXIX; 1379–1390.

45 Ibid. 818.

46 Ibid. 822–823.

47 In the mid-1990s, a research project explored the European influence on the national systems of administrative law. On the ground of a comparative study of 13 countries, several special administrative procedures and institutions were identified where such effects may have been demonstrated, like the withdrawal of the unlawful decision by the decision maker, the duty to give reasons of the administrative acts, or the reception of interim judicial reliefs, Schwartze, n. 4 807–818.

48 See e.g. Anne Meuwese, Ymre Schuurmans and Wim Voermans, 'Towards a European Administrative Procedure Act' (2009) 2 *Review of European Administrative Law* 3–35.

The growing and continuously developing body of the EU law and the jurisprudence of the European courts provide a strong incentive to improve the tools and methods of legal protection, and play prominent role to harmonise the national regulations and practices, not only in the fields of EU law, but in other areas of administrative law as well. The usual way of this harmonisation is that the EU law borrows a legal principle or conception from a Member State (or from the general values of the legal systems of its members), transforms it for Community objectives and goals, and generalises it, expecting the legal transplant and the uniform implementation of that particular piece of law.

When the appropriate procedures and legal guarantees emerge as special requirements of EU law imposing duties on the Member States, it is plausible to claim that the principle of effective legal protection, as it is defined by the EU legislation or the ECJ case law, has a direct impact on national legal systems. This view might be strengthened by the need for a uniform and coherent application of EU law in the member countries, having regard also to the doctrines of its supremacy and direct effect. Many scholars claim that as a result of the rise of the EU administration, and as a consequence of the convergence of the administrative systems of the nation states, a European Administrative Space has been developed in the recent two decades based on commonly shared principles of administrative law, constituting a so-called '*Ius Commune Europeaum*'.[49]

The supranational nature of EU law together with all of its attributes like its supremacy and direct effect and applicability in the national law, can be overestimated,[50] and can easily make an impression that the national legal systems mechanically follow the principles invented and set by EU law. Even if the spread of some general principles or certain requirements across all Member States was inspired by EU institutions, in most cases, these legal doctrines or methods had been borrowed from national jurisdictions, and, they are applied, apart from the little scope of direct administration of the EU, in the context of national administrative law. Most institutions and mechanisms of rights-protection of EU law are deeply rooted in the national legal cultures. It is true that the European administrative law[51] has achieved real innovations in the areas of EU law requiring Member States to provide effective legal protection for individuals to enforce their rights granted by the EU law. But even in this sphere, the EU institutions, especially the ECJ have always played only a mediating role in the

49 Eberhard Schmidt-Aßmann, 'Europäisches Verwaltungsrecht als Gemeinsame Aufgabe' (2000) 12 *European Review of Public Law* 11, 12; Jarle Trondal and B. Guy Peters, 'A Conceptual Account of the European Administrative Space' in Michael W. Bauer and Jarle Trondal (eds.), *The Palgrave Handbook of the European Administrative System* (Palgrave-MacMillan, Houndmills, Basingstoke 2015) 79–92; H. Hofmann, 'Mapping the European Administrative Space' (2008) 31 *West European Politics* 662–676; J. P. Olsen, 'Towards a European Administrative Space' (2003) 10 *Journal of European Public Policy* 506–531; Eckhard Schröter, 'Europäischer Verwaltungsraum und Reform des öffentlichen Sektors' in Bernhard Blanke, Frank Nullmeier, Christoph Reichard and GöttrikWewer (eds.), *Handbuch zur Verwaltungsreform* (3rd edn., VS Verlag für Sozialwissenschaften, Wiesbaden 2005) 510–518; E. G. Heidbreder, 'Structuring the European Administrative Space: Policy Instruments of Multi-Level Administration' (2011) 18 *Journal of European Public Policy* 709–727.

50 Karl-Heinz Ladeur, 'Conflict and Co-Operation Between European Law and the General Administrative Law of the Member States' in Karl-Heinz Ladeur (ed.), *The Europeanisation of Administrative Law: Transforming National Decision-Making Procedures* (Ashgate, Aldershot 2002) 2.

51 See the thematic issue of Law and Contemporary Problems (2004) 68 (1).

sense that most principles and guarantees of EU law[52,53] were borrowed from national administrative systems and transferred into autonomous Community law doctrines.[54] The basic values and relevant body of EU law rests upon the common public law traditions of the various legal systems.[55] In addition, most administrative and judicial institutions mainly serve national rather than Community purposes, so if we look at the real workloads of these organisations, the vast majority of cases they administer is national matter guided by national standards of administrative law. As a matter of fact, the national administrative law governs the most part of day-by-day administration, and it is hard to imagine how it could be otherwise.

Nevertheless, the influence of European administrative law can hardly be underestimated for several reasons. Even though these principles are widely known and used in modern Europe, their recognition has not been universal, and they have been used in different ways in the national administrative jurisdictions. Today, the EU institutions have a separate role in shaping and harmonising the common European standards of legal protection. They establish a minimum level of legal protection, while the national regimes of administrative law are the main sources of all tools and instruments. The ECtHR and ECJ have defined and required the minimum standards for legal protection of individual rights and legitimate interests fermenting rapprochement of the national traditions to each other and to the common European principles. The jurisprudence of the European courts is deeply rooted in the national legal systems in the field of administrative law too, and is indeed the synthesis of the different national public law cultures and traditions.

As a consequence, under the umbrella of EU law, there is an undeniable convergence between the administrative jurisdictions of the Member States, whatever the original source of the various principles and institutions was. So national systems of administrative law continuously converge as a result of the inspiration of the principles and rules of EU law, or global administrative law.[56] There is vivid scholarly discourse, however, on the convergence versus divergence of the national administrative jurisdictions and the European administration.[57] It is sure, notwithstanding, that the

52 Jürgen Schwarze, 'Rules and General Principles of European Administrative Law' (2004) 14 *Rivista Italiana de Diritto Publico Comunitario* 1219–1241; Claudio Franchini, 'European Principles Governing National Administrative Proceedings' (2004) 68 *Law and Contemporary Problems* 190; Jürgen Schwarze, *European Administrative Law* (Sweet & Maxwell, London 2006) cxx–cliv; Carol Harlow and Richard Rawlings, 'National Administrative Procedures in a European Perspective: Pathways to a Slow Convergence' (2010) 2 *Italian Journal of Public Law* 218–226.

53 For the types and peculiarities of European administrative procedures, see e.g. Schwarze (n. 53) (2006) 1173; Sabino Cassese, 'European Administrative Proceedings' (2004) 68 *Law and Contemporary Problems* 21–36.

54 Ton Heukels and Jamila Tib, 'Towards Homogeneity in the Field of Legal Remedies: Convergence and Divergence' in Paul Beaumont, Carole Lyons and Neil Walker (eds.), *Convergence and Divergence in European Public Law* (Hart Publishing, Oxford 2002) 114, 121.

55 Jorge Agudo González, 'The Evolution of Administrative Procedure Theory in "New Governance" Key Point' (2013) 6 *Review of European Administrative Law* 84.

56 Bernardo Giorgio Mattarella, 'The Influence of European and Global Administrative Law on National Administrative Acts' in Edoardo Chiti and Bernardo Giorgio Mattarella (eds.), *Global Administrative Law and EU Administrative Law: Relationships, Legal Issues and Comparison* (Springer-Verlag, Berlin, Heidelberg 2011) 66.

57 For a review of the pros and cons, see Chris Himsworth, 'Convergence and Divergence in Administrative Law' in Paul Beaumont, Carole Lyons and Neil Walker (eds.), *Convergence and Divergence in European*

EU law has a harmonising effect in the application of certain legal methods,[58] including the instruments of legal protection.

6.5 Other trends

Certainly, there are some other developments and trends concerning the effective legal protection which raise only in one or two countries. Still, they can be really important or interesting for others as well, like the mixed character of the decision making bodies in administrative cases at high level.

One of these tendencies is that certain privileges that central government traditionally exercised in some countries (like the participation of a special commissioner of government in the administrative, or even in judicial proceedings) have been abolished. The spread of tribunals and quasi-judicial bodies (special commissions) appears to be another trend, based on the general aim to reduce the heavy caseload of (administrative) courts preserving the judicial way for the really important cases and as ultimate forums for legal remedy. These bodies often well combine the expertise and professionalism of administrative organs and the independence and impartiality of courts. The judicialisation of the tribunals is also a common trend in the countries where these bodies are employed. The use of tools of the so-called alternative dispute resolution, which have long been used in other fields, is a fairly new idea in administrative matters as well.

Lastly, we can refer to the use of certain techniques and mechanisms which can actually substitute the traditional instruments of legal protection. Although most national experts have reported about the minor importance of the forms of alternative dispute resolution, the special methods of resolving administrative disputes have probably a great significance in practice. However, it is difficult to assess the actual role of the mechanisms based on cooperation between the administrative authorities and their clients since their aim is just to avoid the formalised controversies in which the instruments of legal protection are used.

7 Conclusions

After a careful examination and description and in-depth analysis of the national systems of legal protection in administrative law of their countries, most authors of this book concluded that the rights of procedural fairness, and the legal institutions, as they are enshrined in the domestic law, provide an effective legal protection for individual rights and legitimate interests. The national experts have reported that, although there are certain deficiencies and shortcomings in the national jurisdictions, and there are ups and downs in the development or practice of legal protection, the basic institutions and mechanisms of rights-protection exist in the national administrative law. According to their assessment, the level of effectiveness of legal remedies corresponds to the constitutional requirements and the standards of the

---

Public Law (Hart Publishing, Oxford 2002) 99–110. For a sceptic view, see Pierre Legrand, 'European Legal Systems are not Converging' (1996) 45 *International & Comparative Law Quarterly* 52–81.

58 Silvia Mirate, 'The ECrtHR Case Law as a Tool for Harmonization of Domestic Administrative Law sin Europe' (2012) 5 *Review of European Administrative Law* 47–60.

EU law and the ECHR. Most of them hold that the national level of rights-protection is higher than the common European standards demand.

Still, forms and tools, availability and effectiveness of legal protection are subjects of vivid political, professional and public debates and I think it is so good. The effective legal protection of rights and legitimate interests of individuals, and the efficient and effective performance of public administration are all real values, even if they are frequently in conflict with each other. Thus, whatever particular systems and solutions exist in the various countries, it is certain that a delicate balance between the administrative justice and the effective government is an indispensable condition of the good government and the modern state in the twenty first century.

Index